Upper harmonics

Piccolo

A-440

	G₄	A₄	B₄	C₅	D₅	E₅	F₅	G₅	A₅	B₅	C₆	D₆	E₆	F₆	G₆	A₆	B₆	C₇	D₇	E₇	F₇	G₇	A₇	B₇	C₈				
	369.99	415.30	466.16		554.37	622.23		739.99	830.61	932.33		1108.7	1244.5		1480.0	1661.2	1864.7		2217.5	2489.0		2960.0	3322.4	3729.3					
349.23	392.00	440.00	493.88	523.25	587.33	659.26	698.46	783.99	880.00	987.77	1046.5	1174.7	1318.5	1396.9	1568.0	1760.0	1975.5	2093.0	2349.3	2637.0	2793.0	3136.0	3520.0	3951.1	4186.0	5000.0	6000.0	7000.0	10,000.0

| 5 | 47 | 49 | 51 | 52 | 54 | 56 | 57 | 59 | 61 | 63 | 64 | 66 | 68 | 69 | 71 | 73 | 75 | 76 | 78 | 80 | 81 | 83 | 85 | 87 | 88 |

www.wadsworth.com

wadsworth. com is the World Wide Web site for Wadsworth/Thomson Learning and is your direct source to dozens of online resources.

At *wadsworth.com* you can find out about supplements, demonstration software, and student resources. You can also send e-mail to many of our authors and preview new publications and exciting new technologies.

wadsworth.com
Changing the way the world learns®

Audio IN
Media

From the Wadsworth Series in Production

Albarran, Alan B., *Management of Electronic Media,* 2nd ed.

Alten, Stanley, *Audio in Media,* 6th ed.

Armer, Alan A., *Writing the Screenplay*, 2nd ed.

Craft, John, Frederic Leigh, and Donald Godfrey, *Electronic Media*

Eastman, Susan Tyler, and Douglas A. Ferguson, *Broadcast/Cable/Web Programming: Strategies and Practices,* 6th ed.

Gross, Lynne S., and Larry W. Ward, *Electronic Moviemaking,* 4th ed.

Hausman, Carl, Philip Benoit, and Lewis B. O'Donnell, *Modern Radio Production,* 5th ed.

Hausman, Carl, Lewis B. O'Donnell, and Philip Benoit, *Announcing: Broadcast Communicating Today,* 4th ed.

Hilliard, Robert L., *Writing for Television and Radio,* 7th ed.

Hilmes, Michele, *Only Connect: A Cultural History of Broadcasting in the United States*

Hilmes, Michele, *Connections: A Broadcast History Reader*

Kaminsky, Stuart, and Jeffrey Mahan, *American Television Genres*

MacDonald, J. Fred, *Blacks and White TV: African-Americans in Television Since 1948,* 2nd ed.

MacDonald, J. Fred, *One Nation Under Television: The Rise and Decline of Network TV*

Mamer, Bruce, *Film Production Technique: Creating the Accomplished Image,* 2nd ed.

Meeske, Milan D., *Copywriting for the Electronic Media,* 3rd ed.

Viera, Dave, *Lighting for Film and Electronic Cinematography*

Zettl, Herbert, *Sight Sound Motion,* 3rd ed.

Zettl, Herbert, *Television Production Handbook,* 7th ed.

Zettl, Herbert, *Television Production Workbook,* 7th ed.

Zettl, Herbert, *Video Basics 3*

Zettl, Herbert, *Zettl's VideoLab 2.1,* CD-ROM

Audio IN Media

SIXTH EDITION

Stanley R. Alten

Syracuse University

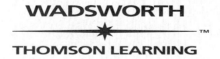

WADSWORTH

THOMSON LEARNING

Australia ■ Canada ■ Mexico ■ Singapore
Spain ■ United Kingdom ■ United States

Mass Communication Editor: Karen Austin
Executive Editor: Deirdre Cavanaugh
Publisher: Clark Baxter
Assistant Editor: Nicole George
Editorial Assistant: Mele Alusa
Executive Marketing Manager: Stacey Purviance
Marketing Assistant: Neena Chandra
Technology Project Manager: Jeanette Wiseman
Project Manager: Cathy Linberg
Print Buyer: Robert King
Permissions Editor: Stephanie Keough-Hedges
Production Service: Ideas to Images
Text Designer: Gary Palmatier
Photo Researcher: Roberta Broyer
Copyeditor: Elizabeth von Radics
Illustrator: Robaire Ream
Cover Designer: Gary Palmatier
Cover Images: © 2001 PhotoDisc, © Digital Vision
Cover Printer: Phoenix Color
Compositor: Ideas to Images
Printer: R. R. Donnelley & Sons, Crawfordsville

Printed in the United States of America

2   3   4   5   6   7   05   04   03   02

For permission to use material from this text, contact us by

    Web: http://www.thomsonrights.com

    Fax: 1-800-730-2215

    Phone: 1-800-730-2214

Library of Congress Cataloging-in-Publication Data
Alten, Stanley R.
  Audio in media / Stanley R. Alten. — 6th ed.
    p.   cm.
  Includes bibliographical references and index.
  ISBN 0-534-54804-0
  1. Sound—Recording and reproducing.   I. Title.

  TK7881.4 .A46   2001
  791.45'024—dc21   2001017975

Wadsworth/Thomson Learning
10 Davis Drive
Belmont, CA 94002-3098
USA

For more information about our products, contact us:
Thomson Learning Academic Resource Center
1-800-423-0563
http://www.wadsworth.com

International Headquarters
Thomson Learning
International Division
290 Harbor Drive, 2nd Floor
Stamford, CT 06902-7477
USA

UK/Europe/Middle East/South Africa
Thomson Learning
Berkshire House
168-173 High Holborn
London WC1V 7AA
United Kingdom

Asia
Thomson Learning
60 Albert Street, #15-01
Albert Complex
Singapore 189969

Canada
Nelson Thomson Learning
1120 Birchmount Road
Toronto, Ontario M1K 5G4
Canada

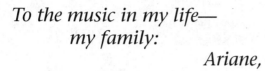

To the music in my life—
my family:
Ariane,

Renee,

and "the
sweetest sound,"

Claudette.

Brief Contents

Contents

CHAPTER **19**

Mixing and Rerecording   412

Preface

Audio in Media takes a generic, nontechnical approach to audio production. It subsumes audio in radio, television, film, music recording, and the Internet under the rubric *sound*. Content is designed for the beginner, yet the experienced practitioner will also find it beneficial. The organization facilitates using the book in total or in parts and reading chapters in or out of sequence, based on need and level of background, with no disruption in continuity.

New to this edition are expanded coverage of digital audio editing techniques; the digital versatile disc (DVD); mixing and rerecording; surround-sound production, including miking, mixing, and monitoring; a chapter about Internet production; and appendices on occupations in the field of audio and pertinent Web sites for reference.

Topics worthy of coverage such as Musical Instrument Digital Interface (MIDI) and audio in such multimedia areas as game sound and CD-ROM production are not included because they would require more space than even an expanded book would permit. Several fine publications about MIDI are available, and many of the production techniques relevant to audio in media also apply to audio in multimedia. Please consult the Wadsworth Communication Café Web site for helpful links to information on MIDI:

http://communication.wadsworth.com

STRUCTURE OF THE BOOK

The sixth edition of *Audio in Media* is divided into five parts, organized to reflect processes: Principles, Equipment, Sound Design, Production, and Postproduction.

In Part One, "Principles," the first chapter, "Ears," emphasizes the importance of healthy hearing and discriminating listening. Chapter 2, "Physics and Psychophysics of Sound," introduces the physical behavior of sound and its relationship to our psychophysical perception of sound stimuli. Chapter 3, "Acoustics and Psychoacoustics," develops the material in Chapter 2 as it applies to the objective behavior of received sound, its subjective effect on those who hear it, and how these factors affect studio and control room design and construction.

Part Two, "Equipment," begins with Chapter 4, "Microphones," which discusses their principles, types, characteristics, and accessories. Chapter 5, "Mixers and Consoles," covers basic signal flow and design of mixers, broadcast consoles, and production consoles—both analog and digital. Patching and console automation are also covered. Chapter 6, "Analog Recording," covers the characteristics of analog audiotape and recorders. Chapter 7, "Digital Recording," does the same with digital audiotape and recorders; the chapter also covers basic digital theory and disk-based recording/editing systems. Chapter 8, "Synchronization," covers this fundamental aspect of most production and postproduction. Chapter 9, "Signal Processing," discusses the general principles of signal processors and their effect on sound, including digital signal processing plug-ins for disk-based systems. Chapter 10, "Loudspeakers and Monitoring," deals with the relationship between loudspeaker selection and control room monitoring of stereo and surround sound.

Part Three, "Sound Design," consists of a single chapter of the same title. It sets a context for Parts Four and Five, "Production" and "Postproduction," by describing the nature and aesthetics of sound design; the basic structure of sonic communication; the cognitive and affective functions of speech, sound effects, and music; and the sound/picture relationship.

Part Four includes Chapters 12 through 15— "Studio Production: Live and Live-on-Tape," "Field Production: Live and Live-on-Tape," "Staged Productions," and "Music Production"—which cover microphone and production techniques as they apply to those various production environments. (For readers who want full coverage of studio-based music production, see *Audio in Media: The Recording Studio,* also available from Wadsworth.) The new Chapter 16, "Internet Production," covers sound quality on the Internet and producing sound in the "virtual studio."

Part Five begins with Chapter 17, "Dialogue, Sound Effects, and Music in Postproduction," which details the techniques used in automated dialogue replacement, sound-effect production, and producing music underscoring from music libraries. Chapter 18, "Editing," describes the techniques of electronic audio editing and digital hard-disk editing. It also addresses organizing the edit tracks; drive management; the aesthetic considerations that apply to editing speech, dialogue, sound effects, and music; and the uses of transitions. Chapter 19, "Mixing and Rerecording," covers the final stage in audio production, when sounds are combined and processed into stereo or surround sound. Coverage includes the specific requirements of radio, music recording, television, and film in mixing and rerecording.

ACKNOWLEDGMENTS

Audio in Media has been a staple in the literature of sound production since 1981. This is due in great part to the interest, advice, and guidance of teachers and practitioners in the field who have been so forthcoming with their expertise over the years. Whatever success the sixth edition enjoys is due in no small measure to their continued good advice and guidance.

To the following reviewers of the sixth edition, I offer my sincere gratitude for their insightful contributions: David C. Cox, Baylor University; Michael J. Dalby, Emerson College; Josh Hecht, San Francisco State University; Steven E. Metze, University of Texas, Austin; Douglas Mitchell, Middle Tennessee State University; and William D. Moylan, University of Massachusetts, Lowell.

In the Preface to the fifth edition, recognition was given to the reviewers of the previous editions. In this sixth edition, the grateful author would like to recognize those academic and industry professionals who have provided their assistance to this and previous editions. Some of the affiliations of these fine people are listed as they were at the time of their good counsel: Dick Alexander, rerecording mixer; Ray Angel, sound supervisor, BBC-TV; Steve Baldwin, head of sound effects, Walt Disney Productions; Bruce Bartlett, author; Rick Belt, Sennheiser Electronic Corporation; Peter Berkos, sound editor, Universal Pictures; Rick Berman, senior audio engineer, NBC-TV; Ben Burtt, sound designer; James Biddle, adjunct professor of television-radio-film, Syracuse University; the late John Bonner, former chief engineer, Goldwyn Sound Facility; Jerry Bruck, president, Posthorn Recordings; Benjamin Buchalter, Metric Halo; Jessica Casavant, ADR and Foley recordist, McClear Pathe; Arul Chib, Internet and multimedia consultant; Bob Costas, NBC-TV Sports; Carl Countryman, Countryman Associates; Peter D'Antonio, president, RPG Diffusor Systems; Lee Dichter, rerecording mixer, Sound One; Martin Dombey, district manager for commercial audio, Yamaha Corporation of America; Larry Elin, professor of multimedia and multimedia producer,

Syracuse University; Michael Epstein, professor of communications law, Syracuse University; Ron Estes, audio engineer and mixer; David Faulkner, vice president of broadcasting, High Definition Audio; Akira Fukada, NHK Broadcast Center; Rob Getty, dialogue editor; David Gibson, director, California Recording Institute; Luke Giles, Sound-Field; Doc Goldstein, chief engineer, Universal Pictures; Larry Gordon, assistant head of television sound, BBC-TV; Ed Greene, Greene, Crowe Productions; Joe Grimaldi, rerecording mixer, McClear Pathe; Bill Hatch, postproduction consultant, Applied Technical Systems; Mike Hertlein, dialogue editor; Tom Holden, radio systems design engineer, CBC; Tomlinson Holman, president of THM Corporation and professor of cinema-television, University of Southern California; Robert L. Hoyt, former head rerecording mixer, Universal Pictures; Gordon Hunt, voicing director, Hanna-Barbera; Dilys Jones, director of Communications House Ear Institute; Joseph Kelly, former president of Glen Glenn Sound; Skip Lievsay, sound editor; Jonathan Lory, postproduction mixer, ABC-TV; Doug Magyari, chief engineer, High Definition Audio; Dan Metivier, Metric Halo; Scott Millan, rerecording mixer; William Miller, engineering vice-president, ABC-TV; Dan Milner, producer, StudioWest; Chuck Morris, chief engineer, KIRO, Inc.; Walter Murch, sound designer; William Murphy, director of broadcast promotion, WTIC-TV; Shawn Murphy, scoring producer and rerecording mixer; Matt Nelson, Metric Halo; Chris Newman, production mixer; Don Peebles, vice-president, broadcast and postproduction, Solid State Logic; Jim Perry, chief engineer, WTIC-TV; Skip Pizzi, multimedia consultant and editor, *BE Radio;* Richard Portman, rerecording mixer and professor, Florida State University; Stuart Provine, sound designer and postproduction mixer; Tom Ray, chief engineer, WTIC AM and FM; Ron Remschel, national sales and marketing manager, Sony Education Systems; Donald Rogers, former director of sound, Warner Hollywood Studios; Dave Ryan, sportscaster, ESPN; Gary Rydstrom, sound designer; Manny Salcedo, sound transfer manager, Paramount; Mark Schnell, audio engineer, Syracuse University; Larry Schneider, audio postproducer, CBS-TV; Howard Schwartz, president, Howard Schwartz Recording; Bob Seiderman, principal mixer, Fox Sports; Frank Serafine, composer and sound designer, Serafine Productions; Mike Shane, Wheatstone Corporation; John Sherrard, audio engineer, ABC-TV; Tom Shipton, studio manager, Glenn Gould Theater, CBC; Wylie Stateman, co-founder, Soundelux; John Storyk, Walters-Storyk Design Group; Richard Stumpf, vice-president of sound, Universal Pictures; John Sullivan, senior audio engineer, NBC-TV; Bruce Swedien, music producer/engineer; John Terrelle, audio producer, Hothead Productions; Anthony Vadala, freelance mixer for network sports; Bill Varney, director of sound, Universal Pictures; Jack Wadsworth, music editor, Walt Disney Productions; W. O. Watson, former director of sound, Universal Pictures; Damon Whittemore, audio producer, Awakening Productions; and Herbert Zettl, professor of broadcast communication arts, San Francisco State University.

Thanks to Karen Austin, Wadsworth communication editor, for being a pleasure to work with and for her understanding.

A special salute to Gary Palmatier and his creative crew at Ideas to Images, who brought the design of the sixth edition to life and demonstrated that producing a book can be an art form.

Grateful thanks also to Elizabeth von Radics for her perception, attention to detail, and polished editing.

To David Rubin, dean of the Newhouse School of Public Communications, Syracuse University, my continued gratitude for his continuing support.

Stanley R. Alten

Credits

Acoustic Sciences Corporation: 3-22

ADC Telecommunications, Inc.: 5-15

AKG: 4-13, 4-33b, 4-34, 4-38a, 4-46b, 4-46c, 4-61d, 4-61e

Alpha Audio: 3-13

Aphex Systems: 9-8

Arrakis Systems, Inc.: 5-20

Atlas Sound: 4-52, 4-54

Audio Engineering Associates: 4-16

Audio Services Corporation: 14-8

Audio-Technica: 4-32

beyerdynamic: 4-3b, 4-14, 4-33a, 4-39

James Biddle: 12-9, 18-1

Broadcast Engineering Magazine: 10-9, © Intertec Publishing Corporation. All rights reserved.

Comrex: 13-5

Cooper Sound Systems: 5-2

Countryman Associates: 4-29, 15-28

Crown International, Inc.: 4-36, 4-38

dbx: 9-3

digidesign: 7-12, 9-21, 18-2, 18-24

Denecke, Inc.: 8-3

Digital Audio Labs: 18-4

Dorrough Electronics: 5-8

Dan Dugan Sound Design: 13-20

Electro-Voice, Inc.: 4-7, 4-8, 4-49 (center left, center right), 4-58b

Ron Estes: 15-46

Esto Photographic: 12-8

Etymotic Research: 1-8

Euphonix: 6-16

Eventide: 9-20a

J. L. Fisher: 4-55

Focusrite: 5-4

Fostex: 6-11

Garner Industries: 6-9b

Bob Ghent, "Healthy Hearing," *Mix,* March 1994, p. 153: 1-1

David Gibson, *The Art of Mixing.* Emeryville, Calif.: MixBooks, 1997: 19-3 to 19-10

Gotham Audio Corporation: 9-10

Lynne Gross and Larry Ward, *Electronic Moviemaking,* 4th ed. Belmont, Calif.: Wadsworth Publishing, 2000: 11-1

Joseph E. Hawkins, Kresge Hearing Research Institute, University of Michigan, and National Hearing Conservation Association: 1-3

Michael Hertlein: 18-12 to 18-21

HHB Communications, Ltd.: 7-4, 7-10

High Definition Audio: 4-19

Holophone® H-17 Channel Surround Sound Microphone System: 4-23

Ikegami: 13-7

David Immer, "Phone It In," *Mix,* February 1994, p. 88: 7-13

International Tapetronics Corporation: 12-14

JK Audio: 13-3, 13-9

Rattling off equipment models and types isn't that impressive or revealing. What's more important is knowing what to do with them.

—*Anonymous*

You need to be comfortable with the technology so you can ignore it. Because if you're thinking about SCSI drives and file management, then you're not thinking about the story and the feel of the sounds.

—*Roger Pardee, Field Recordist*

Much of what you think you're seeing in a film or video, you're actually hearing.

—*Anonymous*

Because we lived in a world of sounds and tones before we could even see light, our emotions are unconsciously linked to the sounds that surround us every day. Choosing the right sound for the right emotion is truly an art.

—*Claude Letessier, Sound Designer*

One

Principles

1

"Ears"

What is sound? A physicist will tell you that sound is both a disturbance of molecules caused by vibrations transmitted through an elastic medium (such as air) and the interaction of those vibrations with an environment. That definition does not mean much to the psychologist, however, who thinks of sound as a human response.

To put the question another way: If a tree falls in a forest and there is no one to hear it, does the falling tree make a sound? The physicist would say yes, because a falling tree causes vibrations, and sound is vibration. The psychologist would probably say no, because without a perceived sensation there can be no human response; hence, there is no sound. In practical terms both the physicist and the psychologist are correct. Yet, interesting as this argument may be, it is unproductive.

What is of greater significance about sound is its effect on our aural perception, a subject often weighted as secondary in importance to our visual perception. Consider: It is sound that brings the world into a person; the ear points inward. What we see takes a person into the world; the eye points outward.

Sight and sound are not alternatives, however. The senses function as a democracy, a concept that has been lost because of the dominance of the eye. Each one serves its own "constituency" and is uniquely suited to its role in the sensorial realm. The senses are also interdependent. To overlook the function of one is to miss their overall impact on a human being's relationship to, and perception of, the physical world, particularly when it comes to the contributions of audio in media.

We continue to ask, "Do you *see* what I mean?" when we converse. We admire people for their fore*sight,* in*sight,* and *vision.* Because we, of course, also possess these attributes, it is with such people that we *see eye-to-eye* and en*vision* doing so for the fore*see*able future. On the other hand, *hear*say is something not to be believed; playing a song "by *ear*" has a pejorative connotation; children should be *seen* and not *heard;* and the term *phony* was used in the early days of the telephone, when conversants could not see one another's face to determine if what they were hearing was genuine. And if "seeing is believing," what does that imply about "hearing"?

We refer to film and television as visual media. We speak of *seeing* a film and *watching* TV, suggesting that sound is subordinate to picture. So it follows, although mistakenly, that in its supporting role sound has less import and impact than picture. Even radio and music recordings, which are clearly aural media, often accompany other engrossments. They do not have to be watched, ergo they do not require the same level of attention as visual media. Worse, radio and recordings are frequently used as background to create atmosphere or for "company."

Sound is a force: emotional, perceptual, physical. It can excite feeling, convey meaning, and, if it is loud enough, resonate the body. The late renowned film director Akira Kurosawa has said, "The most exciting moment is the moment when I add the sound . . . [Then] I tremble."

Sound is omnidirectional; it is everywhere. The human eye can focus on only one view at a time. When the eye shifts, the original view is displaced. Sound can be layered—one sound can be added to another without displacement. Sound is attention demanding. Comprehending and assimilating aural information requires active listening. Sonic communication is a dynamic activity.

What also enhances the power of sound, paradoxically, is its visual component. As one sage observed, "He who has ears to hear sees!" For decades radio drama created pictures in the "theater of the mind." Today sound adds visual dimension to radio news and documentary. Songs stir images (with no help needed from music videos). Sound in film and television, even from off-screen, often excites an image. A shot can show a cowboy sauntering down the boardwalk on a street in the Wild West, but the sounds of a blacksmith's hammering, a saloon's player-piano, a buckboard, and horses' hooves put a town around him in the mind's eye.

Sound provides all sorts of *cognitive information*—information related to mental processes of knowledge, reasoning, memory, judgment, and perception—and *affective information*—information related to emotion, feeling, and mood. Sound is elemental.

This is all moot, however, especially for the audio professional, without "ears." In the parlance of audio, this means having healthy hearing and the ability to listen perceptively.

THE HEALTHY EAR

The human ear is divided into three parts: the **outer ear**, the **middle ear**, and the **inner ear** (see Figure 1-1). Sound waves first reach and are collected by the *pinna* (or *auricle*), the visible part of the outer ear. The sound waves are then focused through the *ear canal,* or *meatus,* to the *eardrum (tympanum)* at the beginning of the middle ear.

The tympanic membrane is attached to another membrane, called the *oval window,* by three small bones—the *malleus, incus,* and *stapes*—called *ossicles* and shaped like a hammer, anvil, and stirrup. The ossicles act as a mechanical lever, changing the small pressure of the sound wave on the eardrum into a much greater pressure. The combined action of the ossicles and the area of the tympanum allow the middle ear to help protect the inner ear from pressure changes (loud sounds) that are too great. It takes about one-tenth of a second to react, however, and therefore provides little protection from sudden loud sounds.

The inner ear contains the *semicircular canals,* which are necessary for balance, and a snail-shaped structure called the *cochlea.* The cochlea is

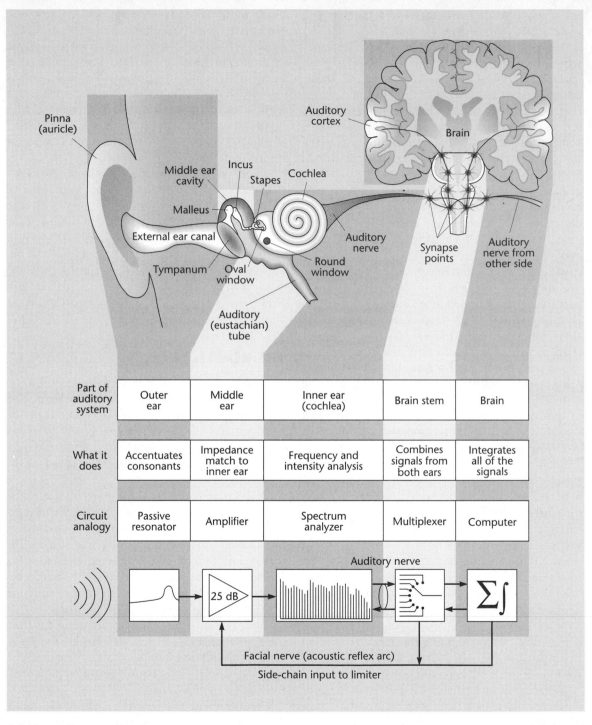

The following labels appear in the illustration:

Pinna (auricle)

Middle ear cavity
Incus
Stapes
Cochlea
Malleus
External ear canal
Tympanum
Oval window
Round window
Auditory nerve
Auditory (eustachian) tube

Auditory cortex
Brain
Synapse points
Auditory nerve from other side

Part of auditory system	Outer ear	Middle ear	Inner ear (cochlea)	Brain stem	Brain
What it does	Accentuates consonants	Impedance match to inner ear	Frequency and intensity analysis	Combines signals from both ears	Integrates all of the signals
Circuit analogy	Passive resonator	Amplifier	Spectrum analyzer	Multiplexer	Computer

25 dB

Auditory nerve

∑∫

Facial nerve (acoustic reflex arc)

Side-chain input to limiter

1-1 The auditory system

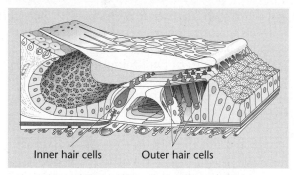

1-2 Artistic representation of the organ of Corti, showing the symmetrical layout of the outer and inner sensory hair cells

Inner hair cells   Outer hair cells

filled with fluid whose total capacity is a fraction of a drop. It is here that sound becomes electricity in the human head. Running through the center of the cochlea is the *basilar membrane,* resting upon which are sensory hair cells attached to nerve fibers composing the *organ of Corti,* the "seat of hearing." These fibers feed the auditory nerve, where the electrical impulses are passed on to the brain. It is estimated that there may be as many as 16,000 sensory hair cells at birth. In the upper portion of each cell is a bundle of microscopic hairlike projections called *stereocilia,* or *cilia* for

short, which quiver at the approach of sound and begin the process of transforming mechanical vibrations into electrical and chemical signals, which are then sent to the brain. In a symmetrical layout, these sensory hair cells are referred to as "outer" and "inner" sensory hair cells (see 1-2). Approximately 12,000 outer hair cells amplify auditory signals and discriminate frequency. About 140 cilia jut from each cell. The 4,000 inner hair cells are connected to the auditory nerve fibers leading to the brain. About 40 cilia are attached to each inner cell. Continued exposure to high *sound-pressure levels (SPLs)* can damage the sensory hair cells, and, because they are not naturally repaired or replaced, hearing loss results. The greater the number of damaged hair cells, the greater the loss of hearing (see 1-3).

HEARING LOSS

We are a nation of the hard-of-hearing, because of the everyday, ever louder noise around us—noise from traffic, airplanes, lawnmowers, sirens, vacuum cleaners, hair dryers, blenders, can openers, snow mobiles, even children's toys. In modern homes with wood floors, cathedral ceilings, brick or stucco walls, and many windows, sound is reflected and

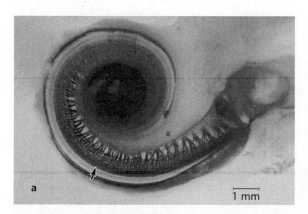
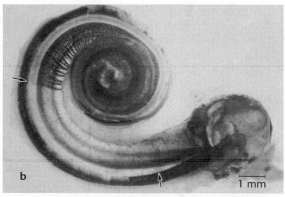

1-3 Normal and damaged human cochlea (a) The cochlea in the normal ear shows the densely stained nerve fibers. (b) The cochlea of the damaged ear shows the degenerated sensory and supporting cells and nerve fibers. The lower arrow points to the basal tip of the cochlea, where some sensory hair cells and nerve fibers are still preserved. What this damaged cochlea means in hearing loss is little or no sensitivity to frequencies above 2 kHz with a maximum loss of 80 dB at 4 kHz. The preserved hair cells and nerve fibers at the base of the cochlea account for improved hearing sensitivity at 8 kHz.

therefore intensified because there is little to absorb it. It is becoming increasingly rare to find a quiet neighborhood. Parks and campgrounds are inundated with the annoying sounds of RVs, boisterous families, and blaring boom boxes. At beaches the lap and wash of gentle surf has been drowned out by the roar of jet skis. There are Walkmans, rock concerts, and parties and bars where sound levels are so loud it is necessary to shout to be heard, increasing the din even more. In one Manhattan bistro, it is so loud that orders from customers have to be relayed to a person standing on the bar.

More people suffer from hearing loss than from heart disease, cancer, multiple sclerosis, and kidney disease combined. It afflicts one out of every nine people in the United States and one out of every five teenagers. Because it is usually not life threatening, hearing loss is possibly America's most overlooked physical ailment. For the audio professional, however, it is an ailment that is career threatening.

In industrialized societies some hearing loss is a natural result of aging, but it is not an inevitable consequence. In societies less technologically advanced than ours, people in their eighties have normal hearing. Short of relocating to such a society, for now the only defense against hearing loss is prevention.

Usually, when hearing loss occurs, it does so gradually, typically without warning signs, and it occurs over a lifetime. When there are warning signs, they are usually due to overstimulation from continuous, prolonged exposure to loud sound. You can tell there has been damage when there is ear discomfort after exposure; it is difficult to hear in noise; it is difficult to understand a child's speech or an adult's speech at more than a few feet away; music loses it color; quiet sounds are muffled or inaudible; it is necessary to keep raising the volume on the radio or TV; and your response to a question is usually, "What?"

Hearing damage caused by exposure to loud sound varies with the exposure time and the individual. Prolonged exposure to loud sound decreases the ear's sensitivity. Decreased sensitivity creates the false perception that sound is not as loud as it actually is. This usually necessitates an increase in levels to compensate for the hearing loss, thus making a bad situation worse.

After exposure to loud sound for a few hours, you may have experienced the sensation that your ears are stuffed with cotton. This is known as *temporary threshold shift (TTS)*—a reversible desensitization in hearing that disappears in anywhere from a few hours to several days; TTS is also called *auditory fatigue*. With TTS the ears have, in effect, shut down to protect themselves against very loud sounds.

Prolonged exposure to loud sounds can bring on **tinnitus**, a ringing, whistling, or buzzing in the ears, even though no loud sounds are present. Tinnitus is a danger signal that the ears may already have suffered—or soon will—*permanent threshold shift* with continued exposure to loud sound.

One audiologist's good advice is: If it's loud, turn it down. If you can't turn it down, keep your distance (or wear earplugs). If your ears are ringing, answer them!*

How Loud Is Loud?

This raises the question: How loud is loud? Humans have the potential to hear an extremely wide range of loudnesses. The ratio between the quietest sounds—at the **threshold of hearing**—and the loudest sounds—at the **threshold of pain**—is 1 to 10,000,000 and greater. Figure 1-4 shows the relative loudness of various sounds, many common in our everyday lives. (For a full discussion of Figure 1-4, see Chapter 2.)

Safeguards Against Hearing Loss

As gradual deterioration of the auditory nerve endings occurs through the aging process, it usually results in a gradual loss of hearing first in the mid-high-frequency range, at around 3,000 to 6,000 **hertz (Hz)**, and then in the lower-pitched sounds. The ability to hear in the mid-high-frequency range is important to understanding speech, because

---

*Richie Moore, Ph.D., "Tips from the Doctor," *EQ*, February 1993, p. 44.

Apparent Loudness	Ratio to dB	dB-SPL	
		220	12' in front of cannon below muzzle
		200	
Deafening		180	Rocket engines
		160	Jet engine, close up
		150	Permanent damage to hearing
	10,000,000	140	Inside a bass drum / Airport runway
	3,162,000	130	Rock band—on stage; symphony orchestra, triple forte, 30' away
	1,000,000	120	Threshold of pain; loud vocals in front of mouth / Thunder
Very loud	316,200	110	Electric guitar amp at maximum volume, 6" away / Power tools
	100,000	100	Subway; loud vocals, 6" away
	31,620	90	Heavy truck traffic; baby crying; trombone, 16" away
	10,000	80	Acoustic guitar, 1' away
Loud	3,162	70	Busy street
	1,000	60	Average conversation
	316	50	Average office
Moderate	100	40	Subdued conversation
	32	30	Quiet office / Recording studio
Faint	10	20	Furnished living room
Very faint	3	10	Insect noises at night, open field *whisper*
	1	0	Threshold of hearing

1-4 Sound-pressure levels of various sound sources

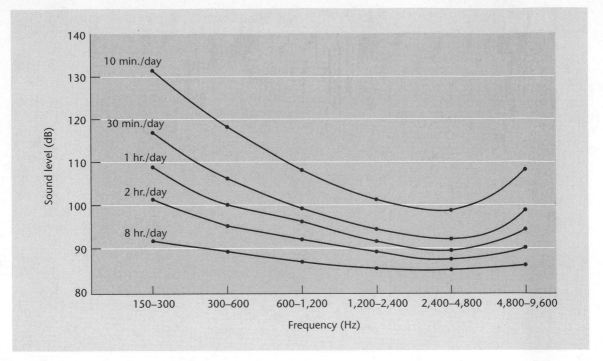

1-5 Damage risk criteria for a single-day exposure to various sound levels

consonants are mostly composed of high frequencies. Hearing loss in the lower-pitched sounds makes it difficult to understand vowels and lower-pitched voices. Prolonged exposure to loud sounds hastens that deterioration. To avoid premature hearing loss, the remedy is simple: Do not expose your ears to excessively loud sound levels for extended times (see Figure 1-5, Table 1-1, and Figures 1-6 and 1-7).

Hearing impairment is not the only detrimental consequence of loud sound levels. They also produce adverse physiological effects. Sounds transmitted to the brain follow two paths. One path carries sound to the auditory center, where it is perceived and interpreted. The other goes to the brain centers that affect the nervous system. Loud sound taking the latter path can increase heart rate and blood pressure, constrict small blood vessels in the hands and feet, contract muscles, release stress-related hormones from adrenal glands, disrupt certain stomach and intestinal functions,

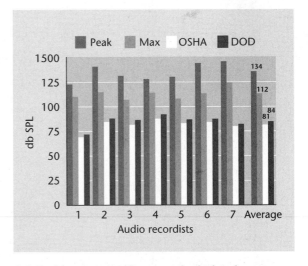

1-6 Peak, average maximum, and calculated average SPL exposures by OSHA and Department of Defense (DOD) standards. These results are in relation to the daily exposure to loudness of seven different audio recordists. It is estimated that recordists work an average of eight to 10 hours a day.

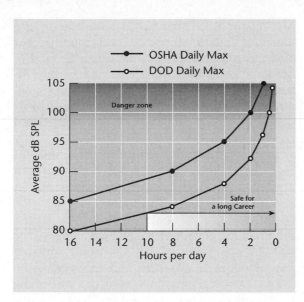

1-7 Allowable daily exposure of sound pressure levels plotted in relation to OSHA and DOD permissible exposure levels

and create dry mouth, dilated pupils, tension, anxiety, fatigue, and crankiness.

When you are in the presence of loud sound, including amplified music, wear earplugs designed to reduce loudness without seriously degrading frequency response. Some options among available earplugs are custom-fit earmolds, disposable foam plugs, reusable silicon insert plugs, and industrial headsets. The custom-fit earmold is best to use because, as the term suggests, it is made from a custom mold of your ear canal. It provides 15 to 20 **decibels (dB)*** of balanced sound-level reduction and attenuates all frequencies evenly. The disposable foam plug is intended for onetime use. It provides noise reduction from 12 dB to 20 dB, mainly in the high frequencies. The reusable silicon insert plug is a rubberized insert cushion that covers a tiny metal filtering diaphragm. It reduces sound levels by approximately 17 dB. The silicon insert plug is often used at construction sites and firing ranges. The industrial headset has a cushioned headpad and tight-fitting earseals. It provides maximum sound-level attenuation, often up to 30 dB, and is particularly effective at low frequencies. This is the headset commonly used by personnel around airport runways and in the cabs of heavy-construction equipment (see 1-8).

The human ear is a very sophisticated electromechanical device. As with any device, regular maintenance is wise, especially for the audio professional. Make at least two visits per year to a qualified ENT (ear, nose, and throat) specialist to have your ears inspected and cleaned. The human ear secretes wax to protect the eardrum and cochlea from loud sound-pressure levels. Let the

---

*The *decibel*, abbreviated *dB*, is a measure of relative power values and is discussed in Chapter 2.

Table 1-1 Hours of exposure to high sound levels permitted by the U.S. government and the British Occupational Hygiene Society

U.S. Government—Occupational Safety and Health Administration (OSHA)		British Occupational Hygiene Society	
Sound Level (dB-SPL)	*Daily Permissible Hours of Exposure*	*Sound Level (dB-SPL)*	*Daily Permissible Hours of Exposure*
90	8	90	8
92	6	91	6
95	4	93	4
97	3	94	3
100	2	96	2
105	1	99	1
110	½	102	½
115	¼	105	¼

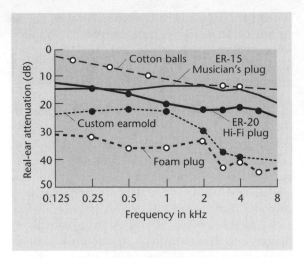

1-8 Attenuation effects of selected hearing protection devices. Notice that compared with a variety of commonly used hearing protectors, the Musician's and Hi-Fi plugs have relatively even attenuation across the frequency spectrum. (The ER-15 and ER-20 are products of Etymotic Research.™)

doctor clean out the wax. Do not use a cotton swab. You risk the chance of infection and jamming the wax against the eardrum, which obviously exacerbates the situation. If you must clean your ears between visits, ask the ENT doctor about the safest way to do it.

The implications of all this should be obvious, especially if you are working in audio. Not only is your hearing, in particular, and your physiological well-being, in general, at risk, but so is your livelihood.

THE EDUCATED EAR

For the audio professional, having healthy ears is one major requirement. Another is having *educated* ears—the ability to listen with careful discrimination to style, interpretation, nuance, and technical quality in evaluating the content, function, characteristics, and fidelity of a sound.

Most day-to-day aural stimuli we take for granted. We may pay attention to a particular song, to a siren, to an explosion, or to a victim's scream in a TV or film drama, but sound generally functions as little more than background to our comings and goings. To the person in audio, however, such a lack of awareness is a liability. An audio professional must be sensitive to all sound, pleasant and unpleasant, exciting and unexciting, significant and insignificant, well performed and poorly performed.

Innate sensitivity to sound varies, and not everyone has the same perceptual acuity. You can acquire certain skills, however, through training in audio and music courses. Ear-training tapes and CDs also help (see Bibliography). Study the natural sounds of the environment. Take advantage of the vast and rich resources from the audio worlds of film sound tracks, TV, radio, and music on digital discs. By not listening, sound remains part of the landscape—it does not become part of your consciousness.

Developing an ear involves discrimination—the ability to shut out all sounds but the one you are listening to, to hear one sound among many. This is known as "putting your ear to it."

It can be argued that many sounds offer so little aesthetic satisfaction that they are not worth listening to. Many sounds even annoy, such as a loud TV from an adjacent apartment, music in an elevator, the sonic assault from sound systems in stores as you shop, hedge cutters, sirens, and blaring horns. It is all enough to desensitize aural acuity and make it difficult to enjoy worthwhile sound. Hence, it seems reasonable to conclude that listening should be selective. Such a conclusion might be appropriate for most people, but it does not apply to the audio professional.

Listening

Training the ear takes time. It comes with years of perceptive listening. You begin by learning how to listen, paying attention to sound wherever and whenever it occurs: in conversation, in traffic, at sporting events, at a concert or movie, or when showering, getting dressed, dining, walking, watching television, or just lying in bed. Remember, exposure to sound goes on during every waking hour, and even during sleep.

You learn what to listen for by studying a sound both in context and by itself. That means the ability to listen analytically and critically. "Analytical listening is the evaluation of the content and function of the [sound] . . . Critical listening is the evaluation of the characteristics of the sound itself and the integrity of . . . [its] technical quality."*

Analytical Listening

In speech, words may denote meaning, but sound often defines it. On paper, the meaning of the phrase *Have a nice day* is clear. But the meaning changes when the stress on certain words changes or when the words are spoken with a lilt; in a monotone, whine, or drawl; or by an old man, young woman, or child. Sound in speech conveys such qualities as confidence, fear, anxiety, arrogance, humor, and concern. In an interview a person may appear confident, but if there are unnatural pauses between words or phrases, or if there is a parched quality to the speech, the person's sound will belie the appearance. In dialogue a charming, good-looking character conveys a sense of menace when his words are delivered in a harsh and guttural voice. A character whose voice rises at the end of sentences conveys a vulnerability, regardless of what is being said. *Analytical listening* is the evaluation of such sound, the interpretation of the nuances and connotations of the sound quality in addition to—or in spite of—the words being spoken.

Take the sound of a dog barking. A bark is generally harsh and abrupt. But barks vary widely in pitch, loudness, rhythm, and context. For example, low-pitched barks last longer than high-pitched barks, and some barks begin with a gurgling-type sound rather than with a sharp attack. Within a bark may be a whine, yelp, growl, howl,

---

*William Moylan, *The Art of Recording* (New York: Van Nostrand Reinhold, 1992), p. 53.

or boom. Also some barks have regular rhythms, whereas others shift beats and produce irregular tempos. Each of these sounds tells you something about the dog and the situation.

The sound a chick makes while hatching may seem obvious: gradual cracking of the eggshell and then peeping. But listening to a hatching reveals more: The chick peeps inside the egg before cracking it; the peeping is muffled. The shell begins cracking slowly with short, tentative splitting sounds that increase in force. With the increase in force and slightly longer cracking sounds, peeping increases in clarity, loudness, and rapidity. The final cracks of the shell sound more like crunches as the chick stumbles into the world. Once out of the shell, the peeping is unmuffled, steady, and strong, but not quite so loud as it was just before emergence.

In television, sound varies from program to program, even of the same genre. In sitcoms laughter may come from a live audience or from a recorded laugh track. It may be more robust, or less, with a preponderance of elderly female or young male voices. In football there are different approaches to mixing the announcers' sounds with crowd sounds. Some audio operators like to keep the level of crowd sounds and the announcers' voices nearly the same to maintain excitement. Others prefer to keep the level of crowd noise relatively low so that, when the action justifies it, the level can be increased to accent the excitement.

Music presents the greatest challenge in listening. Its sonic combinations are infinite, and its aesthetic value fulfills basic human needs. Musical taste is intensely personal; two people listening to the same music may respond in two different ways, both valid.

Take two recordings of, say, Beethoven's Fifth Symphony. Keep constant as many factors as possible, such as the quality of the digital discs, the recording format (stereo, surround sound, digital, analog), the audio system, and the room. You may be surprised at the differences in sound and interpretation. You may prefer the sound in one recording and the interpretation in another. That does not mean that one recording is necessarily better; it means that, based on your perceptions, one is preferable to another for certain reasons. Someone else may disagree.

Critical Listening

In listening to those two recordings of Beethoven's Fifth Symphony, you may prefer the sound of one recording to the other because of its technical quality: the clarity of detail, the inflection of a particular range of frequencies, the balance of orchestral instruments, or the spatial imaging. Or in listening to a song, you may decide that it is darker sounding than it should be because the bass drum is muddying the mix or there is a buildup of too many frequencies in the low midrange or there is an absence of color in the treble range.

Critical listening is the evaluation of the characteristics of the sound itself: when the vocalist enters a bit early or late to counterpoint the lyric against the accompaniment; when a sound effect has too much wheeze and not enough whine; music underscoring that fades up at the wrong time, masking dialogue; the polyrhythms that play off one another to enhance the rhythmic excitement of an action scene; the annoying surges in crowd sound during pauses in a sportscaster's game call, because the ratio and/or threshold settings on a compressor are set too severely; the sonic differences between an acoustic and an electric bass, or acoustic drums and a drum machine; the unique sound of a Zildjian™ cymbal or a Stratocaster™ electric guitar; a concert grand piano with a percussive tonality or a tonality that "sings"; the musicians' technical proficiency; the acoustics that enrich sound or dull it; stylistic differences among artists; the sonic difference between analog and digital sound or between 16-bit and 24-bit mastered CDs.

Critical ears hear differences in sound between microphones, changes in tone color from different microphone placements, coloration of a microphone preamplifier, subtle phase cancellation, and the right frequency or frequency range to fix an equalization problem.

This is not to overwhelm you with detail or suggest that serious listening is entirely clinical. Feeling the sound and sensing what works are also critical to active analysis, as is being aware of the relationship between your taste and mood and your response.

Reading reviews also provides insight into why critics think a work does or does not succeed. In fact, it is equally instructive to know why a recording or film sound track does not work as it is to know why it does, perhaps even more so.

Develop a sound vocabulary. Sound is nonverbal; it is difficult to describe. Coining words that are descriptive of the effect you are trying to achieve not only hones your own perceptions, but also provides others on the sound team with an indication of what you are going for. There are hundreds of such terms used for sound effects, such as *twung, squidge, whibble, wubba, boink, kabong, zuzz,* and so on. In music there are terms such as *honky, mellow, warm, bright, hollow, and zitsy* (also see Chapter 19). Such terms are inexact, of course, and will need some objective association to make them clear to others.

Because response to sound is personal, standards and guidelines are difficult to establish, and so listening is the key to improving aural discrimination. The ear is capable of constant improvement in its ability to analyze sound. As your aural sensitivity improves, so will your level of auditory achievement.

► Physically, sound is both a disturbance of molecules caused by vibrations transmitted through an elastic medium and the interaction of these vibrations with an environment.

► Psychologically, sound is a perceived sensation.

► With aural perception, as opposed to visual perception, sound brings the world into a person, whereas what we see takes a person into the world.

► Sound is a force: emotional, perceptual, and physical.

► Sound is omnidirectional; it is everywhere. The human eye can focus on only one view at a time.

► Sound, paradoxically, has a visual component; it can create pictures in the "theater of the mind."

► In the parlance of audio, having "ears" means having healthy hearing and the ability to listen perceptively.

► The human ear is divided into three parts: the outer ear, the middle ear, and the inner ear.

► In the basilar membrane of the inner ear are bundles of microscopic hairlike projections called cilia attached to each sensory hair cell. They quiver at the approach of sound and begin the process of transforming mechanical vibrations into electrical and chemical signals, which are then sent to the brain.

► Temporary threshold shift (TTS), or auditory fatigue, is a reversible desensitization in hearing caused by exposure to loud sound over a few hours.

► Prolonged exposure to loud sounds can bring on tinnitus, a ringing, whistling, or buzzing in the ears.

► Exposure to loud sound for extended periods of time can cause permanent threshold shift—a deterioration of the auditory nerve endings in the inner ear. In the presence of loud sound, use an ear filter designed to reduce loudness.

► Humans have the potential to hear an extremely wide range of loudnesses between the threshold of hearing and the threshold of pain.

► Having educated ears means the ability to listen with careful discrimination to style, interpretation, nuance, and technical quality in evaluating the content, function, character-istics, and fidelity of sound.

► Learning how to listen begins with paying attention to sound wherever and whenever it occurs.

► Analytical listening is the evaluation of the content and function of sound.

► Critical listening is the evaluation of the characteristics of the sound itself.

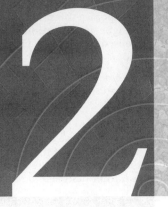

Physics and Psychophysics of Sound

The term *sound* can denote (1) the physical phenomenon of vibrations that set into motion longitudinal waves of compression and rarefaction propagated through molecular structures such as gas, liquids, and solids; (2) the physiological phenomenon that stimulates the sense of hearing; or (3) the psychophysical perception of sound stimuli. Chapter 1 discussed the sense of hearing; this chapter addresses the physical and psychophysical aspects of sound.

THE SOUND WAVE

Sound begins when an object vibrates and sets into motion molecules in the air closest to it. These molecules pass on their energy to adjacent molecules, starting a reaction—a *sound wave*—which is much like the waves that result when a stone is dropped into a pool. The transfer of momentum from one displaced molecule to the next propagates the original vibrations longitudinally from the vibrating object to the hearer. What makes this reaction possible is air or, more precisely, a molecular medium with the property of elasticity. *Elasticity* is the phenomenon in which a displaced molecule tends to pull back to its original position after its initial momentum has caused it to displace nearby molecules.

As a vibrating object moves outward, it compresses molecules closer together, increasing pressure. *Compression* continues away from the object as the momentum of the disturbed molecules displaces adjacent molecules and so produces a crest in the sound wave. When a vibrating object moves inward, it pulls the molecules farther apart and thins them, creating a **rarefaction**. This rarefaction also travels away from the object in a manner similar to compression, except that it decreases pressure, thereby producing a trough in the sound wave (see Figure 2-1). As the sound wave moves away from the vibrating object, the individual molecules do not advance with the wave; they vibrate at what is termed their *average resting place* until their motion stills or they are set in motion

by another vibration. Inherent in each wave motion are the components that make up a sound wave: frequency, amplitude, velocity, wavelength, and phase (see 2-1, 2-2, and 2-7).

FREQUENCY AND PITCH

When a vibration passes through one complete up-and-down motion, from compression through rarefaction, it has completed one cycle. The number of cycles that a vibration completes in one second is expressed as its **frequency**. If a vibration completes 50 **cycles per second (cps)**, its frequency is

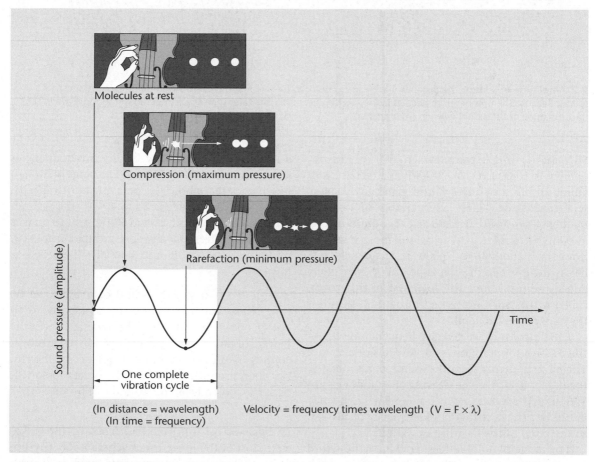

2-1 Components of a sound wave. The vibrating object causes compression in sound waves when it moves outward (causing molecules to bump into each other). The vibrating object causes rarefaction when it moves inward (pulling the molecules away from each other).

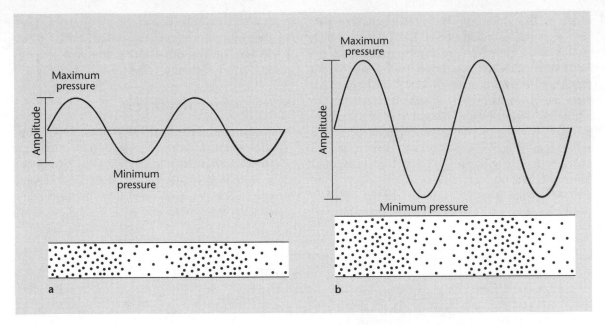

2-2 Amplitude of sound. The number of molecules displaced by a vibration creates the amplitude, or loudness, of a sound. Because the number of molecules in the sound wave in (b) is greater than the number in the sound wave in (a), the amplitude of the sound wave in (b) is greater.

50 hertz (Hz); if it completes 10,000 cps, its frequency is 10,000 Hz, or 10 kilohertz (kHz). Every vibration has a frequency, and generally humans with excellent "ears" are capable of hearing frequencies from 20 to 20,000 Hz. The limits of low- and high-frequency hearing for most humans, however, is about 35 to 16,000 Hz. Frequencies just below the *low end* of this range, called *infrasonic,* and those just above the *high end* of this range, called *ultrasonic,* are sensed more than heard, if they are perceived at all.

Psychologically, we perceive frequency as *pitch—* the relative tonal highness or lowness of a sound. The more times per second a sound source vibrates, the higher its pitch. The G string of a guitar vibrates 196 times per second, so its fundamental frequency is 196 Hz. The A string has a frequency of 110 Hz, so the pitch of the G string is higher.

The range of audible frequencies, or the *sound frequency spectrum,* is divided into sections, each having a unique and vital quality. The usual divisions in Western music are called octaves. An *octave* is the interval between any two frequencies that have a tonal ratio of 2 to 1. The range of human hearing covers about 10 octaves. Starting with 20 Hz, the first octave is 20 to 40 Hz; the second, 40 to 80 Hz; the third, 80 to 160 Hz; and so on (see inside back cover). Octaves are grouped into bass, midrange, and treble and further subdivided as follows.

■ *Low bass*—first and second octaves (20 to 80 Hz). These are the frequencies associated with power, boom, and fullness. The lowest notes of the piano, organ, tuba, and bass are in this range. Sounds in these octaves need not occur often to maintain a sense of fullness. If they occur too often, or at too loud a level, the sound can become thick or muddy.

■ *Upper bass*—third and fourth octaves (80 to 320 Hz). Most of the lower tones generated by rhythm and other support instruments such as drums, piano, bass, cello, and trombone are in this range. They establish a balance in musical structure. Too many frequencies from this range make it sound boomy; too few make it thin. When properly proportioned, pitches in the second, third, and fourth octaves are very satisfying to the ear, because we perceive them as giving sound an anchor, that is, fullness or bottom. Frequencies in the upper bass range serve aural structure the way the horizontal line serves visual structure—by providing a foundation.

■ **Midrange**—fifth, sixth, and seventh octaves (320 to 2,560 Hz). The midrange gives sound its intensity. It contains the fundamental and the rich lower harmonics and overtones of most sound sources.* The midrange does not necessarily generate pleasant sounds, however. Too much emphasis of sixth-octave frequencies is heard as a hornlike quality; too much emphasis of seventh-octave frequencies is heard as a tinny quality. Extended listening to midrange sounds can be annoying and fatiguing.

■ **Upper midrange**—eighth octave (2,560 to 5,120 Hz). We are most sensitive to frequencies in the eighth octave, a rather curious range. The lower part of the eighth octave (2,560 to 3,500 Hz) contains frequencies that, if properly emphasized, improve the intelligibility of speech and lyrics. These frequencies are roughly 3,000 to 3,500 Hz. If these frequencies are unduly emphasized, however, sound becomes abrasive and unpleasant; and vocals, in particular, become harsh and lispy,

---

*A **fundamental**, also called the *first harmonic* or *primary frequency,* is the lowest, or basic, pitch of a musical instrument. Its **harmonics** are exact multiples of the fundamental; and its **overtones**, also known as **inharmonic overtones**, are pitches that are not exact multiples of the fundamental. If a trumpet sounds a low G, the fundamental is 392 Hz, its harmonics are 784 Hz, 1,568 Hz, 3,136 Hz, and so on, and its overtones are the frequencies in between (see section on timbre later in this chapter). Sometimes in usage, harmonics also assume overtones. Another term for harmonics and overtones is *partials*. A harmonics-related term that is sometimes confused with inharmonic is **enharmonic**. Enharmonic notes are two different notes that sound the same. For example, C♯ and D♭, D♯ and E♭, and G♯ and A♭.

making some consonants difficult to understand. The upper part of the eighth octave (above 3,500 Hz), on the other hand, contains rich and satisfying pitches that give sound definition, clarity, and realism. Listeners perceive a sound source frequency in this range (and also in the lower part of the ninth octave, up to about 6,000 Hz) as being nearby, and for this reason it is also known as the *presence range.* Increasing loudness at 5,000 Hz, the heart of the presence range, gives the impression that there has been an overall increase in loudness throughout the midrange. Reducing loudness at 5,000 Hz makes a sound seem transparent and farther away.

■ **Treble**—ninth and tenth octaves (5,120 to 20,000 Hz). Although the ninth and tenth octaves generate only 2 percent of the total power output of the sound frequency spectrum, and most human hearing does not extend much beyond 16,000 Hz, they give sound the vital, lifelike qualities of brilliance and sparkle, particularly in the upper-ninth and lower-tenth octaves. Too much emphasis above 6,000 Hz makes sound hissy and brings out electronic noise. Too little emphasis above 6,000 Hz dulls sound.

AMPLITUDE AND LOUDNESS

We have noted that vibrations in objects stimulate molecules to move in pressure waves at certain rates of alternation (compression/rarefaction) and that rate determines frequency. Vibrations not only affect the molecules' rate of up-and-down movement but also determine the number of displaced molecules that are set in motion from equilibrium to a wave's maximum height *(crest)* and depth *(trough).* This number depends on the intensity of a vibration; the more intense it is, the more molecules are displaced. The greater the number of molecules displaced, the greater the height and depth of the sound wave. The number of molecules in motion, and therefore the size of a sound wave, is called **amplitude** (see 2-2). Our subjective impression of amplitude is a sound's loudness or softness. Amplitude is measured in decibels.

The Decibel

The *decibel (dB)* is a dimensionless unit used to compare the ratio of two quantities usually in relation to acoustic energy, such as sound pressure, and electric energy, such as power and voltage. In mathematical terms it is 10 times the logarithm to the base 10 of the ratio between the powers of two signals: $dB = 10 \log (P_1 / P_0)$. P_0 is usually a reference power value with which another power value, P_1, is compared. It is abbreviated *dB* because it stands for one-tenth *(deci)* of a *bel* (from Alexander Graham Bell). The bel was the amount a signal dropped in level over a 1-mile distance of telephone wire. Because the amount of level loss was too large to work with as a single unit of measurement, it was divided into tenths for more-practical application.

Sound-Pressure Level

Acoustic sound pressure is measured in terms of *sound-pressure level (dB-SPL)*, because there are periodic variations in atmospheric pressure in a sound wave. Humans have the potential to hear an extremely wide range of these periodic variations, from 0 dB-SPL, the threshold of hearing, to 120 dB-SPL, the threshold of pain, and beyond (see 1-4). The range of the difference in decibels between the loudest and quietest sound a vibrating object makes is called *dynamic range*. Because this range is so wide, a logarithmic scale is used to compress loudness measurement into more-manageable figures. (On a linear scale, a unit of 1 adds an increment of 1. On a logarithmic scale, a unit of 1 multiplies by a factor of 10.)

Humans have the capability to hear loudness at a ratio of 1 to 10,000,000 and greater. Sound at 60 dB-SPL is 1,000 times louder than sound at 0 dB-SPL; at 80 dB-SPL it is 10 times louder than at 60 dB-SPL. If the amplitude of two similar sounds is 100 dB-SPL each, their amplitude, when added, would be 103 dB-SPL. Nevertheless, most people do not perceive a sound level as doubled until it has increased anywhere from 3 to 10 dB, depending on their aural acuity.

There are other acoustic measurements of human hearing based on the interactive relationship between frequency and amplitude. These measurements are discussed in "Frequency and Loudness," later in this chapter.

Sound in Electrical Form

For sound (acoustic) energy to be processed through electrical equipment, it must be *transduced,* or converted, into electric energy. Electric energy is measured in decibels in relation to power—dBm—and voltage—dBu or dBv, and dBV. It is difficult to discuss these measurements here fully, because they involve mathematical formulas and technical terminology that are beyond the scope of this book (see Table 2-1).

In measuring an electric circuit, a foremost concern is *impedance*—that property of a circuit, or an element, that restricts the flow of *alternating current (AC)*. Impedance is measured in *ohms (Ω),* a unit of resistance to current flow. The lower the impedance in a circuit, the better.

Table 2-1 Power and voltage measurements in dB

dBm is the original electrical measurement of power. It is referenced to 1 milliwatt (mW) as dissipated across a 600-ohm (Ω) load. 600 ohms is the standard circuit resistance of a telephone line. (A *resistor* is a device that opposes the flow of current.) Any voltage that results in 1 milliwatt is 0 dBm, which is the same as 0.775 volt across a 600-ohm impedance. +30 dBm is 1 watt; +50 dBm is 100 watts.

dBu, or *dBv,* is a unit of measurement for expressing the relationship of decibels to voltage—0.775 volt to be exact.* The *u* stands for "unterminated." The figure comes from 0 dBm, which equals 0.775 volt. *dBu* is a more flexible reference than *dBm,* because it permits use of the decibel scale to obtain a relative level without regard to a standard impedance, that is, 600 ohms. It is a measurement most useful in professional audio.

dBV is also a measure of voltage but with decibels referenced to 1 volt. This measurement is used where the dBm—600 ohm/1 milliwatt—value is impractical, as it is with the measurement of microphone sensitivity where the zero reference is 1 volt. +10 dBV is equal to 20 volts. Otherwise, dBV is not often used in professional audio.

*Originally, the reference symbol *dBu* was designated *dBv,* but because *dBv* was often confused with *dBV,* it was changed to *dBu.* Both are still used— *dBu* mainly in the United States, and *dBv* mainly in Europe.

FREQUENCY AND LOUDNESS

Frequency and amplitude are interdependent. Varying a sound's frequency also affects perception of its loudness, and varying a sound's amplitude affects perception of its pitch.

Equal Loudness Principle

The response of the human ear is not equally sensitive to all audible frequencies (see 2-3). Depending on loudness, we do not hear low and high frequencies as well as we hear middle frequencies. In fact, the ear is relatively insensitive to low frequencies at low levels. Oddly enough, this is called the *equal loudness principle* rather than that of unequal loudness (see 2-4).

As you can see in Figures 2-3 and 2-4, at low frequencies the ear needs about 70 dB more sound level than it does at 3 kHz to be the same loudness. The ear is at its most sensitive at around 3 kHz. At frequencies of 10 kHz and higher, the ear is somewhat more sensitive than it is at low frequencies but not nearly as sensitive as it is at the midrange frequencies.

In other words, if a guitarist, for example, plucks all six strings equally hard, you do not hear each string at the same loudness level. The high E string (328 Hz) sounds louder than the low E string (82 Hz). To make the low string sound as loud, the guitarist would have to pluck it harder. This suggests that the high E string may sound louder because of its higher frequency. But if you sound three tones, say, 50 Hz, 1,000 Hz, and 15,000 Hz, at a fixed loudness level, the 1,000-Hz tone sounds louder than either the 50-Hz or the 15,000-Hz tone.

In a live concert, sound levels are usually louder than they are on a home stereo system. Live music often reaches levels of 100 dB-SPL and higher. At home, levels are as high as 70 to 75 dB-SPL and, alas, too often much higher. Sound at 70 dB-SPL requires more bass and treble boost than does sound at 100 dB-SPL to obtain equal loudness. Therefore the frequency balances you hear at 100 dB-SPL will be different when you hear the same sound at 70 dB-SPL.

In a recording or mixdown session, if the loudness level is high during recording and low during playback, both bass and treble frequencies could be considerably reduced in volume and may

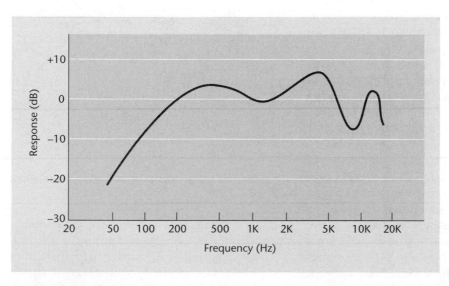

2-3 Responses to various frequencies by the human ear. This curve shows that the response is not flat and that we hear midrange frequencies better than low and high frequencies.

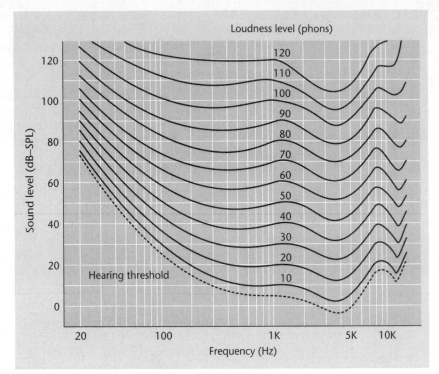

2-4 Equal loudness curves. These curves illustrate the relationships in Figure 2-3 and our relative lack of sensitivity to low and high frequencies as compared with middle frequencies. A 50-Hz sound would have to be 50 dB louder to seem as loud as a 1,000-Hz sound at 0 dB. To put it another way, at an intensity, for instance, of 40 dB, the level of a 100-Hz sound would have to be 10 times the SPL of a 1,000-Hz sound for the two sounds to be perceived as equal in loudness. Each curve is identified by the SPL at 1,000 Hz, which is known as the "phon of the curve."

(This graph represents frequencies on a logarithmic scale. The distance from 20 to 200 Hz is the same as from 200 to 2,000 Hz or from 2,000 to 20,000 Hz.) (Based on Robinson-Dadson.)

be virtually inaudible. The converse is also true: If sound level is low when playing back, the bass and treble frequencies could be too loud relative to the other frequencies and may even overwhelm them.

Because sensitivity of the ear varies with frequency and loudness, meters that measure sound-pressure level are designed to correspond to these variations by incorporating one or more weighting networks. A *weighting network* is a filter used for weighting a frequency response before measurement. Generally, three weighting networks are used: A, B, and C. The A and B networks bear close resemblances to the response of the human ear at 40 and 70 phons, respectively. (A *phon* is a dimensionless unit of loudness level related to the ear's subjective impression of signal strength. For a tone of 1,000 Hz, the loudness level in phons equals the sound-pressure level in decibels.) The C network corresponds to the ear's sensitivity at 100 phons and has an almost flat frequency response (see 2-5). Decibel values for the three networks are written

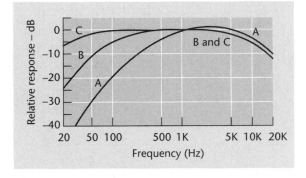

2-5 Frequency responses of the A, B, and C weighting networks

as dBA, dBB, and dBC. The level may be quoted in dBm, with the notation "A weighting."

The A weighting curve is preferred for measuring lower-level sounds. The B weighting curve is usually used for measuring medium-level sounds. The C weighting, which is essentially flat, is used for very loud sounds (see Table 2-2).

Table 2-2 Sound-level ranges of the A, B, and C weighting networks

Weighting Network	dB
A	20–55
B	55–85
C	85–140

Masking

Another phenomenon related to the interaction of frequency and loudness is *masking*—the hiding of some sounds by other sounds when each is a different frequency and they are presented together. Generally, loud sounds tend to mask softer ones, and lower-pitched sounds tend to mask higher-pitched ones.

For example, if a 100-Hz tone and 1,000-Hz tone are sounded together at the same level, both tones will be audible, but the 1,000-Hz tone will be perceived as louder. Gradually increasing the level of the 100-Hz tone and keeping the amplitude of the 1,000-Hz tone constant will make the 1,000-Hz tone more and more difficult to hear. If an LP (long-playing) record has scratches (high-frequency information), they will probably be masked during loud passages and audible during quiet ones. A symphony orchestra playing full blast may have all its instruments involved at once; however, flutes and clarinets will probably not be heard over trumpets and trombones, because woodwinds are generally higher in frequency and weaker in sound level than are the brass.

VELOCITY

Although frequency and amplitude are the most important physical components of a sound wave, another component—*velocity,* or the speed of a sound wave—should be mentioned. Velocity usually has little impact on pitch or loudness and is relatively constant in a controlled environment; sound travels 1,130 feet per second at sea level when the temperature is 70° Fahrenheit. The denser the molecular structure, the greater the vibrational conductivity. In water sound travels 4,800 feet per second. In solid materials such as wood and steel, it travels 11,700 and 18,000 feet per second, respectively.

In air, sound velocity changes significantly in very high and very low temperatures, increasing as air warms and decreasing as it cools. For every change of 1°F, the speed of sound changes 1.1 feet per second.

WAVELENGTH

Each frequency has a *wavelength,* determined by the distance a sound wave travels to complete one cycle of compression and rarefaction; that is, the physical measurement of the length of one cycle is equal to the velocity of sound divided by the frequency of sound ($\lambda = v/f$) (see 2-1). Therefore frequency and wavelength change inversely with respect to each other. The lower a sound's frequency, the longer its wavelength; the higher a sound's frequency, the shorter its wavelength (see Table 2-3).

Table 2-3 Selected frequencies and their wavelengths

Frequency (Hz)	Wavelength	Frequency (Hz)	Wavelength
20	56.5 feet	1,000	1.1 feet
31.5	35.8	2,000	6.7 inches
63	17.9	4,000	3.3
125	9.0	6,000	2.2
250	4.5	8,000	1.6
440	2.5	10,000	1.3
500	2.2	12,000	1.1
880	1.2	16,000	0.07

ACOUSTICAL PHASE

Acoustical phase refers to the time relationship between two or more sound waves at a given point in their cycles. Because sound waves are repetitive, they can be divided into regularly occurring intervals. These intervals are measured in degrees (see 2-6).

If two identical waves begin their excursions at the same time, their degree intervals will coincide and the waves will be *in phase*. If two identical waves begin their excursions at different times, their degree intervals will not coincide and the waves will be *out of phase*.

Waves that are in phase reinforce each other, increasing amplitude (see 2-7a). Conversely, waves that are out of phase weaken each other, decreasing amplitude. When two sound waves are exactly in phase (0-degree phase difference) and have the same frequency, shape, and peak amplitude, the resulting waveform will be twice the original peak amplitude.

Two waves that are exactly out of phase (180-degree phase difference) and have the same frequency, shape, and peak amplitude cancel each other (see 2-7b). These two conditions rarely occur in the studio, however.

It is more likely that sound waves will begin their excursions at different times. If the waves are partially out of phase, there would be *constructive interference*, increasing amplitude, where compression and rarefaction occur at the same time, and *destructive interference*, decreasing amplitude, where compression and rarefaction occur at different times (see 2-8).

TIMBRE

For the purpose of illustration, sound is often depicted as a single, wavy line (see 2-1). Actually, a wave that generates such a sound (known as a *sine wave*) is a *pure tone*—a single frequency devoid of harmonics and overtones.

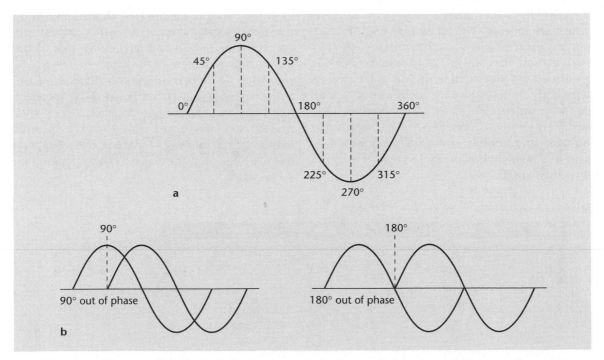

2-6 Sound waves. (a) Phase is measured in degrees, and one cycle can be divided into 360 degrees. It begins at 0 degrees with 0 amplitude, then increases to a positive maximum at 90 degrees, decreases to 0 at 180 degrees, increases to a negative maximum at 270 degrees, and returns to 0 at 360 degrees. (b) Selected phase relationships of sound waves.

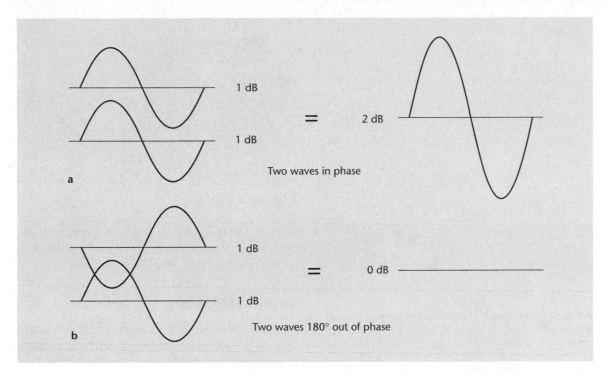

2-7 Sound waves in and out of phase. (a) In phase: Their amplitude is additive. Here the sound waves are exactly in phase—a condition that rarely occurs. It should be noted that decibels do not add linearly. These values have been assigned only to make a point. The actual additive amplitude here would be 6 dB. (b) Out of phase: Their amplitude is subtractive. Sound waves of equal amplitude 180 degrees out of phase cancel each other. This situation also rarely occurs.

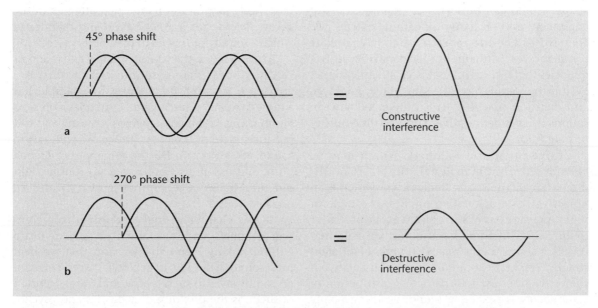

2-8 Waves partially out of phase (a) increase amplitude at some points and **(b)** decrease it at others

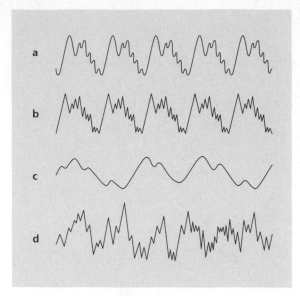

2-9 Waveforms showing differences between musical sounds and noise. (a) The pitch C from a piano. (b) The pitch C from a clarinet. (c) The waveform of an oboe. (d) The waveform of a noise. Notice its irregular pattern compared with the regular pattern of musical sounds.

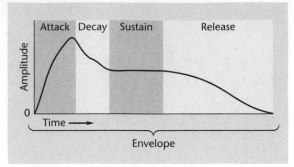

2-10 Sound envelope

Most sound, though, consists of several different frequencies that produce a complex **waveform**—a graphical representation of a sound's characteristic shape, which can be seen, for example, on test equipment and on hard-disk editing systems (see Figures 10-13 and 18-5). Each sound has a unique tonal mix of fundamental and harmonic frequencies that distinguishes it from all other sound, even if the sounds have the same pitch, loudness, and duration (see 2-9). This difference between sounds is what defines their **timbre**—tone quality or tone color.

Unlike pitch and loudness, which may be considered unidimensional, timbre is multidimensional. The sound frequency spectrum is an objective scale of relative pitches; the table of sound-pressure levels is an objective scale of relative loudnesses. But there is no objective scale that orders or compares the relative timbres of different sounds. The best we can do is try to articulate our subjective response to a particular distribution of sonic energy. For example, sound consisting mainly of lower frequencies played by cellos may be perceived as mellow, mournful, or quieting; these same lower frequencies played by a bassoon may be perceived as raspy, honky, or comical.

SOUND ENVELOPE

Another factor that influences the timbre of a sound is its shape, or envelope, which refers to changes in loudness over time. A **sound envelope** has four stages: attack, initial decay, sustain, and release (ADSR). **Attack** is how a sound starts after a sound source has been vibrated. **Initial decay** is the point at which the attack begins to lose amplitude. **Sustain** is the period during which the sound's relative dynamics are maintained after its initial decay. **Release** refers to the time and manner in which a sound diminishes to inaudibility (see 2-10).

Two notes with the same frequency and loudness can produce different sounds within different envelopes. A bowed violin string, for example, has a more dynamic sound overall than does a plucked violin string. If you take a piano recording and edit out the attacks of the notes, the piano will start to sound like an organ. Do the same with a French horn, and it sounds similar to a saxophone. Edit out the attacks of a trumpet, and it creates an oboelike sound.

In this chapter we have examined the components of a sound wave and how they are heard without taking into consideration that we hear most sound in built-up or enclosed spaces. Behavior of sound waves in such spaces, and our perception of them, is the province of acoustics and psychoacoustics, which is the subject of Chapter 3.

- A sound wave is a vibrational disturbance that involves mechanical motion of molecules transmitting energy from one place to another.

- A sound wave is caused when a body vibrates and sets into motion the molecules nearest to it; the initial motion starts a chain reaction. This chain reaction creates pressure waves through the air, which are perceived as sound when they reach the ear and brain.

- The pressure wave compresses molecules as it moves outward, increasing pressure, and pulls the molecules farther apart as it moves inward, creating a rarefaction by decreasing pressure.

- The components that make up a sound wave are frequency, amplitude, velocity, wavelength, and phase.

- Sound acts according to physical principles, but it also has a psychological effect on humans.

- The number of times a sound wave vibrates determines its frequency, or pitch. Humans can hear frequencies between, roughly, 20 and 20,000 Hz—a range of 10 octaves. Each octave has a unique sound in the frequency spectrum.

- The size of a sound wave determines its amplitude, or loudness. Loudness is measured in decibels.

- The decibel (dB) is a dimensionless unit used to compare the ratio of two quantities usually in relation to acoustic energy, such as sound-pressure level (SPL), and electric energy, such as power—dBm—and voltage, such as dBu (dBv) and dBV.

- Impedance is that property of a circuit, or an element, that restricts the flow of alternating current (AC). Impedance is measured in ohms (Ω), a unit of resistance of current flow.

- Humans can hear from 0 dB-SPL, the threshold of hearing, to 120 dB-SPL, the threshold of pain, and beyond. The scale is logarithmic, which means that adding two sounds each with a loudness of 100 dB-SPL would bring it to 103 dB-SPL. The range of difference in decibels between the loudest and quietest sound a vibrating object makes is called dynamic range.

- The ear does not perceive all frequencies at the same loudness even if their amplitudes are the same. This is the equal loudness principle. Humans do not hear lower- and higher-pitched sounds as well as they hear midrange sounds.

- Masking—covering a weaker sound with a stronger sound when each is a different frequency and both vibrate simultaneously—is another perceptual response dependent on the relationship between frequency and loudness.

- Velocity, the speed of a sound wave, is 1,130 feet per second at sea level and 70°F. Sound increases or decreases in velocity by 1.1 feet per second for each change of 1°F.

- Each frequency has a wavelength, determined by the distance a sound wave travels to complete one cycle of compression and rarefaction. The length of one cycle is equal to the velocity of sound divided by the frequency of sound. The lower a sound's frequency, the longer its wavelength; the higher a sound's frequency, the shorter its wavelength.

- Acoustical phase refers to the time relationship between two or more sound waves at a given point in their cycles. If two waves begin their excursions at the same time, their degree intervals will coincide and the waves will be in phase, reinforcing each other and increasing amplitude. If two waves begin their excursions at different times, their degree intervals will not coincide and the waves will be out of phase, weakening each other and decreasing amplitude.

- Timbre is the tone quality or color of a sound.

- A sound's envelope refers to its changes in loudness over time. It has four stages: attack, initial decay, sustain, and release (ADSR).

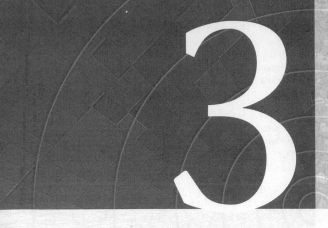

3

Acoustics and Psychoacoustics

In the broad sense, ***acoustics*** is the study of auditory sensation in the ear and the sound waves that cause that sensation; ***psychoacoustics*** deals with the perception of those sensations. *Acoustics* is also used to describe the physical behavior of sound waves in a room. In that context psychoacoustics is concerned with the relationship of our subjective response to such sound waves.

SPATIAL HEARING

As noted in Chapter 1, sound is omnidirectional. Our auditory system can hear acoustic space from all around—360 degrees—in any direction, an ability our visual system does not have. More noteworthy is that from the many sounds bombarding us from everywhere, we are able not only to isolate and recognize a particular sound but to tell from what direction it is coming. To do this the brain processes (1) the *time differences* between when the sound reaches each ear and (2) the *intensity differences* at each ear. These time and intensity differences occur because the head separates the ears and, depending on which way the head is turned and from what direction the sound is coming, the sound will reach one ear before it reaches the other. The brain compares these differences and tells the listener the sound's location. Processing these differences also makes it possible to hear sound three-dimensionally—from any angle, height, and distance. This is known as *binaural hearing*. Whereas *stereo,* for example, is essentially one-dimensional sound that creates the illusion of two-dimensional sound.

Stereo has two static sound sources—the loudspeakers—with nothing in between. Although each ear receives the sound at a different time and intensity—the left ear from the left loudspeaker earlier and louder than the right ear and vice versa—the sounds are a composite of the signals from both loudspeakers. Here the brain adds the two signals together, creating the illusion of an image in the middle. Processing of surround-sound imaging is somewhat different, but its spatial illusion is still not binaural. Basically, this is why recorded sound cannot quite reproduce the definition, fidelity, and dimension of live sound, even with today's technology. The only way a recording can sound similar to live sound is to record and play it back binaurally (see Chapter 4).

X **Precedence Effect**

When a sound is emitted in a sound-reflectant space, *direct sound* reaches our ears first, before it interacts with any other surface. Indirect sound, or *reflected sound,* on the other hand, reaches our ears only after bouncing off of one or more surfaces. If similar sounds reach the ear within about 20 *milliseconds (ms)* of one another, the reflected sounds and the direct sound are usually perceived as coming from the same direction, even if the immediate repetitions coming from another direction are louder. This is known as the *precedence effect*, or *Haas effect*. As the time between the direct and indirect sounds reaching the ears increases beyond 20 ms, localization becomes increasingly difficult.

Another aspect of the precedence effect is that direct and reflected sounds reaching the ear approximately 10 to 20 ms after the original waves are perceived as a single sound; the ear does not distinguish among them. This is called *temporal fusion*. This effect gradually disappears as the time interval between direct and reflected sounds increases from roughly 30 to 50 ms.

DIRECT, EARLY, AND REVERBERANT SOUND

When a sound is emitted in a room, its acoustic "life cycle" can be divided into three phases: direct sound, early sound, and reverberant sound (see Figure 3-1).

Direct sound reaches the listener first, before it interacts with any other surface. Depending on the distance from the sound source to the listener, the time, T_0, is 20 to 200 ms. Direct waves provide information about a sound's origin, size, and tonal quality.

The same sound reaching the listener a short time later, after it reflects from various surfaces, is *indirect sound*. Indirect sound is divided into *early sound*, also known as *early reflections*, and reverberant sound (see 3-2). Early reflections

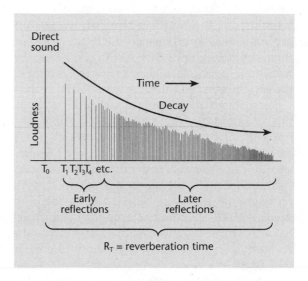

3-1 Anatomy of reverberation in an enclosed space.
At time₀ (T_0) the direct sound is heard. Between T_0 and T_1 is the initial time delay gap—the time between the arrival of the direct sound and the first reflection. At T_2 and T_3, more early reflections of the direct sound arrive as they reflect from nearby surfaces. These early reflections are sensed rather than distinctly heard. At T_4 repetitions of the direct sound spread through the room, reflecting from several surfaces and arriving at the listener so close together that their repetitions are indistinguishable.

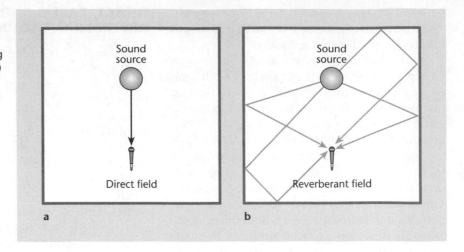

3-2 Acoustical behavior of sound in an enclosed room. (a) The direct sound field is all the sound reaching the listener (or microphone) directly from the sound source without having been reflected off any of the room's surfaces. (b) The indirect sound is all sound reaching the listener (or microphone) after being reflected off any of the room's surfaces.

Sound source

Direct field

a

Sound source

Reverberant field

b

reaching the ear within 20 ms of when the direct sound is produced are heard as part of the direct sound. *Reverberant sound,* or **reverberation** (*reverb* for short), is the result of the early reflections becoming smaller and smaller and the time between them decreasing until they combine, making the reflections indistinguishable. They arrive outside of the ear's integration time.

Early sound adds loudness and fullness to the initial sound and helps create our subjective impression of a room's size. Reverb creates acoustical spaciousness and fills out the loudness and body of a sound. It contains much of a sound's total energy. Also depending on the *decay time,* or *reverberation time* (the time it takes a sound to decrease 60 dB-SPL after its steady-state sound level has stopped), reverb provides information about the absorption and reflectivity of a room's surfaces, as well as about a listener's distance from the sound source. The longer it takes a sound to decay, the larger and more hard-surfaced the room is perceived to be and the farther from the sound source the listener is or senses him- or herself to be.

Reverberation and Echo

Reverberation and *echo* are often used synonymously—but incorrectly so. Reverberation is densely spaced reflections created by random, multiple, blended repetitions of a sound. The time between reflections is imperceptible. If a sound is delayed by 35 ms or more, the listener perceives *echo,* a distinct repeat of the direct sound.

In large rooms discrete echoes are sometimes perceived. In small rooms these repetitions, called *flutter echoes,* are short and come in rapid succession. They usually result from reflections between two parallel surfaces that are highly reflective. Because echoes usually inhibit sonic clarity, studios and concert halls are designed to eliminate them.

MATCHING ACOUSTICS TO PROGRAM MATERIAL

Although the science of acoustics is highly developed, there is no such thing as a sound room with perfect acoustics. The sonic requirements, for example, of rock-and-roll and classical music are different, as they are for a radio studio and a studio used for dialogue rerecording in film and television.

A reverberant studio might be suitable for a symphony orchestra, because the reflections add needed richness to the music, as they do in a concert hall. The extremely loud music a rock group generates would swim amid too many sound reflections, becoming virtually unintelligible. At the same time, a studio with relatively few reflections, and therefore suitable for rock-and-roll, would render the sound of a symphony orchestra lifeless.

A radio studio is relatively quiet, but does have some room tone, or atmosphere, so the sound is not too closed down or closetlike. In radio it is important to maintain the intimate sonic rapport between announcer and listener that is essential to the personal nature of the medium. Rerecording dialogue in postproduction for a film or TV drama requires a studio virtually devoid of room tone, to prevent acoustics from coloring the dialogue, and so room tone appropriate to a scene's setting can be added later.

Rooms with reverberation times of one second or more are considered to be "live." Rooms with reverberation times of one-half second or less are considered to be "dry," or "dead" (see 3-3). Live rooms reinforce sound, making it relatively louder and more powerful, especially, although not always, in the lower frequencies. They also tend to diffuse detail, smoothing inconsistencies in pitch, tonal quality, and performance.

In dry rooms sound is reinforced little or not at all, causing it to be concentrated and lifeless. Inconsistencies in pitch, tonal quality, and other aspects of undesirable performance are readily

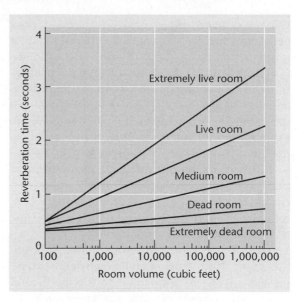

3-3 Room liveness in relation to reverberation time and room size

apparent. In instances where dry rooms are required for recording, signal processing is used to provide appropriate reverberation (see 3-4 and Chapter 9).

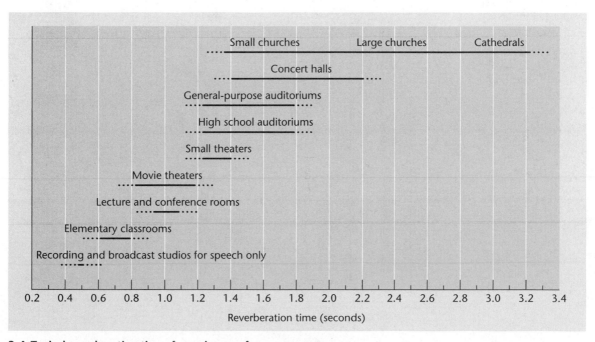

3-4 Typical reverberation times for various performance spaces

Liveness can be added by increasing the frequencies between, roughly, 500 and 2,000 Hz and adding reverberation in the range of one to two seconds.

Intimacy and warmth are two other considerations in the acoustics of a room or recording. *Intimacy* relates to the closeness of the listener to the sound source and the ability to hear sonic detail. Intimacy results from early reflections that follow the direct sound by no more than 15 to 20 ms.

Warmth is a sonic quality usually associated with the lower frequencies and increased reverberation time—specifically, the frequencies between, roughly, 125 and 250 Hz—and a high reverb time relative to the midrange frequencies.

Acousticians have calculated optimum reverb times for various types of audio material that have proved suitable for emulation in the production room (see 3-5). That said, preference for the amount of reverberation and reverb time is a matter of individual taste, as all judgments in sound should be.

STUDIO DESIGN

The behavior of sound waves in an acoustic environment and how that behavior affects aural perception leads logically to a consideration of the four factors that influence this behavior: (1) sound isolation, (2) room dimensions, (3) room shape, and (4) room acoustics. These factors are directly related to one overriding concern: *noise*.

Noise

Noise—unwanted sound—is the number one enemy in audio production. As noted in Chapter 1, noise is everywhere. Outside a room it comes from traffic, airplanes, jackhammers, thunder, rain, and so on. Inside a room noise is generated by fluorescent lights, ventilation and heating/cooling systems, computers, and appliances. And these are only the more obvious examples. A few not so obvious examples include the "noise" made by the

3-5 Optimum reverberation times for various types of music and speech produced indoors

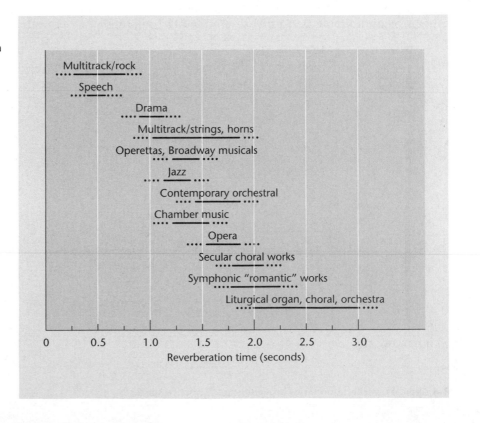

random motion of molecules, by our nervous and circulatory systems, and by our ears. In short, noise is part of our existence and can never be completely eliminated. (Audio equipment also generates *system noise*, and analog recording tape generates *tape noise*.)

Even though unwanted sound is always present, in producing audio it must be brought to well within tolerable levels so that it does not interfere with the desired sound, particulary with digital sound. Among other things, noise can mask sounds, make speech unintelligible, create distraction, cause annoyance, and reduce if not ruin the aesthetic listening experience.

To this end acousticians have developed *noise criteria (NC)* that identify, by means of a rating system, background noise—also called *ambient noise*—levels (see 3-6). From this rating system, NC levels for various types of rooms are derived (see Table 3-1). This raises the question: Once NC levels for a particular sound room are known, how is noise control accomplished?

Sound Isolation

Sound studios must be isolated to prevent outside noise from leaking into the room and to keep loud sound levels generated inside the room from

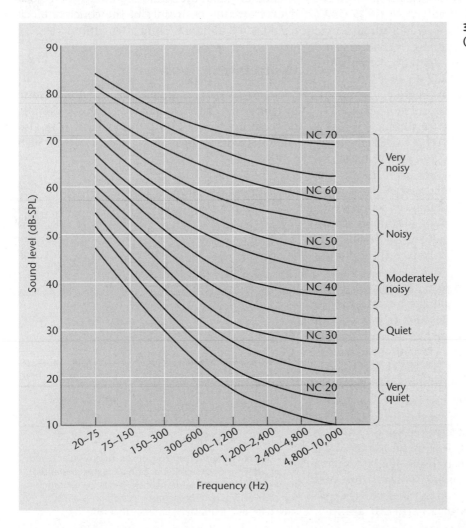

3-6 Noise criteria (NC) curves

Table 3-1 Recommended noise criteria levels for selected rooms

Type of Room	Recommended NC Curve	dB
Broadcast and recording studios	NC 15–25	25–35
Concert halls	NC 20	30
Drama theaters	NC 20–25	30–35
Motion picture theaters	NC 30	40
Sports arenas	NC 50	60

disturbing neighbors. This is accomplished in two ways. The first is by determining the loudest outside sound level against the minimum acceptable NC level inside the studio. This is usually between NC 15 and NC 25 (approximately 25 to 35 dBA), depending on what type of sound the studio is used for. It is also done by determining the loudest sound level inside the studio against a maximum acceptable noise floor outside the studio.

For example, assume that the maximum measured noise outside a studio is 90 dB-SPL and the maximum acceptable noise level inside a studio is 30 dB-SPL at, say, 500 Hz. (These values are always frequency-dependent but are usually based on 500 Hz.) This means that the construction of the studio must reduce the loudness of the outside sound level by 60 dB. If the loudest sound inside a studio is 110 dB-SPL and the maximum acceptable noise outside the studio is 45 dB-SPL, the studio's construction must reduce the loudness level by 65 dB.

The amount of sound reduction provided by a barrier—wall, floor, or ceiling—is referred to as *transmission loss (TL)*. Because TL works both ways, determining barrier requirements is equally applicable to sound traveling from inside to outside the studio and vice versa. Therefore the barriers constructed to isolate the studio in this example would have to reduce the loudness level by at least 65 dB (500 Hz).

Just as it is convenient to define a noise spectrum by a single NC number, it is useful to measure a barrier on the basis of its transmission loss; such a measurement is called *sound transmission class (STC)*. Sound transmission class varies with the type and mass of materials in a barrier. If a 4-inch

concrete block has an STC of 48, it indicates that sound passing through it will be attenuated by 48 dB. An 8-inch concrete block with an STC of 52 attenuates 4 dB more sound than the 4-inch block does. Plastering both sides of the concrete block would add 8 dB more sound attenuation.

Room Dimensions

Sometimes a studio's dimensions accentuate noise by reinforcing certain frequencies, thereby altering, or "coloring," the natural sound. This may also affect the response of a sound's decay (see 3-7). Such

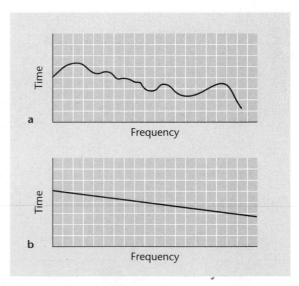

3-7 Reverberation decay responses. (a) Irregular reverb decay, which is undesirable because it creates unwanted sound coloration. (b) Desirable reverb decay illustrating no resonant coloration. This acoustic condition is always strived for but, in practice, is rarely attained.

Table 3-2 Simplified table of reinforced frequencies in a room 10 by 20 by 30 feet. If this table were continued, each frequency that occurs in the height dimension would recur in the other two dimensions.

	Height: 10 Feet	Width: 20 Feet	Length: 30 Feet
Fundamental	150 Hz	75 Hz	50 Hz
Second harmonic	300 Hz	150 Hz	100 Hz
Third harmonic	450 Hz	225 Hz	150 Hz
Fourth harmonic	600 Hz	300 Hz	200 Hz
Fifth harmonic	750 Hz	375 Hz	250 Hz
Sixth harmonic	900 Hz	450 Hz	300 Hz
Seventh harmonic	1,050 Hz	525 Hz	350 Hz
Eighth harmonic	1,200 Hz	600 Hz	400 Hz

coloration affects perception of tonal balance, clarity, and imaging as well. Audio mixed in a control room with these problems will sound markedly different when played in another room. Other factors related to the shape of a studio and construction materials used therein (discussed in the following two sections) may also affect coloration.

Rooms have particular resonances at which sound will be naturally sustained. These are related to the room's dimensions. **Resonance** results when a vibrating body with the same natural frequencies as another body causes it to vibrate sympathetically and increases the amplitude of both of them at those frequencies if the vibrations are in acoustical phase.

The story is told of soldiers on horseback galloping across a wooden bridge. The sound created by the hoofbeats on the wood generated the resonant frequency of the bridge, causing it to collapse. In another incident wind excited the resonant frequency of a modern steel-and-concrete bridge, increasing amplitude until it was torn apart.* These are interesting examples, but they are extreme for our purpose.

Resonances occur in a room at frequencies whose wavelengths are the same as or a multiple of one of the room's dimensions. These resonances are called

---

*Tacoma Narrows Suspension Bridge at Puget Sound, Washington, in 1940.

eigentones, or, more common, **room modes**—increases in loudness at resonant frequencies that are a function of a room's dimensions. When these dimensions are the same as or multiples of a common value, the resonance amplitude is increased. Such a room's dimensions may be 10 by 20 by 30 feet, or 15 by 30 by 45 feet (see Table 3-2). This creates unequal representation of the frequencies generated by a sound source. In other words certain frequencies will be reinforced while others will not be. To avoid additive resonances, room dimensions should not be the same, nor be integer multiples of one another. Dimensions of, say, 9 by 10.1 by 12.5 feet or 15 by 27 by 31.5 feet, would be satisfactory (see Table 3-3). It should be noted, however, that although perfect dimensions are the ideal, they are rarely a reality. Most studios will have some resonant frequencies.

Resonance is not always bad, however. The tubing in wind and brass instruments, the pipes in an organ, and the human mouth, nose, chest, and throat are resonators. Air columns passing through them excite resonant frequencies, creating sound. Without resonators such as the "box" of a guitar or violin, weak sound sources would generate little sound. Some studios use this principle to construct resonators that help amplify certain frequencies to enhance the type of sound being produced. As we shall see in the section headed "Room Acoustics" later in this chapter, resonators are also used to absorb sound.

Table 3-3 Simplified table of frequencies in a studio with dimensions that are not the same as or multiples of a common value. In this example only one frequency, 300 Hz, recurs in another dimension.

	Height: 9 Feet	Width: 10.1 Feet	Length: 12.5 Feet
Fundamental	150 Hz	136 Hz	60 Hz
Second harmonic	300 Hz	272 Hz	85 Hz
Third harmonic	450 Hz	409 Hz	128 Hz
Fourth harmonic	600 Hz	545 Hz	171 Hz
Fifth harmonic	750 Hz	681 Hz	214 Hz
Sixth harmonic	900 Hz	818 Hz	257 Hz
Seventh harmonic	1,050 Hz	954 Hz	300 Hz
Eighth harmonic	1,200 Hz	1,090 Hz	342 Hz

Room Shape

Acoustics is a science of interacting relationships. Although studio walls, floors, and windows may have been properly constructed and their dimensions conform to a set of preferred standards, the room's shape is also important to good noise reduction and sound dispersion.

Except for bass frequencies, sound behaves like light; *its angle of incidence is equal to its angle of reflectance* (see 3-8). If a studio has reflective parallel walls, sound waves reinforce themselves as they continuously bounce between opposing surfaces

(see 3-9). If there are concave surfaces, they serve as collecting points, generating unwanted concentrations of sound (see 3-10a). A studio should be designed to break up the paths of sound waves (see 3-10b and 3-10c).

Typical studio designs have adjacent walls at angles other than 90 degrees and different-shaped wall surfaces, such as spherical, cylindrical, and serrated, to help disperse the sound waves (see 3-11). Even the glass between the studio and the control room is angled toward the floor for sound dispersal (and also to avoid light reflections), but it is not

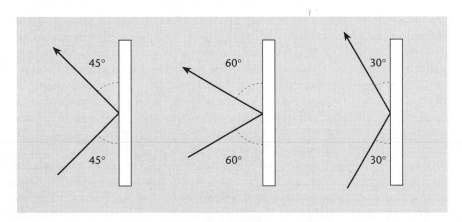

3-8 Angle of incidence and angle of reflectance. In sound, as in light, these angles are equal.

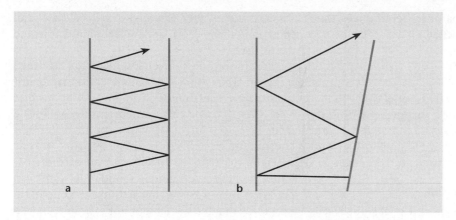

3-9 Parallel walls. (a) Sound waves reflect back along their original paths of travel, thereby generating standing waves which are reinforced, creating echoey sound. (b) Slightly changing the angle of one wall reduces the possibility of the reflections' following repeated paths.

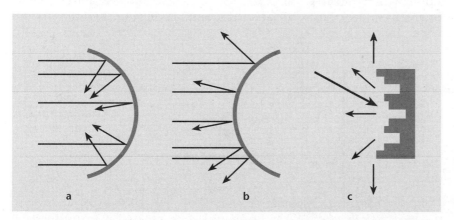

3-10 Shape of a room's surface affecting direction of sound reflections. (a) Concave surfaces concentrate sound waves by converging them. (b) Convex surfaces are more suitable in studios because they disperse sound waves. (c) A quadratic residue diffusor also disperses waves at many different angles.

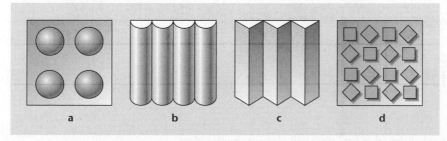

3-11 Examples of studio walls with different surface shapes: (a) spherical, (b) cylindrical, (c) serrated, and (d) a combination of square and diamond

enough to break up the paths of sound waves; they must be controlled once they hit a surface.

Room Acoustics

When sound hits a surface, one thing—or a combination of five things—happens, depending on the surface's material, mass, and design. Sound is absorbed, reflected, partially absorbed and reflected, diffracted, or diffused.

Absorption and Reflection

When sound hits a surface and is absorbed, it is soaked up. There is little or no reflection; hence, the sonic result is lifeless, or dry. When sound hits a surface and is reflected, it bounces off the surface and is perceived as reverberation or echo, depending on its interaction with other live surfaces in the vicinity. Conditions under which sound is completely absorbed or reflected are rare. Most materials absorb and reflect sound to some degree (see 3-12).

The amount of indirect sound energy absorbed is given an acoustical rating called a *sound absorption coefficient,* also known as a *noise reduction coefficient (NRC).* Theoretically, on a scale from 1.0 to 0.0, material with a sound absorption coefficient of 1.0 completely absorbs sound, whereas material with a sound absorption coefficient of 0.0 is completely sound reflectant. Soft, porous materials absorb more sound than do hard, nonporous materials. Drapes, for example, have a higher absorption coefficient than does glass. Sound absorption ratings for the same material vary with frequency, however (see Table 3-4).

Three types of acoustic absorbers are porous absorbers, diaphragmatic absorbers, and Helmholtz absorbers. Examples of *porous absorbers* are

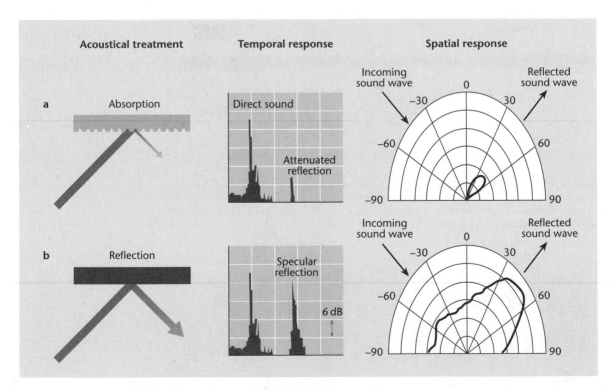

3-12 Absorption and reflection in relation to temporal and spatial response

Table 3-4 Absorption coefficients of common building materials and finishes

Floor materials	125 Hz	250 Hz	500 Hz	1 kHz	2 kHz	4 kHz
Carpet (indoor/outdoor)	0.01	0.02	0.06	0.15	0.25	0.45
Concrete or terrazzo (unpainted, rough finish)	0.01	0.02	0.04	0.06	0.08	0.10
Concrete or terrazzo (sealed or painted)	0.01	0.01	0.02	0.02	0.02	0.02
Marble or glazed tile	0.01	0.01	0.01	0.01	0.02	0.02
Vinyl tile or linoleum on concrete	0.02	0.03	0.03	0.03	0.03	0.02
Wood parquet on concrete	0.04	0.04	0.07	0.06	0.06	0.07
Wood flooring on joists	0.15	0.11	0.10	0.07	0.06	0.07
Seating materials	**125 Hz**	**250 Hz**	**500 Hz**	**1 kHz**	**2 kHz**	**4 kHz**
Benches (wooden, empty)	0.10	0.09	0.08	0.08	0.08	0.08
Benches (wooden, ⅔ occupied)	0.37	0.40	0.47	0.53	0.56	0.53
Benches (wooden, fully occupied)	0.50	0.56	0.66	0.76	0.80	0.76
Benches (cushioned seats and backs, empty)	0.32	0.40	0.42	0.44	0.43	0.48
Benches (cushioned seats and backs, ⅔ occupied)	0.44	0.56	0.65	0.72	0.72	0.67
Benches (cushioned seats and backs, full)	0.50	0.64	0.76	0.86	0.86	0.76
Theater seats (wood, empty)	0.03	0.04	0.05	0.07	0.08	0.08
Theater seats (wood, ⅔ occupied)	0.34	0.21	0.28	0.53	0.56	0.53
Theater seats (wood, fully occupied)	0.50	0.30	0.40	0.76	0.80	0.76
Seats (fabric, upholstered, empty)	0.49	0.66	0.80	0.88	0.82	0.70
Seats (fabric, upholstered, fully occupied)	0.60	0.74	0.88	0.96	0.93	0.85
Reflective wall materials	**125 Hz**	**250 Hz**	**500 Hz**	**1 kHz**	**2 kHz**	**4 kHz**
Brick (natural)	0.03	0.03	0.03	0.04	0.05	0.07
Brick (painted)	0.01	0.01	0.02	0.02	0.02	0.03
Concrete block (coarse)	0.36	0.44	0.31	0.29	0.39	0.25
Concrete block (painted)	0.10	0.05	0.06	0.07	0.09	0.08
Concrete (poured, rough finish, unpainted)	0.01	0.02	0.04	0.06	0.08	0.10
Doors (solid wood panels)	0.10	0.07	0.05	0.04	0.04	0.04
Glass (¼" plate, large pane)	0.18	0.06	0.04	0.03	0.02	0.02
Glass (small pane)	0.04	0.04	0.03	0.03	0.02	0.02
Gypsum board (½" paneling on studs)	0.29	0.10	0.06	0.05	0.04	0.04
Plaster (gypsum or lime, on masonry)	0.01	0.02	0.02	0.03	0.04	0.05
Plaster (gypsum or lime, on wood lath)	0.14	0.10	0.06	0.05	0.04	0.04
Plywood (⅛" paneling over 1¼" air space)	0.15	0.25	0.12	0.08	0.08	0.08
Plywood (⅛" paneling over 2¼" air space)	0.28	0.20	0.10	0.10	0.08	0.08
Plywood (³⁄₁₆" paneling over 2" air space)	0.38	0.24	0.17	0.10	0.08	0.05
Plywood (³⁄₁₆" panel, 1" fiberglass in 2" air space)	0.42	0.36	0.19	0.10	0.08	0.05
Plywood (¼" paneling, air space, light bracing)	0.30	0.25	0.15	0.10	0.10	0.10
Plywood (⅜" paneling, air space, light bracing)	0.28	0.22	0.17	0.09	0.10	0.11
Plywood (¾" paneling, air space, light bracing)	0.20	0.18	0.15	0.12	0.10	0.10

Table 3-4 Absorption coefficients of common building materials and finishes *(continued)*

Absorptive wall materials	125 Hz	250 Hz	500 Hz	1 kHz	2 kHz	4 kHz
Drapery (10 oz./yd.^{2}, 340 g/m^2, flat against wall)	0.04	0.05	0.11	0.18	0.30	0.35
Drapery (14 oz./yd.^{2}, 476 g/m^2, flat against wall)	0.05	0.07	0.13	0.22	0.32	0.35
Drapery (18 oz./yd.^{2}, 612 g/m^2, flat against wall)	0.05	0.12	0.35	0.48	0.38	0.36
Drapery (14 oz./yd.^{2}, 476 g/m^2, pleated 50%)	0.07	0.31	0.49	0.75	0.70	0.60
Drapery (18 oz./yd.^{2}, 612 g/m^2, pleated 50%)	0.14	0.35	0.53	0.75	0.70	0.60
Fiberglass board (1" thick)	0.06	0.20	0.65	0.90	0.95	0.98
Fiberglass board (2" thick)	0.18	0.76	0.99	0.99	0.99	0.99
Fiberglass board (3" thick)	0.53	0.99	0.99	0.99	0.99	0.99
Fiberglass board (4" thick)	0.99	0.99	0.99	0.99	0.99	0.97
Open brick pattern over 3" fiberglass	0.40	0.65	0.85	0.75	0.65	0.60
Pegboard over 1" fiberglass board	0.08	0.32	0.99	0.76	0.34	0.12
Pegboard over 2" fiberglass board	0.26	0.97	0.99	0.66	0.34	0.14
Pegboard over 3" fiberglass board	0.49	0.99	0.99	0.69	0.37	0.15
Ceiling materials	**125 Hz**	**250 Hz**	**500 Hz**	**1 kHz**	**2 kHz**	**4 kHz**
Gypsum board (½" in suspended ceiling grid)	0.15	0.11	0.04	0.04	0.07	0.08
Lay-in perforated metal panels (1" batts)	0.51	0.78	0.57	0.77	0.90	0.79
Metal deck (perforated channels, 1" batts)	0.19	0.69	0.99	0.88	0.52	0.27
Metal deck (perforated channels, 3" batts)	0.73	0.99	0.99	0.89	0.52	0.31
Plaster (gypsum or lime, on masonry)	0.01	0.02	0.02	0.03	0.04	0.05
Plaster (gypsum or lime, rough finish on lath)	0.14	0.10	0.06	0.05	0.04	0.04
Sprayed cellulose fiber (⅝" on solid backing)	0.05	0.16	0.44	0.79	0.90	0.91
Sprayed cellulose fiber (1" on solid backing)	0.08	0.29	0.75	0.98	0.93	0.76
Sprayed cellulose fiber (1" on lath)	0.47	0.90	1.10	1.03	1.05	1.03
Sprayed cellulose fiber (1¼" on solid backing)	0.10	0.30	0.73	0.92	0.98	0.98
Sprayed cellulose fiber (3" on solid backing)	0.70	0.95	1.00	0.85	0.85	0.90
Wood tongue-and-groove roof decking	0.24	0.19	0.14	0.08	0.13	0.10
Miscellaneous surface materials	**125 Hz**	**250 Hz**	**500 Hz**	**1 kHz**	**2 kHz**	**4 kHz**
People—adults (per ¹⁄₁₀ person)	0.250	0.350	0.420	0.460	0.500	0.500
People—high school students (per ¹⁄₁₀ person)	0.220	0.300	0.380	0.420	0.450	0.450
People—elementary students (per ¹⁄₁₀ person)	0.180	0.230	0.280	0.320	0.350	0.350
Ventilating grilles	0.300	0.400	0.500	0.500	0.500	0.400
Water or ice surface	0.008	0.008	0.013	0.015	0.020	0.025

acoustical tiles, carpet, fiberglass, and urethane foams (see 3-13). The thicker and denser the absorbent, the greater the sound absorption. Porous absorbers are most effective with high frequencies. Because the wavelengths of high frequencies are short, they tend to get trapped in the tiny air spaces of the porous materials.

Diaphragmatic absorbers are generally flexible panels of wood or pressed wood mounted over an air space (see 3-14). When a sound wave hits the

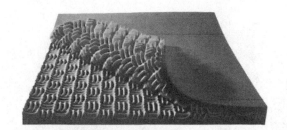

3-13 Polyurethane-foam sound absorber

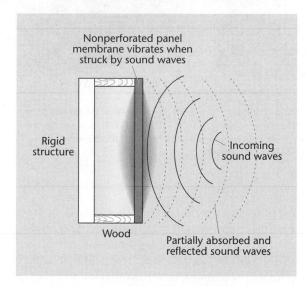

3-14 Diaphragmatic absorber. The approaching sound wave strikes the cover panel or diaphragm, setting it into motion and canceling resonant frequencies and reflecting nonresonant frequencies.

panel, it resonates at a frequency (or frequencies) determined by the stiffness of the panel and the size of the air space. Other sound waves of the same frequency (or frequencies) approaching the panel, therefore, are dampened. Diaphragmatic absorbers are used mainly to absorb low frequencies; for this reason they are also called *bass traps*. This principle can also be applied to absorbing high frequencies. Because it is difficult to completely dissipate standing waves, especially in small rooms and even with optimal acoustics, bass traps are usually designed to introduce significant absorption for frequencies between 30 and 100 Hz.

A **Helmholtz absorber**, also called a *Hemholtz resonator,* is a tuned absorber designed to remove sound at specific frequencies or within specific frequency ranges, usually the lower-middle frequencies. It functions, in principle, not unlike the action created when blowing into the mouth of a soda bottle. The tone created at the frequency of the bottle's resonance is related to the air mass in the bottle. By filling the bottle with water, the air mass is reduced, so the pitch of the tone is higher.

Diffraction

When sound reaches a surface, in addition to being partially absorbed and reflected, it *diffracts*—spreads or bends around the surface. The amount of **diffraction** depends on the relation between wavelength and the distances involved. You will recall that each frequency has a wavelength; bass waves are longer, treble waves shorter. Hence, the diffraction of bass waves is more difficult to control acoustically than the diffraction of treble waves.

Diffusion

The overriding challenge for the acoustician is controlling the physical behavior of sound waves in a studio. The goal is the uniform distribution of sound energy in a room so that its intensity throughout the room is approximately equal (see 3-15). This is called *diffusion*. No matter how weak or strong the sound and regardless of its wave-

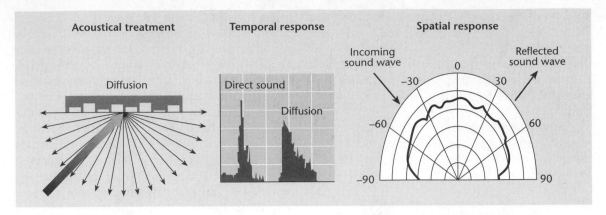

3-15 Diffusion in relation to temporal and spatial response

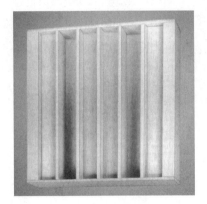

3-16 Abffusor.™ Provides reflection control by simultaneously using absorption and diffusion down to 100 Hz for all angles of incidence.

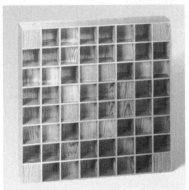

3-17 Omniffusor.™ Sound diffusor that scatters sound into a hemisphere; useful when omnidirectional coverage and high sound attenuation are desired.

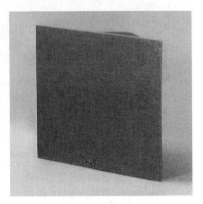

3-18 B.A.S.S. Trap.™ Bass-absorbing soffit system to control low-frequency reverberation in small rooms.

length, the diffused energy is reduced in amplitude and spread out in time, falling off more or less exponentially. Figures 3-16 through 3-18 display various forms of diffusors to meet specific needs.

Adjustable Acoustics

Basic principles of acoustics apply to any room in which sound is generated. As noted earlier, however, a room's purpose has a great deal to do with how those principles are applied. If a studio is used for rock music and speech, the acoustics must absorb more sound than they diffuse so that there is minimal interference from other sounds or from reverberation—or both. On the other hand, studios used for classical music and some types of jazz should diffuse more sound than they absorb to maintain a balanced, blended, open sound imaging.

Theoretically, this means that a studio designed to fulfill one sonic purpose is inappropriate for another. In fact, to be more functional, some studios are designed with variable acoustics. They have adjustable panels, louvers, or partitions and portable baffles, or *gobos*, to alter diffusion, absorption, and reverb time (see 3-19 through 3-22).

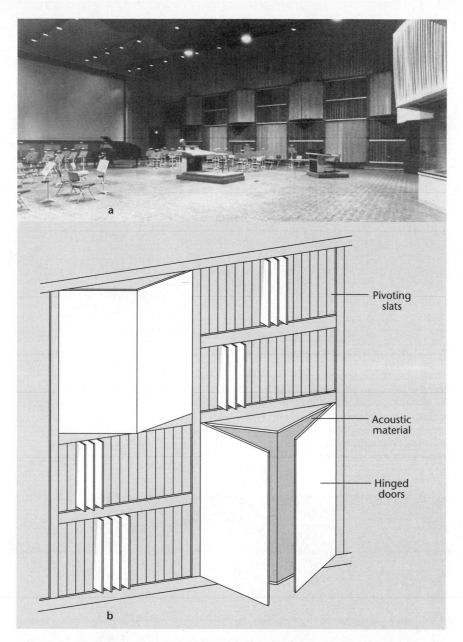

3-19 Example of acoustic treatment along walls. (a) Scoring stage with alternating doors and slats that can be opened or closed to vary acoustics. (b) Detail of doors and slats shown in (a).

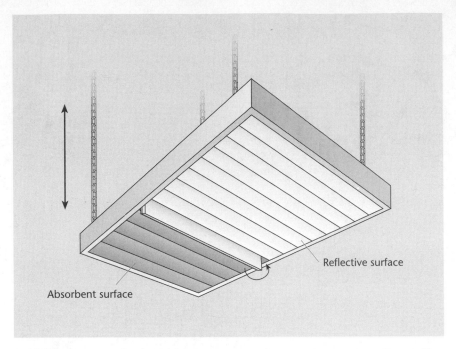

Reflective surface

Absorbent surface

3-20 Sketch of a variable, adjustable acoustic partition used in one recording studio. This partition is connected to the ceiling and can be raised or lowered to vary studio reverberation time between two and four seconds. Reverb times can be further refined by turning the bottom panels to their reflective or absorbent surfaces. For example, in recording an orchestra, the panels over the strings and woodwinds could be turned to their reflective side to enhance these weaker-sounding instruments, and the panels over the brass and timpany could be turned to their absorptive side to help control these stronger-sounding instruments.

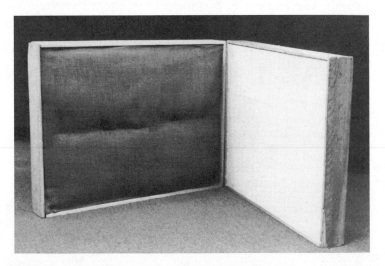

3-21 Movable baffles, or gobos, showing absorbent and reflective surfaces

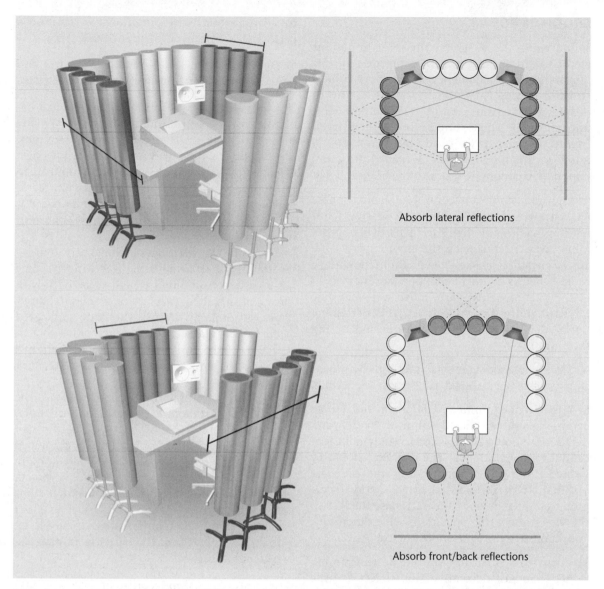

3-22 Acoustic treatment for rooms with less-than-desirable acoustics. One way of handling such a situation is with the Attack Wall,™ a portable array of reflective/absorptive acoustic traps that can be positioned in various ways around the console and recordist.

Absorb lateral reflections

Absorb front/back reflections

CONTROL ROOM DESIGN

Purpose also affects design differences between studios and control rooms. Studios are designed for sound that is appropriate for microphone pickup, whereas control rooms are designed for listening to loudspeakers. Therefore, to accurately assess the reproduced sound in a control room, the main challenge is to reduce the number of unwanted reflections at the stereo and surround-sound monitoring locations so that they are relatively reflection-free zones. (Control room monitoring is discussed in Chapter 10, "Loud-speakers and Monitoring.")

ERGONOMICS

Sound control is obviously the most important factor in studio and control room design, but human needs should not be ignored. Production is stressful enough without personnel having to endure poor lighting, hard-to-reach equipment, uncomfortable chairs, and so on. Designing an engineering system with the human element in mind is called *ergonomics*. A few of the more important ergonomic considerations are as follows.

■ **Lighting** Studio and control room atmosphere are important in a production session, and lighting—adjustable lighting in particular—goes a long way in enhancing the environment. One audio operator may like a lot of light in the control room, whereas another audio operator may prefer it dim. Talent, particularly musicians, may like low-key lighting, assorted colored lights, or flashing lights, depending on the emotional bolstering they may need.

■ **Size** Ample room for personnel and equipment should prevent a cramped, claustrophobic feeling.

■ **Position of equipment** Equipment and remote controls should be situated within arm's reach, and easy access should be provided to equipment that cannot be so positioned. The operator should be located at the point where hearing and seeing are optimal. If there is a dedicated section for a producer, director, and observers, raise the area so the views of console operations, video monitors, and studio activities are unobstructed.

■ **Furniture** Furniture should be functional, rather than just decorative, and reflect as little sound as possible. Chairs should be comfortable and move around easily on wheels without squeaking. A chair should be adjustable, have a five-point base so it does not tip, and flexibility when sliding or leaning. Most people prefer armrests and even flexible headrests. A chair should give back support, particularly in the lower back, and not cut off blood circulation in the legs. Cushions should be firm and shaped to support the body. If different contoured chairs are needed to accommodate the regular control room personnel, they're worth the investment.

■ **Floor covering** Rugs should be static-free and permit anything on wheels to move about easily.

■ **Computer workstation** With the proliferation of hard-disk recording and editing systems, many hours a day are spent at computer workstations. The repetitive nature of computer operations over extended periods of time can lead to chronic pain in the fingers, hands, arms, shoulders, and back, ranging from mild discomfort to serious disability, a condition known as *repetitive strain,* or *stress, injury (RSI).*

The main RSI risk factors include: performing a repetitive motion in the same way with the same body part; performing a repetitive activity with force; putting direct pressure on nerves, tendons, bones, or joints by keeping the body part rested against a hard surface; maintaining, or holding an object in, a fixed position; and keeping a joint in a forced position away from its normal centered or neutral position.

There are ways to prevent or reduce RSI. At the computer workstation, keep feet flat on the floor, arms horizontal at the elbow, and eyes lined up with the top one-third of the monitor. Employ cushioned tabletop surfaces. To avoid mouse-related strain, switch among a trackball, mouse, and/or keyboard. There are mice and trackballs available that allow you to plug into an external switch, such as a foot pedal. Do simple stretching and flexing exercises with the adversely affected body parts. Take regular breaks and just relax.*

■ **Access** Studios and control rooms are busy places. Production and performance personnel should not be disturbed by the comings and goings of clients and other observers. Access into and out of production rooms should be easy, allowing activities to continue without distraction or interruption.

---

*From Philip DeLancie, "Engineering Without Pain," *Mix,* February 1999, p. 80.

When the ergonomics in a production venue are lacking, it puts undue mental and physical strain on personnel, reducing concentration and perceptual acuity, thereby increasing the risk of a subpar product. Production is demanding enough: *Make it as efficient and easy on yourself as possible.*

▶ Acoustics is the study of auditory sensation in the ear and the sound waves that cause that sensation. The term is also used to describe the physical behavior of sound waves in a room. Psychoacoustics deals with the perception of auditory sensations in the ear and our subjective response to the behavior of sound waves in a room.

▶ By processing the time and intensity differences of sound reaching the ears, the brain can isolate and recognize the sound and tell from what direction it is coming.

▶ Processing these time and intensity differences also makes it possible to hear sound three-dimensionally. This is known as binaural hearing.

▶ Direct sound reaches the listener first, before it interacts with any other surface. The same sound reaching the listener, after it reflects from various surfaces, is indirect sound.

▶ If similar sounds reach the ear within about 20 ms of one another, the reflected sounds and the direct sound are usually perceived as coming from the same direction, even if the immediate repetitions coming from another direction are louder. This is known as the precedence, or Haas, effect.

▶ The acoustic "life cycle" of a sound emitted in a room can be divided into three phases: direct sound, early sound, and reverberant sound.

▶ Indirect sound is divided into early reflections (early sound) and reverberant sound (reverb).

▶ Early reflections reach the listener within about 20 ms of when the direct sound is produced and are heard as part of the direct sound.

▶ Reverberant sound is the result of the early reflections becoming smaller and smaller and the time between them decreasing until they combine, making the reflections indistinguishable.

▶ Reverberation is densely spaced reflections created by random, multiple, blended reflections of a sound.

▶ Reverberation time, or decay time, is the time it takes a sound to decrease 60 dB-SPL, after its steady-state sound level has stopped, usually from average loudness—85 dB-SPL—to, generally, inaudible—25 dB-SPL.

▶ If sound is delayed by 35 ms or more, the listener perceives echo, a distinct repeat of the direct sound.

▶ Direct sound provides information about a sound's origin, its size, and its tonal quality. Early reflections add loudness and fullness to the initial sound and help create our subjective impression of room size. Reverberation adds spaciousness to sound, fills out its loudness and body, and contains most of its tonal energy.

▶ No one sound room is acoustically suitable for all types of sound. Therefore it is important to match studio acoustics to sonic material.

▶ Rooms with reverberation times of one second or more are considered to be "live." Rooms with reverberation times of one-half second or less are considered to be "dry," or "dead."

▶ Four factors influence how sound behaves in an acoustic environment: (1) sound isolation, (2) room dimensions, (3) room shape, (4) and room acoustics.

▶ Noise is any unwanted sound (except distortion) in the audio system, the studio, the environment, and so on.

▶ The noise criteria (NC) system rates the level of ambient, or background, noise.

▶ Sound isolation in a room is measured in two ways: by determining the loudest outside sound level against the minimum acceptable NC level inside the room, and by determining the loudest sound level inside the studio against a maximum acceptable noise floor outside the room.

▶ Transmission loss (TL) is the amount of sound reduction provided by a barrier—a wall, floor, or ceiling. This value is given a measurement called sound transmission class (STC).

▶ The dimensions of a sound room—height, width, and length—should not equal nor be exact multiples of one another. It creates additive resonances, reinforcing certain frequencies and not others, thereby coloring the sound.

▶ Resonance, another important factor in studio design, results when a vibrating body with the same natural frequencies as another body causes that body to vibrate sympathetically, thereby increasing the amplitude of both of them at those frequencies if the variables are in acoustical phase.

▶ The shape of a studio is significant for good noise reduction and sound dispersion.

▶ When sound hits a surface, one or a combination of reactions occurs: It is absorbed, reflected, partially absorbed and reflected, diffracted, or diffused.

▶ The amount of indirect sound energy absorbed is given an acoustical rating called a sound absorption coefficient, also known as a noise reduction coefficient (NRC).

▶ Three classifications of acoustic absorbers are porous absorbers, diaphragmatic absorbers, and Helmholtz absorbers or resonators.

▶ When sound reaches a surface, in addition to being partially absorbed and reflected, it diffracts—spreads or bends around the surface.

▶ Diffusion is the uniform distribution of sound energy in a room so that its intensity throughout the room is approximately equal.

▶ To be more acoustically functional, many studios are designed with adjustable acoustics—movable panels, louvers, walls, and gobos to alter reverberation time.

▶ Studios are designed for sound that is appropriate for microphone pickup. Control rooms are designed for listening through loudspeakers.

▶ To accurately assess the reproduced sound in a control room, the main challenge is to reduce the number of unwanted reflections at the monitoring location(s) so it is a relatively reflection-free zone.

▶ Ergonomics addresses the design of an engineering system with human comfort and convenience in mind.

Equipment

4

Microphones

The analogy can be made that microphones are to audio production what colors are to painting. The more colors and hues available to a painter, the greater the possibilities for coloration in a visual canvas. In recording sound the more models of microphones there are, the greater variety of tones in the sonic palette and, hence, the greater the possibilities for coloration in designing an aural canvas.

When choosing a **microphone**, or *mic,* there are three basic features to consider: operating principles, directional characteristic(s), and sound response. Appearance may be a fourth feature to consider if the mic is on-camera. Cost and durability may be two other considerations.

OPERATING PRINCIPLES

The microphone is a **transducer**—it converts one form of energy into another: acoustic energy into electric energy. (Another example of a transducer is the loudspeaker, which converts electric energy into acoustic energy.) The electric energy flows through a circuit as voltage. You will recall from Chapter 2 that resistance to the flow of voltage is called *impedance.*

Impedance

Microphones used in professional audio are low impedance. Low-impedance microphones (and equipment) have three advantages over high-impedance mics: (1) They generate less noise, (2) they are much less susceptible to hum and electrical interference, such as static from motors and fluorescent lights, and (3) they can be connected to long cables without increasing noise. Professional mics usually range in impedance from 150 to 600 ohms.

Transducing Elements

The device that does the transducing in a microphone is mounted in the mic head and is called the *element*. Each type of microphone gets its name from the element it uses. The elements in professional microphones operate on one of two physical principles: *magnetic induction* and *variable capacitance*.

Magnetic Induction

Magnetic induction uses a fixed magnet and a movable diaphragm to which a small, lightweight coil is attached. The coil is placed in the magnetic field and moves when sound hits the diaphragm. When the coil moves, voltage is generated. Such mics are called ***moving-coil microphones*** (see Figure 4-1).

Another type of mic employing magnetic induction is the ***ribbon microphone*** (see 4-2). Instead of a moving coil, it uses a metal ribbon

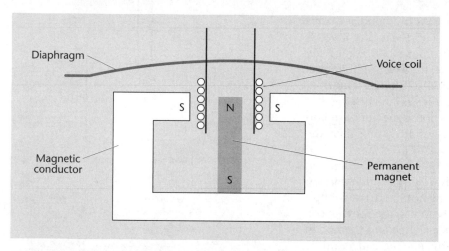

4-1 The element of a moving-coil microphone

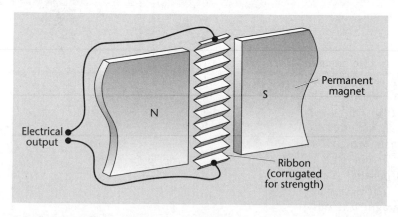

4-2 The element of a ribbon microphone

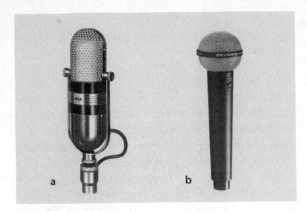

4-3 Ribbon microphones. (a) Older model with vertical ribbon. (b) New model with small, longitudinal ribbon.

attached to a fixed magnet. As the ribbon vibrates from the pressure of the sound waves, voltage is generated. Generally, in older ribbon mics the ribbon is situated vertically; in newer ribbon mics, it is positioned horizontally. The longitudinal positioning and more advanced ribbon design has helped make it possible to house the newer ribbon mics in a smaller, lighter-weight casing than the older ribbon mics (see 4-3).

Microphones that use the magnetic induction principle are classified as **dynamic microphones**. This includes the moving-coil and the ribbon transducers. In practice, however, the moving-coil mic is referred to as a *dynamic* mic and the ribbon as a *ribbon* mic; the term *moving coil* is rarely used. Throughout this book, however, the term *moving coil,* instead of *dynamic,* will be used to avoid confusion.

Variable Capacitance

Microphones operating on the variable capacitance principle transduce energy using voltage (electrostatic) variations, instead of magnetic (electromagnetic) variations, and are called **capacitor microphones**. They are also referred to, incorrectly, as *condenser microphones*, which is a holdover from the past.

The element consists of two parallel plates separated by a small space (see 4-4). The front plate is a thin, metalized plastic diaphragm, the only moving part in the mic head, and the back plate is

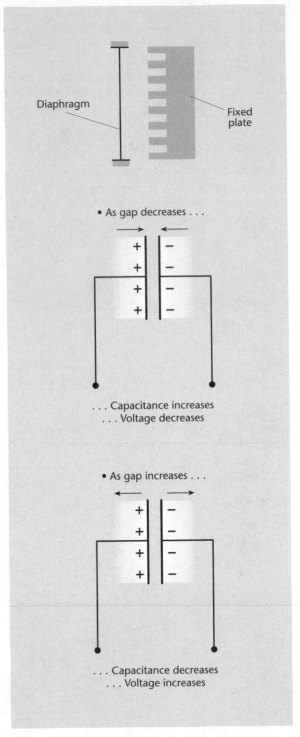

4-4 Element and operation of a capacitor microphone

fixed. Together these plates or electrodes form a *capacitor*—a device that is capable of holding an electric charge. As acoustic energy moves the diaphragm back and forth in relation to the fixed back plate, the capacitance change causes a voltage change, varying the signal. The signal output, however, is delicate and has a very high impedance requiring a preamplifier (mounted near the mic capsule) to bring it to useable proportions.

Most preamps in capacitor microphones use a transistor circuit which, generally, produces a clean sound. But a number of capacitor mics use a tube circuit in the preamp instead. This is due to the particular sonic characteristic that **tube microphones** give to sound, which many perceive as being more present and livelier than the transistorized capacitors.

Because the capacitor requires polarizing voltage and the preamplifier requires power voltage to operate, capacitor mics must have a separate power supply either from batteries contained inside the microphone or from an external, or so-called *phantom*, power supply. External power eliminates the need for batteries and may be supplied from the console, studio microphone input circuits, or portable units.

Some capacitor microphones have an electret diaphragm. An electret is a material (high-polymer plastic film) that can hold a charge permanently, thus eliminating the need for external polarizing voltage. Because a small battery is all that is required to power the preamp, *electret microphones* can be made more compact, which facilitated the design of lavalier and mini-mics.

GENERAL TRANSDUCER PERFORMANCE CHARACTERISTICS

Each type of microphone is unique. It is not a matter of one microphone being better than another, but that one microphone may be more suitable for a particular application than another.

Moving-coil microphones are rugged, generate low self-noise, tend to be less susceptible to humidity and wide temperature variations, and handle high sound-pressure levels without distortion. They are usually less expensive than the other professional types and come in a wide variety of makes and models.

The element of a moving-coil mic has more mass than that of a ribbon or capacitor microphone and, therefore, has greater inertia in responding to sound vibrations. This results in a slower response to **transients**—sounds that begin with a quick attack, such as a drum hit or breaking glass, and then quickly decay. (Capacitor microphones have the lowest mass of the three types of professional mics, which makes them best suited to handle transient sounds. The ribbon mic has relatively low mass; its transient response is between the moving-coil and capacitor mics.) The inertia of the moving-coil element has another affect on pickup: With increased mic-to-source distance, high-frequency response is reduced. Generally (there are a number of exceptions), the frequency response of moving-coil mics is transparent; they tend not to color sound.

Ribbon microphones are not widely used today, except in music recording and for the speaking voice. They are more expensive than many moving-coil mics and have to be handled with care, particularly when it comes to loud sound levels.

Older-type ribbon mics have mediocre high-frequency response, which can be turned into an advantage because it gives sound a warm, mellow quality. Modern ribbon mics have a more extended high-frequency response. Generally, ribbon mics have low self-noise but have the lowest output level of the three major types. This means a poorer signal-to-noise ratio if the mic is too far from the sound source or if the cable run is too long.

Capacitor microphones are high-performance instruments. They reproduce clear, detailed sound and are the choice among professional-quality microphones when it is necessary to record sounds rich in harmonics and overtones. Capacitor mics have high sensitivity, which makes them the preferred microphone for distant miking; high-end response is not hampered by extended mic-to-source distances. They also have the highest output level, which gives them a wide signal-to-noise ratio. These advantages come at a cost, however; capacitors are generally the most expensive type of microphone.

DIRECTIONAL CHARACTERISTICS

A fundamental rule of good microphone technique is that a sound source should be *on-mic*—at an optimal distance from the microphone and directly in its pickup pattern. *Pickup pattern*, also known as *polar response pattern*, refers to the direction(s) from which a mic hears sound. Depending on the design, a microphone is sensitive to sound from (1) all around—*omnidirectional*, (2) its front and rear—*bidirectional*, or (3) its front only—*unidirectional* (see 4-5). Omnidirectional mics are also called *nondirectional*, and unidirectional mics are also called *directional*. *Cardioid* is still another commonly used name for a unidirectional microphone, because its pickup pattern is heart-shaped. Five unidirectional patterns are in common use: *subcardioid* (also referred to as *wide-angle cardioid*), *cardioid*, *supercardioid*, *hypercardioid*, and *ultracardioid* (see 4-6).

A microphone's pickup pattern and its transducer classification are unrelated. Moving coil mics are available in all pickup patterns except bidirectional. Ribbon mics are bidirectional, hypercardioid, or multidirectional—providing more than one pickup pattern. Capacitor microphones come in all available pickup patterns, including multidirectional.

Figures 4-5 and 4-6 show basic microphone directionalities. The precise pattern varies from mic to mic. To get a better idea of a microphone's pickup pattern, study its polar response diagram (see the following section).

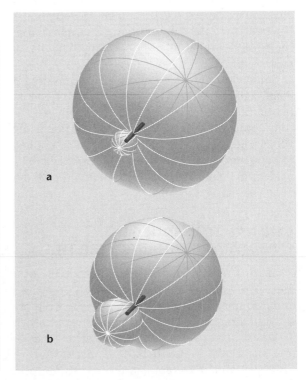

4-5 Pickup patterns: (a) Omnidirectional, (b) bidirectional, and (c) unidirectional, or cardioid.

4-6 Pickup patterns: (a) Supercardioid and (b) hypercardioid.

A microphone's unidirectionality is facilitated by ports at the side and/or rear of the mic that cancel sound coming from unwanted directions. (For this reason you should not cover the ports with a hand or with tape.) In relation to the ports, directional mics are referred to as *single-entry-port micro-phones,* or *single-D*™—having ports in the capsule; or *multiple-entry-port microphones,* also called *variable-D*™—having ports in the capsule and along the handle. In a single-entry directional mic, the rear-entrance ports handle all frequencies (see 4-7). A multiple-entry directional mic has several ports, each tuned to a different band of frequencies (see 4-8). The ports closer to the diaphragm process the higher frequencies; the ports farther from the diaphragm process the lower frequencies. Ports also influence a microphone's proximity effect, which is discussed later in this chapter.

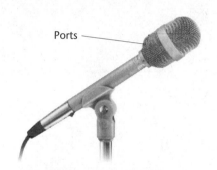

4-7 Microphone with single-entry ports. *Note:* This figure and Figure 4-8 indicate the position of the ports on these microphones. The actual ports are concealed by the mic grille.

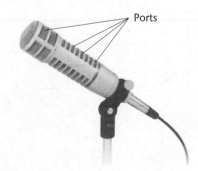

4-8 Microphone with multiple-entry ports

Polar Response Diagrams

A microphone's directional sensitivity, or polar response pattern, can be displayed on a graph. The graph consists of concentric circles, usually divided into segments of 30 degrees. Reading inward, each circle represents a decrease in sound level of 5 dB. The graph depicts response sensitivity in relation to the angle of sound incidence.

The omnidirectional polar pattern shows that sound is picked up almost uniformly from all directions (see 4-9a). The bidirectional polar pattern is most sensitive to sound coming from the front and rear and least sensitive to sounds entering the sides (see 4-9b).

The cardioid polar pattern illustrates sensitivity to sounds arriving from the front and front-sides. It shows a reduced sensitivity of about 6 dB at the sides and least sensitivity, 15 to 25 dB, in the rear (see 4-9c). The subcardioid has a wider front and front-side, and therefore a less directional pickup pattern, than does the cardioid. The supercardioid is more directional at the front than the cardioid. At the sides it is about 9 dB less sensitive and least sensitive at 125 degrees away from the front (see 4-9d). The hypercardioid polar pattern illustrates its highly directional frontal pickup, a 12 dB reduced sensitivity at the sides, and its areas of least sensitivity 110 degrees away from the front (see 4-9e).

To compare the cardioid, supercardioid, hyper-cardioid, and ultracardioid pickup patterns: The cardioid mic has a wide-angle pickup of sound in front of the mic and maximum sound rejection at its rear. The supercardioid mic has a somewhat narrower on-axis response and less sensitivity at the rear sides than the cardioid mic. It has maximum difference between its front and rear hemisphere pickups. The hypercardioid mic has a far narrower on-axis pickup and has its maximum rejection at the sides compared with the supercardioid mic. Its rear rejection is poorer than that of the supercardioid mic, however. The ultracardioid microphone has the narrowest on-axis pickup and widest off-axis sound rejection of the directional mics (see 4-9f).

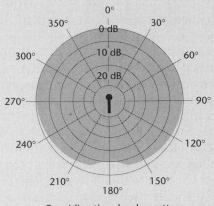

a. Omnidirectional polar pattern

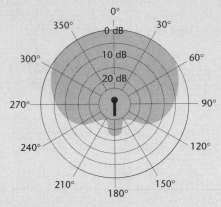

b. Bidirectional polar pattern

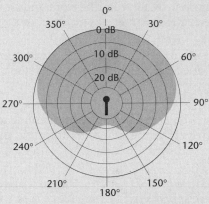

c. Unidirectional, or cardiod, polar pattern

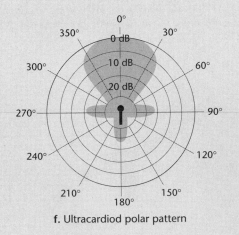

d. Supercardiod polar pattern

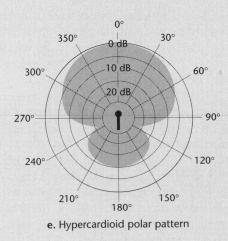

e. Hypercardioid polar pattern

f. Ultracardiod polar pattern

4-9 Principal microphone polar patterns

The polar pattern diagrams shown here are ideals. In actual use a microphone's directional sensitivity varies with frequency. Because treble waves are shorter and bass waves are longer, *the higher the frequency, the more directional a mic becomes, and the lower the frequency, the less directional a mic becomes, regardless of pickup pattern.* Even omnidirectional microphones positioned at an angle to the sound source tend not to pick up higher frequencies coming from the sides and rear, thus making the nondirectional pattern somewhat directional at these frequencies. Figure 4-10 shows an example of a polar pattern indicating the relationship of on- and off-axis pickup to frequency response.

It should be noted that a microphone's polar pattern is not an indication of its *reach*—the working distance from the microphone that the sound source can be and still remain on-mic. Reach also relates to a mic's relative effectiveness in rejecting reverberation (see 4-11).

A word of caution about polar patterns: Don't believe everything you read. Looking good on paper is not enough. The microphone has to be put to the test in use to determine its actual response, particularly off-axis.

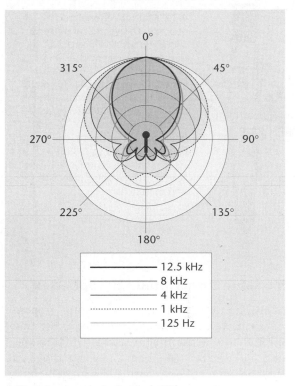

4-10 Polar pattern indicating differences in directionality at certain frequencies. Notice that the lower the frequency, the less directional the pickup.

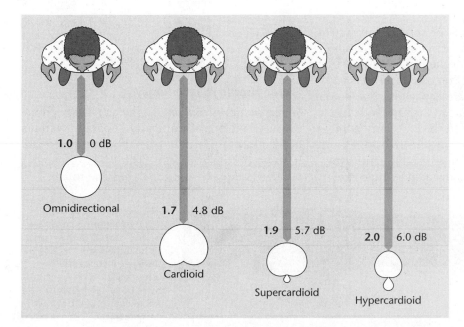

4-11 Differences in relative working distances among omnidirectional, cardioid, supercardioid, and hypercardioid microphones and their relative effectiveness in rejecting reverberation

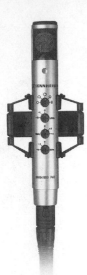

4-12 Multidirectional microphone with five pickup patterns: Omnidirectional, subcardioid, cardioid, supercardioid, and bidirectional. This microphone also has a three-position pad (0, –6 dB, and –12 dB) (second control from top), a three-position treble boost at 10 kHz (0, +3 dB, and +6 dB) (third control from top), and a bass roll-off at 50 Hz (–3 dB and –6 dB) (bottom control). See "Overload" and "Proximity Effect" later in this chapter.

Variable Directional Microphones

Microphones with a single directional response have one fixed diaphragm (or ribbon). By using more than one diaphragm, and a switch to select or proportion between them, or by including more than one microphone capsule in a single housing, a mic can be made **multidirectional** (or **polydirectional**), providing two or more ways to pick up sound from various directions (see 4-12).

System Microphones

One multidirectional mic of sorts is the **system microphone**, which uses interchangeable heads or capsules, each with a particular pickup pattern, that can be mounted onto a common base (see 4-13). Because these systems are capacitors, the power supply and preamplifier are in the base, and the mic capsule simply screws into the base. Any number of directional capsules—omnidirectional and bidirectional, cardioid, supercardioid, and hypercardioid—can be interchanged on a single base.

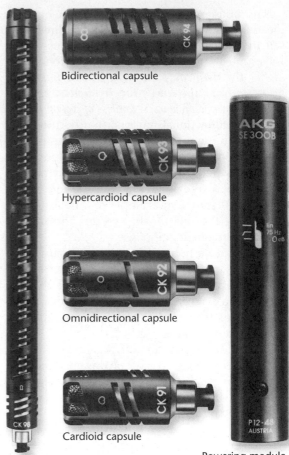

Bidirectional capsule

Hypercardioid capsule

Omnidirectional capsule

Cardioid capsule

Shotgun capsule

Powering module with preamplifier and bass roll-off

4-13 Example of a system microphone

Stereophonic Microphones

Stereophonic microphones are actually microphone capsules with electronically separate systems housed in a single case (see 4-14). The stereo mic has two distinct elements. The lower element is usually stationary, and the upper one rotates 180

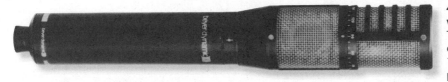

4-14 Stereo microphone with two separate capsules. The end capsule in this model can be turned 360 degrees, in 10-degree increments. The pattern selectors on the microphone body can be set to *R* for remote control of the capsule configurations.

to 360 degrees, depending on the mic, to facilitate several different stereo pickup patterns. Some stereo mics can be remote-controlled.

Middle-Side Microphones

Most **middle-side (M-S) microphones** consist of two mic capsules housed in a single casing. One capsule is designated as the midposition microphone aimed at the sound source to pick up mostly direct sound; it is usually cardioid. The other capsule is designated as the side-position microphone. It is usually bidirectional with each lobe oriented 90 degrees laterally to the sides of the sound source to pick up mostly ambient sound. The outputs of the cardioid and bidirectional capsules are combined into a sum-and-difference matrix through a controller (see 4-15, 4-16, and 4-17).

The systems in Figures 4-15 and 4-16 make it possible to remote-control the ratio of mid-to-side

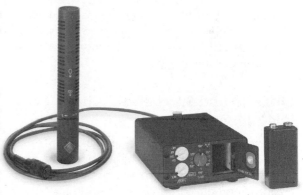

4-15 Middle-side microphone and matrix controller

information to adjust the stereo width of the direct-to-ambient sound. It is also possible to adjust for only left-to-right stereo imaging (also called *XY stereo*). In addition to its advantage in recording

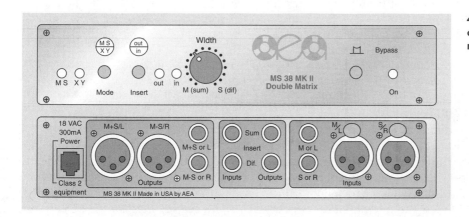

4-16 Another matrix controller, front and rear views

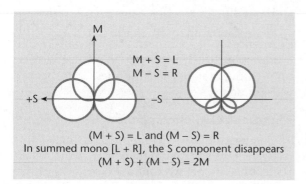

$M + S = L$
$M - S = R$

$(M + S) = L$ and $(M - S) = R$
In summed mono [L + R], the S component disappears
$(M + S) + (M - S) = 2M$

4-17 M-S pickup pattern and capsule configuration

stereo sound, the M-S microphone's matrixed stereo signal is completely *mono-compatible,* that is, the stereo signal can be played in mono with no distortion of sonic imaging.

Binaural and Surround-Sound Microphone Systems

Binaural microphony picks up sound in three, instead of two, dimensions. The addition of vertical, or height, information to the sonic depth and breadth reproduced by conventional stereo and M-S mics makes sound quite spacious and localization very realistic. Surround sound adds greater front-to-rear depth and side-to-side breadth (assuming side placement of the loudspeakers) than stereo, but not quite the vertical imaging or sonic envelopment of binaural sound.

Binaural Microphone Head

The **binaural microphone head** (also known as *artificial head* or *dummy head* [Kunstkopf] *stereo*) consists of an artificial head with an omnidirectional capacitor microphone or microphone capsule placed in each ear canal (see 4-18). Some binaural microphone systems go so far as to construct the head and upper torso based on statistical averaging and variations in real humans. Some even feature felt hair and shoulder padding to simulate the characteristics of hair and clothing.

There are three essential differences between the way a stereo microphone "hears" sound and the way humans hear it. (1) With stereo there is no solid object, like the head, between the microphones. When sound comes from the left, particularly midrange and high frequencies, it reaches the left ear sooner and with greater intensity than it does the right ear. The sound reaching the right ear is delayed, creating a *sound shadow.* The converse is also true: Sound coming from the right is louder in the right ear and casts a sound shadow in the left ear. The listener's shoulders and torso also reflect sound. (2) With the low frequencies, this shadow is largely neutralized because the longer wavelengths diffract around the head. Therefore, we depend on their time of arrival—relative phases— for perceptual clues. (See also "Spatial Hearing" in

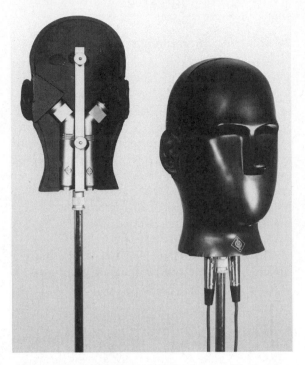

4-18 Binaural microphone head. Two omnidirectional capacitor microphones mounted in "ear" cavities reproduce binaural sound. To hear the binaural effect, it is necessary to listen with headphones.

Chapter 3.) (3) The human ear itself also modifies sound. The folds in the outer ear (pinna) resonate and reflect sounds into the ear canal, causing phase cancellations at certain frequencies. Combined, these *head-related transfer functions (HRTF)* are the theoretical bases for binaural head construction and recording.

Binaural sound is an extraordinary listening experience. It has not been commercially viable, however, because it is possible to get its full effect only through stereo headphones; loudspeakers will not do.

High-Definition Microphone

The high-definition microphone is a single-point, coincident stereo receptor that differs operationally from conventional microphones (see 4-19). It has a triad of operating systems—two electronic and

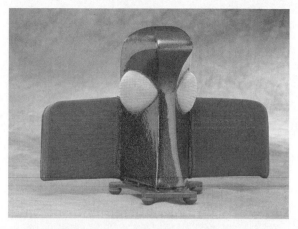

4-19 High-definition audio microphone. This device is a single-point, coincident stereo receptor that picks up the sound of a live event in its natural state and without loss of dimension or detail.

one a function of geometry. The result is a pickup that is virtually binaural without loss of dimension or detail and which can be reproduced on most stereo systems.

In hearing binaurally, humans hear sound with more than just ears. We hear as an integrated sum of direct airborne ear signals, bone conduction, meaty tissue absorption (skin over skull), fluid dynamics, interaural delays, as well as anatomical

head-related transfer functions (HRTFs). It is the combination of all of this sonic information that differentiates a high-definition microphone.

The first electronic operating system utilizes a unique capacitor-coupling methodology to capture airborne sonic information for the widest possible frequency response, at least 20 Hz to 20 kHz, and sound-pressure level—155 dB-SPL and louder. The second electronic operating system captures all the non-ear-related sonic information, collectively called the *body component.* This is useful for any recording where considerable detail and definition are required.

The geometry of the high-definition microphone solves two of the serious drawbacks of the binaural mic: monaural incompatibility and the need for headphones to accurately hear the reproduced three-dimensional sound. The geometry also gives accurate spatial information in the three dimensions—depth, width, and height. Reproduction requires no specific playback equipment or headphones, and mic output is compatible with surround-sound processing.

SoundField Microphone System

The *SoundField microphone system* is a method of recording an entire soundfield as defined by absolute sound pressure and three pressure gradients of the left/right, front/rear, and up/down directions. The microphone contains four mic capsules mounted as a tetrahedron. The outputs of these elements are fed into a matrix network that can be controlled to reproduce a number of different pickups (see 4-20, 4-21, and 4-22).

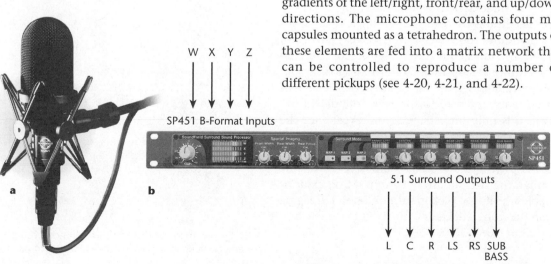

W X Y Z

SP451 B-Format Inputs

5.1 Surround Outputs

L C R LS RS SUB BASS

a   b

4-20 (a) SoundField microphone and (b) 5.1 controller. The arrows indicate inputs for the basic pickup arrays shown in Figure 4-22a and the outputs for 5.1 surround sound.

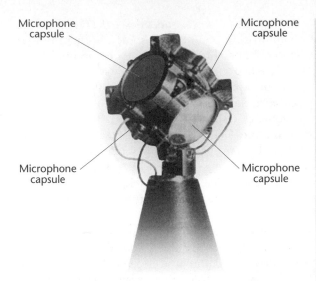

Microphone capsule

Microphone capsule

Microphone capsule

Microphone capsule

4-21 Four rotating capsules of the SoundField microphone

The four outputs, known as the A-format, feed the high left-front-right-rear and the low right-front-left-rear information into the matrix network. After the signals are mixed, they are converted into the so-called B-format, from which they can be manipulated to produce a variety of pickups. The operation is complex but worth the trouble. The resulting three-dimensional sound is quite spacious, and localization is realistic although it does not provide quite the enveloping sonic experience of binaural sound. But SoundField recordings do not require headphones for listening; they do, however, require four loudspeakers, two in front of the listener and two to the rear. SoundField has given this fully immersing sound experience the name *ambisonic.*

The SoundField's 5.1 controller provides the means to record surround sound (see 4-20b). By configuring the Mic Array Pattern (MAP) cards, it enables the mic to pickup surround-sound imaging from the front left, center, front right, rear left, and rear right (see 4-22b).

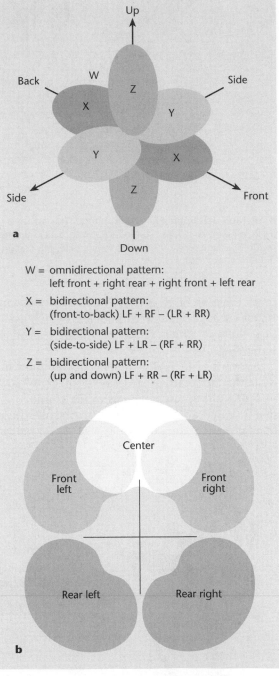

W = omnidirectional pattern:
    left front + right rear + right front + left rear

X = bidirectional pattern:
    (front-to-back) LF + RF − (LR + RR)

Y = bidirectional pattern:
    (side-to-side) LF + LR − (RF + RR)

Z = bidirectional pattern:
    (up and down) LF + RR − (RF + LR)

4-22 Pickup arrays of the SoundField microphone system. (a) Basic pickup arrays and (b) 5.1 surround-sound pickup array.

Holophone™ Microphone System

The *Holophone™ microphone system* consists of seven miniature omnidirectional microphone elements housed in a 7.5-by-5.7-inch fiberglass epoxy ellipsoid that is shaped like a giant teardrop (see 4-23). Five microphones are for front-left-right-left surround and right-surround pickup, with the front (or center) element at the tip of the teardrop. Another mic is positioned on top for height. The seventh microphone is dedicated to low-frequency pickup. This configuration is consistent with the 5.1 surround-sound protocol which, in reproduction, calls for frontal loudspeakers left, center, and right, plus a loudspeaker for low-frequency enhancement (LFE), and two loudspeakers left-rear and right-rear (see Chapters 10, 15, and 19). The Holophone comes with a control module that allows for manipulating the seven signals.

Atmos 5.1 Surround Microphone System

The *Atmos 5.1 surround microphone system* consists of a control console and an adjustable surround microphone (see 4-24). The console is the command center for the microphone's various

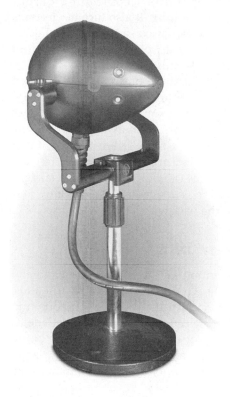

4-23 Holophone microphone system

4-24 Atmos 5.1 surround-sound microphone and control console

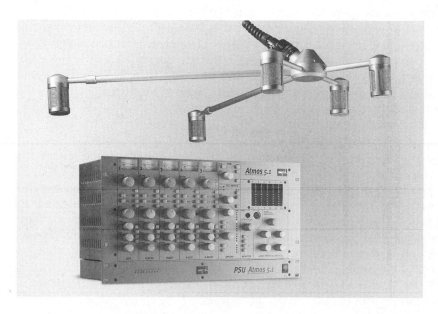

surround configurations controlling output assignment and panning. It also includes features found on conventional consoles, such as microphone amplifiers, pads, phase reversal, phantom power, filters, and sends (see Chapter 5).

The microphone unit consists of five matched cardioid capsules mounted on a spiderlike stand. The capsules can be manually rotated 90 degrees and the pickup patterns remotely controlled. The left, center, and right capsules are positioned in a triangle, with each microphone 6.9 inches from the center. These mics can be positioned in a straight line if desired. The two rear mic capsules are about 24 inches to the back with a 60-degree offset.

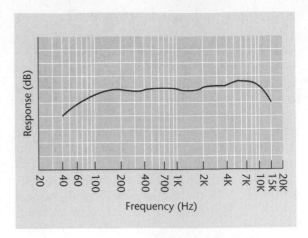

4-25 Response curve of the Electro-Voice 635A mic

SOUND RESPONSE

Clearly, a microphone's operating principle and directional characteristics affect the way it sounds. The particular sonic features that are important to consider when selecting a microphone include its frequency response, overload limit, maximum sound-pressure level, sensitivity, self-noise, signal-to-noise ratio, proximity effect, and humbucking.

Frequency Response

A microphone's *frequency response* is the range of frequencies that it reproduces at an equal level, within a margin of ±3 dB. That is, at a given level, a frequency will not be more or less than 3 dB off.

A microphone's *response curve* is displayed in a graph with the vertical line indicating amplitude (dB) and the horizontal line indicating frequency (Hz) (see 4-25). It shows the tonal balance of the microphone pickup at a designated distance from a sound source, usually two or three feet.

When the curve is reasonably straight or *flat*, response has little coloration—all frequencies are reproduced at relatively the same level. But flat is not necessarily desirable. In looking at a response curve, it is important to know for what purpose the microphone was developed and what your sonic requirements are. In Figure 4-25, for example, the bass begins "rolling off" at 150 Hz, there is a boost in the high frequencies between 4,000 and

10,000 Hz, and the high end rolls off beyond 10,000 Hz. Obviously, this particular microphone would be unsuitable for instruments such as the bass drum, organ, and cello, because it is not very sensitive to the lower frequencies from these instruments. It is also unsuitable for high-frequency sound sources, such as the female singing voice, cymbals, and the piccolo, because it is not that sensitive to their higher frequencies or harmonics. The microphone was not designed for these purposes, however; it was designed for the speaking voice, and for this purpose it is excellent. Reproduction of frequencies through the critical upper bass and midrange is flat, the slight boost in the upper midrange adds presence, and the roll-offs in the bass and treble are beyond the ranges of most speaking voices.

Overload Limit

All microphones will distort if sound levels are too high—a condition identified as *overload*—but some mics handle it better than others. Moving-coil and capacitor microphones are not as vulnerable to distortion caused by excessive loudness as are ribbon mics. Moving-coil mics can take high levels of loudness without internal damage. Using a ribbon mic when there may be overload risks damaging the element, particularly with the older-type ribbon mics.

In the capacitor system, although loud sound-pressure levels may not create distortion at the diaphragm, the output signal may be great enough to overload the electronics in the mic. To prevent this, many capacitors contain a built-in pad. Switching the pad into the mic system eliminates overload distortion of the mic's preamp, thereby reducing the output signal so many decibels (see 4-12).

Maximum Sound-Pressure Level

Maximum sound-pressure level is the level at which a microphone's output signal begins to distort, that is, produces a 3 percent *total harmonic distortion (THD)*. *Harmonic distortion* occurs when an audio system introduces harmonics into the output signal that were not present originally. If a microphone has a maximum sound-pressure level of 120 dB-SPL, it means that the mic will audibly distort when the level of a sound source reaches 120 dB-SPL. A maximum SPL of 120 dB is good, 135 dB is very good, and 150 dB is excellent.

Sensitivity

Sensitivity measures the voltage that a microphone produces (dBV), which indicates a microphone's efficiency. Sensitivity does not affect a mic's sound quality, but it can affect a recording's overall sound quality. The lower the output voltage, the less sensitive the microphone. The less sensitive the microphone, the closer it has to be to a sound source to maintain a decent signal-to-noise ratio, or the more level gain the signal needs at the console, or both. Increased level often means increased noise. Ribbon and small moving-coil mics have low sensitivity (–85 dBV); larger moving-coil mics have medium sensitivity (–75 dBV); capacitor mics have high sensitivity (–65 dBV).

Self-noise

Self-noise is the electrical noise, or hiss, a microphone (or any electronic device) produces. Self-noise measurement is in dB-SPL, A-weighted.

A fair self-noise rating is around 40 dB-SPL, a good rating is around 30 dB-SPL, and an excellent rating is 20 dB-SPL or less.

Signal-to-Noise Ratio

Signal-to-noise ratio (S/N) is the difference between the signal and the noise levels in an electronic component and is measured in decibels.* In relation to microphones, S/N is the difference between sound-pressure level and self-noise. For example, if the microphone's maximum SPL is 94 dB and the self-noise is 30 dB-SPL, the signal-to-noise ratio is 64 dB. The higher the S/N, the more noise-free the signal. An S/N of 64 dB is fair, 74 dB is good, and 84 dB and higher is excellent.

Proximity Effect

When any microphone is placed close to a sound source, bass frequencies increase in level relative to midrange and treble frequencies. This response is known as *proximity effect* or *bass tip-up* (see 4-26).

Proximity effect is most pronounced in pressure-gradient (ribbon) microphones—mics in which both sides of the diaphragm are exposed to incident sound. Response is generated by the pressure differential, or gradient, between the sound that reaches the front of the diaphragm relative to the sound that reaches the rear. As mic-to-source

---

*Signal-to-noise (S/N) is the ratio of audio signal compared with the level of noise measured at some point in an audio system. In audio equipment S/N is expressed as the ratio of the weighted noise floor compared with a standard reference level. For example, an analog tape recorder's signal-to-noise ratio may be given as the ratio of noise present when compared with a reference level of a 1-kHz tone recorded at the tape's optimum recording level. Signal-to-noise ratios for various audio components give an indication of their ability to reproduce a sound cleanly and are expressed in negative numbers. Professional-quality analog tape recorders may have an S/N ratio of about –65 dB. Digital audio recorders have an S/N ratio of about –95 dB and better. Hence, the S/N of a digital audio recorder is considerably better than that of an analog tape recorder.

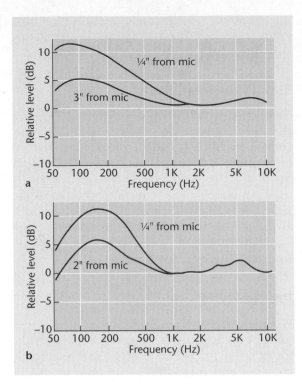

4-26 Proximity effect. (a) A typical cardioid moving-coil mic and (b) a cardioid capacitor mic.

distance decreases, acoustic pressure on the diaphragm increases. Because pressure is greater at lower frequencies and the path between the front and rear of the diaphragm is short, bass response rises.

Response of directional microphones is, in part, pressure-gradient and, therefore, also susceptible to

proximity effect, but not to the extent of ribbon mics. Omnidirectional microphones are not subject to proximity effect unless the mic is close enough to the sound source as to be almost touching it.

Proximity effect can be a blessing or a curse, depending on the situation. For example, in close-miking a bass drum, cello, or thin-sounding voice, proximity effect can add power or solidity to the sound source. Where a singer with a deep bass voice works close to the mic, proximity effect can increase boominess, masking middle and high frequencies.

To neutralize unwanted proximity effect (rumble, or 60-cycle hum), most microphones susceptible to the effect include the feature, called *bass roll-off*, of a limited in-mic equalizer (see 4-12). When turned on, the roll-off attenuates bass frequencies several decibels from a certain point and below, depending on the microphone, thereby canceling or reducing any proximity effect (see 4-27).

Because bass roll-off has so many advantages, it has become a common feature even on microphones that have little or no proximity effect. In some models bass roll-off has been extended to include several different frequency settings at which attenuation can occur, or different levels of attenuation at the same roll-off frequency (see 4-28).

Another way to reduce proximity effect is to use a multiple-entry directional microphone, because these mics have some distance between the rear-entry low-frequency ports and the sound source. At close mic-to-source distances, however, most multiple-entry microphones have some proximity effect.

4-27 Example of bass roll-off curves

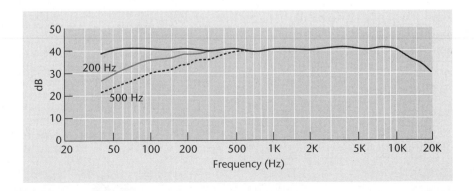

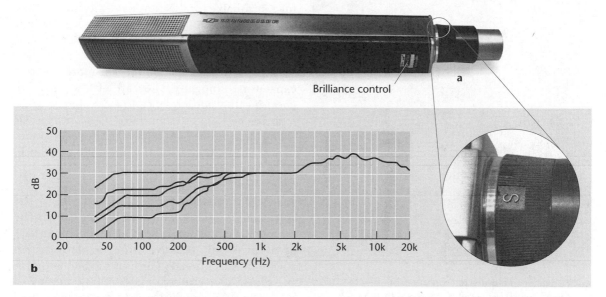

Brilliance control

4-28 (a) **Five-position roll-off control and** (b) **its effect on bass response.** S = speech, M (not shown) = music. This particular microphone also has a brilliance control. The response curve (b) shows the curve when the high-frequency boost is switched into the pickup.

To avoid proximity effect at close working distances down to a few inches, directional microphones have been designed that are frequency independent. One such mic uses two transducers, one to process high frequencies, the other to process low frequencies. This *two-way system* design also produces a more linear response at the sides of the microphone.

Humbucking

Humbucking is not so much a response characteristic as it is a feature built into many microphones. Hum is an ever-present concern in audio, in general, and in microphone pickup, in particular. To minimize this problem, microphones are designed with a **humbuck circuit**—a circuit that reduces hum by several decibels. It is built into the microphone system and requires no special operation to activate it. The amount of hum reduction varies with the microphone.

SPECIAL-PURPOSE MICROPHONES

In addition to a microphone's operating principle, directional characteristic(s), and sound, certain mics have also been designed to meet specific production needs. Some of these mics were discussed in "Variable Directional Microphones" earlier in the chapter; the following discussion addresses some other popular special-purpose microphones.

Lavalier Microphones (Mini-mics)

The first TV microphone created primarily for looks was the small and unobtrusive **lavalier microphone** (see 4-29), although by today's standards it was not so small and unobtrusive. The microphone was hung around the neck, hence the name (*lavaliere* is French for *pendant*). Today these mics are, indeed, quite small and are also known as *miniature microphones,* or **mini-mics**. They are attached to a tie, to the front of a dress in the sternum area or at the neckline, or to a lapel. When they have to be

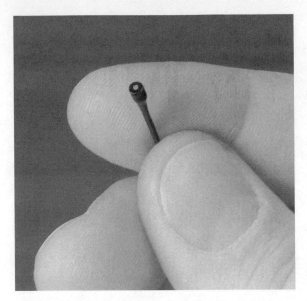

4-29 Lavalier miniature microphone. This model measures ¹⁄₁₀-inch in diameter. It features three protective caps that both keep moisture out and alter the mic's color and frequency response to match desired applications. Frequency responses using the three protective caps are flat, +0 dB; bright, +4 dB; and very bright, +8 dB.

concealed, they are placed under clothing, behind the ear, and in the hair.

Mini-mics designed for use under the chin have two things in common: (1) Most are omnidirectional, although directional minis are available and used under certain conditions (see Chapter 13), and (2) many have a built-in high-frequency boost. The omnidirectional pickup is necessary because, with the mic being mounted away from the front of the mouth, a speaker does not talk directly into it but across it. A directional response would not pick up much room presence and would sound too dead. In addition, as a speaker talks, high frequencies, which are directional, travel straight ahead. The chin cuts off many of the less directional high frequencies with longer wavelengths that otherwise would reach the mic. The built-in high-frequency boost compensates for this loss. If you hold in front of your mouth a mini-mic that was designed for use under the chin, its response will be overly bright and hissy. Their sensitivity to

breathing and popping sounds also makes mini-mics unsuitable for use in front of the mouth; they have no pop filter, although windscreens come with many models (see "Windscreens and Pop Filters" later in this chapter).

The mini-mics in common use are electret capacitors. Sonically, they are either *proximity oriented*—they add presence to close speech while reducing background sound—or *transparent*—their sound blends more naturally with the overall sound, which means that they pick up more ambience.

Microscopic Microphones

A new concept in mic design and size is the **microscopic microphone** (see 4-30). Called the *Microflown,* it measures the velocity of air particles across two tiny, resistive strips of platinum on silicon nitride, instead of measuring fluctuating air pressure as conventional mics do. (The motion of gas or liquid is called *flow* in the science of fluid dynamics, hence the name *Microflown,* which is serendipitous in its sonic relationship to the word *microphone.*) The strips are heated to about 200°C. When air flows across the strips, heat is carried from one to the other, causing a temperature differential between them and generating a very small voltage. With a sound wave, the air flows across the strips and alternates according to the waveform, resulting

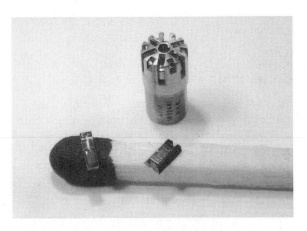

4-30 Microflown microphone. Two Microflowns compared in size with a wooden match and a conventional mini-mic.

in a corresponding voltage. The Microflown measures about ³⁄₂₅ inch wide, about ²⁄₂₅ inch long, and ¹⁄₁₀₀ inch thick. The sensor strips are so small that they cannot be seen with the naked eye.

Shotgun Microphones

Television created the need for a good-looking on-camera microphone, but the need for an off-camera mic first became apparent in sound motion pictures. The problem was to record performers' voices without a microphone being visible. Directors had many ingenious ways to hide a mic on the set; they used flowerpots, vases, lamps, clothing, and virtually anything else that could conceal a microphone. These attempts only made more obvious the need for a microphone capable of picking up sound from a distance.

The solution was the *shotgun microphone* (see 4-49, right). The basic principle of all shotgun mics is that they attenuate sound from all directions except a narrow angle at the front. This creates the perception that they have greater reach. Compared with an omnidirectional microphone, mic-to-source distances can be 1.7 times greater with a cardioid, 1.9 times greater with a supercardioid, and 2.0 times greater with a hypercardioid and not affect on-mic presence (see 4-11). Some shotguns are better than others, so be careful when you choose one, especially for use in mediocre acoustic environments. The main consideration should be how well it discriminates sound, front-to-back, in a given situation.

The comparison can be made between a shotgun mic and a telephoto lens on a camera. A telephoto lens compresses front-to-back space. Shot with such a lens, an auditorium, for example, would appear smaller with the rows of seats closer together than they really are. A shotgun mic does the same thing with acoustic space: It brings the background and foreground sounds closer together. The extent of this spatial compression depends on the mic's pickup pattern. Of the three types of shotgun pickups—super-, hyper-, and ultracardioid—the supercardioid compresses front-to-rear sound the least and the ultracardioid compresses it the most.

Shotgun mics can sacrifice quality for greater reach. The shotgun becomes less directional at lower frequencies, as do all directional mics, because of the inability to deal well with wavelengths that are longer than the length of its tube, called the *interference tube*. Interference tubes come in various lengths from 6 inches to 3 feet and longer. The longer the interference tube, the more highly directional the microphone. If the tube of a shotgun mic is 3 feet long, it will maintain directionality for frequencies of 300 Hz and higher—that is, wavelengths of approximately 3 feet and less. For 300 Hz and lower, the mic becomes less and less directional, canceling fewer and fewer of the lower frequencies. Many shotgun mics do have bass roll-off, however.

Parabolic Microphone System

Another microphone that is used for long-distance pickup, mainly outdoors at sporting events, film and video shoots, and in gathering naturalistic recordings of animals in the wild, is the *parabolic microphone system*. It consists of either an omni- or a unidirectional microphone facing inward and attached to a parabolic reflector (see 4-31).

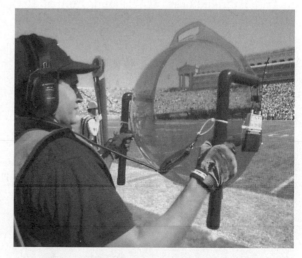

4-31 Parabolic microphone system. This particular system is using a wireless lavalier microphone with the transmitter attached to the parabolic reflector.

Fine-tuning the pickup is done by moving the device that holds the mic forward or backward. More than canceling unwanted sound, the parabolic dish, which is concave, concentrates the sound waves from the sound source and directs them to the microphone. As with the shotgun mic, the parabolic mic is most effective within the middle- and high-frequency ranges; its sound quality is not suitable for critical recording.

Adaptive Array Microphone System

The *Adaptive Array microphone system* is a uniquely configured mic system designed to increase long-distance pickup while substantially reducing background (unwanted) sound. It is intended for use at sporting events, location recordings, and for handheld interviews in high-noise environments.

The microphone system, which is 14 inches long and weighs 16 ounces, consists of five mic elements housed in a single casing, and a control pack (see 4-32). The five mics are a conventional capacitor shotgun interference tube plus four cardioid elements mounted in a co-planar diamond configuration along with their mic preamps. The purpose of the cardioid capsules is to pick up sounds that are *not* to be heard. The sounds from all five mics are fed to the control pack; if the cardioid array

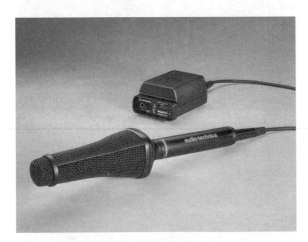

4-32 Adaptive Array microphone system with controller

hears sounds that the shotgun does not hear and/or sounds that the shotgun does hear, those sounds are digitally suppressed at the output. The Adaptive Array microphone system offers three modes of polar pattern operation: a full-field adaptive mode for the narrowest response angle, a planar-adaptive mode for a narrow pattern in only the vertical plane, and the line+ gradient mode for a wider pickup in less noisy environments.

Headset Microphones

Sports broadcasting led to the development of the *headset microphone*—a mic mounted to headphones. The microphone is usually a moving-coil type, with built-in pop filter, because of its ability to handle the loud sound-pressure levels that sports announcers project (see 4-33). It may be unidirec-

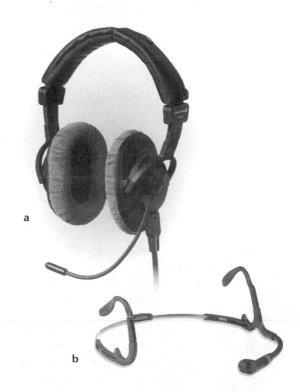

4-33 (a) Headset microphone system with omnidirectional mic. (b) Small headset microphone system with cardioid mic for vocalists, singing instrumentalists, and radio talk-show hosts. Headset microphone systems can be wired or wireless.

tional to keep background sound to a minimum or omnidirectional for added event ambience.

The headphones can carry two separate signals; the program feeds through one headphone and the director's cues through the other. The headset system frees the announcer's hands and frontal working space. Another benefit is that the announcer's distance from the mic does not change once the headset is in place. Smaller and more lightweight headset mics than those used in sports broadcasting are also available. They are particularly popular with singers doing TV and live concerts.

Contact Microphones

Not to quibble about semantics, but some lavaliers, particularly the miniature models, can be classified as *contact microphones* and vice versa. Essentially, the difference between the two is that a contact mic has been specially designed to attach to a vibrating surface (see 4-34). Exact positioning of a contact mic is important if the sound is to be free of standing-wave resonance from the vibrating surface, especially if it is a musical instrument.

Contact mics come in various impedances, so it is important to select low-impedance models for professional recording. They also come in different designs. One electret capacitor version is enclosed in a strip and is flexible enough to adhere to almost any surface, flat or curved.

Boundary Microphones

When a conventional microphone is placed on or near a surface, such as a wall, floor, or ceiling, reflections from that surface so close to the mic can create a *comb-filter effect*—additive and subtractive phase shifts that give sound an unnatural, hollow coloration (see 4-35). The *boundary microphone* positions a mini-capacitor mic capsule very close to, but at an optimal distance from, a sound-reflecting plate—the boundary (see 4-36). It picks up direct and reflected sound at the same time, in phase. Any comb filtering occurs out of the range of human hearing.

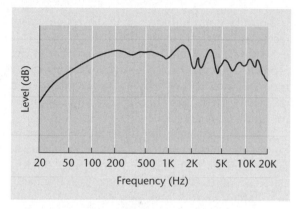

4-35 Comb-filter effect. Delayed reflected sound combined with direct sound can create this effect.

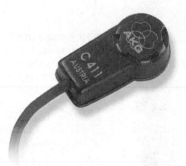

4-34 Contact microphone, also called *acoustic pickup mic*. This particular contact mic is designed for attachment to string instruments. Its size is 1 by 0.50 by 0.03 inch.

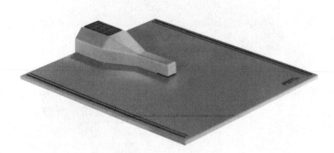

4-36 Boundary microphone

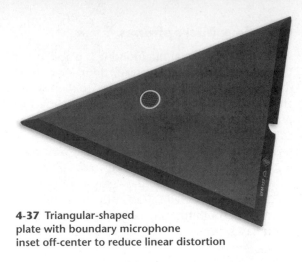

4-37 Triangular-shaped plate with boundary microphone inset off-center to reduce linear distortion

Boundary microphones may be mounted on rectangular, square, or circular plates. If the mic is positioned centrally on a symmetrical plate, acoustical phasing from the edges of the plate may interfere with pickup and cause irregularities in response. Therefore, boundary mics are often positioned off-center (see 4-37).

Boundary microphones have an electret transducer. Their pickup pattern is half-omnidirectional or hemispheric, half-cardioid, half-supercardioid, or stereophonic (see 4-38). Their response is open and, in suitable acoustics, spacious.

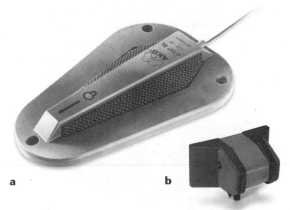

a   b

4-38 Boundary mics with (a) hypercardioid pickup and (b) stereo pickup. The stereo boundary mic is a PZM™ (pressure zone microphone) called SASS,™ for Stereo Ambient Sampling System. It uses two boundary-mounted mics, with a foam barrier between them, to make each mic directional.

Noise-Canceling Microphones

As stated earlier a shotgun mic is designed for long-reach pickup and in so doing focuses sound by reducing unwanted background noise. The *noise-canceling microphone* is also intended to reject unwanted ambient sound, but is designed for use close to the mouth (see 4-39). Because of its particular electronics, the noise-canceling mic must be used close to the sound source. If it is held even a short distance away, the performer's sound may be clipped, and the pickup may be off-mic entirely.

Wireless Microphone System

The *wireless microphone system*, also called a *radio mic, FM mic, transmitter mic,* or *cordless mic,* consists of three components (four, if you count the mic): transmitter, antenna, and receiver. A standard mic is used with the system in one of two ways: lavalier and handheld. The lavalier system uses a mini-mic connected to a battery-powered bodypack transmitter. The handheld wireless mic operates with the transmitter and microphone in a single housing (see 4-40 and 4-41). An alternative to the single-housed handheld mic is the plug-on transmitter, a wireless transmitter with an XLR connector that plugs into the end of the microphone (the XLR connector is discussed later in this chapter) (see 4-42; see also 14-8).

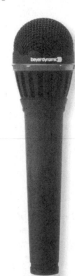

4-39 Noise-canceling microphone. This particular mic is hypercardioid and designed to be handheld in venues with very loud background noise. It is equipped with a built-in pop filter, shock mount, and convenient on/off switch. Handling noise is insignificant.

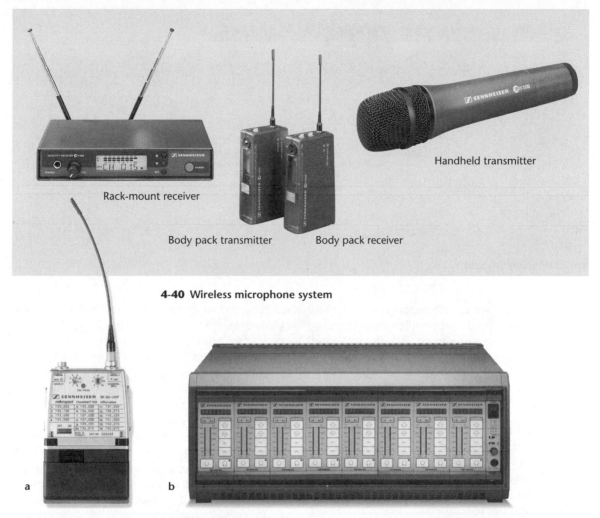

Rack-mount receiver

Body pack transmitter

Body pack receiver

Handheld transmitter

4-40 Wireless microphone system

a

b

4-41 Multichannel wireless microphone system with (a) tunable multichannel bodypack transmitter and (b) multichannel receiver system

The microphone's signal is sent to the transmitter, which relays the signal to a receiver anywhere from several feet to many yards away, depending on the system's power. Wireless microphone systems operate in the VHF (very high frequency) and UHF (ultrahigh frequency) bands. The frequency of each system is approved by the Federal Communications Commission (FCC) because its transmissions may be subject to interference from other transmitting devices in a given vicinity.

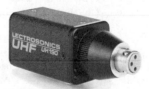

4-42 Plug-on wireless microphone transmitter

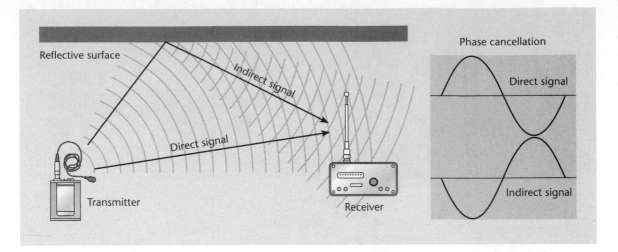

4-43 Multipath dropout

Before using a wireless microphone system, there are a few operational and performance criteria to consider: frequency assignment, diversity reception, companding, transmission range, antenna, sound quality, and power supply.

■ **Frequency assignment and usage** Wireless microphone systems transmit on frequencies in or near the VHF and UHF television bands. In the VHF band, the frequencies are between 169 and 216 *megahertz (MHz);* in the UHF band, they are between 470 and 806 MHz.*

The differences between VHF and UHF wireless mic systems relate to bandwidth, flexibility, power, multipath reception, and cost. Because the VHF bandwidth is far narrower than UHF, there is much less room for available frequencies. This limits both its use in large metropolitan areas, where the spectrum is crowded with VHF TV and FM radio stations, and its flexibility in operating a number of wireless systems simultaneously. Although maximum operating power for UHF wireless systems is greater than for VHF wireless systems, the shorter UHF wavelengths can exhibit more instances of multipath reception. *Multipath* is a physical phenomenon in which more than one *radio frequency (RF)* signal from the same source arrives at the receiver's front end, creating phase mismatching (see 4-43). The area affected by each null in UHF systems is small compared with larger, albeit fewer, nulls in VHF wireless microphone reception. As for cost, VHF wireless systems are usually far less expensive.

■ **Diversity reception** A wireless microphone system transmits radio waves from a transmitter, through the air, to a receiver. Because VHF and UHF waves are transmitted "line-of-sight," there is the danger that the radio waves will encounter obstructions on the way to the receiver. Another potential hindrance to signal reception could result from the transmitter's being out of range. The problem with multipath reception may be a third difficulty. Any of these three problems creates a dropout or null in the transmission. *Dropout* is a momentary loss of the signal at the receiver. The technique used to deal with dropout is known as *diversity reception.*

---

*With the implementation of digital television (DTV), some wireless microphone channels have been reallocated to DTV and public safety. The 764–776 MHz and 794–806 MHz bands are assigned to public safety, with transition to be complete by December 31, 2006. After that the TV channel bands 746–764 MHz and 776–794 MHz bands will be released for wireless microphone systems. During the transition period, wireless microphone systems may continue to operate on these frequencies but may incur interference.

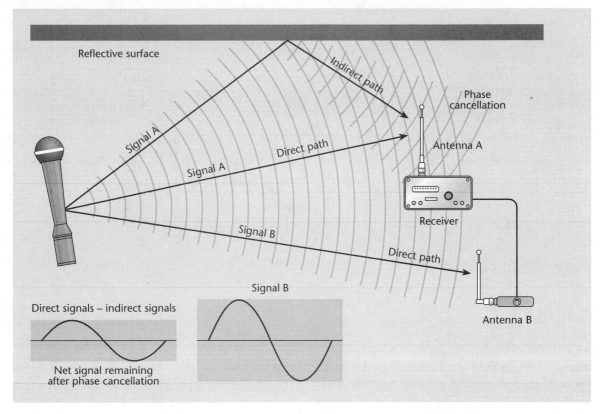

Reflective surface

Indirect path

Phase cancellation

Signal A

Signal A

Direct path

Antenna A

Signal A

Receiver

Signal B

Direct path

Signal B

Direct path

Antenna B

Direct signals – indirect signals

Net signal remaining after phase cancellation

4-44 Diversity reception

There are three types of diversity reception. *Space diversity* places antennas far enough apart so that at least one receives an unobstructed signal (see 4-44). *Phase-switching diversity* shifts phase in the receiver so that one antenna's signal phase shifts to reinforce the other, rather than cancel it. *Audio-switching diversity* uses two receivers and switches to the one getting the stronger signal. It is the fastest and quietest of the three types of diversity reception.

When a wireless system is used in a controlled environment where dropout is not a problem, a **nondiversity receiver** can be used. Nondiversity systems have a single antenna mounted on the receiver. They are generally less expensive than diversity systems.

To check if a wireless system is operating correctly, walk the signal path from the transmitter to the receiver, speaking into the microphone as you go. If you hear dropout, buzzing, or any other sonic anomaly, note the location(s). First check the system to make sure it is in proper working order. If it is, change microphone placement or receiver location if you can and retest the signal transmission.

■ **Companding** To increase dynamic range and reduce noise inherent in the transmission system, wireless mics use ***companding***—a contraction of the terms *compressing* and *expanding.* The audio signal is compressed during transmission and expanded at the receiver. Even though companding sometimes creates noise, coloration, and the audible pumping sound caused by compander mistracking, particularly in less expensive systems, a wireless mic is always better off with a compander than without one (see 4-45; see also "Double-Ended Noise Reduction" in Chapter 9).

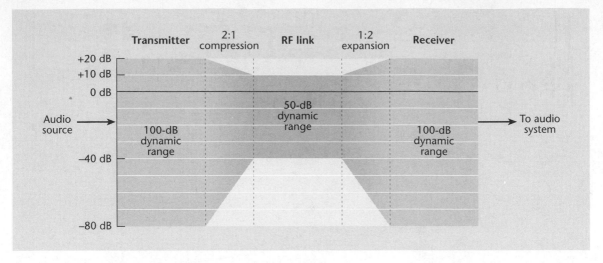

4-45 Compander action

■ **Transmission range** Because the FCC limits the output power of wireless systems, transmission range for high-quality systems is virtually the same: about 250 feet effective in mediocre conditions and up to 1,500 feet effective in optimum conditions. In most controlled studio environments, 150 feet is sufficient operating distance.

Inexpensive wireless systems are 100-feet effective. In optimum conditions their range can increase up to 250 feet.

■ **Antenna** The antenna should be fully extended and several feet away from any obstruction, including the floor. With transmitters avoid taping "whip" antennas (and bodypacks) to the skin, as perspiration inhibits signal transmission.

Both the transmitter and receiver antennas should be oriented either vertically or horizontally. If they are not, it hinders reception. Because performers usually stand, the most common antenna position is vertical. Some antennas are more effective than others. To improve system performance, a dipole antenna could increase signal pickup by 3 dB or more.

■ **Sound quality** Wireless microphone systems vary widely in quality. Clearly, in professional audio only a system with wide frequency response and dynamic range should be used. Frequency response should be well beyond the frequency range of the sound being recorded. Good wireless systems are now capable of dynamic ranges up to 115 dB. A system with poorer dynamic range needs more compression at the transmitter and more expansion at the receiver, creating an annoying squeezed sound that results from companding loud levels.

■ **Power supply** Battery lifetime varies widely. The better systems operate up to eight continuous hours on a new 9-volt alkaline battery, even longer with a lithium battery. Some newer systems use AA batteries. Regardless of the voltage a system requires, install only the highest-quality batteries, preferably lithium for added lifetime. To reduce power-supply problems, batteries should be replaced before they have a chance to run down. It simply is not worth holding up a production session to save a few cents, trying to squeeze maximum life out of a battery.

Other Types of Special-Purpose Microphones

Two other types of special-purpose microphones warrant mention: the *ice zone mic* and the *underwater mic,* or *hydrophone.* The ice zone mic is designed for implantation in an ice rink to pick up the skating sounds. The underwater mic is designed

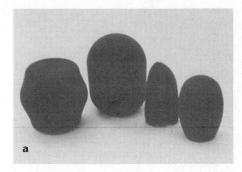

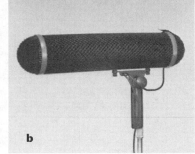

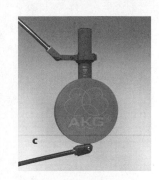

a

b

c

4-46 Windscreens. (a) Various windscreens for conventional microphones. (b) So-called zeppelin windscreen enclosure for shotgun microphones. (c) Stocking (fabric) windscreen designed for use between the sound source and the microphone. This particular model has two layers of mesh material attached to a lightweight wooden ring. (d) Windscreen cover, or windjammer, to cover zeppelin-type windscreens.

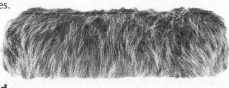

d

for recording sound underwater. Incidentally, if the need arises to record underwater sound, in the absence of the specially designed underwater mic, wrapping a small, conventional mic in a thin, airtight plastic cover will work. Of course, the connector cannot be submerged.

MICROPHONE ACCESSORIES

Microphones come with various accessories. The most common are windscreens and pop filters, shock mounts, cables, connectors, and stands and special-purpose mounts.

Windscreens and Pop Filters

Windscreens and *pop filters* are designed to deal with distortion that results from blowing sounds caused by breathing and wind, the sudden attack of transients, the hiss of sibilant consonants *s* and *ch,* and the popping plosives of consonants like *p* and *b.* (In practice, the terms *windscreen* and *pop filter* are used interchangeably, but for clarity of discussion here, they have been given slightly different applications.)

Windscreens are mounted externally and reduce the distortion from blowing and popping but rarely eliminate it from particularly strong sounds (see

4-46). A pop filter is built-in and is most effective against blowing sounds and popping (see 4-47). It allows very close microphone placement to a sound source with little fear of this type of distortion.

Windscreens also slightly affect response, somewhat reducing the crispness of high frequencies (see 4-48). Many directional microphones with pop filters are designed with a high-frequency boost to compensate for reduced treble response.

Pop filters are mainly found in moving-coil, newer ribbon, and some capacitor microphones, particularly directional models, because they are more susceptible than omnidirectional mics to breath and popping noise, due to their partial pressure-gradient response. (They are also more likely to be used closer to a sound source than are other microphone types.) An omnidirectional mic is about 15 dB less sensitive to wind noise and popping than a unidirectional microphone of similar size.

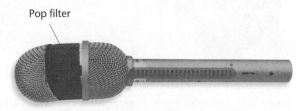

Pop filter

4-47 Built-in pop filter

4-48 The effect on frequency response of various windscreens

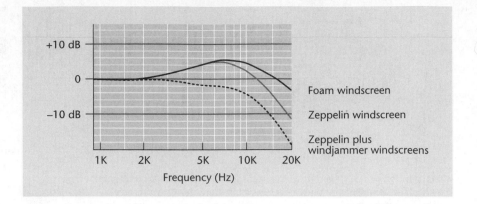

+10 dB

0

−10 dB

1K 2K 5K 10K 20K

Frequency (Hz)

Foam windscreen

Zeppelin windscreen

Zeppelin plus windjammer windscreens

Another way to minimize distortion from sibilance, transients, blowing sounds, and popping is through microphone placement. (These techniques are discussed throughout Part Four "Production.")

Shock Mounts

Because solid objects are excellent sound conductors, the danger always exists that unwanted vibrations will travel through the mic stand to the microphone. To reduce noises induced by vibration, place the microphone in a *shock mount*—a device that suspends and mechanically isolates the mic

from the stand (see 4-49). Some microphones are designed with a shock absorber built-in.

Cables

A microphone cable is either a *balanced line*—consisting of two conductors and a shield—or an *unbalanced line*—consisting of one conductor with the shield serving as the second conductor. A quad mic cable uses a four-conductor design for added noise control. As with all professional equipment, the balanced line is preferred because it is less susceptible to electrical noise.

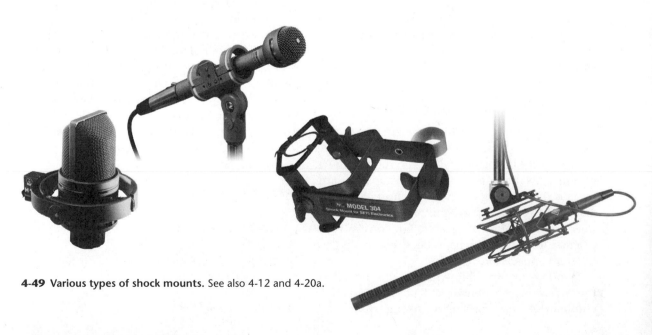

4-49 Various types of shock mounts. See also 4-12 and 4-20a.

When winding mic cable, do not coil it around your arm, and be careful not to make the angle of the wrap too severe or it can damage the internal wires. It is also a good idea to secure the cable with a clasp specially made for this purpose to prevent it from getting tangled (see 4-50).

Connectors

Most professional mics and mic cables use a three-pin plug that terminates the two conductors and shield of the balanced line. These plugs are generally called **XLR connectors** (*X* is the ground or shield, *L* is the lead wire, and *R* is the return wire). Usually, the female plug on the microphone cable connects to the mic, and the three-prong male plug connects to the console (see 4-51).

It is always important to make sure that the three pins in all microphones being used in a session are connected in exactly the same way. If pin 1 is

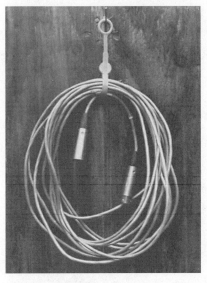

4-50 Microphone cable. To keep cable intact and avoid damage to internal wires and connections, coil and secure cable when not in use.

Safety lock

Female wall receptacle microphone input to console

Safety lock

Male microphone connector

Female microphone connector on cable

Male microphone connector on cable

4-51 Microphone connectors. The female cable connector plugs into the male microphone connector; the male cable connector plugs into the female wall receptacle, which is connected to the microphone input on the console.

ground, pin 2 is positive, and pin 3 is negative, all mics must be wired in the same configuration, otherwise the mismatched microphones will be electrically out of polarity and reduce or null the audio level.

Microphone Mounts

Just as there are many types of microphones to meet a variety of needs, numerous microphone mounts are available for just about every possible application. Commonly used microphone mounts are shown in Figures 4-52 to 4-61.

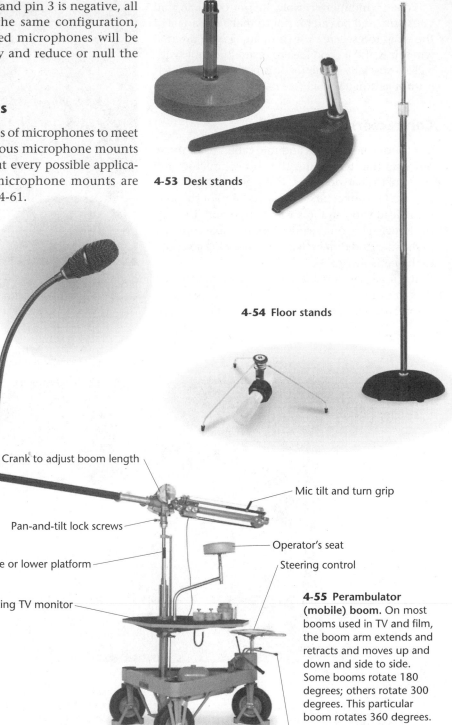

4-52 Gooseneck stand

4-53 Desk stands

4-54 Floor stands

Crank to adjust boom length

Mic tilt and turn grip

Pan-and-tilt lock screws

Operator's seat

Control to raise or lower platform

Steering control

Platform for mounting TV monitor

4-55 Perambulator (mobile) boom. On most booms used in TV and film, the boom arm extends and retracts and moves up and down and side to side. Some booms rotate 180 degrees; others rotate 300 degrees. This particular boom rotates 360 degrees.

Brake and gear change

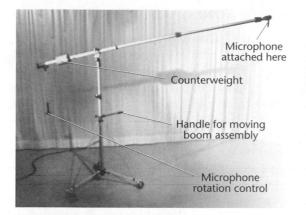

Microphone
attached here

Counterweight

Handle for moving
boom assembly

Microphone
rotation control

4-56 Tripod or "giraffe" mobile boom

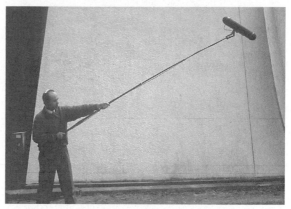

4-57 Handheld "fishpole" boom

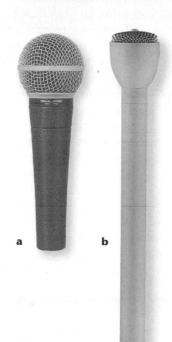

a   b

4-58 Handheld microphones. (a) Microphone with thin tube. It is easily handheld and is also shock resistant and has a pop filter. All are essential in a handheld microphone. (b) Handheld mic with a long handle for added control in broadcast applications.

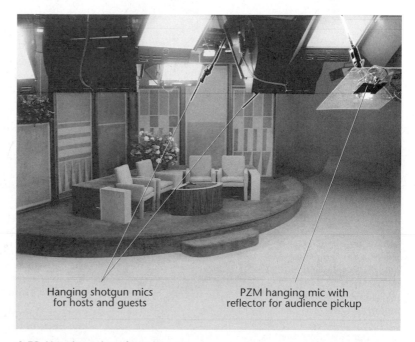

Hanging shotgun mics
for hosts and guests

PZM hanging mic with
reflector for audience pickup

4-59 Hanging microphones

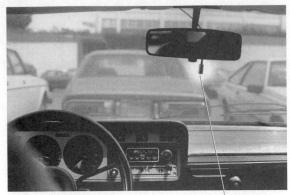

4-60 Hidden microphone

Lavalier mic taped to rear-view mirror

MICROPHONE CARE

Poor care of audio equipment adversely affects sound quality—this cannot be stressed enough. Moisture from high humidity or breath can greatly shorten a microphone's life. When moisture is a problem, a windscreen will help protect the microphone element. Avoid blowing into a mic to check if it is on. There is not only the problem of moisture, but the force can drive particles through the grille screen and onto the diaphragm.

Ribbon mics are especially sensitive to the force of air pressure from blowing into the grille. Capacitor mics are also sensitive to air turbulence, not only from blowing but from fans and blowers. In fact, a breath blast can result in perforating a capacitor mic's diaphragm. Be sure to turn off phantom power when a capacitor mic is not in use. The electric charge attracts dust to the mic's diaphragm. Do not plug or unplug the mic cable while the phantom power is on. The abrupt power change could damage the mic's preamp.

Dirt, oil from hands, cigarette smoke, and jarring also reduce microphone efficiency. Microphones should be cleaned and serviced regularly and kept in carrying cases when not in use. Microphones left on stands between sessions should be covered with a cloth or plastic bag but not so tightly as to create a condensation problem. The working environment should be temperature- and humidity-controlled, kept clean, and vacuumed regularly.

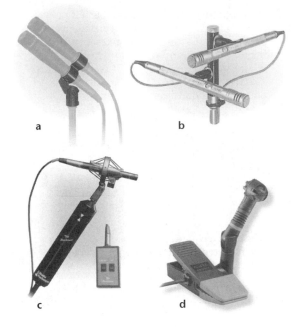

a

b

c

d

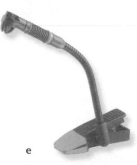

e

4-61 Special microphone mounts. (a) Redundant mono microphone mount, (b) stereo microphone mount, (c) remote panner boom mount and control module, (d) hypercardioid microphone and mount for attachment to drums, (e) hypercardioid microphone and mount for attachment to brass and woodwind instruments.

MAIN POINTS

▶ Microphones are transducers that convert acoustic energy into electric energy. The device that does the transducing is called the element.

▶ The elements in professional microphones operate on one of two physical principles: magnetic induction and variable capacitance.

▶ Professional microphones (and equipment) are low impedance.

▶ The two types of professional microphones that use magnetic induction are the moving-coil and the ribbon mics. The type of professional microphone using variable capacitance is the capacitor mic.

- Capacitor microphones require a power supply to operate.

- Each type of microphone is unique. One type is not so much better than another as it is more suitable for a particular application.

- Microphones pick up sound from essentially three directions: all around—omnidirectional; front and rear—bidirectional; and front—unidirectional.

- The unidirectional, or cardioid, design has even narrower pickup patterns. They are supercardioid, hypercardioid, and ultracardioid.

- A microphone's directional sensitivity can be displayed graphically in a polar response diagram.

- A microphone's unidirectionality is facilitated by ports at the side and/or rear of the mic that cancel sound coming from unwanted directions.

- Directional sensitivity in a unidirectional microphone varies with frequency: The higher the frequency, the more directional the pickup; the lower the frequency, the less directional the pickup.

- Multidirectional microphones have more than one pickup pattern.

- Other types of mics with variable pickup patterns are the system, stereophonic, and middle-side (M-S) microphones.

- Among the mics used for binaural and surround-sound imaging are the binaural microphone head, and the High-Definition, SoundField, Holophone, and Atmos 5.1 surround microphone systems.

- A microphone's frequency response is the range of frequencies that it produces at an equal level, within a margin of ±3 dB, and can be displayed in a response curve graph.

- All microphones will distort if sound levels are too high—a condition identified as overload.

- Maximum sound-pressure level is the level at which a microphone's output signal begins to distort.

- To help protect against loudness distortion, many capacitor microphones are equipped with a pad to reduce overloading the mic's electronics.

- Sensitivity measures the voltage that a microphone produces (dBV), which is an indication of a microphone's efficiency.

- Self-noise is the electrical noise, or hiss, a microphone (or any electronic device) produces.

- Signal-to-noise ratio (S/N) is the difference between the signal and the noise levels in an electronic component; it is measured in decibels.

- Bidirectional and most directional microphones are susceptible to proximity effect—an increase in the level of bass frequencies relative to midrange and treble frequencies—when they are placed close to a sound source. To neutralize proximity effect, most of these microphones are equipped with bass roll-off.

- To minimize the problem of hum, some microphones are designed with a humbuck circuit.

- Microphones have been developed for special purposes: the lavalier, mini, and microscopic mics to be unobtrusive; the shotgun, parabolic, and adaptive array mics for long-distance pickup; the headset mic to keep background sound to a minimum by maintaining a close mic-to-source distance; the contact mic to be attached to a vibrating surface; the boundary mic for use on a boundary (a hard, reflective surface) so that all sound pickup at the microphone is in phase; the noise-canceling mic for use close to the mouth with excellent rejection of ambient sound; the wireless mic for greater mobility and flexibility in plotting sound pickup regardless of camera-to-source distance; the ice zone mic to pick up ice-skating sounds; and the underwater mic, or hydrophone, to record underwater sounds.

- When using a wireless microphone system, consider: frequency assignment and usage; diversity reception; companding; transmission range; antenna positioning; sound quality; and the power supply.

- Windscreens and pop filters are used to reduce distortion caused by wind and transients. An external shock mount, or a built-in shock absorber, is used to prevent unwanted vibrations from reaching the microphone element.

- Standard accessories used for professional microphones include the following: twin conductor cables called balanced lines, XLR connectors, and various types of stands and clips for microphone mounting.

- Proper care is very important to the functioning and sound quality of a microphone.

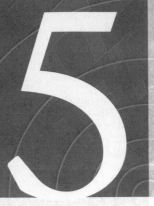

Mixers and Consoles

Mixers and *consoles* take input signals and amplify, balance, process, combine, and route them to broadcast or recording. Many consoles also store operational data. The differences between them are that a mixer is small, quite portable, and performs limited processing functions. The console is larger, substantially so in many models, more complex, and performs numerous processing functions. In many systems these functions are computer-assisted. Their purposes and differences notwithstanding, mixers and consoles, from the most fundamental to the most elaborate, whether analog or digital, have at least three basic control sections: input, output, and monitor.

Signals from a sound source, such as the microphone, feed to the ***input section,*** which routes them to the output section. The ***output section*** routes the signals to a recorder or broadcast, or both. The ***monitor section*** enables the signals to be heard. Consoles designed for multichannel recording usually have a master section as well. In those consoles the output section routes signals to a multitrack recorder, and the ***master section*** routes the final mix to its recording destination.

MIXERS

The mixer is used when audio need not or cannot be complex, as is often the case with news, local sports broadcasts, and disc-jockey programs done on location (see Chapter 13). The most basic type

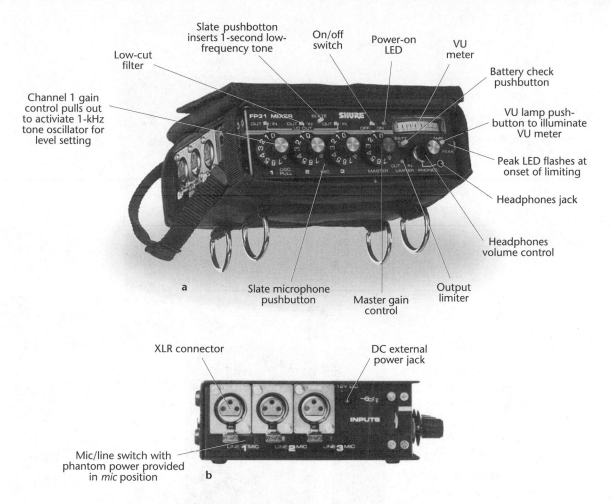

Channel 1 gain control pulls out to activiate 1-kHz tone oscillator for level setting

Low-cut filter

Slate pushbotton inserts 1-second low-frequency tone

On/off switch

Power-on LED

VU meter

Battery check pushbutton

VU lamp push-button to illuminate VU meter

Peak LED flashes at onset of limiting

Headphones jack

Headphones volume control

Output limiter

Master gain control

Slate microphone pushbutton

a

XLR connector

DC external power jack

Mic/line switch with phantom power provided in *mic* position

b

5-1 Microphone mixer. (a) Front, (b) side.

of mixer is the *microphone mixer,* which, as the name suggests, handles only mics. The format can be mono or stereo, and operation can be manual or automatic (see Figure 5-1). Signal flow is straight-forward: Microphones are plugged into the mixer's input channels, where their signals are preamplified and their loudness levels are controlled by *faders*—usually rotary. A fader is also known as an *attenuator, gain* or *volume control,* or **pot** (short for **potentiometer,** a device that regulates the level coming from a preamp). The signals are then routed to the output channel, where they are combined, and a *master fader* controls their overall loudness level before they are sent on to broadcast or recording.

In the field monitoring is usually done through headphones. In the studio it is done through loudspeakers.

Mic mixers may have other features, such as pan control, high-pass filter, oscillator, and slate microphone. These features are discussed in "Production Consoles" later in this chapter.

Somewhat more elaborate portable mixers are designed to accommodate a limited number of additional inputs, such as recorders and CD players. They may include a few functions found in larger consoles as well, such as equalization, sends and returns, and patching (see 5-2). These functions are also covered in the "Production Consoles" section.

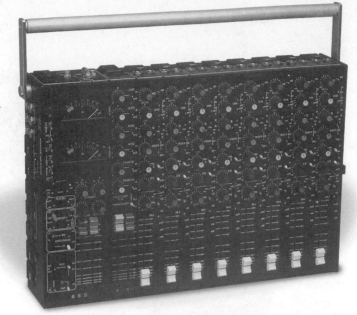

5-2 Portable mixer designed for recording or broadcasting in the field and its functions

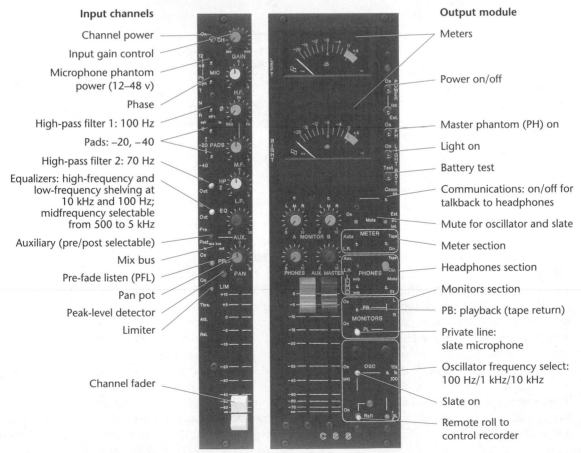

Input channels

- Channel power
- Input gain control
- Microphone phantom power (12–48 v)
- Phase
- High-pass filter 1: 100 Hz
- Pads: –20, –40
- High-pass filter 2: 70 Hz
- Equalizers: high-frequency and low-frequency shelving at 10 kHz and 100 Hz; midfrequency selectable from 500 to 5 kHz
- Auxiliary (pre/post selectable)
- Mix bus
- Pre-fade listen (PFL)
- Pan pot
- Peak-level detector
- Limiter
- Channel fader

Output module

- Meters
- Power on/off
- Master phantom (PH) on
- Light on
- Battery test
- Communications: on/off for talkback to headphones
- Mute for oscillator and slate
- Meter section
- Headphones section
- Monitors section
- PB: playback (tape return)
- Private line: slate microphone
- Oscillator frequency select: 100 Hz/1 kHz/10 kHz
- Slate on
- Remote roll to control recorder

ANALOG CONSOLES

The basic differences between analog and digital consoles are in the way signals are processed and routed. These differences are more easily explained once the operational features of analog consoles are understood.

Analog consoles come in a variety of designs to meet particular needs. Basically, they fall into two categories: on-air broadcast consoles and production consoles.

On-Air Broadcast Consoles

Operationally, on-air consoles are simple compared with production consoles. They are mainly used in radio to handle, in addition to the announcer(s), program materials that have already been produced, such as commercials, news reports, and music CDs.

In on-air broadcast consoles, the input, output, and monitor sections are usually separate (see 5-3). Consoles with separate input, output, and monitor functions are called *split-section consoles*. With production consoles the input and output, and some monitor, functions are located in a single module and are known as *in-line consoles* (see "The In-line Production Console" later in this chapter).

The input section takes an incoming signal from a microphone, CD player, recorder, or phone-in caller. Each input channel is configured for either low-level sound sources, such as microphones, or high-level sound sources, such as CD players and recorders. The loudness level of each channel is regulated by a fader (sliding or rotary). A delegation switch on each channel can either turn off the signal flow or route it to one of three destinations: *program,* which sends it to the console's output; *monitor,* so it can be heard; or to a second monitor system, called *audition* or *cue.* The audition or cue system makes it possible to listen to program material while preparing it for broadcast, without it being heard on the air.

At the output section, there is a master fader to adjust the level of the combined signals feeding to

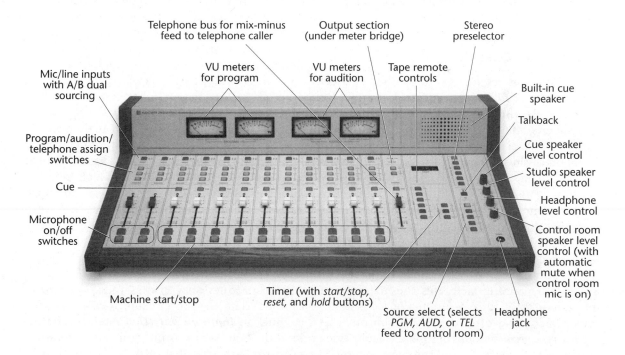

5-3 Example of an on-air radio broadcast console

it from the input channels. This is the last stop at the console before the output signal is sent on its way to transmission.

For stereo, faders usually carry a tandem left/right stereo signal. Some on-air consoles may use stereo pairs, with the left fader carrying the left signal and the right fader carrying the right signal.

Input and output signals are heard as sound through monitor loudspeakers. As they pass through the console, however, they are in the form of voltage. Therefore meters are necessary to measure the voltages in the input and output sections, respectively. By using the fader, these voltages can be kept within acceptable limits. The meter most commonly used with on-air broadcast consoles in the United States is the *volume unit (VU) meter* (see 5-6). The *peak program meter (ppm)* is generally preferred in Europe, although it is found on production consoles here and abroad. Both meters are discussed in the following section.

A console designed for broadcast may be a production console as well and do double duty. Figure 5-19 displays a digital version of one such radio broadcast console.

Production Consoles

Production consoles are used to produce a variety of demanding and complex audio applications for commercials, film and television sound tracks, sports, news, and music recordings. They therefore require a greater number of inputs, outputs, and signal-processing functions than do on-air consoles for radio. They are also designed to meet specific needs.

For example, production is so complex these days that consoles with computer-assisted automation are a necessity, allowing operational data from production sessions to be stored on and retrieved from disk. In film and television, automated panning facilitates the matching of movement to picture. A production console for music recording often requires a number of *submixers* to *premix* groups of similar voicings, such as strings, backup vocals, and the components of a drum set. Network TV news is essentially a one-

mic show, yet with recorded music intros, reports from the field, and interviews, it can easily occupy a 36-input production console. Specialized, compact consoles with integrated machine interface systems are required to handle the unique requirements of automated dialogue replacement and Foley recording (see 17-1). Consoles used for music and postproduction mixes in film and television must have the output capabilities to handle surround sound.

Input/Output Specifications

Two indications of a console's layout and capabilities are provided by the number of input sources it can accommodate at the same time and the number of discrete output signals it can send to its master bus. A *bus* is a common junction of several different signal paths. It can be accessed by more than one stream of audio, which can be sent to one or more destinations. Analog consoles are often specified by their number of inputs and master outputs. For example, an 8×2 (or 8-in, 2-out), has 8 inputs and 2 master (stereo) outputs; a 32×4 (or 32-in, 4-out), has 32 inputs and 4 master outputs. Clearly, an 8×2 console is limited to a few sound sources, but as an on-air console for a stereo radio station it may be adequate. By contrast a 32×6 console is designed for larger-scale recording assignments that require many inputs as well as stereo and surround-sound output capability. Indeed, consoles are available with an even greater number of inputs—several dozen and counting. Production consoles may have a three-number specification, such as $36 \times 8 \times 2$, which indicates 36 inputs, 8 submasters (for submixes, in which selected channels are combined before they reach the master outputs, where all signals are combined), and 2 master outputs.

The In-line Production Console

Analog production consoles today are *in-line consoles*. The in-line console locates in each channel an *input/output (I/O) module*. The I/O module houses the input, output, and some monitor controls, bringing these functions vertically "in a line."

This makes it possible to route a signal from, say, the input of channel 4 either directly to track 4 of a multitrack recorder or to the master output(s). The signal is then routed back into channel 4's input section, passing through the equalizer (and/or other effects modules) for delegation either to the monitor section or the master section. Such signal routing is possible during both recording and **mixdown**.

There are two parallel signal paths, *channel* and *monitor*. In the I/O section, *equalization (EQ)* and other signal processing can be delegated to the monitor system for auditioning without affecting the signal being sent to the multitrack recorder, or the signal can be sent to the multitrack recorder, or both.

Although features of the in-line console differ from model to model, the basic design includes four main sections: input/output, master, monitor, and communications. The patch bay may be considered a fifth section. As noted, in the I/O design each section may include some functions belonging to another section.

In most production consoles, the following are typical functions of each section. Some consoles may have fewer or more features and, depending on the design and manufacturer, the sequence of functions, signal flow, sections designations, groupings, and terminology may differ.

Input/Output Section During recording, the input/output section processes and delegates incoming signals and sends them to the multitrack recorder. During mixdown the I/O section processes

signals from the multitrack recorder and routes them to the master section, where they are combined into mono, stereo, or surround channels and sent to the master recorder.

■ **Microphone-line input selector** You will recall that two types of signal sources feed to input modules: low-level, such as microphones, and high-level, such as recorders. The *microphone-line input selector* controls which signal source enters the input section.

■ **Microphone preamplifier** A microphone signal entering the console is weak. It requires a *mic preamplifier* to increase its voltage to a usable level.

A word about mic preamps in consoles: Whether the audio is analog or digital, each component in the signal flow must be as noise-free as possible. Given the low-noise, high-sensitivity, and high-SPL specifications of many of today's microphones, it is important that the mic preamp be capable of handling a mic's output without strain. If the console's preamp is inadequate to meet this requirement, it is necessary to use an outboard mic preamp (see 5-4).

Inboard or outboard, a good-quality mic preamp must deliver high gain, low circuit noise (hiss), high *common-mode rejection ratio (CMRR)*—the ratio between signal gain and interference rejection— freedom from *radio frequency (RF)* interference, and freedom from ground-induced buzz or hum.

Console preamps may be located many feet from a microphone. The more circuitry a signal navigates,

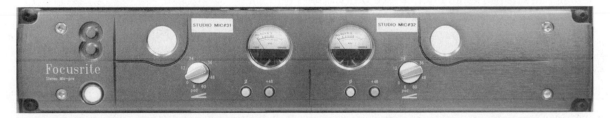

5-4 Microphone preamplifier. This mic preamp provides two independent preamplifiers, each available as a separate channel. It includes: a switchable 12-position gain control (each gain increase is 6 dB, up to a maximum of 60 dB); a phase button that reverses phase of the channel; and phantom power.

the greater the chance for increased noise. By placing a mic preamp in close proximity to a microphone and amplifying mic signals to the required levels before they travel very far, noise can be dramatically reduced. A mic preamp should be stable at very low and/or very high gain settings. The CMRR values should be at least 80 to 90 dB at crucial frequencies, such as 50 to 60 Hz and above 10 kHz—not just at 1 kHz, the only frequency at which many mic preamps are measured.

■ **Phantom power** Just ahead of the microphone preamplifier is the *phantom power* supply (48 volts DC). When activated it provides voltage for capacitor mics, thus eliminating the need for batteries.

■ **Trim** The *trim* is a gain control that changes the input sensitivities to accommodate the nominal input levels of various input sources. Trim boosts the lower-level sources to usable proportions or prevents overload distortion in higher-level sources.

■ **Overload indicator** The *overload indicator* tells you when the input signal is approaching or has reached overload and is clipping. It is usually a *light-emitting diode (LED)*. In some consoles the LED flashes green when the input signal is peaking in the safe range and flashes red either to indicate clipping or to warn of impending clipping.

■ **Pad** A *pad* reduces the power of a signal. On a console it is placed ahead of the mic input transformer to prevent overload distortion of the transformer and mic preamplifier. It is used when the trim, by itself, cannot prevent overload in the mic signal. The pad should not be used otherwise, because it reduces signal-to-noise ratio.

■ **Channel assignment switches** This is a group of switches on each I/O channel used to direct the signal from that channel to one or more outputs; or several input signals can be combined and sent to one output. For example, assume that three different microphone signals are routed separately to channels 1, 3, and 11 and the recordist wishes to direct them all to channel 18. By pressing assignment switch 18 on channels 1, 3, and 11, the

signals are fed to channel 18's active combining network and then on to recorder track 18.

An *active combining network (ACN)* is an *amplifier* at which the outputs of two or more signal paths are mixed together to feed a single track of a recorder. To save space the assignment switches are sometimes paired, either alternately—1 and 3, 2 and 4, and so on—or adjacently—1 and 2, 3 and 4, et cetera. In relation to stereo, odd numbers are left channels and even numbers are right channels.

■ **Direct switch** The *direct switch* connects the channel signal to the channel output, directing the signal to its own track on the recorder, bypassing the channel ACN and thus reducing noise. For example, using the direct switch routes the signal on, say, channel 1 to recorder track 1, the signal on channel 2 to recorder track 2, and so on.

■ **Equalizer and filter** An *equalizer* is an electronic device that alters a signal's frequency response by boosting or attenuating the level of selected portions of the audio spectrum. A *filter* alters frequency response by attenuating frequencies above, below, or at a preset point. Most production consoles have separate equalizer controls for selected frequencies grouped in the low, middle, and high ranges. Filters are usually high-pass and low-pass. (Equalizers and filters are discussed in Chapter 9.)

■ **Dynamics section** High-end production consoles usually include a *dynamics section* in each I/O module for added signal processing. It often includes, at least, compression, limiting, and noise gating (see Chapter 9).

■ **Channel/monitor control** The *channel/monitor control* switches the equalizer, dynamics, and usually selected *send* functions (discussed later in this section) into either the channel signal path to the recorder, or the monitor signal path to the monitor section.

■ **Polarity reversal** *Polarity* (sometimes referred to as *phase*) *reversal* is a control that inverts the polarity of an input signal 180 degrees. It is used to reverse the polarity of miswired equipment, usually

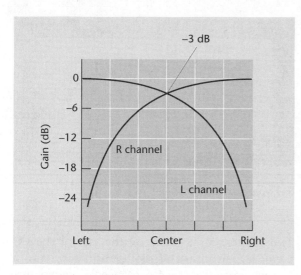

5-5 Effect of a typical pan pot

microphones, whose signal is out of phase with the signal from a piece of similar equipment correctly wired. Sometimes, intentional polarity reversal is helpful in canceling leakage from adjacent microphones or in creating *electroacoustic* special effects by mixing together out-of-phase signals from mics picking up the same sound source.

▣ **Pan pot** A *pan pot* (short for *panoramic potentiometer*) is a control that can shift the proportion of sound to any point from left to right between two output buses and, hence, between the two loudspeakers necessary for reproducing a stereo image (see 5-5). Panning is also necessary in surround sound to delegate signals left-to-right, front-to-rear (or to rear-side), and rear side-to-side. To hear a signal louder in one bus than in the other, the pan pot varies the relative levels being fed to the output buses. This facilitates the positioning of a sound source at a particular place in the stereo or surround field between or among the loudspeakers.

▣ **Cue send (pre- or postfader)** *Cue send* is a monitor function that routes a signal from an input channel to the headphone, or foldback, system. *Foldback* is a monitor system that feeds signals from the console to the headphones. The cue send level control adjusts the loudness of the headphone signal before it is sent to the master cue sends in the monitor module.

At the input channel, the cue send can be assigned before or after the channel fader. Before, or *prefader cue,* means that the level control at cue send is the only one affecting the loudness of the channel's cue send. After, or *postfader cue,* means that the main channel fader also affects the cue send level. In the postfader mode, the level control at cue send is still operational but the main channel fader overrides it.

Pre- and postfader controls add flexibility in providing a suitable headphone mix to performers. In music recording, for example, if the musicians were satisfied with their headphone mix and did not want to hear channel fader adjustments being made during recording, cue send would be switched to the prefader mode. On the other hand, if the musicians did want to hear changes in level at the channel fader, cue send would be switched to the postfader mode.

▣ **Aux send (pre- or postfader)** The *aux* (auxiliary) *send* control (also called *effects [EFX or FX] send, reverb send,* or *echo send*) feeds the input signal to an external (outboard) signal processor, such as a reverberation unit, compressor, or harmonizer (see Chapter 9). Aux send can feed a signal to any external signal processor so long as it is wired to the console's patch bay (see "Patching" later in this chapter).

After the "dry" send signal reaches the outboard signal processor, it returns "wet" to the reverb return in the master section for mixing with the main output. The wet signal may also feed to a monitor return system.

The send function also has pre- and postfader controls whereby any signal can be sent from before or after the channel fader.

▣ **Solo and prefader listen** Feeding different sounds through several channels at once can create an inconvenience if it becomes necessary to hear one of them to check something. Instead of shutting off or turning down all the channels but the one you wish to hear, by activating the *solo* control, located in each input module, you automatically cut off all other channels feeding the monitor system; this has no effect on the output system. More than one solo can be pushed to audition several channels at once and still cut off the unwanted channels.

The solo function is usually prefader. On some consoles, therefore, it is called *prefader listen (PFL)*. In consoles with both solo and prefader listen functions, PFL is prefader and solo is postfader.

■ **Mute (channel on/off)** The *mute* function, also called *channel on/off,* turns off the signals from the I/O channel. During mixdown when no sound is feeding through an input channel for the moment, it shuts it down or mutes it. This prevents unwanted channel noise from reaching the outputs.

■ **Channel and monitor faders** The *channel and monitor faders* control the channel level of the signal being recorded and its monitor level, respectively. During recording channel levels to the multitrack recorder are set for optimal signal-to-noise ratio. On a VU meter, for example, levels would be set to reach or slightly exceed 0 VU (see "Meters" below). Level balances are made during mixdown. To enable the recordist to get a sense of what the balanced levels will sound like, the monitor faders are adjusted to taste, with no effect on the signal being recorded.

Meters

It is a paradox in sound production that the only way to determine levels in mixers and consoles (and recorders) is visually—by watching a meter that measures the electric energy passing through an input or output. Audio heard through a monitor system is acoustic, but it passes through the console as voltage, which cannot be heard and, therefore, must be referenced in another way. A number of different meters are in use today. The most familiar are the volume unit meter and the peak program meter.

VU Meter The *volume unit (VU) meter* is a voltage meter originally designed to indicate level as it relates to the human ear's perception of loudness.

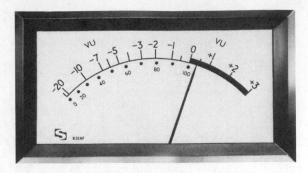

5-6 Volume unit (VU) meter

Two calibrated scales are on the face of the VU meter: a percentage of modulation scale and a volume unit scale (see 5-6). A needle, the volume indicator, moves back and forth across the scales, pointing out the levels. The needle responds to the electric energy passing through the VU meter. If the energy level is excessively high, the volume indicator will *pin*—slam against the meter's extreme right-hand side. Pinning can damage the VU meter's mechanism, rendering the volume indicator's reading unreliable.

Percentage of modulation is the percentage of an applied signal in relation to the maximum signal a sound system can handle. It is a linear scale defined such that 100 percent of modulation is equal to 0 VU on the volume unit scale. Therefore 30 percent of modulation is equal to slightly less than –10 VU, 80 percent of modulation is equal to –2 VU, and so on.

Any sound below 20 percent of modulation is too quiet, or *in the mud*, and levels above 100 percent of modulation are too loud, or *in the red*. (The scale to the right of 100 percent is red.) As a guideline, the loudness should "kick" between about –5 and +1, although the dynamics of sound make such evenness difficult to accomplish, if not aesthetically undesirable. Usually, the best that can be done is to *ride the gain*—adjust the faders from time to time so that, on average, the level stays out of the mud and the red. Fader movements can also be automated (see "Console Automation" later in this chapter).

When manually operating the faders, ride the gain with a light, fluid hand and do not jerk the faders up and down or make adjustments at the slightest fall or rise in loudness. Changes in level should be smooth and imperceptible, because abrupt changes are disconcerting to the listener, unless an abrupt change is called for in, say, a transition from one shot to another.

When the VU meter is in the red, it is a warning to be cautious of loudness distortion. All modern consoles are designed with headroom so that a signal peaking a few decibels above 0 VU will not distort. *Headroom* is the amount of level equipment can take, above working level, before overload occurs. The problem is that although the console may have sufficient headroom, other equipment in the sound chain, such as the recorder, may not be able to handle the additional level. In digital recording there is no such thing as headroom; when you have run out of room, there is nothing left (see Chapter 7).

Because a VU meter is designed to reflect a signal's perceived loudness, it does a poor job of indicating transient peaks. To help remedy the problem, modern production consoles build in a headroom of +4 dB or more; although the signal is in the red, there is still leeway before *clipping*— distortion—occurs.

Peak Program Meter

The *peak program meter (ppm)* was specifically designed to indicate transient peaks (see 5-7). As signal levels increase, there is a warning of impending overload distortion. The level indicator makes this easier to notice, because its rise time is rapid and its fallback is slow.

The ppm's scale is linear and in decibels, not volume units. The scale's divisions are 4-dB intervals, except at the extremes of the range, and zero level is 4, in the middle of the scale. Advocates of the ppm think that it gives a more accurate indication of a signal's actual level of loudness than does the VU meter. The argument is that although humans may not hear momentary peaks in loudness, the electronics do. The ppm is therefore better insurance against signal distortion, particularly in digital audio. Consoles are available with both the VU and peak program meters.

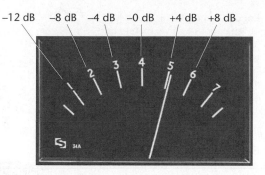

−12 dB −8 dB −4 dB −0 dB +4 dB +8 dB

5-7 Peak program meter (ppm) with equivalent dB values. Dual-movement ppms with two indicators are for two-channel stereo applications.

Bargraph Meters

Whereas VU and peak program meters are mechanical, *bargraph meters* are electronic. Their rise time is quite fast, because there is no mechanical inertia to overcome. This can create problems riding gain. Two popular types of bargraph meters are LED and plasma displays.

LED meters *LEDs* (light emitting diodes) are small light sources. The meters are arranged horizontally or vertically. Usually, green LEDs indicate safe levels and red ones register in the overload region. On professional equipment the LEDs are about 2 dB apart, so resolution is fair. The advantages of LED meters are that they take up little space and are easy to see. Their disadvantage is that, generally, they are not as accurate as the VU and peak program meters.

Plasma displays *Plasma displays* are columns of light that display safe levels in one color, usually green, and overload levels in red. They are more complex than LED meters and have excellent resolution, with an accuracy of 1 dB. One version of a plasma display meter is roughly analogous to a VU meter and ppm combined, thereby establishing a relationship between average and peak levels (see 5-8).

Master Section

The *master section* contains the master controls for the mixing bus outputs, reverb send and reverb return, master fader, and other functions.

5-8 Loudness meter. This meter is roughly analogous to a VU meter and ppm combined. It establishes a relationship between the root mean square (RMS) and peak content of a signal. When riding the gain for balanced loudness, peaks should be driven to the brink of the top set of three LEDs (red), while the RMS should be driven to the brink of the center set of three LEDs (red). This is defined as relative loudness, in 1-dB steps. When the signal peaks in the red, the levels should be reduced slightly.

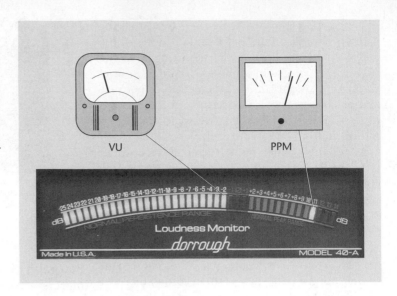

VU   PPM

Loudness Monitor
dorrough

Made In U.S.A.   MODEL 40-A

■ **Master buses** After a signal leaves an input/output module, it travels to its assigned *bus(es)*. In many consoles these signals may be grouped for premixing at submaster buses before being finally combined at the master bus(es).

There may be any number of submaster buses, but usually there are only a few master buses, because final output signals are mixed down to a few channels, such as two-channel stereo and six-channel surround sound.

■ **Master fader** The *master fader* controls the signal level from the master bus to the master recorder. Most master faders are configured as a single fader carrying a tandem left/right stereo signal; some are configured as a stereo output pair with the left fader carrying the left signal and the right fader carrying the right signal. A console may have two, four, eight, or more such faders or sets of faders to handle stereo and surround sound. There is often a mono master fader as well.

■ **Aux send (EFX send, reverb send, echo send)** The *aux sends* from the I/O channels are first routed to the master aux sends before being output to an outboard signal processor.

■ **Aux return (EFX return, reverb return, echo return)** Signals routed to an outboard signal processor from the master sends are returned at the master returns and mixed with the main program signal.

■ **Level, mute, PFL, solo, and pan pot** Each master aux send and return usually has a level control and a mute switch. The master returns also usually have PFL, solo, and pan controls.

■ **Meters** Most in-line production consoles have a VU meter (and/or peak program meter) for each master fader; a mono meter to indicate the level of a summed stereo signal; a phase meter to show the phase relationship between the left and right stereo signals or among the surround signals; metering to monitor surround-sound levels; and metering to display master send and/or return levels. Some consoles also have meters for the control room monitor outputs.

Monitor Section Monitor functions, such as setting monitor level and panning for each channel, may be performed by the I/O module. The monitor module, among other things, allows monitoring of the line or recorder input, selects various inputs to the control room and studio monitors, and controls their levels.

■ **Recorder select switches** These switches select a recorder (other than multitrack) for direct feed to the monitor system, bypassing the I/O controls. There may also be *aux in* switches for direct feeds to the monitor system from other sound sources such as a CD player or digital cassette recorder.

■ **Send switches** These route signals from the sends to the input of the control room or studio monitors, or both.

■ **Mix switches** These select the mix input (i.e., stereo or surround sound) for the monitor system.

■ **Speaker select switches** These select the control room or studio loudspeakers for monitoring. There is a level control for each set of loudspeakers. Monitor sections also have a *dim* switch for the control room monitors. Instead of having to turn the monitor level down and up during control room conversation, the dim function reduces monitor level by 15 dB or more at the touch of a button.

■ **Mono switch** Directs a left + right mono signal to the control room monitors.

A monitor section may also have a pan pot, mutes for the left and right channel signals to the control room, and a phase coherence switch. The *phase coherence switch* inverts the left channel signal before it combines with the right channel signal. If the stereo signals are in phase, sound quality should suffer and, in particular, the sonic images in the center (between the two loudspeakers) should be severely attenuated. If the phase coherence check improves the mono signal, there is a problem with the stereo signal's mono compatibility.

Communications Section As the name suggests, the communications section facilitates communication between the control room and the studio. It also contains the modules used for cueing and equipment calibration.

■ **Talkback** The *talkback* permits the recordist in the control room to speak into a console microphone to the studio performers or music conductor, or both. The talkback may be directed through the studio monitor, headphones, or slate system.

■ **Slate/talkback** Multichannel consoles also have a *slate* feature that automatically feeds to the recorder anything said through the talkback. It is a convenient way to transcribe information about the name of the recording, the artist, the take number, and so on.

■ **Oscillator** An *oscillator* is a signal generator that produces pure tones or sine waves (sound waves with no harmonics or overtones) at selected frequencies. On a console it is used to (1) calibrate the console with the recorder so that their meters indicate the same levels and (2) put reference tone levels on recordings.

■ **Patch bay** The inputs and outputs of console components are wired to jacks in the *patch bay*—a central routing terminal—to facilitate the routing of sound through pathways not provided in the normal console design (see 5-9 and "Patching" later in this chapter).

As noted earlier, in-line consoles differ in their array of features, complexity, and signal flow. Figure 5-9 displays a relatively basic example of an in-line production console and should give you an idea of how the modules function and interrelate. The purpose of the subsequent figure (see 5-10) is to correlate the functions of selected modules in Figure 5-9 to the way they are symbolized in a flowchart. Knowing how to read a flowchart helps you master console operation more quickly. It also helps you track down operational problems when they occur. Having said this, flowcharts vary in technical complexity. The diagrams a technician requires to install a console are quite different from those a nontechnical person needs to understand signal flow.

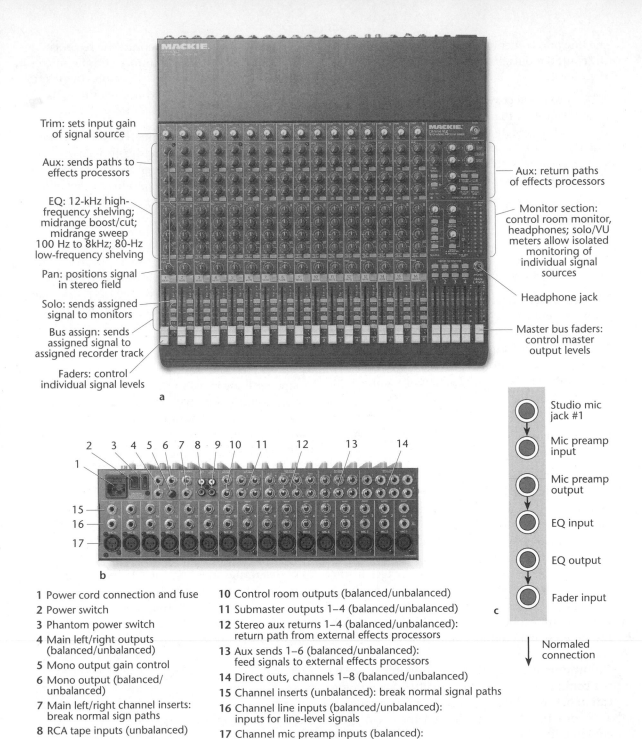

Trim: sets input gain of signal source

Aux: sends paths to effects processors

EQ: 12-kHz high-frequency shelving; midrange boost/cut; midrange sweep 100 Hz to 8kHz; 80-Hz low-frequency shelving

Pan: positions signal in stereo field

Solo: sends assigned signal to monitors

Bus assign: sends assigned signal to assigned recorder track

Faders: control individual signal levels

Aux: return paths of effects processors

Monitor section: control room monitor, headphones; solo/VU meters allow isolated monitoring of individual signal sources

Headphone jack

Master bus faders: control master output levels

a

Studio mic jack #1

Mic preamp input

Mic preamp output

EQ input

EQ output

Fader input

c

Normaled connection

b

1 Power cord connection and fuse
2 Power switch
3 Phantom power switch
4 Main left/right outputs (balanced/unbalanced)
5 Mono output gain control
6 Mono output (balanced/unbalanced)
7 Main left/right channel inserts: break normal sign paths
8 RCA tape inputs (unbalanced)
9 RCA tape outputs (unbalanced)

10 Control room outputs (balanced/unbalanced)
11 Submaster outputs 1–4 (balanced/unbalanced)
12 Stereo aux returns 1–4 (balanced/unbalanced): return path from external effects processors
13 Aux sends 1–6 (balanced/unbalanced): feed signals to external effects processors
14 Direct outs, channels 1–8 (balanced/unbalanced)
15 Channel inserts (unbalanced): break normal signal paths
16 Channel line inputs (balanced/unbalanced): inputs for line-level signals
17 Channel mic preamp inputs (balanced): inputs for mic-level signals

5-9 Basic in-line console. (a) Front view, (b) rear view with patch bay, (c) patch bay signal flow. Patch bays in large production consoles are far more extensive than the one shown here, but the principles are the same.

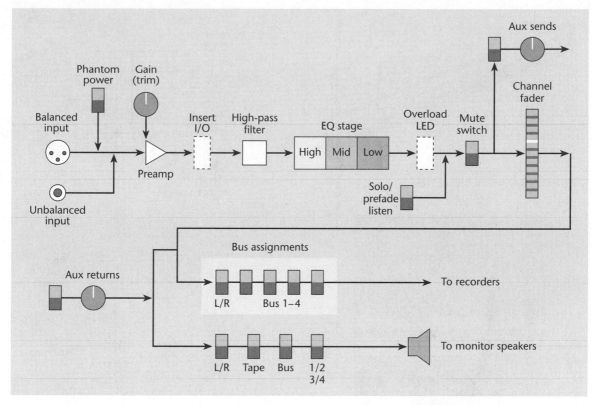

5-10 Flowchart of the console in Figure 5-9

PATCHING

Regardless of how elaborate the console or the studio, signal flow—the paths a signal takes from its source to its destination—is restricted by how active components are wired. When components are wired directly to one another (for example, a microphone to a recorder, or the outputs of a microphone, CD player, and recorder to the input of another recorder), they are considered *hardwired*. The signal can travel only one route. In a small production control room with little equipment, hardwiring may not present a problem.

Multichannel production consoles, however, require flexibility in routing signals to various components within the console and to and from outboard equipment in the control room and other areas in a facility, if necessary. In these circumstances the multiple routes a signal may have to take make hardwiring impractical.

Active components are therefore not wired directly to one another but to the console or studio patch bays, or both. Each hole in the bay (or panel), called a *jack*, becomes the connecting point to the input or output of each electronic component in the sound studio (see 5-11). *Patching* is the interconnecting of these inputs and outputs using a *patch cord* (see 5-12; also see 5-15). In this context a patch bay is more like an old-fashioned telephone switchboard.

But such flexibility is not without potential problems. In a well-equipped and active facility, the patch bay could become a confusing jungle of patch cords. In all studios, regardless of size and activity, a signal travels some paths more often than others. For example, it is more likely that a signal in a console will travel from mic (or line) input to pan pot to equalizer to assignment control to fader,

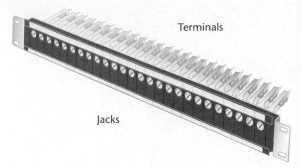

5-11 Patch bay with a row of jacks

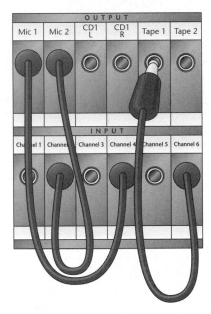

5-12 Use of patch bay. Any sound source wired to the patch panel can be connected to any other one with a patch cord plugged into the appropriate jacks.

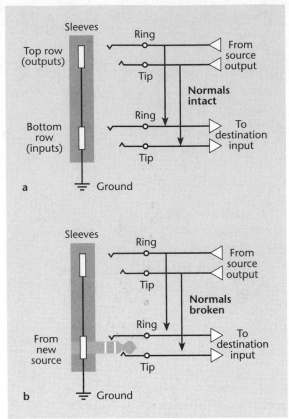

5-13 Normaling. (a) With no patch cords inserted, output of source equipment is automatically normaled to the input of another piece of equipment (tip = high, ring = low, sleeve = grounded shield). (b) When a patch cord is inserted in the bottom-row (input) jack, the normals are interrupted, breaking the original signal routing. The new source signal will now feed the destination.

rather than directly from mic (or line) input to output bus. It is also more likely that a signal will travel from mic to console to recorder than directly from one recorder to another.

As a way of both reducing the clutter of patch cords at the patch bay and simplifying production, terminals wired to certain equipment can also be wired, or *normaled,* to one another. A *normal* connection is one that permits a signal to flow freely among components without any patching. To route a signal through components that have terminals

not normaled or wired to one another, patch cords are put in the appropriate jacks to *break normal*— that is, interrupt the normal signal flow—thus rerouting the signal (see 5-13).

The ability to reroute a signal is also advantageous when equipment fails. Suppose a microphone is plugged into studio mic input 1, which connects directly to console channel 1, and channel 1 becomes defective. With all inputs and outputs connected at the patch bay, the defective console channel 1 can be bypassed by patching the output from studio mic input 1 to any other working console channel.

Some other features of patch bays include the following.

■ **Input/output** Most patch bays are wired so that a row of input jacks is directly below a row of output jacks. By reading a patch bay downward, it is possible to get a good idea of the console's (or studio's) signal flow.

■ **Full-normal and half-normal** Input jacks are wired so that a patch cord always interrupts the normal connection. These connections are called *full-normal*. Output jacks may be wired as either full-normal or *half-normal*—connections that continue rather than interrupt signal flow. Hence, a half-normal connection becomes a junction rather than a switch (see 5-14).

■ **Multiple** Most patch bays include jacks called **multiples** (or *mults*) that are wired to one another instead of to any electronic component. Multiples provide the flexibility to feed the same signal to several different sources at once.

■ **Tie line** When the only patch bay in a control room is located in the console, the other control room equipment, such as recorders, CD players, and signal processors, have to be wired to it to maintain flexibility in signal routing. *Tie lines* in the patch bay facilitate the interconnecting of outboard devices in the control room. When a control room has two patch bays, one in the console and one for the other control room equipment, tie lines can interconnect them. The tie line is also used to interconnect separate studios, control rooms, or any devices in different locations.

General Guidelines for Patching

☑ Do not patch microphone-level signals into line-level jacks and vice versa. The signal will be barely audible in the first instance and will distort in the latter one.

☑ Do not patch input to input or output to output.

☑ Unless jacks are half-normaled, do not patch the output of a component back into its input, or feedback will occur.

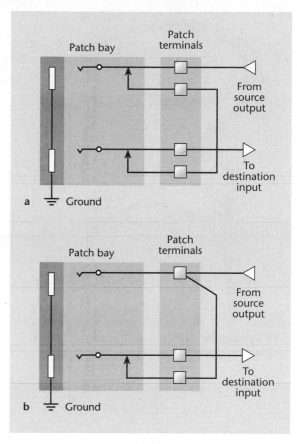

5-14 (a) Full-normal and (b) half-normal patch configurations

☑ When patching microphones make sure the fader controls are turned down. Otherwise, the loud popping sound that occurs when patch cords are inserted into jacks with the faders turned up could damage the microphone or loudspeaker element.

Plugs

While we are on the subject of patching, something more should be said about the plugs on the end of the patch cords. The plugs most commonly used in professional facilities are the ¼-*inch phone plug* and the *bantam* (also called *mini* and *tiny telephone*) *phone plug*. The bantam plug, and the smaller patch panel with which it is used, has all but replaced

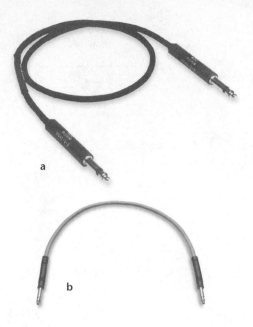

5-15 Patch cords with (a) ¼-inch phone plugs and (b) bantam (mini) phone plugs

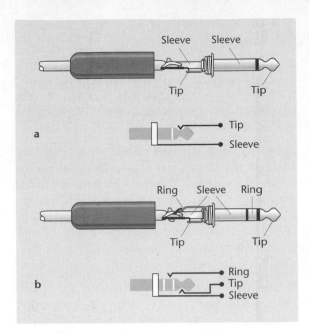

5-16 (a) Mono unbalanced phone plug; (b) stereo balanced phone plug

the larger ¼-inch phone plug and its patch panel (see 5-15).

These plugs are either unbalanced—tip and sleeve—or balanced—tip, ring, and sleeve (see 5-16). An unbalanced audio cable has two conductors: a center wire and a braided shield surrounding it. A balanced audio cable has three conductors: two center wires and a braided shield. The balanced line is preferred for professional use, because it is not so subject to electrical interference and can be used in long cable runs without undue loss in signal-to-noise ratio.

CONSOLE AUTOMATION

Given today's complex production consoles and the myriad procedures involved in mixing many tracks to a few, console automation has become indispensable. It greatly facilitates operations by automatically keeping track of the various mixer settings and storing the information for recall at any time.

Types of Automation Systems

Four types of console automation systems are in use today: voltage-controlled automation, moving-fader automation, software-controlled automation, and MIDI-based automation.

Voltage-Controlled Automation

In voltage-controlled automation, fader levels (and other functions) are regulated by *voltage-controlled amplifiers (VCAs)* or by *digitally controlled amplifiers (DCAs)*. The VCA amplifier is used to decrease level, unlike conventional amplifiers that become unstable if operated with loss. It is regulated by DC voltage. In a typical VCA-equipped console, faders vary the DC control voltage that changes the VCA's gain in relation to the fader movement. This control voltage is digitized and stored for later retrieval. In addition to fader levels, it is possible to automate channel and group mutes, solo functions, and in-board signal processors, such as the equalizer. DCA is an amplifier whose gain is remotely controlled by a digital control signal.

Moving-Fader Automation

Moving-fader, also called *flying-fader, automation,* drives a small servo-motor which is attached to the fader, instead of using DC voltage to control a VCA. As the control voltages are regenerated, it activates the motor, which moves the fader automatically; no hand-operated assistance is necessary. It is possible to control automatically one fader or groups of faders at the same time.

Software-Controlled Automation

Software-controlled automation uses specially designed computer programs for console automation. It is usually employed in hard-disk recording and editing systems (see Chapter 7).

Adjustments are made through *virtual faders* displayed on a video monitor. A *virtual* control is simulated on a computer monitor and adjusted at the computer keyboard or with a mouse or by using a touchscreen. More-complex programs, in addition to automated level control, also allow automated control of all in-board signal processing, such as equalization, panning, compression, and effects.

MIDI-Based Automation

MIDI, short for **Musical Instrument Digital Interface,** is a communications protocol. The *digital* refers to a set of instructions in the form of digital (binary) data, like a computer program, that must be interpreted by an electronic sound-generating or -modifying device, such as a synthesizer, that can respond to the instructions. *Interface* refers to the hardware connection that permits the control signals generated by one device to be transmitted to another. A specified system of digital commands and hardware interface allow musical instruments and other devices to communicate with one another.

In the same way that MIDI can automate musical instruments, it can also be used to automate console operations, such as fader levels, send and return levels, EQ, and pans. MIDI-automated consoles may physically resemble consoles with conventional automation or may be "black boxes" with input and output jacks. These boxes may use either a virtual console computer graphic interface or dedicated controllers with slides and knobs that control the box through MIDI commands.

MIDI console automation has limitations in handling the large amounts of data that other types of automation do not have. But because many conventional console automation systems are so complex, some recordists turn to MIDI-based automation systems as a simpler alternative.

Snapshot and Continuous Automation Two methods are used to handle data changes in console automation: snapshot control and continuous control. With *snapshot control,* the automation system takes an instant reading of the console settings for recall from storage. The reading reflects the state of the console at a particular moment. With *continuous* (also called *dynamic*) *control,* the motion of the mixer controls is recorded. Gradual changes of parameters, from small adjustments in level to larger changes such as fades, are stored as they are made over time.

Operating Modes

Console automation systems have at least three basic operating modes: write, read, and update. All functions may be used independently on any or all channels.

■ **Write mode** The **write mode** is used to create an automated mix. In the write mode, the automation system monitors and stores data from the faders. Only current fader movements are stored in the write mode.

■ **Read mode** The **read mode** plays back or recalls the stored automation data. In the read mode, the console's faders are inoperative. They take their control voltage information only from the stored data on the disk to reproduce the "recorded" fader movements in real time.

■ **Update mode** The **update mode** allows the operator to read the stored information at any time and make changes simply by moving the appropriate fader. A new data track is generated from the original data track with the changes that have been made.

Advantages of Console Automation

Mixing various sounds once they are recorded can be exacting and tedious. It requires dozens, maybe hundreds, of replays and myriad adjustments to get the right equalization, reverberation, blend, spatial balance, timing of inserts, and so on. Comparing one mix with another is difficult unless settings are written down (which is time-consuming) so that controls can be returned to previous positions if necessary. It is not uncommon to discard a mix because someone forgot to adjust one control or decided after a few days to change a few settings without noting the original positions. Then the controls have to be set up all over again. Mixing one song can take many hours or even days; a production can take months.

Console automation has greatly facilitated the recordkeeping and accuracy of mixing; it has made the engineer's arms "longer." Many productions are so involved that they would be nearly impossible without automation. But it has its disadvantages.

Disadvantages of Console Automation

As necessary as automation is in so much of audio production today, it also has some disadvantages. It tends to be confusing, even to experienced operators. Some systems are so complex that it is easy to lose track of the many operations necessary to perform a mix, which defeats the purpose of console automation. Some systems may not play back exactly what the operator wrote. If the mix is complex, a difference of a few decibels, overall, may not be perceptible. That would not be the case, however, in more-subtle mixes.

Automation systems, like all computer systems, are vulnerable to crashing. Getting the system operational again, even assuming that you had the forethought to make a backup copy of the mix before completion, often involves a frustrating loss of production time and continuity, to say nothing of the financial cost.

An aesthetic concern with automation is "sameness." Unless an automated mix is done with skill, its dynamics can sound the same from beginning to end.

DIGITAL CONSOLES

Aside from their differences in technologies, the main innovation in digital consoles compared with analog consoles is the divorcing of circuitry from panel controls. The control surface is still made up of the familiar controls—faders, EQ, sends, returns, and so on—but there is no physical connection between the controls on the console surface and the audio circuit elements, nor are specific controls necessarily dedicated to particular channels.

The digital console consists of *actuators*. Although they look like the familiar controls, when activated they send out digital commands that operate the faders, EQ, sends, returns, and other switches. These commands are stored for instant recall at any time and are assignable.

The *assignable* concept was first developed in analog production consoles as a way to reduce their ever increasing size and improve manageability. Assignable consoles use two basic approaches. In one configuration, instead of each input module carrying its own set of functions, only one control module is used. This system works in combination with a group of controls, each one corresponding to an input channel. This means that instead of routing a signal through an existing input channel and making individual adjustments—such as EQ, cue and aux send, and bus assignment at that channel—the various controls of an input channel are grouped into separate, centralized panels. From these panels a signal is assigned to a channel, processed, and routed. Routing assignments are entered into a central control panel and stored on disk.

A second configuration uses as many modules as there are input channels. But each module has only one control fader that works in conjunction with a group of function buttons. All required effects are distributed among the function buttons. In this system you choose a module and assign one or more functions to the control fader of that particular module. In both assignable approaches, a given control set may be used to perform either the same set of functions for a variety of channels or different functions for a single channel.

The assignable console design has several advantages over large, conventional production consoles: (1) It makes many more operations possible in a more compact chassis; (2) an operator can remain in the central listening location without having to move back and forth to adjust controls; (3) signals can be handled more quickly and easily, because functions are grouped and, with fewer controls, there are fewer operations to perform; and (4) the reduced number of controls lessens the chance of error and makes console layout easier on the eye.

Digital consoles are available in three configurations. One configuration is actually an analog console that is digitally controlled. The signal path is distributed and processed in analog form, but the console's control parameters are maintained digitally.

The all-digital console uses two approaches. The analog input signal is first encoded into a digital signal or it is directly accepted as digital information. In either case, the data are distributed and processed digitally. The output might be either decoded back into analog or remain in digital form, depending on its destination (see 5-17, 5-18, and 5-19).

A third type of digital mixer is actually a virtual console. As the term suggests, a virtual console is not a console per se, but an integrated system that combines a hard-disk computer and specialized software to record and process audio direct to disk. Instead of feeding a sound source to a conventional console, it is fed directly to the computer. On the computer monitor are displayed the console

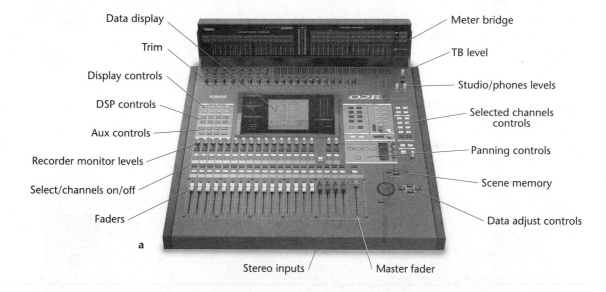

5-17 Example of a digital console and its functions.
(a) Front view, (b) rear view.

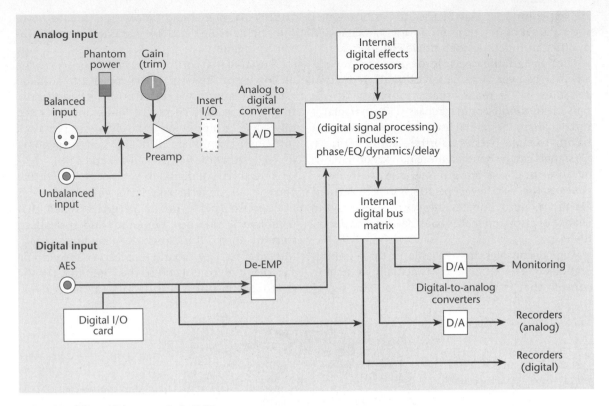

5-18 Signal flow of the console in 5-17

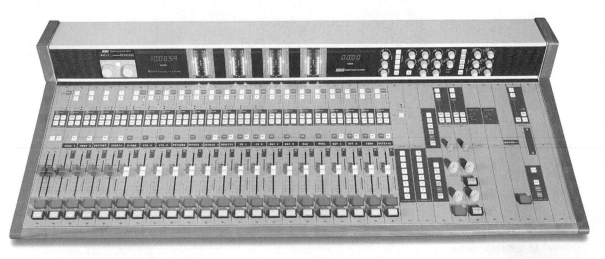

5-19 (a) Digital radio console

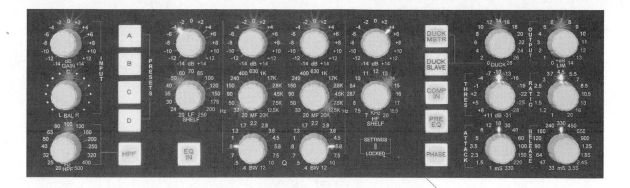

Stereo mode switches—allows stereo, left, or right channels to be summed to mono

A/B select switches—selects one of two alternate audio sources for each channel

Mix-minus select—selects which bus generates mix-minus (the monitor audio sent to callers and remote locations)

Tape transport control module—provides transport control for outboard recording devices (DAT, MD, cassette, reel to reel)

DSP controller—provides editing for the individual channel DSP functions (EQ, compression, ducking, EQ presets, HPF, pan, attenuation)

Bus assign switches—route module audio to any of the four main output busses

Select switch—assigns channel to DSP controller so module settings may be edited

Cue—assigns input audio to cue bus

Channel alpha display—displays current input source for each module; may be controlled by external devices such as automation systems and routers

Module fader—controls audio level for each input

Module on/off buttons activate module and associated logic (machine commands, studio speaker muting)

Preselector—allows switching of multiple inputs to feed one console module

Control room monitor module—provides line level audio feed to drive control room speakers and headphones

Studio monitor module—provides line level audio feed to drive speakers and headphones in a second and third studio; includes a talkback interrupt function

Programmable sends section—provides two programmable aux sends per channel for additional mixes and effects sends

Preset select function—controls recall of the 99 console presets (A preset stores all console settings, levels, and source selections in one of 99 memory locations.)

Timer controls—provides controls for the elapsed time counter

Local/remote switch—enables/disables the serial control port on the console

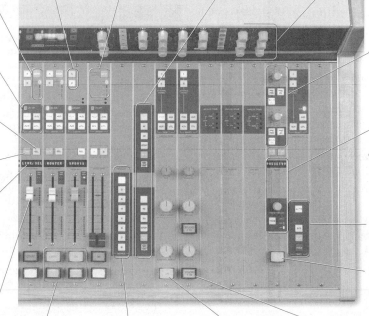

5-19 (b) Functions of the digital radio console with close-up view of the DSP controller

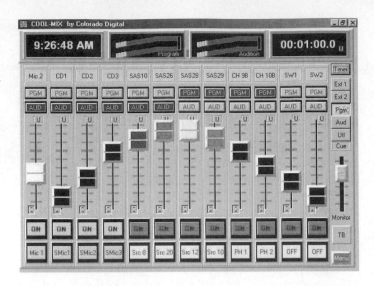

5-20 Touchscreen of virtual broadcast console. This model is a 12 channel, 24 input, PC-controlled console and can be used for air, production, and news. The touchscreen is a high-resolution LCD monitor mounted on a pedestal (not shown) that takes up little desk space.

controls—faders, EQ, panning, and so on—which are maneuvered by a mouse, keyboard, or touchscreen (see 5-20 and Chapter 7).

The digital console has several advantages over its all-analog counterpart: (1) It is virtually distortion- and noise-free; (2) every control move, manual or preprogrammed, is stored and retrieved accurately; (3) operating one control can direct several preprogrammed functions to occur simultaneously; (4) in-board patch bays are unnecessary; and (5) in-board visual displays show the status of various control settings.

MAIN POINTS

▶ Mixers and consoles take input signals and amplify, balance, process, combine, and route them to broadcast or recording.

▶ The differences between a mixer and a console are that a mixer is small, highly portable, and performs limited processing functions, whereas a console is larger and performs numerous processing functions. In many consoles these functions are computer-assisted.

▶ Mixers and consoles have at least the three basic control sections: input, output, and monitor. Many consoles have an additional master control section.

▶ The input section takes incoming signals and routes them to the output section.

▶ The output section routes signals to broadcast or recording.

▶ The master section contains, among other things, the master output bus (or buses) that routes the final mix to the master recorder.

- The monitor section enables signals to be heard.

- On-air broadcast consoles, particularly for radio, are not as elaborate as production consoles, because most of the audio they handle has been produced already.

- Split-section consoles have separate input, output, master, and monitor sections. In-line consoles bring the input and output functions vertically in line, enabling any signal processing to be routed to the monitor or master system.

- The main sections of an in-line console are: input/output, master, monitor, and communications.

- The input/output section includes: microphone-line input selector, microphone preamplifier, phantom power, trim, overload indicator, pad, channel assignment switches, direct switch, equalizer and filter, dynamics section, channel/monitor control, polarity reversal control, pan pot, cue send, aux (or effects) send, solo and prefader listen (PFL), mute, channel and monitor faders, and meters.

- The volume unit (VU) meter is a voltage meter that measures the amount of electric energy flowing through the console. The meter has two scales: percentage of modulation and volume units. Percentage of modulation is the percentage of an applied signal in relation to the maximum signal a sound system can handle.

- The VU meter responds to average sound intensity, unlike another popular meter, the peak program meter (ppm), which is designed to indicate transient peaks.

- The master section includes: master buses, master fader, aux (or effects) send, aux (or effects) return, and meters.

- The monitor section includes: recorder select, send, mix, loudspeaker select, and mono switches. It may also have a pan pot and phase coherence switch.

- The communications section includes: talkback, slate/talkback, and oscillator.

- Most analog production consoles include a patch bay, a central routing terminal to which are wired the inputs and outputs of the console or the equipment in a studio, or both. The patch bay makes multiple signal paths possible. Patch cords plugged into jacks connect the routing circuits.

- The signal paths that are used most often are wired together at the terminals of the patch bay. This normals these routes and makes it unnecessary to use patch cords to connect them. It is possible to break normal and create other signal paths by patching.

- Plugs at the end of patch cords are either unbalanced, comprising a tip and a sleeve, or balanced, comprising a tip, ring, and sleeve.

- Console automation makes it possible to automate fader functions, decoding positional information as adjustments in level are made. The data is stored on and retrieved from a computer disk.

- There are four types of console automation systems in use: voltage-controlled automation, moving-fader automation, software-controlled automation, and MIDI-based automation.

- Console automation systems have at least the three basic operating modes: write, read, and update.

- Digital consoles use the assignable concept in three configurations: in an analog console that is digitally controlled, in an all-digital console, and in a virtual console which is not a console per se, but an integrated system that combines a hard-disk computer and specialized software to record and process audio direct to disk.

- With digital consoles, instead of individual controls for channel-to-track routing on each channel strip, these functions have been centralized into single sets so they can be assigned to any channel. Once assigned, the commands are stored in the console's computer, so different functions can be assigned to other channels. There is no physical connection between the controls on the console surface and the audio circuit elements.

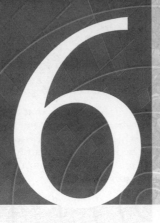

6

Analog Recording

The wonderful thing about audio is that, in the final analysis, it's all a matter of taste. "Ears" are uniquely individual, which leaves ample room for a wide range of sensibilities and varied opinion. Nowhere has this been more apparent than in the debate over analog versus digital sound.

On one hand, advocates of analog recording claim that it produces a warmer sound and that it is a more forgiving production format—technical problems are not as apparent as they are with digital; it is a less intensive production process than digital; it is more complementary to music; and it is the better medium for preserving archived recorded material. On the other hand, proponents of digital recording praise its virtually noise-free, crystal clear sound; its technology, which greatly increases data storage and production flexibility; and the fact that it allows many copies of an original recording to be made without loss in sound quality.

Implicit in the analog versus digital debate is that one format is not so much superior to the other, but simply different. Each has its positive and negative attributes. So far predictions of analog's demise have been premature. Analog recording remains robust, and equipment and tape sales are holding their own. Undoubtedly, however, the speed, data storage capacity, electronic convenience, flexibility, durability, and sound quality of the digital domain will replace analog as *the* audio

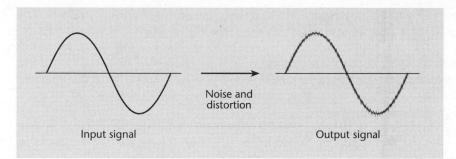

Input signal

Noise and distortion

Output signal

production platform. But for a while at least, coexistence of both formats ensures expansive sonic prospects. Besides, comparing analog with digital sound is like comparing apples with oranges; they are both distinctive and delicious, but different.

ANALOG AUDIOTAPE RECORDING

In audiotape recording, electrical signals are transduced into magnetic signals at the recording stage and encoded onto tape. At the playback stage, these taped magnetic signals are reconverted into electrical signals. This process is accomplished in two different ways: using the analog or the digital method.

In *analog recording*, the waveform of the signal being processed resembles the waveform of the original sound; they are analogous. The frequency and amplitude of an electrical signal changes continuously in direct relationship to the original acoustic sound waves; it is always "on." If these continuous changes were examined, they would reveal an infinite number of variations, each instant different from any adjacent instant. During processing, noise—electrical, electronic, or tape— may be added to the signal. Hence the processed signal is analogous to the original sound plus any additional noise (see Figure 6-1). Although the digital recording process is entirely different (see Chapter 7), the tape medium and some of the tape recorders used in analog and digital recording have a number of features in common.

Physical Characteristics of Audiotape

If tape is your storage medium, and therefore preserves the record of your creative output, it is important to be aware of its properties and composition.

Composition

Audiotape is a thin plastic ribbon consisting of (1) hard, needle-like magnetic particles composed of iron (ferric) oxide, chromium dioxide, cobalt-doped iron oxide, or pure metal particles; (2) a plastic base material that supports the oxide; (3) a binder of synthetic varnish that holds the magnetic particles and adheres them to the base; and (4) a back coating to reduce slippage and buildup of magnetic charges (see 6-2).

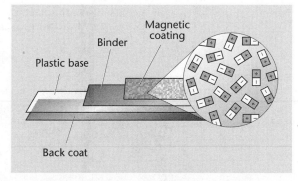

Magnetic coating

Binder

Plastic base

Back coat

6-2 The four layers that make up audiotape and the random distribution of magnetic domains on the microscopic magnetic particles

The plastic material used for a tape's backing is strong, supple, and resistant to temperature extremes and humidity. Its one significant drawback is that it stretches when placed under too much tension or when used too often. Once a tape is stretched, so is the recording.

To reduce the possibility of stretching, use only the highest-quality tape, make sure that tape recorders have the proper tension when spooling, and use new tape for each project.

Dimensions

The two physical dimensions of magnetic audiotape worth noting are thickness and width.

Thickness Open-reel audiotape comes in two thicknesses, measured in *mils* (thousandths of an inch): 1 and $1\frac{1}{2}$ mil. (Measurement is taken from the plastic base; the plastic base plus the magnetic coating is actually slightly thicker.) A tape's thickness determines the amount that can be spooled onto a given size of reel as well as the playing time. Open-reel sizes come in 5-, 7-, $10\frac{1}{2}$-, and 14-inch reels (see Table 6-1).

In analog recording $1\frac{1}{2}$ mil is used for two reasons: (1) It is the thickest and most durable tape available and is therefore the least likely to crease, snap, stretch, or shrink; and (2) print-through is considerably lessened. *Print-through* usually occurs in storage, when a signal from one layer of tape "prints" a low-level replica of itself on an adjacent layer. When the tape is played back, you can hear both signals, one strongly and one faintly. The thicker the tape, the less chance of sound "spilling" from layer to layer. Other factors that affect print-through are discussed later in this chapter. (In digital open-reel recording, $\frac{1}{4}$-, $\frac{1}{2}$-, and 1-mil tapes are available.)

Width Open-reel audiotape is available in four widths: $\frac{1}{4}$, $\frac{1}{2}$, 1, and 2 inches (see 6-3). Analog cassette tape is roughly $\frac{3}{20}$-inch wide.

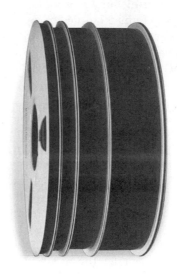

6-3 Open-reel audiotape in $\frac{1}{4}$-, $\frac{1}{2}$-, 1-, and 2-inch widths

Table 6-1 Recording times for open-reel analog tape.
Times are not exact because extra tape is provided to spool around the takeup and feed reels.

Reel Size (inches)	Tape Thickness (mils)	Tape Length (feet)	Playing Time (minutes)			
			30 ips*	15 ips	7½ ips	3¾ ips
7.0	1.5	1,200	7.50	15.0	30.0	60.0
7.0	1.0	1,800	11.25	22.5	45.0	90.0
10.5	1.5	2,500	16.60	33.3	66.6	133.2
14.0	1.5	5,000	33.30	66.6	133.3	266.4

*Inches per second

Magnetic Properties of Audiotape

Tape used in professional audio is designed to provide particular response characteristics to meet certain needs. For example, the type normally used to record popular music is **high-output tape** capable of handling higher levels than is standard tape. The louder recording levels make print-through more noticeable, however. **Low-output tape** is used for archiving to preserve program material for long periods of time with reduced print-through.

Certain measures are used to determine how suitable a tape is for a particular recording. Three ways to determine a tape's ability to retain magnetic information are to check (1) how strong a force field must be to change the magnetic charge of a given particle, (2) how well the tape retains magnetization once the force field is removed, and (3) how great an output level the tape can reproduce. The terms used to describe these measures are *coercivity, retentivity,* and *sensitivity.*

Coercivity

Coercivity indicates the magnetic force (current) necessary to fully erase a tape. It is measured in *oersteds*—units of magnetic intensity. Professionally used analog open-reel tapes usually have oersted measurements between 360 and 380. The oersted measurements of digital open-reel tapes are in the 700s. Digital audiocassette tape is 1,500 oersteds.

The higher the coercivity, the more difficult it is to erase the tape. A tape recorder should be able to completely erase the tape being used. If it does not, some part of a previously recorded signal may be heard with a newly recorded signal.

Retentivity

Retentivity is a measure of the tape's magnetic field strength remaining after an external magnetic force has been removed. Retentivity is measured in *gauss*—a unit of magnetic density. A higher gauss rating means greater retentivity, which in turn indicates that a tape has a greater potential output level. Greater is not necessarily better; what is better depends on what you are recording and why. Gauss ratings between 1,200 and 1,700 are typical in professionally used open-reel tapes, analog and digital. Digital audiocassette tape has gauss ratings between 2,300 and 2,500.

Sensitivity

Sensitivity is similar to retentivity in that it indicates the highest output level a tape can deliver; sensitivity is measured in decibels, however, and the test must be made against a reference tape. If the maximum output level of a reference tape is 0 dB and the output of the tape you are testing is +3 dB, the tape is capable of handling 3 dB more loudness before it *saturates,* or becomes fully magnetized.

Care of Tape

Because the entire tape-recording process ultimately depends on the magnetic tape, it is important to exercise proper care when handling and storing it.

Handling

☑ Never handle the tape surface—front or back. The oil from a fingerprint can catch dust and grime that can damage the tape surfaces. If touching the tape cannot be avoided, use lint-free gloves. This is especially important when using digital tape.

☑ Do not smoke or eat in the tape area. Smoke and food particles can contaminate the tape and also cause damage.

☑ Carry the tape reel by the hub.

☑ Trim damaged tape ends to avoid depositing debris on the tape transport and record heads.

☑ Always store tape in a dust-proof container when it is not in use.

☑ Do not stack tapes on top of one another. Store tapes vertically so they will be supported by the hub.

☑ Keep tape away from heat-generating equipment and magnetic fields when not in use.

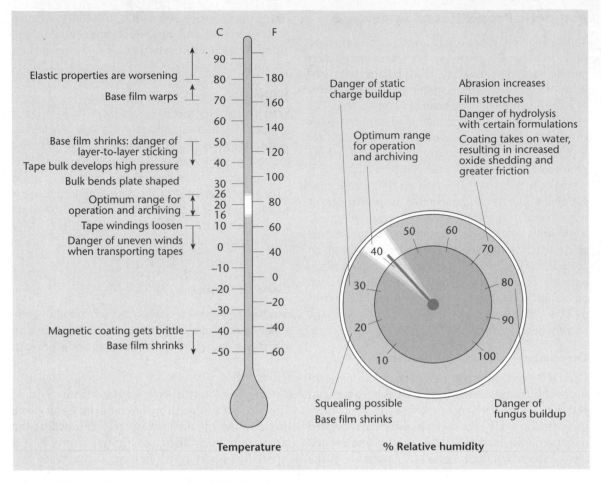

6-4 **Recommended environment for magnetic tape storage**

Storage

If you intend to keep a recording for any length of time, take the following precautions against alteration of the magnetically encoded signal.

☑ Use low-print-through tape 1½ mils thick.

☑ Store the tape in a controlled environment. The Audio Engineering Society (AES) and the Society of Motion Picture and Television Engineers (SMPTE) have established that the optimum temperature for an archive is 68°F, plus or minus 5 degrees, and a relative humidity of 40 percent, plus or minus 5 percent (see 6-4).

☑ Play, as opposed to fast-forward, the tape *tails out*—with the end of the recording on the outside of the reel. If print-through does occur, the weaker signal or sound decay will be post-echo (transferred into the stronger signal), thus masking the print-through, instead of pre-echo (before the signal), thus being audible.

☑ Beware of exposed edges that result from *scattered wind* or *stepping* of tape due to uneven winding (see 6-5).

☑ If the tape is in long-term storage, play it at least once every year or two as an added precaution. Even

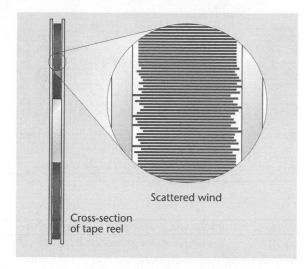

Scattered wind

Cross-section
of tape reel

6-5 Scattered wind. Individual tape strands are exposed and vulnerable to damage.

if print-through has occurred, rewinding reduces it somewhat. If, for some reason, the temperature in the storage area has changed by more than 10 degrees, the tape may expand and contract. Rewinding prevents uneven pressure distribution in the tape pack.

OPEN-REEL AUDIOTAPE RECORDERS

Open-reel audiotape recorders, and *audiotape recorders (ATRs)* in general, have three essential elements: (1) the tape transport system, (2) magnetic heads, and (3) record and playback electronics. You may consider the recording tape as a fourth element (see 6-6). Of interest here are the tape transport system and the magnetic heads.

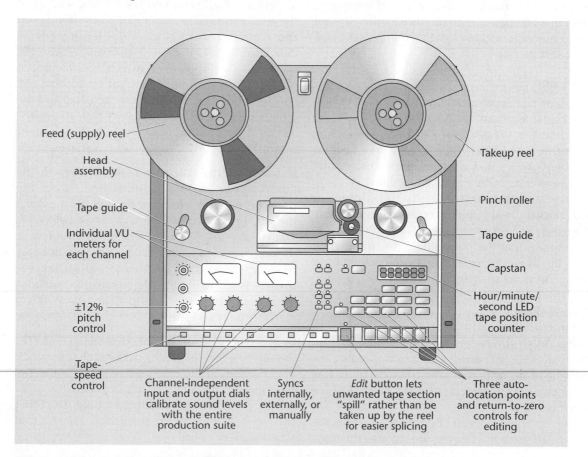

Feed (supply) reel

Head assembly

Tape guide

Individual VU meters for each channel

±12% pitch control

Tape-speed control

Takeup reel

Pinch roller

Tape guide

Capstan

Hour/minute/second LED tape position counter

Channel-independent input and output dials calibrate sound levels with the entire production suite

Syncs internally, externally, or manually

Edit button lets unwanted tape section "spill" rather than be taken up by the reel for easier splicing

Three auto-location points and return-to-zero controls for editing

6-6 Example of an open-reel analog audiotape recorder and its functions

Tape Transport System

Tape transports are designed to pull the tape across the magnetic heads at a constant speed and tension without causing fluctuations in the tape movement. In a typical *tape transport system*, a tape is prepared for recording or playback by placing it on the *feed (supply) reel*, threading it past the *tape guide*, across the *head assembly*, and between the *capstan* and *pinch roller*, through another tape guide to the takeup reel. (Some newer ATR models have a pinch roller–free transport for gentler handling of tape.) The tape guides correctly position the tape on the heads during spooling.

The **capstan** is a precision drive shaft that regulates the tape speed. When you put the machine in play mode, the tape is forced against the motor-driven shaft by the **pinch roller**. The pinch roller is usually rubber, and as the spinning capstan comes into contact with it the capstan drives the roller and the two together pull the tape at a constant rate of speed.

Wow and Flutter

Constant tape movement and tension are critical to acceptable recording. If a problem results from any change in the constant transport speed during recording or playback, the sound may take on audible changes in frequency. Slow changes are called **wow**; faster changes are called **flutter**.

Wow and flutter are usually not a problem with regularly maintained professional equipment. If either or both are present in a recording, however, it may be not audible on the original tape. But as analog tape is **dubbed**—copied—from one generation to another, noise builds up and the wow or flutter becomes audible. (There is also noise buildup.)

Most professional open-reel ATRs come with **scrape flutter filters** to reduce flutter. Scrape flutter filters are installed between the heads to reduce the amount of unsupported tape, thereby restricting the degree of tape movement as it passes across the heads (see 6-7).

The lower the wow and flutter specification, the better. Although it is beyond the scope of this book

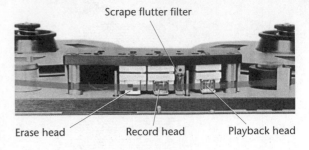

6-7 Audiotape recorder with three magnetic heads. These are half-track heads (see Figure 6-10).

to explain the following wow and flutter measurements, they are cited here for reference: 0.05 percent WRMS (weighted root mean square) is very good; 0.04 percent WRMS is excellent.

■ **Tension (reel-size) control** Electric current to the feed and takeup motors keeps the torque on the reels constant, but it does not control differences in tension created when tape winds from one reel to a different-sized reel. Today's professional ATRs use a microprocessor for reel-tension control. Older models that are designed to take different-sized reels have a *tension* or *reel-size* switch so that the tape wind from reel to reel is constant regardless of tape distribution and reel sizes.

■ **Safety control** The *safety control* or *idler arm* (the term may vary among manufacturers) stops the transport when it senses the absence of tape along the guide path because the tape ran out or broke. The control may be a light beam interrupted by the presence of tape in its path, or the control may be incorporated in the tape-tension sensor. Because the safety control stops the transport without turning off the entire recorder, it cuts down on machine wear and tear.

■ **Tape speeds** Professional open-reel analog ATRs usually have one or more of the following speeds: 7½, 15, and 30 *inches per second (ips)*. Two other tape speeds, 1⅞ and 3¾, are not used for high-quality recording. In analog recording, the faster the speed, the better the frequency response and signal-to-noise ratio.

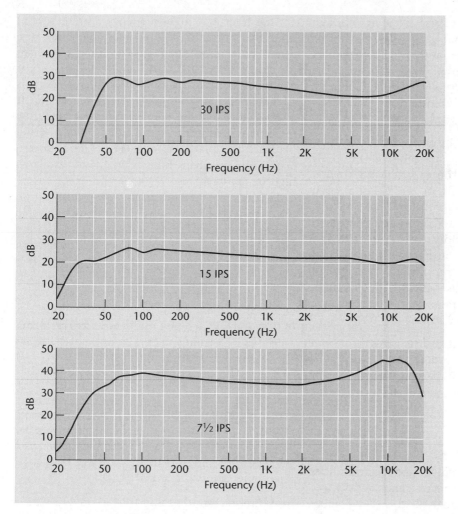

6-8 How tape speed affects frequency response

Professionals generally use 7½ ips as a common speed when distributing or airing tape recordings, but they often work at 15 or 30 ips for improved sound quality and ease of editing. In any case, it is not wise to use speeds lower than 7½ ips (see 6-8). (A speed of 1⅞ ips is standard for analog audiocassette recorders; digital ACRs run at ¼ ips.) A record/play frequency response of 40 Hz to 18 kHz is considered excellent for an open-reel analog ATR.

Faster speeds also make it easier to edit—cut and splice—tape. The more tape that passes across the heads per second, the more spread out the sound is on the tape.

Tape Transport Controls

Several different controls operate the tape transport system (see 6-6). Some of their functions are obvious, such as the on/off power switch, play and record, and so on. The following explanations are of those functions that may not be so obvious.

■ **Variable-speed control** Modern multispeed audiotape recorders have a control that adjusts tape speed to a rate that is ±5 to 50 percent of the machine's set speeds. This *variable-speed control* comes in handy when you want to change the pitch of a sound for a special effect or to correct slight anomalies in pitch resulting from AC voltage changes or batteries that gradually lose power during recording. The variable-speed control also permits a shortening or lengthening of material that may be desirable and acceptable if the change in frequency and rate is unimportant.

■ **Fast-forward and rewind** The function of these controls is evident by their names, but their importance warrants a comment about their purpose: to disengage the capstan/pinch roller when the tape is winding or rewinding at high speed. In either mode tape lifters hold the tape away from the heads to avoid the increased friction that would rapidly wear both tape and heads and to mute the annoying high-pitched squeal that comes when running the tape at high speed. If that high-pitched squeal is loud enough, by the way, it can damage the tweeter(s) in a loudspeaker (see Chapter 10).

■ **Edit control** This control disengages the takeup reel while allowing the rest of the tape transport to continue functioning. This permits the spooling off of unwanted tape without the takeup reel turning.

Magnetic Heads

Professional open-reel analog tape recorders have at least three heads: erase, record, and playback (see 6-7). A good way to identify them is to remember that the erase head is always closest to the feed reel, the record head is in the middle, and the playback head is closest to the takeup reel. Machines with four heads use the fourth as a synchronization head for time code (see Chapter 8).

Bias

Before examining the function of each magnetic head, it is necessary to discuss **bias**. The response of magnetic particles on recording tape (and magnetic film) is nonlinear—their magnetic energy is not a perfect analog of the signal from the record head. A method is needed to force the magnetic properties of the particles as the audio current directs.

That force is a high-frequency current several times that of the highest recorded frequency and, therefore, far above the frequency limits of human hearing (100,000 Hz and higher). This high-frequency current, referred to as **bias current**, is added to the audio signal during recording. It affects the magnetic tape particles so that they respond and conform to the audio signal. During playback the bias frequency is not reproduced, because the playback head is unable to read such high frequencies.

In addition to making magnetic recording linear, the strength of the bias current also affects frequency response, distortion, and signal-to-noise ratio. A particular amount of bias current will work best with a particular type of recording tape. It is therefore critical that the tape recorder you use has been *biased* for the specific tape that you are using. Otherwise, a bias current set too high results in loss of high frequencies, and one set too low results in increased distortion and background noise. Always check with a technician to be sure.

Types of Heads

Erase Head The *erase head* is activated during recording. Its function is to neutralize the polarities of the magnetic particles—to remove sound from the tape with a high-frequency current before the tape passes across the record head.

Bulk Erasers Another way to erase tape is with a *bulk eraser* (also known as a *degausser*)—a large magnet that can erase an entire reel at once (see 6-9). It is fast and easy to use but generally gives a poorer signal-to-noise ratio than does the erase head. When using a bulk eraser with no conveyor belt, take the following precautions.

☑ Keep the tape (and your watch) away from the demagnetizer when it is switched on or off, because the tape could get a surge of magnetism that may be difficult to remove with an erase head.

☑ Before (and after) degaussing, slowly move the tape into (and away from) the bulk eraser's field.

☑ Rotate the tape over the degausser slowly at a rate not more than 2 inches per second. Faster rates

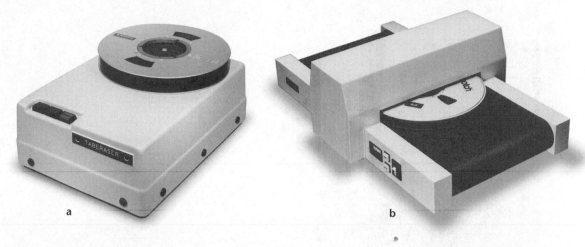

6-9 High-quality bulk erasers. (a) This model erases open-reel tapes from 150-mil to 2-inch widths, as well as cartridges, cassettes, and magnetic film. The erase field electronically diminishes at the end of each 20-second cycle. A fan blower protects the eraser from overheating. (b) High-energy bulk eraser for high-coercivity tapes.

will leave residual magnetism on the tape. Do not scrape the tape too hard or jerk it across the surface of the bulk eraser or it will reduce signal-to-noise ratio and increase tape noise in the form of periodic noise surges—known as *spoking*—as the tape plays. Be sure to erase *both* sides of the entire reel.

☑ Know the use time of the demagnetizer; older models tend to heat up quickly and will burn out if left on too long.

Record Head The *record head* transduces electric energy into the magnetic force that magnetizes the tape. It carries two signals: the record bias current and the audio current—the signal fed to the recorder from the original sound.

Playback Head The *playback head* transduces the magnetic field from the tape back into electric energy.

Head Sizes and Track Formats

The amount of surface area on a magnetic head (or *headstack,* as it is called on multitrack heads) varies with the width of the head. Heads on open-reel analog tape recorders are manufactured today in

¼-inch and 2-inch widths. The ¼-inch head actually houses two separate heads and is used for stereo recording. Each head records or plays back a separate tape track. Two-inch headstacks house 16 or 24 separate heads and can record or play back 16 or 24 tape tracks. Each head is separated by a **guard band** that considerably reduces the chance of **crosstalk**—leakage of a signal from one track into an adjacent track (see 6-10).

Do not confuse the term *channel* with *track;* they are not synonyms. A *channel* is a conduit through which signal flows. The path the signal makes on the tape is the *track*.

Head Care

Magnetic heads require very careful treatment. Scratches, wear, magnetic buildup, the slightest change in their alignment, or any accumulation of dust, dirt, or magnetic particles adversely affects sound quality.

Demagnetizing the Heads Before using a tape recorder (and once or twice during long sessions), make sure the heads are free of any magnetization that may have been left from previous use. When heads build up enough permanent magnetism, they

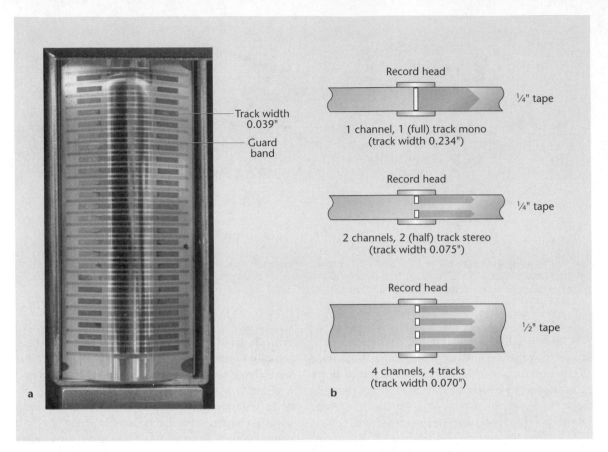

Track width 0.039"

Guard band

Record head

¼" tape

1 channel, 1 (full) track mono
(track width 0.234")

Record head

¼" tape

2 channels, 2 (half) track stereo
(track width 0.075")

Record head

½" tape

4 channels, 4 tracks
(track width 0.070")

a

b

6-10 (a) 24-track headstack used with 2-inch tape and (b) channel and track formats of selected standard-gauge open-reel analog recorders

can partially erase a recording; higher frequencies are particularly susceptible. Recordings so affected sound muddy, often lacking presence and brilliance.

Various types of head demagnetizers are available (see 6-11). Choose one that does not produce too strong a magnetic field, or it can permanently magnetize a head instead of demagnetizing it. Turn off the tape recorder before demagnetizing. Also, when turning the demagnetizer on and off, do so away from the heads; otherwise, the surge or cut in power could leave remnant magnetization on the heads. Make sure that the demagnetizer does not touch or scrape the heads, or they could be scratched and permanently damaged. An etched head acts like sandpaper, scraping magnetic particles off of tape.

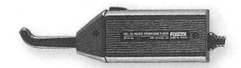

6-11 Head demagnetizer. This model has a curved lip for hard-to-reach places.

Aligning the Heads Although a technician usually aligns the heads, you should be aware of the five adjustments that are made and some problems that can result when the heads are out of alignment (see 6-12).

■ *Zenith* The vertical angle of the heads is important in maintaining uniform tape tension

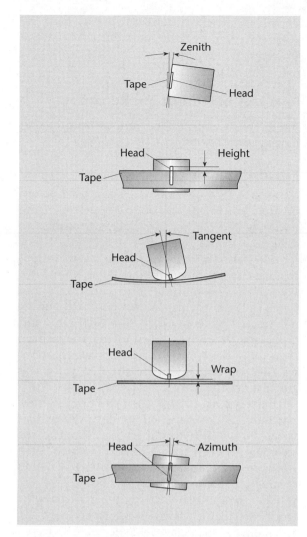

6-12 Five alignment adjustments to a magnetic head

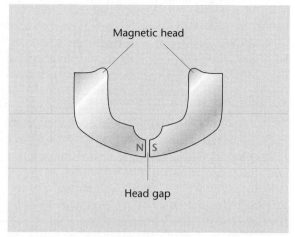

6-13 The poles and head gap of a magnetic head

across the entire width of the tape-to-head contact. If a head is tilted and the top or bottom portion applies greater pressure to the tape than the other, it causes the tape to *skew*—ride up or down on the head. In less severe cases, the lack of pressure can cause degraded performance.

■ *Height* The heads must present themselves to the tape at exactly the right height. Otherwise, the result could be signals that are only partially recorded or reproduced, crosstalk between tracks, more noise, or poor erasure.

■ *Tangency* The head-to-tape contact at the head gap must be at the right pressure. The *head gap* is the space between the poles of a magnetic head (see 6-13). The farther forward the head, the greater the pressure. Too little or too much pressure noticeably degrades a signal by reducing high-frequency response and causing dropout.

■ *Wrap* The angle at which the tape curves around the head must ensure proper contact at the gap. Without firm tape-to-head contact, as with poor tangency, there is sound dropout and high-frequency loss.

■ *Azimuth* Adjustment of the gap must be exactly perpendicular to the length of the tape. Heads that are not in azimuth alignment record and reproduce out-of-phase stereo signals.

It is difficult to visually spot heads that are out of alignment, but you can hear many of the problems caused by misaligned heads. Most studios have a routine schedule of preventive maintenance that includes head alignment. If you are getting poor sound from a tape recorder, have a technician check the heads.

Aligning the Heads Electronically Another important procedure in ATR preventive maintenance is *electronic alignment* (or *calibration*). Because specifications such as bias requirements, frequency response, and sensitivity vary from one tape formulation to another, audiotape recorders have various electronic adjustments so that they all operate at a given standard. Without such a standard, tapes recorded on one ATR may not have the identical response as a recording made on another ATR.

The National Association of Broadcasters (NAB) has established standards for 3¾ ips, 7½ ips, and 15 ips that are in use throughout the United States and much of the world. Europe conforms to the DIN standard set by Deutsche Institute Norme. The Audio Engineering Society has established the standard for 30 ips.

To perform a physical alignment, you need to use the appropriate alignment tape and follow playback and record alignment procedures. These procedures are available in a number of technical audio books and from the NAB and the AES.

Cleaning the Heads Dust, dirt, and magnetic particles collect on the heads and tape guides even in the cleanest studios. Some of these particles are abrasive; when the tape picks them up and drags them across the heads, they can scratch both the heads and the tape's magnetic coating. If the particle buildup is substantial, sound quality suffers noticeably. For example, if oxide particle buildup is ¹⁄₁₀₀₀ inch on the playback head, a recording running at 15 ips will have a loss of 55 dB at 15 kHz.

The best preventive maintenance is to clean the heads and tape guides each time you use a tape recorder, especially when high-output tape is used, because it is prone to shedding. Dense-packed cotton swabs and an approved head cleaner or easy-to-obtain and inexpensive 99 percent (anhydrous) isopropyl or denatured alcohol will do. Do not use rubbing alcohol. It contains water and can leave a film on the head. Commercial head cleaner is available, but it may be too potent for some heads and dissolve part of the plastic. Check with a technician if you are in doubt. Use a water-based cleaner on rubber parts, such as pinch rollers. Even if the label indicates "rubber cleaner," make sure it is water-based, otherwise it could swell and crack the rubber. Use one cotton swab for each head and guide (two or more if the cotton turns brown) and swab gently.

Features of Audiotape Recorders

Audiotape recorders have various features that increase their flexibility in production.

Selective Synchronization (Sel Sync)

Multitrack recorders were developed to permit greater control of the sound sources during recording and playback by making it possible to assign each one to its own track. Multitrack recorders also make it possible to record various sound sources at different times by *overdubbing*— recording new material on open tracks and synchronizing it with material on tracks already recorded. The technology that facilitates this production technique, called by the trademarked term *Sel Sync* (short for *selective synchronization*), was developed by Ampex; the innovator was guitarist Les Paul.

Under normal conditions, if you first recorded, say, only the instrumental accompaniment to a vocal, the vocalist would have to listen to the recording (through headphones) to synchronize the words to the music. A distance of a few inches separates the record and playback heads, however, which creates a delay between the music and the lyrics when they are played back together (see 6-14). To eliminate this delay, Sel Sync uses the record head as a playback head for the previously recorded tracks and plays them in sync with the new material being recorded (see 6-15).

Tape Timing

A *tape timer* reads out actual tape time in hours, minutes, and seconds and/or with *time code* that reads out in hours, minutes, seconds, and frames. With time code each "frame" of audiotape is coded with a different number. Tape timers provide an easy and, in most cases, indispensable way not only to locate recorded material but also to synchronize it (see Chapter 8).

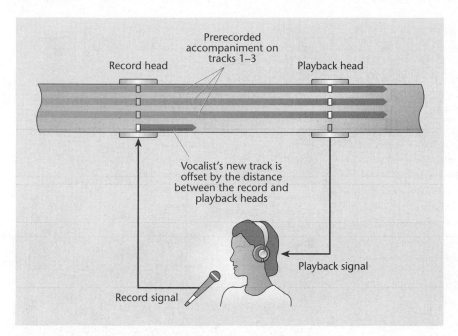

6-14 Overdubbing Without Sel Sync. This method creates an offset between the sound being played back and the sound being recorded.

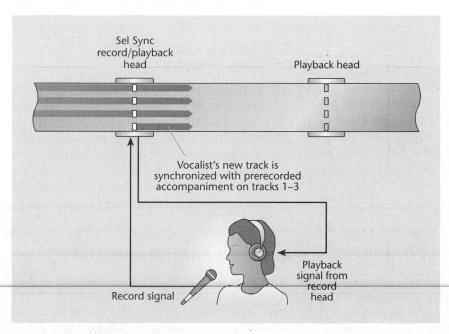

6-15 Overdubbing with Sel Sync. Playback and record are synchronized.

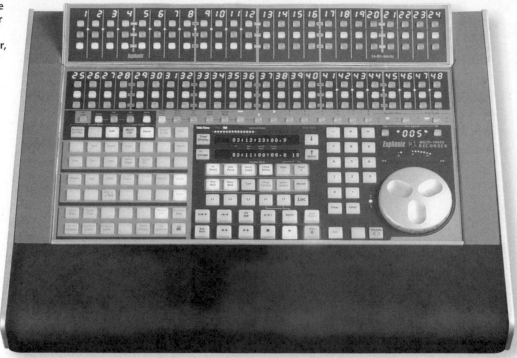

6-16 Remote controller for a multitrack tape recorder, including auto-locator features

Auto-Locator

Even with a tape timer and time-coded tape, locating specific cue points can be time-consuming. An accessory that is part of most professional ATRs, analog and digital, known as an *auto-locator,* makes it possible to program cues and store them in memory. At the touch of a few buttons, the tape transport automatically spools to a precise location on the tape (see 6-6 and 6-16).

With an auto-locator specific cue points on a tape are coded and entered into memory using a keypad. The code number is usually in time code, or in tape time, and is interchangeable between the two. To recall the cue point from memory, the coded number is reentered via the keypad. By pressing a *search* button, the auto-locator shuttles the tape to the desired position. At that point the transport either stops, places itself into *play,* or cycles. *Cycling* loops the tape between two cue points in a play-relocate-play sequence.

CARTRIDGE AND CASSETTE TAPE RECORDERS

The analog cartridge and cassette tape recorders revolutionized audio production techniques and have been a mainstay in audio since their appearance in 1958 and 1963, respectively. But since the development of the digital cartridge and cassette recorder, their analog counterparts are being phased out. Cartridge and cassette recorders are therefore covered in their digital incarnations in Chapter 7.

AUDIO ON ANALOG VIDEOTAPE

The digital revolution has made analog *videotape recorders (VTRs)* obsolescent, but given the heavy investment many TV stations and production houses have in analog VTRs and the cost of changeover to digital VTRs, conversion is ongoing. The few analog VTR formats that remain in use merit some discussion here.

Analog Videotape Formats

Analog VTRs encode analog video as well as audio that may be analog, frequency modulated, or digital. The three analog formats still in use are Betacam SP, S-VHS, and Hi8.

Betacam SP

The *Betacam SP* (*SP* stands for *superior performance*) is a ½-inch format VCR developed for used in TV news and field production. It has two fixed audio heads for conventional longitudinal analog recording. The two tracks can be used separately for monaural recording or for stereo. Although there is Dolby C noise reduction, sound quality is mediocre (see discussion of noise reduction in Chapter 9).

The Betacam SP also has two additional *AFM (audio frequency modulation)* tracks that deliver high-fidelity sound. AFM tracks are recorded by audio heads on the spinning video head drum in the larger video portion of the tape, without interfering with the video signal (see 6-17). The higher tape-to-head speed and the larger recording area help improve audio quality; noise reduction and the use of metal particle tape (coercivity: 1,500 oersteds) also help. The trade-off is that audio and video cannot be recorded separately on AFM tracks.

Betacam SP uses cassettes ranging from 10 to 30 minutes. It can also accommodate large cassettes that provide 60 and 90 minutes of recording time.

S-VHS

S-VHS is the high-grade version of the well-known VHS consumer system. It is used in news, corporate video, and schools that teach video production. The format is ½ inch, with two longitudinal analog audio channels and two AFM channels with noise reduction.

Even with AFM audio, S-VHS sound quality is not up to Betacam SP standards. One reason is because it uses cobalt-doped iron oxide tape with lower coercivity than metal particle tape. Cassette record time can be up to 120 minutes.

Hi8

Hi8 gets its name from the 8-mm width of the cassette tape it uses. It is used in news, industrial production, and production classes in schools.

It has one AFM channel, stereo is optional, and, unlike the Betacam SP and S-VHS VCRs, it has optional two-channel digital sound (see 6-18). A Hi8 cassette can record up to 120 minutes.

The problem with Hi8, in relation to sound and picture, is that with multiple dubs the audio lags behind the video. The digital audio tracks are recorded by the video heads in spurts. This "segmented" audio has to be reconstructed into a continuous analog audio signal. The process, which takes up to 1/30 second, creates an increasingly more noticeable delay of audio behind picture with each dub. Hi8 must therefore be dubbed up to a higher-quality format for extensive postproduction editing.

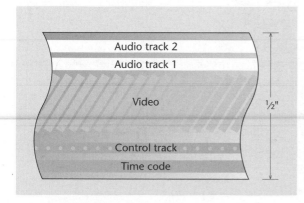

6-17 Betacam format

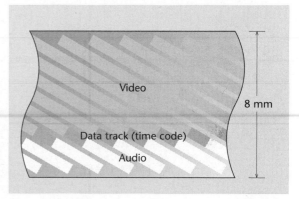

6-18 Hi8 format

AUDIO ON FILM

There are three basic types of film—silent, sound, and magnetic—and they come in two gauges: 35 mm and 16 mm (see 6-19). **Silent film** carries no sound information; it consists of the picture area and two columns of sprocket holes, one on each edge of the film. It is used during shooting when picture and sound are recorded separately—picture with a camera, and sound with an audio recorder

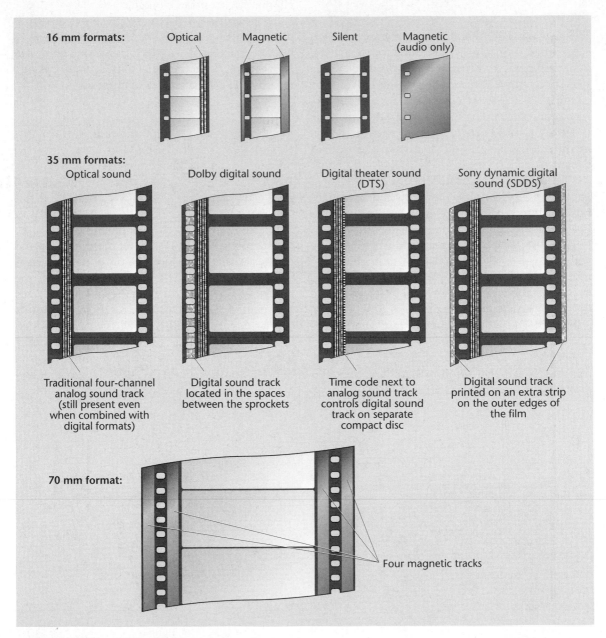

16 mm formats: Optical   Magnetic   Silent   Magnetic (audio only)

35 mm formats:
Optical sound   Dolby digital sound   Digital theater sound (DTS)   Sony dynamic digital sound (SDDS)

Traditional four-channel analog sound track (still present even when combined with digital formats)

Digital sound track located in the spaces between the sprockets

Time code next to analog sound track controls digital sound track on separate compact disc

Digital sound track printed on an extra strip on the outer edges of the film

70 mm format:

Four magnetic tracks

6-19 Various film stock formats

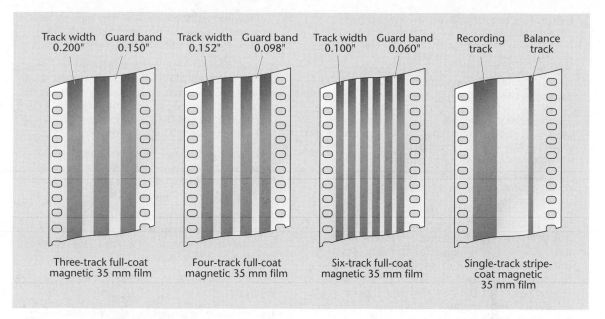

6-20 Types of 35 mm magnetic film

(see "Synchronizing Sound and Picture on Film" in Chapter 8). **Sound film** carries both picture and optical sound. The optical process is used for release prints and done photographically in a laboratory. In 16 mm optical film, the optical audio track replaces the sprocket holes on one edge of the film.

Magnetic film is similar to audiotape in that it contains all sound and no picture, and it has similar magnetic characteristics, but it is the same size as regular film stock and contains sprocket holes. Magnetic film is available either full coat or stripe coat and it records analog sound.

With **full coat** the oxide coating covers most or all of the film width (see 6-20). The 16 mm variety is usually full width for single-track monaural audio; 35 mm full coat has three, four, or six magnetic stripes, with clear base between, for three-, four-, or six-channel recording.

In 35 mm **stripe coat**, there are two stripes of oxide: a wide stripe for recording single-track mono and a narrow balance stripe to ensure that the film wind on reels is smooth. In 16 mm the oxide stripe coat is either down the edge of the film (*edge track*) or down the center of the film (*center track*).

Sound quality—dynamic range, signal-to-noise ratio, and frequency response—in 16 mm magnetic film is mediocre; in 35 mm it is a little better. But with such enhancements as Dolby processing and digital audio, 35 mm sound quality is excellent.

MAIN POINTS

▶ In audiotape recording, electrical signals are transduced into magnetic signals during the recording phase. During playback the magnetic signals are transduced back into electrical signals.

▶ In analog recording, signals are oriented on the tape in patterns analogous to the waveform of the original signal. The signal is continuous—it is always "on."

▶ Most recording tape is composed of a thin, plastic ribbon of polyester; microscopic needlelike magnetic particles; a binder of synthetic varnish so the particles adhere to the polyester; and a back coating to reduce slippage.

▶ Analog audiotape comes in two thicknesses: 1 and 1½ mil. The 1½-mil tape is preferred because it is least likely to crease, snap, or stretch, and it

- reduces the chance of print-through. Digital audiotape is available in ¼, ½, and 1 mil.

- Audiotape comes in five widths—¼, ½, 1, and 2 inches (and ³⁄₂₀ inch, for analog cassette tape)—to accommodate the various formats used in recording today.

- There are several measures of a tape's ability to reproduce sound: coercivity, the magnetic force it takes to fully erase a tape; retentivity, a measure of the tape's magnetic field strength remaining after an external magnetic force has been removed; and sensitivity, the output level a tape can reproduce.

- Some tape is made for specific purposes. Low-print-through tape has lower retentivity and sensitivity so it can handle lower energy levels, thus reducing the chance of magnetic information transferring from one tape layer to another. High-output tape has higher coercivity and sensitivity and, therefore, is capable of reproducing higher output levels.

- Tape should be handled carefully. The tape surface can be sullied by fingerprints, smoke, and dust, and the tape reels can be damaged by being stacked one upon the other. Tape should be stored tails out in a controlled environment of 68°F, plus or minus 5 degrees, and 40 percent humidity, plus or minus 5 percent.

- The three essential sections of a tape recorder are the tape transport system, the magnetic heads, and the record and playback electronics.

- A number of controls operate the transport: the power switch, select and variable-speed control, play, record, stop, fast-forward, rewind, and the tape edit control.

- An important function of the transport system is to maintain the tape movement at a precise, constant speed. A change in the transport speed could result in audible changes in a recording's frequency. Slow changes are called wow; faster changes are called flutter.

- Most professional analog tape recorders run at one or more speeds: 7½, 15, and 30 inches per second (ips). Generally, the faster the speed, the better the sound quality.

- Professional analog tape recorders have at least three heads: erase, record, and playback. Most models also have a fourth head for time code.

- Because the magnetic particles on tape respond to magnetization nonlinearly (they cannot make sense of the information carried by the input signal), the record head has a high-frequency bias current that linearizes the magnetic information so it can be encoded on the tape.

- A ¼-inch head houses two separate heads and is used for stereo recording. A 2-inch headstack houses 16 or 24 separate heads and can record or play back 16 or 24 tape tracks.

- The position of the heads is critical, and any change in their physical alignment—zenith, height, tangency, wrap, or azimuth—adversely affects sound quality.

- Heads must also be electronically aligned regularly.

- Heads should be demagnetized and cleaned before each session and during long sessions.

- Multitrack tape recorders have a variety of features, including Sel Sync, which temporarily changes selected tracks on the record head into the playback mode. This permits various elements in a recording to be taped synchronously at different times.

- Analog videotape recorders encode analog video as well as audio that may be analog, frequency modulated, or digital.

- Basically, analog videotape recording encodes a video track, usually two audio tracks, a control or cue track, and an address or time code track.

- There are three types of film: silent, sound, and magnetic.

- Silent film carries no sound information. Sound film carries both picture and optical sound. Magnetic film contains all sound and no picture.

- Magnetic film comes in either full coat or stripe coat.

- Sound quality in 16 mm magnetic film is mediocre; in 35 mm it is a little better. But with such enhancements as Dolby processing and digital audio, 35 mm sound quality is excellent.

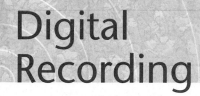

Digital Recording

Compared with analog recording, digital recording virtually eliminates noise, distortion, crosstalk, wow and flutter, print-through, and degeneration of sound quality in dubbing. Dynamic range is at least 96 dB and better. Although the popularity of analog remains stable, and its sonic characteristics are unique, audio is headed toward a digital future—and that future is upon us.

DIGITAL AUDIO

Instead of an analogous relationship between the acoustic sound and the electronically processed signal, *digital recording* uses a numerical representation of the audio signal's actual frequency and amplitude. In analog, *frequency* is the time component and *amplitude* is the level component. In digital, *sampling* is the time component and *quantization* is the level component.

Sampling

Sampling takes periodic samples (voltages) of the original analog signal at fixed intervals and converts them into digital data. The rate at which the fixed intervals sample the original signal each second is called the *sampling frequency*. For example, a sampling frequency of 48 kHz means that samples are taken 48,000 times per second, or each sample period is $\frac{1}{48,000}$ second. Because sampling and the component of time are directly related, a system's sampling rate determines its upper frequency limits. Theoretically, the higher the sampling rate, the greater a system's frequency range.

It was determined several years ago that if the highest frequency in a signal were to be digitally encoded successfully, it would have to be sampled at a rate at least twice its frequency.* In other words, if high-frequency response in digital recording is to reach 20 kHz, the sampling frequency must be at least 40 kHz. Too low a sampling rate would cause loss of too much information (see Figure 7-1).

Think of a movie camera that takes 24 still pictures per second. A sampling rate of 1/24 second seems adequate to record most visual activities.

---

*This concept was developed by a Bell Laboratories researcher named Harry Nyquist. To honor this discovery, the sampling frequency has been named the Nyquist frequency.

Although the camera shutter closes after each 1/24 second and nothing is recorded, not enough information is lost to impair perception of the event. A person running, for example, does not run far enough in the split second the shutter is closed to alter the naturalness of the movement. If the sampling rates were slowed to 1 frame per second, the running movement would be quick and abrupt; if it were slowed to 1 frame per minute, the running would be difficult to follow.

A number of sampling rates are used in digital audio. The five most commonly employed are: 32, 44.056, 44.1, 48, and 96 kHz. The international sampling rate, 32 kHz, is used for broadcast digital audio. Because the maximum bandwidth in broadcast transmission is 15 kHz, the 32 kHz sampling rate is sufficient. For laser disc, compact disc, and digital tape recording 44.056, 44.1, and 48 kHz, respectively, are used. Generally, standards

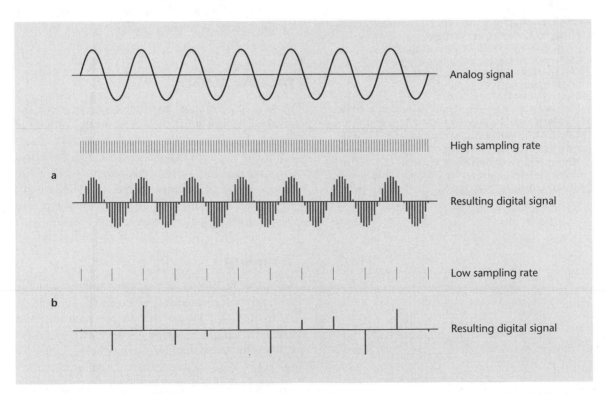

7-1 Sampling. (a) A signal sampled frequently enough contains sufficient information for proper decoding. (b) Too low a sampling rate loses too much information for proper decoding.

for the *digital versatile disc (DVD)* are 48 and 96 kHz. DVD consists of several formats, however, some of which use higher sampling rates, as does the **Super Audio Compact Disc (SACD)** (see "Digital Versatile Disc" later in this chapter).

Quantization

As samples of the waveform are taken, these voltages are converted into discrete quantities and assigned values, a process known as **quantization**. The assigned value is in the form of *binary digits*, or *bits*. Most of us learned math using the decimal, or base 10, system, which consists of 10 numerals—0 through 9. The binary, or base 2, system uses two numbers—0 and 1. In converting the analog signal to digital, when the voltage is off, the assigned value is 0; when the voltage is on, the assigned value is 1.

A quantity expressed as a binary number is called a *digital word:* 10 is a two-bit word, 101 is a three-bit word, 11010 is a five-bit word, et cetera. Each *n*-bit binary word produces 2^n discrete levels. Therefore, a one-bit word produces two discrete levels—0,1; a two-bit word produces four discrete levels—00, 01, 10, and 11; a three-bit word produces eight discrete levels—111, 110, 101, 100, 011, 010, 001, and 000; and so on. So the more quantizing levels there are, the longer the digital word must be. The longer the digital word, the better the sonic resolution. For example, the number of discrete voltage steps possible in an 8-bit word is 256; in a 16-bit word, it is 65,536; in a 20-bit word, it is 1,048,576; and in a 24-bit word it is 16,777,216. The greater the number of these quantizing levels, the more accurate the representation of the analog signal and the wider the signal-to-noise ratio (see 7-2).*

---

*In quantizing the analog signal into discrete binary numbers (voltages), noise, known as *quantizing noise,* is generated. The signal-to-noise ratio in an analog-to-digital conversion system is 6 dB for each bit. A 16-bit system is sufficient to deal with quantizing noise. This gives digital sound a signal-to-noise ratio of 96 dB (6 dB × 16-bit system), which is pretty good by analog standards; but by digital standards, 20-bit systems are better at 120 dB, and 24-bit systems are dramatically better at 144 dB.

This raises a question: How can a representation of the original signal be better than the original signal itself? Assume that the original analog signal is an ounce of water with an infinite number of values (molecules). The amount and "character" of the water changes with the number of molecules; it has one "value" with 500 molecules, another with 501, still another with 2,975, and so forth. But all together the values are infinite. Moreover, changes in the original quantity of water are inevitable: Some of it may evaporate, some may be lost if poured, and some may be contaminated or absorbed by dust or dirt.

But what if the water molecules are sampled and then converted to a stronger, more durable form? In so doing, a representation of the water would be obtained in a facsimile from which nothing would be lost. But sufficient samples would have to be obtained to ensure that the character of the original water is maintained.

For example, suppose that the molecule samples were converted to ball bearings and a quantity of 1 million ball bearings was a sufficient sample. In this form the original water is not vulnerable to evaporation or contamination from dust and dirt. Even if a ball bearing is lost, they are all the same; therefore, losing one ball bearing does not affect the content or quality of the others.

THE DIGITAL RECORDING/ REPRODUCTION PROCESS

The digital recording/reproduction process essentially involves two complementary procedures in the encoding and decoding of a signal.

The Recording Process

Converting analog signals into a digital format for recording occurs in five basic steps: anti-aliasing, sample and hold, analog-to-digital conversion, data coding, and data storage (see 7-3).

To keep unwanted high frequencies from *aliasing*—becoming audible when the analog signal begins its passage through the digital sampling system—they are rolled off using a low-pass filter. The process is called *anti-aliasing*.

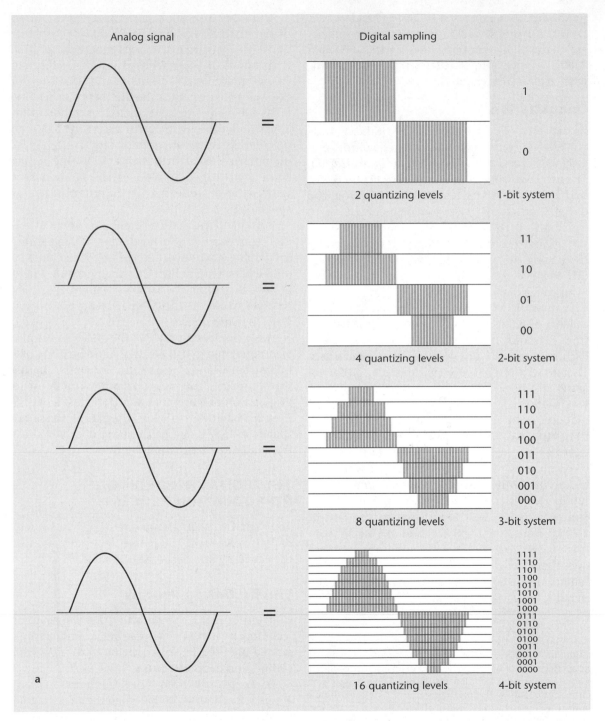

Analog signal   Digital sampling

1
0
2 quantizing levels   1-bit system

11
10
01
00
4 quantizing levels   2-bit system

111
110
101
100
011
010
001
000
8 quantizing levels   3-bit system

1111
1110
1101
1100
1011
1010
1001
1000
0111
0110
0101
0100
0011
0010
0001
0000
16 quantizing levels   4-bit system

a

7-2 Quantizing. (a) As the number of quantizing levels increases, the digital sample of the analog signal becomes more accurate. In 16-bit systems, the audio spectrum is divided into 65,536 values in a single sample. A 20-bit system captures 1,048,576 values in a single sample. A 24-bit system captures 16,777,216 values in a single sample.

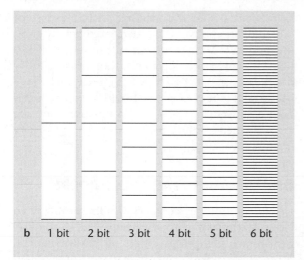

7-2 Quantizing. *(continued)* (b) The addition of a single bit doubles the data a digital device can capture.

After anti-aliasing, a *sample-and-hold* circuit temporarily holds the analog voltage level for the duration of a single sampling period. This allows enough time for the analog-to-digital converter to generate a digital word that corresponds to the sampled voltage.

During *analog-to-digital conversion,* the signal is sampled and quantized in a remarkable operation. For example, in a 16-bit system at a sampling rate of 48 kHz, as the signal is sampled and held, 16 successive approximations are performed within $\frac{1}{48,000}$ second.

Once the signal has been converted into digital form, it is coded. This process involves data coding, error correction, and record (or data) modulation. *Data coding* prevents ambiguity by making it easier to identify the beginning of each digital word in the bit stream. Data coding serves much the same purpose as spaces between words in a sentence. *Error correction* is necessary to minimize the effect of storage defects. Because digital data is packed at very high density, storage defects are inevitable. These defects would degrade the quality of digital audio, especially with digital audiotape recorders and compact disc formats. Data error rates for hard disks and optical disks are very low. Error correction minimizes the number of errors during the storage process. *Record* (or *data*) *modulation* is the final processing of digital data before storage. Although the data is in the form of 1s and 0s, binary code is not an efficient way to store data. It is therefore modulated and stored as pulses of magnetic energy. Data may be stored on any recording medium, such as tape, digital disc, or computer hard disk.

The Reproduction Process

The basic steps in the digital reproduction process are: demodulation, error correction, digital-to-analog conversion, sample and hold, and low-pass filtering.

Demodulation performs three important functions: (1) It amplifies the signals, which are at a

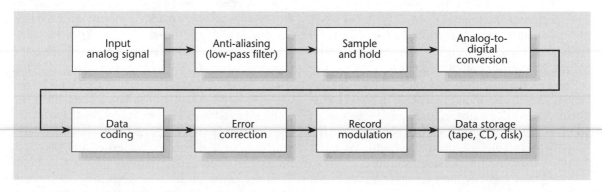

7-3 Basic steps in analog-to-digital conversion

very low level; (2) it takes the waveforms, which are inevitably distorted by the conversion process, and reshapes them into their original modulated states; and (3) it returns the modulated signals to their original binary form of 1s and 0s. *Error correction* compensates for errors introduced during storage. In *digital-to-analog conversion,* the digital word is converted to an analog voltage that is analogous to the original signal before sampling. The output *sample-and-hold* circuit removes irregular signals, called *switching glitches,* from the reproduction chain. *Low-pass filtering* at the output smooths in the final waveform any nonlinearity that was introduced by the digital sampling process.

OPEN-REEL DIGITAL AUDIOTAPE

There are three essential differences between the type of audiotape used for analog recording and that used for digital. First, digital tape in general and the magnetic coating in particular do not have to be as thick as that used for analog recording. In the analog system, varying signal strengths recorded on the tape correspond to the different levels from the input signal. To a great extent, the thickness of the oxide coating determines the tape's signal-to-noise ratio. Moreover, saturating the tape with too much signal must be avoided.

In digital recording, the sampling frequency is constant, and at each sample the tape is saturated with a series of pulses. There is no resultant distortion, because the digital system has to deal only with the presence (1) or absence (0) of a pulse. Therefore, tape thickness is not a factor in the tape's ability to reproduce dynamic range. The total thickness of open-reel digital tape (base, back, and magnetic coating) is about 1 mil.

Second, the coercivity of nonmetal tape used for digital recording is about twice that of analog tape. Greater coercivity is needed to retain the very short wavelengths of the higher frequencies and the densely packed digital information, which is about 10 times that stored in analog recording.

Third, any tape requires care in handling, but digital tape requires more care than analog does.

It is essential that the working area be as free of dust and dirt as possible. Moderate temperature and low humidity should be kept within ranges of ±10 percent. Oils from the hands can cause quality degradation of both the magnetic and back coatings. If tape is soiled, it should be wiped gently with a soft cloth. Cleaning liquids used on tape recorder heads must be completely dry before digital tape is used.

DIGITAL AUDIOTAPE RECORDERS

Digital audiotape recorders (DTRs) come with either stationary or rotary heads. The stationary-head machines professionals use are open reel. Professional- and consumer-grade rotary-head recorders are cassettes.

Stationary-Head Digital Audio Recording

Although the **stationary-head digital audiotape (S-DAT) recorder** is similar in looks and operation to the open-reel analog machine, its recording format and head configuration are different.

DASH Format

Most S-DAT recorders used today conform to the **Digital Audio Stationary Head (DASH) format**. The **DASH format** specifies sampling frequency, tape format, track geometry, packing density, and error correction for 24- and 48-channel digital tape recorders. DASH also specifies protocols for two-channel, open-reel DTRs, although these machines are no longer actively marketed in the United States.

Tape width for both the 24- and 48-track machines is ½ inch; tape speed is 30 ips; and sampling rates are 44.1, 44.056, and 48 kHz. Playing time for a 10½-inch reel is 30 minutes; a 12½-inch reel is 45 minutes; and a 14-inch reel is 60 minutes.

DASH machines have either two or three heads. On two-head machines, the heads are record and playback. In addition to the record and playback heads, the three-head machines have a *sync record* head for insert or Sel Sync recording. Both configurations also include an analog erase head.

Rotary-Head Digital Audio Recording

Storing video information on tape requires a different recording system than the one used to record sound with stationary-head recorders. Due to the considerable bandwidth it takes to store video, very high tape speeds are necessary. In a stationary-head format, the tape speed would have to be many times faster than the 30 ips of today's fastest ATRs, and it would take thousands of feet of tape to make a video recording. Therefore, instead of increasing longitudinal tape speed in video recording, the videotape head rotates at very high speed—2,000 *revolutions per minute (rpm)* in stereo rotary-head recorders, and more than 14,000 rpm in modular digital multitrack recorders. This creates the tape-to-head velocity essential for the wide bandwidth to store the video information without requiring faster longitudinal tape speeds. This technique is called **helical scanning**, due to the somewhat spiral shape of the tape when it is threaded around the head assembly (the Greek word for *spiral* is *helix*). Helical videotape recording has made it possible not only to record picture on tape, but to produce digital sound on audio- and videocassette as well.

Rotary-Head Digital Audiotape Recorder

The **rotary-head digital audiotape (R-DAT) recorder** has the wide dynamic range, low distortion, and immeasurable wow and flutter common to digital audio. Although the R-DAT uses cassette tape, it equals or exceeds many standard digital specifications.

At the very least, professional R-DATs operate at two sampling frequencies: 44.1 kHz and 48 kHz. Many models also include 32 kHz. Recording and playback can be done at all three sampling rates. Longitudinal tape speed is about ⅓ ips, one-sixth the speed of analog cassette recorders. The very slow speed does not affect sound quality, however, due to the high speed of the head drum and the digital processing of the audio signal. The recording format is two-channel stereo.

R-DAT has other advantages. For example, the encoding of nonaudio data permits automatic cueing to a particular selection, skipping over selections, and numbering selections. A high-speed search function facilitates quick search-to-cue spooling. R-DATs in professional use have time code. R-DAT machines are available in portable, lightweight cassette-size units, as well as in rack-mountable studio models (see 7-4).

R-DAT Audiocassette Tape

Digital audiotape (DAT) is about ⅐ inch wide, slightly wider than the standard analog audio-cassette; tape thickness is about ¼ mil. The cartridge itself is half the size of an analog cassette, and the length of tape in a cartridge is one-fourth that of an analog cassette. Cassettes are available in different lengths up to two hours at 48 and 44.1 kHz and four hours at 32 kHz. As in analog recording, the slower the speed, the poorer the sound quality, the digital format notwithstanding. Most digital audiocassette tape is metal particle, not lower than 1,500 oersteds.

Although the tape is enclosed in a plastic cartridge, its thinness and the density of the encoded information (114 million bits per square inch) make the tape and data extremely susceptible to damage from dirt, dust, and mishandling, especially because the track width of the encoded data is about one-tenth the thickness of a human hair.

Bulk erasing cannot totally eliminate the recorded signal on the high-density DAT surface. A recorded signal can be completely removed only by rerecording.

Many R-DATs have a moisture prevention cutoff to help protect the tape. Any moisture entering the unit from the tape stops the recorder, which then heats up to evaporate the moisture. When the unit is dry, it begins to function again.

Problems with DAT

It is natural to assume that because the digital recording process converts analog signals into a more durable format, the sonic results are relatively

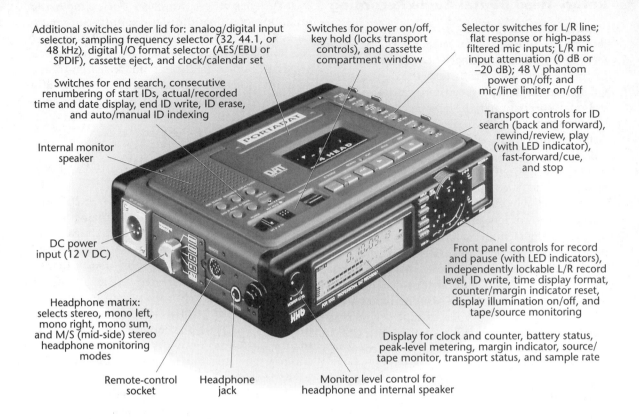

Additional switches under lid for: analog/digital input selector, sampling frequency selector (32, 44.1, or 48 kHz), digital I/O format selector (AES/EBU or SPDIF), cassette eject, and clock/calendar set

Switches for end search, consecutive renumbering of start IDs, actual/recorded time and date display, end ID write, ID erase, and auto/manual ID indexing

Internal monitor speaker

Switches for power on/off, key hold (locks transport controls), and cassette compartment window

Selector switches for L/R line; flat response or high-pass filtered mic inputs; L/R mic input attenuation (0 dB or −20 dB); 48 V phantom power on/off; and mic/line limiter on/off

Transport controls for ID search (back and forward), rewind/review, play (with LED indicator), fast-forward/cue, and stop

DC power input (12 V DC)

Headphone matrix: selects stereo, mono left, mono right, mono sum, and M/S (mid-side) stereo headphone monitoring modes

Front panel controls for record and pause (with LED indicators), independently lockable L/R record level, ID write, time display format, counter/margin indicator reset, display illumination on/off, and tape/source monitoring

Remote-control socket

Headphone jack

Monitor level control for headphone and internal speaker

Display for clock and counter, battery status, peak-level metering, margin indicator, source/ tape monitor, transport status, and sample rate

7-4 R-DAT. This particular model is portable. Its head configuration allows both monitoring of the source material and monitoring directly from tape; most R-DATs permit only monitoring of the source material. This machine comes with a separate time code unit; most time code R-DATs have the time code generator built-in.

invariable, regardless of the digital cassette tape used. Such is not the case. Qualitative differences exist among the various brands of DAT.

■ **Wear** The R-DAT's rotary head spins at 2,000 rpm which, over time, can create a molecular breakdown that could lead to tape shedding and head clogging. Interference with tape-to-head contact is of much greater consequence in digital recording than in analog recording, due to the densely packed digital information, among other things. Before recording, fast-forward and rewind the DAT to distribute the tape lubricants more evenly and help align the tape with the tape guides.

■ **Error concealment** In R-DAT errors result from tape noise, tape defects, head-to-tape contact problems, and sullied or creased tape. To the extent that it can, the system tries to conceal them. But if there are more errors than it can handle, they become audible. Certain brands of DAT are better able to deal with concealment than are others. Computer-grade *DDS (digital data storage)* DATs are more error-free than are audio-grade DATs.

■ **Cassette shells** Like cassette tape, the plastic cassette shell is also subject to wear. A worn tape shell could create audible error rate variations caused by problems with tape rotation, accelerated tape wear, debris that could roughen the running of the tape, timing errors, and tape vibration.

■ **Erasure** Some DATs have a higher **remnance**—residual magnetization from a previous recording after erasure. In rerecording, this could create a significant error rate.

■ **Aging** Because an increasing number of recordings are being mastered onto DAT, tape aging has become a concern. When DAT is in good condition, digital copies can be made with no sonic degradation. But if a DAT has deteriorated, the inevitable increased error rate creates a loss in sound quality that would be quite audible.

Storage in a scrupulously controlled cool-temperature and low-humidity environment is necessary. Warm temperatures and high humidity accelerate tape deterioration. Indeed, high humidity can lead to water penetration into the gaps of wound tape after long storage periods, causing tape layers to stick or the magnetic particles to rust, or both. Rusting is particularly notable because R-DATs are subject to buildup of condensation and, unless the tape's magnetic particles are protected in some way, rusting could be accelerated.

Features of R-DATs

R-DATs have a number of features that enhance ease of operation and production control. They include subcodes, transport and assignment controls, and visual indicators.

Subcodes A *subcode* is taped information that is independent of the audio. With R-DATs, subcodes facilitate cueing. They include *start IDs,* which mark the beginning of each audio segment; *program numbering,* which numbers each audio segment; and a *skip ID,* which makes the machine skip an audio segment. A subcode can be erased and recorded without affecting the program material.

Transport and Assignment Controls Subcodes make it possible to auto-locate segments. *Search* enables the machine to fast-forward to the selected program number; *return to zero* rewinds the tape to

a preset "0" position; and *renumber* automatically renumbers the start IDs consecutively from 1 upward. Other controls choose sampling frequency, which can be 44.1 or 48 kHz, and in some units 32 kHz also; select between analog and digital input signals; and copy-protect to prevent the recording from being digitally dubbed.

Visual Indicators R-DATs have display windows that show recording level; various timings, such as total time, elapsed time for the selection being played, and remaining tape time; sampling rate; subcodes; and an error indicator that flashes when there is a loss of data.

Care of R-DATs

Among the considerations in R-DAT care are alignment and cleaning.

Aligning an R-DAT Proper alignment is critical to the operation of all tape recorders, particularly the R-DAT. The mechanisms are quite delicate and require extremely fine tuning.

R-DATs are designed to correct errors due to noise, slight mistracking, and dropout. But if there is significant mistracking, error correction cannot handle it, and the audio mutes.

Of particular importance are the tape guides. If they are not properly adjusted, the tape will not track correctly as it passes around the head drum's scanner. A reference tape is used for alignment of the guides.

Proper tape tension is also important to alignment, because it affects track angle and, therefore, must be checked before making adjustments to the drum. Usually, a specially designed cassette with a tension gauge built into each hub is used. The amount of tension is read off a scale in the body of the cassette. Tension is adjusted for normal play, reverse, and shuttle.

Proper track spacing in record mode is determined by checking the frequency-generating wheel on the capstan shaft to make sure the frequency is correct. This is done with a scratch tape.

Tracks recorded at the proper angle and spacing and with correct timing will play back accurately on another R-DAT. If timing is off, however, the recorder will be able to play its own tapes, but they may not play back accurately on another machine. Recording begins when a sensor generates one pulse for each revolution of the scanner. A reference tape is used to adjust the relative timing between the event on the reference tape and the sensor pulse.

Cleaning an R-DAT The importance of having a regular equipment maintenance schedule cannot be overemphasized. With R-DATs that is almost as easily done as said, using cleaning tapes especially made for them. These tapes are nonabrasive, gentle to the heads, and good at removing small, loose particles in the tape path. It is wise to clean an R-DAT after about 20 hours of use. It takes five to 10 seconds to run a cleaning tape.

Cleaning tapes usually will not remove grime and debris that get into the nooks and crannies of the small working parts. To do this you have to get inside the R-DAT and clean the tape path and heads, if you are technically able. For this operation use a lint-free lens-cleaning cloth, a chamois, foam-tipped cleaner dipped in an approved VCR cleaning solvent, or a small, round wooden stick soaked in VCR cleaning solvent. The wood should be strong enough to dislodge the debris but soft enough to not scratch the drum surface. Do not use anything that could clog the tape path and heads, such as cotton swabs, tissue, or cotton cloth.

Rotary-Head Open-Reel Digital Audiotape Recorder

The rotary-head format is also used in the open-reel design. The Nagra-D II, for example, is a 24-bit, two- or four-channel, ¼-inch tape recorder designed for use in the field (see 7-5). The four-channel recording system consists of pairs of tracks. Data for channels 1 and 2 are on one track; data for channels 3 and 4 are on the other track. This configuration allows simple lockout of either pair. There are also three longitudinal tracks for cue, control, and time code. Sampling frequencies are 32, 44.1, 48, 88.2, and 96 kHz; tape speeds are about

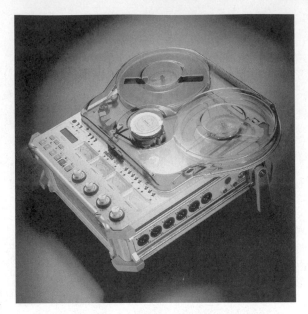

7-5 Rotary-head open-reel digital audiotape recorder. This machine uses ¼-inch digital tape. Tape speeds are 3.9 ips for 4 channels at 48 kHz or 2 channels at 96 kHz and 1.95 ips for 2 channels at 48 kHz. Three other sampling frequencies are 32, 44.1, and 88.2 kHz. Recording times are 2 hours for 2 channels and 1 hour for 4 channels using a 5-inch reel, and 4 hours for 2 channels and 2 hours for 4 channels using a 7-inch reel. Recording is 24-bit. Signal-to-noise ratio is better than 110 dB. In addition to the rotary heads, there are longitudinal Cue and Time Code heads. It is possible to lock several of these machines together for extended multitrack recording.

1.9 ips for two channels at 48 kHz, and about 3.9 ips for four channels at 48 kHz or two channels at 96 kHz; signal-to-noise ratio is better than 110 dB.

Modular Digital Multitrack Recorder

The *modular digital multitrack (MDM) recorder* also uses rotating heads to record audio. But instead of using an R-DAT transport with digital audio-cassette tape, the MDM uses a videocassette transport with videocassette tape. It can record up to eight channels and be linked to multiple units, thereby expanding track capability in eight-channel increments (see 7-6). As many as 16 MDMs (of

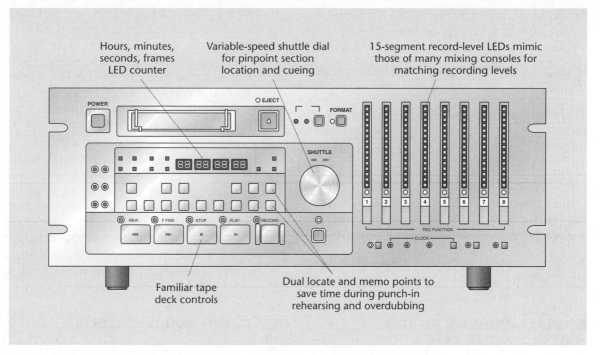

7-6 Modular digital multitrack tape recorder. This model has eight tracks and can record 108 minutes on a standard 120-minute Hi8 videotape. A single cable can lock up and synchronize two machines for 16-track recording. This modular approach allows up to 16 of these MDMs to be interlocked, providing 128 tracks (in eight-track increments) of recording capability. In addition to the usual transport functions such as *play, record,* and so on, there are controls for tape shuttle, sample rate selection, locator points, rehearse and auto-punch, clock source selection, time code generate/record, and soft keys that are used in conjunction with a display button that allows the setting of preroll and crossfade times.

the same format) can be stacked with a cable loop-through, and run synchronously, to provide a total of 128 tracks. This capability is what the *modular* refers to.

The two formats of MDMs are distinguished by the tape and transport used. One format, the ***digital tape recording system (DTRS)*** uses Hi8 video-cassette tape. The other format, ***ADAT*** (the *A* stands for Alesis, its developer), uses S-VHS. Although standard Hi8 and S-VHS tape can be used, versions of these tapes optimized for MDM are available. Currently, Sony and Tascam support DTRS; Alesis, Fostex, and Panasonic support ADAT.

One operational difference between the two formats is the maximum recording time. The tape speed of DTRS is just slightly faster than stan-dard-play speed, which yields 108 minutes per 120-minute cassette. ADAT runs at about three times normal speed, for a recording time of 67 minutes per tape.

There are a number of features of MDMs that facilitate production, although they vary with make and model. Features such as location memories, auto-loop/rehearse in both record and playback, digital crossfade times, time code, variable-pitch change, 16- or 24-bit high-resolution audio, and dynamic range over 100 dB.

MDMs have several advantages:

■ They provide an inexpensive way for a studio to have digital multitrack capability that is expandable in eight-channel increments, and at relatively low cost.

■ Sound quality is not sacrificed with multiple tracks, because the widest portion of the tape, the video portion, is used to encode the audio.

■ Dubbing can be done between recorders, in sync if necessary.

■ Operational data such as locate points, time code, frame rate, and other information can be stored and retrieved.

■ An MDM makes it convenient to record six mixed surround-sound tracks (assuming the 5.1 format's full-frequency channels plus the low-frequency channel) and have the remaining two tracks for the stereo downmix (see Chapter 19).

■ MDMs take up comparatively little space, even when several units are stacked.

DIGITAL AUDIO ON DIGITAL VIDEOCASSETTE TAPE

It is somewhat ironic that it became possible to digitize an audio signal on videotape before it was possible to digitize a video signal. In the late 1980s, the first *digital videotape recorder (DVTR)* was introduced. It was not too many years ago that five systems were in use. Today there are twice that number.

The major differences among these systems have more to do with the way they process video than with their audio processing. There are also differences in compatibility among systems, tape width, and cassette recording time.

Sound in DVTRs is digital quality. The differences in audio among the various systems come down to bit rate and number of audio channels.

Due to the number of DVTR systems available and the fact that their principal advantages and disadvantages have more to do with video than audio, a discussion of these systems is better left to the television production books. Table 7-1, however, gives a brief summation of the similarities and differences among their audio formats.

DISK-BASED AUDIO SYSTEMS

Disk-based systems have several advantages over tape-based systems: All data are digital; recording, playback, and signal processing are possible in a self-contained unit; information retrieval is nonlinear and virtually instantaneous; encoded

Table 7-1 Digital videotape formats

Type	Tape Width	Number of Digital Audio Channels	Sound Channel Coding*
D-1	About ¾ inch	4	16–20-bit @ 48 kHz
D-2	About ¾ inch	4	16-bit @ 48 kHz
D-3	½ inch	4	20-bit @ 48 kHz
D-5†	½ inch	4	20-bit @ 48 kHz
D-6	About ¾ inch	10	20-bit @ 48 kHz
Digital Betacam	½ inch	4	20-bit @ 48 kHz
Betacam SX	½ inch	4	16-bit @ 48 kHz
Digital S (or D-9)	½ inch	4	16-bit @ 48 kHz
DVCPRO (or D-7)	¼ inch	2	16-bit @ 48 kHz
DVCAM	¼ inch	2 4	16-bit @ 48 kHz 12-bit @ 32 kHz

*In the 20-bit machines, the coding tape can handle this quantization, but some may not be equipped with 20-bit converters. 18-bit converters are more common.

†There is no D-4 because in Japanese culture the number *4* has a negative stigma attached.

data can be nondestructive; synchronization options are extensive; and storage capacity is substantial. Not to be overlooked are the greatly increased creative and technical possibilities disk-based systems afford.

Disk-based systems can be divided into two groups: record/playback and distribution. Record/playback systems are used in production and postproduction. Distribution systems are what the final product is transferred to for release to the marketplace. Examples of distribution systems are the compact disc (CD), Super Audio Compact Disc (SACD), CD-ROM, digital versatile disk (DVD), and High-Definition Compatible Digital (HDCD) technology.* Two of these distribution systems, the CD and DVD, can also be used like tape for recording and playback during production. Because this book deals with the audio production process,

---

*HDCD is a process developed for use with release formats to increase the amount of audible information on DVD-Audio, DVD-Video, compact disc, and surround digital recordings while significantly reducing distortions that occur during analog-to-digital and digital-to-analog conversion.

only disk-based record/playback systems are addressed in this chapter.

Disk-Based Record/Playback Systems

Record/playback production systems include the magneto-optical disc, mini disc, digital cartridge disk, recordable and rewritable compact discs, solid-state digital recorder/editor, digital versatile disc, and hard disk.

Magneto-Optical Disc

Magneto-optical (MO) recording, like magnetic digital tape recording, uses tiny magnetic particles to encode digital information. But unlike magnetic tape recording: (1) the MO recording medium is disc-based; (2) instead of magnetic heads to orient the particles, a laser beam is used; and (3) to orient the magnetic particles, they must be heated to extremely high temperatures.

The MO disc's advantages are: (1) it is erasable and can be used like tape; (2) it is two-sided to increase playing time; and (3) perhaps most significant of all, it uses an optical instead of a

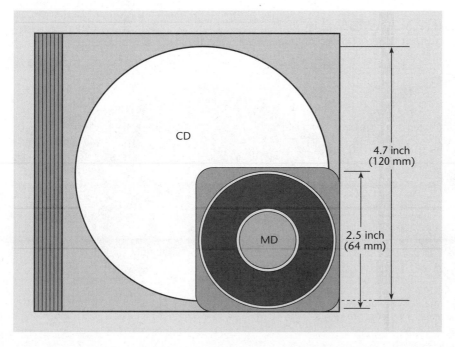

7-7 Comparison of mini disc and compact disc

CD

MD

4.7 inch
(120 mm)

2.5 inch
(64 mm)

mechanical process, which makes it wear resistant. Its main disadvantages are that it is not interchangeable with ordinary CD players and, compared with other disk-based formats, even with two-sided recording, playing time is limited. Stereo recording times are approximately 12, 20, 50, or 60 minutes using 128, 230, 540, or 640 *megabyte (MB)* disks at a sampling rate of 44.1. Eight-track recording time is 15 minutes at a 17-bit, 44.1 sampling rate on a 640 MB disk. MO recorders can be linked like MDMs to provide additional tracks for simultaneous recording.

Mini Disc

The *mini disc™ (MD™),* originally intended for the consumer market, has become a popular, inexpensive alternative to higher-priced disk-based systems, particularly in radio and project studios, and for sound effects playback automation (see Chapter 12). The mini disc is a 2½-inch-wide magneto-optical disc with a recording time of 148 minutes in mono, 74 minutes in stereo, 37 minutes of four-track recording, and 18 minutes of eight-track recording (see 7-7). The mini disc format uses a sampling rate of 44.1 kHz. Audio is digital quality with low distortion, low noise, and a dynamic range of 105 dB.

The MD system uses two types of media: audio discs and data discs. The *audio disc* (MD) is a consumer format, two-channel CD-type medium for prerecorded material. *Data discs* (MDD) are blank, recordable magneto-optical media. The mini disc comes in two-channel stand-alone units, rack-mountable and portable, or multitrack recording/mixing systems (see 7-8). Stand-alone units can be linked to provide additional tracks. The mini disc is also used in cartridge disk systems (see the following section). Mini disc recorders offer instantaneous random locate capability, easy portability, and, depending on the system, some editing capabilities. Its data compression scheme, however, limits its use for critical recording.*

Digital Cartridge Disk System

The *digital cartridge disk system* is the successor to the analog tape cartridge system. Like the tape cart, the disk cart can be a recorder/player unit or a

---

*Data compression is a scheme that allows more information to be encoded on a disk by, as the term suggests, compressing it. It is what allows formats such as the mini disc and DVD to carry significantly greater amounts of data than they otherwise would be able to do. The compression process reduces the size of audio files by removing redundancy in the data, thereby using as little file space as possible to store and accurately reproduce the audio data. For a full discussion of data compression and the protocols involved see Chapter 16, "Internet Production."

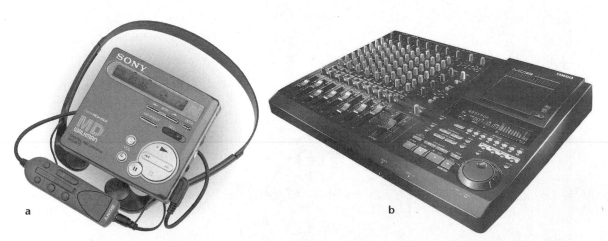

7-8 Mini disc recorders. (a) Portable Walkman® stereo used in field news reporting (see Chapter 13). (b) Multitrack MD combination recorder/console. Recording times are : eight-track, 18 minutes; four-track, 37 minutes; stereo, 74 minutes; mono, 148 minutes.

player-only unit. Unlike the tape cart, which used only audiotape, the disk cart's record/play medium can be a compact disc, magneto-optical disc, mini disc, Zip™ disk, or hard disk. The cartridge is the plastic container that holds the disk.

The cartridge disk is used for short program materials, such as songs, spot announcements, station IDs, program "intros" and "outros," jingles, and bumpers (music lead-ins or lead-outs that immediately precede or follow a program segment); playlist assembly for automatic cueing; and for starting the various audio segments. A playlist comprises any combination of audio program materials, including their length and time of broadcast. It facilitates tight and reliable production with its instant start, automatic recueing, and a variety of other features that include back cueing, track selection, automatic fade-in, editing, and an information display (see 7-9).

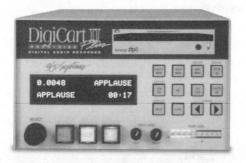

7-9 Digital cartridge disk system. This hard-disk cartridge machine includes an internal hard disk offering up to 49 hours of storage and the capability to also use removable 100 MB Zip disks for recording. Transport controls emulate conventional analog carts with *record, play,* and *stop.* The menu keys include: *Utility menu* for disk and file management; *Setup menu* for record format, sample rate, threshold record level, count up/down, and restart; *Edit menu* for head trim, tail trim, output gain, fade-in, fade-out, and preroll; *SEC* for control of an external device; *D-NET XFER* for activation of the D-NET file transfer network menu; position arrows for selecting menu options, drive, and directories; *Enter* to confirm the current selection/operation; *Pause* to interrupt playback or to preselect or preview a cut; *View List* to view the contents of a playlist; and *Loop* to continuously loop a cut.

Recordable and Rewritable Compact Discs

In one sense the *recordable compact disc (CD-R)* is not a production tool because, once encoded, the information cannot be manipulated—edited, equalized, remixed, and so on. In another sense it is a record/playback medium and as such has become a valuable production tool that has made in-studio CD premastering possible and affordable.

The CD-R makes the compact disc somewhat similar to recording tape in that it has unlimited playback, but until recently it could be recorded on only once and could not be erased. Even false starts were there for good, so many users assembled their audio on DAT or hard disk and then transferred it to CD-R.

The recordable compact disc conforms to the standards document known as *Orange Book.* According to this standard, data encoded on a CD-R does not have to be recorded all at once but can be added to whenever the user wishes, making it more convenient to produce sequential audio material. But CD-Rs conforming to the Orange Book standard are not compatible with standard CD players. To be playable on any standard CD player, the CD-R must conform to the *Red Book* standard, which requires that a table of contents (TOC) file be encoded onto the disc.* A TOC file is written at the start of the disc and includes information related to subcode and copy prohibition data, index numbering, and timing information. The TOC,

---

*In addition to the Orange and Red Book standards, there are Yellow, Green, White, Blue, and Scarlet Book, standards. The *Yellow Book* format describes the basic specifications for computer-based CD-ROM (compact disc–read-only memory). The *Green Book* format describes the basic specifications for CD-I (compact disc–interactive), also designated CD-ROM XA (the *XA* is short for extended *a*rchitecture). It is aimed at multimedia applications that combine audio, graphic images, animation, and full-motion video. The *White Book* describes basic specifications for full-motion, compressed videodiscs. The *Blue Book* format provides specifications for a high-density compact-disc (HDCD) format, such as DVD-A (audio). The *Scarlet Book* includes the protocol for the Super Audio CD.

which is written onto the disc after audio assembly, tells the CD player where each cut starts and ends. Once it is encoded, any audio added to the disc will not be playable on standard CD players due to the write-once limitation of CD-R. It is therefore important to know the types of "color book" standards with which a CD recorder is compatible.

Compact-disc recorders are available in different recording speeds. For example, single- (1×), double- (2×), quad- (4×), and 6× speed. Single-speed machines record in real time, that is, at the CD's playback speed, 2× machines record at twice the playback speed, reducing by half the time it takes to create a CD, and so on.

CD-R technology has revolutionized premastering, particularly in music recording, by making it convenient and relatively inexpensive to produce a finished, customized, music CD at the end of a recording session—in the studio.

As revolutionary as the CD-R technology has been, the rewritable CD is one step better (see 7-10). The **rewritable CD (CD-RW)** is like audiotape in that it can be recorded on, erased, and used again for another recording. If the driver program supports it, erase can even be random. Like the CD recorders, CD-RW drives operate at different speeds to shorten recording time, but they include the

added abilities to play CD-ROMs and to record and play CD-Rs. CD-RWs, however, must be read in either CD-RW drives or new CD-ROM drives that support MultiRead, a specification set by the Optical Storage Technology Association (OSTA) and agreed to by the major manufacturers of CD-R, CD-RW, CD-ROM, and DVD-ROM discs and drives.

Solid-State Digital Audio Recorder/Editor

The *solid-state digital audio recorder/editor* is a 16-bit recorder/player with built-in virtual editing that uses *PCMCIA (Personal Computer Memory Card International Association)* cards as the storage medium (see 7-11). The machine shown in Figure 7-11 is designed for use in broadcast news reporting from the field. Recording capacity is 40 minutes (mono) on one PCMCIA card; there is a double card holder for continuous, extended recording time. The recording method is digital compression. Sampling rates are 16, 24, 32, and 48 kHz.

Digital Versatile Disc

When the *DVD* first appeared on the scene in 1996, it was known as the "digital video disc." With its potential for expandability and the relatively quick realization of that potential, it was redubbed *digital versatile disc (DVD)*. And versatile it is. It is

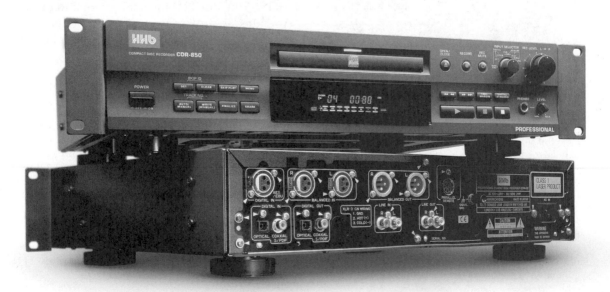

7-10 Recordable and rewritable compact disk recorder. Front and rear views.

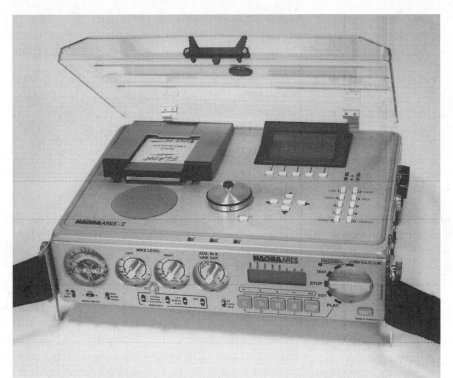

7-11 Solid-state digital audio recorder/editor. This machine uses PCMCIA cards as the recording medium, uses D-size batteries, weighs about six pounds (with the pack), and provides up to five hours of recording time with a four-cell pack and up to 15 hours of continuous operation with an eight-cell pack.

expected to replace the CD-ROM as a common storage medium and may even supplant other disc formats, such as the CD and MD, as well. One indication of its versatility is the alphabet soup of DVD formats. It may therefore provide a clearer perspective of the medium to include a few of DVD's distribution formats before discussing the production formats, with the understanding that DVD is still a developing technology.

The DVD is the same diameter and thickness as the compact disc, but it can encode a much greater amount of data. The storage capacity of the current CD is 650 MB. The storage capacity of the DVD can be on a number of levels (see Table 7-2), each one far exceeding the CD.

Currently the DVD formats are: DVD-ROM, DVD-Video, DVD-Audio, DVD-Recordable (DVD-R), DVD-RAM, DVD-Rewritable (DVD-RW), and another rewritable format, DVD-R+W. Of interest for our purposes are DVD-Audio and the recordable and rewritable formats.

DVD-Audio *DVD-Audio (DVD-A)* is a distribution medium with extremely high quality audio. To get a better idea of DVD-A, we can compare it with *DVD-Video (DVD-V)*, the first DVD format marketed. DVD-V is a high-quality motion picture/ sound delivery system. The audio portion can have up to eight audio tracks. They can be one to eight channels of linear digital audio; one to six channels of Dolby 5.1 surround sound; or one to eight channels (5.1 or 7.1 surround) of MPEG-2 audio.* There are provisions for *Digital Theater Sound (DTS)* and *Sony Dynamic Digital Sound (SDDS),* as well. Sampling rates can be 44.1, 48, or 96 kHz, with a bit depth of 16, 20, or 24 bits. Although these digital specifications yield high-quality audio, the transfer bit rate for audio is limited to 6.144 *megabits per second (Mbps)*. This means that there is room

---

*MPEG-2 is a compression protocol. This and other compression schemes are explained in Chapter 16, "Internet Production."

Table 7-2 DVD protocols

Type	Physical Format	Capacity (billions of bytes)	Equivalent to
DVD-5	Single side/single layer	4.7	7 CD-ROMs
DVD-9	Single side/dual layer	8.5	13 CD-ROMs
DVD-10	Double side/single layer	9.4	14 CD-ROMs
DVD-14	Double side/one dual layer side, one single-layer side	13.2	20 CD-ROMs
DVD-18	Double side/dual layer	17.0	26 CD-ROMs

for only two audio channels at a sampling rate of 96 kHz and a bit depth of 24 bits (abbreviated 96/24). The best multichannel audio be 48/20.

DVD-A differs from DVD-V in that there is more storage room for audio data on the DVD-A. The DVD-A can hold 9.6 Mbps. This provides six channels of 96/24 audio. To accomplish the increased storage room, *MLP (Meridian Lossless Packing)* data compression is used. It gives a compression ratio of about 1.85 to 1. (**Lossless compression** means that no data is discarded during the compression process; during **lossy compression** data that is not critical is discarded.)

DVD-A is also flexible. It is possible to choose the number of channels—1 to 6; the bit depth—16, 20, 24; and the sample rating—44.1, 48, 88.2, 96, 176.4, or 192 kHz. Another advantage of DVD-A is that it is *extensible,* meaning that it is relatively open-ended and can utilize any future audio coding technology. DVD-A's recording time is 74 minutes, but it can hold up to seven hours of audio on two channels with lesser sound quality. DVD-A can also encode text, graphics, and still pictures. It should be noted that DVD-A discs are not compatible with CD players, and some DVD-A discs will not play in some current DVD players, because DVD-A was specified well after DVD-V.*

Recordable and Rewritable DVDs The recordable DVD (DVD-R) is the high-density equivalent of the CD-R. It is a write-once format that can store 3.95 gigabytes (GB) on a single-sided disc and 7.9 gigabytes on a double-sided disc. It takes about 50 minutes to record a single-sided

DVD-R disc. It provides both DVD flexibility and program quality. DVD-R is compatible with DVD-V and DVD-ROM players.

There are three basic types of rewritable DVD: DVD-RW, DVD-RAM, and DVD-R+W.

DVD-RW DVD-RW is the rewritable version of DVD-R. Two differences between DVD-RW and CD-RW are the way they are written and storage capacity. DVD-RW employs phase-change technology, which means that the phase of the laser light's wavefront is being modulated to write to the medium. In the erase mode, the material (a photopolymer medium) is transferred back into its original crystalline state, allowing data to be written to the disc again and again. The other way to write to DVD is the organic-dye process, a nonreversible

---

*The DVD-A raises the question of how it differs from the Super Audio Compact Disc (SACD). Briefly, the SACD is a distribution medium intended for the audiophile market, as opposed to the mass market. The disc is the same size as the DVD, with a data capacity of 7.4 gigabyes. It is one-sided and two-layered. One layer is dedicated to normal Red Book CD-type audio and the second to a high-density layer for extremely high-quality two-channel stereo and seven-channel surround sound. It utilizes a proprietary format called *direct stream digital (DSD)*. DSD samples a wave many more times each second than during conventional analog-to-digital conversion, and the wave is digitized on the basis of a simple distinction: whether it goes up (encoded as a 1), or down (encoded as a 0), relative to the previous sample. SACD's specifications are a sampling rate of about 2.8 MHz (29 times 96 kHz), a frequency response up to 100 kHz, and a dynamic range of 120 dB. SACD discs are compatible with CD players but not with DVD players.

method. In essence, rewritable discs using this process are write-once media. DVD-RW has a capacity of 4.7 GB and is compatible with DVD-R and DVD-ROM players. Currently, the primary application for DVD-RW is authoring media for content development of DVD-ROM and DVD-V.

DVD-RAM DVD-RAM also employs phase-change technology but is not compatible with current DVD players and DVD-ROM drives. It comes in single- and double-sided versions. Data capacity is 4.7 GB on a single-sided disc and twice that on a double-sided disc. Discs are enclosed in protective cartridges for recording purposes. Single-sided discs can be removed from the cartridge for playback in a DVD player or PC drive, but double-sided discs cannot be.

DVD-R+W DVD-R+W is an erasable format using phase-change technology that has been developed to compete with DVD-RAM. Data capacity for a single-sided disc is 3 GB, with expectations that it will increase to 4.7 GB and 9.4 GB for a double-sided disc. DVD-R+W drives can write CD-Rs and CD-RWs and read CDs, DVD-ROMs, DVD-Rs, DVD-RWs.

With the almost confusing number of different disc formats available, and possibly others on the way, and the concerns with compatibility, to say nothing of their differences in cost and ease of use, undoubtedly the marketplace will sort things out. Otherwise, we'll all need a program to keep track of the players. We may already need such a program!

Hard-Disk Recording

What once took various types of equipment— console, tape recorder, editing gear, and signal processor, to name the most obvious—located in different areas of the control room to do a production, now can be done at a central location with a hard-disk recorder.

Hard-disk recording resembles tape recording in that it encodes, stores, and reproduces a signal, which can be edited, on a few or several different tracks. But there the resemblance ends. Unlike tape recording, hard-disk recording has a different, more versatile channel/track configuration; information access is random and quick; storage capacity is far greater; data is nondestructive; editing is nonlinear (see Chapter 18); and it is possible to do signal processing, such as equalization, reverberation, and delay (see Chapter 9).

On a professional analog open-reel tape recorder, one input, one output, and one channel are dedicated to each track. Once a track has been magnetically encoded, that information is tied to that track; it cannot be moved to another track or slipped out of time without being rerecorded.

With hard-disk recording the relationships of channels to inputs, outputs, and tracks are not directly linked. Once the computer-based audio data is recorded and stored, it can be assigned to any output(s) and moved in time. For example, a hard-disk recorder may have four inputs, eight outputs, 16 channels, and 256 virtual tracks. This means that up to four inputs can be used to record up to four channels at one time; up to eight channels at one time can be used for internal mixing or routing; up to 16 channels (real tracks) are simultaneously available during playback; and up to 256 separate *soundfiles** can be maintained and assigned to a virtual track. *Virtual tracks* provide all the functionality of an actual track, but cannot be played back simultaneously. For example, in a 16-channel system with 256 virtual tracks, only 16 tracks can play back at once. Think of 16 stacks of index cards totaling 256 cards. Assume that each stack is a channel. A card can be moved from anywhere in a stack to the top of the same stack or to the top of another stack. There are 256 cards, but only 16 of them can be on top at once. In other words, any virtual track can be assigned to any channel(s) and slipped along that channel or across channels.

---

*Audio that is encoded onto the disk takes the form of a *soundfile*. The soundfile contains information about the sound such as amplitude and duration. When the soundfile is opened, most systems display that information on a monitor.

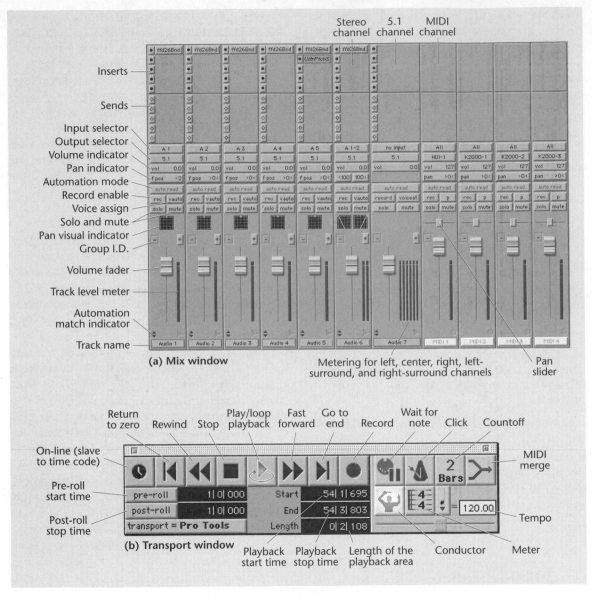

Inserts
Sends
Input selector
Output selector
Volume indicator
Pan indicator
Automation mode
Record enable
Voice assign
Solo and mute
Pan visual indicator
Group I.D.
Volume fader
Track level meter
Automation match indicator
Track name

Stereo channel
5.1 channel
MIDI channel

(a) Mix window

Metering for left, center, right, left-surround, and right-surround channels

Pan slider

Return to zero · Rewind · Stop · Play/loop playback · Fast forward · Go to end · Record · Wait for note · Click · Countoff

On-line (slave to time code)
Pre-roll start time
Post-roll stop time

MIDI merge

Tempo

(b) Transport window

Playback start time · Playback stop time · Length of the playback area · Conductor · Meter

pre-roll 1| 0| 000 · Start 54| 1| 695
post-roll 1| 0| 000 · End 54| 3| 803
transport = **Pro Tools** · Length 0| 2| 108

2 Bars · 4/4 · 120.00

7-12 (a) Mix and (b) transport windows of a hard-disk recording and editing system

There are two basic types of hard-disk recorders: modular (stand-alone) and computer-based. Both types also have signal processing and editing capability.

It is difficult to discuss recording operations generically, because terms, configurations, and visual displays differ from system to system, but Figure 7-12 should give you a sense of the procedures.

Digital Audio Workstation

A hard-disk recorder/editor is also known as a ***digital audio workstation (DAW)***, although some purists make a distinction between the two. A DAW

Table 7-3 Digital interfaces

- The *AES/EBU* interface is a professional digital audio connection standard specified jointly by the Audio Engineering Society (AES) and the European Broadcast Union (EBU). Its standard calls for two audio channels to be encoded in a serial data stream and transmitted through a balanced line using XLR connectors.

- *SPDIF (Sony/Philips Digital Interface)* is the consumer version of the AES/EBU standard. It calls for an un-balanced line using phono connectors. SPDIF is implemented on consumer audio equipment such as CD players.

- *SCSI (Small Computer Systems Interface)* is the standard for hardware and software command language. Pronounced "scuzzy," it allows two-way communication between, primarily, hard-disk and

CD-ROM drives to exchange digital data at fast speeds. SCSI can also be used with other components, such as scanners.

- *MADI (Multichannel Audio Digital Interface)* is the standard used when interfacing multichannel digital audio. It allows up to 56 channels of digital audio to be sent down one coaxial cable.

- *ADAT Optical* is a proprietary digital-connection format designed for use with the Alesis MDM digital tape recorder. It is designed to carry eight channels of digital audio on a single fiber-optic cable.

- *TDIF (Tascam Digital Interface Format)* is Tascam's proprietary digital audio format. It is a bidirectional interface; that is, it carries eight channels of audio in both directions.

---

combines a host computer with specialized hardware and software and can be upgraded and expanded. Modular units do not require a desktop computer as host, and the choice of supported peripherals for expansion is limited.

A DAW can be integrated with and networked to a collection of devices, such as other audio, video, and MIDI sources, within or among facilities in the same or different locations. A DAW's systemwide communication with other external devices, and communication between devices in general, is facilitated through the distribution of digital interfaces such as *AES/EBU, SPDIF, SCSI, MADI, ADAT Optical,* and *TDIF* (see Table 7-3).

DIGITAL AUDIO NETWORKING

Recording has come a long way since the days when overdubbing provided a way to manipulate time and space. Signal processing added to that capability with effects such as delay, reverberation, time compression, and pitch shifting. Digital technology provided the means to access data

randomly and nonlinearly. Workstations facilitated speedy interstudio interchange of encoded, digital-quality audio. Now, through telephone lines, a recording can be produced in real time between studios across town or across the country with little or no loss in audio quality and at relatively low cost.

Integrated Services Digital Network (ISDN) is a public telephone service that allows cheap use of a flexible, wide-area, all-digital network (see 7-13). With ISDN it is possible to have a vocalist in New York, wearing headphones for the foldback feed, singing into a microphone whose signal is routed to a studio in Los Angeles. In L.A. the singer's audio is fed through a console, along with the accompaniment from, say, the L.A. studio (it could be from elsewhere), and recorded. When necessary, the singer in New York, the accompanying musicians (from wherever), and the recordist in L.A. can communicate with one another through a talkback system. Commercials are now being done with the announcer in a studio in one city and the recordist adding the effects in another city. And unlike much of today's advanced technology, ISDN is a relatively uncomplicated service to use.

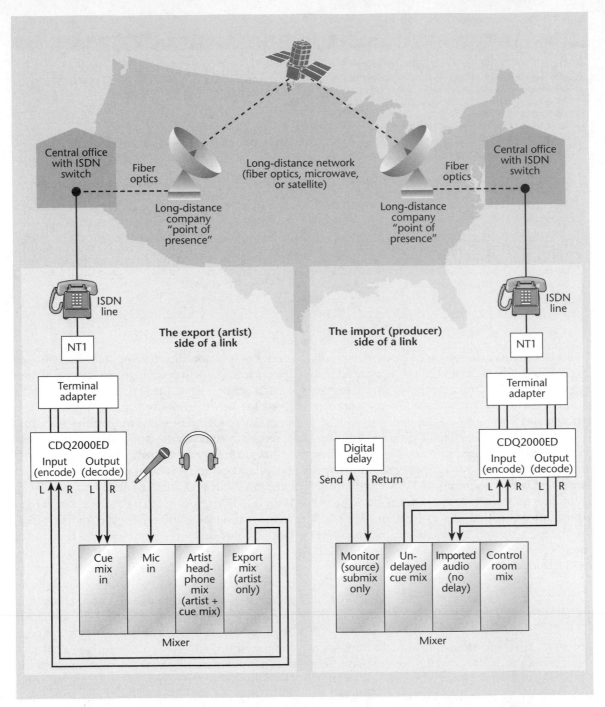

7-13 Long-distance recording. In this illustration NT1 is a network terminator that protects the network from electrical malfunctions. CDQ2000ED code enables you to send a cue mix to an artist in another location, delay the mix sent to your monitors, not delay the received artist's solo signal, mix the two, give direction, and make production judgments in real time.

▶ Digital audio uses a numerical representation of the sound signal's actual frequency and amplitude. In analog, frequency is the time component, and amplitude is the level component. In digital, sampling is the time component, and quantization is the level component.

▶ Sampling takes periodic samples (voltages) of the original analog signal at fixed intervals and converts them into digital data. The rate at which the fixed intervals sample the original signal each second is call the sampling frequency.

▶ As samples of the waveform are taken, these voltages are converted into discrete quantities and assigned values. This process is known as quantization.

▶ There are five basic steps in the digital recording process: anti-aliasing, sample and hold, analog-to-digital conversion, signal coding, and data storage.

▶ The basic steps in digital reproduction are: demodulation, error correction, digital-to-analog conversion, sample and hold, and low-pass filtering.

▶ Tape used for digital recording is different from tape used for analog recording. It is thinner, has about twice the coercivity, must be used in an environment whose temperature and humidity are more closely controlled, and must be handled with greater care.

▶ Digital audiotape recorders (DTRs) fall into two categories: stationary head and rotary head.

▶ Stationary-head digital audiotape (S-DAT) recorders are similar in operation to analog audiotape recorders (ATRs). They differ, however, in recording format and head configuration.

▶ Most stationary-head digital audiotape recorders conform to the DASH (Digital Audio Stationary Head) format.

▶ The rotary-head digital audiotape (R-DAT) recorder uses the principle of the videotape recorder's spinning heads to encode audio onto tape.

▶ Generally, R-DATs operate at three sampling speeds: 32 kHz, 44.1 kHz, and 48 kHz. Longitudinal tape speed is $1/3$ ips (inch per second), one-sixth the speed of analog cassette recorders.

▶ Audiocassette tape for R-DAT is about $1/7$-inch wide and is similar in thickness to a 90-minute analog cassette (about $1/4$ mil). The cartridge is half the size of an analog cassette, and the tape length is one-fourth that of an analog cassette.

▶ When selecting and using digital cassette tape, be wary of problems with wear, error concealment, the cassette shell, erasure, and aging.

▶ R-DATs have a number of features that enhance ease of operation and production control, including subcodes, transport and assignment controls, and visual indicators.

▶ Even though the digital format is robust, R-DATs and digital cassette tape require regular maintenance and cleaning to ensure proper tape tracking, tape tension, and track spacing and to prevent the buildup of grime and debris that could wreak havoc on encoding and error correction.

▶ Modular digital multitrack (MDM) tape recorders use a videocassette transport with videotape, instead of an R-DAT transport, to record up to eight channels of audio per unit. Units can be linked, expanding track capability in eight-channel increments.

▶ MDMs come in two formats: the digital tape recording system (DTRS), which uses Hi8 videocassette tape; and ADAT, which uses S-VHS videocassette tape.

▶ Digital videotape recorders (DVTRs) come in a variety of formats, which differ more in the way they process video than the way they process audio. The differences in audio among the various systems come down to bit rate and number of audio channels. All sound in DVTRs is digital quality.

▶ Disk-based audio record/playback systems include the magneto-optical disc, mini disc, digital cartridge disk, recordable and rewritable compact discs, solid-state digital recorder/editor, digital versatile disc, and hard disk.

▶ Magneto-optical (MO) recording, like magnetic digital tape recording, uses tiny magnetic particles to encode digital information. But unlike magnetic tape recording, MO recording is a disc-based optical process; a laser beam orients the magnetic particles, and the magnetic particles are heated to extremely high temperatures.

- The mini disc (MD) is a 2½-inch-wide compact disc. The MD system uses MO media for recordable blank discs and CD-type optical media for prerecorded software. The encoded data is compressed.

- The digital cartridge disk system is the successor to the analog tape cartridge system. The disk cart can be a recorder/player unit or a player-only unit. The disk cart's medium can be a compact disc, magneto-optical disc, mini disc, Zip disk, or hard disk.

- The recordable compact disc (CD-R) is a write-once medium with unlimited playback. The rewritable CD (CD-RW) is like recording tape in that it can be recorded on, erased, and used again for another recording.

- The solid-state digital audio recorder/editor is designed for use in broadcast news reporting from the field. Its recording medium is the PCMCIA card.

- The digital versatile disc (DVD) is the same diameter and thickness as the compact disc, but it can hold a much greater amount of data.

- DVDs come in a variety of formats: DVD-ROM, DVD-Video (DVD-V), DVD-Audio (DVD-A), DVD-Recordable (DVD-R), DVD-RAM, and two rewritable formats: DVD-RW and DVD-R+W.

- DVD-Audio differs from DVD-Video in that there is much more storage room for audio data. DVD-A can provide a greater number of extremely high quality audio channels.

- Recordable and rewritable DVDs are high-density versions of the CD-R and CD-RW.

- Hard-disk recording encodes, stores, and reproduces a signal on a multitrack hard-disk recorder. The channel/track configuration is versatile; information access is nonlinear, random, and quick, and storage capacity is far greater than with tape.

- The digital audio workstation (DAW) is an expandable recording, mixing, signal-processing, and editing system that is integrated with and networked to a collection of devices, such as other audio, video, and MIDI sources, within or among facilities.

- Communication between electronic devices, such as audio, video, and MIDI sources, is facilitated through digital interfaces such as: AES/EBU, SPDIF, SCSI, MADI, ADAT Optical, and TDIF.

- Digital audio networking makes it possible to produce a recording in real time between studios across town or across the country with little or no loss in audio quality and at relatively low cost.

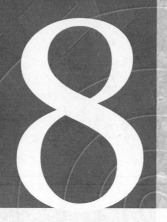

Synchronization

Today little in production and postproduction can be accomplished without **synchronization**—the ability to lock two or more devices that have microprocessor intelligence so that they operate at precisely the same rate. That includes almost any combination of audio and video equipment, from a simple audio-to-audio or audio-to-video recorder interface—analog or digital, tape or disk—to a complete studio system that interfaces a digital audio workstation, console, synthesizer, sequencer,* effects processors, and recorders (see Figure 8-1).

Accurate synchronization requires a system to code the recording media as well as a *synchronizer* to read the codes, compare them, and adjust the positions and speeds of machine transports so that they run at exactly the same rate.

TIME CODES

Time code is changed into different forms depending on the application, but each adheres to the same basic rules of counting time. Consequently, the forms are compatible with one another for synchronization so long as the proper translation device is used. There are three basic time codes: **longitudinal time code (LTC)** and vertical interval time code (VITC), both of which

---

*A *sequencer* is a device that can record performance data for synthesizers and other electronic instruments and, during playback, pass on that data to the instruments so that they play what has been recorded.

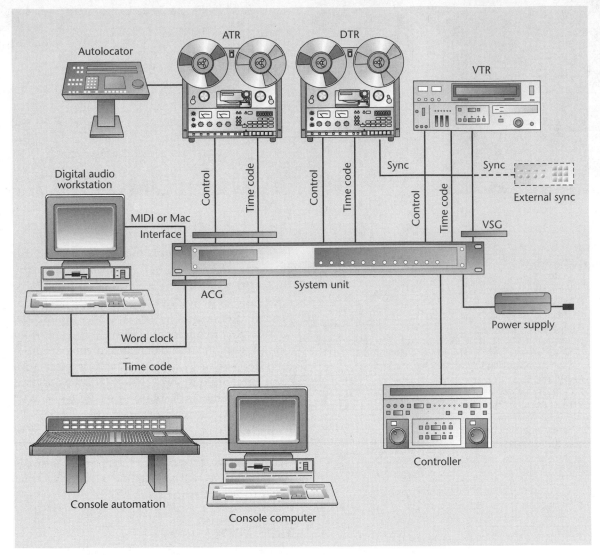

8-1 Example of a synchronization system flowchart. ACG = audio clock generator; VSG = video sync generator.

are forms of SMPTE time code; MIDI time code (MTC); and the IEC (International Electrotechnical Commission) standard.

SMPTE Time Code

SMPTE time code (pronounced "semp-ty") is a high-frequency electronic digital signal consisting of a stream of pulses produced by a time code generator. It is recorded along the length of a tape or film track in the same way a conventional audio track is recorded.

Time code was originally developed to make videotape editing more efficient; hence, its identifying code numbers are broken down into hours, minutes, seconds, and frames. The code number 01:22:48:15 is read as 1 hour, 22 minutes, 48 seconds, and 15 frames. (Videotape has 30 frames per second, or 29.97, to be exact.) Each ¹⁄₃₀ second of audiotape or each frame of videotape is tagged with a unique identifying code number called a **time code address**. By decoding the time code address with a time code reader, an operator can select the appropriate code numbers that instruct recorders to locate a certain point and begin playing in sync from there. SMPTE LTC time code is a digital signal converted to audio frequencies so it can be recorded on an audio track.

Many recorders have a built-in time code generator and reader as well as a time code head. SMPTE code may be recorded during or after production.

Vertical Interval Time Code

Vertical interval time code (VITC) (pronounced "vit-see") carries the same information as SMPTE code but it is used with videotape and encodes its information vertically within the video signal, outside the visible picture area. Because VITC is part of the video signal, it can be read at slow speeds and in still-frame, with the time code displayed through a *window burn* or *window dub* (see 8-2). Two other advantages are that it does not require a dedicated audio track and it can be converted to SMPTE code for equipment that requires it.

There are also some disadvantages to VITC. Many VCR systems cannot read the code at all

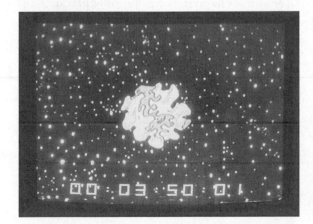

8-2 Window dub with SMPTE time code "burned in"

shuttle speeds and, unlike SMPTE, which can be recorded at any time, VITC must be recorded simultaneously with the video image.

Of the two time code systems, SMPTE is more popular, but both are usually employed in complex video production.

MIDI Time Code

MIDI time code (MTC) was developed as a way to translate SMPTE time code into MIDI messages. An absolute timing reference, SMPTE time code remains constant throughout a program. In MIDI recording, timing references are relative and vary with both tempo and tempo changes. Because most studios use SMPTE time code addresses (as opposed to beats in a musical bar) as references, trying to convert between the two timing systems to cue or trigger an event would be tedious and time-consuming. MIDI time code allows MIDI-based devices to operate on the SMPTE timing reference independent of tempo. In MIDI devices that do not recognize MTC, integrating an MTC sequencer is necessary. Converting SMPTE to MIDI time code is straightforward: SMPTE comes in and MIDI goes out.

With SMPTE-to-MIDI time code conversion, the recorder sets the pace; the sequencer follows the recorder. But it would be desirable in some situations for the recorder to follow the sequencer. The problem is that devices such as synthesizers, drum machines, signal processors, and consoles are electronic, and tape recorders use mechanical transports. Moreover, MIDI timing references are relative, based on tempo; but for automation, tape decks require an absolute reference, such as SMPTE. To deal with this problem, the *MIDI Machine Control* protocol was developed. It includes provisions for virtually any recorder command, including *start*, *stop*, *record*, *shuttle*, *chase*, and *locate*.

The IEC Standard

The *IEC standard*, established by the International Electrotechnical Commission, is the most recent addition to time codes. As the term suggests, it is an attempt to standardize time coding. The IEC standard code is the system used in digital audiocassette recorders as agreed to by all manufacturers of R-DATs, thus ensuring compatibility among all R-DAT equipment.

The main difference between the IEC R-DAT code and other time codes is that the IEC code provides more flexibility in adjusting frame rates during playback. IEC time code R-DATs extract time code information and put it on tape without it being contained in the frame rate. This makes it possible to set the playback machine's output to whatever frame rate you want. If a playback machine is equipped with an auto-detect mode, it will automatically output the recorded time information at the same frame rate that the code came in.

USING TIME CODE

When encoding SMPTE time code, set the generator to the preferred starting time. Although time code readout is in hours, minutes, seconds, and frames, it is easy to confuse them if any numbers are duplicated on the same tape or on other tapes belonging to the same production. To avoid this confusion, time code is used employing either the zero-start or the time-of-day logging method.

Zero start indicates the lapsed time of a recording. The first tape begins at zero, and each successive reel begins at 01:00:00:00, then 02:00:00:00, 03:00:00:00, et cetera. For example, if the first tape segment starts at zero and ends at 00:00:02:46, the second segment could start at 00:00:02:47. It would be wiser to spool the tape ahead several frames, however, to make the segments easier to access and also to avoid accidental erasure.

Time-of-day numbering is synchronized with clock time. This is a handy way to keep track of when material is recorded, but tapes used day to day must be clearly marked with the date to avoid any confusion about inevitable duplication of coding times.

Recording SMPTE Time Code on Audio- and Videotape

On audiotape record time code on the highest-number edge track: On an 8-track tape, that would be track 8; on a 24-track tape, that would be track 24, and so on. Record level is usually –5 VU to –10 VU. To prevent crosstalk between the time code signal and program material, leave the track adjacent to the time code blank: On an 8-track tape, that would be track 7; on a 24-track tape, that would be track 23. Do not record the time code signal at a lower level; otherwise synchronization is adversely affected.

In fact, recording time code onto analog tape can be difficult, even at recommended levels, because it tends to distort. The problem becomes particularly acute when dubbing tapes. By the second or third generation, distortion can be so great that the code becomes unreadable. Most time code generators have features designed to reduce or alleviate problems in reading time code. The two most commonly used are called jam sync and freewheel.

Jam sync produces new time code during dubbing, either to match the original time code or to regenerate new address data, thereby replacing defective sections of code. *Freewheel* mode allows the bypassing of defective code without altering the speed of the synchronized tape transports.

Frame rate is usually set next (see "Frame Rates" later in this chapter). For audio-only productions, use 30 frames per second, nondrop frame rate. Start recording time code 20 to 30 seconds before the program material begins, to allow sufficient time for the tape machines to interlock. Once recording commences, it must be continuous—without pause. Tapes should be coded simultaneously. If that is not possible, a time code editor will be needed to correct offsets in the synchronization.

Videocassette recorders include a dedicated cue/time code track. As for time code levels, because of the differences between analog and digital audio and the number of different VCR formats, it is best to consult the recorder and tape specifications and then run tests to determine the optimum time code level.

If a tape recorder has an *automatic gain control (AGC)*, it should *not* be used for recording time code, or the time code signal will distort; gain should be set manually. In video time code must be synchronized to the picture material, and, as with audiotape, encoding should begin before the program material starts.

Time Formats with Hard-Disk Recorder/Editors

Hard-disk recorder/editors incorporate SMPTE time code, at least. Many systems also include other time formats for internal use, such as real time, music time, and film time. These format names differ among programs, but their functions are essentially comparable.

Real time displays the time scale in actual minutes and seconds. Many systems are able to refine real time to tenths, hundredths, and thousandths of a second.

Music time is in bars and beats and usually requires tempo data on which to base it. It can be adjusted to preserve relative timing to a variety of values, such as ¼ note, ¼ triplet, ⅛ note, ⅛ triplet, and so on.

Film time displays the time scale in feet and frames.

Synchronizing Digital Equipment

Synchronizing digital equipment presents a problem that synchronizing analog equipment does not: keeping the digital data synchronized in the digital domain. This requires the digital interconnectivity of the data to be compatible. Time code alone cannot accomplish this. Every digital audio system has a signal generated inside the device that controls sampling rate. This signal is commonly known as a **word clock**; it is sometimes also referred to as a *sample clock* or *digital clock*. The word clock is an extremely stable synchronization signal that is used to control the rate at which digital audio data is converted or transmitted. Hence it is responsible for the timing associated with moving audio data from one digital device to another. If the word clocks of different audio devices are not identical, resulting problems in the data transfer process can seriously degrade the audio signal.

In making digital transfers, it is worthwhile to keep in mind the following procedures:

☑ Digital audio data cables and word clock lines need to be the same length. Cable length affects timing, which affects the phase relationship of the word clock to the digital audio data.

☑ Make sure that all signals—time code, digital audio, and word clock—are flowing from the source machine to the destination machine(s). Set the destination machine to *input* and the source machine to *play* to check signal flow and to make sure there are no pops or clicks.

☑ Avoid using *wild* time code during formatting. Wild time code originates from a generator not locked to the device that made the original recording.

☑ Make sure there is plenty of preroll and keep the transfer start point consistent.

FRAME RATES

Four frame rate standards are used within SMPTE time code: 30, 29.97, 25, and 24 *frames per second (fps)*. **Frame rate** refers to the number of frames that pass in one second of real time.

Drop Frame and Non–Drop Frame

In the days before color television, the frame rate of American black-and-white TV was 30 fps. With color TV the rate was reduced to 29.97 fps to allow easier color syncing of new programs and reproduction of black-and-white programs. Today American television and videotape recorders run at 29.97 fps.

The problem is that 30-fps time code running at 29.97 fps comes up 108 frames short every hour. To correct this problem, a time code format called *drop frame* was developed. Drop frame skips the first two frame counts in each minute, except for each tenth minute (00, 10, 20, etc.), to force the time code to match the clock time.

Solving one problem, however, created another. A frame rate of 29.97 fps for, say, a 1-minute commercial will show as exactly 1 minute on a clock but will read 00:00:59:28 on a SMPTE display. One hour of real time will read out as 00:59:56:12. In editing, not working with whole numbers can be bothersome, to say nothing of trying to get an exact program time in broadcasting. To resolve this problem, the 30-fps and 29.97-fps frame rates can be adjusted between drop frame and *non–drop frame*.

Drop frame is necessary when precise timing is critical and when synchronizing audio to video. But in most other production—audio and video—non–drop frame is used because it is easier to work with. It is worth remembering that tapes used in any given production must employ one mode or the other; the two modes are not interchangeable.

As for the 25- and 24-fps frame rates, European video and film shot for television use 25 fps; 24 fps is the frame rate used for pure film applications in the United States, although 24 fps is little used once a film is shot. After production, material is usually transferred to hard disk for postproduction.

SYNCHRONIZING SOUND AND PICTURE ON FILM

The problem in recording sound and picture synchronously in film production is that audiotape recorders and disk-based media do not have sprocket holes like film does; moreover, they run at different speeds. The solution to the problem is the technique known as *double-system recording:* Sound and picture are recorded separately and in sync; the camera records the picture, and an audio recorder handles the sound.

Single-system recording records both sound and picture on the same medium, which today is either videotape or disk. It is particularly convenient and

efficient in TV news, where time is of the essence (see Chapter 13). But if extensive postproduction is necessary and sound quality is important, double-system recording is used.

In film the two methods of synchronizing sound and picture in double-system recording are with a crystal synchronizing oscillator in both camera and recorder or with time code.

Crystal Synchronization

Crystal synchronization regulates the camera and tape recorder motors to run at the same speed so they stay in sync. The oscillator in the tape recorder regulates tape speed to camera speed and also puts the synchronizing tone onto the tape.

Sync Tones

The tones that help synchronize sound and picture—known as *sync tones*—are recorded in various ways, depending on the system employed. Nagra analog tape recorders that use sync tones employ the *neo-pilottone* system. It records a 60-Hz signal with its sync head on two narrow center tape tracks superimposed over the main audio signal. During playback the sync head reads the sync signal, but at the playback head the tones are 180 degrees out of phase, so they cancel each other and do not interfere with the sound on the main track. *Synchrotone* is used for stereo recording. It has a separate third track for pulse tone recorded down the center of the tape. This type of recording, however, is obsolete and has been all but supplanted by time code synchronization using digital recorders (see "Time Code Synchronization" later in this chapter).

Slating

An important but often underestimated synchronizing procedure in double-system recording is *slating*. Although picture and sound are shot in sync, to match them properly the editor has to know the precise point at which recording began. For this purpose a *clapslate* (clapstick attached to a slate) is used (see 8-3). The clapslate is filmed just before each take, after the camera and recorder have

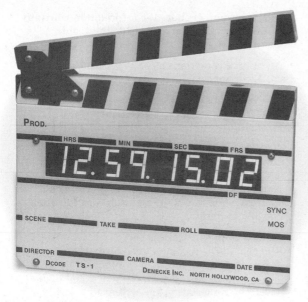

8-3 Time code clapslate

begun rolling. It serves two purposes: First, it displays the names of the production, director, and cameraperson; the number of the scene and take; the number of the sound take; the date; and whether the shot is interior or exterior. Second, on top of the slate is a clapstick, which can be opened and then closed quickly to produce a loud, snapping sound. This sound is the sync mark that tells the editor at exactly what point to begin synchronizing sound with picture.

Once sound has been recorded, it is transferred to magnetic film, multitrack tape, or a hard-disk system, a process called *resolving*.

Resolving

Although the double-system method records the sound and picture in synchronization, there is no way to align the audio recording and film for postproduction because of their physical differences. In resolving, as the audio is transferred to magnetic film or, most common, hard disk, the sync signal is interpreted so that each "frame" of sound is exactly the same length as each frame of picture so that they can be aligned frame-to-frame.

During transfer the sync pulse on the audiotape, or time code, controls the synchronization of the transfer machine so that it matches that of the camera motor.

In addition to the sound transfer, resolving also provides an opportunity to clean up audio quality by removing audible technical glitches. This helps make processing a bit easier for the audio folks down the postproduction line.

Time Code Synchronization

In time code synchronization for film, a SMPTE clapslate is used. It includes a time code generator that runs parallel to a time code generator in the audio recorder. If the recorder is multitrack, the generator is external. The clapslate displays a running time code (see 8-3). At the moment the clapstick closes, the time code showing at that instant freezes; that is the start point. Audio that is time code synchronized can be transferred directly to hard disk for postproduction.

SYNCHRONIZERS

Although time code permits the accurate interlocking of recorders, anytime two or more transports must run together simultaneously, frame-for-frame, a device called a *synchronizer* is necessary. It controls the position and speed of the "slave" transport(s) to lock to the "master" machine's transport using time code as its reference. Synchronization systems using time code vary widely in sophistication, from those that synchronize one master machine to one slave, to those that synchronize several transports at once and perform a variety of other computer-assisted functions as well (see 8-1).

Most synchronizers have available two types of locking modes: frame lock and phase lock. *Frame lock* locks the master and the slave units using time code so that any variations in the master reference are passed on to the slave. *Phase lock* (also referred to as *sync lock*) prevents sudden speed variations in the master, such as wow and flutter, from being passed to the slave.

Other synchronizer features include automatic switching from play mode to cue mode that allows the slave transport to "chase" the master whenever it is rewound and to resync to it when it is again put into play. Offsets can be set between machines, allowing a recording to be "slipped" out of sync, by less than one frame if necessary. Synchronizers control transport record/edit functions, enabling in- and out-points to be repeated accurately to as little as $\frac{1}{100}$ of a frame in some units. To isolate themselves from speed changes during time code dropouts, synchronizers can *freewheel*, passing over time code loss at a constant speed.

A note of caution: When time code is recorded during production, it is continuous. When the material is dubbed to an edit master for editing, any discontinuity in time code will confuse the synchronizer. Therefore, a continuous time code should be recorded onto the edit master(s). This, however, creates two sets of time code numbers, one for the production and one for the edited material. Good recordkeeping is essential to avoid mixups.

MAIN POINTS

▶ Synchronization allows the locking of two or more devices that have microprocessor intelligence so that they operate at precisely the same rate.

▶ Accurate synchronization requires a system to code the recording media as well as a synchronizer to read the codes, compare them, and adjust the positions and speeds of machine transports so that they run at exactly the same rate.

▶ There are three basic time codes: longitudinal time code (LTC) and vertical interval time code (VITC), both of which are forms of SMPTE time code; MIDI time code (MTC); and the IEC (International Electrotechnical Commission) standard.

▶ SMPTE time code is a high-frequency electronic digital signal consisting of a stream of pulses produced by a time code generator. Its identifying code numbers are broken down into hours, minutes, seconds, and frames.

▶ Vertical interval time code carries the same information as SMPTE code but it is used with videotape and encodes the information vertically within the video signal, outside the visible picture area.

▶ MIDI time code translates SMPTE time code into MIDI messages.

▶ The IEC standard is the time code system used in digital audiocassette recorders to ensure compatibility among all R-DAT equipment.

▶ Because all time code readouts are in the same form, it is easy to confuse them if any numbers are duplicated on the same tape or on other tapes in a production. Two ways to avoid this confusion are to use the zero-start or time-of-day logging method.

▶ In recording SMPTE time code, be careful to record it at the recommended level. If the signal is recorded at too low a level, synchronization is adversely affected. If it is recorded at too high a level, the time code signal will distort.

▶ Every digital audio system has a signal, known as a word clock, generated inside the device that controls sampling rate.

▶ Four frame rate standards are used within SMPTE time code: 30, 29.97, 25, and 24 frames per second (fps).

▶ Frame rates for television are in either drop frame or non–drop frame format.

▶ In double-system recording, sound and picture are recorded separately and in sync; the camera records the picture, and an audio recorder handles the sound.

▶ In single-system recording, both sound and picture are recorded on the same medium.

▶ Two methods used to synchronize the camera and audio recorder in double-system recording are crystal synchronization and time code synchronization.

▶ In double-system recording, a clapslate is used to make a visible and audible sync mark on the film and audio recording, respectively. This helps identify and synchronize scenes during their transfer from the audio recording to magnetic film and in editing.

▶ Time code permits the accurate interlocking of two or more recorders, but a synchronizer is necessary to ensure that their transports run together simultaneously.

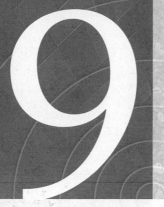

Signal Processing

Signal processors are devices used to alter some characteristic of a sound. Generally, they can be grouped into four categories: spectrum processors, time processors, amplitude processors, and noise processors. A ***spectrum processor,*** such as the equalizer, affects the spectral balances in a signal. A ***time processor,*** such as a reverberation or delay device, affects the time interval between a signal and its repetition(s). An ***amplitude***, or ***dynamic***, ***processor,*** such as the compressor-limiter, affects a signal's dynamic range. A ***noise processor,*** such as the Dolby system, does not alter a signal so much as it makes the signal clearer by reducing noise.

Some signal processors can belong to more than one category. For example, the equalizer also alters a signal's amplitude and, therefore, can be classified as an amplitude processor as well. The flanger, which affects the time of a signal, also affects its frequency response. A de-esser alters amplitude and frequency. In other words, many effects are variations of the same principle.

Digital effects processors are typically multi-effects units rather than discrete processors. Because the technology facilitates it, the processing engine can be configured in a variety of ways. A single unit can, for example, limit, compress, and noise-gate, or reverb, delay, flange, chorus, and pitch-shift. In the interest of organization, the signal processing covered in this chapter has been arranged by category.

SPECTRUM SIGNAL PROCESSORS

Spectrum signal processors include equalizers, filters, and psychoacoustic processors.

Equalizers

The best-known and most often used signal processor is the **equalizer**—an electronic device that alters frequency response by increasing or decreasing the level of a signal at a specific portion of the spectrum. This alteration can be done in two ways: by *boost* or *cut* (also known as *peak* or *dip*) or by *shelving*.

Boost/cut increases or decreases the level of a band of frequencies around a **center frequency**, the frequency at which maximum boost or cut occurs. This type of *equalization (EQ)* is often referred to as *bell curve* or *haystack,* due to the shape of the response curve (see Figure 9-1).

Shelving also increases or decreases amplitude but gradually flattens out or shelves at the maximum selected level when the chosen (turnover) frequency is reached. Level then remains constant at all frequencies beyond that point (see 9-2).

In other words, with boost/cut EQ, when a frequency is selected for boost or cut by a certain amplitude, that frequency is the one most affected. Adjacent frequencies are also affected but by

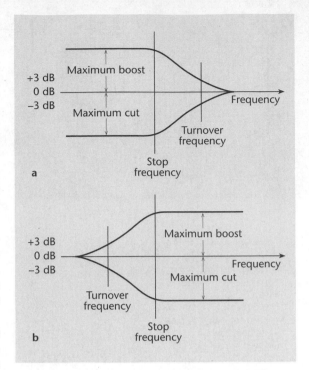

a

b

9-2 (a) Low-frequency shelving equalization and (b) high-frequency shelving equalization. The turnover frequency is that frequency where the gain is 3 dB above (or below) the shelving level—in other words, the frequency where the equalizer begins to flatten out. The stop frequency is the point where the gain stops increasing or decreasing.

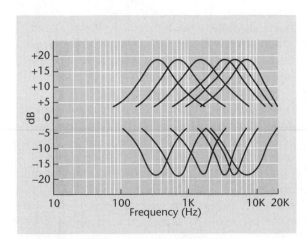

9-1 Bell or haystack curves showing 18-dB boost or cut at 350, 700, 1,600, 3,200, 4,800, and 7,200 Hz

gradually lesser changes in level. With shelving EQ all frequencies above (high-frequency shelving) or below (low-frequency shelving) the selected frequency are equally increased or decreased by the level selected.

The number of frequencies on equalizers varies. Generally, the frequencies are in full-, half-, and third-octave intervals. If the lowest frequency on a full-octave equalizer is, say, 50 Hz, the other frequencies ascend in octaves: 100 Hz, 200 Hz, 400 Hz, 800 Hz, and so on, usually to 12,800 Hz. A half-octave equalizer ascends in half octaves. If the lowest frequency is 50 Hz, the intervals are at or near 75 Hz, 100 Hz, 150 Hz, 200 Hz, 300 Hz, 400 Hz, 600 Hz, and so on. A third-octave equalizer would have intervals at or near 50 Hz, 60 Hz, 80 Hz,

100 Hz, 120 Hz, 160 Hz, 200 Hz, 240 Hz, 320 Hz, 400 Hz, 480 Hz, 640 Hz, and so on. Obviously, the more settings, the better the sound control—but at some cost. The more settings there are on an equalizer (or any device, for that matter), the more difficult it is to use correctly, because problems such as added noise and phasing may be introduced.

Two types of equalizers are in general use: fixed-frequency and parametric.

Fixed-Frequency Equalizer

The *fixed-frequency equalizer* is so called because it operates at fixed frequencies usually selected from two (high and low) or three (high, middle, and low) ranges of the frequency spectrum. Each group of frequencies is located at a separate control, but only one center frequency at a time per control may be selected. At or near each frequency selector is a level control that boosts or cuts the selected center and band frequencies. On consoles where these controls are concentric to save space, the outer ring chooses the frequency, and the inner ring increases or decreases level.

A fixed-frequency equalizer has a preset *bandwidth*—a range of frequencies on either side of the center frequency selected for equalizing that is also affected. The degrees of amplitude to which these frequencies are modified form the *bandwidth curve*. If you boost, say, 350 Hz a total of 18 dB, the bandwidth of frequencies also affected may go to as low as 80 Hz on one side and up to 2,000 Hz on the other. The peak of the curve is 350 Hz—the frequency that is boosted the full 18 dB (see 9-1).

The adjacent frequencies are boosted also, but to a lesser extent, depending on the bandwidth. Because each fixed-frequency equalizer can have a different fixed bandwidth and bandwidth curve, it is a good idea to study the manufacturer's specifications before you use one.

Usually, the high and low fixed-frequency equalizers on consoles are shelving equalizers. The midrange EQs are center-frequency boost/cut equalizers.

Graphic Equalizer

The *graphic equalizer* is a type of fixed-frequency equalizer. It consists of sliding, instead of rotating, controls that boost or attenuate selected frequencies. It is called "graphic" because the positioning of these controls gives a graphic display of the frequency curve set. (The display does not include the bandwidth of each frequency, however.) Because each frequency on a graphic equalizer has a separate sliding control, it is possible to use as many as you wish simultaneously (see 9-3).

Parametric Equalizer

The main difference between a *parametric equalizer* (see 9-4) and a fixed-frequency equalizer is that the parametric has continuously variable frequencies and bandwidths, making it possible to change a bandwidth curve by making it wider or narrower, thereby altering the affected frequencies and their levels (see 9-5). This provides greater flexibility and more precision in controlling equalization.

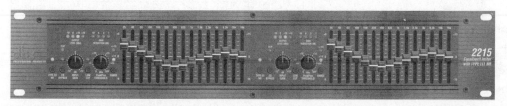

9-3 Graphic equalizer. This model is a dual 15-band graphic equalizer with two-thirds octaves frequency centers ranging from 25 to 16 kHz. Boost and cut ranges are switchable from ±6 to ±15 dB. Also included are a high-pass (low-cut) filter, limiting, and dbx Type III™ noise reduction, providing up to 20 dB of broadband noise reduction.

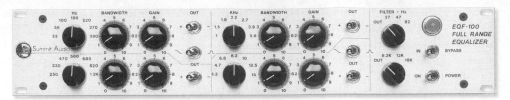

9-4 Parametric equalizer. This model uses both tube and solid-state technologies. There are four bands of seven switch-selectable frequencies, plus high- and low-pass filters with three frequencies each.

9-5 Selectable bandwidths of a parametric equalizer. In this example the boost curves are broad and the cut curves are tight. Other parametric equalizers use the same range of adjustment for the boost and cut curves.

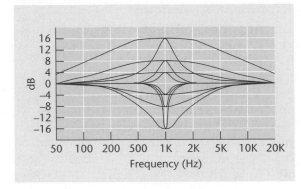

Paragraphic Equalizer

A *paragraphic equalizer* combines the sliding controls of a graphic equalizer with the flexibility of parametric equalization (see 9-21).

Filters

A *filter* is a device that attenuates certain bands of frequencies. It is a component of an equalizer. There are differences between attenuating with an equalizer and attenuating with a filter, however. First, with an equalizer attenuation affects only the selected frequency and the frequencies on either side of it, whereas with a filter all frequencies above or below the selected frequency are affected. Second, an equalizer allows you to vary the amount of drop in loudness; with a filter the drop is usually preset and relatively steep.

Among the most commonly used filters are high-pass, low-pass, band-pass, and notch filters.

High- and Low-Pass Filters

A *high-pass (low-cut) filter* attenuates all frequencies below a preset point; a *low-pass (high-cut) filter* attenuates all frequencies above a preset point (see 9-6).

Suppose in a recording that there is a bothersome rumble between 35 and 50 Hz. By setting a high-

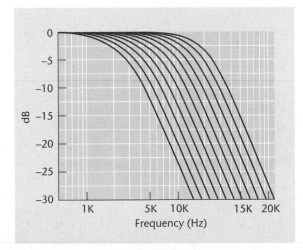

9-6 Example of low-pass filter curves

pass filter at 50 Hz, all frequencies below that point are cut and the band of frequencies above it continues to pass—hence the name "high-pass (low-cut)" filter.

The low-pass (high-cut) filter works on the same principle but affects the higher frequencies. If there

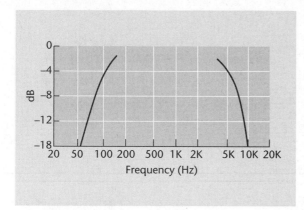

9-7 Band-pass filtering. The frequencies below 120 Hz and above 5,000 Hz are sharply attenuated, thereby allowing the frequencies in the band between to pass.

is hiss in a recording, you can get rid of it by setting a low-pass filter at, say, 10,000 Hz. This cuts the frequencies above that point and allows the band of frequencies below 10,000 Hz to pass through. But you should keep in mind that *all* sound above 10 kHz—the program material, if there is any, along with the hiss—will be filtered.

Band-Pass Filter

A *band-pass filter* is a device that sets high- and low-frequency cutoff points and permits the band of frequencies between to pass (see 9-7). Band-pass filters are used more for corrective rather than creative purposes.

Notch Filter

A *notch filter* is also used mainly for corrective purposes. It can cut out an extremely narrow band, allowing the frequencies on each side of the notch to pass. For example, a constant problem in audio is AC (alternating current) hum, which has a frequency of 60 Hz. A notch filter can remove it without appreciably affecting adjacent frequencies.

Psychoacoustic Processors

A *psychoacoustic processor* is designed to add clarity, definition, overall presence, and life or "sizzle" to program material. Some units add tone-

generated odd and even harmonics* to the audio; others are fixed or program-adaptive high-frequency equalizers. A psychoacoustic processor might also achieve its effect by adding comb filtering and by introducing narrow-band phase shifts between stereo channels. One well-known psychoacoustic processor is the Aural Exciter™ (see 9-8).

TIME SIGNAL PROCESSORS

Time signal processors are devices that affect the time relationships of signals. These effects include reverberation and delay.

Reverberation

Reverberation, you will recall, is created by random, multiple, blended repetitions of a sound or signal. As these repetitions decrease in intensity, they increase in number. Reverberation increases average signal level and adds depth, spatial dimension, and additional excitement to the listening experience.

A common principle is basic to reverberation and, hence, reverb systems. Think of what it takes to produce an echo: A sound has to be sent, hit a reflective object, and then bounce back. In the parlance of audio, it is sent as *dry sound*—without reverb—and is returned as *wet sound*—with reverb.

Actually, as defined, remember that there is a difference between echo and reverb. *Echo* is one or, at most, a few discrete, discernable repetitions of a sound (or signal); *reverb* consists of many blended repetitions (see Chapter 3). To produce either, the dry sound must be sent, "reflected," and returned

---

*Each harmonic or set of harmonics adds a characteristic tonal color to sound, although they have less effect on changes in timbre as they rise in pitch above the fundamental. In general, even-number harmonics—second, fourth, and sixth—create an open, warm, filled-out sound. Odd-number harmonics—third and fifth—produce a closed, harsh, stopped-down sound. The second harmonic, an octave above the fundamental, can be barely audible yet it adds fullness to sound. The third harmonic (called musical twelfth, or quint) softens sound. Harmonics above the seventh give sound edge, bite, and definition.

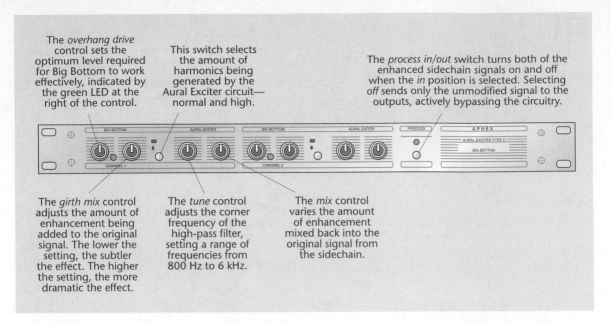

The *overhang drive* control sets the optimum level required for Big Bottom to work effectively, indicated by the green LED at the right of the control.

This switch selects the amount of harmonics being generated by the Aural Exciter circuit— normal and high.

The *process in/out* switch turns both of the enhanced sidechain signals on and off when the *in* position is selected. Selecting *off* sends only the unmodified signal to the outputs, actively bypassing the circuitry.

The *girth mix* control adjusts the amount of enhancement being added to the original signal. The lower the setting, the subtler the effect. The higher the setting, the more dramatic the effect.

The *tune* control adjusts the corner frequency of the high-pass filter, setting a range of frequencies from 800 Hz to 6 kHz.

The *mix* control varies the amount of enhancement mixed back into the original signal from the sidechain.

9-8 One type of Aural Exciter™ and its functions

wet. Three reverb systems in current use are digital, plate, and acoustic chamber reverberation.

Digital Reverberation

Digital reverberation is the most commonly used today. The *digital reverberation (reverb) unit* is a device that artificially reproduces the sound of different acoustic environments. The reverb is accomplished electronically. Generally, when fed into the circuitry and digitized, the signal is delayed for several milliseconds. The delayed signal is then recycled to produce the reverb effect. The process is repeated many times per second, with amplitude reduced to achieve decay.

Specifically, in digital reverb there are numerous delay times that create discrete echoes, followed by a repetition of these initial delays many times to create the ambience which continues with decreasing clarity and amplitude. High-quality digital reverb units are capable of an extremely wide range of effects, produce high-quality sound, and take up relatively little room.

Digital reverb systems can simulate a variety of acoustical and mechanical reverberant sounds, such as small and large concert halls, bright- and dark-sounding halls, small and large rooms, and small and large reverb plates (see "Plate Reverberation" in the next section). With each effect it is also possible to control individually the attack; decay; diffusion (density); high-, middle-, and low-frequency decay times; and other sonic colorings.

One important feature of most digital reverbs is *predelay*—the amount of time between the onset of the direct sound and the appearance of the first reflections. Predelay is essential for creating a believable room ambience, because early reflections arrive before reverberation. It also helps create the perception of a room's size: Shorter predelay times give the sense of a smaller room, and vice versa.

Most digital reverb systems are programmed and programmable. They come with preprogrammed effects but also permit new ones to be programmed in and stored for reuse (see 9-9).

Plate Reverberation

The *reverberation plate* is a mechanical-electronic device consisting of a thin, steel plate suspended under tension in an enclosed frame (see 9-10). It is

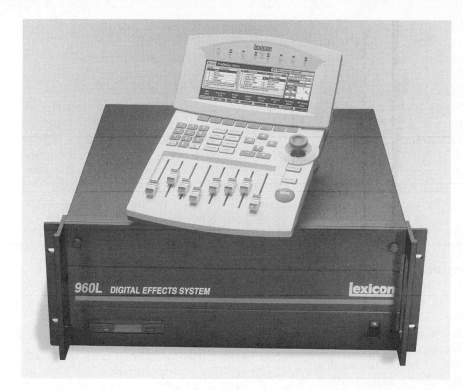

9-9 Digital reverberation and effects system with controller. This system provides a wide sonic palette of programs including Halls, Chambers, Rooms, Plates, Ambiences, and Wild Spaces. It can store up to 500 additional user-defined programs. Its multiple digital reverb processing configurations include: stereo, 5.1 surround sound, multiple-stereo, and stereo plus 5.1 surround. Sampling rates are 44.1, 48, 88.2, and 96 kHz. The system is capable of 24-bit performance.

large and heavy and requires isolation in a separate room. A moving-coil driver, acting like a small speaker, vibrates the plate, thus transducing the electrical signals from the console into mechanical energy. A contact microphone (two for stereo) picks up the plate's vibrations, transduces them back into electric energy, and returns them to the console. The multiple reflections from the vibrating plate create the reverb effect.

The reverberation plate is capable of producing a complex output, but it is difficult to change its characteristics. Generally, plates have long reverb times (more than two seconds) at high frequencies that produce a crisp, bright decay. They are susceptible to overload, however. With louder levels, low frequencies tend to increase disproportionately in reverb time compared with the other frequencies, thus muddying sound. Rolling off the unwanted lower frequencies helps, but too much roll-off reduces a sound's warmth.

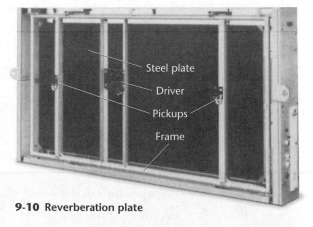

9-10 Reverberation plate

Acoustic Chamber Reverberation

The *acoustic reverberation chamber* is the most natural and realistic type of simulated reverb, because it works on acoustic sound in an acoustic environment. It is a room with sound-reflective surfaces and nonparallel walls to avoid *flutter echo*—multiple echoes at a rapid, even rate—and *standing waves*—apparently stationary waveforms created by multiple reflections between opposite, usually parallel, room surfaces. It usually contains two directional microphones (for stereo), placed off room center, and a loudspeaker, usually near a corner at angles to or back-to-back to the mic(s) to minimize the amount of direct sound picked up by the mic(s). The dry sound feeds from the console through the loudspeaker, reflects around the chamber, is picked up by the mic(s), and is fed back wet into the console for further processing and routing.

Reverb times differ from chamber to chamber. Generally, however, reverb time should be about 3.5 seconds at 500 Hz, and about 1.25 seconds at 10,000 Hz. Reverb times can be varied by using movable acoustic baffles.

Although an acoustic chamber creates very realistic reverberation, it is expensive to build. It must be at least 2,000 cubic feet in size (too small a room is poor for bass response), it requires good soundproofing, and it must be isolated. Even with a chamber, studios use other reverb devices to provide additional sonic alternatives.

Choosing a Reverberation System

In choosing a reverberation system, personal taste notwithstanding, the system should sound natural. The high end should be bright and lifelike, and the low end should not thicken or muddy the sound. Good diffusion is essential; repeats should be numerous and random, and decay response should be smooth. There should be an absence of flutter, twang, "boing," and tinniness.

A good test to check for muddy sound is to listen to a singer. If the reverb system makes the lyrics more difficult to understand, it is not clear or transparent enough. To check for density and randomness of the early reflections, try a transient sound such as a sharp drumbeat or handclap. Poorer reverb systems will produce a sound like an acoustic flutter. To check for randomness of the later reflections, listen to a strong male voice completely wet—with no dry feed from the reverb send on the console. If the lyrics are clear, the combined wet and dry signals will probably be muddy.

Delay

Delay is the time interval between a sound or signal and its repetition. By manipulating delay times, it is possible to create a number of echo effects (see the following section on uses of delay). Today this is most commonly done with an electronic digital delay.

Digital Delay

Digital delay is generated by routing audio through an electronic buffer. The information is held for a specific period of time, which is set by the user, before it is sent to the output. A single-repeat delay processes the sound only once; multiple delays process the signal over and over. The amount and number of delay times vary with the unit (see 9-11 and 9-12).

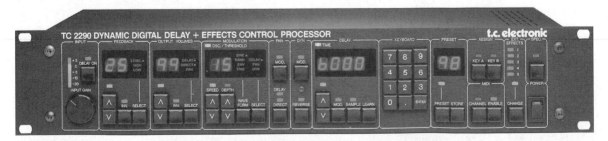

9-11 Digital delay. In addition to a wide range of delay effects, this unit provides real-time echo looping, tap tempo control, chorus, gating, and panning. It is also programmable.

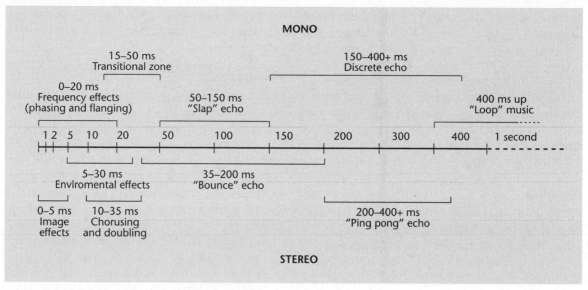

9-12 Example of time delay values and effects

The two parameters important to understand about delay are delay time and feedback. *Delay time* regulates how long a given sound is held and, therefore, the amount of time between delays. *Feedback* controls how much of that delayed signal is returned to the input. Raising the amount of feedback increases the number of repeats and the length of decay. Turning it down completely generates only one repeat.

The better digital delays have excellent signal-to-noise ratio, low distortion, good high-frequency response with longer delay times, and an extensive array of effects. They are also excellent for prereverb delay. Lower-grade units are not as clean-sounding, and high-frequency response is noisier with longer delay times.

Uses of Delay

Delay has a number of creative applications. Among the frequently used effects are doubling, chorus, slap back echo, and prereverb delay.

◼ **Doubling** One popular use of delay is to fatten sound. The effect gives an instrument or voice a fuller, stronger sound and is called *doubling*. It is created by setting the delay to about 10 to 35 ms.

These short delays are like early sound reflections and lend a sense of openness or ambience to dead-sounding instruments or voices.

Doubling can also be done live by recording one track and then overdubbing the same part on a separate track in synchronization with the first. Because it is not possible to repeat a performance exactly, variations in pitch, timing, and room sounds add fullness or openness to sound. By continuing this process, it is possible to create a chorus effect.

◼ **Chorus** The *chorus effect* is achieved by recirculating the doubling effect. The delay time is about the same as in doubling—15 to 35 ms—but is repeated. This effect can make a single voice sound like many and add spaciousness to a sound. Two voices singing in a relatively dead studio can be made to sound like a choir singing in a hall by chorusing the original sound.

◼ **Slap back echo** A *slap back echo* is a delayed sound that is perceived as a distinct echo, much like the discrete Ping-Pong sound emitted by sonar devices when a contact is made. Slap back delay times are generally short, about 50 to 150 ms.

■ Prereverb delay As was pointed out in the discussion of digital reverberation earlier in this chapter, there is a definite time lag between the arrival of direct waves from a sound source and the arrival of reflected sound in acoustic conditions. In some reverb systems, there is no delay between the dry and wet signals. Therefore by using a delay unit to delay the input signal before it gets to the reverb unit, it is possible to improve the quality of reverberation, making it sound more natural.

Flanging

Flanging is a time-delay effect that gets its name from the way in which it was first produced. The same signal was fed to two different tape recorders and recorded simultaneously. The playback from both was fed to a single output, but one playback was delayed, by applying some pressure to the flange of the supply reel to slow it down.

Today these effects are produced electronically using digital flangers. The delay time is relatively short, from 0 to 20 ms. Ordinarily, the ear cannot perceive time differences between direct and delayed sounds that are this short. But due to phase cancellations when the direct and delayed signals are combined, the result is a series of peaks and dips in the frequency response (called the *comb filter effect*). This creates a filtered tone quality that sounds vibratolike, similar to the sound of speaking underwater.

In addition to the various delay times, flangers typically provide feedback rate and depth controls. Feedback rate determines how quickly a delay time is modulated. For example, a feedback rate setting of 0.1 Hz performs one cycle sweep every 10 seconds. Depth adjusts the spread between minimum and maximum delay times and is expressed as a ratio.

Many flangers provide controls to delay feedback in phase or out of phase. In-phase flanging is "positive," meaning that the direct and delayed signals have the same polarity. Positive flanging accents even harmonics, producing a metallic sound. Out-of-phase flanging is "negative," meaning that the two signals are opposite in polarity. Negative flanging works on odd

harmonics, producing a warm sound. It can also create strong, sucking effects like a sound being turned inside out.

Phasing

Phasing and flanging are similar in the way they are created. In fact, it is sometimes difficult to differentiate between the two. Instead of using a time-delay circuit, however, phasers use a phase shifter. Delays are very short, between 0 and 10 ms. The peaks and dips are more irregular and farther apart than in flanging, which results in something like a wavering vibrato that pulsates or undulates. Phasers provide a less pronounced pitched effect than flangers do, because their delay times are slightly shorter.

Phasers use two parameters that control modulation of the filters: rate (or speed) and depth (or intensity). Rate determines the sweep speed between the minimum and maximum values of the frequency range. Depth defines with width of that range between the lowest and highest frequencies.

Morphing

Morphing is the continuous, seamless transformation of one effect (aural or visual) into another. For example, in Michael Jackson's video *Black and White,* a Chinese woman is transformed into an African American man, who is transformed into an Irishman, who is transformed into a Hispanic woman, and so on. In *Terminator II* the silver terminator could melt, slither through cracks, and transform into various objects; and in *Matrix* characters change shape and form as though they were made of plastic. These effects are more than sophisticated dissolves (the sonic counterpart of dissolve is crossfade). Morphing is a complete restructuring of two completely different and independent effects. Because most audio morphing effects are delay-based, audio-morphing devices can be classified as time signal processors.

A few examples of audio morphing are: spinning vowel-like sounds, varying their rate and depth, and then freezing them until they fade away; flanging cascades of sound across stereo space, adding echo, and varying the envelope control of rates; adding echoing rhythms to a multivoice chorus which become more dense as they repeat, with the effect growing stronger as the notes fade away; and taking a musical instrument and adding pitch sweeps that dive into a pool of swirling echoes that bounce from side to side or end by being sucked up.

AMPLITUDE (DYNAMIC) SIGNAL PROCESSORS

Amplitude, or *dynamic, signal processors* are devices that affect dynamic range. These effects include such functions as compressing, limiting, de-essing, expanding, noise gating, and pitch shifting.

Compressors

The *compressor* is a processor whose output level increases at a slower rate as its input level increases (see 9-13). It is used to restrict dynamic range: because of the peak signal limitations of an electronic system; for artistic goals; due to the surrounding acoustical requirements; or any combination of these factors.

Compressors usually have four controls—for compression ratio, compression threshold, attack time, and release time—each of which can affect the others. Some compressors also include a makeup gain control.

The *compression ratio* establishes the proportion of change between the input and output levels. The ratios are usually variable, and, depending on the compressor, there are several selectable points between 1.1 to 1, and 20 to 1. Some recent compressor designs change ratios instantaneously depending on the program's dynamic content and the range of control settings. If you set the compression ratio for, say, 2 to 1, it means that for every 2-dB increase of the input signal, the output will increase by 1 dB; at 5 to 1, a 5-dB increase of the input signal increases the output by 1 dB. In other words it "reins in" excessive program dynamics. This is how sound with a dynamic range greater than the equipment can handle is brought to usable proportions before distortion occurs.

The *compression threshold* is the level at which compression takes effect. It is an adjustable setting

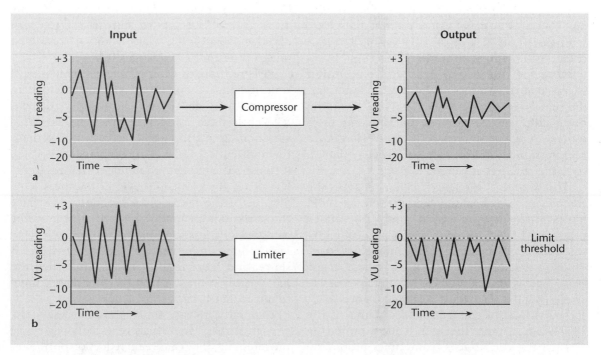

9-13 Effect of (a) compression and (b) limiting

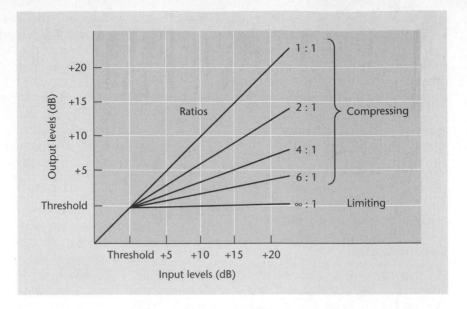

9-14 A representation of the relationship of various compression ratios to a fixed threshold point. The graph also displays the difference between effects of limiting and compressing.

and usually selected based on a subjective judgment of where compression should begin. It is difficult to predetermine what settings will work best for a given sound at a certain level; it is a matter of listening and experimenting. The compressor has no effect on the signal below the threshold level setting. (For an idea of the relationship between compression ratio and threshold, see 9-14.)

Once the threshold is reached, compression begins, reducing the gain according to the amount the signal exceeds threshold level and according to the ratio set. The moment that the compressor starts gain reduction is called the **knee. Hard knee compression** is abrupt; **soft knee compression** is smoother and less apparent.

Attack time is the length of time it takes the compressor to start compressing after the threshold has been reached. In a good compressor, attack times range from 500 microseconds to 100 milliseconds (ms). Depending on the setting, an attack time can enhance or detract from a sound. If the attack time is long, it can help bring out percussive attacks, but if it is too long, it can miss or overshoot the beginning of the compressed sound. If the attack time is too short, it reduces punch by attenuating the attacks, sometimes producing

popping or clicking sounds. When it is controlled, a short attack time can heighten transients and add a crisp accent to sound. Generally, attack time should be set so that signals exceed the threshold level long enough to cause an increase in the average level. Otherwise, gain reduction will decrease overall level. Again, your ear is the best judge of the appropriate attack time setting.

Release time (or *recovery time*) is the length of time it takes a compressed signal to return to normal (unity gain) after the input signal has fallen below the threshold. Typical release times vary from 20 ms to several seconds. It is perhaps the most critical variable in compression, because it controls the moment-to-moment changes in the level and, therefore, the overall loudness. One purpose of the release-time function is to make the variations in loudness level caused by the compression imperceptible. For example, longer release times are usually applied to music that is slower and more legato (that is, smoother and more tightly connected), and shorter release times to music that is fast.

Generally, release times should be set long enough that if signal levels repeatedly rise above the threshold, they cause gain reduction only once.

If the release time is too long, a loud section of the audio could cause gain reduction that continues through a soft section.

These suggestions are not to imply rules—they are only guidelines. In fact, various release times produce various effects. Some enhance sound, others degrade it, as the following list of potential effects suggests:

▨ A fast release time combined with a low compression ratio makes a signal seem louder than it actually is.

▨ Too short a release time with too high a ratio causes the compressor to pump or breathe. You actually hear it working when a signal rapidly returns to normal after it has been compressed and quickly released.

▨ A longer release time smoothes a fluctuating signal.

▨ A longer release time combined with a short attack time gives the signal some of the characteristics of a sound going backward. This effect is particularly noticeable with transients.

▨ A release time longer than about half a second for bass instruments prevents harmonic distortion.

▨ Too long a release time creates a muddy sound and can cause the gain reduction triggered by a loud signal to continue through a soft one that follows.

Makeup gain allows adjustment of the output level to the desired optimum. It is used for example, when loud parts of the signal are so reduced that the overall result sounds too quiet.

Limiters

The *limiter* is a compressor whose output level stays at or below a preset point regardless of its input level. It has a compression ratio between 10 to 1 and infinity; it puts a ceiling on the loudness of a sound at a preset level (see 9-13). Regardless of how loud the input signal is, the output will not go above this ceiling. This makes the limiter useful in situations where high sound levels are frequent or where a performer or console operator cannot prevent loud sounds from going into the red.

The limiter has a preset compression ratio but a variable threshold; the threshold sets the point where limiting begins. Attack and release times, if they are not preset, should be relatively short, especially the attack time. A short attack time is usually essential to a clean-sounding limit.

Unlike compression, which can have little effect on the frequency response, limiting can reduce high-frequency response. Also, if limiting is severe, the signal-to-noise ratio drops dramatically. What makes a good limiter? One that is used infrequently but effectively, that is, except in broadcasting, where limiting the signal before transmission is essential to control peak levels and, hence, overload distortion.

De-essers

The *de-esser* is basically a fast-acting compressor that acts on high frequencies by attenuating them. It gets rid of the annoying hissy consonant sounds such as *s, z, ch,* and *sh* in speech and vocals. A de-esser may be a stand-alone unit or, more common, built into compressors and voice processors.

Uses of Compressors and Limiters

Compressors and limiters have many applications, several of which are listed here.

▨ Compression minimizes the wide changes in levels of loudness caused when a performer fails to maintain a consistent mic-to-source distance.

▨ Compression smoothes the variations in attack and loudness of instruments with wide ranges or wide sound-pressure levels, such as the guitar, bass, trumpet, French horn, and drums. It can also smooth percussive sound effects such as jangling keys, breaking glass, and crashes.

▨ Compression can improve the intelligibility of speech in an analog tape recording that has been rerecorded, or dubbed, several times.

▨ Compressing speech or singing brings it forward and helps it jump out of the overall mix.

■ Compression reduces apparent noise if the compression ratios are low. Higher ratios add more noise.

■ Limiting prevents high sound levels, either constant or momentary, from saturating the recording.

■ The combination of compression and limiting can add more power or apparent loudness to sound.

■ The combination of compression and limiting is often used by AM radio stations to prevent distortion from loud music and to bring out the bass sounds. This adds more power to the sound, thus making the station more obvious to someone sweeping the dial.

■ Compression in commercials is used to raise average output level and thus sonically capture audience attention.

Expanders

An *expander*, like a compressor, affects dynamic range (see 9-15a). But whereas a compressor reduces it, an expander increases it. Like a compressor, an expander has variable ratios and is triggered when sound reaches a set threshold level. The ratios on an expander, however, are the inverse of those on a compressor, but usually gentler: 1 to 2, 1.5 to 2, and so on. At 1 to 2, each 1 dB of input expands to 2 dB of output; at 1 to 3, each 1 dB of input expands to 3 dB of output. Because an expander is triggered when a signal falls below a set threshold, it is commonly used as a noise gate.

Noise Gates

Like the compressor, the expander/*noise gate* has the same dynamic determinants, but they act

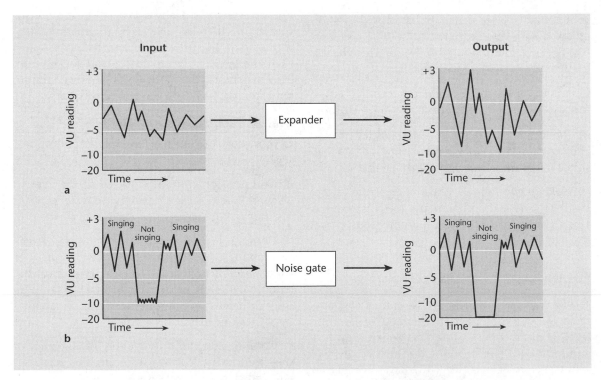

9-15 Effect of (a) expansion and (b) noise gating. Without noise gating, ambient noise is masked during singing and audible when singing is not present. Noise gating eliminates the ambient noise when there is no singing.

inversely to those of the compressor. In addition to ratio settings, there is threshold: When the input signal level drops below the threshold, the gate closes and mutes the output. When the signal level exceeds the threshold, the gate opens. Attack time determines how long it takes for the gate to go from full off to full on once the input level exceeds the threshold. Attack times are usually quite short— 1 ms or even less. Longer attacks tend to chop off fast transients on percussive sounds. Release time sets the time required for the gate to go from full on to full off once the signal level falls below the threshold. Another control is the *key input,* sometimes called a *side chain input,* which allows a different signal to be patched in to govern the gating action, such as using a bass drum as the key signal to turn another sound on and off in time with the bass drum's rhythm.

The noise gate is used primarily as a fix-it tool to reduce or eliminate unwanted low-level noise from amplifiers, ambience, rumble, noisy tracks, and leakage. It also has its creative uses to produce dynamic special effects. As an example of a practical application, assume that you have two microphones, one for a singer and one for an accompanying piano. When the singer and pianist are performing, the sound level will probably be loud enough to mask unwanted low-level noises. But if the pianist is playing quietly and the vocalist is not singing, or vice versa, the open, unused microphone may pick up these noises (see 9-15b).

An obvious solution to this problem is to turn down the fader when a microphone is not being used, cutting it off acoustically and electronically. But this could become hectic for a console operator if there are several sound sources to coordinate. Another solution is to set the expander's threshold level at a point just above the quietest sound level that the vocalist (or piano) emits. When the vocalist stops singing, the loudness of the sound entering the microphone falls below the threshold point of the expander, which shuts down, or gates, the mic.

The key to successful noise gating is in the coordination of the threshold and ratio settings. Because there is often little difference between the low level of a sound's decay and the low level of noise, you have to be wary that in gating noise you do not cut off program material as well. Always be careful when you use a noise gate; unless it is set precisely, it can adversely affect response.

Noise gates are also used to create effects. Shortening decay time of the drums can produce a very tight drum sound. Taking a 60-Hz tone and feeding it so that it is keyed or triggered by an electric bass can produce not only a simulated bass drum sound but also one that is synchronized with the bass guitar.

Pitch Shifters

A *pitch shifter* is a device that uses both compression and expansion to change the pitch of a signal. It is used to correct minor off-pitch problems, create special effects, or change the length of a program without changing its pitch. The latter function is called *time compression/expansion.* For example, if a singer delivers a note slightly flat or sharp, it is possible to raise or lower the pitch so that it is in tune. A pitch shifter also allows an input signal to be harmonized by mixing it with the harmonized signal at selected pitch ratios.

A pitch shifter works by compressing and expanding audio data. When the audio is compressed, it runs faster and raises pitch. It also shortens the audio segment. When the audio is expanded, it lowers pitch and lengthens the audio data. During processing, therefore, the pitch shifter is also rapidly cutting and pasting segments of data at varying intervals.

The basic parameter for pitch shifting is transposition. *Transposing* is changing the original pitch of a sound into another pitch, and in music, therefore, another key. Transposition sets the harmony-line interval, typically within a range of ±1 or 2 octaves. A pitch shifter may also include a delay line with feedback and predelay controls.

As a time compressor, a pitch shifter can shorten recorded audio material with no editing, no deletion of content, and no alteration in pitch (see 9-16 and 9-20).

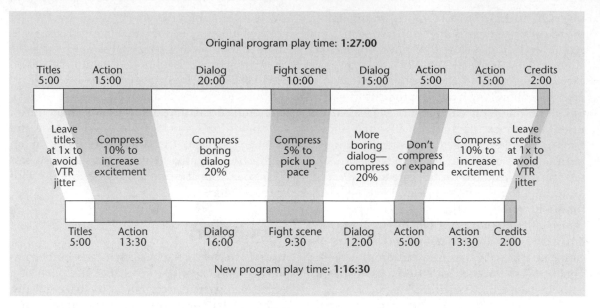

Original program play time: **1:27:00**

| Titles 5:00 | Action 15:00 | Dialog 20:00 | Fight scene 10:00 | Dialog 15:00 | Action 5:00 | Action 15:00 | Credits 2:00 |

| Leave titles at 1x to avoid VTR jitter | Compress 10% to increase excitement | Compress boring dialog 20% | Compress 5% to pick up pace | More boring dialog— compress 20% | Don't compress or expand | Compress 10% to increase excitement | Leave credits at 1x to avoid VTR jitter |

| Titles 5:00 | Action 13:30 | Dialog 16:00 | Fight scene 9:30 | Dialog 12:00 | Action 5:00 | Action 13:30 | Credits 2:00 |

New program play time: **1:16:30**

9-16 Example of time compression of an event sequence

NOISE PROCESSORS

Noise processors reduce or eliminate noise from an audio signal. Let's take analog audiotape as one example of their application.

You will recall that the dynamic range of human hearing is 120 dB-SPL and beyond. The best analog recording produces a dynamic range of 80 to 90 dB. Some analog recording is in the 65- to 70-dB range, half as much as humans are capable of hearing and far less than the dynamic range of digital recording (see 9-17). Recording at high levels improves dynamic range but could also increase distortion. And there is the problem of tape noise.

The inherent unevenness of a tape's magnetic coating, even in the highest-quality tapes, always leaves a slight polarization of the magnetic particles in the coating after erasure, regardless of how complete the erasure is. Each time a tape is used, some of the magnetic coating is worn away, thus decreasing the signal-to-noise ratio. Poor dispersion of the magnetic particles creates sound dropout and noise. Residual magnetization after erasure due either to an improper erase current or to a poor bulk-erasing technique increases tape noise. A problem with the record current will result in a recording that is not uniformly magnetized. A tape recording made at a level that is too quiet will underpolarize the magnetic particles, thereby creating hiss. Multitrack tape brings an associated increase in tape noise.

To improve dynamic range and reduce noise, the signal must be processed before it is encoded on tape and after it is decoded from tape. Such a process is called *double-ended noise reduction*. Noise reduction that occurs either just before recording or just after playback is called *single-ended noise reduction*.

Double-Ended Noise Reduction

A compressor can process noise "before the fact"— during recording—and the expander can process noise "after the fact"—during playback. During recording, the input signal is compressed; that is, dynamic range is reduced. Where quiet passages occur in the sound, they are recorded at a higher-than-normal level. During playback the signal is expanded—returned to its original dynamic range— but with one difference: The level is reduced, and so is the noise, in all of the places where it was increased during recording (see 9-18).

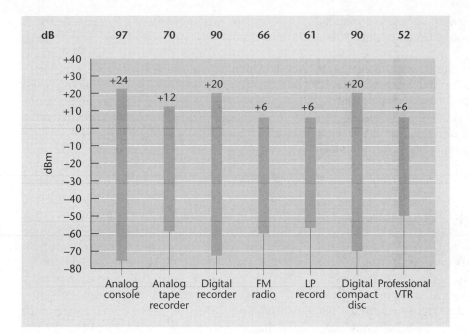

9-17 Dynamic ranges of various audio devices in dBm (an electrical measurement of power) and in dB

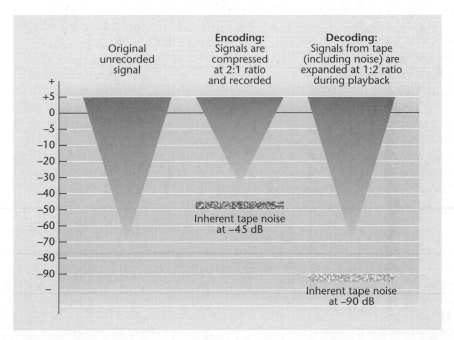

9-18 Companding dynamic range. Compression treats dynamic range before recording, so the program material is above the noise floor. During playback expansion restores the original dynamic range with reduced tape noise.

Of course, using the compressor and expander for noise reduction would be extremely time-consuming and costly. It would involve setting the appropriate thresholds and ratios on each unit for each tape track being produced; a 24-track recording would require 24 compressors and 24 expanders to reduce overall tape noise. So the double-ended process of noise reduction has been incorporated into a single unit called a **compander** (from its functions, *com*pression and ex*pan*sion). The compander is more popularly known as a *noise reducer*.

In double-ended noise reduction, a tape encoded with noise reduction must be decoded during playback. If it is not, the increased signal and noise level that was encoded during recording will be annoyingly perceptible. The most commonly used double-ended noise reduction systems are Dolby and dbx. These systems are not compatible, so tapes made with one are not interchangeable with the other.

The Dolby System

The Dolby company has a number of systems currently in use. The one most prevalent in professional analog recording is *SR (spectral recording)*.

Spectral recording uses the principle of least treatment to the audio signal (see 9-19). At the lowest levels or when no signal is present, SR applies a fixed gain/frequency characteristic that reduces noise and other low-frequency disturbances. Noise reduction is applied to those regions that contain low- and medium-level signal components. Similar to the response of the human hearing system, SR responds to changing amplitudes in various regions of the frequency spectrum, rather than to instantaneous variations in the signal's overall waveform. To put it another way, SR changes the gain only by the amount required and only at frequencies where the change is needed, thereby achieving as nearly optimal a level as possible at all frequencies. Spectral recording increases dynamic range as much as 24 dB at high frequencies and 10 dB at low frequencies, increasing headroom to the point where the risk of underrecording analog tape and overrecording digital tape is reduced considerably.

Other Dolby noise reduction systems are the S, B, and C. *Dolby S* is based on the SR process. It is less complex and less costly than SR and is used in audiocassettes and semipro multitrack recorders. It uses three fixed and two sliding bands to lower the midrange and high-frequency noise floor by about 24 dB and the low-frequency noise floor by about 10 dB. The *Dolby B* and *C* systems are used in consumer cassette decks and semipro recorders. Dolby C is also used with some videotape formats. Dolby B reduces high-frequency noise 10 dB. It uses a single sliding band that starts at 500 Hz, and it achieves maximum noise reduction from 1,500 to 20,000 Hz. There is no operating effect on lower-frequency noises. Dolby C uses two sliding bands that start at about 125 Hz and provide 20-dB reduction upward from 375 Hz. (Other Dolby systems, such as Dolby Digital and Dolby E, have more to do with encoding and decoding multichannel formats like surround sound to make them reproduceable in their release media.)

The dbx System

The dbx system reduces noise 30 dB across a single, full-frequency-range band from 20 to 20,000 Hz. There is no division of noise reduction among frequency bands. The compression ratio is 2 to 1, so sonic material with a dynamic range of, say, 90 dB is compressed to 45 dB during recording and expanded to 90 dB during playback; dbx is not level-dependent.

The original dbx noise reduction system, designated Type I, was developed for use in professional recording studios. Broadcast cartridges and telephone transmission lines do not offer the excellent frequency response available in professional tape recorders, however; the low end and high end fall off considerably. To meet the needs of broadcasters, the dbx Type II noise reduction system was developed. The Type I and Type II systems are incompatible; a tape encoded with one system cannot be decoded by the other.

There is also a dbx Type III noise reduction system. When any equalizer is in the signal chain, movement of controls—fader, send, EQ, and so

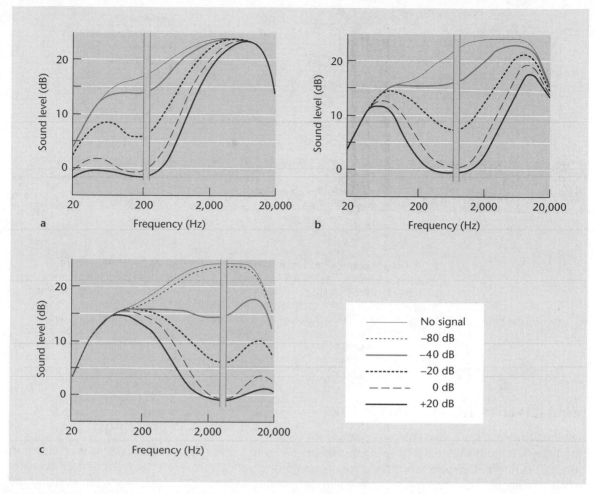

9-19 Examples of Dolby SR noise reduction at (a) 200 Hz, (b) 800 Hz, and (c) 3,000 Hz

on—usually adds noise to the signal. Type III noise reduction is a simultaneous encode/decode process that is built into dbx equalizers and designed to neutralize such noise (see 9-3).

Single-Ended Noise Reduction

Double-ended noise reduction systems do not remove noise from a signal—they prevent it from entering. Single-ended noise reduction systems work to reduce source noise in one pass. These units are generally applied to microphones, guitar amplifiers, and synthesizers. They may also be applied to the main left/right stereo signal during a mixdown, but on a professional level this is rarely done.

Single-ended systems use one of two techniques to reduce noise: dynamic filtering or downward expansion. With *dynamic filtering* a variable filter is applied during quiet passages and usually to noise that changes with the level of the signal, such as noisy synthesizer patches. *Downward expansion* works like an expander by reducing the level of any signal that drops below a preset threshold. It is used for ambient noise and relatively constant noise, such as the buzz from guitar amps and 60-Hz hum. Some single-ended noise reduction systems incorporate both techniques.

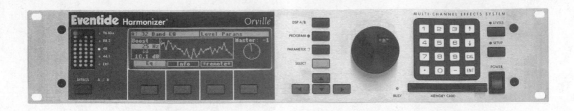

a

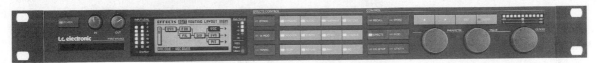

b

9-20 Examples of multieffects processors. (a) This device uses real-time adaptive resynthesis, which allows natural-sounding pitch shifts, extensive modification of the original signal, or both. It includes presets that emulate ring modulators, cinema filter sets, graphic and parametric EQs, intercoms, telephones, tube preamps, fuzz boxes, boom boxes, someone pulling the plug on a record player, twang guitars, and the sound of a 16 mm film projector, among the 800-plus effects. In addition to the presets, effects can be created and programmed. (b) This device features a vocoder, equalizer, filter, dynamics processor, pitch shifter, synthesizer generator, delay, reverb, chorus, pan, and distortion.

MULTIEFFECTS SIGNAL PROCESSORS

A *multieffects signal processor* combines several of the functions of individual signal processing in a single unit. The variety and parameters of these functions vary with the unit, but because most multieffects processors are digital, they are powerful audio processing tools albeit, in some cases, dauntingly complicated. Figure 9-20 displays two examples of multieffects processors.

DIGITAL SIGNAL PROCESSING PLUG-INS

Digital signal processing (DSP) has been incorporated into hard-disk recorder/editors. The processing most commonly used, such as EQ, compression, and reverb, comes with most systems as part of the software program. What is not included can be added as a plug-in, which makes just about every signal processing function available to a hard-disk recorder/editor (see 9-21).

Noise Reduction with Digital Signal Processing

A considerable advantage of DSP is its potency in noise reduction, particularly when converting analog recordings to digital (see 9-22). Virtually any unwanted sound can be eliminated. In fact, because noise reduction with digital processing is such a powerful production tool, getting rid of recorded noise has become much less of a problem than it once was.

In addition to the conventional noise reduction associated with Dolby, for example, digital noise reduction can act on other noises as well. There is declicking for removal of clicks, pops, thumps, electrostatic ticks, and other impulse noises; decrackling for automatic click and scratch detection and removal; and broadband denoising to eliminate hiss, surface noise, and unwanted background noise.

Digital noise reduction is able to remove constant, steady noises. For example, in a vocal

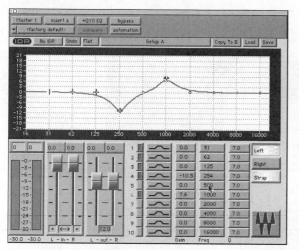

Paragraphic equalizer

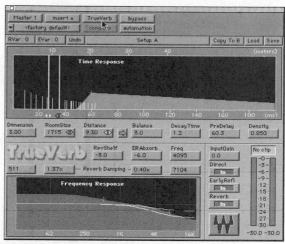

Reverb system

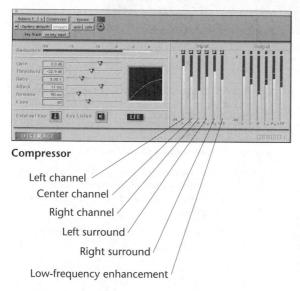

Compressor

Left channel

Center channel

Right channel

Left surround

Right surround

Low-frequency enhancement

9-21 Examples of DSP menus

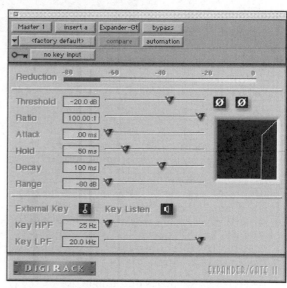

Expander/noise gate

track with high-level background noise from lights, ventilating fans, and studio acoustics, almost all of the noise can be removed without affecting voice quality.

In digital noise reduction, there are parameters to control and balance. It is important to consider the amount of noise being removed from the signal, the amount of signal being removed from the program material, and the amount of new sonic colorations being added to the signal. Failure to coordinate these factors can be sonically detrimental to the program material, if not exacerbate the original noise problem.

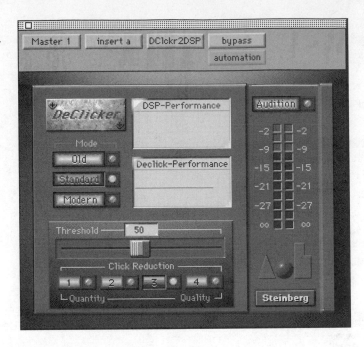

9-22 Example of DSP noise reducer. This plug-in, designed for a hard-disk recording/editing system, removes unwanted clicks from a recording without altering the undamaged sound immediately before and after a click.

▶ Signal processors are devices used to alter some characteristic of a sound. They can be grouped into four categories: (1) spectrum, (2) time, (3) amplitude, or dynamics, and (4) noise.

▶ The equalizer and filter are examples of spectrum processors, because they alter the spectral balance of a signal. The equalizer increases or decreases the level of a signal at a selected frequency by boost or cut (also known as peak and dip), or by shelving. The filter attenuates certain frequencies above, below, between, or at a preset point(s).

▶ Two types of equalizers in common use are the fixed-frequency and the parametric.

▶ The most commonly used filters are high-pass (low-cut), low-pass (high-cut), band-pass, and notch.

▶ Psychoacoustic processors add clarity, definition, and overall presence to sound.

▶ Time signal processors affect the time relationships of signals. Reverberation and delay are two such effects.

▶ The three most common types of reverberation systems used today are (1) digital, (2) plate, and (3) acoustic chamber.

▶ Digital reverb reproduces the sound of different acoustic environments electronically.

▶ An important feature of most digital reverb units is predelay—the amount of time between the onset of the direct sound and the appearance of the first reflections.

▶ Delay is the time interval between a sound or signal and its repetition.

▶ Most delay effects today, such as doubling, chorus, and slap back echo, are produced electronically using a digital delay device.

▶ Flanging and phasing split a signal and slightly delay one part to create controlled phase cancellations that generate a pulsating sound. Flanging uses a time delay; phasing uses a phase shifter.

▶ Amplitude (dynamic) signal processors affect a sound's dynamic range. These effects include compressing, limiting, de-essing, expanding, noise gating, and pitch shifting.

- With compression, as the input level increases, the output level also increases but at a slower rate, reducing dynamic range. With limiting, the output level stays at or below a preset point regardless of its input level. With expansion, as the input level increases, the output level also increases but at a greater rate, increasing dynamic range.

- A de-esser is basically a fast-acting compressor that acts on high-frequency sibilance by attenuating it.

- A noise gate is used primarily to reduce or eliminate unwanted low-level noise, such as ambience and leakage. It is also used creatively to produce dynamic special effects.

- A pitch shifter uses both compression and expansion to change the pitch of a signal or the running time of a program.

- Noise processors are designed to reduce or eliminate noise from an audio signal. Most are double-ended; they prevent noise from entering a signal. Single-ended noise processors reduce existing noise in the signal.

- Multieffects signal processors combine several of the functions of individual signal processors in a single unit.

- Digital signal processing (DSP) is available in hard-disk recorders/editors either as part of the software program or as plug-ins. This makes it possible to use virtually every signal processing function in hard-disk production.

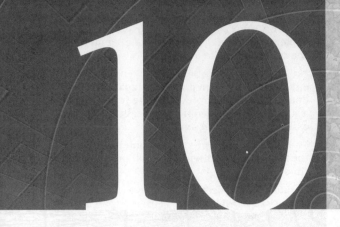

10 Loudspeakers and Monitoring

Each component in the *sound chain*—microphone, console, signal processor, and recorder—is important. But, analog or digital, no matter how good these components are in listening to their product, *the quality of every sound evaluated is based on what you hear from the loudspeaker,* the last link in the chain. The tendency is to underestimate the importance of the loudspeaker. Perhaps there may be a subconscious correlation between last and least.

The point seems straightforward: Always use the best loudspeaker. But which is best? Is it the most expensive? The largest? The loudest? The one with the widest, flattest frequency response? The one suitable for symphonic music or hard rock? Although a loudspeaker is critical to every audio operation, choosing the one most suited to your needs is not so straightforward. It involves several decisions; each influences later ones, and most are mainly subjective.

In deciding which loudspeaker is "best," consider several factors: frequency response, linearity, amplifier power, distortion, output-level capability, sensitivity, polar response, arrival time, and phase. Placement also affects the sound. These factors are discussed later in this chapter.

Like the microphone, the loudspeaker is a transducer, but it works in the opposite direction: Instead of changing acoustic energy into electric energy, it changes electric energy back into acoustic energy. Unlike microphone usage, only one type of loudspeaker is in common use—the *moving-coil loudspeaker*.

LOUDSPEAKER SYSTEMS

The function of a loudspeaker is to convert the electric energy that drives it into mechanical energy and in turn into acoustic energy. Theoretically, a loudspeaker should be able to reproduce all frequencies linearly—that is, having an output that varies proportionally with the input. In reality this does not happen. A loudspeaker that is large enough to generate low-frequency sound waves most likely will not be able to efficiently reproduce the high frequencies. Conversely, a speaker capable of reproducing the shorter waves may be incapable of reproducing the longer wavelengths.

To illustrate the problem, consider that many radio and television receivers contain a single speaker; even many stereo radios and tape recorders contain only one loudspeaker in each of the two loudspeaker enclosures. Because a single speaker has difficulty coping with the entire range of audible frequencies, a compromise is made: The long and the short wavelengths are sacrificed for the medium wavelengths that a single, mid-sized loudspeaker can reproduce more efficiently. Therefore, regardless of a recording's sound quality, a receiver with just one loudspeaker cannot reproduce it with full-frequency response.

Crossover Network and Drivers

To widen the loudspeaker's frequency response and make reproduction of the bass and treble more efficient, the *crossover network* was created. Also, individual speaker elements, called *drivers,* were developed to handle the different physical requirements necessary to emit the long, powerful bass frequencies and the short, more directional treble frequencies.

The crossover network divides the frequency spectrum between the low and high frequencies. The actual point, or frequency, where the bass and treble divide is called the *crossover frequency*. A driver large enough to handle the low frequencies is dedicated to the bass, and a driver small enough to handle the high frequencies is dedicated to the treble. Informally, these drivers, or loudspeakers, are called the *woofer* and the *tweeter*. Low- and high-frequency drivers are contained in a single cabinet. The size of the drivers is related to the power output of the loudspeaker system.

If a loudspeaker system divides the frequency spectrum once, it is called a *two-way system loudspeaker*. The crossover frequency in a two-way system is in the neighborhood of 1,500 to 2,000 Hz. The frequencies below the crossover point are assigned to the woofer, and the frequencies above the crossover are assigned to the tweeter. A loudspeaker may have more than one driver for each frequency range.

A loudspeaker system that uses two crossover frequencies is called a *three-way system loudspeaker,* and one that has three crossover frequencies is called a *four-way system loudspeaker.* Three-way systems divide the frequency spectrum at roughly 400 to 500 Hz and 3,500 to 5,000 Hz. Four-way systems divide it at anywhere between 400 to 500 Hz, 1,500 to 2,000 Hz, and 4,500 to 6,000 Hz.

SELECTING A MONITOR LOUDSPEAKER

Loudspeakers are like musical instruments in that they produce sound. They are not like purely electronic components such as consoles, which can be objectively tested and rationally evaluated. No two loudspeakers sound quite the same. Comparing the same make and model of loudspeakers in one room tells you only what they sound like in that acoustic environment; in another room they may sound altogether different. Furthermore, a loudspeaker that satisfies your taste might be unappealing to someone else.

A loudspeaker's specifications can be used only as a reference. No matter how good a speaker looks on paper, keep in mind that the measurements are based on tests made in an *anechoic chamber*—a room with no reflections of any kind. Clearly, that will not be the case in actual use.

Thus it is extremely difficult to suggest guidelines for selecting a studio monitor. Nevertheless, all loudspeakers used for professional purposes should meet certain requirements.

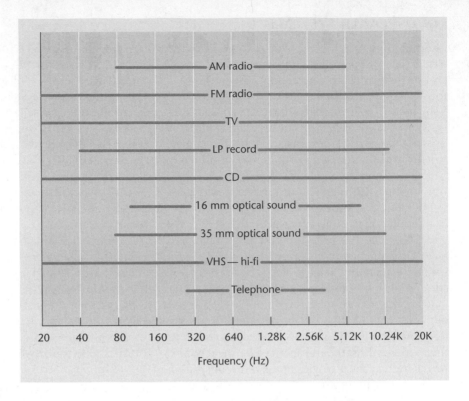

10-1 Frequency responses of various reproducing systems

AM radio

FM radio

TV

LP record

CD

16 mm optical sound

35 mm optical sound

VHS — hi-fi

Telephone

20   40   80   160   320   640   1.28K   2.56K   5.12K   10.24K   20K

Frequency (Hz)

Frequency Response

Evaluating *frequency response* in a loudspeaker involves two considerations: (1) how wide it is and (2) how flat, or linear, it is. Frequency response ideally should be as wide as possible, from at least 40 to 20,000 Hz, especially with digital sound. But the relationship between the sound produced in the studio and the sound reproduced through the audience's receiver/loudspeaker becomes a factor when selecting a monitor loudspeaker (see Figures 10-1 and 10-2).

For example, TV audio can carry the entire range of audible frequencies. You may have noticed during a televised music program, however, that you see certain high- and low-pitched instruments being played but you hear them only faintly or not at all. Overhead cymbals are one example. Generally, their frequency range is between 300 and 12,000 Hz (including overtones), but they usually begin to gain good definition between 4,500 and 8,000 Hz, which is well within the frequency of television transmission. The highest response

of many home TV receivers is about 6,000 Hz, however, which is below a good part of the cymbals' range.

Assume that you wish to boost the cymbal frequencies that the home TV receiver can barely reproduce. Unless you listen to the sound over a monitor comparable in output level and response to the average TV speaker, you cannot get a sense of what effect the boost is having. But that monitor will not give you a sense of what viewers with upgraded TV sound systems, such as stereo and surround sound, are hearing. (The audio in *high-definition television [HDTV]* has great potential to level the playing field between the sonic fidelity of the transmission and that of the reception, but it depends on the audio quality of the commercial TV tuner and the willingness of the consumer to purchase an HDTV set.)

Due to the differences between the potential sound response of a medium and its actual response after processing, transmission, and reception, most professional studios use at least two types of studio

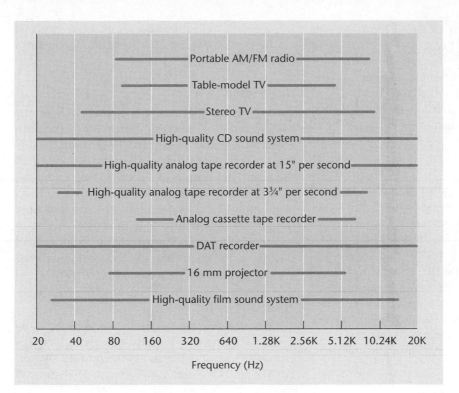

10-2 Frequency responses of various receiver/loudspeaker systems

Portable AM/FM radio

Table-model TV

Stereo TV

High-quality CD sound system

High-quality analog tape recorder at 15" per second

High-quality analog tape recorder at 3¾" per second

Analog cassette tape recorder

DAT recorder

16 mm projector

High-quality film sound system

20 40 80 160 320 640 1.28K 2.56K 5.12K 10.24K 20K

Frequency (Hz)

monitors: one to provide both wide response and sufficient power to reproduce a broad range of sound levels, and the other with response and power that reflect what the average listener hears. Many studios use three sets of monitors to check sound: (1) low-quality loudspeakers with only midrange response and limited power output, such as those in portable and car radios, portable and desktop TVs, and cheap tape decks; (2) average-quality loudspeakers with added high and low response, such as moderately priced component systems; and (3) high-quality loudspeakers with a very wide response and high output capability.

Linearity

The second consideration in evaluating frequency response in a loudspeaker is how linear it is. *Linearity* means that frequencies being fed to a loudspeaker at a particular loudness are reproduced at the same loudness. If they are not, it is very difficult to predetermine what listeners will hear.

If the level of a 100-Hz sound is 80 dB going in and 55 dB coming out, some—if not most—of the information may be lost. If the level of an 8,000-Hz sound is 80 dB going in and 100 dB coming out, the information may be overbearing.

Loudspeaker specifications include a value that indicates how much a monitor deviates from a flat frequency response, either by increasing or decreasing level. This variance should be no greater than ±3 dB.

Amplifier Power

To generate adequately loud sound levels without causing distortion, the loudspeaker amplifier must provide sufficient power. At least 30 watts for tweeters and 100 watts for woofers is generally necessary. Regardless of how good the rest of a loudspeaker's components are, if the amplifier does not have enough power, efficiency suffers considerably. There is a commonly held and seemingly plausible notion that increasing amplifier power means a proportional increase in loudness; for example, that a 100-watt amplifier can play twice as loud as a 50-watt amplifier. In fact, if a 100-watt and a 50-watt amp are playing at top volume, the 100-watt amp will sound only slightly louder. What the added wattage gives is clearer and less distorted reproduction in loud sonic peaks.

Distortion

Discussion of amplifier power naturally leads to consideration of *distortion*—appearance of a signal in the reproduced sound that was not in the original sound. Any component in the sound chain can generate distortion. Because distortion is heard at the reproduction (loudspeaker) phase of the sound chain, regardless of where in the system it was generated, and because loudspeakers are the most distortion-prone component in most audio systems, it is appropriate to discuss briefly the various forms of distortion: intermodulation, harmonic, transient, and loudness.

Intermodulation Distortion

The loudspeaker is perhaps most vulnerable to *intermodulation distortion (IM)*, which results when two or more frequencies occur at the same time and interact to create combination tones and dissonances that are unrelated to the original sounds. Audio systems can be most vulnerable to intermodulation distortion when frequencies are far apart, as when a piccolo and a baritone saxophone are playing at the same time. Intermodulation distortion usually occurs in the high frequencies, because they are weaker and more delicate than the low frequencies.

Wideness and flatness of frequency response are affected when IM is present. In addition to its obvious effect on perception, even subtle distortion can cause listening fatigue.

Unfortunately, not all specification sheets include percentage of IM, and those that do often list it only for selected frequencies. Nevertheless, knowing the percentage of IM for all frequencies is important to loudspeaker selection. A rating of 0.5 percent IM or less is considered good for a loudspeaker.

Harmonic Distortion

You will recall that *harmonic distortion* occurs when the audio system introduces harmonics into a recording that were not present originally. Harmonic and IM distortion usually happen when the input and output of a sound system are *non-linear*—that is, when they do not change in direct proportion to each other. A loudspeaker's inability to handle amplitude is a common cause of harmonic distortion. This added harmonic content is expressed as a percentage of the total signal or as a component's *total harmonic distortion (THD)*.

Transient Distortion

Transient distortion relates to the inability of an audio component to respond quickly to a rapidly changing signal, such as that produced by percussive sounds. Sometimes transient distortion produces a ringing sound.

Loudness Distortion

Loudness distortion, also called *overload distortion*, occurs when a signal is recorded or played back at a level of loudness that is greater than the sound system can handle. The clipping that results from loudness distortion creates a fuzzy, gritty sound.

Output-Level Capability

Overly loud signals give a false impression of program quality and balance; nevertheless, a loudspeaker should be capable of reproducing loud sound levels without distorting, blowing fuses, or damaging its components. An output capability of 110 dB-SPL is desirable for studio work. Even if studio work does not often call for very loud levels, the monitor should be capable of reproducing them, because it is sometimes necessary to listen at a loud level to hear subtlety and quiet detail.

Sensitivity

Sensitivity is the on-axis sound-pressure level a loudspeaker produces at a given distance when driven at a certain power (about 3.3 feet with 1 watt of power). A monitor's sensitivity rating gives you an idea of the system's overall efficiency. Typical ratings range from 84 dB to more than 100 dB.

In real terms, however, a sensitivity rating of, say, 90 dB indicates that the loudspeaker could provide 100 dB from a 10-watt input and 110 dB from a 100-watt input, depending on the type of driver. The point is that it is the combination of sensitivity rating and power rating that tells you whether a monitor loudspeaker will be loud enough to suit your production needs. Generally, a sensitivity rating of 93 dB or louder is required for professional applications.

Polar Response

Polar response indicates how a loudspeaker focuses sound at the monitoring position(s). Because it is important to hear only the sound coming from the studio or the recorder, without interacting reflections from the control room walls (vertical surfaces) and ceiling or floor (horizontal surfaces), dispersion must be controlled at the monitoring locations so it is a relatively reflection-free zone (see 10-3).

This is easier said than done, particularly with bass waves, which are difficult to direct because of their long wavelengths. Therefore bass traps and other low-frequency absorbers are included in control room design to handle those bass waves not focused at the listening position (see 10-4; see also 3-22).

Frequencies from the tweeter(s), on the other hand, are shorter and easier to focus. The problem with high frequencies is that as the wavelength shortens, the pattern can narrow. Therefore the *coverage angle,* defined as the off-axis angle or point at which loudspeaker level is down 6 dB compared with the on-axis output, may not be wide enough to include the entire listening area.

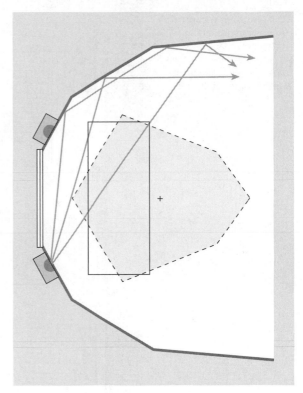

10-3 The shaded area in this control room design is a reflection-free zone

To help in selecting a loudspeaker with adequate polar response, specifications usually list a monitor's horizontal and vertical coverage angles. These angles should be high enough and wide enough to cover the listening position and still allow the operator or audience some lateral movement without seriously affecting sonic balance (see 10-5).

Arrival Time

Even if coverage angles are optimal, unless all reproduced sounds reach the listening position(s) at relatively the same time they were produced, aural perception will be impaired. When you consider the differences in size and power requirements among drivers and the wavelengths they emit, you can see that this is easier said than done.

10-4 Improving control room acoustics. Using strategically placed absorbers, diffusers, and bass traps can help control unwanted room reflections.

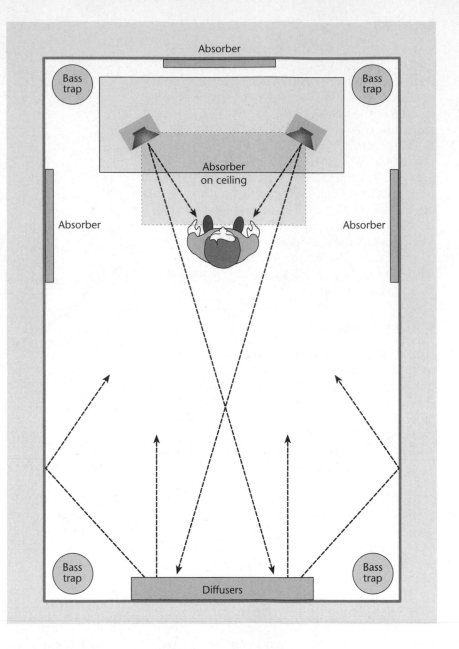

In two-, three-, and four-way system loudspeakers, the physical separation of each speaker in the system causes the sounds to reach the listener's ears at different times. Arrival times different by more than 1 ms are not acceptable in professional applications.

Phase

Sometimes, although dispersal and arrival time are adequate, sound reaching a listener may not be as loud as it should be or the elements within it may be poorly placed. For example, a rock band may be generating loud levels in the studio, but the sounds

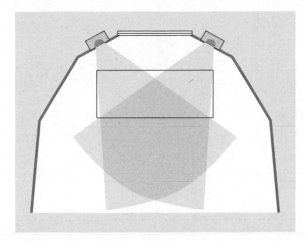

10-5 Desirable coverage angle of monitor loudspeakers

in the control room are, in relative terms, not so loud; or an actor is supposed to be situated slightly left in the aural frame but is heard from the right loudspeaker.

These problems may be the result of out-of-phase loudspeakers: One loudspeaker is pushing sound outward (compression), and the other is pulling sound inward (rarefaction). **Phase** problems can occur between woofer and tweeter in the same loudspeaker enclosure or between two separate loudspeakers. In the latter case, it is usually because the connections from loudspeaker to amplifier are improperly wired; that is, the two leads from one loudspeaker may be connected to the amplifier positive-to-negative and negative-to-positive whereas the other loudspeaker may be connected positive-to-positive and negative-to-negative. If you think that sound is out of phase, check the VU meters. If they show a similar level and the audio still sounds skewed, the speakers are out of phase; if they show different levels, the phase problem is probably elsewhere.

MONITOR PLACEMENT

Where you place monitor loudspeakers also affects sound quality, dispersal, and arrival time. Loud-speakers are often designed for a particular room

location and are generally positioned in one of four places: (1) well toward the middle of a room, (2) against or flush with a wall, (3) at the intersection of two walls, or (4) in a corner at the ceiling or on the floor. Each position affects the sound's loudness and dispersion differently.

A loudspeaker hanging in the middle of a room radiates sound into what is called a *full sphere* (or *full space*), where, theoretically, the sound level at any point within a given distance is the same (see 10-6). If a loudspeaker is placed against a wall, the wall concentrates the radiations into a *half sphere,* thereby theoretically increasing the sound level by 3 dB. With loudspeakers mounted at the intersection of two walls, the dispersion is concentrated still more into a *one-quarter sphere,* thus increasing the sound level another 3 dB. Loudspeakers placed in corners at the ceiling or on the floor radiate in a *one-eighth sphere,* generating the most-concentrated sound levels in a four-walled room. A significant part of each increase in the overall sound level is due to the loudness increase in the bass (see 10-7).

For informal listening one of these monitor positions is not necessarily better than another; placement may depend on a room's layout, furniture position, personal taste, and so on. In professional situations it is preferable to flush-mount loudspeakers in a wall or soffit. The most important thing in monitor placement is to avoid any appreciable space between the loudspeaker and the wall and any protrusion of the loud-speaker's cabinet edges. Otherwise, the wall or cabinet edges, or both, will act as secondary radiators, degrading frequency response. Flush-mounting also improves low-frequency response through avoiding back-wall reflections.

Monitoring Stereo

Stereo sound is two-dimensional: It has depth—front-to-back—and width—side-to-side. It therefore requires two discrete loudspeakers for monitoring. In placing these loudspeakers, it is critical that they be positioned to reproduce an accurate and balanced stereo image. The monitoring system should be set up symmetrically within the room.

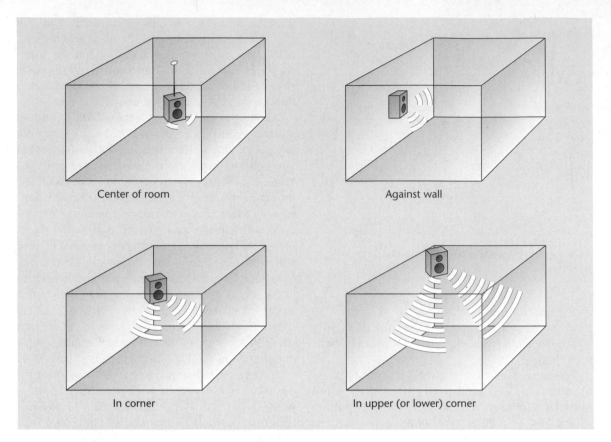

10-6 Four typical loudspeaker locations in a room and the effects of placement on overall loudness levels

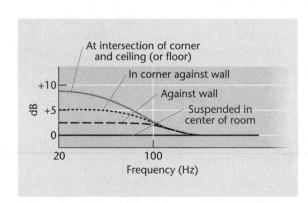

10-7 An example of the effects of loudspeaker placement on bass response

The distance between the speakers should be the same as the distance from each speaker to your ears, forming an equilateral triangle with your head.

Also, the center of the equilateral triangle should be equidistant from the room's side walls (see 10-8).

The location of the front-to-back and side-to-side sound sources are where they should be. If the original material has the vocal in the center (in relation to the two loudspeakers), the first violins on the left, the bass drum and bass at the rear center, the snare drum slightly left or right, and so on, these should be in the same spatial positions when the material is played through the monitor system.

Near-Field Monitoring

Even in the best of monitor–control room acoustic environments, the distance between wall-mounted loudspeakers and the listening position is often wide enough to generate sonic discontinuities from unwanted control room reflections. To

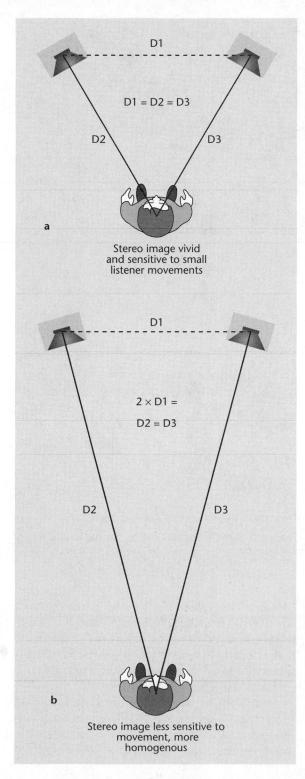

10-8 To help create an optimal travel path for sound from the loudspeakers to the listening position, carefully measure the loudspeaker separation and the distance between the loudspeakers and the listening position. (a) The distance between the acoustic center (between the loudspeakers) and the listening position is equal. In this arrangement head movement is restricted somewhat and the stereo image will be emphasized or spread out, heightening the sense of where elements in the recording are located. Shortening D2 and D3 will produce a large shift in the stereo image. (b) The distance between the acoustic center and the listening position is about twice as long. With this configuration the movement of the head is less restricted and the stereo image is reduced in width, although it is more homogeneous. The more D2 and D3 are lengthened, the more monaural the stereo image becomes (except for hard-left and hard-right panning).

reduce these unwanted reflections, another set of monitors is placed on or near the console's meter bridge (see 10-9).

Near-field monitoring reduces the audibility of control room acoustics by placing loudspeakers close to the listening position. Moreover, near-field monitoring improves source localization, because most of the sound reaching the listening position is direct; the early reflections that hinder good source localization are reduced to the point where they are of little consequence. At least, that is the theory; in practice, problems with near-field monitoring remain (see 10-10).

Among the requirements for near-field monitors are: loudspeakers that are small enough to put on or near the console's meter bridge without the sound "blowing you away"; a uniform frequency response from about 70 to 16,000 Hz, especially smooth response through the midrange; a sensitivity range from 87 to 92 dB; sufficient amplifier power; and good vertical dispersion for more-stable stereo imaging.

Monitoring Surround Sound

Surround sound differs from stereo by expanding the dimension of depth, thereby placing the listener more in the center of the aural image than in front of it. Accomplishing this requires additional audio channels routed to additional loudspeakers.

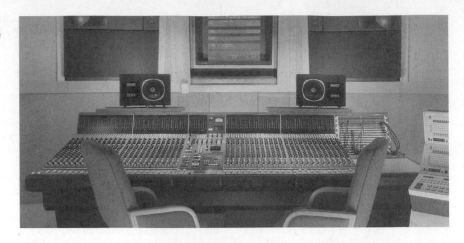

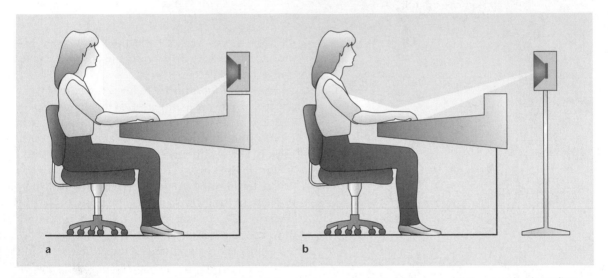

10-10 Near-field monitoring. (a) If a meter bridge is too low, early reflections will bounce off the console, degrading the overall monitor sound reaching the operator's ears. (b) One way to minimize this problem is to place the near-field monitors a few inches or so in back of the console.

The most common surround-sound format (for a while, at least) uses six discrete audio channels, five full-range and one limited to low frequencies (typically below 125 Hz), called the *subwoofer*. Hence the format is known as **5.1**. The loudspeakers that correspond to these channels are placed front left and right, like a stereo pair; a center-channel speaker is placed between the stereo pair; and another stereo pair—the surround speakers—are positioned to the left and right sides, or left and right rear, of the listener. The subwoofer can be placed almost anywhere in the room, because low frequencies are relatively omnidirectional, but it is usually situated in the front, between the center and the left or right speaker (see 10-11). Sometimes it is positioned in a corner to reinforce low frequencies.

A problem in positioning the center-channel speaker is the presence of a video monitor if it is situated on the same plane as the loudspeakers. Mounting the center speaker above the monitor is

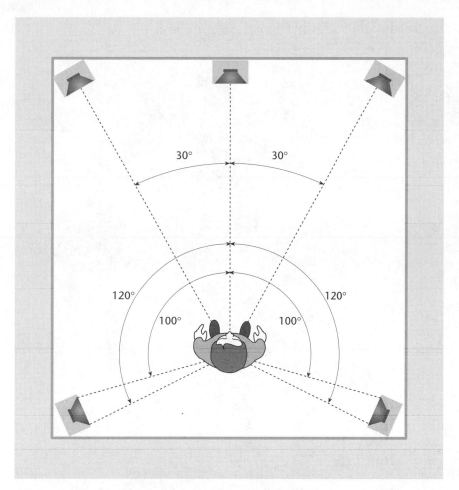

10-11 ITU (International Telecommunications Union) guideline for arranging loudspeakers in a surround-sound setup. In a 5.1 system, the front-left and front-right speakers form a 60-degree angle with the listener at the apex, and the center-channel speaker is directly in front of the listener. The surround speakers are usually placed at an angle between 100 and 120 degrees from the front-center line.

not the best location. If it is unavoidable, however, keep the tweeters close to the same plane as the left and right speakers, which may require turning the center speakers upside down. If the image is being projected, it becomes possible to mount the center speaker behind a micro-perforation screen, as they do in movie theaters.

The three front speakers are typically direct-radiating designs. A *direct radiator* is a speaker that is coupled directly to the air in front of it. The surrounds are either direct radiator or bipolar. In a bipolar loudspeaker, there are two sets of drivers mounted into a cabinet, each set firing in an opposite direction. They are usually placed to the sides of the listener and situated so that one set of drivers radiates toward the front of the room and the other set radiates toward the rear. A bipolar speaker produces a greater sense of envelopment than does a direct radiator, but makes it more difficult to localize an individual sound source. This

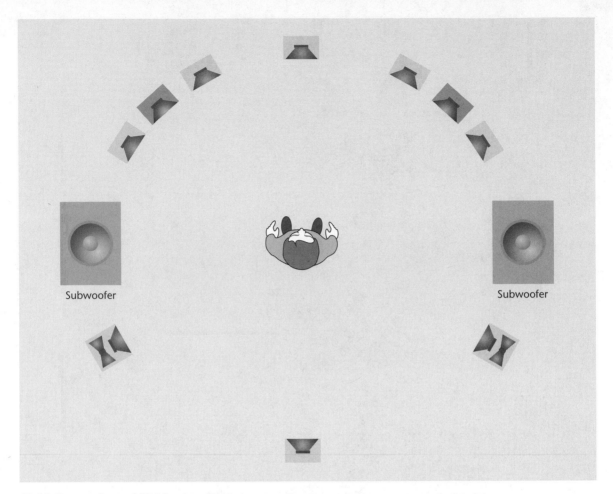

Subwoofer

Subwoofer

10-12 Surround-sound 10.2 loudspeaker arrangement

type of imaging is desirable in mixing film and television sound tracks, but in music recording it could be a disadvantage when it is aesthetically preferable to place a voice more precisely.

Another consideration in dealing with surround-sound setups, perhaps the primary one, is making sure the room is large enough, not only to accommodate the additional equipment and loudspeaker placement specifications but also to handle the relatively high loudness that is sometimes necessary when monitoring surround sound. There is also the factor of new surround-sound systems that go beyond the 5.1 configuration, such as 6.1 and 7.1, up to 10.2 (see 10-12). Also see Chapter 19 for a discussion of mixing for surround sound.

ADJUSTING MONITOR SOUND TO ROOM SOUND

As important as the "ear" and personal taste are to monitor selection and evaluation, it is critical to obtain an objective measure of the correlation between monitor sound and room sound. This is done using a *real-time analyzer*—a device that, among other measurements, displays response curves on an instantaneous basis and at different amplitudes (see 10-13).

When problems with frequency response show up, particularly serious ones, avoid the temptation to offset them with equalization. For example, if control room acoustics boost loudspeaker sound by,

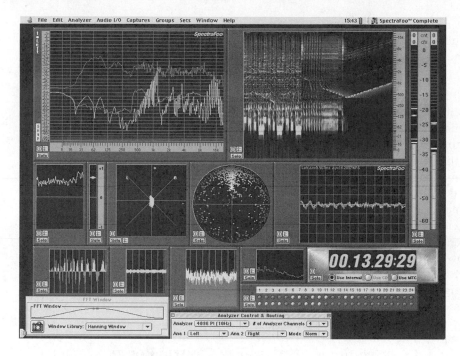

10-13 Audio analysis and monitoring system. This system provides a range of measurement and visualization tools. It includes an audio spectrum analyzer; audio frequency oscilloscope; left/right stereo power balance meter; frequency-sensitive phase meter; correlation meter to show the phase correlation between two audio channels; signal generator that generates concurrent sine waves with independently adjustable frequencies, amplitudes, and phases; and the tracking histories of the various measurement analyses.

say, 6 dB at 250 Hz, try not to equalize the monitors by, in this case, attenuating their response 6 dB at 250 Hz. Aside from adding noise by running the signal through another electronic device, an equalizer can change the phase relationships of the audio that passes through it.

To deal with discontinuities in monitor–control room interface, look to the source of the problem and correct it there. It may be necessary to change or modify the monitor, monitor position, power amplifier, or sound-diffusing materials or correct an impedance mismatch between sections of the monitor system. Whatever it takes, "natural" provides a truer sonic reference than "artificial," especially if the recording has to be evaluated or further processed in a different control room.

EVALUATING THE MONITOR LOUDSPEAKER

The final test of any monitor loudspeaker is how it sounds. Although the basis for much of the evaluation is subjective, there are guidelines for determining loudspeaker performance:

☑ Begin with rested ears. Fatigue alters aural perception.

☑ Sit at the designated listening position—the optimal distance away from and between the loudspeakers. This position, known as the *sweet spot*, should allow some front-to-back and side-to-side movement without altering perception of loudness, frequency response, or spatial perspective. It is important to know the boundaries of the listening position(s) so that all sound can be monitored on-axis within this area (see 10-3, 10-5, and 10-11).

☑ Use material with which you are intimately familiar for the evaluation, preferably on a high-quality digital disc or tape. Otherwise, if some aspect of the sound is unsatisfactory, you will not know whether the problem is with the original material or with the loudspeaker.

☑ Listen at a comfortable loudness level; 85 dB-SPL is often recommended.

☑ Listen for sounds you may not have heard before, such as hiss, hum, or buzz. Good monitors may reveal what inferior monitors cover up, or it could indicate that the monitors you are listening to have problems. In either case, you have learned something.

☑ In listening for spatial balance, make sure that the various sounds are positioned in the same places relative to the original material. As an additional test for stereo, put the monitor system into mono and check to make sure that the sound appears to be coming from between the two loudspeakers. Move toward the left and right boundaries of the sweet spot. If the sound moves with you before you get near the boundaries, reposition the monitors; then recheck their dispersion in both stereo and mono until you can move within the boundaries of the listening position without the sound following you or skewing the placement of the sound sources. If monitor repositioning is necessary to correct problems with side-to-side sound placement, make sure that it does not adversely affect front-to-back sound dispersion to the listening position.

☑ In evaluating monitor loudspeakers for surround sound, consider the following: Is the imaging of the sound sources cohesive or disjointed? Does the sound emanate from the appropriate loudspeaker location or does it seem detached from it? In moving around the listening environment, how much of the positional information, or sonic illusion, remains intact? How robust does that illusion remain in another listening environment? If there are motion changes—sound moving left-to-right, right side–to–right front, and so on—are they smooth? Does any element call unwanted attention to itself?

☑ In evaluating treble response, listen to the cymbal, triangle, flute, piccolo, and other high-frequency instruments. Are they too bright, crisp, shrill, or dull? Do you hear their upper harmonics?

☑ In testing bass response, include instruments such as the tuba and bass, as well as the low end of the organ, piano, bassoon, and cello. Sound should not be thin, boomy, muddy, or grainy.

☑ Assess the transient response, which is also important in a loudspeaker. For this, drums, bells, and triangle provide excellent tests, assuming they are properly recorded. Good transient response reproduces a crisp attack with no distortion or breakup.

☑ If you are evaluating a number of different loudspeakers, compare only a few at a time and take notes. Trying to remember, for example, how different speakers color the presence range; their differences in low-end warmth, or their degree of darkness or brightness, is unreliable. Our ability to retain precise auditory information is limited, particularly over time and when comparison testing.

Other important elements to evaluate, such as intermodulation, harmonic, and loudness distortion, were touched upon earlier in this chapter.

Monitoring in an Unfamiliar Control Room

When you do a session in a facility you have not worked in before, it is essential to become thoroughly familiar with the interaction between its monitor sound and its room sound. A relatively quick and reliable way to get an objective idea of that interaction is to do a real-time analysis. It is also crucial to put the real-time analysis into perspective with reference recordings and your ears.

Reference recordings on CD, CD-ROM, or DAT can be commercial recordings with which you are entirely familiar, or discs specially designed to help assess a listening environment, or both. Knowing how a recording sounds in a control room whose monitors and acoustics you are intimately familiar with is a good test in determining the sonic characteristics of, and among, the monitors and acoustics in a new environment. For example, if you know that a recording has clear high-end response in your own control room but the high end sounds thinner in another control room, it could indicate, among other things, that the other studio's monitors have inadequate treble response; the presence of harmonic distortion; a phase problem; the room's mediocre sound diffusion; or any combination of these factors.

Digital discs specially produced for referencing are also available. They are variously designed to test monitor and/or room response to a particular instrument, such as a drum set; individual or groups of instruments, such as the voice and clarinet, or strings, brass, and woodwinds; various sizes and types of ensembles, such as orchestras, jazz bands, and rock groups; room acoustics; spatial positioning; and spectral balances (see Bibliography).

HEADPHONES

Headphones (also referred to as "cans") are a too-often-overlooked but important part of monitoring, especially in field production. Five considerations are basic when using headphones for professional purposes: (1) frequency response should be wide, flat, and uncolored; (2) you must be thoroughly familiar with their sonic characteristics; (3) they should be *circumaural* (around-the-ear)—as airtight as possible against the head for acoustical isolation—and comfortable; (4) the fit should stay snug even when you are moving; and (5) although it may seem obvious, stereo headphones should be used for stereo monitoring, and headphones capable of multichannel reproduction should be used for monitoring surround sound.

Headphones are usually indispensable in field recording, because monitor loudspeakers are often unavailable or impractical. In studio control rooms, however, there are pros and cons to using headphones. The pros are that: (1) sound quality will be consistent in different studios; (2) it is easier to hear subtle changes in the recording and the mix; and (3) there is no aural smearing due to room reflections. The cons are that: (1) the sound quality will not be the same as with the monitor loudspeakers; (2) the aural image forms a straight line between your ears and is unnaturally wide; (3) in panning signals for stereo, the distance between monitor loudspeakers is greater than the distance between your ears—left and right sounds are directly beside you; (4) there is no interaction

between the program material and the acoustics, so the tendency may be to mix in more artificial reverberation than necessary; and (5) if open-air, or *supra-aural,* headphones are used, bass response will not be as efficient as with circumaural headphones, and outside noise might interfere with listening.

MAIN POINTS

▶ Loudspeakers are transducers that convert electric energy into sound energy.

▶ The moving-coil loudspeaker is the type most often used.

▶ A single, midsized speaker cannot reproduce high and low frequencies very well; it is essentially a midrange instrument.

▶ For improved response, loudspeakers have drivers large enough to handle the bass frequencies and drivers small enough to handle the treble frequencies. These drivers are called, informally, woofers and tweeters, respectively.

▶ A crossover network separates the bass and treble frequencies at the crossover point, or crossover frequency, and directs them to their particular drivers.

▶ Two-way system loudspeakers have one crossover network, three-way system loudspeakers have two crossovers, and four-way system loudspeakers have three crossovers.

▶ Each medium that records or transmits sound, such as a CD or TV, and each loudspeaker that reproduces sound, such as a studio monitor or home receiver, has certain spectral and amplitude capabilities. For optimal results audio should be produced with an idea of how the system through which it will be reproduced works.

▶ In evaluating a monitor loudspeaker, frequency response, linearity, amplifier power, distortion, output-level capability, sensitivity, polar response, arrival time, and phase should also be considered.

▶ Linearity means that frequencies being fed to a loudspeaker at a particular loudness are reproduced at the same loudness.

- Amplifier power must be sufficient to drive the loudspeaker system, or distortion, among other things, will result.

- Distortion is the appearance of a signal in the reproduced sound that was not in the original sound. Various forms of distortion include inter-modulation, harmonic, transient, and loudness.

- Intermodulation distortion (IM) results when two or more frequencies occur at the same time and interact to create combination tones and disso-nances that are unrelated to the original sounds.

- Harmonic distortion occurs when the audio system introduces harmonics into a recording that were not present originally.

- Transient distortion relates to the inability of an audio component to respond quickly to a rapidly changing signal, such as that produced by percussive sounds.

- Loudness distortion, or overload distortion, results when a signal is recorded or played back at an amplitude greater than the sound system can handle.

- The main studio monitors should have an output-level capability of 110 dB-SPL.

- Sensitivity is the on-axis sound-pressure level a loudspeaker produces at a given distance when driven at a certain power. A monitor's sensitivity rating provides a good overall indication of its efficiency.

- Polar response indicates how a loudspeaker focuses sound at the monitoring position(s).

- The coverage angle is the off-axis angle or point at which loudspeaker level is down 6 dB compared with the on-axis output.

- A sound's arrival time at the monitoring position(s) should be no more than 1 ms; otherwise, aural perception is impaired.

- Where a loudspeaker is positioned affects sound dispersion and loudness. A loudspeaker in the middle of a room generates the least-concentrated sound; a loudspeaker at the intersection of a ceiling or floor generates the most.

- Stereo sound is two-dimensional; it has depth and breadth. In placing loudspeakers for monitoring stereo, it is critical that they be positioned sym-metrically within a room to reproduce an accurate and balanced front-to-back and side-to-side sonic image.

- Near-field monitoring enables the sound engineer to reduce the audibility of control room acoustics, particularly the early reflections, by placing loud-speakers close to the monitoring position.

- Surround sound differs from stereo by expanding the depth dimension, thereby placing the listener more in the center of the aural image than in front of it. Therefore, using the 5.1 surround-sound format, monitors are positioned front-left, center, and front-right, and the surround loud-speakers are placed left and right behind, or to the rear sides of, the console operator. A sub-woofer is usually positioned in front, between the center and the left or right speaker.

- In adjusting and evaluating monitor sound, objective and subjective measures are called for. Devices, such as a real-time analyzer, measure the relationship of monitor sound to room sound. Although part of testing a monitor loudspeaker involves subjectivity, there are guidelines for determining performance.

- Headphones are an important part of monitoring, particularly on location. Five considerations are vital in using headphones: (1) frequency response should be wide, flat, and uncolored; (2) you must be thoroughly familiar with the headphones' sonic characteristics before you use them; (3) the headphones should be airtight against the head for acoustical isolation; (4) the fit should stay snug even when you are moving; and (5) stereo headphones should be used for stereo monitoring, and multichannel headphones should be used for monitoring surround sound.

Three

Sound Design

CHAPTER 11   Sound Design

11

Sound Design

Sound design is the process of creating the overall sonic character of a production. In terms of film and video, it is to producing the sound track what cinematography is to producing the picture. Responsibility for it falls to a designated sound designer, who advises the audio team and, ordinarily, has a hands-on role during one or more stages of the sound track's production.

THE SOUND DESIGNER

The term *sound designer* was first used as a professional craft designation in theatrical film in 1979 when an academy award for sound design was given to Walter Murch for *Apocalypse Now.* Over the years, the term has been diluted to include just about anyone on the audio production team, particularly creators of sound effects and sound-effect editors, who has a hand in producing the audio. Using the preferred meaning, the **sound designer** is the one person responsible for creative control of the audio. Like the cinematographer, who is responsible for the overall look of the picture, it is the sound designer's function to put a coherent sonic stamp on the production—and the one member of the audio team who has the director's ear.

Regardless of whether there is a designated sound designer, all members of the audio team contribute creatively to the sound in a production. Hence, the material in this chapter applies to sound design in general and the various components of audio in particular, rather than to a specific role carried out by a particular member of the audio production team.

ELEMENTS OF SOUND STRUCTURE AND THEIR EFFECTS ON PERCEPTION

There are three domains to work with in creating a sound design: speech, sound effects, and music. Paradoxically, sound's ability to evoke a picture, and silence, may be considered two other sonic components. This may not seem to be an impressive arsenal, especially when compared with the number of elements available in pictorial design—light, color, picture composition, scenery, costumes, physical dimension, focal length, camera angle, depth of field, and so on. As you will discover, however, few though these aural elements are, they are powerful agents in creating, supplementing, and complementing cognitive and affective information.

All sound—speech, sound effects, and music— are made up of the same basic elements: pitch, loudness, timbre, tempo, rhythm, attack, duration, and decay. During audio production everyone involved is dealing with these elements, consciously or subconsciously, and assessing their effects on perception. Because each element contains certain characteristics that affect our response to sound, understanding those effects are fundamental to sound design.

Pitch refers to the highness or lowness of a sound. High-pitched sound often suggests something delicate, bright, or elevated; low-pitched sound may indicate something sinister, strong, or peaceful.

Loudness describes sound in terms of how loud or soft it is. Loud sound can suggest closeness, strength, or importance; soft sound may convey distance, weakness, or tranquility.

Timbre is the characteristic tonal quality of a sound. It not only identifies a sound source—reedy, brassy, tympanic—but also sonic qualities such as rich, thin, edgy, or metallic. Reedy tonal qualities produced by a clarinet or oboe, for example, can suggest something wistful, lonely, or sweet. A brassy sound can imply something cold, harsh, fierce, bitter, forceful, martial, or big. A tympanic or percussive sound can convey drama, significance, or power.

Tempo refers to the speed of a sound. Fast tempos agitate, excite, or accelerate; slow tempos may suggest monotony, dignity, or control.

Rhythm relates to a sonic time pattern. It may be simple, constant, complex, or changing. A simple rhythm can convey deliberateness, regularity, or lack of complication. A constant rhythm can imply dullness, depression, or uniformity. Rhythmic complexity suggests complication or elaborateness. Changing rhythms can create a sense of uncertainty, vigor, or the erratic.

Attack—the way a sound begins—can be hard, soft, crisp, or gradual. Hard or crisp attacks can suggest sharpness, excitement, or danger. Soft or gradual attacks can imply something gentle, muted, or blasé.

Duration refers to how long a sound lasts. Sound short in duration can convey restlessness, nervousness, or excitation; more-sustained sounds can create a sense of peace, persistence, or tiredness.

Decay—how fast a sound fades from a certain loudness—can be quick, gradual, or slow. Quick decays can create a sense of confinement, closeness, or definiteness; slow decays can convey distance, smoothness, or uncertainty.

Other aspects of sound, such as changing pitch, changing loudness, and acoustic interactions, also affect response. Of course, these elements are not heard individually but in combination.

Someone speaking in a loud, high-pitched voice at a rapid rate conveys excitement, whatever meaning the words may have. Lowering pitch, reducing loudness, and slowing tempo may also convey excitement, but this combination of sounds suggests something more profound and deeply felt. Words spoken at a deliberate tempo in a reverberant—that is, acoustically live—room may suggest a weightier content than those same words spoken in an acoustically drier environment.

These same factors can be applied to music and sounds. A trumpet or violin played loudly and rapidly at a high pitch could also suggest excitement, agitation, or gaiety—perhaps agitation in dryer acoustics and gaiety in livelier acoustics.

Striking a wooden door or metal barrel loudly and rapidly can also suggest agitation or gaiety. And again, lowering pitch, reducing loudness, and slowing tempo changes the response to something more serious, whether the sound source is a trumpet, violin, wooden door, or metal barrel.

That these characteristics are elemental in sonic structure is not to suggest that sound design is prescriptive or developed by applying formulas; the basic components of sound structure do not occur separately, but together in myriad forms. Rather, it is to introduce and define the building blocks of sound from which the sound designer shapes aural structure and meaning.

In thinking about the character of a sound, the key is to ask yourself: *Is it interesting? Is it involving? Does it do any good?*

FUNCTIONS OF SOUND

As essential as sound is, in relation to picture its "great power is conditional. It places the image in an emotional and physical context, helping us to decide how to take the image and how it integrates itself into everything else."* The sound/picture relationship is not a contest of superiority. It is a symbiotic relationship; they are two different "organisms" that are mutually beneficial to the whole.

Speech

Speech interpretation is the responsibility of the director and performer, not the sound designer. Nevertheless, it is important for those involved in audio production to know the various ways in which speech—verbal and nonverbal—affects

---

*Kevin Hilton, "Walter Murch: The Sound Film Man," *Studio Sound,* May 1998, p. 77.

meaning. Speech has basically two functions, narration and dialogue, and conveys nonverbal meaning primarily through emphasis, inflection, and aural mood.

Narration

Narration is usually descriptive and voiced-over; that is, a narrator describes events from outside the action, not as a participant but as an observer. Three types of narration are direct, indirect, and contrapuntal.

Direct narration describes what is being seen or heard. If we see or hear an automobile coming to a stop, a car door opening and closing, footsteps on concrete and then on stairs, and a wooden door opening and closing, and are told as much, the narration is direct. If, on the other hand, the narrator tells us that the person emerging from the car and going into the building is an ambassador on an urgent mission and is meeting with his counterparts from other countries who are waiting in the building, this is *indirect narration*. What you are being told is not evident in what is being shown. Indirect narration adds more information to the picture. *Contrapuntal narration,* as the term suggests, counterpoints narration and action to make a composite statement not explicitly carried, or suggested, in either element. For example, the action may contain people happily but wastefully consuming a more-than-ample meal, while the narration comments on the number of starving people in the world. The conflict between the two pieces of information makes a separate, third, comment.

These examples may suggest that indirect and contrapuntal narration are better than direct narration because they supplement and broaden information and, therefore, provide more content. Indirect and contrapuntal narration are preferable if the action is somewhat obvious. But direct narration is useful in radio when sounds may not convey the necessary meaning. It is also helpful in educational or instructional programs, when information requires reinforcement to be remembered and understood.

Narration provides nonverbal information as well. If the style of the delivery is formal and unemotional, the content comes across as impersonal and objective. If the sound is heavily inflected and personalized, the content takes on a more emotional and subjective quality.

Although the particular narrational approach depends on the script, understanding the influences of narration on content in general results in a better-conceived sound design.

Dialogue

Dialogue is a conversation between two or more people. Obviously, the verbal content of the conversation is essential to meaning, but nonverbal sound in dialogue also shapes meaning. Some examples follow.

Accent An accent can tell you if a character is cultured or crude, an American from rural Minnesota or someone from England, France, or India. It can also color an entire drama. A story set in Russia depicting events that led to the 1917 Bolshevik Revolution with an all-British cast may have superb acting and dialogue, but the refined, rounded, mellifluous British sound may not be so effective as the more guttural Slavic sound and may not give the necessary edge to people and events. Shakespeare played by actors with deep Southern drawls would sound unnatural. Films rerecorded from one language to another rarely sound believable.

Pace The pace of dialogue can convey nonverbal information about the passion, urgency, or boredom of a situation. For example:

> *She:* Go away.
> *He:* No.
> *She:* Please.
> *He:* Can't.
> *She:* You must.
> *He:* Uh-uh.

Certainly, there is not much verbal content here apart from the obvious. But by pacing the dialogue in different ways, meaning can be not only defined but also changed. Think of the scene played deliberately, with each line and the intervening pauses measured, as opposed to a rapid-fire delivery and no pauses between lines. The deliberately paced sound design can convey more stress or, perhaps, more inner anguish than the faster-paced version. On the other hand, the faster pace can suggest nervousness and urgency.

Patterns Dialogue patterns are important to natural-sounding speech and believable characterization. Although dialogue patterns are inherent in the script, a writer must be equally aware of how words should sound. If a character is supposed to be highly educated, the vocabulary, sentence structure, and speech rhythms should reflect erudition. If a character is being formal, vocabulary and sentence structure should be precise, and speech rhythms should sound even and business-like. Informality would sound looser, more relaxed, and more personal. An actor playing a nineteenth-century character should speak with a vocabulary and syntax that evokes that period to modern ears. That is, unless the character has a modern outlook and temperament, which would make the sound of contemporary vocabulary and sentence structure appropriate.

Emphasis Emphasis—stressing a syllable or word—is important to all speech—narration and dialogue. It often conveys the meaning of what is being said. On paper the words "How are you?" suggest concern for someone's welfare. But often the words are used as another way of saying "Hello," or making a perfunctory recognition with no expression of concern. Emphasis is what tells you so. Moreover, it is possible to emphasize the *how,* the *are,* or the *you* and communicate three different meanings. The words remain the same; the aural emphasis alters the message.

Take the line, "He'd kill us if he got the chance." If it were delivered with the emphasis on *us*—"He'd kill *us* if he got the chance"—the meaning conveyed would be defensive, that is, unless we kill him first. If the emphasis was on *kill*—"He'd *kill* us if he got the chance"—it suggests that the "us" did something to him first or that the "us" did something that would provoke him if he found it out.

Inflection Inflection—altering the pitch or tone of the voice—can also influence verbal meaning. By raising the pitch of the voice at the end of a sentence, a declarative statement becomes a question. Put stress on it, and it becomes an exclamation. Take the sentence "And the bombing continued." As a declarative statement, it is a fact. As a question, it introduces skepticism or perhaps even anguish. As an exclamation it becomes a statement of impact or pride.

"So help me God" is usually said at the end of an oath, as a declarative statement with almost equal emphasis on "help me God." But if the inflection rose at the end of the sentence, it would become a plea, perhaps underscoring the weight of responsibility now borne by the new office holder.

Mood Sound affects the mood or feeling of words and sentences. Aside from meaning, the sound of *dine* is more refined than the sound of *eat*. If the idea is to convey an edge to the action, *eat* is the better choice. *Lounge* has a softer, more gradual sound than *bar*. *Bestial* conveys more of a sense of the word's meaning than *barbaric,* because of its harder sounds and shorter, more staccato attacks at the beginning of its two syllables.

In the lines "lurid, rapid, garish, grouped" by poet Robert Lowell and "Strong gongs growing as the guns boom far" by G. K. Chesterton, the sounds in the words not only contribute to the overall meaning but are contained in the other words to further enhance the mood of the line.

Consider the following translations of the same line from Dante's *Purgatorio:*

"I go among these with my face down."

"Among these shades I go in sadness."

The first sounds graceless and heavy-handed. The sound of the second is more emotional, rhythmic, and vivid.

Sound Effects

Sound effects can be classified as anything sonic that is not speech or music. They are essential to storytelling, helping amplify the reality created in a production. It is worth noting that the art of sound is not only about creating big or bizarre effects, but also about creating subtle, low-key moments. Generally, sound effects perform two functions—contextual and narrative—although these functions are not mutually exclusive.

Contextual Sound

Contextual sound emanates from and duplicates a sound source as it is. It is also referred to as *diegetic sound*—coming from within the story space. (*Nondiegetic sound* comes from outside the story space. Music underscoring is an example of nondiegetic sound.) If a rocket fires, a horse gallops, or paper rustles, that is what you hear; the sound is natural or normal in structure and perspective. In other words, contextual sound is like direct narration.

Narrative Sound

Narrative sound adds more to a scene than what is apparent and so performs an informational function. It can be descriptive or commentative.

Descriptive sound, as the term suggests, describes sonic aspects of a scene, usually those not directly connected with the main action. A conversation in a hot room with a ceiling fan slowly turning is contextual sound. Descriptive sound would be the buzzing about of insects, oxcarts lumbering by outside, and an indistinguishable hubbub of human activity. A child leaves the house on the way to school, and you hear descriptive sounds of the neighborhood: birds chirping, one neighbor calling to another, a car turning down the street, and the grinding sound of the school bus growing louder.

Commentative sound also describes, but it makes an additional statement, one that usually has something to do with the story line. For example: A longtime athlete is released from the team. As he walks across the playing field for the last time, the wind comes up. Infused in the wind sound is the faint sound of cheering, giving the scene a wistful quality as the athlete reflects on the crowds that will be rooting for him no longer. Or behind the scene of a verdant, halcyon countryside is heard machinery and building to comment on the inevitable encroachment of industrialization.

Functions of Sound Effects

Sound effects also have specific functions within the general contextual and narrative categories. They break the screen plane, define space, focus attention, establish locale, create environment, emphasize and intensify action, depict identity, set pace, provide counterpoint, create humor, symbolize meaning, and unify transition.

Breaking the Screen Plane A film or video without sounds, natural or produced, detaches an audience from the on-screen action. The audience becomes an observer. In documentaries, for example, this has been a relatively common approach used to convey the sense that a subject is being treated objectively and so there is less possible distraction. The presence of sounds changes the audience relationship to what is happening on-screen; it becomes part of the action, in a sense. The audience becomes a "participant" in that there is no longer a separation between it and the screen plane. Therefore, it can also be said that sound effects add realism to the picture.

Defining Space Sound defines space by establishing distance, direction of movement, position, openness, and dimension. Distance—how close to or far from you a sound seems to be—is created mainly by relative loudness, or *sound perspective*. The louder a sound, the closer to the listener-viewer it is. A person speaking from several feet away will not sound as loud as someone speaking right next to you. Thunder at a low sound level tells you that a storm is some distance away; as the storm moves closer, the thunder grows louder.

By varying sound level, it is also possible to indicate direction of movement. As a person leaves a room, sound will gradually change from loud to soft; conversely, as a sound source gets closer, level changes from soft to loud.

With moving objects, frequency also helps establish distance and direction of movement. As a moving object such as a train, car, or siren approaches, its pitch gets higher; as it moves away or recedes, its pitch gets lower. This phenomenon is known as the *Doppler effect* (named for its discoverer, C. J. Doppler, an early-nineteenth-century Austrian physicist).

Sound defines relative position—the location of two or more sound sources in relation to one another, whether close, distant, side-to-side (in stereo), or to the rear-side or behind (in surround sound). Relative position is established mainly through relative loudness. If two people are speaking and a car horn sounds, the loudness of the three sound sources tells you their proximity to one another. If person A is louder than person B, and person B is louder than the car horn (assuming monaural sound), person A will sound closest, person B farther away, and the car horn farthest away. If the car horn is louder than person B, it will be perceived as being between persons A and B. If the aural image is in stereo, relative position will be influenced by how far left or right the sounds are. Here, too, imaging is mainly due to loudness, as lateral perspective is changed by panning. Once the lateral perspective is established, a further change in loudness moves the sound closer or farther away.

Openness of outdoor space can be established in a number of ways—for example, thunder that rumbles for a longer than normal period of time and then rolls to quiet; wind that sounds thin; echo that has a longer than normal time between repeats; background sound that is extremely quiet—all these effects tend to enhance the size of outdoor space.

Dimension of indoor space is usually established by means of reverberation (see Chapter 3). The more reverb, the larger the space is perceived to be. For example, Grand Central Station or the main hall of a castle would have a great deal of reverb, whereas a closet or an automobile would have little.

Focusing Attention In shots, other than close-ups, in which a number of elements are seen at the same time, how do you know where to focus attention? Of course, directors compose shots to direct the eye, but the eye can wander. Sound, however, draws attention and provides the viewer with a focus. In a shot of a large room filled with people, the eye takes it all in, but if a person shouts or begins choking, the sound directs the eye to that individual.

Establishing Locale Sounds can establish locale. A cawing seagull places you at the ocean; the almost derisive, mocking cackle of a bird of paradise places you in the jungle; honking car horns and screeching brakes place you in city traffic; the whir and clank of machinery places you in a factory; the crack of a bat hitting a ball and the roar of a crowd place you at a baseball game.

Creating Environment Establishing locale begins to create an environment, but more brush strokes are often needed to complete the picture. Honky-tonk saloon music may establish the Old West, but sounds of a blacksmith hammering, horses whinnying, wagon wheels rolling, and six-guns firing create environment. A prison locale can be established in several ways, but add the sounds of loudspeakers blaring orders, picks and shovels hacking and digging, grunts of effort, dogs barking, and whips cracking and you have created a brutal prison environment. To convey a sense of alienation and dehumanization in a high-tech office, the scene can be orchestrated using the sounds of ringing telephones with futuristic tonalities, whisper-jet spurts of laser printers, the buzz of fluorescent lights, machines humming in monotonous tempos, and synthesized Muzak in the background.

Emphasizing Action Sounds can emphasize or highlight action. A person falling down a flight of stairs tumbles all the harder if each bump is accented. A car crash becomes a shattering collision by emphasizing the impact and sonic aftermath—including silence. Creaking floorboards underscore someone slowly and methodically sneaking up to an objective. A saw grinding harshly through wood, rather than cutting smoothly, emphasizes the effort involved and the bite of the teeth.

Intensifying Action Whereas emphasizing action highlights or calls attention to something important, intensifying action increases or heightens dramatic impact. As a wave forms and then crashes, the roar of the buildup and loudness of the crash intensifies the wave's size and power. The slow, measured sound of an airplane engine becoming increasingly raspy and sputtery heightens the anticipation of its stalling and then crashing. In cartoons sound (and music) intensify the extent of a character's running, falling, crashing, skidding, chomping, and chasing.

Depicting Identity Depicting identity is, perhaps, one of the most obvious uses of sound. Barking identifies a dog, slurred speech identifies a drunk, and so on. But on a more informational level, sound can also give a character or object its own distinctive sound signature: the rattle sound of a rattlesnake to identify a slippery villain with a venomous intent; thin, clear, hard sounds to convey a cold character devoid of compassion; labored, asthmatic breathing to identify a character's constant struggle in dealing with life; the sound of a dinosaur infused into the sound of a mechanical crane to give the crane an organic character; or the sound of a "monster" with the conventional low tonal grunting, breathing, roaring, and heavily percussive clomping infused with a whimpering effect to create sympathy or affection for the "beast."

Setting Pace Sounds, or the lack of them, help set pace. The incessant, even rhythm of a machine creates a steady pace to underscore monotony. The controlled professionalism of two detectives discussing crucial evidence becomes more vital if the activity around them includes such sonic elements as footsteps moving quickly, telephones ringing, papers being shuffled, and a general hubbub of voices. Car-chase scenes get most of their pace from the sounds of screeching tires, gunned engines, and shifting gears. Sounds can also be orchestrated to produce a rhythmic effect to enhance a scene. In a gun battle, bursts can vary from *ratta tat tat* to *ratta tat,* then a few pauses, followed by *budadadada*. Additionally, sounds of the bullets hitting or ricocheting off different objects can add to not only the scene's rhythm but also its sonic variety.

Providing Counterpoint Sounds provide counterpoint when they are different from what is expected, thereby making an additional comment on the action. A judge bangs a gavel to the accompanying sound of dollar bills being peeled off, counterpointing the ideal of justice and the reality of corruption; or a smiling leader is cheered by a crowd, but instead of cheers, tortured screams are heard, belying the crowd scene.

Creating Humor Sounds can be funny. Think of *boings, boinks,* and *plops;* the swooping of a penny whistle; and the *chuga-chuga-burp-cough-chuga* of a steam engine trying to get started. Comic sounds are indispensable in cartoons in highlighting the shenanigans of their characters.

Symbolizing Meaning Sound can be used symbolically. The sound of a faucet dripping is heard when the body of a murder victim killed in a dispute over water rights is found. An elegantly decorated, but excessively reverberant, living room symbolizes the remoteness or coldness of the occupants. An inept ball team nicknamed "the Bulls" gathers in a parking lot for a road game. As the bus revs its engine, the sound is infused with the sorry bellow of a dispirited bull, comedically symbolizing the team's incompetence. A condemned prisoner walks through a steel gate that squeaks when it slams shut. Instead of just any squeak, the sound is mixed with an agonized human groan to convey his anguish.

Unifying Transition Sounds provide transitions and continuity between scenes, linking them by overlapping, leading-in, segueing, and leading out. *Overlapping* occurs when the sound used at the end of one scene continues, without pause, into the next. A speech being delivered by a candidate's spokesperson ends one scene with the words "a candidate who stands for . . ."; the next scene begins with the candidate at another location, saying "equal rights for all under law." Or the sound of a cheering crowd responding to a score in an athletic contest at the end of one scene overlaps into the next scene as the captain of the victorious team accepts the championship trophy.

A *lead-in* occurs when the audio to the next scene is heard before the scene actually begins and establishes a relationship to it. As a character thinks about a forthcoming gala event, the sounds of the gala are heard before the scene changes to the event itself. While a character gazes at a peaceful countryside, an unseen fighter plane in action is heard, anticipating and leading into the following scene, in which the same character is a jet pilot in an aerial dogfight.

A *segue*—cutting from one effect (or recording) to another with nothing in between—links scenes by abruptly changing from a sound that ends one scene to a similar sound that begins the next. As a character screams at the discovery of a dead body, the scream segues to the shriek of a train whistle; a wave crashing on a beach segues to an explosion; the sound of ripping cloth segues to the sound of a jet roar at takeoff.

Lead-out sound is audio to an outgoing scene that carries through the beginning of the following scene, but with no visual scene-to-scene relationship. A cop-and-robber car chase ends with the robber's car crashing into a gasoline pump and exploding, the repercussions of which carry over into the next scene and fade out as the cop walks up the driveway to his home. Wistful, almost muted sounds of the countryside play under a scene in which boy meets girl, with love at first sight, and fade out under the next shot showing them in a split screen sitting in their cubicles in different office buildings, staring into space.

Music

Although music has the same basic structural elements common to all sound, such as pitch, loudness, tempo, tone color, and envelope, it also contains other characteristics that broaden its perceptual and aesthetic meaning, such as melody and tonality; harmony and its qualities of consonance, dissonance, and texture; dynamic range that is quite wide compared with speech and sounds; and style in limitless variety.

Music in a production can have three uses: as production source, source, and for underscoring. *Production source music* emanates from an on-screen singer or ensemble and is produced live during shooting or in postproduction. *Source music* is background music from a stereo, radio, jukebox, and so on, and is added during post. *Underscore music* is original or library music added to enhance the informational or emotional content of a scene. Underscore music is the focus of the following discussion.

Underscoring serves picture in a number of ways. As composer Aaron Copland observed many years ago, and which still holds up today: Underscoring creates a more convincing atmosphere of time and place; it underlines psychological refinements—the unspoken thoughts of a character or situation; it serves to fill pauses between conversation; it builds a sense of continuity; it underpins dramatic buildup and gives finality to a scene.*

Functions of Music

Music performs many of the same functions in audio design that speech and sound effects perform, plus a few others, but in very different ways. One essential difference between sound effects and music in sound design is that sound effects are generally associated with action and music with reaction. This generality can be argued, of course, but it serves to provide insight into their different roles and effects. There is also the unique language, vast vocabulary, and universal resonance of music that make it so powerful and so widely applicable in aural communication.

Establishing Locale Many musical styles and themes are indigenous to particular regions. By recalling these styles and themes or by simulating a reasonable sonic facsimile, music can establish a locale such as Asia, the American West, old Vienna, Mexico, Hawaii, the city, the country, the sea, outer space, and other environments.

Emphasizing Action Music emphasizes action by defining or underscoring an event. The crash of a chord defines the impact of a fall or collision. A dramatic chord underscores shock or a moment

---

*Aaron Copland. *Our New Music* (New York: McGraw-Hill, 1941).

of decision. A romantic theme highlights that flash of attraction between lovers when their eyes first meet. Tempo increasing from slow to fast emphasizes impending danger.

Intensifying Action Music intensifies action, usually with crescendo or repetition. The scariness of sinister music builds to a climax behind a scene of sheer terror and crashes in a final, frightening chord. The repetition of a short melody, phrase, or rhythm intensifies boredom, the threat of danger, or an imminent action.

Depicting Identity Music can identify characters, events, and programs. A dark, brooding theme characterizes the "bad guy." Tender music indicates a gentle, sympathetic personality. Strong, evenly rhythmic music suggests the relentless character out to right wrongs. A particular theme played during an event identifies the event each time it is heard. Themes also have long served to identify radio and television programs, films, and personalities.

Setting Pace Music sets pace mainly through tempo and rhythm. Slow tempo suggests dignity, importance, or dullness, whereas fast tempo suggests gaiety, agility, or triviality. Changing tempo from slow to fast accelerates pace and escalates action; changing from fast to slow decelerates pace and winds down or concludes action. Regular rhythm suggests stability, monotony, or simplicity, whereas irregular (syncopated) rhythm suggests complexity, excitement, or instability.

Providing Counterpoint Music that provides counterpoint adds an idea or feeling that would not otherwise be obvious. Revelers flitting from party to party are counterpointed with music that is monotonous and empty to belie their apparent good cheer. Football players shown blocking, passing, and running are counterpointed with ballet music to underscore their grace and coordination. A man proposing to a woman is accompanied by skittish music to counterpoint the seriousness of the occasion with the insincerity of the man's intent.

Creating Humor A sliding trombone, clanking percussion, a galumping bassoon, or a cackling heckelphone can define a comic highlight or underscore its humor. For example, a bumbling jungle explorer is made all the more ridiculous by the mocking caw of a bird of paradise, or a fight is made silly, instead of violent, by adding the sounds of boings, bonks, and splats.

Unifying Transition Music is used to provide transitions between scenes for the same reasons that sounds are used: to overlap, lead in, segue, and lead out. *Overlapping* music provides continuity from one scene to the next. *Leading-in* music establishes the mood, atmosphere, locale, pace, and so on, of the next scene before it actually occurs. *Segued* music changes the mood, atmosphere, pace, subject, and so on, from one scene to the next. By gradually lowering and raising levels, music can also be used to *lead out* of a scene. A complete fade-out and fade-in makes a definite break in continuity; hence, the music used at the fade-in would be different from that used at the fade-out.

Smoothing Action Scenes In kinetic action scenes filled with quick cuts and rapid-fire sound effects, music is often used to smooth the abruptness of the shots and sounds and to create continuity.

Fixing Time Among the many uses for musical style is fixing time. Depending on the harmonic structure, the voicings in the playing ensemble, or both, it is possible to suggest the Roman era, Elizabethan England, the Roaring Twenties, the Jazz Age, the future, morning, noon, night, and so on.

Recalling or Foretelling Events If music can be used to fix a period of time, it can also be used to recall a past event or foretell a future occurrence. A theme used to underscore a tragic crash is repeated at dramatically appropriate times to recall the incident. A character begins to tell or think about the first time she saw her future husband at a party as the music that was playing during that moment is heard. A soldier kisses his girl good-bye as he goes off to war, but the background music indicates that he will not return. A budding composer looks wistfully at a secondhand piano through a pawnshop window as the strains of his most famous composition, yet to be written, are heard.

Evoking Atmosphere, Feeling, or Mood Perhaps no other form of human communication is as effective as music in providing atmosphere, feeling, or mood. There is a musical analogue for virtually every condition and emotion. Music can evoke atmospheres that are thick, unsavory, cold, sultry, and ethereal. It can evoke feelings that are obvious and easy to suggest, such as love, hate, and awe, and also subtle feelings such as friendship, estrangement, pity, and kindness. Music can convey the most obvious and the subtlest of moods: ecstasy, depression, melancholy, and amiability.

Music in Spot Announcements

Because of the effects of music on memory and emotion, it is a staple in *spot announcements*—commercials, public service announcements (PSAs), promotional announcements (promos), and jingles. The majority of *spots* incorporate music in some way. But too often, due to lack of imagination, time, or understanding of its potency, music for spots is chosen or composed carelessly, to the detriment of the message. For example, a producer using a music bed will simply grab a CD, start it playing at the beginning of the copy, and fade it out when the copy ends. Such shortsightedness is a particular handicap in a medium like radio, which has one primary sensory channel to exploit.

Well-selected music can enhance the effectiveness of a spot announcement in a number of ways:

■ Music creates mood and feeling. The purpose of most spots is to have emotional appeal. Nothing reaches the emotions as quickly or as comprehensively as music.

■ Music is memorable. Music in spots should have a simple, short, melodic line or lyric, or both—something that sticks in the mind and can be easily, even involuntarily, recalled.

■ Music gets the audience's attention. A musical spot should grab attention at the start with a compelling musical figure. It can be a catchy rhythm or phrase, percussive accents, an electronic effect, a sonic surprise, or a lyrical statement that impels an audience to listen to its resolution.

▆ Music is visual—it provokes visual images. It can set scenes in the country, at the seashore, on shipboard, on the ski slopes, and so on. By so doing, music saves precious copy time spent evoking such scenes verbally.

▆ Music can be directed to the taste of a specific audience. The type of music in a spot announcement can be suitable both to the audience to which the message is aimed and, if appropriate, to the radio station's musical format. This makes the sound of the spot at once comfortable and familiar.

▆ Music style can be matched with the product. Music for an airline can be open, spacious, and establish a floaty feeling; for a car commercial, it can evoke the feeling of power, speed, or luxury; for a perfume it can be romantic, sensuous, or elegant.

▆ Music unifies. In a series of spots emphasizing different copy points about a single product or message, the same music can be used as a thematic identifier to unify the overall campaign. Music also bonds the various elements in spots with, say, multiple copy points and two or more voices.

All that said, music in spot announcements is not always recommended—for a few reasons: (1) More copy points can be covered in a spoken announcement than in one that is sung; (2) a spot with music usually has to be aired several times before the music is remembered; and (3) music can place an announcement in a less serious light than can the spoken word.

Silence

A producer was once asked why he chose to show the explosion of the first atomic bomb test with no sound. He replied, "Silence was the most awesome sound that I could find." Silence is not generally thought of as "sound"—that seems like a contradiction in terms. But it is the pauses or silences between words, sounds, and musical notes that help create rhythm, contrast, and power—elements important to sonic communication.

In situations where we anticipate sound, silence is a particularly powerful element. Thieves break into and rob a bank with barely a sound. As the burglary progresses, silence heightens suspense to an oppressive level as we anticipate an alarm going off, a tool clattering to the floor, or a guard suddenly shouting "Freeze!" A horrifying sight compels a scream—but with the mouth wide open there is only silence, suggesting a horror that is unspeakable. Birds congregate on telephone wires, rooftops, and TV aerials and wait silently; absence of sound makes the scene eerie and unnatural.

The silence preceding sound is equally effective. Out of perfect quiet comes a wrenching scream. In the silence before dawn, there is the anticipation of the new day's sounds to come.

Silence is also effective following sound. An explosion that will destroy the enemy is set to go off. The ticking of the bomb reaches detonation time. Then, silence. Or the heightening sounds of passion build to resolution. Then, silence.

The Visual Ear

For more than four decades, the sounds of radio drama created pictures in the audience's "theater of the mind" (a characterization coined by poet Stephen Vincent Benét). Understood in the context of synaesthesia, this is not so unusual a reaction. *Synaesthesia* is the phenomenon whereby a sensory stimulus applied in one modality causes a response in another. For example, hearing a particular sound creates a distinct mental image, or seeing a certain color mentally triggers a specific sound. (There are other synaesthetic reactions not appropriate to this discussion, such as a certain smell stimulating the mental image of a particular color, or a certain sound stimulating a specific taste.) For our purpose what the synaesthetic phenomenon demonstrates is that the ear sees and the eye hears.

The implications of the power of sound to stimulate visual images is another formidable consideration in sound design. Among other things, it allows expanding the screen's dimensions. Sound is not bound by screen size as picture is. Off-screen sounds can provide added "picture" to what is seen on-screen, such as atmosphere, environment, and action, especially with surround sound. Even on-screen sound can add greater "visual" dimension to a shot. The on-screen shot shows soldiers hunkered down, waiting for the attack, but in the off-screen audio, is the rumble of tanks and the splintering of trees as the armored column crashes through woods advancing on the soldiers. (See also "Strategies in Designing Sound," later in this chapter.)

FUNCTIONS OF SOUND IN RELATION TO PICTURE

A good bit of the foregoing discussion is applicable to any audio or audiovisual medium. It has not necessarily assumed the presence or absence of picture. When picture is present, however, the sound/picture relationship creates certain dynamics that affect overall meaning. Generally, there are five relationships: (1) Sound parallels picture, (2) sound defines picture, (3) picture defines sound, (4) sound and picture define effect, and (5) sound counterpoints picture.

Sound Parallels Picture

When sound parallels picture, neither the aural nor the visual element is dominant. This function of audio in relation to picture may be the best known, because it is often misunderstood to be sound's only function. In other words, what you see is what you hear. A character knocks on a door and you hear it. An orchestra plays and you hear the music. On-screen is a raging typhoon, with mountainous waves crashing on a shore and trees bent almost horizontal by fierce winds, and in the sound track are the sounds of the storm.

This sound/picture relationship should not be dismissed as unworthy just because it is so common; not all shots require sonic augmentation.

Sound Defines Picture

When sound defines picture, audio is not only dominant, but it also determines the point of view—the subjective meaning of the image(s). Take a scene in which prison guards are standing battle-ready in front of a cellblock. A sound track consisting of crashing, breaking, yelling sounds suggests a prison riot and casts the guards as "good guys," as protectors of law and order. If the same scene were accompanied by the song "Freedom," the music then casts the prisoners sympathetically and the guards as their oppressors. The same scene augmented by a dissonant, distorted rendering of "The Star-Spangled Banner" not only conveys the idea of the guards as oppressors but also adds an element of irony.

Consider a picture showing a man apologizing to a woman for his many wrongs. Her look is stern and unforgiving. The music underscoring the scene is gentle and sympathetic, indicating her true feelings. In the same scene, if the music were light and farcical, both his past wrongs and his pleading would be defined as not very serious. Change the music to dissonant and derisive sound, and the woman's stern, unforgiving look becomes nasty and gloating.

Picture Defines Sound

Picture helps define sound by calling attention to particular actions or images. In a scene where a person walks down a city street, with traffic sounds in the background, cutting to close-ups of the traffic increases the impact of the sounds. The sound of metal wheels on a horse-drawn wagon clattering down a cobblestone street is intensified all the more when the picture changes from a medium shot of the carriage to a close-up of one of the wheels.

Sound and Picture Define Effect

When sound and picture define effect, the aural and visual elements are different yet complementary. Together they create an impact that neither could alone. Take the obvious example of a wave building and then breaking on a beach, accompanied by the swelling and crashing sounds. Separately, neither sound nor picture conveys the overall impact of the effect. Together they do. Neither sound nor picture is dominant, and although they are parallel they are reinforcing each other to produce a cumulative effect. Another example would be an elderly man sitting on a park bench, watching a mother playing with her child, lovers walking hand-in-hand, and teenagers playing touch football, accompanied by a music track that evokes a feeling first of pleasure, then of loneliness, and finally of futility. Sound and picture are complementary, with both contributing equally to an effect that would not be possible if one element were dominant or absent.

Sound Counterpoints Picture

When sound counterpoints picture, both elements contain unrelated information that creates an effect or meaning not suggested by either element alone. For example, the audio conveys the sounds of different groups of happy, laughing people, while the picture shows various shots of pollution. The audio/video counterpoint suggests an insensitive, self-indulgent society. Or consider the shot of an empty hospital bed, with the music evoking a sense of unexpected triumph. The audio/video counterpoint creates the idea that whoever had been in the bed is now, by some miracle, recovered. Change the music to sound spiritual and ascending, and the person who had been in the bed will have died and "gone to heaven."

STRATEGIES IN DESIGNING SOUND

Sound influences how we react to picture. Try watching a film or television, first with the sound off and then with the sound on but without the picture. Usually, you will find that more information comes from the sound than from the picture. Two different sound tracks for the same picture will produce two different meanings. In a very real sense, creating a sound design is often tantamount to defining a production's conceptual and emotional intent.

There is no set procedure for designing sound. At the outset the most important thing to do is study the script, determine its overall sonic concept,

if there is to be one, and analyze its auditory requirements line-by-line. When there is a director, of course it is necessary to consult. There is no right or wrong method in this type of creative decision making. For the director or sound designer, or both, decisions are often made on the intuitive basis of what "feels" best, of what "works." This is not to suggest that sound design is simply "touchy-feely." Reasoned bases should underlie determinations.

Script Analysis

Script analysis involves two things: (1) determining the overall sound design to various scenes or to an entire work and (2) *spotting*—deciding on the placement of sound effects and music.

In deciding on a sound design, the overriding questions are: How is the audience to think or feel about a particular story, character, action, or environment? And from what point of view? Moreover, is the sound design to be carried out mainly in the sound effects, the music, or both?

Some examples:

■ In a story about a reclusive, paranoid, unsuccessful writer, his environment, where there should be various sounds of life and living things, has only a few sounds, and those are spare, disjointed, reverberant, and mechanical.

■ In a story about a musician whose life and music were one, the music is constantly intertwined throughout the scenes of the musician's story.

■ In a story about the Amish, who are forbidden to use man-made, synthetic products, backgrounds and ambiences are devoid of any sounds that would be generated by those products.

■ In a story about a completely self-involved person, not hearing any background sounds wherever he is, regardless of the locale, would underscore his psychic isolation.

■ In a story that takes place in the 1930s, using audio equipment from that time to produce authentic effects and music tracks would sonically frame the story in that period.

■ In a story about the fourteenth century, using musical instruments and styles from that period in the underscoring would add to the story's authenticity.

■ In a scene showing a raging fire, designing the sonic effect of a fire on a building, such as the sound of metal warping, pipes creaking, puffy explosive *whomps,* and the roaring crackle of the fire itself would intensify the scene.

■ In a scene taking place on a neighborhood street on the hottest day of the year, the ambience is dense and the sounds of sparse traffic, people strolling, and children playing halfheartedly are muted and slowed slightly.

■ In a scene about building a car, tying the rhythm of the machines to the rhythm of the music underscoring creates a unifying gestalt.

The following radio commercial and the film or video shot provide examples of how sound design can influence meaning and, therefore, reaction.

Radio Commercial Example

The following radio commercial is for the Opulent 3QX, an expensive, full-sized luxury sedan. The target audience is affluent, suburban, college-educated, and in their late thirties to early sixties. The Modest MV is a mid-priced, family-type minivan. The target audience is in the socio-economic middle class, urban-suburban, with at least a high school education, and in their midtwenties to late thirties.

> MUSIC: UP AND UNDER
>
> ANNOUNCER:
>
> Today is a big day at your [Opulent/Modest] dealer. The exciting new [year] [Opulent 3QX/Modest MV] is on display. And as a way of saying "Come on down," your [Opulent/Modest] dealer will include an eight-year, 100,000-mile, full power-train warranty free when you purchase a new [Opulent 3QX/Modest MV] before October first. Even if you decide not to buy, there's a free gift for you just for coming down and saying hello. That's at your [Opulent 3QX/Modest MV] dealer now.
>
> MUSIC: UP TO FINISH

The commercial is straightforward, indeed routine. Yet sound can not only bring it to life, but change its impact to suit the two different audiences, even though the copy is the same.

The spot calls for an announcer and music. But what type of announcer? What kind of music? First let's discuss the announcer.

It is not enough for an announcer to have a "good" voice. The announcer's voice quality and delivery must be compatible with the content of the message. If the message is "having a good time," the announcer should sound that way, delivering the copy with a smile in the voice and buoyancy in the intonation. If the message is lighthearted or comedic, the announcer's sound should be playful, whimsical, or offbeat. A serious message is better served with a composed, perhaps cultured, delivery from a performer who sounds that way. Good announcers (and narrators) are also actors.

In selecting the announcers for the Opulent and Modest commercials, the sound designer must first consider the products themselves. The Opulent is an expensive luxury automobile usually affordable to upper-middle- and upper-class professionals with a college education and social position. The Modest, on the other hand, is generally a lower-middle- to middle-class automobile affordable to a broad group of people including blue- and white-collar workers, some with a high school education and some college educated, some with and some without social position. These two groups of consumers call for two different announcing approaches.

The announcer delivering the commercial for the Opulent may have a cultured sound: rounded-sounding vowels, deliberate pacing, stable rhythm, somewhat aloof but friendly. Among the important words to be emphasized are *new, gift,* and, of course, the product's name.

The sound for the Modest commercial would be brisker and more excited. The announcer might sound younger than the announcer for the Opulent and more like the person next door—warm, familiar, and friendly. Pacing might be quicker and rhythms syncopated. The important words to emphasize are, at least, *big, exciting, free, come on down,* and the product's name.

No doubt there are other, equally valid approaches to the commercial. The point is that, through sound design, the same words take on different meanings and address different audiences just by changing the announcer and the announcer's delivery.

Music can emphasize the differences even more. For the Opulent, perhaps an orchestra playing a bright but melodic, sophisticated theme in moderate tempo, or a small jazz ensemble playing in a light, laid-back, "cool" style would be appropriate. This would not only complement the product's image but also provide compatible counterpoint to the announcer's sound and delivery. What would not be appropriate is a rock group or a large jazz band. For the Modest, however, these alternatives might make more sense. Again, we have the same commercial, but with two different sound designs and two different messages.

The commercial could also include sound effects: a smooth-running car engine to indicate quiet comfort (Opulent) or a more aggressive sounding engine to indicate power (Modest); the approving murmur (Opulent) or the excited hubbub (Modest) of celebrants at the dealerships to complement the occasion; a sonorous (Opulent) or cheerful (Modest) car horn to punctuate a sales point.

Film or Video Example

For this example let's use one simple shot.

FADE IN

INTERIOR. BEDROOM. MAN AND WOMAN IN THEIR MIDTHIRTIES ARE SLEEPING. A DIGITAL CLOCK SHOWS 6:00. FAINT SUNLIGHT IS COMING THROUGH AN OPEN WINDOW HUNG WITH LACE CURTAINS FLUTTERING IN A BREEZE. THE CAMERA SLOWLY ZOOMS IN.

Clearly, the script's story and director's decision would govern the sound design for this shot. But the intent of this example is to demonstrate sound's significant influence on picture. Consider the shot with the following sound patterns and how each pattern influences its meaning and feel.

■ Gentle breaking of waves, sea gulls cawing listlessly

■ Gentle breaking of waves, sea gulls cawing listlessly, a squeaky door slowly opens, footsteps move deliberately over groaning floorboards

■ Waves crashing heavily against a barrier, sea gulls screeching excitedly

■ Sleeping man's breathing is labored and wheezy, reverberant battle sounds are gradually slowed in speed and lowered in pitch

■ A rooster announces the new dawn, followed by a pounding on the door

■ Increasingly gusty wind sound, thunder, and footsteps running up stairs

■ The rumble of traffic sounds, a baby's wail, the clank of a pan, and splat of something hitting the floor

■ A distant howl, a scream, then silence

■ Excited hubbub coming from outside, faint crackle of flames, horses whinnying

■ Only the sound of the faint breeze fluttering the curtains

These examples have other thematic possibilities, of course. Instead of using organic sounds, nonorganic sounds processed electronically could create different textures, moods, and environments. Nonorganic sounds are less realistic and have an otherworldly detachment; they tend to make a sound track less emotional. Conversely, organic sounds are more realistic and tend to make a sound track more emotional.

Now consider what underscoring does to the meaning of each example above, with or without the sound effects. With music that is, say, celestial, mysterious, sinister, playful, comedic, romantic, melancholy, blissful, animated, and threatening, notice how the idea and feel of each shot changes still again.

Another important factor in the sound design of this shot is how the audio cues are mixed. Mixing layers the sonic elements and establishes their balance and perspective, aspects of sound that are discussed at length in Chapter 19.

Part Three: Sound Design

Spotting

Spotting takes place at different times in the production process, because sound effects can be produced during and after shooting, whereas music is usually spotted after the picture is edited. Regardless, its purpose is the same: to decide on the placement of sound effects and music in a production.

Spotting Sound Effects

Spotting sound effects involves going through the script or edited work print and specifically noting on a spotting sheet each effect that is called for. A *spotting sheet* not only indicates the sound effect, but also whether the effect is synchronous or nonsynchronous, its in- and out-times, and its description. If the sounds have been recorded, notes about their dynamics, ambience, the way they begin and end, and any problems that require attention are also noted (see Figure 11-1).

Spotting also has to take into consideration how the effects should be "played." If there are surf sounds in a beach scene, how active and dense-sounding are the waves? In a love scene, how much clothes rustle is to be heard? At a dance is the background *walla* to be murmured, lively, or punctuated with shouts? In a dinner scene, do the sounds of plates, glasses, and cutlery continue through the scene and the various shot changes from long, to medium, to close-up? If not, to what extent do they change?

Spotting Music

In deciding when and where to spot music, there are several questions to consider:

■ How much music is there in the production?

■ Where is it used? How is silence used?

■ Where does the music enter?

■ What is the dramatic motivation for each cue?

■ Is the music used to play scenes that have important dramatic or psychological text or subtext, or is it used as filler to keep scenes from seeming too empty?

■ How does it enter—does it sneak in softly or enter loudly?

■ How does it end? What is the dramatic motivation for ending the music?*

In the process of spotting music in a production, decisions are made about the music design overall and in various segments and scenes. Overall, is the music to complement, supplement, or counterpoint the production? In action and romantic films, music generally plays a major role in underscoring events. In fact, in action stories there is often more reliance on music (and sound effects) than there is on dialogue to generate the impact. In a love story, is the music to be emotionally "hot" and aggressive or "cool" and restrained? By what type of an ensemble—orchestral, jazz, chamber—is it to be played and therefore colored?

In choosing to use music already familiar to an audience from commercial recordings, for example, for the sake of the story it is wise to have an aesthetic rationale. Familiar music carries with it the baggage of association, which can detract from a drama's impact. Of course, the rationale to use popular music may be motivated solely by the financial prospect of selling CDs of the sound track, which does not necessarily serve the story. Regardless, when familiar music is used, songs in particular, it makes a big difference to the success of the storytelling when the music is interpretive and not just a commercial embellishment.

Decisions related to segments include the main title and pivotal scenes throughout a production. Main title music usually provides clues about what type of story it is going to be or what type of characters are in it. Lively, quirky main title music tells you to expect a comedy. If it is a horror story, spooky-sounding music is appropriate. Perhaps the main title theme is neutral so as not to tip off the audience about the psychological thriller to come. Maybe there is no main title music, or little music throughout a drama, to allow the audience to

---

*From Fred Karlin, *Listening to Movies* (New York: Schirmer Books, 1994).

SPOTTING SHEET

Project Title _____ *The Event* _____ Page Number __4 of 6__

Spotter _____ *A.M.* _____ Date Prepared __10/21__

Item	Syn/Nonsync	In-time	Out-time	Description
1	NS	01:42:15:10	01:43:12:09	Airplanes taking off
2	NS	01:45:26:29	01:46:15:12	Muddled voices
3	S	01:49:52:12		Door slamming
4	NS	01:49:52:12	01:53:05:05	Traffic noises
5	NS	01:54:03:27	01:56:22:17	Restaurant noises
6	S	01:56:13:25		Gunshot
7	NS	02:03:14:23	02:04:03:10	Phone ringing
8	NS	02:10:52:12	02:11:01:24	Glass breaking
9	NS	02:11:27:03	02:12:04:19	Dog barking
10	S	02:12:46:18		Glass breaking
11	NS	02:15:33:16		Thunder
12	NS	02:16:12:15	02:19:22:04	Rain, wind, and thunder
13	S	02:21:45:23		Car backfiring
14	NS	02:21:50:20	02:23:47:04	Children playing
15	NS	02:23:47:04	02:26:33:12	Ocean waves
16	NS	02:24:55:23		Thunder
17	NS	02:26:10:10		Thunder
18	S	02:30:12:14		Hit glass
19	NS	02:33:05:06	02:34:55:07	Dogs barking
20	NS	02:35:12:14		Door slamming
21	S	02:36:36:11		Door slamming

11-1 Example of a spotting sheet listing the sound effects required for a production

develop their own opinions about where the events are taking them.

In spotting individual scenes, decisions are made about whether music should enter before or after a character says a line; whether it should carry through the scene or punctuate its most dramatic aspects; whether it should be melancholy, stirring, romantic, threatening, heroic, and so on.

When and Where to Place Music Deciding where music cues should start, fade under, and stop is perhaps the most challenging decision of all. There are no rules, only guidelines, in underscoring music, so decisions about when and where to incorporate it are as varied as the productions that use music and the creativity of spotting teams. With that caveat, in the most general way, spotters have made certain observations about when and where to place music:

■ It is better to bridge into a scene from a previous line of dialogue, or come into the scene a bit later under a line of dialogue or under an action from a character, than it is to start music on a scene change.

■ If music starts within a scene, usually it should not be fragmented; it should play through the scene. There are scenes, however, in which stopping the music can heighten a dramatic action, after which the underscoring may continue, not continue, or change.

■ It is less obvious, less intrusive, and more effective to start music at the moment when emphasis shifts, such as a scene change, a camera movement, or a reaction shot.

■ In covering the entrance of a music cue so that it is unobtrusive, it can be sneaked in or distracted from by some visual action.

■ In action scenes with music and considerable sound effects, either the sound effects should play over the music or vice versa to avoid sonic muddle and confusing the action's emphasis and point of view.

■ Perhaps music is easiest to spot when it covers scenes without dialogue. Simplified, this means: music up when they kiss and down when they talk.

■ Trust your instincts. Look at the piece many times, until you have some kind of response—cerebral or emotional. If after many viewings nothing occurs to you, maybe instinct is suggesting that the scene does not need music.

When spotting music it is always best to do it with the composer, music editor, and director present. Whether the score is original or taken from a music library, underscoring is so much a matter of intuition, taste, and biases that final decisions are better made in consultation than individually. Even when one person has the final say, the ideas, reactions, and perspectives from the other spotters provide a far more wide-ranging basis for decision making.

MAIN POINTS

▶ Sound design is the process of creating the overall sonic character of a production (usually in relation to picture).

▶ The sound designer is responsible for creative control of the audio—to put a coherent sonic stamp on a production—although all members of the audio team make creative contributions to the sound.

▶ Sound can be grouped into three categories: speech, sound effects, and music. All sound is made up of the same basic components: pitch, loudness, timbre, tempo, rhythm, attack, duration, and decay.

▶ Meaning in speech can be communicated verbally and nonverbally.

▶ Speech has two basic functions: narration—direct, indirect, or contrapuntal—and dialogue.

▶ Nonverbal meaning in speech can be communicated through accent, pace, dialogue patterns, emphasis, inflection, and aural mood.

▶ Sound effects perform two general functions: contextual and narrative. Contextual sound is also known as diegetic sound. Narrative sounds can be descriptive or commentative.

▶ Sound effects and music can define space, focus attention, establish locale, create environment, emphasize and intensify action, depict identity, set pace, provide counterpoint, create humor, symbolize meaning, and unify transition.

- A production may have three types of music: production source, source, and underscore.

- Production source music emanates from a primary on-screen source. Source music is background music from an on-screen source. Underscore music is original or library music added to enhance a scene's content.

- Well-selected music in spot announcements can enhance the effectiveness of the message in a number of ways. There are instances, however, when music in spots can distract from the message.

- Silence can be used to enhance sonic effect, particularly in situations where sound is expected or anticipated.

- Sound also has a visual component in that it can create pictures in "the theater of the mind."

- Sound has several functions in relation to picture: Sound can parallel picture; sound can define picture; picture can define sound; sound and picture can define effect; and sound can counterpoint picture.

- There is no set procedure for designing sound, but thorough script analysis goes a long way in facilitating decision making.

- Script analysis involves determining the overall sound design for various scenes or for an entire work, and spotting—deciding on the placement of sound effects and music in a production.

- Determining a sound design involves consideration of how the audience is to think or feel about a particular story, scene, character, or action; from what point of view; and whether that is to be carried out mainly in the sound effects or music or both.

- Determining a sound design also requires the awareness that doing so is often tantamount to defining a production's conceptual and emotional intent.

12

Studio Production: Live and Live-on-Tape

The principal difference between live programs and those done *live-on-tape*—recorded but run as though it were a live show—and material produced for later release, aside from the broadcast or distribution date, is postproduction. Live programs are processed, "edited," and mixed during broadcast or recording. Audio is similarly handled during live-on-tape production, but with some leeway for post, although postproduction time is limited due to an imminent or relatively imminent broadcast deadline. Material for later release is produced with postproduction in mind.

This chapter focuses on live and live-on-tape studio production for radio and multicamera television. Chapter 13 covers live and live-on-tape field production for radio, single-camera, and multicamera television. Chapter 14 deals with multi- and single-camera staged productions for TV and film, which are usually produced for later release.

SOUND AND THE SPEAKING VOICE

The production chain generally begins with the performer—announcer, disc jockey, newscaster, actor, interviewer/interviewee, and so on—and therefore involves considerations that relate to producing speech. How that speech is handled depends on four factors: (1) the type of program or production—disc jockey, news, commercial, drama, and so on; (2) whether it is produced on radio or, as in the case of film and television, using the single- or multicamera technique; (3) whether it is done in the studio or in the field; and (4) whether it is live, live-on-tape, or produced for later release.

Frequency Range

The frequency range of the human speaking voice, compared with that of some musical instruments, is not wide (see the diagram on the inside front cover). Fundamental voicing frequencies produced by the adult male are from roughly 80 to 240 Hz; for the adult female they are from roughly 140 to 500 Hz. Harmonics and overtones carry these ranges somewhat higher. (Ranges for the singing voice are significantly wider—see Chapter 15.)

Despite these relatively narrow ranges, its harmonic richness makes the human voice a highly complex instrument. Frequency content varies with the amount of vocal effort used. Changes in loudness and intensity change pitch. Loud speech boosts the midrange frequencies and reduces the bass frequencies, thus raising overall pitch. Quiet speech reduces the midrange frequencies, lowering overall pitch.

In relation to the recording/playback process, if speech (and audio in general) is played back at a level louder than originally recorded, as is possible in radio and film, the lower-end frequencies will be disproportionately louder. If speech (and audio in general) is played back at a quieter level than originally recorded, as is possible in radio and TV, the lower-end frequencies will be disproportionately quieter.

Regardless of the dynamic range in voicing sounds, speech must be intelligible while maintaining natural voice quality. Moreover, in audio production speech must also be relatively noise-free. Although background noise does not affect speech intelligibility when the noise level is 25 dB below the speech level, such a signal-to-noise (S/N) ratio is still professionally unacceptable. Even when the S/N ratio is adequate, other factors, such as distance between speaker and listener, the listener's hearing acuity, and other sounds, can adversely affect speech intelligibility. These factors as they relate to aural perception in general are discussed elsewhere in this book. Two other influences on speech intelligibility—sound level and distribution of spectral content—are covered in the following sections.

Sound Level

Speech intelligibility is at a maximum when levels are about 70 to 90 dB-SPL. At higher levels intelligibility declines slightly. It also declines below 70 dB-SPL and falls off rapidly under about 40 dB-SPL. Distance between speaker and listener also affects intelligibility: As distance increases, intelligibility decreases (see the discussion of the inverse square law in Chapter 13).

Distribution of Spectral Content

Each octave in the audible frequency spectrum contributes a particular sonic attribute to a sound's overall quality (see Chapter 2 and the diagram on the inside back cover). In speech certain frequencies are more critical to intelligibility than others. For example, an absence of frequencies above 600 Hz adversely affects the intelligibility of consonants; an absence of frequencies below 600 Hz adversely affects the intelligibility of vowels.

Various procedures have been developed to evaluate and predict speech intelligibility. One such procedure is based on the relative contribution to intelligibility by various frequencies across one-third and full-octave ranges (see Table 12-1).

BASIC CONSIDERATIONS IN MIKING SPEECH

One of the most important and generally subjective influences on sound shaping is microphone selection and placement. Microphones directly affect the quality of recorded or transmitted sound. But because no two audio people achieve their results in exactly the same way, there can be no hard-and-fast rules about selecting and positioning microphones. The purpose of discussing microphone technique in this and subsequent chapters is to suggest possible approaches, nothing more,

Table 12-1 Percentage of contribution to speech intelligibility by various frequency ranges

Band Center Frequency (Hz)	Percentage of Contribution	
	One-third Octave	Full Octave
200 and below	1.2	
250	3.0	7.2
315	3.0	
400	4.2	
500	4.2	14.4
680	6.0	
800	6.0	
1,000	7.2	22.2
1,250	9.0	
1,600	11.2	
2,000	11.4	32.8
2,500	10.2	
3,150	10.2	
4,000	7.2	23.4
5,000 and above	6.0	

Source: From the American National Standards Institute (ANSI).

using as examples the types of situations you are most likely to encounter.

Phase and Polarity

Before moving on, it is necessary to say a word about phase and polarity. In acoustics *phase* is the time relationship between two or more sound waves at a given point in their cycles (see Chapter 2). In electricity *polarity* is the relative position of two signal leads—the high (+) and the low (–)—in the same circuit.

Phase

Phase is an important acoustic consideration in microphone placement. If sound sources are not properly placed in relation to microphones, sound waves can reach the mics at different times and be out of phase. For example, sound waves from a source (performer or musical instrument) that is slightly off center between two spaced microphones will reach one mic a short time before or after they reach the other mic, causing some cancellation of sound. Perceiving sounds that are considerably out of phase is relatively easy: When you should hear sound, you hear little or none. Perceiving sounds that are only a little out of phase is not so easy.

By changing relative time relationships between given points in the cycles of two waves, a *phase shift* occurs. Phase shift is referred to as *delay* when it is equal in time at all frequencies. Delay produces a variety of out-of-phase effects that are useful to the recordist (see Chapter 9). To detect unwanted phase shift, however, listen for the following: unequal levels in frequency response, particularly in the bass and midrange; slightly unstable, wishy-washy sound; or a sound source that is slightly out of position in relation to where it should be in the aural frame.

One way to avoid phase problems with microphones is to follow the *three-to-one rule*—place no two microphones closer together than three times the distance between one of them and its sound source. If one mic is 2 inches from a sound source, for example, the nearest other mic should be no closer to the first mic than 6 inches; if one mic is 3 feet from a sound source, the nearest other mic should be no closer than 9 feet to the first; and so on (see Figure 12-1).

If a sound source emits loud levels, it might be necessary to increase the ratio between microphones to 4 to 1 or even 5 to 1. Quiet levels may facilitate microphone placement closer than that prescribed by a ratio of 3 to 1.

Phasing problems can also be caused by reflections from surfaces close to a microphone bouncing back into the mic's pickup. This condition is discussed in "Miking Speech in Radio" later in this chapter.

Polarity

Signals in a microphone circuit that are electrically out of polarity, depending on degree, considerably reduce sound quality or cancel the sound altogether. A common cause of mics being out of polarity is incorrect wiring of the microphone plugs. Male and female XLR connectors used for most mics have three pins: a ground, a positive pin for high output,

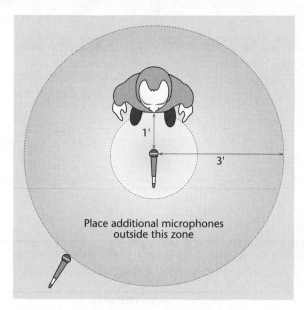

12-1 The three-to-one rule. Most phasing problems generated by improper microphone placement can be avoided by placing no two microphones closer together than three times the distance between one of them and its sound source.

In the figure: 1' · 3' · Place additional microphones outside this zone

and a negative pin for low output. (XLR five-pin connectors are used for stereo microphones.) Mic cables house three coded wires. All mics in the same facility must have the same-number pin connected to the same-color wire. If they do not and are used simultaneously, they will be electrically out of polarity.

To check the polarity of two mics, first make sure that both are delegated to the same output channel. Adjust the level for a normal reading as someone speaks into a mic. Turn down the fader and repeat the procedure with another mic. Then open both mics to the normal settings. If the meter reading decreases when the levels of both mics are turned up, there is a polarity problem.

The obvious way to correct this condition is to rewire the equipment, assuming the problem is not in the mic itself. If there is no time for that, most multichannel consoles have a polarity reversal control that reverses polarity by 180 degrees (see 5-2).

Moving-Coil Versus Capacitor Microphones

In deciding what type of microphone to use, the choice, usually, will be between a moving-coil and a capacitor mic. Often circumstances make the decision for you. For example, if it is necessary to record at a high loudness, the moving-coil would likely be the mic of choice; if transient sounds are important, the likely choice is the capacitor mic. If there is an option between choosing either type of mic, remember that each has particular attributes (see "General Transducer Performance Characteristics" in Chapter 4).

Omnidirectional Versus Unidirectional Microphones

Another common decision in microphone selection is deciding what directional pattern to choose. Usually, the choice is between an omnidirectional and a unidirectional mic. Again, circumstances sometimes make the decision for you. In a noisy environment, a unidirectional microphone discriminates against unwanted sound better than does an omnidirectional mic; to achieve a more open sound, the omnidirectional mic is the better choice. If there is an option of choosing either pickup pattern, each has certain advantages and disadvantages, depending on the demands of a given situation (see Tables 12-2 and 12-3).

Based on the differences detailed in Tables 12-2 and 12-3, the omnidirectional pickup pattern seems to be the more useful of the two. In fact, unidirectional mics are far more widely used, which does not necessarily suggest that they are better. As it is with the choice between moving-coil and capacitor mics, so it is with deciding between an omni- and a unidirectional mic: A microphone's suitability depends on sonic need, not on favoritism.

MIKING SPEECH IN RADIO

Radio performers are for the most part stationary. Whether they are seated or standing, microphone positioning during a broadcast changes relatively

Table 12-2 The omnidirectional microphone

Advantages	Disadvantages
Does not have to be held directly in front of the mouth to provide adequate pickup	Does not discriminate against unwanted sound
Does not reflect slight changes in the mic-to-source distance	Is difficult to use in noisy environments
Gives a sense of the environment	Presents greater danger of feedback in reverberant location
Is less susceptible to wind, popping, and handling noises	
Is not subject to the proximity effect	
Is natural sounding in rooms with good acoustics	

Table 12-3 The unidirectional microphone

Advantages	Disadvantages
Discriminates against unwanted sound	Must be angled correctly to the mouth, or the performer will be off-mic
Gives little or no sense of the environment (which could also be a disadvantage)	May be subject to the proximity effect
Significantly reduces the danger of feedback in reverberant locations	Is susceptible to wind and popping, unless there is a pop filter
	Is more susceptible to handling noises
	Requires care not to cover the ports, if handheld
	Is less natural sounding in rooms with good acoustics

little. When performers do change it, it is usually to adjust for a small shift in their position. Under these apparently straightforward circumstances, however, there are a number of miking techniques to consider.

Single Speaker

In radio, positioning a microphone in front of a seated or standing performer—disc jockey, newscaster, talk-show host, guest—is the most common miking placement. The mic usually is mounted on a flexible swivel stand suspended in front of the performer (see 12-2); sometimes it is on a table stand (see 12-3).

In selecting and positioning the mic, it is important to keep excessive sound that is reflected from room surfaces, furniture, and equipment from reaching the mic. This can result in comb filtering, creating a hollow sound quality.

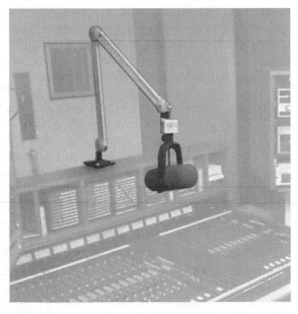

12-2 Microphone mounted on a flexible swivel stand

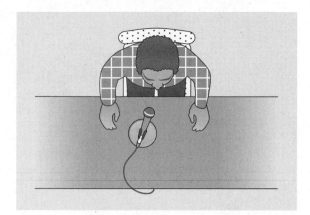

12-3 Performer speaking into a microphone mounted on a desk stand

To minimize sound reflections reaching the microphone, a performer should work at a relatively close mic-to-source distance and use a directional microphone. How directional depends on how much front-to-rear sound rejection is needed. Keep in mind that the more directional the mic, the more restricted the side-to-side movement. Because radio studios are acoustically quiet, there is little need for highly directional mics, unless more than a few speakers are using microphones in close proximity. Therefore, the cardioid pattern is most commonly used. It allows relatively wide side-to-side movement, yet its directional pickup produces the intimate sound essential to creating radio's lip-to-ear rapport with the listener. A problem with using too directional a mic is the usually drier and more closed sound it produces.

It is difficult to suggest an optimal mic-to-source working distance, because voice projection and timbre vary from person to person. Here are a few guidelines:

☑ Always stay within the mic's pickup pattern.

☑ Maintain voice level between 60 and 100 percent of modulation; some stations like it between 80 and 100.

☑ Working too close to a microphone may create sound that is devoid of ambience and is oppressive and unnatural.

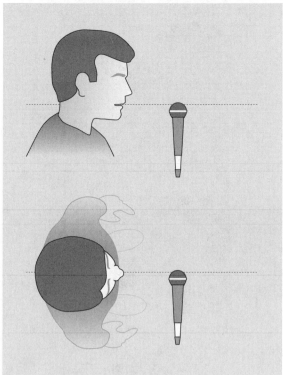

12-4 Directional microphone positioned so that the performer speaks across the mic face. This placement may reduce popping and sibilance, but it also reduces the frequency response. Sound reaches the microphone from off-axis.

☑ Working too close to a mic emphasizes tongue movement, lip smacking, and teeth clicks. It could also create proximity effect.

☑ Working too far from a mic diffuses the sound quality, creating spatial distance between performer and listener.

Sometimes a microphone is positioned to the side of or under a performer's mouth, with the performer speaking across the mic face (see 12-4). Usually this is done to reduce the popping and sibilance that often occur when a performer talks directly into a mic.

Speaking across a directional microphone can reduce these unwanted sounds. Unless the mouth-to-mic angle is within the microphone's pickup

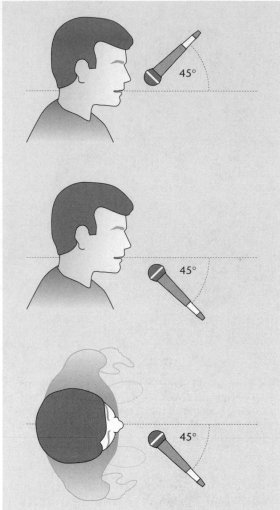

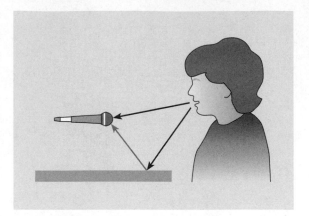

12-6 Incorrect placement of microphone. Indirect sound waves reflecting back into a mic cause phase cancellations that degrade the response. To avoid this, a microphone should not be placed parallel to or more than a few inches from a reflective surface.

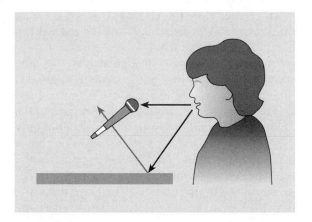

12-5 Speaking at a 45-degree angle into a directional mic. This reduces popping and sibilance.

12-7 Correct placement of microphone. Placing a microphone at an angle to a reflective surface reduces indirect sound bouncing back into the mic.

pattern, however, talking across the mic degrades the response. To eliminate popping and reduce sibilance without overly degrading the response, (1) use a windscreen, (2) use a microphone with a built-in pop filter, or (3) point the mic at about a 45-degree angle above, below, or to the side of the performer's mouth, depending on the mic's pickup pattern (see 12-5).

In positioning a mic, make sure that its head is not parallel to or facing the tabletop. Remember that the angle of a sound's incidence is equal to its angle of reflectance in midrange and treble frequencies (see 3-8). Therefore sound waves bouncing from the table will reflect back into the mic's pickup pattern, creating the comb-filter effect. Any hard surface that is close to a mic, such as a table, console, computer monitor, or window, should be angled so that the sound waves do not reflect directly into the mic (see 12-6 and 12-7). When changing the microphone's angle presents a problem, if possible cover the hard surface with a soft material to absorb most of the unwanted reflections.

It is also a good idea to mount the microphone in a shock absorber, if it does not have one built-in. This reduces or eliminates jarring and handling noises.

Space and Perspective: Monaural and Stereo Sound

AM and FM radio are broadcast in stereo, yet talent is still miked monaurally. In monaural sound, aural space is one-dimensional—that is, perceived in terms of depth—so perspective is near-to-far. Reverberation notwithstanding, the closer a microphone is placed to a sound source, the closer to the audience the sound source is perceived to be; the farther a microphone is placed from a sound source, the farther from the audience the sound source is perceived to be. If the microphone is omnidirectional, both the closer and more distant sounds are perceived as more open than if the mic is directional; a directional microphone reproduces a closer, tighter sound.

In stereo sound, aural space is two-dimensional—that is, perceived in terms of depth and breadth—so perspectives are near-to-far and side-to-side. Moreover, stereo space includes more ambience than does monaural space. Stereo miking involves using either two microphones or a stereo mic (see "Stereo Microphone Technique" in Chapter 14 and "Off-Miking with Stereo Microphone Arrays" in Chapter 15).

Stereo radio transmission and reception have little effect on single-speaker miking; talent is still miked with one microphone. If the performer is not sonically "stage-center," localization is disconcerting to the listener. Stereo sound in stereo radio is in the music and often in the spot announcements as well, but not in the spatial positioning of the talent.

Interview and Panel

When there is more than one speaker, as in interview and panel programs, it is customary today to mike each participant with a separate microphone for better sonic control. Directional

microphones, usually cardioid or supercardioid, are preferred. If the participants are sitting opposite one another, the cardioid is sufficient because it is least sensitive at 180 degrees off-axis. If the participants are sitting side-by-side, facing the host, the supercardioid could be a better choice. Its on-axis response allows sufficient side-to-side head movement, and it is less sensitive at the sides than the cardioid. The hypercardioid mic would also work in the latter situation, but there are the potential problems of restricted head movement, due to its quite narrow on-axis pickup, and of reduced sound quality, because of its poorer rejection at 180 degrees. In any case, microphones are commonly fixed to flexible mic mounts to free frontal working space and to make minor positioning adjustments easier (see 12-8).

When more than one microphone is used, they must have the same directional pattern. Mics with different polar patterns, say, a cardioid mic used with a supercardioid mic, will have perceptible sonic differences. With the cardioid and supercardioid mics, for example, the cardioid will produce a more open sound than the supercardioid; or, to put it

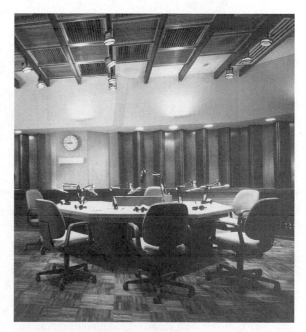

12-8 Radio talk/interview studio

another way, the supercardioid will sound tighter than the cardioid.

In miking a radio program with two or more participants, usually the host and guests are in the studio and an operator is in the control room, or the host operates the control panel in the studio at the table where the guests are sitting. The studio control panel can usually handle telephone feeds for listener call-in, as well. Some radio stations even put a simple control console at the guest stations. In both situations, host and guests have their own directional microphones or, as is often the case with telephone call-in programs, headset mics. A headset mic facilitates the feeding and balancing of all program information to each participant, reduces problems of microphone placement, allows host and guests more freedom of movement, and clears desk space for scripts and note taking. Because it is radio, appearance is of no concern, except that the participants must be comfortably and sensibly arranged for optimal interaction (see 12-9).

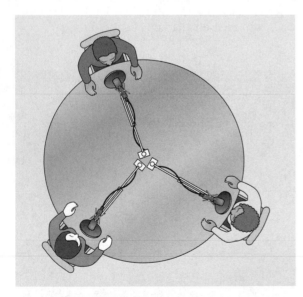

12-9 Example of an arrangement for a radio panel program. Because in radio there is less concern for appearance on the set, microphones can be selected and arranged primarily for sound quality, without inconveniencing the panelists, of course. This illustration is based on an actual arrangement using high-quality Neumann U-87 multidirectional microphones, set on the cardioid pickup pattern, and fabric windscreens.

PRODUCING A RADIO STATION'S SOUND

The overall sound of a station is another aspect of studio production in radio. It involves the particular music or talk format, announcer's delivery style, production style of the spot announcements and jingles, and how tightly presented they all are. There are far too many radio formats—roughly 30 and counting—to deal with all of them here (see Table 12-4). To provide a sense of how format and production approach interrelate to give a station its distinctive sound, here is a brief profile of four popular music formats: contemporary hit radio, adult contemporary, country, and easy listening.

Contemporary Hit Radio

A typical contemporary hit radio (CHR) station (also known as *current hit radio* and *Top 40*) plays only top-selling songs announced by dynamic, fast-paced, but friendly disc jockeys, with songs, spot announcements, and chatter presented at a tight, brisk clip. Spots and the music beds in them are energetic.

Adult Contemporary

Adult contemporary (AC) stations play pop standards, called *currents,* recent hits, *recurrents,* and *oldies.* Usually, there is no hard rock or any music with a driving, pronounced beat, although some stations adapt their AC format to soft rock. Disc jockeys are bright and pleasant, with chatter kept to a minimum. The tempo of spot announcements and their music beds is sonically consistent with the format's overall sound. Most AC formats are blocked; that is, music is grouped in uninterrupted segments, and spots are clustered among the music sweeps. How long the grouped music segments are, within an hour, is determined by the number of spots there are to be aired.

Country

Obviously, country stations highlight country-and-western music. But any similarities in format

Table 12-4 Popular radio formats

Adult contemporary (AC)	Modern adult contemporary
Adult hits (hot adult contemporary)	New rock/modern rock
Adult standards	News/talk
Alternative rock	Oldies
Black gospel	Preteen
Classic hits	Rap
Classic rock	Religion (teaching, variety)
Classical, fine arts	Rock
Comedy	Soft adult contemporary
Contemporary Christian	Southern gospel
Contemporary hit radio (CHR)	Spanish
Country	Sports
Easy listening	Top 40
Gospel	Urban rhythm-and-blues (R&B)
Jazz	Variety
Lite adult contemporary	

approaches end there. Some country stations feature fast-paced music, others use music that is more deliberately paced; some emphasize air personalities, others deemphasize them. In most cases, announcing is warm and friendly and, for the most part, kept free of southern accents or other pronounced regionalisms. Because the format has widespread appeal, spot announcements do not conform to a "rural" sound, but to whatever sells to the station's particular audience demographics. Production is usually tight, but not hyped or aggressive.

Easy Listening

As the term suggests, easy listening stations play melodic, slow- to medium-tempo music. Disc jockeys are warm, friendly, and credible. Chatter is easygoing and kept to a minimum. Spots are more soft sell than hard sell. Pronounced hard rhythms or beats in bed music are rare, as are heavily produced spots using sound effects, multiple voices, and so on. Production is smooth, with no jarring transitions from song to song or spot to spot. In

fact, music is often programmed so that segued songs are in compatible keys (see 18-22).

MIKING SPEECH FOR MULTICAMERA TELEVISION

Television productions aired live or live-on-tape generally use the multicamera approach. By employing two or more cameras and feeding the signals to a switching console, a shot from one camera can be broadcast (or taped) while other cameras prepare the next shots—in essence, "editing as you go." Sound is similarly handled during live or live-on-tape production. Post-production time is limited due to an imminent or relatively imminent broadcast deadline. Programs such as news, sports, interview, panel, talk, and game shows, awards shows, and parades are carried live or live-on-tape and use the multicamera production technique.

Productions that do not have an imminent release deadline, such as theatrical TV dramas, films made for television, magazine programs, and commercials, frequently use the single-camera production method. Scenes are shot one at a time—first from a general perspective and then from various individual perspectives. These different views are edited during postproduction into a meaningful sequence of events to build the structure and create the pace. It is also in postproduction that dialogue and sound effects are recorded or rerecorded, if necessary, and music is added.

This categorizing is not to imply hard-and-fast production conventions; they are simply generalizations. For example, episodes of soap operas are shot well in advance of their broadcast dates yet use the multicamera camera approach. Commercials shot in studios, as opposed to on location, often use the multicamera technique.

News and Interview Programs

In news and interview programs, the participants are usually seated at a desk or in an open set. The mic almost universally used in these situations is the omnidirectional capacitor mini-mic. It is unobtrusive and easy to mount; its sound quality with speech is excellent; and the omnidirectional pickup pattern ensures that ambience is natural and that a performer will stay on-mic regardless of head movement. If background sound is troublesome, which is unlikely in a broadcast studio, the directional mini-mic is a suitable alternative. Generally, for optimal sound pickup, the recommended placement for a mini-mic is in the area of the wearer's sternum—hooked to a tie, shirt, or dress—6 to 8 inches from the chin. Frequently, the mic is attached to the lapel, but beware of getting it too close to the mouth or the sound may be too dry.

Although the mini-mic is unobtrusive, a few directors prefer to make it even more low profile by hiding the mic cord underneath the performer's clothing. This is usually done with a specially designed belt clip to keep the mic in position, isolate it from the rest of its cord, and reduce the sound of clothes rustling, which the cord often picks up through mechanical conductance. Most directors, however, are unconcerned about the mic cord showing, because today's audiences accept it as a natural part of the picture.

Sometimes the mic itself is hidden underneath clothing. Unless it is important that the mic not be seen, as in drama, this is usually not a good idea. Clothing inhibits higher frequencies (shorter wavelengths) from reaching the mic and, thereby, can degrade the sound quality. Also, some mini-mics are even more sensitive to the sound of clothes rustling than is the cord. (See also "Using Wireless Body Microphones" in Chapter 14.) These problems can be avoided if performers wear the proper clothing. Cotton clothing does not make much rustling sound; polyester, rayon, and dacron do. Test different clothing samples to determine which generate the least rustling noise. It is also important to keep a mini-mic from knocking against jewelry, such as tie clips or necklaces, that performers may wear.

Because the mini-mic's cord can pick up rubbing sounds from movements, be careful when miking a performer, such as a weathercaster, who moves about within a small set. The performer should use a belt clip, leave enough play in the mic cord so it drags across the floor as little as possible, and avoid sudden, wrenching motions. If the mic cord is put underneath a pant leg or dress to keep it out of sight, it is a good idea to tape it to the leg to reduce rustling sounds.

Why, then, do some newscasters wear two mini-mics, when the general goal is to keep them unobtrusive? Because the microphones are capacitors, and one is simply for backup in case the on-air mic fails.

Having said all this, directors avoid most of the problems associated with wired mini-mics—belt clips, visible mic cords, constrained movement, and so on—by using wireless microphone systems on the set, if not for seated talent then certainly for the moving performers, such as the weathercaster. The wireless mic system is cordless, it can be easily used with a mini-mic, and, in a controlled studio environment, it is normally free of interference problems (see Chapter 4).

In interview programs the host sometimes sits behind a mic mounted on a desk stand. In many instances the mic is not live. It is being used as a set piece to create a closer psychological rapport between the host and the television audience or to fill the open table space in front of the host, or both. Otherwise, with a few exceptions, desk mics are seldom used.

If you do use a live desk mic, select one that is good-looking so it does not call attention to itself; use one with a built-in shock mount to isolate the mic from desk noises; and make sure the mic-to-source angle is on-axis.

Panel and Talk Programs

Television panel and talk programs employ a few basic set arrangements. When the host or moderator is seated, guests sit in a line either diagonal to and facing the host, or, if an audience is participating in the show, the guests sit in a horizontal line facing the audience and the host moves between them and the audience. Sometimes the set design is in the shape of an inverted ∪. The moderator sits at the top center of the ∪, with the interviewers usually to the moderator's right and the guest(s) to the moderator's left across from the interviewers. Or panel participants might sit in a semicircle with the moderator opposite them at the center of the semicircle.

Choosing a Microphone

In most circumstances, for host and guest alike, the mini-mic's multiple advantages make it the microphone of choice:

■ It is unobtrusive and tends to disappear on-camera.

■ It is easy to mount.

■ It is easily adaptable to use with a wireless system, which is how it is usually employed.

■ It keeps the mic-to-source distance constant.

■ It reduces the need for frequent loudness adjustments once the levels have been set.

■ It requires no special lighting or additional audio operator, as does a boom mic.

■ It enables participants to be placed comfortably in a set without concern for keeping the mic, such as a boom mic, out of the picture.

The mini-mic's main disadvantage is that it's a single-purpose microphone. It rarely sounds good used away from the body.

There are situations in panel and talk programs in which microphone mounts, other than the body-positioned mini-mic, are preferred. For a host moving about a set among guests or going into the audience for questions, the handheld mic is the popular choice. In situations where the studio is very large and the audience is seated amphitheater-style, except for overall coverage mics of the audience sound, handheld mics are the only choice for host, guests, and audience participants.

The handheld microphone has these advantages:

■ It allows the host to control the audience questioning.

■ It allows the host to control mic-to-source distances.

■ Like the desk mic, it helps the host generate a closer psychological rapport with the television audience.

When using the handheld microphone, it should have a built-in pop filter to minimize sibilance and popping, and an internal shock mount to eliminate handling noise. Optimal position is about 6 to 12 inches from the mouth, pointing upward at about a 45-degree angle (see 12-10).

A disadvantage of the handheld mic is that it ties up one of the host's hands. This is not a problem with the boom mic, and for some situations that is the mic of choice.

When guests are coming and going during the course of a show, for example, the boom mic is often used once they are seated. It is less awkward than having a guest put on and take off a mini-mic on camera, or having a guest hold a mic. Usually no more than a few guests are seated on the set at any one time, which allows one boom to cover the group adequately. Generally, in this type of situation, the host uses a live desk mic for several reasons: (1) to set the host apart from the guests, (2) to enhance, psychologically, the rapport with the television audience, and (3) to avoid the lighting and logistical problems that result from having two booms on a set in close proximity.

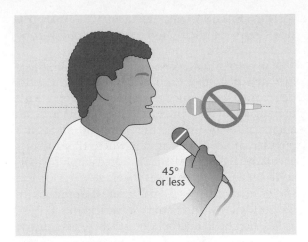

12-10 Handheld microphone positioning. Ideally, a handheld microphone should be positioned 6 to 12 inches from the user's mouth, at an angle of 45 degrees or less. Positioning the microphone at an angle of about 90 degrees may result in popping sounds when consonants like *p* and *t* are pronounced.

Whenever one boom covers two or more people in conversation, the boom operator has to make sure that none of the program's content is inaudible or off-mic. A good boom operator must therefore quickly learn the speech rhythms and inflections of the people talking, listen to their conversations, anticipate the nonverbal vocal cues that signal a change in speaker, and, when the change occurs, move the mic from one speaker to another quickly and silently.

If performers are seated, there is little need to do anything but rotate the mic itself. If performers are mobile, moving the boom arm and extending and retracting it are also important aspects of good boom operation (see Chapter 14).

Controlling Multiple Sound Sources

Individually miking several program participants can be a challenge for the console operator trying to control various levels simultaneously, especially when other sound sources such as the announcer, bumper (intro and outro) music, and recorded spot announcements are also part of the operator's program responsibilities. It is best to use as few mics as possible in a given situation to reduce system noise, phasing, and coordination problems. But with the multichannel console and sophisticated signal processing, many recordists prefer separate control of each sound source to more conservative miking techniques. To help reduce the problems associated with controlling multiple, simultaneous microphone voice feeds, the console operator has a number of options.

One option is to put a moderate limit or some compression on each mic, once levels are set. With the mini-mic and handheld mics, the proximity of the mic to the speaker's mouth is close enough to be a potential problem with loud sound surges and, hence, overloading. Limiting keeps such surges under control, thereby helping maintain more-uniform levels. Also, because mic-to-source distance with a mini-mic is close, there is little problem with voice levels being too quiet; such may not be the case with the boom. With the boom microphone, compression helps keep quieter voices above the noise floor and louder voices from overloading, although there is some risk with this technique. If compression values are not properly set, the compressor's effects on the signals could result in an audible pumping sound.

When omnidirectional mini-mics are used closer than the recommended three-to-one ratio, phasing problems can create the hollow, "tin can" sound that results from comb filtering. Compression is definitely needed to reduce the dynamic range of each mic. If that is not sufficient, it might be necessary to put adjacent microphones out of phase with each other. When adjacent microphones are out of phase, a null is created between them, which keeps the same sound from reaching an adjacent mic at slightly different times by canceling the delayed sound. This technique works only if the participants are not mobile and do not lean into the null. Omnidirectional mini-mics can also be a problem in less than acceptable studio acoustics. Many TV studios are designed primarily with picture in mind, at the expense of sound. Also, in TV studio sets, walls are often concave and hard, which focuses and reflects sound.

A way to avoid the problems created by omnidirectional mini-mics is to use directional mini-mics. They interact less and can be left at or near operating levels without having to keep riding gain. Directional mics also help with **upcuts,** where a participant's first few utterances are barely heard until the audio operator responds. But keep in mind that directional mini-mics, and directional mics in general, produce a drier, more closed sound than omnis, which some directors tend not to like for speaking. They also require that participants control head movements to stay on-mic.

Using a noise gate is yet another way to handle these phasing problems, although it can be a solution that is more trouble than it is worth. Setting precise thresholds takes time, and the gating effect may be audible as microphones are open and closed.

Still another alternative to controlling multiple sound sources is to use an automatic microphone mixer. For a discussion of the automatic mic mixer, see Chapter 13.

Miking the Audience

When a talk show (or almost any entertainment program) takes place before an audience, the crowd response becomes integral to the program's presentation. Applause, laughter, and other reactions contribute to the show's spontaneity and excitement. The presence of an audience creates two challenges for the sound designer: (1) the people at home must be able to hear them, and (2) the audience must be able to hear the participants, wherever they are in the studio.

For the home viewer, the studio audience should sound relatively close and uniform so that the viewer feels a part of the action. No single voice or cadence or group of similar-sounding voices (that is, high-pitched cackle, halting laugh, children, elderly women, and so forth) should predominate, unless that is the intention. (Some game shows, for example, whose viewers make up the majority of a particular demographic group like to have that group sonically evident in its audience reaction.)

One way to achieve these ends is to mount directional shotgun microphones several feet above the audience and distribute them in equal quadrants throughout the audience area for uniform pickup (see 12-11; see also 4-58). The type of shotgun—cardioid, supercardioid, or hyper-cardioid—depends on how broad or focused you

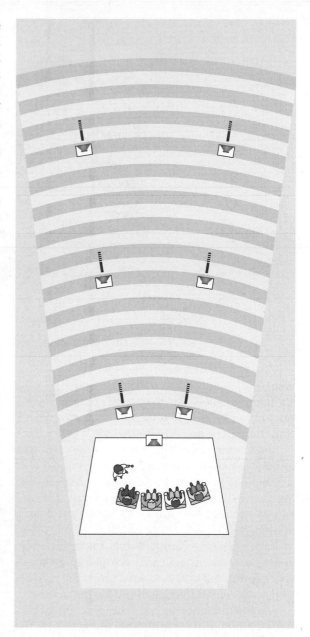

12-11 Talk-show studio with audience area. Shotgun microphones are placed above the audience in quadrants for uniform and controlled directional pickup. Above and behind the mics are small directional loudspeakers situated to avoid feeding back into the mics and to cover specific audience areas. A small loudspeaker above the stage feeds audience sound to the guests during questioning. Depending on the layout and studio size, this loudspeaker may be phased so that it covers a narrow stage area or to avoid interference with the studio loudspeakers, or both.

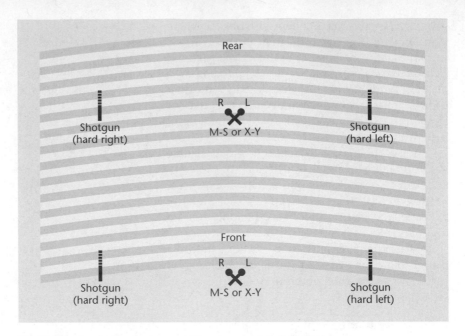

12-12 Theater audience stereo miking for a variety/talk show

want the pickup to be. Keep in mind that with shotguns good off-axis frequency response is vital; poor off-axis response results in unwanted coloration that can be quite pronounced in inferior mics.

Sometimes, depending on the studio acoustics and the size of the audience, omnidirectional mics or boundary mics with hemispheric pickup patterns are also used to help blend the overall audience sound. Figures 12-12 and 12-13 display a few other approaches.

To free the operator's hands for other audio control operations, audience microphones are sometimes controlled by a foot pedal under the console. The pedal is used to open and close the mics.

For the audience to hear the program participants, loudspeakers must be mounted in the audience area of the studio. This places microphones and loudspeakers close together, creating the potential for *feedback*—that high-pitched squeal from a signal feeding from a mic to a loudspeaker, around and around. To avoid feedback the loudspeakers are placed so that their sound is off-axis to the microphone's pickup pattern (see 12-11).

If the loudspeaker is too loud, however, feedback will occur anyway. To minimize this risk, smaller, more directional loudspeakers are used, and their levels are kept moderate. If the danger of feedback still exists, still smaller loudspeakers may be employed or their sound may be compressed, or both.

A small loudspeaker above the stage feeds audience sound to the guests during questioning. Depending on the layout and studio size, this loudspeaker may be phased so that it covers a narrow stage area or to avoid interference with the studio loudspeakers, or both.

"Producing" Audience Response

Audiences usually react in two ways: by laughing and by applauding. Raising the levels of these sounds when they occur adds to their uplift and to the program's overall fun and excitement. This is known as *milking the audience*. But such level adjustments have to be accomplished gracefully; they cannot be abrupt. Skillfully done, increasing the level of laughter can add to its infectiousness, thus reinforcing the impact of a funny line or joke,

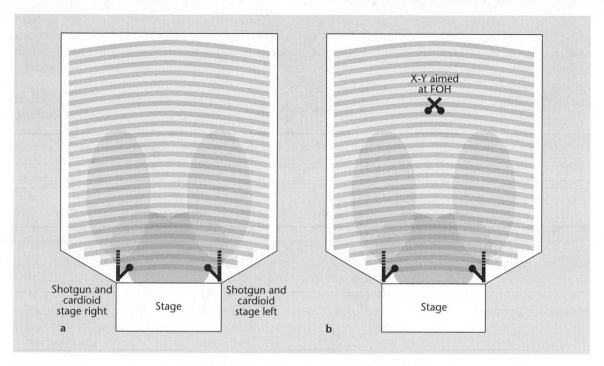

12-13 Two other examples of audience miking. (a) Pairs of cardioid and shotgun microphones are placed stage-left and stage-right. The cardioids are aimed at the nearest segment of the audience. The shotguns are aimed farther back in the hall. (b) This microphone arrangement supplements the mics in (a) with another pair of cardioid mics arranged in an X-Y pattern aimed toward the front of the hall (FOH).

or, in the case of applause, it can heighten its intensity, perhaps even its enthusiasm.

The audience sound may be controlled by a limiter. When the audience microphones reach the limit level, the limiter kicks in to increase apparent loudness but not the actual peak level.

Audiences do not always react as expected, however. When a funny line or a climactic moment is not greeted with the anticipated intensity of laughter or applause, recorded applause and laugh tracks are sometimes used to reinforce or "sweeten" audience reactions. Cartridge tapes or disks with different types and degrees of audience reactions are run continuously, but are played with the faders off, a technique known as *deadpotting*. Or they can be played on a digital program repeater, which performs the same looping function as cart machines and can record and store effects as well (see 12-14 and 7-9).

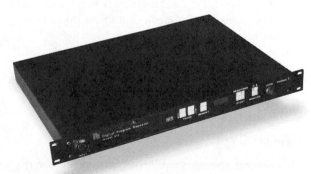

12-14 Digital program repeater. This device is used to record and reproduce repetitively occurring program material. In this model *track* and *start* buttons control program reproduction, and an LED readout selectively indicates track selection, reproduction time of that selection, or the amount of memory utilized or available.

Laughter and applause sometimes occur relatively close together. When this happens, because applause is louder than laughter, the general guideline is to decrease the loudness level of the recorded applause and increase the level of the recorded laughter.

RECORDING SPEECH

Speech sounds are harmonically and dynamically complex. Producing vocal sound involves the lungs, chest, diaphragm, larynx, hard and soft palates, nasal cavities, teeth, tongue, and lips. There is also the dynamic interaction of all these elements through time. The obvious essentials, therefore, are selecting a microphone that is most complementary to the performer's voice; setting the optimum mic-to-source distance; taking care to avoid plosives, sibilance, breathiness, and fluctuations in on-mic presence; making the performer comfortable; and, if the session is a long one, giving consideration to pacing the takes so as not to cause fatigue.

Speech recording also requires suitable acoustics, which seems obvious. But suitable acoustics are more important to speech than to singing. For one thing, the spectral density and energy the singing voice generates can somewhat overcome mediocre acoustics. For another, in multitrack recording other tracks can mask less than acceptable acoustics on a vocal track, to say nothing of the "distraction" of a good lyric or performance, or both. In recording speech, most often suitable acoustics are dry acoustics. The less the ambient coloration, the easier it is mix the voice with other elements.

Voice-Over

Recording speech generally involves either the voice-over or dialogue. *Voice-over (V.O.)* is the term used when a performer records copy to which other materials, such as sound effects, music, dialogue, and visuals, are added, usually at another time. There are two types of voice-over material: *short form,* such as spot announcements; and *long form,* such as documentaries and audiobooks.

Recording the voice-over may not seem particularly demanding, especially given the multifarious nature of today's production. But producing a solo performer and a microphone is a considerable challenge: There is no place to hide.

Most performers prefer doing a voice-over when standing. It allows for better vocal control, because the diaphragm is free to move, and it helps the body language, which often makes for a better performance. Long-form readings are usually done sitting, mainly due to the endurance factor.

The high-quality capacitor is the microphone of choice for voice-overs because of its ability to reproduce vocal complexities and handle transient sounds. Directional pickup patterns are preferred, because they reduce ambience and produce a more intimate sound. Sometimes shotgun mics are used for added punch.

Mic-to-source distance depends on the strength and intensity of the performer's delivery, but it is usually close enough to retain intimacy without sounding too close or oppressive.

For standing performers, scripts are usually placed on music stands, padded and angled to avoid reflections back into the mic. Seated performers generally use desktop copy stands, also padded and angled. In both cases the stands are high enough that the performer does not have to look down at the script, thereby going off-mic.

Avoiding plosives, sibilance, breathiness, and tongue and lip smacks is handled in two ways: (1) by placing the mic capsule on line with, or slightly above, the performer's upper lip so the pickup is not directly in the slip stream yet still on-mic and (2) by using a windscreen. The fabric windscreen is preferred over the conventional windscreen for the better high-frequency response (see 4-46c).

In dealing with recording levels, the practice is to set them below 0 VU to preserve headroom and not run the risk of overload distortion, especially in digital recording. How much below zero-level the setting is depends on the recordist's taste, the material being recorded, the equipment used for the recording, other interacting equipment which may be used later during production, and the demands of the overall mix.

Recording is usually done flat; that way, there's no sonic "baggage" to deal with in the mix or if the recording has to be continued on another day or in a different studio. If any signal processing is done at all during recording, it may be to use a high-pass filter to remove low end that creates unwanted density and eats up headroom, or to add a bit of presence in the 5,000-Hz range, or to compress the signal.

Some compressing of speech is almost always done, mostly during the mix, but sometimes during the recording as well. This is especially so with spot announcements to make them punchier so they stand out from the other broadcast program materials.

In producing a voice-over, it is sometimes necessary to record the ambience separately, after the performer finishes recording, by letting the tape or disk *overroll*—keeping it running for a while. This makes it possible to maintain a consistent background sound in the mix, if it is required, by editing in the recorded ambience during the pauses in the voice-over and, in so doing, avoiding ambience "drop outs" in the voice-over track. Such changes may be subtle, but they are perceptible as differences in the openness and closeness of the aural space.

It is also essential to maintain consistency in voice quality from take to take. This is especially challenging during a long session and when sessions run into two or more days. Not to do so makes it difficult to match recorded segments during editing.

One time-consuming factor often overlooked in recording speech is the editing: how long it often takes to repair plosives, breath gasps, sibilance, and mouth noises that get through, even with a windscreen; fluffs of words or phrases which require retakes; and the segments that must be deleted, from letting a reading and rereading continue through passages less than well delivered to help the performer establish a rapport with the mood and pulse of the copy (see Chapter 18).

Dialogue

Recording dialogue is handled in two ways: It is either done during production and then processed from the original recording in postproduction, or it is rerecorded after production in a facility known as a *dialogue rerecording studio*. Recording dialogue during production is discussed in Chapter 14; dialogue rerecording in postproduction is covered in Chapter 17.

STUDIO INTERCOMMUNICATION SYSTEMS

Vital to coordinating the functions of the production team during broadcast or recording is the director's ability to talk to them and their ability to talk to one another without the sound going to air or recording. This is done through an audio intercommunication (intercom) system. Three types of studio intercom systems are in general use: the PL (private line or phone line), SA (studio-address), and IFB (interruptible foldback) systems.

The PL System

The *PL (private line) system*, also known as the *phone line system*, connects production and technical personnel. It consists of a headset with an earpiece and a small microphone. The headsets may be wireless or wired and connected to wall or camera outlets. In instances where it is necessary to hear both the director's cues and the program feed, as is often the case for the boom operator, a double headset with two earpieces is used. If surroundings are noisy or there is a loud sound source such as a rock band, circumaural PL headsets are available.

PL systems can also provide for separate communication lines. For example, audio personnel can confer with one another on one channel while the director talks to, say, the camera operators.

The SA System

The *SA (studio-address) system*, also called a *talkback*, is used like a public-address system to communicate with people in the studio not connected to a PL, such as the performers, and for general instructions to all studio personnel. It consists of a small microphone at or in a console close to the director, a spring-loaded switch to activate it, and a small studio-address loudspeaker.

The IFB System

The *IFB (interruptible foldback) system* connects the director, producer, and other control room personnel with the performer(s), through an earpiece, to convey directions before and during a broadcast. The earpiece is small enough to be inserted into the ear canal and carries program sound, the performer's voice included. When the director, or anyone else connected to the system, has an instruction for the performer, the program feed to the performer's earpiece is interrupted for the instruction (see 12-15).

For example, a newscaster delivering a story is about to introduce a field reporter with more details from the scene. If the field reporter is not standing by because of some delay, that information is conveyed to the newscaster via IFB to prevent a premature cue. Then, of course, it is up to the newscaster to "fill" until the director indicates that the field reporter is ready.

Clearly, using IFB effectively requires performers who are able to bifurcate their concentration by thinking about what they are saying while listening to what the director is telling them—and to do both without making it obvious to the audience.

As with all audio equipment, intercom systems vary in quality. It is essential, however, particularly with PL and IFB systems, that they be as noise-free as possible and that the talk be distinct and easily heard, not only at normal speaking levels, but at quiet ones too. Wireless IFB systems are also available.

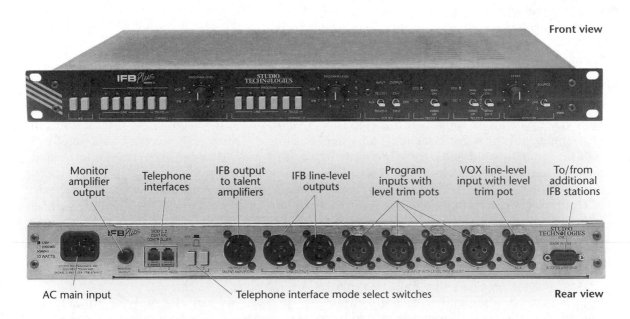

12-15 IFB controller (front and rear views). This model contains two independent IFB channels, each with a complete set of controls. Each IFB output (program and interrupt audio) is sent to four places: the talent amplifier output, a line output, a telephone interface, and a monitor amplifier.

▶ The production chain (in nonmusic production) generally begins with the talking performer and therefore involves considerations that relate to producing speech.

▶ How speech is produced depends on the type of program or production, the method of production, where the production is done, and the production's release time or date.

▶ The frequency range of the human voice is not wide compared with that of other instruments. The adult male's fundamental voicing frequencies are from roughly 80 to 240 Hz; for the adult female, they are from roughly 140 to 500 Hz. Harmonics and overtones carry these ranges somewhat higher. (Ranges for the singing voice are significantly wider.)

▶ Speech intelligibility is at a maximum when levels are about 70 to 90 dB-SPL. Certain frequencies are also more critical to speech intelligibility than others.

▶ Acoustical phase refers to the time relationship between two (or more) sound waves at a given point in their cycles. Electrical phase refers to the relative electrical polarity of two signals in the same circuit. When these waves or polarities are in phase—roughly coincident in time—their amplitudes are additive. When these waves or polarities are out of phase—not coincident in time—their amplitudes are reduced.

▶ The closer a microphone is placed to a sound source, the closer to the audience the sound source is perceived to be, and the warmer, denser, bassier, drier, more intimate, and more detailed is the perceived sound.

▶ The farther a microphone is placed from a sound source, the farther from the audience the sound source is perceived to be, and the more distant, diffused, open, spacious, reverberant, and detached, and the less detailed is the perceived sound.

▶ In selecting and positioning a mic, keep excessive sound that is reflected from room surfaces, furniture, and equipment from reaching the mic, or comb filtering can result. Also, choose a mic and position it to avoid sibilance, plosives, and breath sounds.

▶ In monaural sound, aural space is one-dimensional—measured in terms of depth—so perspective is near-to-far.

▶ In stereo sound, aural space is two-dimensional—measured in terms of depth and breadth—so perspectives are near-to-far and side-to-side.

▶ In stereo miking, the angle or distance between the two microphones (or microphone capsules) determines side-to-side perspective. The smaller the angle or distance between the mics, the narrower the left-to-right stereo image; the larger the angle or distance, the wider the left-to-right image.

▶ In disc jockey, interview, and panel programs, the participants should sound as though they are coming from the front and center of the aural space. With more than one participant, using individual microphones, the loudness levels for the participants must be similar if the sound is to be perceived as coming from the front and center of the aural space.

▶ The overall sound of a radio station involves the particular music or talk format, the announcer's delivery style, the production style of the spot announcements and jingles, and how tightly presented they all are.

▶ The techniques used to mike speech for picture in television and film (and to produce sound, in general) depend on whether the production is broadcast live, or live-on-tape, or is taped/filmed for showing at a later date.

▶ In radio a microphone can be placed anywhere without regard for appearance. In television, if a mic is in the picture, it must be good-looking and positioned so that it does not obscure the performer's face. If it is not in the picture, it must be positioned close enough to the performer so that the sound is on-mic.

▶ Generally, for optimal sound pickup the recommended placement for a mini-mic is in the area of the performer's sternum, about 6 to 8 inches below the chin.

▶ Hiding a mini-mic under clothing requires that the mic and mic cable are or can be made insensitive to rustling sounds and that the clothing be made of material that is less likely to make those sounds.

- In television a desk mic is often used as a prop. If the desk mic is live, make sure it does not block the performer's face, interfere with the performer's frontal working space, or pick up studio noises.

- The handheld mic allows the host to control audience questioning and mic-to-source distance and, like the desk mic, helps generate closer psychological rapport with the audience.

- A boom, like the mini-mic hidden under clothing, is used when mics must be out of the picture. Often one boom mic covers more than one performer. To provide adequate sound pickup, and to move the boom at the right time to the right place, the boom operator must anticipate when one performer is about to stop talking and another starts.

- Different techniques are used in controlling levels, leakage, and feedback of mic feeds from multiple sound sources: following the three-to-one rule, moderate limiting or compression, noise gating, or using an automatic microphone mixer.

- If an audience is present, it must be miked to achieve an overall sound blend and to prevent one voice or group of voices from predominating.

- Increasing audience laughter or applause, or both, by using recorded laughter or applause tracks adds to a program's spontaneity and excitement.

- Recording speech begins with good acoustics. Mediocre acoustics can make speech sound boxy, oppressive, lifeless, ringy, or hollow.

- Recording speech generally involves either the voice-over—recording copy to which other sonic material is added—or dialogue.

- Recording a solo performer and a microphone is a considerable challenge: There is no place to hide.

- Studio intercommunication systems are vital in coordinating the functions of the production team. Three types of studio intercom systems are the private line or phone line—PL; studio address—SA; and interruptible foldback—IFB.

13

Field Production: Live and Live-on-Tape

 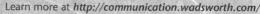

Production is a challenge no matter where it takes place. But in the field, away from a controlled studio environment, it presents its own particular problems, especially given the immediate and relatively immediate demands of live and live-on-tape broadcasting. Yet field production is almost as commonplace as studio production. Producers go on location—or on a *remote*, as broadcasters often refer to field production—to cover news and sports, to do a disc jockey program promoting a sponsor, to heighten realism in a drama, to add authenticity to a setting, or to provide surroundings that are difficult or impossible to reproduce in a studio.

Live and live-on-tape field production for radio and television can be grouped into two basic categories: electronic news gathering (ENG) and electronic field production (EFP). ENG uses highly portable equipment to cover news for live or imminent broadcast. EFP involves more-complex productions, such as sports, parades, and awards programs.

ELECTRONIC NEWS GATHERING

Electronic news gathering (ENG) refers to radio or TV news gathered or broadcast in the field. ENG covers broadcast news as it is happening.

Radio ENG

Radio ENG (often abbreviated *RENG*) is relatively uncomplicated to produce and can be broadcast on the spot with comparative logistical ease. It usually involves a reporter with portable recording and, if necessary, transmitting equipment. At its most basic, all that the radio reporter needs to record a story are a microphone and a recorder. To send the story to the radio station's newsroom, add a transmitting device. Even when somewhat more elaborate production is called for, a microphone mixer or portable console, an edit-capable recorder, or a mobile unit can usually handle it.

Microphone

Because RENG usually involves one reporter delivering a story or doing an interview, or both, the handheld, omnidirectional, moving-coil microphone with pop filter is generally the mic of choice. Capacitor mics are not as rugged, they are susceptible to wind distortion, and they require a power supply. A handheld mic requires no mounting and takes no time at all to set up. Field reporting is often done outdoors, and a pop filter is better at reducing unwanted wind sound than is a windscreen; nevertheless, it does not hurt to use a pop filter *and* a windscreen just to be safe. Using a mic with a built-in shock mount is also a good idea. If wind or traffic rumble is severe, a high-pass filter can be plugged into the mic line to diminish bassy noise (see Figure 13-1). But conditions should justify using the high-pass filter, because it may also attenuate desired low frequencies. When hum and electrical noise from motors, fluorescent lights, and the like are the problems, a quad mic cable, a four-conductor design available from a number of manufacturers, can greatly reduce these sonic nuisances. Field productions that require more-critical noise reduction, and have the time to set up the appropriate equipment, may use a back-ground noise suppressor, or other noise reduction techniques (see "Noise Reduction" in Chapter 14). That said, with the powerful noise reduction available in digital signal processing, this is less of a problem than it once was. With news, of course, dependence on postproduction always assumes time permitting.

An omnidirectional mic maintains a sense of environment. The body blocks sounds coming from behind the reporter, reducing the overall level of background sound. Mic-to-source distance can be adjusted simply by moving the microphone closer to or farther from the mouth to compensate for noisy environments. If a locale is too noisy, try a directional microphone, but be aware that directional mics are more prone to wind noise than are omnidirectional mics. Also, their on-axis response is drier and more concentrated than that of omnis, so working too close to the mic can create a denser, more closed, sound.

Recorder

Digital recorders have all but replaced analog units in RENG. Although digital audio quality is not essential to news, it is not detrimental either, particularly with the advent of digital broadcasting. Aside from this, the reasons for the changeover are the storage and editing capabilities of digital recorders; their faster, more precise cueing; and, with hard-disk systems, their robustness. The preferred digital recorders in RENG, and in news in general, are the mini disc and hard-disk formats (see 13-2). R-DATs are also used by those who still like tape and the sound of uncompressed recording. But because their mechanisms are complex and delicate, they are not ideal for the rough handling and harsh environment of news gathering.

Microphone Mixer/Console

When one microphone is used for field reporting, it is a simple matter to plug it directly into the recorder. If two mics are needed, a recorder with two mic inputs suffices. (Assuming in both cases that the recorder uses balanced connectors.) When there are more microphones than recorder inputs, or if the recorder takes an unbalanced mini- or

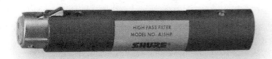

13-1 High-pass filter. This device can be plugged into a microphone line to reduce unwanted low-frequency sounds. A similar-looking low-pass filter is also available to reduce unwanted high-frequency sounds.

phono plug, it calls for a microphone mixer. Remember that mic mixers are available in mono and stereo and have features such as low-cut filters, pan pots, phantom power, tone oscillator, and slate tone (see 5-1). A highly portable, suitcase-sized mini-console would also meet the need for multiple microphone inputs and also provide additional processing features (see 5-2). The mixer and console designed for field use may also be equipped with a telephone jack for direct transmission to the station.

Transmission

In the world of news, where stories must be filed fast and first, field reporters often do not have the luxury of bringing their stories back to the newsroom, nor do they have to, given today's technology. They can easily transmit them to the station from the field for direct broadcast or recording. Various transmitting systems are used, the most common of which are the mobile telephone, cellular telephone, remote transmitter, and codec.

The *mobile telephone* is a radio unit connected to telephone equipment that sends the signal to phone wires for transmission to the station. With mobile telephones it is possible to call anyone, anywhere. Sound quality is mediocre but can be improved with a telephone line interface (see 13-3).

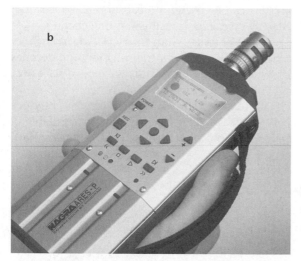

a

b

13-2 Examples of portable hard-disk RAM recorders. (a) This model, which weighs about 3.5 pounds, includes an ISDN codec, telephone line transfer software, a two-channel mixer, and on-board graphical scrub wheel editing. It records on a PCMCIA hard disk, and recordings can be made either uncompressed in the WAV format or with MPEG layer II compression. (b) This "pocket" handheld recorder, which weighs about one pound, also uses the PCMCIA hard disk and data compression. It is equipped with a microphone capsule, screwed directly onto the top of the main body of the recorder. Capsules are available in various directional pickup patterns, from omnidirectional to middle-side (M-S). Five AA batteries give up to four hours of operation.

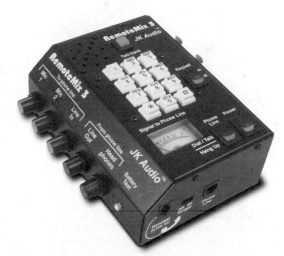

13-3 Telephone line interface. This unit plugs into an analog phone line and combines with the telephone interface an audio mixer and headphone amplifier. It can be used for field reporting and remote broadcasts, such as sporting events.

Mobile telephones are vulnerable to *radio frequency (RF)* and electrical interference from high-voltage lines, transformers, and motors. This is another reason to use an interface, because the better interfaces have a balanced line that helps protect against interference. As an additional safeguard against interference, insulate cables by wrapping them in electrician's tape.

The *cellular telephone* is similar to a mobile telephone, but instead of sending signals over wires, it sends them over radio waves through a computer-controlled network of ground stations. Areas in a locale are divided into cells, and as a mobile unit passes from one cell to another, calls are automatically transferred from one ground station to another. Among the advantages of cell phones are improved sound quality and greater flexibility in feeding material to the station.

The *remote transmitter*, more commonly called a *remote pickup*, *RPU*, or *Marti*, after a leading RPU manufacturer, is a transmitter that allows a reporter freedom of movement. It may be used for direct broadcast from the remote unit, or it can be removed from a news mobile unit and operated on AC current. It also has better sound quality than the other types of mobile transmission; in some units frequency response extends from 20 to 15,000 Hz. Remote transmitters have inputs for at least one microphone and one line source, such as a recorder. Many also include a basic mixer, which, in effect, converts a mobile unit into a ministudio on wheels. The disadvantages of RPUs include their vulnerability to RF and electrical interference; their inability to entirely cover large metropolitan areas, which means they must be supplemented with a cell phone; and, oddly enough, their sound quality, which makes it seem as though reports were done in the studio. (Some news directors feel that location-quality sound in field reports adds authenticity and the sense of "being there.") Fully portable RPUs are also available (see 13-4). In fact, an RPU can be used for local sports broadcasting, thereby saving on transmission line charges.

The *codec* (taken from en*c*oder/*dec*oder) encodes a signal at one end of a transmission and decodes it at another end (see 13-5). This can take place over a POTS (plain old telephone system) line or an ISDN-compatible line. The ISDN tends to produce better sound quality but is not always available. A codec offers one or more mic or line inputs/outputs,

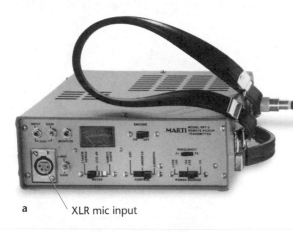

a   XLR mic input

13-4 (a) **Hand-carried transmitter and** (b) **mobile relay receiver.** The transmitter sends the signal to the receiver. This unit weighs 7 pounds and includes 2.5 watts of continuous output, dual frequency provision, internal battery charger and AC supply, compressor-limiter, and one microphone and one line level input with individual mixing controls. The receiver relays a broadcast to the base station, usually in the newsroom. This unit weighs 5.5 pounds and has dual frequency capability, monitor speaker, noise reduction, and terminals for feeding telephone lines.

b

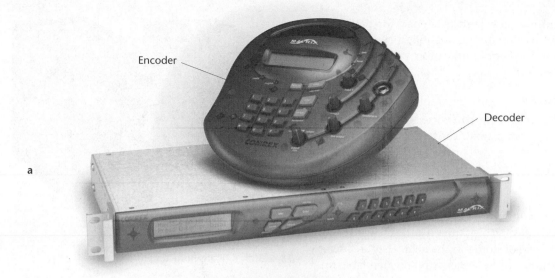

Encoder

Decoder

a

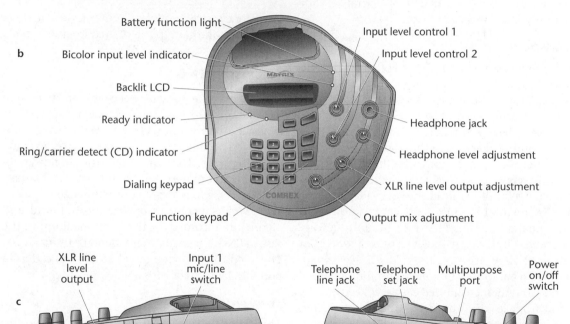

b

Battery function light

Bicolor input level indicator

Backlit LCD

Ready indicator

Ring/carrier detect (CD) indicator

Dialing keypad

Function keypad

Input level control 1

Input level control 2

Headphone jack

Headphone level adjustment

XLR line level output adjustment

Output mix adjustment

c

XLR line level output

Input 1 mic/line switch

Input 2 microphone connector

Input 1 mic/line connector

Tape input −10 dBu mini jack

Telephone line jack

Telephone set jack

Multipurpose port

Power on/off switch

Power connector

Contact closure

Ready closure

13-5 **(a) Codec. (b) View and functions of the top surface of the encoder. (c) Views and functions of the rear and side panels of the encoder.** This unit can be used in a POTS mode or in ISDN using an optional slide-in module. It delivers 15 kHz full-duplex audio on a single standard telephone line. The encoder weighs 2.5 pounds, and the battery kit runs up to seven hours.

a telephone jack, and a keypad for dialing. In addition to signal transmission, a codec provides the ability for communication with personnel at the other end.

Mobile Unit

In radio a *mobile unit* used for news can be anything from a small car to a van. Because even modest radio news operations use more field equipment these days, production flexibility in mobile units is important. In addition to meeting a reporter's typical recording and transmission needs, mobile units are designed to facilitate the producing, editing, mixing, packaging, and broadcasting of stories in the field. They are literally small studios on wheels, with an extendable mast that can be raised to a height of several feet for microwave transmission.

Headphones

Headphones are an important but often overlooked piece of equipment in field production (see Chapter 10). Regardless of the medium—radio, TV, film, or music recording—the purpose of the production, or its scale, headphones are as important on location as loudspeakers are in the studio. Unless there is another way to monitor audio, headphones are the only reference you have to sound quality and balance. Use the best headphones available, study their frequency response, and get to know their sonic characteristics. First-rate headphones are expensive—but worth it. They have a wide, flat response; they are sensitive; they have superb channel separation (for stereo and multichannel sound); and their cushioned earpieces keep outside sound from leaking through. All these characteristics are essential in producing audio on location, when loudspeakers are unavailable.

It is also to your advantage to have a headphone amplifier handy (see 13-6). It provides the ability to monitor a mix at a convenient level without affecting the original signal sources. This is particularly useful when the loudness of background sound makes it difficult to hear program audio. By plugging headphones into a headphone amplifier and plugging the amplifier into the mic

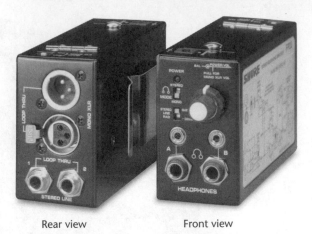

Rear view   Front view

13-6 Stereo headphone amplifier

mixer (or console) headphone output, you can drive the headphone gain to the desired loudness level.

Television ENG

The obvious differences between radio and television ENG are the addition of the camera and equipment necessary to transmit picture as well as sound and the added production considerations that go along with the video. That said, using the single-system recording technique greatly simplifies field coverage of TV news, where time is of the essence.

In *single-system recording*, both sound and picture are recorded on the same medium; in the case of ENG, the medium is videotape or hard disk. The recording device is called a camcorder—a portable TV camera with a video recorder.

Camcorder

The *camcorder* is a combination camera and recorder that is portable, lightweight, and battery-powered and is operated handheld or shoulder-borne. The recorder can be analog, but these days it is more likely to be digital. Camcorders use ½-inch or Hi8 videocassette or a small hard-disk drive built into the camera unit or dockable to it.

Hard-disk camcorders provide at least four digital-quality audio tracks, time code, and cut-and-paste in-camera editing (see 13-7). Disk capacity is

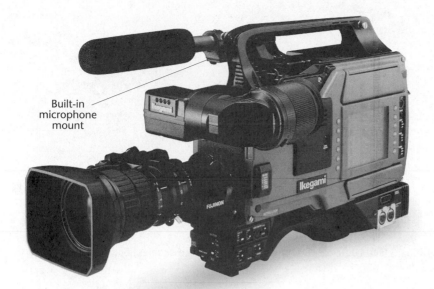

Built-in
microphone
mount

13-7 CamCutter.
This DNG (digital news gathering) camera has a small hard drive attached to it. The hard drive can store up to 20 minutes of digital video and audio material. It is called a CamCutter because it allows "cutting" (editing) in the field.

at least 20 minutes. With videotape camcorders, depending on the format, field recording times per cartridge run from 20 minutes to two hours.

Obviously, sound (and picture) quality is considerably better in digital camcorders than in analog units, and with the advent of the hard-disk field recorder, the era of ENG has become the era of *DNG (digital news gathering)*.

Microphone

As in RENG the handheld, omnidirectional, moving-coil microphone with pop filter and built-in shock mount is still the mic of choice for TV ENG, because the omni pickup pattern provides a sense of sonic environment and the reporter can control mic-to-source distance. If the environment is too noisy, a directional mic may be more suitable. The mic may be wired or, as is more likely today, wireless. The reporter carries the transmitter, and the receiver is usually mounted on the camera.

The convenience of wireless mics is undeniable. That notwithstanding, most audio people advise against using them when a wired mic will do the job. Wireless systems are not as reliable as wired mics; there are problems with interference, dropout, and noise from the camera, motors, cabling, and

so on. This advice is particularly noteworthy when field-recording dramatic material (see Chapter 14).

If you use a wireless mic, be sure to check on RF interference beforehand. This is easy to do using a handheld scanner set to the wireless mic's frequencies. If wireless reception is a problem, putting the beltpack receiver on the front of the reporter instead of on the side or back (out of sight, of course) should improve signal pickup. When camera-to-source distance is wide, placing the receiver closer to the reporter, if possible, minimizes dropout and multipath reflections. In rainy and snowy conditions, mounting the beltpack just above the ankle and placing the receiver as close to the ground as possible can minimize poor reception because of absorption.

Although audiences are accustomed to seeing a microphone in the picture, particularly in news, care still has to be taken to keep the mic from being too obtrusive. In typical stand-up reports and on-the-scene interviews, this usually is not a problem. But if an interview is lengthy, it may be preferable to take the time to body-mount two mini-mics. It could be annoying to the audience (and the person being interviewed) to see one handheld mic moved back and forth between reporter and

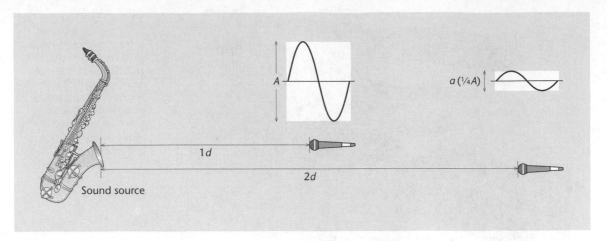

13-8 Illustration of the inverse square law. As the distance *(d)* from a sound source doubles, loudness *(A)* decreases in proportion to the square of that distance.

interviewee for several minutes. On the other hand, if there is nothing to occupy the reporter's hands, using body mics may be more of a distraction. Moreover, unless the camera operator directs the viewer where to look with the video, the viewer may find it distracting without a handheld mic in the picture to help focus attention.

Camcorders also come with a built-in microphone mount (see 13-7), which has numerous advantages: It allows one person to operate audio and video simultaneously; the mic of choice is super- or hypercardioid to pick up sound several feet away; when used in addition to the reporter's mic, it provides another sound pickup; and, when it is the only mic used, it frees the reporter's hands.

The disadvantages of using a microphone fixed to the camera are: The mic may pick up sound from a zoom lens motor or a hum from the monitor; if it is highly directional, which it usually is, it has to be pointed straight at the sound source to reduce unwanted sound; and it cannot adequately handle shots that change from one focal length to another. Unless the camera moves, it is difficult to adjust the sound for a change from, say, a medium shot to a close-up or a long shot. Finally, there is the *inverse square law:* Outdoors, when mic-to-source distance is doubled, the sound-pressure level drops approximately 6 dB, thus reducing loudness to one-fourth. Conversely, cutting the mic-to-source

distance in half increases loudness approximately 6 dB (see 13-8). The precise effect of this law depends on the openness of the area and the directionality of the microphone.

Camcorder Audio Inputs, Outputs, and Controls

Professionally used camcorders have a number of features, which may vary with the model and are known by somewhat different terms. Generally, they include at least two balanced microphone inputs to record two separate audio tracks. There are also line level inputs to receive audio from another VCR, audio recorder, or other line level sound sources. An *audio input selector* tells the recorder whether the signal is coming from the camera or from a microphone or line source.

Camcorders may have an input feature called an *automatic gain control (AGC)*. Avoid using it. AGC automatically boosts sound level when loudness falls below a preset (built-in) level. During recording, when there is no foreground sound for the mic to pick up, the AGC brings up the background sound as it seeks volume. If a reporter makes slight pauses when delivering a story, it may be possible to hear the increases in background sound level as the AGC automatically increases volume. AGC should not be confused with a built-in limiter, which can be useful.

The outputs on a camcorder are for feeding sound to another recorder—audio or video—and for monitoring through headphones. Some camcorders have an RF output that mixes audio and video together and makes it possible to see and hear the recording on a conventional TV set. On recorders with two audio channels, an *audio monitor control* selects which one is heard in the headphones; in the *mix* position, both channels are heard together. Camcorders also have an intercom jack.

In addition to the usual recorder controls—*play, record, stop,* and so on—an *audio dub* function allows the recording of new audio onto a prerecorded tape without erasing the video. Record level controls adjust the loudness of the input, output, and monitor audio. Camcorders also have VU meters. With videocassette recorders there is an *audio mode selector,* which is similar to the bias control on analog audiocassette recorders that adjusts to the type of low-bias or high-bias tape being used, such as iron oxide or metal particle. On camcorders the audio mode selector controls the output of VCRs that are capable of recording "normal" analog audio and "high-fidelity" digital sound.

Despite the convenience and handiness of the audio level controls on camcorders, be aware that they are not as finely "tuned" as similar controls on audio recorders and microphone mixers. The primary function of camcorders, after all, is recording picture. Therefore, whenever possible, feed sound to the camcorder through a mic mixer or use a separate audio recorder. And always monitor the sound through high-quality headphones.

Mobile Unit

ENG mobile units, even at their most basic, obviously require more technical support than do RENG vehicles, not only because of the video component but also because of the transmission requirements. ENG vans require more space and, therefore, may provide additional audio support that includes a small console, signal processors, recorders, and shelf-type loudspeakers.

It is worth noting that what often influences the equipment brought into the field is not production need but how many people are on the production crew.

ENG Production

The main purpose of ENG is to facilitate fast access to the news scene, quick setup time, uncomplicated production, immediate distribution if necessary, and simple postproduction when time permits and production circumstances require. In news the immediacy is more important than the aesthetics, but this is not to say that news producers ignore production values. They simply do the best they can under the circumstances.

Preproduction

Preproduction planning in ENG is obviously difficult because news can occur anywhere, anytime. The best you can do is always be prepared. In audio, preparation means making sure that the following items are available and ready:

☑ AC extension cords

☑ Alligator clips and leads

☑ A backup recorder

☑ Backup phantom power if a capacitor mic is used

☑ Clamp-on mic stands for a podium

☑ Codec

☑ Distribution amplifiers for multiple feeds (see 13-19)

☑ Duct and masking tape

☑ Extra and fresh battery supplies for capacitor mics, recorders, mic mixers, and wireless microphone systems—lithium batteries provide extended operating time

☑ Extra microphone cables, belt clips for body mics, and windscreens

☑ Head cleaner and cotton swabs

☑ High-pass filters to insert into the mic line to cut low-frequency noise

☑ High-quality headphones

☑ Line-to-mic adapters to match impedance from auditorium amplifiers

☑ Log sheet or laptop computer for recordkeeping: time, location, and content of recorded information; problems with audio quality; and suggestions that anticipate editing

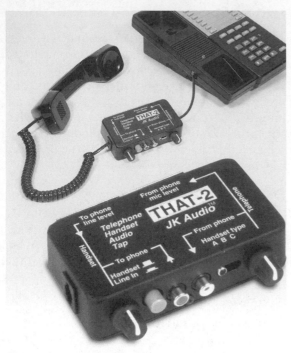

13-9 Phone tap. This device is used as an interface for recording audio from a standard telephone line.

- ☑ Nondirectional and directional handheld and mini microphones
- ☑ Pads (40 dB) if line-to-mic adapters are insufficient to reduce level
- ☑ Phone tap (see 13-9)
- ☑ Plenty of recording tape and/or disks
- ☑ Portable microphone mixer or mini-console
- ☑ Rechargeable battery supply
- ☑ Tool kit
- ☑ XLR, phone, phono, and mini plugs and adapters (see 13-10)

Production

Field production often presents the problem of background sound's interfering with the intelligibility of the on-mic/on-camera reporters. In news, however, sense of locale is important to reports from the field, particularly in radio. In fact, as noted

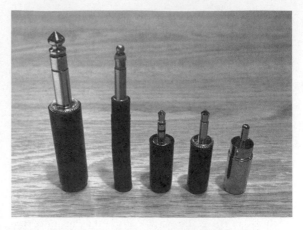

13-10 Commonly used connectors for audio. (Left to right) ¼-inch phone plug (stereo), Bantam phone plug (stereo), mini plug (stereo), mini plug (mono), and RCA or phono plug. (See 4-51 for XLR connectors, not shown here.)

earlier, some news producers do not want the sound quality of actualities—reports from the field—upgraded to studio quality, precisely to preserve location presence.

Miking the Stand-up News Report The omnidirectional, moving-coil, handheld microphone is used most often in stand-up news reports from the field. It picks up enough background sound to provide a sense of environment in normal conditions without overwhelming the reporter's sound. It is possible to control the balance of background-to-reporter sound by moving the microphone closer to or farther from the speaker. The closer the mic-to-source distance, the more the reduction in background sound (see 13-11).

Another advantage of the omnidirectional microphone is that it can be held comfortably below the mouth and in a relatively unobtrusive position on-camera. For interviews, the mic can be situated between reporter and interviewee without necessarily having to move it back and forth for questions and answers (see 13-12).

In noisy environments an omnidirectional microphone may not discriminate enough against unwanted sound even at a close mic-to-source distance. In such a situation, a directional micro-

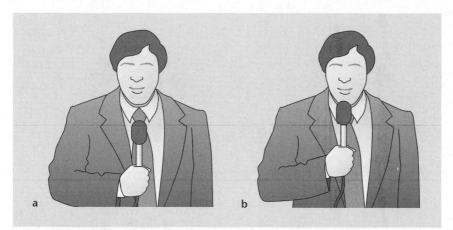

13-11 Reducing background sound. (a) Holding an omnidirectional microphone at chest level usually creates an optimal mic-to-source distance. (b) If background noise is high, its level can be reduced by decreasing the mic-to-source distance.

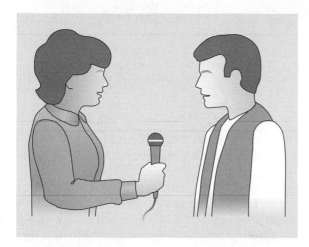

13-12 Using an omnidirectional microphone for on-location interviews. It can be positioned between the principals, usually with little need for repositioning, at least in quiet surroundings.

phone may be suitable. The sound balance between reporter and background can still be maintained by moving the mic closer to or farther from the reporter's mouth. But remember that directional mics must be held at an appropriate angle to be on-axis to the mouth (see 13-13). Moreover, during interviews the microphone must be moved back and forth between interviewer and interviewee if the sound is to be on-mic. In television the microphone should not obstruct the mouth.

To provide a stereo feel to the stand-up report, use a middle-side (M-S) microphone. You will recall that the M-S mic combines a cardioid and a bidirectional pickup in a single casing (see 4-15). By speaking into the front of the mic, the reporter's audio is monaural and on-mic; the bidirectional sides pick up the ambience, providing expanded sonic imaging to the on-scene story. This technique assumes that the environmental sound is not loud enough to overwhelm the reporter's narrative and time permits setting up the M-S mic. If after recording circumstances do not facilitate reproducing the stereo M-S image, the middle, or mono, signal can be separated from the side pickup with no loss in sound or problem with mono compatibility.

Split-Track Recording There is another way to control the audio balances between reporter and background sounds or in an interview, or to enhance stereo imaging. *Split-track recording* employs a recorder with at least two separate audio tracks, such as a stereo recorder, camcorder, or disk recorder. Using two microphones it is possible to feed the output of each to a separate channel. It is like doing a mini-multitrack recording, rather than stereo, to better control the audio quality and mix of two sound sources. If the recorder has more than two mic inputs, it is indeed possible to do a mini-multitrack recording.

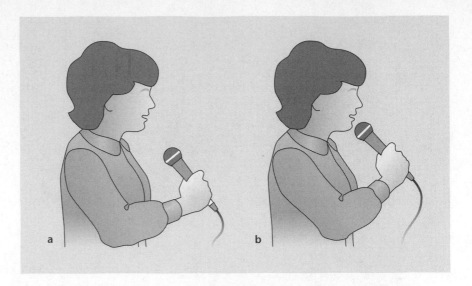

13-13 Miking when on-location background noise is too loud. Use a directional microphone (a) either several inches from the mouth or (b) close to it, depending on the performer's voice projection. Because the microphone is directional, it must be held at the proper angle if the performer is to be on-mic.

In a stand-up report, for example, the speaker can hold the microphone close to the mouth to minimize background sound. The other microphone is used to record just background sound. When each element is separately recorded, they can be balanced properly in the mix under controlled conditions.

In an interview the two principals can be miked separately, or one mic can be used between them, with the second mic used to pick up background sound. In either case, the two microphone feeds facilitate more control over the sound balance. If one voice is dominating the other in an interview, using two mics makes it is possible to employ a polarity reverse cable on the dominant voice to partially cancel it.

Split-track recording may not be possible or necessary on an everyday basis, but the improvement in audio quality and control is worth the time, if you have it. Not only is this technique useful in ENG, but it can also be applied in any type of field recording.

Recording Background Whether you record using the split-track method or put all the audio on one track, make sure you record enough background sound (indoor or outdoor) by running the recorder in *record* for a while either before or after recording—a technique known as **overrolling**. Background sound is useful in postproduction editing to bridge transitions or cover awkward edits.

Analog camcorders used in ENG have at least two audio channels. Recording background may be a problem in TV, however, if it means wasting the picture portion of the videotape unless a number of *cutaways*—shots other than the main action—are taken. It is a good idea, therefore, to bring a second audio recorder with a microphone to record additional background sound separately.

Transmission and Mix-Minus

When the distance between the reporter and the station is thousands of miles or if the signal is being sent via satellite, there will be a slight delay between the time the reporter's words are spoken and the time they reach the station. When the reporter's words are fed back through the IFB earpiece, the reporter and crew will hear the reporter's words after they have been spoken. This is analogous to the disorientation a public-address announcer hears in a stadium when the spoken words are heard a split second after they are delivered. To avoid disorientation, the station sends the incoming report back to the field *mix-minus;* that is, all the audio is returned minus the reporter's words.

Mix-minus can be used in any situation in which sound is being returned via a foldback or IFB system. Some consoles include a mix-minus module, which is particularly useful for call-in programs. It facilitates a variety of mix-minus feeds to studio guests and listeners calling in. It also comes in handy in double remotes, where one personality is broadcasting from, say, an auto show and another performer is taking audience questions in another area of the show while the overall program host is at the station's studio handling phone-in comments from listeners. Mix-minus makes it possible for the talent at the two remote locations to hear one another and the main studio in real time and without echo. Another example is in a music recording when the conductor wishes to hear only the orchestra in the headphones, minus the vocalist, or vice versa.

ELECTRONIC FIELD PRODUCTION

Electronic field production (EFP) refers to video production done on location, involving program materials that take some time to produce. The major differences between ENG and EFP are scale, time, and purpose; in principle they are the same. They both make it possible to produce program material in the field. But whereas ENG is designed to cover news events quickly, EFP is used to produce, more deliberately, material such as entertainment programs, drama, sports, documentaries, and commercials. Therefore EFP generally takes more time in planning, production, and postproduction and usually results in a technically and aesthetically superior product.

Small-Scale EFP

EFP can be divided into small-scale and large-scale productions. The main difference between them is in the complexity of the production and, therefore, in the amount of equipment and personnel required. Commercials, documentaries, disc jockey programs, and local sports can be produced with a minimum of hardware and people, whereas a nationally telecast football game, parade, or the Academy Awards show cannot.

Radio

Electronic field production in radio is usually limited to personality programs such as disc jockey and talk shows, as well as sports. Sometimes it may involve a live concert.

The absence of the visual component in radio drastically cuts down on production needs, compared with TV and film, and on the time needed for preproduction planning. In sports, for example, a few microphones, a mixer or portable mixing console, and a POTS codec are sufficient. A disc jockey program can be mounted with a self-contained remote unit consisting of a microphone, CD and cartridge players, and a small console.

Vans are also used in radio remotes. They may be ENG units equipped with CD players and recorders, or EFP units with removable side panels so the personalities can be seen.

Transmission

Remote radio broadcasts carried by a local station use wired telephone services if they must be transmitted across distances too far for RPU transmission, or if they would be difficult to carry by microwave because of the hundreds of relay stations needed to get the signal from one area to another. Using a satellite to beam signals for long-range transmission also solves this problem, although the solution is not cheap. Generally, satellites are used for global and continental transmission by networks and syndicated programmers.

There are several wired telephone services, analog and digital. They range from an inexpensive and relatively poor quality dial-up voice line for radio remotes; to more-expensive, higher-quality voice lines; to digital transmission with very high quality and greater data capacity. The number of services and their technical parameters are the domain of the engineer and beyond the purview of this book.

There is one useful bit of information to pass on about telephone lines for remote broadcasting: When a line is installed, one terminus will be at the broadcast station. The other terminus—called the *telco drop*—will be at the remote site. Make sure you know where the phone company has left that terminal block, otherwise valuable and frantic time could be spent searching for it.

Television

Small-scale EFP for television is closer to ENG; large-scale EFP is more like a major studio production. Because ENG is covered earlier in this chapter, we'll move on to large-scale EFP.

Large-Scale EFP

Large-scale electronic field production involves recording or broadcasting an event, such as a football or baseball game, a parade, or an awards program, on the spot. As major productions, these events require the same technical support on location that large-scale productions require in the studio. A huge trailer (sometimes more than one)— literally a studio-type technical facility on wheels—and the dozens of engineering and production personnel to go with it provide that support (see 13-14). The trailer contains all the equipment necessary to process and route signals from the many cameras and microphones that cover the event outside the truck and from the video and studio sources, such as instant replay, slow motion, and sound carts, inside the truck.

Increasing attention to the production of high-quality sound and the ever growing audio technology have led to the development of sophisticated audio-only mobile units. These contain the types of equipment found in recording-studio control rooms: multichannel console, multitrack and stereo tape recorders, hard-disk recorders, and signal processors (see 13-15). Audio mobile units are used for on-location concert production and in TV and film shoots to support the video EFP or film unit.

MULTICAMERA EFP

Events produced in the field are either covered or staged. A covered event occurs regardless of media, and production conforms to the event (at least in theory). Sports, parades, and concerts are examples of covered events. Staged events, such as drama, variety, and awards programs, are produced especially for the media and are more tightly controlled. The production approach to an event depends on the type of event it is.

Covered events usually require the multicamera TV approach. Several cameras feed a switcher, several microphones feed a mixer, and all signals feed to recording or broadcast, or both. Shots are selected as the event progresses, and there is little or no postproduction. Staged events can be produced using the multicamera TV or single-camera film approach. The event is constructed in postproduction.

The following sections cover multicamera EFP of speeches, news conferences, and sporting events. Chapter 14 focuses on the single-camera approach to recording staged productions.

Remote Survey

Except for news, field production takes careful planning. The more complex the production, the more detailed the planning has to be. To address the logistics of, among other things, what equipment will be needed and where it will be positioned, a remote, or site, survey is essential. A *remote survey* consists of an inspection of a production location by key production and engineering personnel, and the written plan they draft based on that inspection. The plan helps coordinate the ordering and setting up of pro-

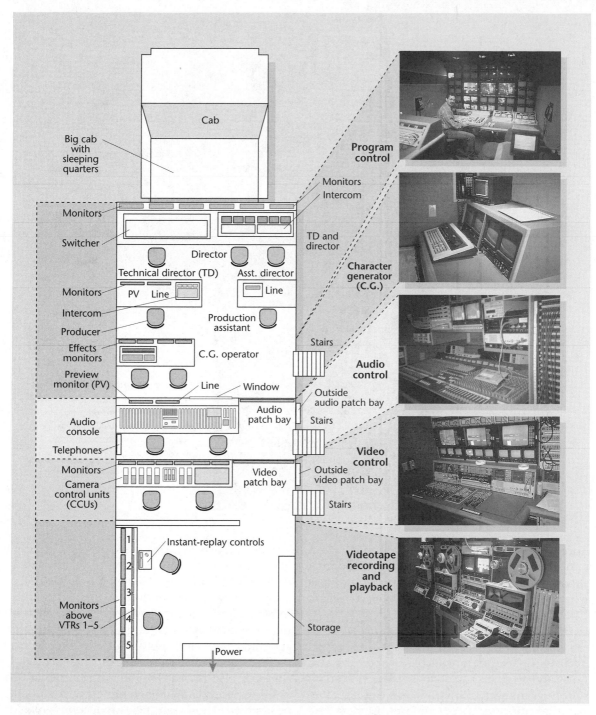

Program control

Character generator (C.G.)

Audio control

Video control

Videotape recording and playback

Cab

Big cab with sleeping quarters

Monitors

Switcher

Technical director (TD)

Director

Asst. director

Monitors
Intercom

TD and director

Monitors

PV   Line

Line

Intercom

Producer

Production assistant

Effects monitors

C.G. operator

Preview monitor (PV)

Line   Window

Stairs

Audio console

Audio patch bay

Outside audio patch bay

Telephones

Stairs

Monitors

Camera control units (CCUs)

Video patch bay

Outside video patch bay

Stairs

Instant-replay controls

1

2

3

Monitors above VTRs 1–5

4

5

Storage

Power

13-14 Control centers in a remote truck

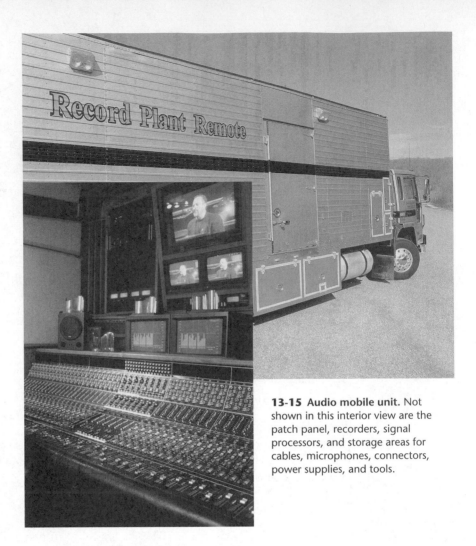

13-15 Audio mobile unit. Not shown in this interior view are the patch panel, recorders, signal processors, and storage areas for cables, microphones, connectors, power supplies, and tools.

duction equipment and the communication hookup among the key production people during shooting or broadcast. A remote survey can take whatever form suits the particular need. Figure 13-16 displays one example.

In surveying a field location, clearing access to the site and acquiring police permits and written permissions from property owners are also necessary. Diagrams and photographs of the various shooting areas at the production site are often required and are always helpful. Camera and microphone positions, cable and power runs, signal feeds, and other equipment locations can be easily determined at a glance.

Production meetings are also essential, particularly after the remote survey has been completed. If something is to go wrong, and it usually does, it is more likely to occur in the field than in a studio. In production meetings key personnel coordinate their responsibilities, explain their needs, discuss audio and video, and resolve problems. The remote production schedule, including setup and rehearsal times, is also planned. Scheduling production meetings seems like common sense, but you would be surprised at how many field productions proceed without them. As you might expect, these particular productions are apt to be more nerve-racking, to run over schedule, to cost more, and to be

REMOTE SURVEY FORM

SURVEY DATE _____   PROGRAM _____
LOCATION SITE _____   AIR DATE & TIME _____
LOCATION SITE ADDRESS _____   PRODUCER _____
_____   DIRECTOR _____
SETUP DATE(S) _____   TD _____

CAMERAS

NUMBER	LOCATION	TYPE	LENS	CABLE RUN

VIDEOTAPE

VTR DESIGNATION	TYPE	FUNCTION	VID FEED	AUD FEED

MICROPHONES

TYPE/MODEL	LOCATION	CABLE RUN/WIRELESS

REMOTE SURVEY FORM (cont.)

PROGRAM _____
_____

LIGHTING

TYPE	LOCATION	AVAILABLE LIGHT IN FC

IFB DELEGATION

DESIGNATION	CHANNEL	LOCATION	FEEDS

POWER

LOCATION ELECTRICIAN CONTACT _____
POWER REQUIREMENTS _____

AC OUTLETS (VOLTAGE/CONNECTOR TYPE/LOCATION)

LOCATION CONTACTS

NAME	TITLE/JOB	NUMBER

SPECIAL INSTRUCTIONS

13-16 Example of a remote survey form for television

aesthetically inferior. In this business of communications, communication is sometimes the element that is overlooked.

How to determine audio needs in a remote survey is, perhaps, better understood in the context of the actual production situation and is therefore explained in the sections on production of speeches and news conferences and of sports programs later in this chapter.

Field Intercom Systems

Intercommunication among personnel is always vital during production. This is particularly so in the field, where crew and facilities are more widely dispersed than in the studio.

Among the intercom systems employed in the field are interruptible foldback (IFB), program sound receiver, paging, intercom, cellular telephone, and walkie-talkie. The IFB system is covered in Chapter 12.

The *program sound receiver,* which looks like a pager, lets you hear the sound portion of the telecast to monitor director's cues.

Paging systems are wireless and similar to the small, belt-clipped receivers used by people who have to be contacted when they are not near a telephone.

Field *intercom systems* are wireless and similar to those used in the studio. They make two-way communication between the remote truck and the field crew possible.

The *cellular telephone* can be used to feed a performer program sound and IFB information, particularly when the performer is beyond a station's transmitting range.

The *walkie-talkie* is a handheld, two-way communications device with adequate reach if the field site is not too widespread. It can also be interfaced with other intercom devices.

Production of Speeches and News Conferences

Recording someone speaking from a podium at an event such as a press conference, dinner, awards ceremony, and the like is almost an everyday assignment in broadcasting. In preparing for such an event, it is important to know whether you will be taking the sound from your own microphone(s), from the house public-address (PA) system, or from a common output feed, other than the PA system, called a *multiple* (also known as a *press bridge*).

Setting Up Your Own Microphones

The directional microphone is usually the best one to use for a speaker at a podium. Its on-axis response focuses the sound from the speaker, and its off-axis cancellation reduces unwanted room and audience noises (see 13-17).

Cardioid microphones are most frequently used at a podium due to their wider on-axis response and because the audience faces the back of the mic, where a cardioid is least sensitive. Super-cardioids may be better, however; though they are slightly more directional at the front than are cardioids, it is not enough to seriously inhibit side-to-side head movement, and their side and rear rejection are superior.

The advantages of setting up and using your own microphones are that you have control of the sound quality and exclusive use of the content. Nevertheless, there are situations in which you have little or no say in these matters and have to take your sound from a common source.

Public-Address Pickups

Talks delivered in many types of rooms and halls require a public-address system so that the audience can hear the speaker. The miking for the PA system is at the podium. On occasion adding your mics to those already at the podium could create clutter that may be visually distracting and also obscure the speaker from some of the audience. In such instances you may have to take the audio feed from the PA system.

This entails patching into an output jack in the PA amplifier or PA control panel and feeding the signal to your mixer. It should not interfere with the loudspeaker sound, because the PA feed from the podium mics is usually split into, at least, two separate routing systems. Because many PA

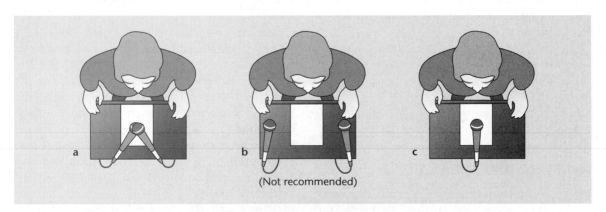

13-17 Commonly used techniques when miking a podium speaker with two directional microphones. (a) This mic placement provides a wide, smooth response and allows comfortable side-to-side head movement, but is often unnecessary. (b) This array is not recommended because it requires the speaker to remain between the mics to ensure smooth response. (c) In many situations a single cardioid or supercardioid is sufficient. Two parallel microphones, one above the other (see 4-61a) or three triangularly arrayed mics are often used in podium setups for redundancy.

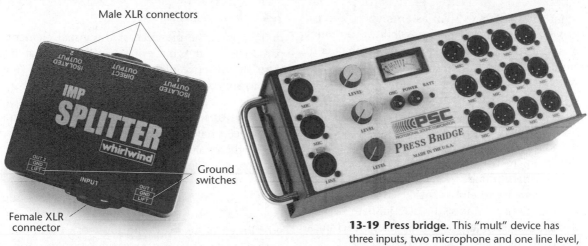

Male XLR connectors

ISOLATED OUTPUT 2 · DIRECT OUTPUT · INPUT · ISOLATED OUTPUT 1

IMP SPLITTER whirlwind

OUT 2 GND LIFT · INPUT · OUT 1 GND LIFT

Ground switches

Female XLR connector

13-18 Transformer-isolated microphone splitter

OSC POWER BATT · LEVEL · LEVEL · LEVEL · LINE · MIC · PSC PRESS BRIDGE MADE IN THE U.S.A. · MIC

13-19 Press bridge. This "mult" device has three inputs, two microphone and one line level, and 12 outputs, providing transformer-isolated, microphone level audio feeds.

loudspeaker systems are not noted for their sound quality, this arrangement gives you some control over the audio. If the house technicians control the sound feed, which is often the case, it is necessary to coordinate your needs with them in advance.

Splitting Microphones

An alternative to public-address pickups is splitting the microphone feed. This is manageable if your station or company is the only one, or one of only a few, covering an event. Otherwise, microphone and cable clutter could result.

Microphone splitting is usually accomplished with a transformer-isolated microphone splitter (see 13-18). It splits the microphone signal to the PA system and your mic mixer, isolating the two feeds, thereby reducing the possibility of hum.

Multiple Pickups

Several stations or networks often cover the same event. If they all set up microphones at the podium, not only would the clutter be unsightly, but also a good sound pickup might depend on how lucky the producer was in getting a mic close enough to the speaker. This often happens at news conferences, sometimes because the speaker believes that a clutter of mics makes the event

appear important. To the audio person, however, this is not ideal or preferred. If the facilities exist, it is better to take the sound from a *multiple,* or *"mult"* for short. A multiple (not to be confused with the *multiple* that interconnects jacks on a patch bay) is a distribution amplifier—an amplifier with several individual line and mic level outputs. Each station then obtains a separate, good-quality sound feed without struggle by patching into one of the amplifier's output connectors. This type of feed is usually agreed upon in advance by those involved and set up either cooperatively by them or by the sound people who operate the in-house audio system. This type of multiple is also known as a *presidential patch* or *press bridge* (see 13-19). Microphones used for questions from the audience are connected to the multiple as well. Thus all networks and stations get the same high-quality feed from the few mics used.

A challenge periodically encountered on remotes is the need to mike several speakers at a conference, symposium, press parley, and the like. The obvious way to produce such a program is to use a multichannel console and control the mic levels of each participant manually. But, depending on the number of participants, this could become unwieldy, especially if the operator has to handle other sound sources such as announcer and cart players. Then too, with the possibility of a number of mics being open at the same time, comb filtering, ambient noise, reverberation buildup, and, if a PA system is operating, feedback could occur.

For several years automatic microphone mixers have been available. Operating like a noise gate, they automatically open and close mics when sound level rises above or below a preset threshold. The problem with using them for broadcast has been the perceptible action of the gating as the mics were opened and closed. Also, it was difficult for some automatic mixers to discriminate between background noise and low-level speech reaching an adjacent mic.

Today, automatic microphone mixers are available in which the gating action is relatively seamless and noise-adaptive threshold settings activate a microphone for speech and not background sound (see 13-20). (These automatic mic mixers can also be used in recording music on location.) An automatic mic mixer can do only so much, however. Table 13-1 lists a few tips to reduce the most common problems associated with having multiple open microphones.

Production of Sports Programs

Sound in sports broadcasting is essential to the excitement of the event. It provides three basic elements—the sound of the announcers, the sound of the crowd, and the sound of the game action—which are handled somewhat differently for television than they are for radio.

Television Sports Audio

In TV sports the presence of the visual element, paradoxically, puts more of a demand on the audio than the absence of picture does in radio. (See "Radio Sports Audio" later in this chapter.)

The Announcers In sports broadcasting the announcers have to be heard clearly, whether they project their voices over the constant din of a large, vocal crowd or speak quietly during a golf or tennis match. In TV no microphone is better suited to meet both of these demands than the headset mic (see 4-33). The mic's design allows it to be positioned close to the announcer's mouth for optimal pickup of normal and quieter-than-normal speech while permitting the announcer to sit or stand. Its moving-coil element and built-in pop filter can withstand loud speech levels without overloading the mic, although limiting or compressing are usually necessary. The unidirectional pickup pattern reduces sound leakages from outside sources, and the omnidirectional pattern adds more background color. Each earpiece can carry separate information—the director's cues on one and the program audio on the other—and the space in front of the announcer can be kept clear for papers, TV monitors, and other paraphernalia.

It is also critical that the announcers can hear themselves in the headphone mix and have a means of communicating with the director through the IFB. To this end headphone and talkback controls are often placed within an announcer's reach, as is a "cough button" to kill the announcer's mic when the throat has to be cleared.

Table 13-1 Suggested solutions for multiple-open-microphone problems

Problem	Indicators	Tips
Comb filtering	Thin, hollow sound	Reduce number of mics Observe three-to-one rule
Excessive ambient noise reverberation	Distant, washed-out sound Loss of clarity and intelligibility	Reduce number of mics Reduce mic-to-source distances
Feedback	Feedback before the system is loud enough for the audience to hear it	Reduce number of mics Reduce mic-to-source distances Increase mic-to-loudspeaker distances

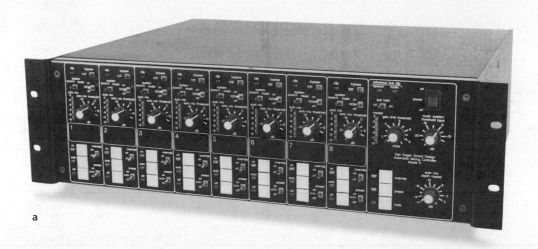

a

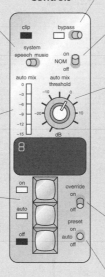

Channel Controls

System speech/music When in the speech mode, the constant equivalent gain of one open channel is distributed over the group of channels according to the pattern of the channels' levels. In the music mode, each channel's gain is expanded with a two-to-one ratio below the threshold. The threshold varies, following the signal level from the music system threshold input.

Auto mix **gain** All lights are on at normal full gain.

On, auto, **and** *off* **keys** These control the automatic mixing. In *on* the VCA is at unity gain. In *auto* the channel performs music or speech automatic mixing. In *off* the channel is fully muted.

Bypass This controls a relay bypassing all circuitry. All channels bypassed when power is off. The amber LED calls attention to a bypassed channel.

NOM (normally on) When off, this allows the channel to be exempted from the *number of open microphones* gain limiting system.

Auto mix threshold In the speech mode, this changes the relative weighting of the channel in the automatic mix without changing its level. Usually left on *0* in this mode. The threshold may be lowered to give less weight to a mic in a noisy location, without changing the gain of the mic when someone is speaking into it. In the music mode, the *threshold* control sets the muting threshold for each channel.

Override This programs the channel's response when the momentary *override* key is pressed in the master section or by remote contact.

Preset This programs the channel's condition on power-up after the *preset* key in the master section is pressed or by remote contact.

b

13-20 (a) Automatic microphone mixer with (b) its channel and master control functions

b (continued)

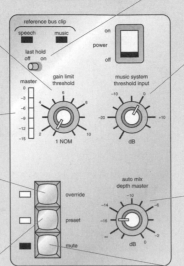

Master Controls

Gain limit threshold This sets the number of active mics at which master gain limiting begins. Gain limiting has nothing to do with the signal levels, loud or soft. It relates only to how many mics are in use.

NOM master This shows the master attenuation applied to all auto mode channels.

Override (momentary) When activated, this makes channels with *override* assign switches on come to normal gain, and all other channels to mute. The LED shows the actuation of the key or remote contacts.

Preset This sets the on/auto/off modes of all channels to the condition of their *preset* switches.

Last hold This keeps the last channel to come to full gain at full until superseded by another. Used with the music system if constant rather than suppressed ambience is desired.

Music system threshold input This controls the gain of the music system threshold input, a line input, typically fed from a preamplified room ambience mic. This signal is used only by the music system, to make the adaptive muting threshold. The pot is a master for the channel *auto mix threshold* controls.

Auto mix depth master This sets how far down auto-mixed channels will go. Less attenuation may be used if more-subtle muting is desired.

Mute (momentary) This switch mutes all channels. The red LED shows actuation of the button or remote contacts.

c

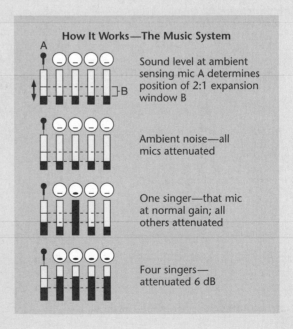

How It Works—The Speech System

Ambient noise—all mics attenuated to equal the gain of one normal mic

One talker—that mic at normal gain; all others attenuated

Another talker—gain shifts instantly to talker

Two talkers—each attenuated 3 dB

How It Works—The Music System

Sound level at ambient sensing mic A determines position of 2:1 expansion window B

Ambient noise—all mics attenuated

One singer—that mic at normal gain; all others attenuated

Four singers— attenuated 6 dB

13-20 (continued) **(b) Channel and master control functions of the automatic microphone mixer and (c) its effects on speech and music mixing**

The Crowd Crowd sound is vital to the excitement of most sporting events. The cheers, boos, and general hubbub punctuate the action, adding vitality to the event and making the audience at home feel a part of things.

Depending on the venue, crowd sound is picked up either by dedicated crowd microphones or the mics that are used to pick up the action sounds, or a combination of both. Dedicated crowd mics are generally employed in outdoor stadiums, because sound is more diffuse in an open space than it is indoors. The microphones—usually an X-Y pair of shotgun mics, a stereo mic, a middle-side mic, or some combination of these arrays—are positioned facing the crowd. They are mounted either low in the stands, aimed toward the crowd; high in the stands at press box level aimed straight ahead; on the field; or a combination of the three.

As with any sound source, proper microphone placement directly influences the quality of the pickup. This makes a location survey mandatory, because each stadium and arena has its own acoustics and seating patterns. For example, some outdoor stadiums are more live than others; the proximity of the crowd to the field may be closer in one stadium than in another; an indoor arena may have a concave roof relatively close to, or farther away from, the playing surface—all of which have a direct effect on the density and loudness of crowd sound.

One famous example of the need for location surveys and testing is a professional football game broadcast by NBC several years ago, without the announcers. It was an experiment to determine how well crowd and actions sounds could sustain the game's excitement. (The experiment was also in response to the still valid criticism that sports announcers talk too much.) The game was at season's end and meaningless, but the experiment failed because it was a sonically dull broadcast: It turns out that the stadium was built on sand, which absorbed much of the action and crowd sounds.

In addition to the typical needs considered in a location survey, such as type of microphones, microphone assignments, length of cable required, and so on, there are a number of steps to take in making decisions related to crowd pickup:

☑ Identify points where sound is more intense or live, or both. Sound-collecting points, usually at the concavities of stadiums and arenas, are good places to begin.

☑ Remember that sound is more concentrated and louder in enclosed venues than in open ones. In domed stadiums sound collects at and bounces from the concave roof to the crown of the playing surface. If microphones near the playing surface are not properly positioned, their sound quality will be degraded.

☑ Avoid dead spots where crowd sound will be hollow, thin, and unexciting.

☑ If attendance is likely to be less than capacity, know which seats will be filled and place the crowd mics in those areas.

☑ Be aware that home-team fans are likely to far outnumber those of a visiting team. To help maintain excitement no matter which team generates it, position a mic in front of or near the section where the visiting fans are seated, particularly if the game is important or involves a heated rivalry, or both.

The Action The sound of the action itself adds impact to a sporting event—the whoosh of the ball crossing the plate on its way to the whomp of it hitting the catcher's mitt or the crack of the bat on the ball in baseball; the signal calling of the quarterback and the crunch of hitting linemen in football; the skating sounds and slamming of bodies against the boards in hockey; the bouncing ball, squeaking sneakers, and swish of the ball through the hoop in basketball; and so on. In fact, many sports producers consider the action sounds as important as—or more important than—the crowd sound. To capture these sounds, separate microphones, other than the crowd mics, are used. The mics are mounted close to the area of play and pointed toward the action.

A synthesis of the various approaches to microphone placement for picking up action and crowd sounds used by the major networks in the various sports are displayed in Figures 13-21 through 13-30. Keep in mind that these illustrations are just that—examples.

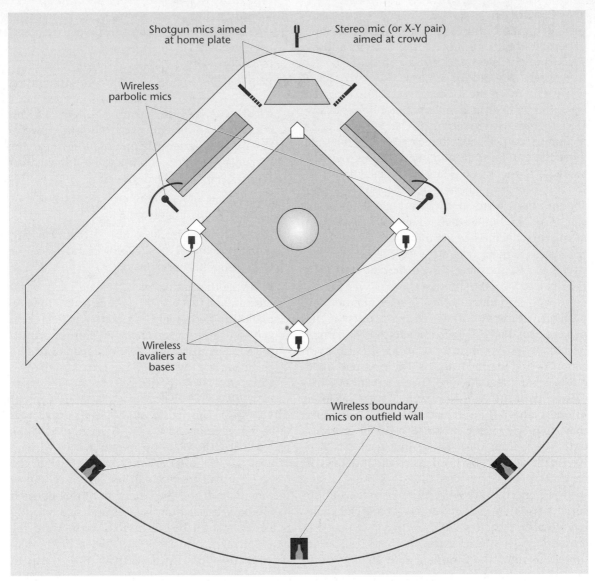

Shotgun mics aimed
at home plate

Stereo mic (or X-Y pair)
aimed at crowd

Wireless
parbolic mics

Wireless
lavaliers at
bases

Wireless boundary
mics on outfield wall

13-21 Miking baseball. Although most baseball sound is broadcast in mono-compatible stereo, only the crowd sound is miked for and reproduced in stereo. The main crowd mic, either a stereo mic or an X-Y pair of shotguns, is usually situated behind home plate, facing the crowd. For additional crowd sound reinforcement, and to help pick up the sound of an outfielder crashing against the wall, wireless boundary mics are mounted on the outfield wall in left, center, and right fields. These mics are panned to enhance the stereo imaging of the crowd sound. Shotgun microphones aimed at the plate pick up action sounds of the ball whooshing across the plate, the umpire's call, and the crack of the bat on the ball. The left shotgun mic (looking in toward home plate) is used when a right-hand batter is at the plate; the right shotgun is used when a left-hand batter is up. Only one shotgun at a time is live. For the whooshing sound of the ball crossing the plate, the level of the working shotgun mic is boosted for that split second of time. Other action sounds from the field are picked up by omnidirectional parabolic mics at the camera locations at first and third bases and wireless lavaliers at the bases. Omnidirectional mics are employed because they reproduce a wider image than do unidirectional microphones. Because all sound sources are mono, except the crowd, too narrow an image of the action sounds would be disconcerting when switching back and forth between them and crowd reaction.

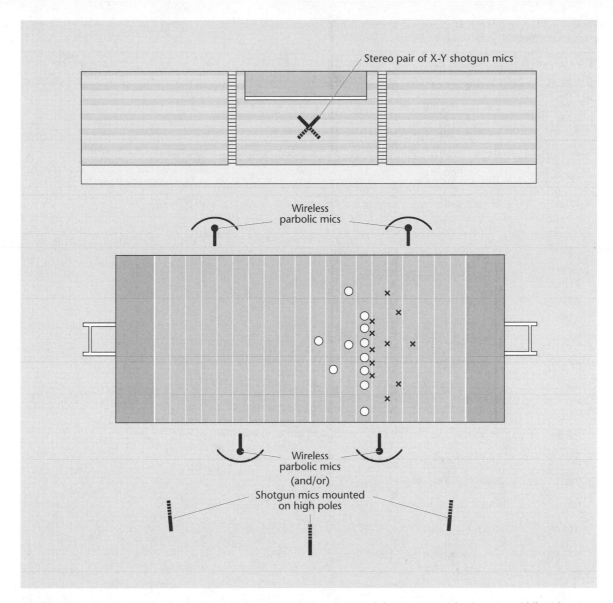

13-22 Miking football. Crowd sound is picked up through a stereo pair of shotgun microphones, or a middle-side mic, placed in the stands usually at press box level and pointed straight across the stadium. Crowd sound is also picked up by shotgun mics mounted on the sideline cameras (not shown) and/or shotguns mounted on high poles, depending on how well or poorly the crowd sound carries. The crowd microphones are mixed for stereo. Wireless parabolic mics pick up the sounds of field action such as the quarterback signals and colliding linemen. Four parabolic mics are usually employed, two on either side of the field, each assigned to cover from the 50-yard line to the end zone. Before the game it is important to make sure that the wireless mics transmit unobstructed sound, with no dropout, over their entire coverage area. Also at field level is a wireless handheld mic for the on-field color/interview announcer.

Miking is not all that the sound crew has to deal with. In the remote truck, the sound sources have to be assigned and mixed. Table 13-2 shows one approach to the audio on a network-level football broadcast.

Table 13-2 Example of sound source assignments in mixing audio for a network professional football game using a 48-channel console

Channel	Source Assignment
1–6	Returns from limiters and effects devices
7–8	Two wireless interview mics on the field
9–14	Left and right of three routers for video playback
15	Wireless field mic for sideline reporter (if not the same person doing interviews)
16–17	Two handheld microphones in the announcer's booth for the game announcers on-camera open
18–20	Three headset mics for the game announcers and any guest who comes by
21	Open
22	Feed from the house public-address system
23	Referee mic, feed from stadium
24–27	Shotgun mics on the sideline handheld cameras
28	Umpire's mic (to pick up sound from the break of the huddle to the snap of the ball, including the linebackers' calling out defensive signals)
29	Feed from the submix of the sideline parabolic mics
30–31	Left and right crowd mix from X-Y shotguns set up high at the 50-yard line
32	Surround channel crowd mics located high in the stadium
33–36	Submasters for the left, center, right, and surround sends to the Dolby encoder
37	Announce submaster
38	Send to the stereo synthesizer
39–44	Music playback devices, such as cart machines, CD players, and cassettes
45–46	Feeds from incoming remotes of other football games
47–48	Return loops for cueing and updating announcers

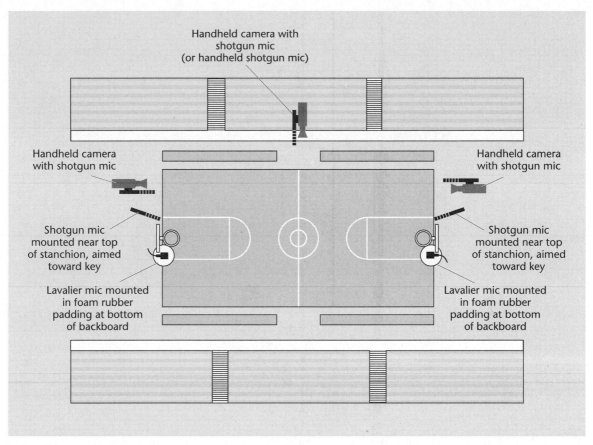

13-23 Miking basketball. Lavalier microphones are mounted to the foam rubber padding at the bottom of each backboard to pick up the sounds of the ball hitting the basket and swishing through the net. Shotgun mics aimed at the key pick up the ball-bouncing and sneaker sounds, grunts and chatter of the players, and calls from the referees. Shotgun mics on handheld cameras also pick up court sounds, as well as the cheerleading and talk from the benches. As the action moves up and down the court, the microphones at either end are opened and closed to avoid undue concentration of crowd sound and the pickup of out-of-shot sounds. A shotgun mic at midcourt, either camera-mounted or handheld, helps fill the transitions as the endcourt mics are opened and closed. The midcourt shotgun is kept open throughout the up- and down-court action. There is no dedicated crowd mic, because the array of microphones around courtside are usually adequate to pick up more-than-sufficient crowd sound due to the highly reflective acoustics in most indoor arenas. There may be an additional shotgun mic behind the backboard (not shown) to pick up the band; but due to the possible copyright infringement of music rights, music licensing agencies such as ASCAP (American Society of Composers, Authors, and Publishers) and BMI (Broadcast Music, Inc.) require a fee from the performing organization or its sponsor to broadcast the music. Therefore miking for such a music pickup should be cleared in advance. The same is true for similar situations in other sports.

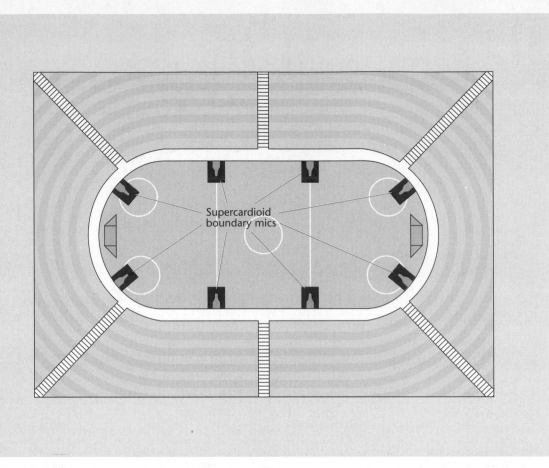

13-24 Miking ice hockey. For the main action and crowd mics, one approach uses eight supercardioid boundary mics on transparent plastic plates mounted on the inside of the glass that surrounds the rink. The mics are positioned on either end of the blue lines and at the end of the rink in the corners, on either side, to pick up the skating and impact sounds. They also pick up sufficient crowd sound due to the concentrated acoustics in enclosed arenas. There may be additional audio pickup from handheld shotgun mics or from the shotguns on handheld cameras. A handheld shotgun may also be assigned to the penalty box. In the American Hockey League, permission is often given to put wireless mics on the goalies, players, and/or coaches. These microphones and the penalty box mic are used for replay in case something interesting happens and to screen foul language.

In mixing hockey audio, the board operator must be adept at following the play-by-play on the monitor and riding levels accordingly, because hockey is so unpredictable. When an action is anticipated, such as a goal or a body slam against the boards, the operator will boost the level to enhance the sound of the play action or crowd reaction.

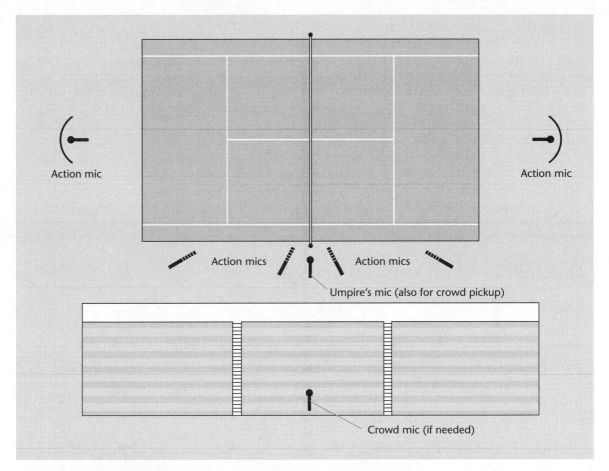

Action mic

Action mics

Action mics

Umpire's mic (also for crowd pickup)

Crowd mic (if needed)

13-25 Miking tennis. In tennis sound is critical because the announcers do not talk when the ball is in play, and the crowd must be quiet. Microphones must, therefore, be strategically placed to pick up the court action. An omnidirectional microphone is set up next to the umpire to hear his calls, the players talking to him, and the crowd sound. Two directional mics are positioned on either side of the net, pointing at the court, to pick up the sounds of the ball when it hits the net on a service, the ball hitting the strings of the tennis racket, and players' comments near midcourt. Directional mics are aimed at the service lines to pick up the whopping sound when the player connects with the ball. Parabolic mics placed behind each baseline pick up the string sound on the racket when the ball is hit deep and the players' grunts when they hit the ball. If the crowd mic at the umpire's location does not pick up enough crowd sound, another crowd mic is mounted from an overhang in the stands.

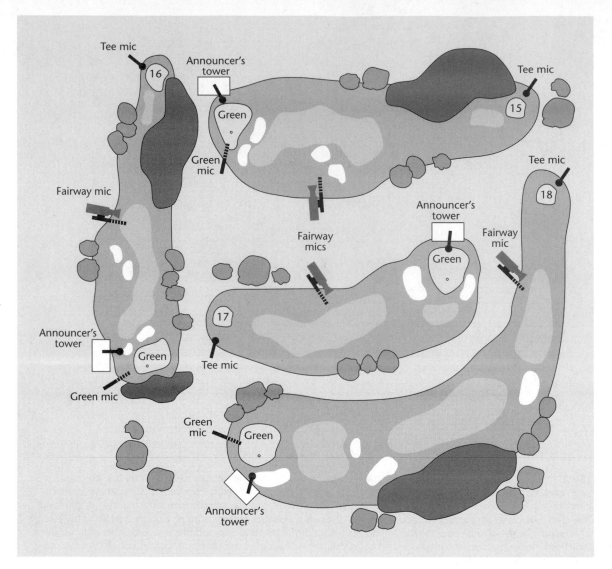

13-26 Miking golf. Omnidirectional or directional microphones are placed near the tees to pick up the sound of the drive and the crowd sound. In the fairways directional mics, either handheld or mounted on minicams, pick up fairway shots and conversation among golfers. At the greens directional mics pick up the sound of the putt and the crowd sound. Wireless mics are placed in the cup, with the transmitter aerial wrapped around the outside, to pick up the sound of the ball falling into the cup. At each hole are announcers' towers with omnidirectional microphones outside to pick up crowd sound and general ambience, or the crowd sound pickup is through the mics already arrayed at the hole. Other wireless operators cover shots where balls are in difficult locations.

Recording and mixing golf presents a unique challenge in that while play at one hole is on the air, play at other holes is being recorded. This requires separate audio effects mixes for the play at each hole.

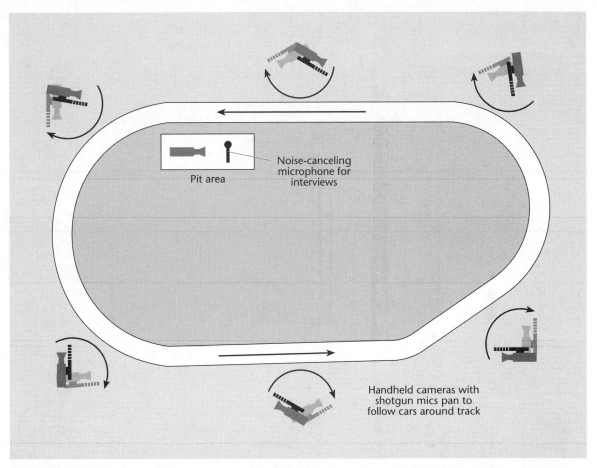

13-27 Miking auto racing. The main audio problem in auto racing is that it is essentially a one-sound sport—the cars as they careen around the track. Announcers' commentary and interviews break up the constancy of the racing car sounds, but the challenge is to vary the racing sounds to make them as interesting as possible. Handheld cameras with shotgun mics, or handheld shotguns, are positioned at strategic points on the racetrack—at the curves and the straightaways. The camera and mics pick up the cars as they come toward the camera position and follow the cars as they race to the next camera position, where that camera picks up the action and the sound, and so on around the track. With the mics in these locations, the Doppler effect of the pitch changes as the cars come toward the camera and move away from it; the shifting gears; the slowing down and speeding up of the engines; the screeching brakes; and, unfortunately, the crashes—all vary the audio and help create sonic perspective. Crowd sound is not the factor in auto racing that it is in other sports. Even when a microphone is placed in the stands, crowd reaction may not be audible above the engine roar. Due to the high levels of track noise, a noise-canceling microphone is usually employed for interviews in the pit area.

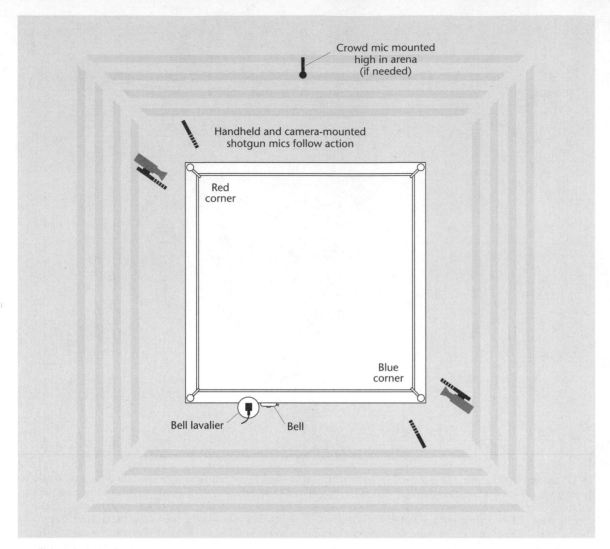

Crowd mic mounted
high in arena
(if needed)

Handheld and camera-mounted
shotgun mics follow action

Red
corner

Blue
corner

Bell lavalier   Bell

13-28 Miking boxing. Two shotgun microphones, one at the red corner, the other at the blue corner, are aimed into the ring to pick up the fight sounds. As the fighters move around the ring, the shotguns follow the action and are opened and closed (although not fully closed) as the fighters move closer to and farther from the mics. Shotgun mics on handheld cameras in the red and blue corners are used between rounds to pick up the exchanges between the fighters and their handlers. Because fights usually take place indoors and the crowd is close to the ring, the shotgun mics are usually adequate to pick up crowd sound as well. If not, a crowd mic, shotgun or omnidirectional, depending on how much reinforcement is needed for the crowd sound, is mounted high in the arena. A lavalier picks up the sound of the bell. The ringside announcers almost always use headset microphones for their commentary and a handheld mic for interviews.

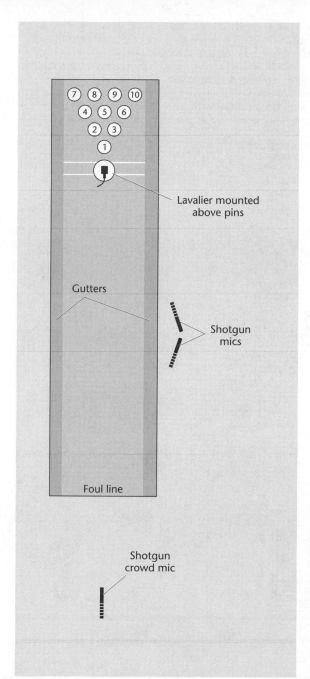

7 8 9 10
4 5 6
2 3
1

Lavalier mounted
above pins

Gutters

Shotgun
mics

Foul line

Shotgun
crowd mic

13-29 Miking bowling. Due to the usually high ambient levels in bowling alleys, directional mics are the microphones of choice. Either two shotguns or directional boundary mics are positioned at the side of the lane, one facing toward the foul line, the other facing toward the pins. This technique captures the sounds of the ball drop, the roll down the alley, and the pin strike. A lavalier may be mounted above the pin pit to reinforce the pin strike and pin fall, and, if wanted, the initial action of the pin setup mechanism. If the action mics are insufficient to deal with crowd sound, an additional mic, usually directional, is aimed toward the crowd from in front and above.

13-30 Miking track and field and gymnastics. Because the action takes place in various locations in the same venue and each event requires a different apparatus, producing audio for track and field and gymnastics requires inventiveness in miking and coordination in mixing. To pick up the action sounds, place a mic anywhere you can put one. When action is moving from one point to another, as in the hurdles, mics should be spaced evenly on side stands between the starting and finish lines to pick up the sound oncoming and passing. With continuous events, such as hurdles and other types of racing, mics should be opened and closed as the action dictates, otherwise the sonic density will mask the audio due not only to the action sounds but to the pickup of crowd sound. Music to accompany gymnastic routines is usually picked up by the action mics. Examples of selected track and field and gymnastic events are shown below and on the next page.

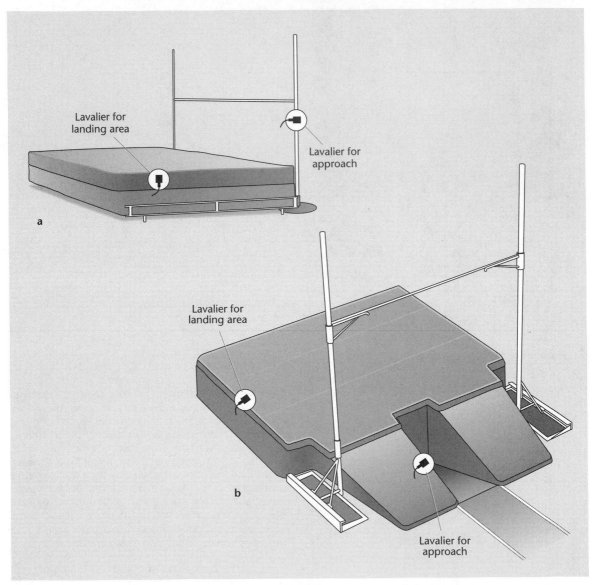

Lavalier for landing area

Lavalier for approach

a

Lavalier for landing area

b

Lavalier for approach

(a) High jump and (b) pole vault. Wireless lavaliers placed at the approach and landing area pick up the sounds of the pole vault or jump, the landing, and any sounds the athlete makes. The mics are opened only for the action they cover. The approach mic opens for the approach and closes after the leap, and the landing mic, which is closed for the approach, opens after the leap. Of course, the mixer must coordinate the levels for a smooth transition.

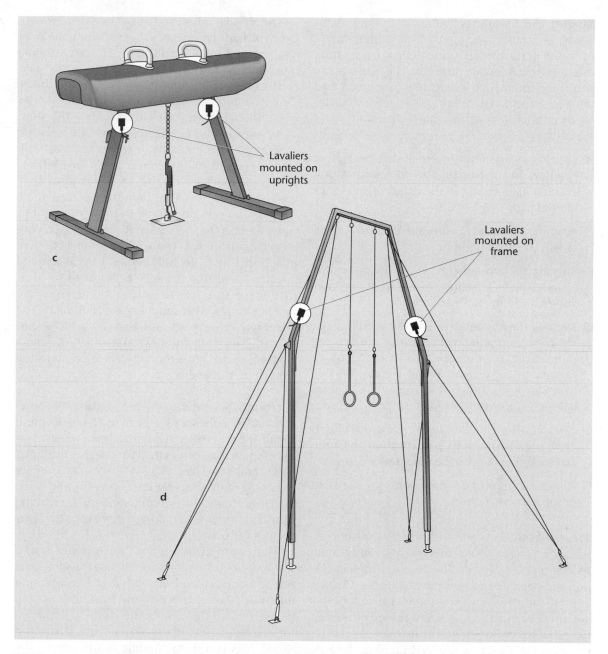

Lavaliers mounted on uprights

Lavaliers mounted on frame

c

d

13-30 *(continued)* **(c) Pommel horse.** Wireless lavaliers mounted near the top of one or both uprights are usually sufficient to pick up the gymnast's sounds. Two mics are used to ensure that hits on the left and right sides of the horse are heard, or to reinforce the action sounds, or both. Mics mounted directly on the underside of the pommel horse could produce a muffled sound because of its padding.

(d) Rings. Wireless lavaliers mounted on one or both sides of the frame not only pick up the action sounds of the gymnast, but any squeaking or metallic creaking sounds as well. Placing the mics between the middle and top of the frame helps pick up the sounds of ring attachments. It is wise to place thin padding between the lavalier and the metal frame to prevent the mic from slipping or from being audibly jarred by the frame's movement.

Mixing the Elements Philosophies vary about how crowd, action, and announcers' sounds should be mixed in the overall sound design of a sporting event. In any approach, however, the play-by-play and color commentary must always be clear and intelligible. Although mixing is covered in Chapter 19, here are a few of the more commonly used approaches:

☑ Keeping crowd level lower during periods of inaction and increasing crowd sound during exciting plays to add to the drama of an event's natural pace

☑ Keeping crowd level constant throughout the broadcast to maintain interest

☑ Burying the announcers' voices in the crowd sound to make the announcers part of the event and to unify overall intensity

☑ Keeping the announcers' voices out in front of the crowd sound to avoid masking the play-by-play and color commentary and to reduce listener fatigue engendered by too much sonic intensity over a long period; sometimes done by compressing crowd sound

☑ Compressing the sounds of the announcers, crowd, and action to control their dynamic ranges and to give each element more punch

☑ Compressing one or more sonic elements to create a layering effect

Stereo Sound As with stereo TV in general, producing stereo sports involves providing sonic spaciousness or depth while dealing with localization and stereo-to-mono compatibility (see Chapter 19). Of the three audio components involved—announcers, crowd, and action—the crowd is often the principal or only stereo element.

Announcers present the least problem. Because they are the primary source of information and are stationary during an event, it is natural that they be positioned in the center of the stereo image, although their voices may be fed through a stereo synthesizer or panned so that they sound more a part of the overall sonic setting instead of separate from it.

The crowd is miked and mixed in stereo. Primary crowd pickup comes from a main microphone array and assigned full left and right. The fan at home must feel that he or she is "sitting in one seat" and close to the action—not moving around with the shot. If additional crowd mics are used, they should be for fill, not for emphasis to coincide with a shot.

Action sounds are handled in two ways: either straight down the middle or somewhat localized. Sound panned to the center gives an up-front feeling to coincide with the generally tighter shot it accompanies. Localized sounds are picked up by one mic and panned slightly to the left or right to coincide with their relative position in the playing area. This means that the action mics must be very directional and precisely aimed to make stereo imaging easier for the mixer. But even in ideal circumstances, trying to localize sound, especially moving sound, with shot changes is difficult. The mixer must constantly anticipate a director's shot change. Even if synchronization is achieved, camera angles may cut across the 180-degree axis, creating "reverse angle" audio.

Surround Sound Due to the logistics, expense, and limited audience capable of receiving surround sound, it has been produced only for selected major sporting events, such as the World Series, the Super Bowl, and the Olympics. With the technology becoming more available, less expensive, and easier to manage, and with consumer interest increasing, surround sound is becoming a more common part of sports telecasting.

The essential difference between stereo and surround sound in sportscasts, beside the additional side and/or rear loudspeakers, is in the crowd sound mix. With stereo, crowd sound is in front of you, imaged left to right, with the panning emphasis toward the sides of the stereo field. Surround sound puts you in the middle of the crowd. The announcers' sound still comes from the front-center, with maybe some slight left-to-right panning to open their space somewhat. The action sounds are pretty much handled as they would be in stereo. The key guideline in surround is the same as it is in stereo: Avoid dislocation. Figure 13-31 is one example of audio coverage in surround sound.

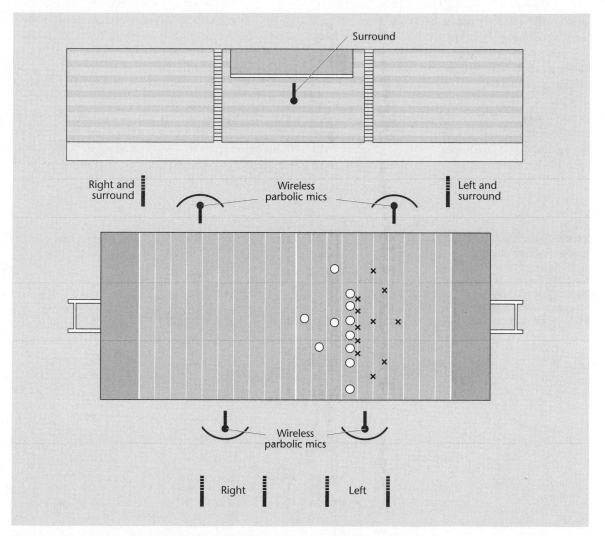

13-31 Surround-sound miking for football. For overall crowd sound, four shotgun mics are positioned on the far side of the field—across from the press box—spaced in pairs on the 20- and 40-yard lines for the main left and right pickups. The near-side shotgun mics are for more-immediate left and right crowd sound and, along with the directional mic at press box level, are fed into the surround channel. The wireless parabolic mics are used to capture field sounds.

Radio Sports Audio

The main difference between radio and TV sports audio, apart from the obvious absence of the visuals, is that radio is less dependent on the action sounds and more dependent on the announcers' word pictures. Because the playing area is not visible in radio, except for a few pronounced and recognizable game sounds like the crack of the bat in baseball, action sounds are more distracting than they are dynamic.

It is up to the announcers to create word pictures of the event; the sonic excitement being provided by their voices and the crowd sound. Good radio sportscasters add their own action descriptors when it is appropriate to do so, by describing the crushing blow, hard hit, board slam, crushed baseball, and so on.

Too often radio sportscasters call a game as if they were doing TV by just summarizing the play, with the color commentator filling in the space between calls. Except for the crowd sound, the broadcast is usually dull and vague.

Miking the sportscasters depends on what is logistically and physically comfortable and practical. In radio it usually comes down to either the headset mic or the desk mic: directional if the announcers' booth or the surrounding area is noisy; omnidirectional if it is not.

For crowd sound the variety of microphone arrays and techniques used in TV are also suitable for radio, although they usually do not have to be as elaborate. In some instances the crowd mics do double duty as action mics, particularly those positioned close to the playing area.

When a radio and a TV sportscast are carried by the same network or by cooperating stations, the radio audio may take part or all of the crowd and action feeds from the TV sound, including the field mics used for interviewing (see 13-32).

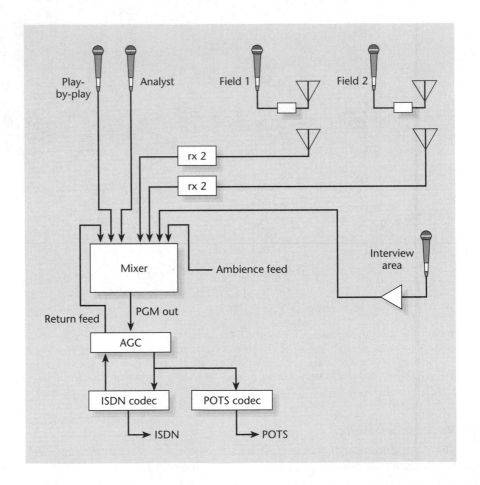

13-32 Signal flow of a sports program chain. With the exception of the radio announcers' microphones, the rest of the radio audio feed is taken from the TV audio.

▶ Producers go on location to cover news and sports, to do a disc jockey program, to heighten realism in a drama, to add authenticity to a setting, or to provide surroundings that are difficult or impossible to reproduce in a studio.

▶ Live and live-on-tape field productions for radio and television can be grouped into two basic categories: electronic news gathering (ENG) and electronic field production (EFP). The main difference between ENG and EFP is that ENG covers news events, whereas EFP is employed with the types of productions that take more time to plan and produce.

▶ Thanks to small, lightweight equipment—such as portable microphone mixers, consoles, handheld cameras, recorders, editors, high-quality headphones, mobile and cellular telephones, remote pickups, codecs, and microwave transmission from a mobile unit—it is relatively easy to transmit from the field to the radio or TV station for recording or direct broadcast.

▶ Field production often presents the problem of background sound's interfering with the intelligibility of the on-mic/on-camera reporters. In news, however, most producers believe that some sonic sense of locale is important to reports from the field.

▶ Mix-minus refers to a program sound feed without the portion supplied by the source that is receiving the feed.

▶ Recording background sound on a separate track is useful in postproduction to bridge transitions or cover awkward edits.

▶ When possible, preproduction planning is essential for most on-location broadcasting or recording. Preparation involves drafting a remote (site) survey; making sure where the power will come from; deciding who will take care of the equipment, program, and administrative details; planning the IFB system; and bringing to the production site the essential tools and backup supplies.

▶ As in studio productions, intercommunication systems are vital in the field, particularly because crew and facilities are usually more widely dispersed. Among the intercom systems used in the field are interruptible foldback (IFB), program sound receiver, paging, intercom, cellular telephone, and walkie-talkie.

▶ Three ways to record someone speaking from a podium are to: (1) set up and use your own microphones, (2) patch into the public-address (PA) system, or (3) patch into a multiple pickup.

▶ When several speakers have to be miked, using an automatic microphone mixer may be more convenient than having one operator try to control all of the mic levels.

▶ Miking sporting events requires sound pickup from the announcers, the crowd, and the action.

▶ In miking and mixing sporting events in stereo, the announcers are centered, action sounds are either centered or somewhat localized, and crowd sound is assigned full left and right. In surround sound announcers and actions sounds are usually delegated as they are in stereo, with the crowd sound assigned to the left, right, and surround channels.

▶ In radio sports broadcasts, the announcers' word pictures, their action descriptors, the sonic enthusiasm in their voices, and the crowd sound all contribute to the excitement and drama of the event.

▶ Philosophies vary about how crowd, action, and announcers' sounds should be mixed in the overall sound design of a sporting event. In any approach, however, the announcers' play-by-play and commentary must always be intelligible.

14

Staged Productions

Staged material—such as commercials, sitcoms, and drama—for radio, television, or film is almost always produced for later release; it is recorded with postproduction in mind. This allows more flexibility during production. Scenes are done in several takes to provide different dramatic perspectives and to give the editor choices in establishing continuity, pace, point of view, and so on.

In audio the principal challenge during production is dialogue recording. Sound effects are usually handled in postproduction; music always is. Regardless of the venue, studio or location, or the medium, *recording dialogue that is clear, intelligible, and as noise-free as possible is the production recordist's goal.* Even when dialogue is to be ultimately recorded or rerecorded in postproduction, it is important to preserve an actor's performance on the set, if for no other reasons than for timing and interpretation. (Also see "Automated Dialogue Replacement" in Chapter 17.)

RADIO DRAMATIZATIONS

Dramatizations produced in radio today are played out mostly in commercials and other types of spot announcements. Except for some drama done on public radio and in some colleges, the days of bona fide radio drama have long since passed. What has carried over, however, are many of the updated microphone and production techniques that were used.

Dramatizations on radio entail creating sound to compel the listener to "see" mental images; to create a "theater of the mind." The stimuli that trigger the imagination are words, sound effects, and music, as well as the methods used to produce these elements. Generating illusions of perspective and movement begin with techniques of miking.

Single-Microphone Technique

Using one microphone in radio dramatization involves positioning performers at the mic and having them play to it as if it were the ear of the audience. This involves selecting an appropriate microphone and properly mounting it. Creating a sense of perspective and, if necessary, movement makes the "visual" illusion effective.

Microphone Selection and Mounting

The best microphone to use for the single-mic technique is a multidirectional capacitor. Capacitors give the human voice a rich, realistic timbre. Ribbon microphones are good for voice, but older models lack the high-frequency response that gives sound its lifelike quality, assuming the medium reproduces those frequencies.

As for moving-coil microphones, several models have excellent voice response, but almost all are either omnidirectional or unidirectional. If the number of performers changes within a dramatization or during a take, it is easier to set up one multidirectional microphone than to change mics every time the situation requires.

The preferred microphone mount for radio dramatizations is the boom. It gives easy access to the mic, there is no floor stand to get in the way, and, with shock mounting, there is less chance of sound conductance from movement across the studio floor.

Another advantage of the boom is that performers deliver their lines standing, which is better for breathing. It also allows some freedom of movement for performers who like to swing an arm to help their delivery, or both arms if one hand is not holding the script.

Creating Perspective

To create perspective acoustically, performers are positioned at appropriate distances relative to the mic and to each other, as the dramatic action dictates. If an actor is close to the mic, the audience perceives the sound as near or the space as small, or both, particularly with a directional microphone. If a performer is farther from the mic, the sense of distance increases and the space becomes larger. If a man and woman are on-mic playing opposite each other in a scenario that calls for them to be equally enthusiastic, position the man farther from the microphone than the woman is to compensate for the (usually) more powerful male voice. If they are equidistant from the mic, the man will sound closer than the woman does (see Figure 14-1). The audience's perspective will be from the performer in the closer position. This assumes a relatively quiet, acoustically controlled studio. In a more open ambience, moving an actor too far from the mic to compensate for a stronger voice would also increase the level of his room tone, thereby placing him in an aural frame that is different from that of the more soft-spoken actor.

Maintaining perspective does not always mean keeping voice levels balanced. If a scene requires one character to call to another from a distance, perspective is created by placing on-mic the actor who is supposed to be closer and off-mic the one who is supposed to be farther away.

Creating Movement

If movement is involved, such as someone leaving or entering a room, there are three ways to create the effect: (1) by moving from the live to the dead side of a directional microphone or vice versa, (2) by turning in place toward or away from the mic, or (3) by walking toward or away from the mic.

Moving the fader up or down—also known as *board fade*—will also create the effect of coming or going, but not so well as having the performers do it. The difference between the two techniques is that using the fader influences not only the actor's voice level but also the room's acoustics. When a

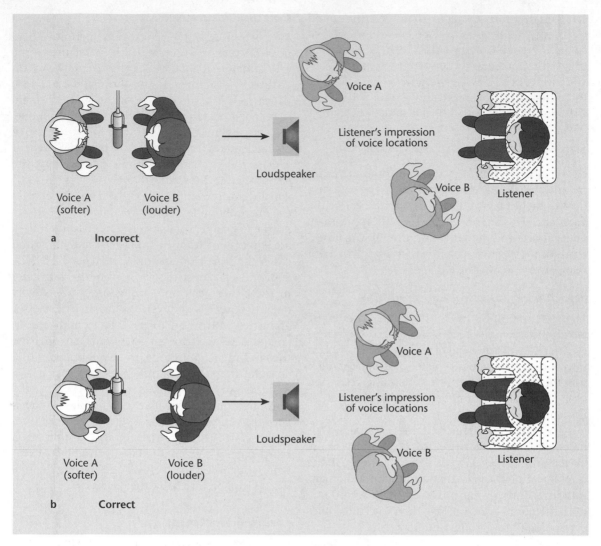

14-1 Balancing two voices with different loudnesses. Positioning the stronger voice farther from the microphone keeps the voices in proper aural perspective relative to the listener. But do not position the stronger voice too far from the mic, or it could take on an ambient quality noticeably different from that of the softer voice.

person enters or leaves a room, the space does not change; only the person's position within it changes.

Once the proper aural balances are determined, it is a good idea to mark or tape the studio floor so the performers will know exactly where to stand and how far to move. Marking the studio floor also assists in traffic control around a microphone when several performers are in a scene and have to yield and take on-mic position.

Multimicrophone Technique

With multitrack recording, producing a dramatization can take advantage of all the flexibility that it affords. Performers can be miked separately to allow greater sound control during recording. Then the various tracks can be processed, edited, and mixed in postproduction. Although added sound control is an advantage of this technique, there are also disadvantages: It is more difficult to obtain natural spatial relationships and perspective between performers and the environment; it reduces the opportunity for talent to interact; and it requires the additional time and expense of a postproduction session.

Deciding whether to use the single- or multimicrophone technique in radio dramatizations depends on your aesthetic philosophy and the complexity of the script. All in all, however, single-microphone production, although old-fashioned, has two major advantages: (1) It produces a more believable performance because the talent can interact and (2) it produces a more realistic sound shape. That said, for the sound shaping of individual performances, particularly when using effects, and for the added flexibility in production, including stereo and surround sound, the multimicrophone approach is the technique of choice.

Stereo Microphone Technique

When stereo placement of the performers is called for, and the multimicrophone technique is employed during recording, spatial placement in the stereo frame is done in postproduction through panning. If the "single" microphone approach is used, the performers must be stereo-miked during recording, otherwise it is quite difficult to position them in stereo space in postproduction.

A number of the production techniques applicable to monaural radio dramatizations also apply to stereo, but stereo does bring its own set of challenges, not the least of which is *mono compatibility.* Although stereo has been around for many years, and AM and FM radio transmit in stereo, much of the audience still listens in mono, particularly to AM radio. This means that material recorded in stereo must be capable of also being reproduced in mono.

Stereo requires two discrete signals, A (left) and B (right). To reproduce these signals in mono, they are summed: A + B. Discrete stereo is also referred to as sum-and-difference stereo, because one channel is summed (A + B), and the other channel is subtracted (A – B). If the stereo signals are in phase when they are added, level can increase 3 to 6 dB; if the signals are out of phase in stereo, they cancel in mono. It is therefore critical during recording to make sure that problems with stereo-to-mono compatibility are anticipated.

Stereo miking uses two microphones (or microphone capsules) to feed each discrete signal to a separate channel. Sound reaches the microphones with intensity and time differences. The difference in arrival time between the signals reaching the two microphones creates phase problems later when combining the signals to mono. The narrower the angle or space between the mics, the less the difference in arrival time between the signals reaching the mics.

There are a number of ways to mike for stereo. One technique—coincident miking—ensures stereo-to-mono compatibility; another—near-coincident miking—can be mono-compatible if the angle or space between the microphones is not too wide. Coincident and near-coincident arrays are also called *X-Y miking.*

Coincident miking positions two microphones, usually directional, in virtually the same space with their diaphragms located vertically on the same axis (see 15-37). This arrangement minimizes the arrival time difference between the signals reaching each mic. Stereo imaging is sharp, and sound localization is accurate.

Near-coincident miking positions two microphones, usually directional, horizontally on the same plane, angled a few inches apart. They may be spaced or crossed (see 15-38). The wider angle or space between the mics adds more depth and warmth to the sound, but stereo imaging is not as sharp as it is with the coincident array. As a guideline in radio dramatizations, keep the angle or space between the mics to 90 degrees or less. At more than 90 degrees, not only could mono compatibility be a problem, but the stereo image would be more diffuse.

In stereo miking, the lateral imaging of the stereo field is also important. If the angle between the microphones is too narrow, sound will be concentrated toward the center (between two loudspeakers). If the angle between the microphones is too wide, sound will be concentrated to the left and right, with little sound coming from the center, a condition referred to as "hole in the middle." The angle between the microphones is contingent on the width of the sound source: the wider the source, the wider the angle; the narrower the source, the narrower the angle. (If a sound source is too wide for the coincident and near-coincident arrays, as may be the case with orchestral ensembles in concert halls, spaced mics are employed—see 15-12.)

In stereo radio dramatizations, performers are usually not widely spaced at a single microphone. The center of the stereo space is where the main action is likely to take place. Too much "ping-ponging" of sound left and right can create dislocation of the sound sources, confusing the listener. If action is played left or right of center, it is usually not too wide afield.

Assuming that there are no acute acoustic problems, the inclusive angle between the microphones should be between 60 and 90 degrees. At the least, that is a good starting point; further positioning depends on the number of people in a scene and the size of the aural "set."

Using the multimicrophone approach, on-mic spacing is not a factor. Stereo imaging is handled in postproduction.

Perspective

In positioning performers take care to ensure that they are in the same positions and perspectives as the associated voices. If a script calls for conversation among performers in various parts of a room, they cannot be grouped around the mics—some closer, some farther—in stereo as they would be in mono. To maintain the stereo perspective, each actor should be in about the same position, relative to the others, as he or she would be if the situation were real (see 14-2).

More studio space is required for stereo radio dramatizations than for mono, because the dead sides of the mics cannot be used for approaches to and recedes from the mics. To produce the illusion of someone walking from left to right, a performer cannot simply walk in a straight line across the stereo pickup pattern. If that happened, the sound at the center would be disproportionately louder than the sound at the left and right, and the changes in level would be too abrupt. To create a more realistic effect, a performer has to pass the microphones in a semicircle. Also, studio acoustics should be dry, because they are much more apparent with stereo than they are with mono.

Surround-Sound Technique

It was noted in Chapter 10 that surround sound adds greater front-to-rear depth and side/rear breadth to aural imaging. A main difference—and advantage—in using surround sound in dramatic radio productions, compared with stereo, is being able to position performers much as they would be on a stage and recording them from those perspectives. This can be done during recording by using surround-sound microphony (see Chapter 4) or by using conventional multitrack-recording techniques and handling the surround-sound placements through panning in postproduction. See Chapters 15 and 19 for more-detailed coverage of surround-sound techniques.

DIALOGUE RECORDING IN MULTI- AND SINGLE-CAMERA PRODUCTION

Recording dialogue that is clear, intelligible, and as noise-free as possible, in the studio or in the field, is the responsibility of the production recordist. *Production recording* preserves the sonic record of a production, regardless of whether the dialogue is to be rerecorded in postproduction. Many things happen in life that are difficult to remember, much less re-create—the precise rhythmic nuance of dialogue, the unplanned cough or sputter that furnished a perfect dramatic highlight, the train that happened to go by at exactly the right moment. The live situation is more real and more delicate than the re-created one.

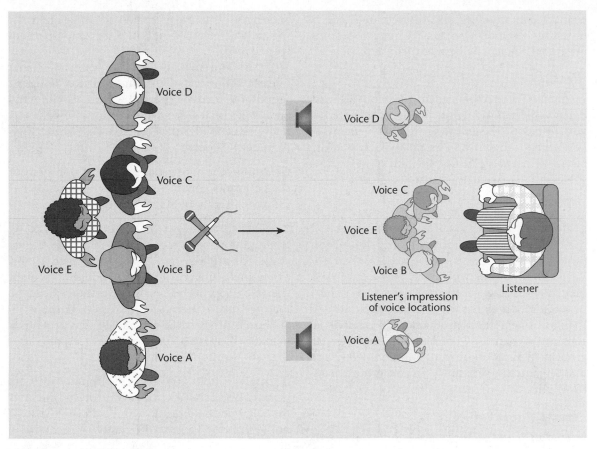

14-2 Effects of stereo-miking technique on listener perception

Capturing dialogue on the set in multicamera or single-camera production usually means employing a boom, body-mounted wireless, or plant microphone, or a combination of the three. The type of mic generally preferred is the capacitor—mini-mic and shotgun.

Using the Boom

The important decisions in using a boom are logistical and aesthetic. They involve (1) plotting the best microphone positions and angles for each scene in a production to ensure optimal aural balance, (2) keeping the boom out of the lighting pattern so that its shadow does not fall across the set, (3) making sure that the boom does not get in the way of the performers, (4) making sure that the boom can move freely, (5) trying to keep cameras and boom out of the audience's line-of-sight as much as possible, and (6) positioning the boom at mic-to-source distances that are relative to the fields of view of the shots to help maintain acoustic perspective between sound and picture.

It is worth noting that because of the logistical and operational concerns associated with using the boom, many directors use the wireless body mic instead, regardless of whatever sonic advantages the boom may have in a given situation (see "Using Wireless Body Microphones" later in this chapter). Their thinking is that easier is better and more economical; any aesthetic shortcomings can be offset in postproduction. Reality notwithstanding, always try to take the best aesthetic approach.

Blocking

In dramatic productions miking decisions are made during the preproduction planning stages when you work out the *blocking*—the movements of performers, cameras, and sound boom(s). Blocking begins with a *floor plan*—a diagram, drawn to scale, showing where scenery, cameras, microphones, and performers will be positioned.

If there is limited physical movement by the performers and the set is small, one boom microphone can usually handle the action, provided the performers are not more than 6 to 9 feet from the mic when they speak. If physical movement is active or the set is large, or both, two booms and sometimes wireless body mics are used. In multicamera staged productions, two booms are standard. When using two booms, one is usually positioned to cover the front and front-left of a set (looking into the set); the other covers the rear and rear-right.

Perambulator Boom

In studios it is also necessary to think about the boom mount when blocking. The *perambulator boom,* for instance, is large, bulky, and difficult to move quickly over extended distances, especially when cameras, cables, and set furniture are in the way (see 4-55). It is easier to leave the boom mount in place and swing, extend, or retract the boom arm to cover the action. If the boom has to be moved, use boom movers, because it is time-consuming and inconvenient to have the operator come down from the boom seat each time the boom has to be repositioned.

An evident but vital concern is making sure the boom mic does not get into the picture. If it is positioned out-of-shot in a close-up, it would obviously show up in a longer shot if not repositioned. The boom should also be out of an audience's line-of-sight as much as possible. Although TV studios have TV monitors for the audience, it is to the program's advantage to make the audience feel like part of the event, especially with comedy.

If the boom stays just above (or below) the frame line, the acoustic mic-to-source distance should be proportionate to the size of the shot, matching the aural and visual space, which is one of the boom's main aesthetic advantages. Here are a few guidelines to using the boom:

☑ Position the boom above and angled in front of the performer's mouth. Remember: Sound comes from the mouth, not from the top of the head.

☑ Establish mic-to-source operating distance by having the performer raise an arm at a 45-degree angle toward the tip of the microphone and extending a finger; the finger should just touch the mic. Appropriate working distances can be planned from there. For example, if the mic-to-source distance in a close-up is 3 feet, in a medium shot it could be about 6 feet, and in a long shot up to 9 feet.

☑ Directional shotgun microphones compress distance between background and foreground. Aim the microphone directly at the performer(s) so as not to increase background sound.

☑ Hypercardioid shotgun microphones have considerable rear sensitivity, so avoid pointing the back end toward a source of unwanted noise such as ventilators, parabolic lights, and so on.

☑ Capacitor shotguns are high-output, high-sensitivity instruments and therefore can be used at somewhat longer mic-to-source distances than moving-coil mics without degrading sound quality. Also, high-frequency response in moving-coil mics falls off with increased mic-to-source distance.

☑ To facilitate learning the shot changes in multicamera production, provide each boom operator with cue sheets and, if possible, place a TV monitor on the boom (assuming a perambulator boom) or near it. Also provide headphones that feed the program sound to one ear and the director's cues to the other ear. Boom dolly movers should also have access to cue sheets. Rehearse each shot so that the exact mic-to-source distances are established.

☑ Rehearse all boom operations. Even the slightest movements such as turning the head while talking or bending down can require complicated boom movements. For example, as a head turns while talking, the boom has to be panned and the mic rotated at the same time.

☑ If a performer has a tendency to do "head whips" while interacting with other guests or because dialogue interaction calls for it, play the mic in front, keeping movement to a minimum so the speech sound and ambience are consistent.

☑ Have preparatory discussions with the sound recordist or mixer.

☑ Learn about lighting. A boom operator has to know what side of a set to work from so that the boom does not throw a shadow. Outside it is necessary to be opposite the sun side so that the shadow falls away from the performer.

☑ Anticipate the performer's movements so that the boom leads, rather than follows, the talent.

☑ Position the boom's base toward the front of the set, not to the side. From the side it is difficult to judge the microphone's height in relation to the cameras, because cameras are usually placed in an arc around the front of the set.

Due to the size of perambulator booms, they may be unwieldy in small sets or difficult to maneuver when relatively frequent repositioning is called for, especially if there is no boom mover. Two alternatives are the tripod (giraffe) boom and the fishpole boom.

Tripod (Giraffe) Boom

The *tripod,* or *giraffe, boom* is smaller and easier to operate than a perambulator boom (see 4-56). But if it has to be adjusted or moved during shooting, it has more disadvantages than advantages. First, because it is lightweight and therefore subject to shock and vibration likely to be picked up by the microphone, it requires a lighter mic and a very good shock mount. Second, it has a limited boom arm reach. Third, once the boom arm has been extended to a particular length, it cannot be extended farther or retracted without interrupting shooting to do so. To change mic-to-source distance during shooting, the entire tripod has to be rolled in or rolled out, and this movement could be audible. Fourth, the height extension is quite limited, presenting the dangers of the boom shadow.

Fishpole Boom

The *fishpole boom* is used in-studio when larger booms cannot negotiate small spaces, but mostly it is the microphone mount of choice in field production. It is more mobile, easier to manage, takes up less space, and requires fewer crew than wheeled booms. A fishpole is handheld and, therefore, can be moved around a set with relative ease (see 14-3).

Fishpole booms come in various lengths, and most of them have a telescoping tube that can be extended or retracted (see 14-4). Shorter fishpoles can extend from 16 inches out to more than 6 feet and weigh as little as 11 ounces; medium-sized fishpoles can extend from 23 inches out to 8 feet and weigh about 14 ounces; longer fishpoles can extend from a little less than 3 feet out to more than 16 feet and weigh a little more than a pound.

The fishpole boom does present a few problems. It gets heavy if it has to be carried about the set or held for any length of time, particularly if the mic is a heavy one. It can be difficult to control precisely, particularly in wider shots when it has to be held high. Furthermore, handling noises can be heard if the fishpole operator is not careful.

The following are some preparational and operational tips when using the fishpole boom, particularly in field production (see also 14-5, 14-6, and 14-7):

☑ It is politic to remember that in field production the boom operator is the sound department's eyes and ears on the set.

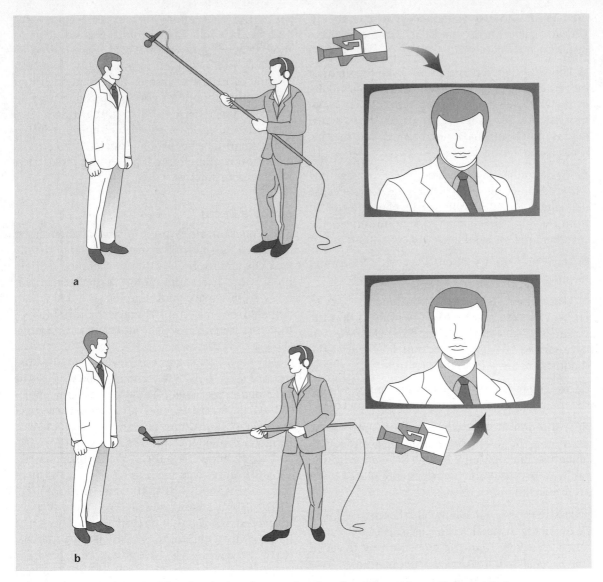

14-3 Using a fishpole with a directional microphone pointed at the performer's mouth from (a) above or (b) below. The mic's position depends on the focal length and angle of the shot. Better sound is usually obtained by positioning the mic above the performer, because sound rises and the bounce from the floor or ground can brighten the pickup.

Two sets of slots accommodate most types of mic cables

Captive collet

Collar with directional dimples

Mushroom pole base

Attach accessories to bottom coupling   Low-handling-noise finish   Telescoping sections

14-4 Fishpole boom and its features

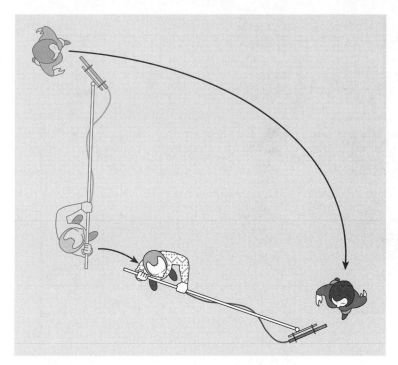

14-5 Boom leading subject. Subject movement requires the boom to lead the subject through a space.

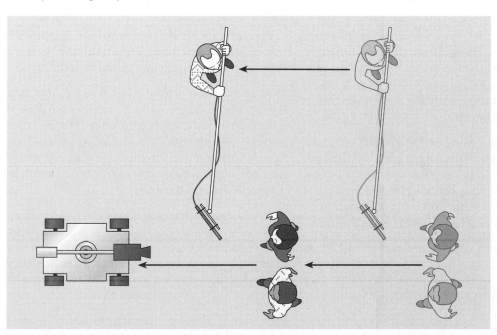

14-6 Moving the boom for broad movements. For broad movements, such as characters moving in front of a dollying camera, the boom operator has to walk backward or sideways when leading.

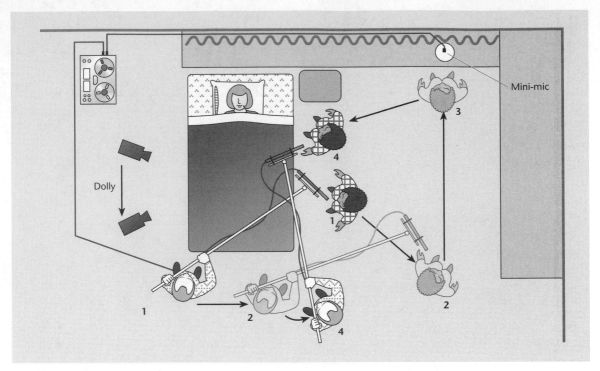

14-7 Miking complicated movement. In cases of complicated movement, a subject may need multiple mic setups.

☑ Operating a fishpole boom is intense and exhausting work. Be well rested and physically conditioned. Build endurance by holding a fishpole for progressively longer periods of time. If one is not available, practice with a bucket or weights at the end of a broom handle.

☑ Wear clothing that is comfortable and relatively loose-fitting. Dark clothes help avoid reflections. Because fishpole miking often involves being on your feet for extended periods of time plus a lot of walking and running, forward and backward, sneakers with thick soles are comfortable and quiet.

☑ Know the script. If one is not available or if last-minute copy changes have been made, learn the body gestures of the performers just before they speak to help anticipate boom movements.

☑ Always use a windscreen, especially with directional capacitors, which are particularly sensitive to even minute air movement; barrier, mesh-style windscreens are quite effective (see 4-46b), especially with a windjammer (see 4-46d).

☑ Always use a shock mount. High-quality microphones, particularly capacitors with high sensitivity, are apt to pick up sound conductance through the metal tube. It is a good idea to tape foam rubber around the tube a few inches above the handgrip and below the microphone mount to inhibit sound conductance.

☑ Use high-quality headphones when operating a fishpole boom mic. Except for the recordist, who may be some distance away, there is no other way to tell what sounds are being picked up or how they are balanced, particularly in relation to the foreground and background sounds.

☑ Be sure that there is enough cable and cleared space on the floor if the fishpole mic must move

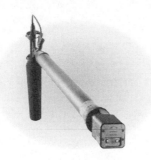

14-8 Wireless boom with mounted transmitter

with the performer(s). To avoid the cable problem altogether, and if it is feasible, boom-mount a wireless mic (see 14-8).

☑ Remove all jewelry before recording and wear gloves to help dampen handling noise.

☑ If the fishpole has to be held for any length of time, secure a flag holder around the waist and sit the pole end in its pocket. Some longer fishpoles come with a handle grip on the pole to help support it against the body.

The advantage of the boom-mounted microphone on location, as in the studio, is that by varying its distance to the sound source you can make it reflect the focal length of shots. This advantage applies especially in the field, where there is more likely to be background sound whose relationship to the principal sound source often helps establish the overall sonic environment. This technique is called *perspective miking*, because it establishes audio viewpoint. Moreover, it helps convey the mood and style of a production.

If a scene takes place in a seedy hotel room, for example, aiming the microphone at a slight angle to the performer's mouth so that it also picks up more room sound will "cheapen" the sound, thereby better articulating the visual atmosphere. If a scene is to convey an anticipatory atmosphere, widening mic-to-source distance even in a tight shot creates an open sound that encompasses background sounds such as a clock ticking, a board

creaking, a drink being poured, an owl hooting, a siren screaming, and so on. (Of course, both of these examples require the director's OK.)

Fishpole booms also permit positional changes to compensate for problems with perspective. In handling a strong voice against a weak one, the mic can be placed closer to the weak voice, but aimed at the strong voice, evening out the overall level. In addition to perspective and flexibility, overhead miking in general tends to provide a crisp, natural sound compared with body mics, which are often sterile in texture.

Perspective

The challenge in operating any boom is to maintain aural perspective while simultaneously keeping the boom mic out of the picture and the performers in the mic's pickup pattern. To create a realistic setting, sound and picture must work together; the aural and visual perspectives should match. If you see two performers talking in the same plane, you should hear them at relatively the same loudness; if you see one performer close up engaged in dialogue with another actor farther away, the performer who is closer should sound louder.

Performers in the Same Plane The easiest way to pick up performers talking in the same plane and to maintain their aural relationship is to position the microphone equidistant between them and close enough so that they are on-mic (see 14-9). If one performer walks a short distance away, blocking will have determined either how far the boom can follow, keeping the performer on-mic yet remaining close enough to get back in time to cover the other performer, or whether a second boom should be used (see 14-10 and 14-11).

Performers in Different Planes During a scene it is typical for shots to change from, say, a medium shot of a group with performer A talking, to a close-up of performer A, to a close-up of performer B responding, to another medium shot of the group, to a close-up of performer C talking, and so on.

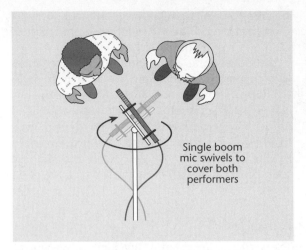

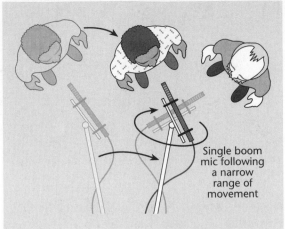

14-9 Two performers on the same plane. The easiest way to boom-mic them is to place the microphone equidistant between them and swivel it back and forth.

14-10 Two performers on the same plane but with some movement. One boom mic can be used when there is some movement between performers on the same plane and the distances between them are not wide.

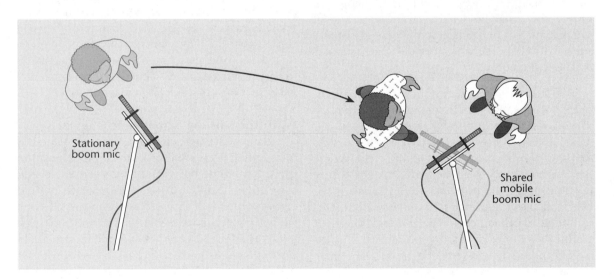

14-11 Two performers on the same plane but with significant movement. Two boom mics may be needed when blocking calls for more-dynamic movement, as it often does.

To keep visual and aural perspective consistent, the sound in the medium shot should not be quite so loud as the sound in the close-up.

In a medium shot compared with a close-up, for example, the boom has to be higher and therefore farther from the actors. In a long shot compared with a medium shot, the mic has to be higher and farther still. The aural difference in the mic-to-source distance, reflected by the acoustic change in the loudness level and the proportion of direct to indirect waves, should match the visual difference in the audience-to-source distance.

Regardless of the visual perspective, however, the audience must hear the performers clearly. Someone

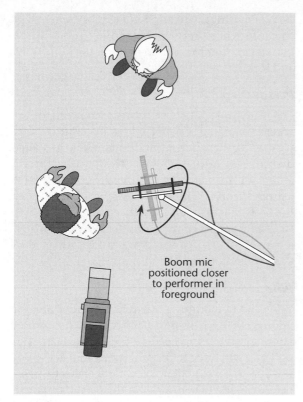

14-12 Two performers on different planes and close enough to be covered by one boom. The microphone should be placed between the performers, but mic-to-source distance should reflect viewer-to-source distance. In other words, the person who looks closer should be louder.

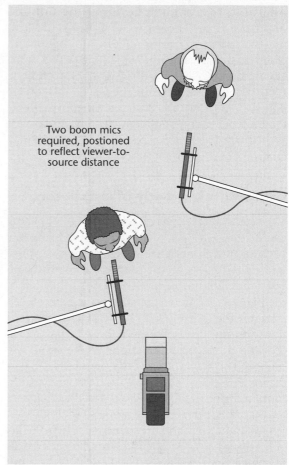

14-13 Two performers on different planes and too far apart to be covered by one boom. Two booms should be used. To some extent mic-to-source distance should complement camera-to-source distance.

close up should sound more present than someone farther away, but only to a certain extent. A performer in a close-up shot should not sound "on top of the audience," and the audience should not have to strain to hear a performer in a long shot. The mic also has to be close enough to a performer so that it does not pick up too much ambience. You have to cheat a bit with mic placement to reduce the unwanted reflections so that the difference in loudness levels is obvious but not disconcerting.

Suppose a scene calls for two performers to talk several feet apart. First, the distance between them has to be within the microphone's range. Second, the mic should be between them but closer to the performer in the foreground (see 14-12). Third, if

further changes in the loudness level are necessary, the range of the boom arm should be increased to get the mic closer or the performers' positions should be changed. If the performers are too far apart to cover with one boom, use two (see 14-13). Remember, within the same scene and locale, differences in loudness levels should be apparent but not marked. Do not worry about the slight discrepancies between the visual and aural perspectives. If the audio sounds realistic enough, the psychological effect of the picture's perspective should make up for the difference between the two.

Adjusting Microphone Levels at the Console

Another way to change the aural perspective is to use the fader; increasing loudness brings sound closer, and decreasing it moves sound farther away. Unless loudness changes are minor, this technique is not recommended. Using the fader to make level adjustments that are obvious not only affects loudness but changes ambient relationships as well. Remember: The relationship of actors on a set may change, but the space itself does not.

Using Wireless Body Microphones

Most audio people agree that if a wired microphone can do the job, it is preferable to a wireless mic because it is more reliable, less subject to interference and noise from motors and cabling, and not vulnerable to dropout. On the other hand, many directors prefer the wireless mic because it liberates the performer from being tethered to a microphone cord. This has been a particular blessing in staged productions where actors are mobile. The advantages of the body mic are that dialogue is clear, intelligible, and present, with a minimum of background sound. The disadvantages are that sonic perspective, regardless of a shot's focal length, is the same and the sound tends to be sterile.

It is possible to compensate for these drawbacks to some extent. There are two basic types of mini-mics used for body miking: proximity-prone and transparent. *Proximity-prone mini-mics* tend to add presence to close dialogue and reject background sound. *Transparent mini-mics* have a more open and natural sound; they pick up more ambience. Their advantage is that sound can be blended more naturally with boom and plant mics. The disadvantage of transparent mini-mics is that they pass more ambience.

Body mics are usually omnidirectional; directional mini-mics have not proved practical. They have to be pointed precisely in the direction of the sound, which, in body-miking actors or in using plant mics, is often not effective. Also remember that sound-canceling ports are what make a mic directional. Clothes or mounting tape could block some of the ports, thereby degrading pickup.

When using a wireless body mic, consider all of the following: aural perspective, microphone placement, number of mics in use at the same time, and sound levels.

Perspective

The main sonic difference between a body-mounted wireless mic and a boom mic is in creating aural perspective. Remember, with a boom, mic-to-source distance is adjusted with the shot, thereby automatically matching aural/visual perspective (at least in theory). When a wireless mic is attached to the body, mic-to-source distance is close and never varies, regardless of the shot's focal length, which means that aural perspective must be adjusted in postproduction.

Placement

When body-mounting a wireless microphone for drama, obviously it must be hidden, so the type of fabric and clothing become important factors in deciding what mic to use and where to place it. For this reason a sound designer should make it a point before miking to consult with the person responsible for wardrobe. Remember that cotton does not make as much rustling sound as do synthetic fabrics such as polyester, rayon, nylon, and dacron. Synthetic fabrics are also more likely to build static electricity, which creates interference, than are wool, suede, cotton, and leather. Leather does, however, make noise.

The design of performers' clothing is also important. A microphone can be hidden inside a tie, in the seam of a shirt or blouse, in a pocket, in the collar of a jacket or turtleneck sweater, behind a scarf, under a bodice, and so on. Certain mics are less susceptible to interference from such noises as rustling, jostling, and static electricity than are others; you have to test to determine which are which. Obviously, a microphone with a windscreen and shock absorbency is better than a mic without one or both, but a windscreen also makes the mic more difficult to hide. Tying a knot in the microphone cable underneath the head of the mic can sometimes, but not always, reduce or eliminate clothing noise. If the proximity of the microphone to the mouth creates problems with sibilance, popping, and *nose blast,* invert the mic (so long as it is omnidirectional).

Clothing style also affects where a mic can be hidden—costumes from different periods and cultures pose different challenges. Hiding a mic on a performer playing an eighteenth-century Austrian prince clothed from neck to ankle in tight-fitting raiment presents one type of problem; hiding a mic on a woman in a low-cut, strapless dress presents another. Here, again, the person handling wardrobe can help. Maybe a pocket for the microphone can be sewn underneath the prince's vest; the bodice of the dress can be tubed and the mic placed inside. It is, of course, easier to hide a microphone in loose-fitting clothes than in tight-fitting ones. Loose-fitting garments also reduce the chance of picking up rustling sounds.

If it can be done, the best thing is to get the microphone in the open as much as possible. Try to mount it in the shadow area of a coat lapel, or sew it to the material, or stick it through material to look like a button, tie clasp, or decorator pin. Use mini-mics that are available in black, which is easier to conceal than gray or shiny metal.

An externally mounted mini-mic can be made inconspicuous by camouflaging it to match wardrobe. Use a marking pen to color small strips of tape or foam windscreens, or both, which are then attached to the mic and clasp, thereby subduing their appearance. An alternative is to use small patches of felt or cloth to cover the mic.

Two types of clothing noise often encountered are contact and acoustic. Contact clothing noise is caused by a garment flapping into or rubbing across the mic capsule. The solution is to carefully immobilize all clothing that may create this problem by taping down everything on either side of the mic. Try sandwiching the mic between two sticky triangles of tape (formed by folding a strip of tape like a flag, sticky side out). Because contact noise can also be caused when clothing rubs against the mic cable, form a loop near the mic for strain relief, and then apply a few lengths of tape along the cable. Try double-faced tape or sticky triangles to immobilize clothing and keep it from rubbing.

Another adhesive is the type of putty used as a weather seal for windows. It bonds to fabric and dampens induced noises from the fabric and cable. Avoid using too much damping material, however; extra material usually means added noise.

Clothing rubbing against itself generates noise; treating the clothing with static guard may solve the problem. A light spray of water can soften starched fabrics. Because synthetic fabrics are much noisier than natural fibers, they should be avoided whenever possible.

It is important never to allow the mic line and the antenna to cross when rigging a wireless body mic, and also to keep the antenna rigid and not looped over itself. A good way to keep the antenna rigid is to affix a rubber band to the tip and then safety-pin the rubber band to the clothing. If the antenna has to run in a direction other than straight up and down or to the side, invert the transmitter pack and let the mic cable, rather than the antenna, loop. Check the performer to make sure that the mic and cable are secure—tape tends to loosen from moisture, and costumes tend to shift from movement—but be careful not to do this too often; many actors are uncomfortable wearing wireless mics, or do not like to be bothered with adjustments, or both. Waterproof sealants and sweat-resistant mics can minimize the moisture problems of loosening tape and degraded transmission.

All of this is well and good, but what can you do when the costume, such as a man's bathing suit or chain mail on a knight, makes it difficult to use a body mic? In the case of the bathing suit, cooperation may be needed from the hairdresser: With skill, a wireless microphone can be hidden in the hair; sound does rise and the body does resonate. For female voices mic placement toward the front hairline is better for their high-frequency response. For the male voice, placing the mic behind the ear or over the ear, attached to a specially made ear clip, is better for low-end pickup. For wigs and hair pieces, there are toupee clips to which a mic can be attached. Avoid placing the mic under the gauze of a wig, however, because of head sweat and reduced high-frequency response. The chain mail, on the other hand, may be too noisy for any successful body miking, in which case either take a more conventional miking approach or rerecord the dialogue in postproduction.

Still another reason for working with wardrobe is to arrange with the costumer when to mount the body mic on the performer. The best time is usually when the performer is dressing at the start of the production day, even if the microphone will not be needed right away. By mounting the mic before production starts, the performer has more time to get used to it, and shooting does not have to be interrupted to put it in place when it is needed. Moreover, a performer has a great deal to think about, and disrupting concentration to body-mount a microphone is not a good idea.

Using Two or More Wireless Microphones

The use of two or more wireless microphone systems in the same immediate area requires that they be on different and, preferably, widely separated frequencies to avoid interference. The wireless systems and microphones should be of similar make and model to ensure sonic consistency. If this is not possible and only different systems and mics are available, each performer should be given the same make and model to use throughout production so at least the individual's sound is uniform.

An ever-present problem with body mics is noise, not only from fabric but also from props in a pocket that may jingle or rustle, such as coins, keys, or paper. For example, suppose two (or more) actors using wireless mics are exchanging dialogue at relatively close proximity. Actor A is nervously jangling coins, and the sound is interfering with the pickup of his dialogue. Assuming the pocket containing the coins is closer to the body mic than it is to the mouth, actor A's dialogue probably is also being picked up by actor B's mic, but with the sound of the coins not as loud. Therefore, in postproduction the recording from actor B's microphone can be used in place of the recording from actor A's mic. This enables continued use of the wireless systems, which may be desirable for logistical or other reasons. This technique also helps solve problems of unwanted or unintelligible overlapping dialogue.

Controlling Levels

A frequent problem in recording dialogue is trying to maintain suitable levels when performers are speaking at different and varying loudnesses. If sound is too loud, level is "in the red"; if sound is too quiet, level is "in the mud." Controlling levels both to avoid distortion, particularly with digital sound, and to keep sound above the noise floor yet still preserve the relative dynamics of the performers is handled in different ways, depending on the miking.

Suppose that in a scene a distraught man is alternately sobbing and shouting at a woman, who is responding in a quiet, controlled voice, trying to calm him. In such a scene, the level changes would be wide and acute and difficult to ride. Putting a limiter on the sound is not always preferred or recommended, because it can reduce sound quality. Nor may it be possible through blocking to place the microphones properly to compensate for the widely fluctuating levels. And it is imprudent to depend completely on postproduction to fix problems that occur in sound recording during production. By then, the sound may be beyond repair, because either it is distorted or the signal-to-noise ratio is unacceptable. Thus, to handle the widely varying sound levels, either boom or body mics may be employed.

When using the boom, recordists in a situation like this may set the level on the loudest sound emitted, in this case the man's shouts. If the shouts are set at, say, zero level (100 percent of modulation), it ensures that, at worst, the peaks will only momentarily get into the red. This makes riding levels less critical in situations where the dynamic range is wide and changes quickly, and it keeps both dialogue and ambience in perspective. Because there is no headroom with digital sound, it may be necessary to set an appropriate limit on the audio level. Or, as was suggested earlier in this chapter, the mic can be placed closer to the weaker voice but aimed at the strong voice, evening out the overall level.

In terms of perspective, by setting a maximum loudness level, the woman's level will be quite a bit lower than the man's, because she has a less powerful voice and is speaking quietly. But increasing her loudness level during the quiet interchanges will also increase her ambience disproportionately to the man's. This creates different background noise levels between the two performers as well as different spatial relationships. If quieter levels are at or below the noise floor, slight adjustments in microphone selection or placement, performer placement, or voice projection can be made, or compression can be used. (Another alternative to using the boom is to shoot and mike the scene entirely from the woman's perspective.)

With the body mic, handling the scene is somewhat easier. Because each performer is individually miked, it is possible to set and control levels separately. If in the scene the woman also has to shout at the man, perhaps to admonish him to stop feeling sorry for himself, another option is to put two wireless mics on each performer. Levels for one pair of mics would be set for the louder dialogue, and levels for the other pair set for the quieter dialogue. The production mixer then has four faders to worry about, but overall sound quality will probably be better, and the editor has more to work with in postproduction.

Here are some other tips to keep in mind when considering or using wireless body mics:

☑ When complex movement is called for, do not automatically choose a wireless body mic before considering whether good boom work can meet the challenge. Remember that a boom-mounted microphone produces a more realistic sound.

☑ Because wireless mics are subject to interference from noise, avoid using them in heavy-traffic areas, such as downtown streets, parking lots, major highways, airports, or in areas where there are frequent RF transmissions.

☑ Place the receiver properly—in line-of-sight with the transmitter and as close to the set as possible.

☑ Check transmission frequencies to make sure that no one else in the area is using your band(s).

☑ Do a sound check by walking around the same area(s) the performers will be using.

☑ Adjust the transmitter's gain control for each performer.

☑ Always power down; that is, do not turn off the transmitter without turning off the receiver. Otherwise, the receiver will keep looking for a signal and could lock into unpleasant VHF white noise. (**White noise** is a wideband noise that contains equal energy at each frequency, as opposed to **pink noise**, which is wideband noise that maintains constant energy per octave. Both types of noise are generally used for testing electronic audio equipment.)

☑ Bring backup wireless systems and plenty of fresh batteries, preferably longer-lasting lithium batteries.

Plant Microphones

Plant microphones, also called *fixed mics*, are positioned around a set to cover action that cannot be easily picked up with a boom or a body mic or to provide fill sound. A plant mic can be either a conventional-size or, preferably, a miniature capacitor. Plant mics can be hidden practically anywhere—in flowers, on a desktop nameplate, in a doorway, on the edge of a windowsill, on an automobile visor, or in a plant, which is where the term comes from.

Because a plant mic is almost always used along with the main boom or body mic, beware of phasing from overlapping sound. Also, if possible, try to match the perspective sound quality of the main and plant mics; that will probably be easier to do with a boom mic than with a body mic.

Multiple Miking with Different Microphone Mounts

It was pointed out earlier that miking dialogue for staged productions might involve using a combination of approaches, incorporating boom, body, and plant microphones.

For example, in single-camera production a master shot and then various perspectives of the shot are recorded in separate takes. A master shot is a single shot of an entire scene from a far-enough distance to cover all the action. Suppose the scene is a party in a large living room, where host and hostess are mingling with guests and exchanging pleasantries. The master shot would be a wide shot of the room and party, taking in all the action. Other takes might consist of a group shot with host, hostess, and a few guests, and three-, two-, and one-shots of the host and hostess in a selected exchange with one person in the group.

To take advantage of all the sonic possibilities, the sound of each take should be recorded. By audio-recording as many takes as possible, the various sonic qualities and perspectives provide the editor with more options in cutting sound and picture. For example, the master shot could be miked from overhead, using boundary mics with hemispheric, or stereo, pickup to capture the overall hubbub. Directional overhead mics could be added for more-selective, but still open, pickup of particular interactions among host and hostess and certain guests or groups of guests. The middle-side (M-S) mic is yet another alternative. The directional capsule can be used to pick up selective sounds, and its side capsules used to pick up the more-open sounds. The advantage of the M-S mic is that middle and side imaging can be handled separately in the mix, so using the M-S mic during production recording does not necessarily commit the mixer to its entire pickup in postproduction. The same is not true with conventional stereo miking.

Wireless mics attached to host and hostess would record their dialogue for close-ups to be shot later. In the group shot, a boom with an omnidirectional or wide-angle pattern could be used for the overall pickup to provide a more open sonic perspective than that provided by the directional overhead mics. For the tighter three-, two-, and one-shots, body-mounted wireless mics provide the sonic complement to these closer cutaways. Also, with a multitrack recorder, there is no reason not to continue using the overhead mics for each take to provide additional recordings of the ambient party sounds.

The point is that in single-camera production, shooting each scene several times to record as many different visual perspectives as possible is part and parcel of the technique. Each shot often requires time to reposition the camera, change the lighting, fluff the performers' clothes, recomb hair, and touch up makeup. If such pains are taken for the picture,

similar time and attention should be given to the sound so that the audio recorded also has as many different perspectives as possible. Enlightened directors do this; the problem is that, even today, too many directors still give sound short shrift, to the detriment of the finished product.*

By the standards of most multicamera production for television, the length of each continuous shot recorded in single-camera production is often relatively short. Long takes are uncommon, because when performer and camera movement change appreciably, it is often also necessary to reposition performers, crew, and equipment. But long takes over relatively far-flung distances are done from time to time.

A key to such takes, in addition to having mics strategically mounted and located, is placement of recorders. Clearly more than one recorder is necessary to handle a long take over some distance. Where the recorders are placed is dictated by the length of mic cable runs or the transmission range of a wireless mic system, or both, and if necessary where recorders and operators can be hidden.

FIELD PRODUCTION

In production always be prepared. Time is money, to say nothing of the physical and psychological angst caused by unnecessary delay. This applies even more so to field production, where away from the security of the studio, if something can go wrong, it will.

---

*It is worth quoting this comment made by one production recordist: "The center stage of film [and video] production is so dominated by visual considerations that the sound department is kind of a mystery to everyone else on the set. Maybe it's because only the sound mixer and the boom operator actually hear what is being recorded, while most visual aspects are obvious to everyone on a . . . set. Whatever the reason, the problem for the sound department is that even the smallest delay for sound adjustments can cause immense irritation . . . (even though an incredible amount of time can be patiently spent fine-tuning lights, rehearsing focus pulls, working out dolly moves, etc.)." From Glen Trew, "Memoirs of a Sound Mixer," *Audio Media,* October 1999, p. 55.

Preproduction Planning

Before actual production gets under way, decisions are made about the production site, the equipment, and any specific needs. Some of these decisions may be out of the sound person's control. But even as a consultant, the sound person can facilitate the preparation and production of audio by anticipating problems and needs and being ready to provide knowledgeable advice when asked. The importance of proper preparation for on-location production cannot be overemphasized. Consider the loss of time and money, to say nothing of the inconvenience to all the people involved, if you have to hold up production because someone brought the wrong microphone, forgot the batteries for the recorder, neglected to pack the tool kit, planned to mount a heavy camera crane on soil too soft to hold it, chose a shooting site several days in advance of production without realizing that a building nearby was slated for demolition on the day of recording, scouted the shooting site at noon although the script called for the scene to take place at dusk, or selected a shooting site filled with ragweed without checking whether any of the key people were allergic to pollen. Planning to shoot on location is a careful, meticulous procedure involving more than just decisions about production and in the long run worth whatever time it takes.

Selecting a Location

In selecting a site, sound designers prefer one with suitable acoustics indoors and no distracting sounds outdoors, although these qualities are rarely found away from the controlled environment of the studio. The first thing to understand about a production site is that directors are interested in what it looks like, not what it sounds like. The second thing to understand is: Be prepared to deal with unwanted sound. If possible, try to reduce the difficulties by suggesting to the director those sites with the fewest sound problems. But keep in mind that where you shoot is determined by the demands of the picture, not of the sound.

Because the main challenge in doing a production on location is to record the principal sound source with little or no sonic leakage from either the acoustics or other sound sources, judge the recording site on what is possible to achieve in neutralizing unwanted sound.

Dealing with Unwanted Sound

Unwanted sound is generated by many sources. Some are obvious; others not so obvious: the low-frequency rumble from traffic that becomes midrange hiss on a wet day, blowing sound from wind, clatter from a nearby office, buzz from fluorescent lights, excessive reverb from rooms that are too live, jet roar from planes that fly over the production area, noise from construction, church bells that ring on the hour, a far-off foghorn, clanking pipes, creaking floorboards, whine from an air conditioner, chirping from birds, barking from dogs, and so on.

Being aware of the problems is not enough, however—you have to know what, if anything, to do about them. For example, you can usually roll off low-frequency rumble from traffic, but the midrange hiss from wet tires on a wet surface is difficult to equalize out. Gentle wind presents little problem for a mic equipped with a pop filter and windscreen. With capacitor mics these filters will not completely offset the effect of noise from strong winds, although the mesh-style zeppelin windscreen and windjammer are quite effective, especially when they are used together. If a room is reverberant, you can make it less so by placing a lot of sound-absorbent material in the area and using tight, highly directional miking; but these techniques may not work in large, extremely reverberant spaces. If the director insists on a site where sound problems cannot be neutralized, plan to rerecord the audio in the studio during postproduction.

Two other considerations in choosing a production site with audio in mind are (1) the available space—make sure the fishpole operator has enough room to move with the action and maneuver the boom; and (2) the power supply—if the production site does not have enough power outlets or wattage, or if the circuits are noisy, plan to bring the main and backup power supplies.

Prerecorded Material

Any prerecorded announcements, sound effects, or music used during production must be included in preproduction planning. Also plan for the equipment to be used to play them: disc player, recorder, cartridge player, and so on.

Other Equipment and Materials

Anticipating the need for less-obvious but nevertheless important equipment and materials is also part of preproduction planning. The following are among the necessary items to have handy, where appropriate (also see Chapter 13):

☑ AC power checker

☑ Adjustable wrench

☑ Backup microphones and mic accessories, such as cables, connectors, windscreens, and shock mounts

☑ Batteries for every piece of equipment using them

☑ C-clamp, pony clips, and various clips for body-mounted mics

☑ Clip leads

☑ Colored acrylic pens to camouflage body-mounted mics

☑ Cotton swabs

☑ Demagnetizer

☑ Disk drives

☑ Drill and drill bits

☑ Flashlight or lantern light

☑ Fuses

☑ Head cleaner

☑ Headphones and headphone amp

☑ Knee bench

☑ Log sheets or a laptop computer to record time, location, and content of production information

☑ Lubes and glues

☑ Multimeter

☑ Nut drivers

☑ Oscillator

☑ Oscilloscope

☑ Pens and paper

☑ Pocket knife

☑ Recording tape

☑ Rope

☑ Scripts and rundown sheets

☑ Soldering pencil

☑ Stopwatch

☑ Time code generator and reader

☑ Tape—duct, masking, and water- (sweat-) proof

☑ Tape measure

☑ Tool kit with ruler, needle-nose and regular pliers, wire cutters, Phillips-head and conventional screwdrivers, hammer, awl, and file/saw

☑ Vise grip

Blocking and Rehearsing

Despite the considerable flexibility that modern technology provides in producing staged material, scenes are still shot one at a time, out of sequence, and often in segments. Each shot is blocked and lit, and camera movements are rehearsed. Just as the visual elements must be painstakingly planned and practiced, so too should the audio. For each shot microphone positions are blocked, movements are rehearsed, and sound balances are determined.

The responsibilities of the sound people, in some ways, are perhaps greater than those of the crew responsible for producing the picture. The sound crew is often left on its own, not because the director does not care (although this is sometimes the case) but because audio is usually the one major production component of film and TV that a director is likely to know least about. As a result, blocking and rehearsing become all the more important for the audio people. The director may proceed with shooting when the pictorial elements are in place and assume that, or not bother to check if, sound is ready. It had better be! As pointed out earlier in this chapter, too many directors who would understand a delay if a light had to be repositioned would have little patience if a similar delay were due to an audio problem.

Production Dialogue Recording

Recording dialogue on the set is known as *production recording*. It was discussed earlier in this chapter, and most of the same considerations that apply to studio recording also apply to field recording, including the challenge of getting the sound right with little leeway for experimentation, refinement, or, should something go wrong, repair. Perhaps one difference between studio and field production recording is the additional pressure that comes from being away from the security of the studio, particularly when a director has an aesthetic distaste for rerecording dialogue in postproduction and indicates a strong desire to use the original sound in the final mix. Being flexible and imaginative in solving problems is essential to good production recording.

Suppose a director wants to shoot a scene with constrained action in a very large stone-and-marble room using a boom, but does not want to rerecord the dialogue in postproduction The reverberation is so dense, however, that the actors cannot pick up cues from one another. Clearly, the walls and ceiling cannot be acoustically treated—the room is far too large. What the production recordist did in this actual situation was devise a canopy secured to four extendable legs and position it over the action. In addition, a rolling, absorbent, 20-foot-high baffle was used to reduce the length of the room and therefore the reverberant space. It should be noted that this type of solution would not have worked had the scene required a lot of movement.

Suppose that a director wants an actor to sing while revving a racecar engine on a racetrack. Clearly, the engine sound will drown out the singing. But with a noise-canceling mic on the actor, the singing can be recorded loud and clear. Because of the inverse square law (see Chapter 13),

if the sound-pressure level of a sound source is high enough, it is possible to close-mike the source and reduce leakage.

These are the success stories. There are conditions in which no amount of ingenuity can make it possible to record much usable dialogue on the set, regardless of a director's intent. For example, in the film *Titanic,* "While shooting was taking place on one side of the ship, building was being done on the other side. There were buzz-saws, beeps from trucks backing up, construction workers yelling at each other, wind machines, wave machines and general background voices . . . for more than seventy-five percent of all the [dialogue] ADR was chosen."* (See "Automated Dialogue Replacement" in Chapter 17.)

That said, actors generally prefer the natural environment and interactions on the set to the sterile environment of the *automated dialogue replacement (ADR)* studio. As good as postproduction can be, most believe that it cannot quite capture the dozens of tiny sounds that correspond to physical movements, such as soft exhales of anxiety, the caress of a touch, the rustling of a shirt, or an arm brushing against a tree branch. Although ADR may save time and money, it is no substitute for the real thing.

Signal Processing and Production Recording

Signal processing is rarely used during production recording except for, perhaps, bass roll-off and a slight midrange boost to help punch dialogue. Anything else, such as compression, heavy equalization, and so on, is usually done in postproduction. Productions shot with a single camera are done out of sequence and with different takes of most scenes; prematurely processing sound on the set could cause myriad matching problems, particularly with stereo and surround sound. Spatial imaging should be left to postproduction. To attempt it during production recording makes little sense, because there is no way to know how a scene will ultimately be edited.

---

*Michael Axinn, "ADR Necessary Evil or Saving Grace?" *Mix* [Sound for Picture section], April 2000, p. 17.

The only "processing" usually done in production recording is riding the mic level and balancing the loudness extremes of each actor. It is important to perform these operations with smooth and imperceptible changes using a top-quality mixer whose controls are easy to see and access. Slight gain adjustments on mixers of mediocre quality are too often apparent in the recording, especially with digital audio.

Recording

Regardless of the microphone used during production, audio pickup is only half the sound equation. Recording is the other half. And the more tracks there are available, the better the chances of both producing usable audio from the set and providing the sound editor with more choices in postproduction.

Today this is less of a problem than ever before. With single-system recording, digital video cameras have at least four high-quality audio tracks available. For double-system recording, a single modular multitrack unit provides eight tracks of digital-quality audio. Road-worthy hard-disk

recorders also furnish multiple tracks (see 14-14). Even R-DATs, with a minimum of two tracks, can be used for split-track recording. In addition to their digital-quality sound, these various recorders are available in models with time code, slate, search-to-cue functions, and 20- or 24-bit audio. One cautionary word about using any recorder for double-system audio: Make sure that the transfer facility has the same type of unit for dubbing the synchronized production recording to whatever medium the sound editor is to work with—tape, film, or hard disk.

The advantages of multitrack recording on the set are obvious: It facilitates various miking arrangements and therefore allows better control of dialogue, background, and even sound-effect recording. For example, take a simple outdoor scene in which a couple is walking in the countryside and focal lengths vary from wide shots to close-ups. One approach could be to use two body mics for the couple and a separate microphone—omnidirectional or boundary mic—to pick up background sound. Recording the three tracks separately not only allows control of each sonic

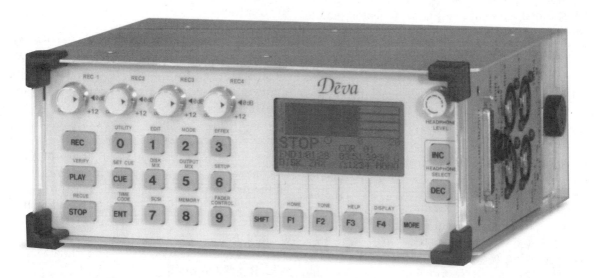

14-14 Portable hard-disk field recorder. This model has four tracks of 20-bit uncompressed digital audio at 48 kHz. It includes preroll cueing that records up to 10 seconds of preroll and time code before program material is actually recorded. The hard drives are removable. A fully charged battery has a 3-hour running time.

element during production and postproduction but also reduces the need for the extra step of dialogue rerecording, potentially at least.

In dramatic productions, because scenes are often shot a few times from different perspectives, the preceding example may be shot as a master scene of the couple, then as close-ups from the man's and woman's perspectives. This allows an editor to cut from shots of the couple to individual shots of their interaction.

As for miking, because the master scene would be shot wider than the one-shot close-ups, clip-on boundary mics could be used as the body microphones. The audio would be more open and would include more background sound than would that of the typical mini-mic, thus better reflecting the wider focal lengths of the shot. During the one-shots the boundary mic could be changed to a mini-mic to sonically articulate the closer focal lengths and reduce background sound. A separate microphone to record background sound could still be employed for added flexibility in mixing. The microphone's pickup pattern may be omnidirectional, directional, or hemispheric, depending on the quality of the background sound required. Indeed, all three pickups may be recorded on separate tracks to further increase flexibility in the mix, but be careful of additive ambience in combining the tracks.

Having the luxury of recording one source per track also presents its own set of challenges. For one, it takes more time to plan and set up. For another, monitoring several inputs at once in multitrack recording is difficult. An approach some recordists take is to adjust and sample all input levels before a shot, establish the headroom level, and then watch the meters during recording, laying down the tracks at optimum loudness. Another approach is to use muting. Even in multitrack production recording, it is unlikely that several tracks will be recorded at the same time. Once a principal track has been recorded, it can be muted during the recording of another track. The danger in this, however, is that if a muted track is being used for cueing purposes, the recordist could miss the cue. A way to avoid this problem is to simply lower the levels of the previously recorded track so that they are audible but not competing with the level of the track being recorded. Even so, this solution still takes bifurcated concentration and nimble fingers.

Production Sound-Effect Recording

Although most sound effects in a staged production are handled in post, some directors prefer to use as many sounds recorded on the set as possible. They feel that because those sounds were recorded in their actual ambient environment and perspective in relation to the sound of the dialogue, they are more realistic than sounds postproduced. Inasmuch as sound-effect production is covered in Chapter 17, albeit in the context of postproduction, in the interest of coherence all sound-effect production is discussed there.

Noise Reduction

Because noise is an ever-present annoyance, the value of noise reduction cannot be overemphasized, especially in relation to dialogue and field recording, particularly with analog audio. Even though *digital signal processing (DSP)* is a powerful ally in eliminating noise from a recording during postproduction, it saves considerable time and expense in the long run if noise reduction is attended to throughout the production process. In addition to DSP, which is implemented "after the fact," there are a number of ways to deal with it "before (and during) the fact."

Use only the highest-quality microphones and recording equipment. With directional mics, make sure they have excellent off-axis rejection. Remember that many capacitor mics have high output, so it is ordinarily unnecessary to increase their levels appreciably during quiet interchanges, thereby avoiding a boost in background noise. The output of moving-coil microphones may be too low to pick up quiet levels without noise. Moreover, capacitor mics do not have to be brought as close to a sound source, and so you avoid the dangers of popping and sibilance.

Equalization also helps. By rolling off the low frequencies, noise from ventilation systems and room rumble are reduced. (Some directors have the air-conditioning turned off during shooting.) Cutting the high frequencies reduces hiss. With dialogue it is possible to use a relatively narrow frequency range, because the speaking voice has little low- and high-frequency content.

Putting gentle compression on a voice raises the quieter levels above the noise floor. Using a noise gate can also reduce ambient noise level, but take care that its action is not perceptible. A de-esser reduces sibilance, but be careful of too much signal processing during recording because (1) once it is part of a recording, it is very difficult to remove, and (2) the more electronic devices in the signal chain, the worse the signal-to-noise ratio. Having said that, use whatever miking technique or signal processing is necessary to reduce rumble, AC hum, buzz, and hiss—they are unacceptable in a recording. Better to deal with these problems during production recording than to leave them to postproduction. Keep in mind, however, that any signal processing during recording should be conservative and knowledgeably applied, otherwise it will create problems in postproduction.

A main source of acoustic noise is the sets. Art directors can eliminate many potential noise problems by following a few principles of acoustic design, such as constructing sets whose walls are not parallel, using absorptive materials (including sound-absorbing paint), and building flooring that does not squeak—unless the director wants this effect.

Directors can also help reduce ambient noise by not blocking action near a flat surface or, worse, a corner. Regardless of the quality of the microphone and the effectiveness of the sound-absorbing materials, it is difficult to avoid signal degradation when sound bounces from walls and corners into a mic at close range. Too much sound absorption is not good either. Heavy carpeting on a set, for example, could make sound lifeless.

In field recording, most venues, no matter how carefully chosen with sound in mind, have background noise problems from wind, traffic, ventilating units, and so on. Although the point has been made before, it bears repeating: Most background noise, once it becomes part of a recording, is difficult if not impossible to remove without altering the sound quality of the program material.

PRODUCTION RECORDING AND THE SOUND EDITOR

Production recordists can be of considerable help in giving sound editors flexibility, by how they record dialogue on the set. This is no small consideration given the pressures, expense, and usually limited time of postproduction. In other words, multitrack recording is often better than split-track recording. If a scene or show uses one or two mics, there is no problem recording split-track. But when a shot uses several mics, a multitrack recorder provides more possibilities for track assignments and for recording dialogue with minimal sonic encumbrance from other pickups.

MAIN POINTS

▶ Staged productions, such as commercials, sitcoms, and drama, are usually produced with postproduction in mind.

▶ The principal challenge during production is recording dialogue that is clear, intelligible, and as noise-free as possible. Sound effects are often handled during postproduction; music always is.

▶ Dramatizations on radio involve creating a "theater of the mind," using sound to impel the listener to "see" the action.

- To create perspective using one microphone in radio dramatization, performers are positioned at appropriate distances relative to the mic and to one another, as the dramatic action dictates.

- Using the multimicrophone technique in radio dramatization, perspective is created in the postproduction mix.

- For stereo radio dramatizations, the coincident or near-coincident microphone arrays are usually employed. Coincident miking positions two microphones, usually directional (or a stereo mic), in virtually the same space, with their diaphragms located vertically on the same axis. Near-coincident miking positions two microphones, usually directional, horizontally on the same plane, angled a few inches apart.

- A main difference and advantage of surround-sound miking radio dramatizations is being able to position performers much as they would be on a stage and recording them from those perspectives.

- Recording dialogue on the set in multi- or single-camera production usually means employing a boom, body-mounted wireless, or plant microphone, or a combination of the three. The microphones of choice are the mini- and shotgun capacitor mics.

- The main sonic difference between the boom and body-mounted microphones is perspective. The boom better reproduces the mic-to-source distances that are relative to the fields of view of the shots. This helps maintain acoustic perspective between sound and picture. On the other hand, the body-mounted mic always picks up dialogue that is clear and present with a minimum of background sound, but sonic perspective remains the same regardless of a shot's focal length.

- Miking decisions are made in preproduction planning during blocking, when the movements of performers and cameras are worked out.

- The challenge in operating a boom is to maintain aural perspective while simultaneously keeping the performers in the mic's pickup pattern and, of course, the mic out of the frame.

- Care must be taken when using a body mic to ensure that it is inconspicuous and that it does not pick up the sound of clothes rustling. Cotton does not make as much rustling sound as do synthetic fabrics.

- Plant, or fixed, microphones are positioned around a set to cover action that cannot easily be picked up with a boom or body mic.

- Preproduction planning is essential in any production, but especially so when working in the field, away from the security and resources of the studio. Preproduction planning involves selecting a location; determining how to deal with unwanted sound; preparing, in advance, prerecorded material; and anticipating all the main and backup equipment needs.

- In production, recording the most intelligible, clearest, noise-free dialogue is the primary challenge of the production recordist, regardless of a director's intention to use it or redo it in postproduction.

- Dealing with unwanted sound on the set is an ever-present challenge to the audio crew. But being of aware of problems is not enough—you have to know what, if anything, to do about them.

- Be wary of employing signal processing during production recording. It affects the dialogue audio throughout postproduction.

- The value of noise reduction throughout the production process cannot be overemphasized, especially in relation to dialogue and field recording.

- Production recordists can be of considerable help in giving sound editors flexibility, by how they record dialogue on the set.

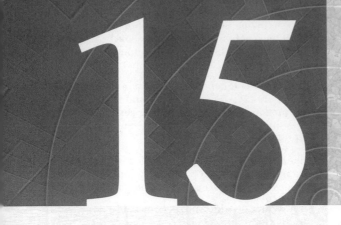

Music Production

The focus of this chapter is studio music production using the close-miking recording technique. There are two basic ways to record musical instruments: distant miking and close miking. ***Distant miking*** uses two or several microphones to record an entire ensemble. ***Close miking*** places a microphone relatively close to each sound source or group of sound sources in an ensemble. Generally, distant miking is employed when all sounds or voicings are recorded at the same time and it is important to preserve the ensemble sound. Orchestral and choral music and certain types of jazz are examples of music that use distant miking. Distant miking attempts to reproduce the aural experience that audiences receive in a live venue by recording in an acoustically suitable studio or by doing it at an actual concert site.

The underlying concept of distant miking is often used in-studio along with the close-miking technique, to enhance a recording with a more acoustically natural, open sound. But because the mic-to-source distances are less considerable, the technique is referred to as ***off-miking***. Off-miking with stereo microphone arrays is covered later in this chapter.

CLOSE MIKING

Close miking is the technique of choice in studio recording for a number of reasons: greater control in recording the nuances of each musical element;

the sound from each instrument, and leakage from other instruments, is better contained; in popular music the difference in loudness between electric and acoustic instruments can be very difficult to balance with distant miking; much of pop music is played loudly, and in even relatively live acoustics close miking helps prevent the music from being awash in reverberation. Reverberation, spatial positioning, and blend are added in the post-production mixdown.

Most of the discussion that follows assumes the use of directional microphones. Remember that among the reasons for close miking are better sound control of each instrument and reduced leakage. If acoustics and recording logistics permit, there are three good reasons why omnidirectional mics should not be overlooked: (1) The better omni capacitors have extraordinarily wide, flat response, particularly in the lower frequencies, and little or no off-axis coloration. (2) Omnis are not as subject to proximity effect, sibilance, plosives, and breathing sounds as are directional mics. (3) Because of the inverse square law, it is possible to close-mike with an omni and still reduce leakage if the instrument's sound-pressure level is high enough.

Before getting into specific applications of close miking, it will be helpful to keep in mind four principles:

■ The closer a microphone is to a sound source, the more detailed, intimate, drier, and, if proximity effect is a factor, bassier the sound; the farther a microphone is from a sound source, the more diffused, open, less intimate, and ambient the sound.

■ The higher the frequency, the more directional the sound wave and, therefore, the mic pickup; the lower the frequency, the more omnidirectional the sound wave and mic pickup, regardless of the mic's directional pattern.

■ Although close miking may employ a number of mics, more may not always be better. Each additional microphone adds a little more noise to the system and means dealing with another input at the console, to say nothing of possible phasing problems.

■ Generally, large-diaphragm microphones are more suitable in reproducing low-frequency instruments, and small-diaphragm mics are more suitable in reproducing high-frequency instruments.

DRUMS

Perhaps no other instrument provides as many possibilities for microphone combinations, and therefore as much of a challenge, as the drums. Several different components make up a drum set—at least a bass drum, floor (low-pitched) tom-tom, medium and high (-pitched) tom-toms, snare drum, hi-hat cymbal, and two overhead cymbals (see Figure 15-1).

Characteristics

Drums consist of at least one membrane (drumhead) stretched over a cylinder and, usually, a second membrane that resonates with the struck head. Drums produce loud sound levels and steep transients. They are not considered pitched instruments, although drumheads can be tuned to a musical pitch, and the pitch relationships of the floor, medium, and high tom-toms must be maintained. Also, various sonic effects can be achieved by tuning the top and bottom heads to different tensions relative to each other.

It is important that tension be uniform across the head to produce a single pitch. When several pitches are produced simultaneously, the sonic result is dissonance.

Drums radiate sound perpendicularly to the heads, particularly the top head. High-frequency transients are most pronounced on-axis, perpendicular to the point where the stick hits the drumhead. This is the sound responsible for most of the drum's "kick." Harmonics and overtones are produced from the tension rings, the shell, and the bottom head.

Bass (Kick) Drum The bass drum is the lowest pitched of the drums. Its fundamental frequencies range from 30 to 147 Hz, with harmonics extending from 1 to 6 kHz. It is commonly called the *kick drum*

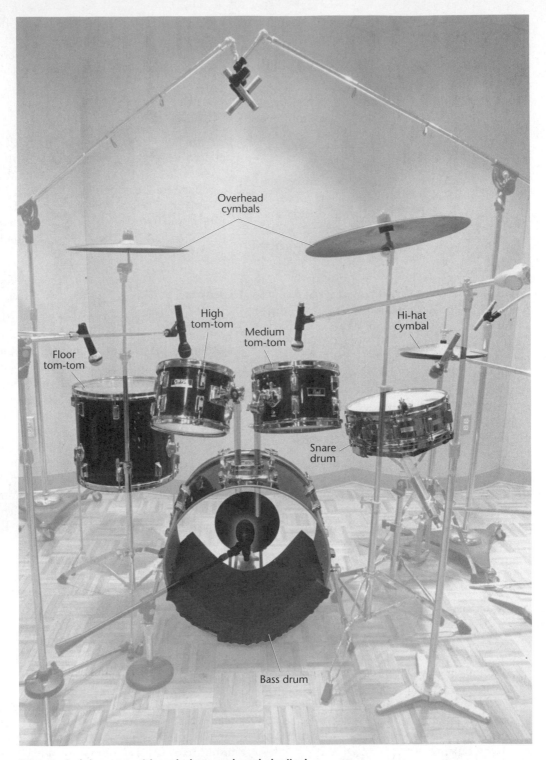

15-1 Typical drum set with each drum and cymbal miked

because it is struck with a beater controlled by the drummer's foot. The drum stands on its side with the "top," or beater, head facing the drummer. The "bottom" head is usually removed or has a hole cut into it because of the low-frequency resonances and very steep transients that the drum can generate. Most of the drum's low frequencies are emitted omnidirectionally, though vibrations from the shell and heads resonate throughout the instrument.

Tom-toms Tom-toms come in a variety of sizes and pitches and usually have two heads. They produce the steep transients and radiating characteristics common to most drums. Lower-pitched toms generate more-omnidirectional waves; higher-pitched toms generate more-directional waves. Because tom-toms are often used to accent a piece, they are tuned to have more sustain than the kick and snare drums.

Snare Drum The snare can be characterized as a tom-tom tuned to a higher pitch and with less sustain. Fundamental frequencies range from 100 to 200 Hz, with harmonics that extend from 1 to 15 kHz. The major difference between a tom-tom and a snare drum are the chainlike *snares,* stretched across the bottom head of the instrument, that give the drum its name, characteristic crispness, and high-frequency cutting power.

Cymbals Cymbals are usually round, metal plates shaped like a flattened bell. They may be struck with a hard, wooden drumstick, a soft mallet, or brushes. The type of striker used is largely responsible for the sound produced. Unlike drums, cymbals have a long decay. The harder the striker, the more high frequencies of the transients are produced. A cymbal tends to radiate sound perpendicularly to its surface, with a ringing resonance near its edge.

A cymbal's pitch is determined by, among other things, size and thickness. Cymbals are also designed to produce different textures; the ring of the ride cymbal or the splash of the crash cymbal are two common examples.

Generally, their fundamentals range from 300 to 587 Hz. Harmonics extend from 1 to 15 kHz.

Hi-hat Cymbal The hi-hat cymbal is actually two cymbals with the open end of the bells facing each other. A foot pedal, controlled by the drummer, raises and lowers the top cymbal to strike the bottom cymbal, or the top cymbal is struck with a drumstick, or both. Different timbres are generated by varying the pressure and distance between the two cymbals. The hi-hat is integral to the drum sound both for its high frequencies that "cut through" a recording and as a timekeeper. For these reasons the high-frequency transients perpendicular to the contact point and the shimmer from the edges are important.

Tuning the Drums

A good drum sound begins with the musicianship of the drummer and the quality and tuning of the drum set. No miking technique will save the drum sound of an incompetent drummer or a low-quality drum set.

Therefore, before drums are miked, they must be tuned. Tuning the drum set is important to the sound of individual drums and also to their overall sound. Many studios have an in-house drum set always tuned and ready to go, not only to ensure the desired drum sound but also to avoid having this necessary and time-consuming procedure cut into recording time.

As you might expect, there are many ways to tune a drum set: in fifths and octaves; in thirds; by tapping on the sides of the drum, finding its fundamental pitch, and then tuning the head to it; or by pitching the bass drum low enough to leave room in the upper bass and midrange for the tom-toms and snare drum. If the bass drum is pitched too high, it pushes too close to the toms, which in turn get pushed too close to the snare drum, making the drum sound smaller. Moreover, by not separating the individual drum sounds, little room is left for such instruments as the bass and guitar.

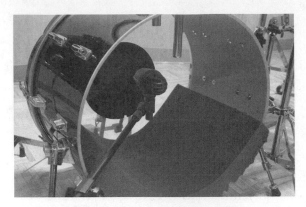

15-2 A directional microphone pointed at the drumhead produces a fuller sound. Foam rubber padding is placed in the drum to reduce vibration.

One problem with even the best drum sets is ringing. Damping the drums helps reduce ringing—and undesirable overtones as well. To damp a bass drum, place a pillow, blanket, foam rubber cushion, or the like inside the drum (see 15-2). To damp a tom-tom and snare, tape a cotton or gauze pad near the edge of the drumhead, out of the way of the drumstick. Specially made drum silencers are also available (see 15-6). Because many drummers do not care to have things taped to their drums, another effective way to damp them is with O-rings placed inside the drumhead.

Make sure the damping does not muffle the drum sound. It helps to leave one edge of the damping material untaped so it is free to vibrate. To reduce cymbal ringing, apply masking tape from the underside of the bell to the rim in narrow radial strips or use specially made cymbal silencers.

Where the drum set is placed in a studio also affects its sound. Isolated in a drum booth (to reduce leakage into other instruments' microphones), the overall sound takes on the acoustic properties of the booth: If the booth is live, the drums will sound live; if it is absorptive, the drums will sound tight or dull. On a hard floor, the drums sound live and bright; on a carpet they sound tighter and drier. In a corner they sound boomier, because the dominant lower frequencies are more concentrated. Often drums are put on a riser that can resonate to reduce low-end leakage.

Miking

Although the drum set consists of several different-sounding instruments, it must be miked so that they sound good individually and blend as a unit. That said, drums are miked in many ways. The approach you take depends on both how much sound control you want and what type of music you are recording. Explaining how to deal with sound control is relatively easy: The more components you want to regulate, the more mics you use (although this can have its drawbacks—possible phasing, for one). Achieving a particular drum sound for a certain type of music involves many variables and is more difficult to explain.

Generally, in rock-and-roll and contemporary pop music, producers like a tight drum sound for added punch and attack. Because this usually requires complete control of the drum sound, they tend to use several microphones for the drums. In jazz many styles are loose and open; hence, producers are more likely to use fewer drum mics to achieve an airier sound.

Bass (Kick) Drum The bass (kick) drum is the foundation of the drum set, because it provides the bottom sound that, along with the bass guitar, supports the other musical elements. Because the bass drum also produces high levels of sound pressure and steep transients, large-diaphragm moving-coil microphones usually work best, although there are a few large-diaphragm capacitor mics that also work well, particularly by adding some midrange coloration.

As for mic placement, the common technique is to use the hole often cut in the front drumhead or to remove the head entirely and place the mic inside. This gives the sound of the bass drum more punch. Pointing the mic perpendicular to the back drumhead produces a fuller sound (see 15-2), and pointing it toward the side of the drum picks up more of the drum's overtones (see 15-3). Placing the mic close to the beater picks up the hard beater sound and, if you are not careful, the action of the beater pedal as well.

Drum mics are usually directional to increase sound separation and reduce leakage from the rest

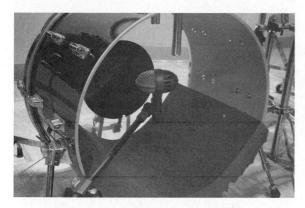

15-3 A microphone pointed to the side of the drum produces more of the drum's overtones

of the drum set, though an omnidirectional mic can be effective in a bass drum. Placing the mic in close proximity to a loud sound source usually prevents leakage from the other drums (remember the inverse square law). To separate the bass drum even more, use a low-pass filter, shelving, or parametric equalizer to cut off or reduce frequencies above its upper range. Be careful, though—the perceived punch of the bass drum goes into the midrange frequencies. In fact, boosting from 1,600 to 5,000 Hz adds a brighter, sharper snap to the bass drum sound. The dull, thuddy, cardboard sound the bass drum tends to produce can be alleviated by attenuating between 300 and 600 Hz.

A word about equalizing during recording: First, equalization should not be used as a substitute for good microphone technique or to correct poor mic technique. Second, if you must equalize, make sure you know exactly what you are doing. Even if mistakes in equalizing during recording can be undone in the mixdown, it may not be possible to undo the additional noise and possible distortion created in passing a signal through an electronic device.

Tom-toms Tom-toms come in a variety of sizes and pitches. Typical drum sets have three toms: the low-pitched, fuller-sounding floor tom; the middle-pitched medium tom, and the higher-pitched, sharper-sounding high tom.

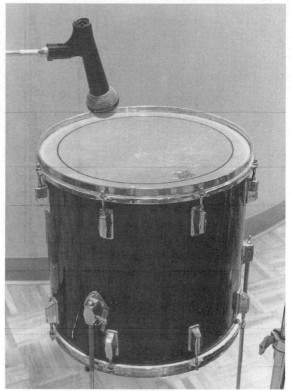

15-4 Miking a floor tom

Although toms produce loud transients (all drums do), they are not as strong as those the bass drum produces; you can therefore mike them with moving-coil, capacitor, or the more rugged ribbon mics. Placement, as always, depends on the sound you want. Generally, the mic is placed from 1 to 10 inches above the tom and is aimed at the center of the skin. It is usually mounted just over the edge of the rim to avoid interfering with the drummer's sticks (see 15-4 and 15-5).

The mic-to-source distance depends on the low-frequency content desired from the drum sound itself. If it has little low-frequency content, try placing a directional mic with proximity effect close to the drum skin to boost the lower frequencies. Placing a mic inside the drum gives the best isolation, but it also produces a closed, dull sound. Whatever technique you use, remember that the sonic relationships of the toms must be maintained;

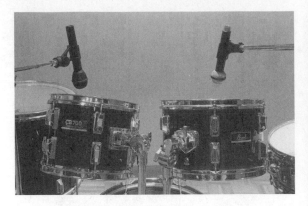

15-5 Miking the high tom (left) and medium tom (right)

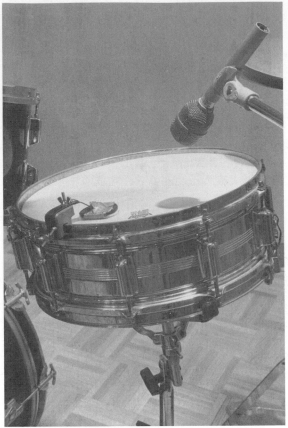

15-6 Miking a snare drum. The pad on the skin of the drum reduces vibrations.

using the same make and model of microphone on each tom helps.

Snare Drum Of all the components in a drum set, the snare usually presents the biggest problem in miking. Most producers prefer a crisp snare drum sound. Miking the snare drum too close tends to produce a lifeless sound, whereas miking it too far away tends to pick up annoying overtones, ringing, and leakage from the other drums.

Another problem is that the snare drum sometimes sounds dull and thuddy. In this instance the problem is most likely the drum itself. Two ways to add crispness to the sound are to use a mic with a high-frequency boost or to equalize it at the console. Boosting at around 4,000 to 5,000 Hz adds crispness and attack. The better alternatives are to retune the drum set and, if that does not work, to replace the drumhead(s).

Moving-coil or capacitor mics work well on the snare drum; the moving-coil mic tends to give it a harder edge, and the capacitor mic tends to make it sound richer or crisper. To find the optimal mic position, begin at a point 6 to 10 inches from the drumhead and aim the mic so that its pickup pattern is split between the head and the side of the drum (see 15-6). This picks up the sounds of the snares and the stick hitting the head. To get the snares' buzz and the slight delay of their snap, use two mics: one over and one under the drum (see 15-7).

Hi-hat Cymbal The hi-hat cymbal produces two sounds: a clap and a shimmer. Depending on how important these accents are to the music, the hi-hat can either share the snare drum's mic or have a microphone of its own. If it shares, place the mic between the hi-hat and the snare and adjust the sound balance through mic placement (see 15-8).

If the hi-hat has a separate mic, the two most common positions for it are 4 to 6 inches above the center stem with the mic pointing straight down (see 15-9), and off the edge (see 15-10). Sound is brightest over the edge of the cymbal. Miking too close off the center produces ringing, and miking off the edge may pick up the rush of air produced each time the two cymbals clap together (see 15-11). Equalize by rolling off the bass to reduce

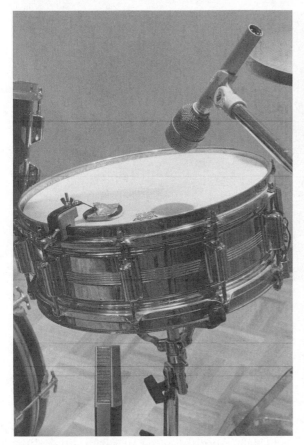

15-7 Miking a snare drum over and under

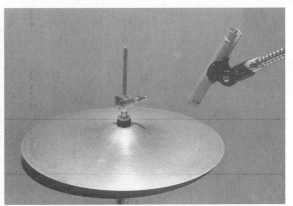

15-9 Miking over the hi-hat cymbal

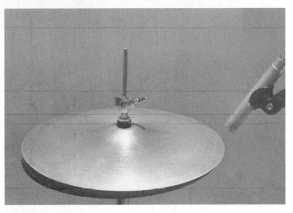

15-10 Miking at the edge of the hi-hat cymbal

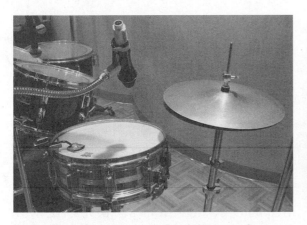

15-8 Miking the hi-hat cymbal and the snare drum

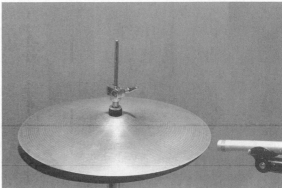

15-11 A mic aimed at the point where the cymbals clap may pick up the rush of air as they come together

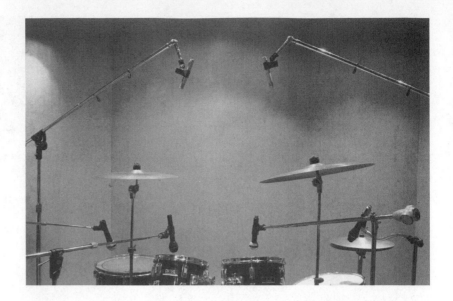

15-12 A spaced pair of directional microphones to pick up the sound of the overhead cymbals and add spaciousness to the overall sound of the drum set

low-frequency leakage, but only if the hi-hat is miked separately. If the mic is shared with the snare drum, rolling off the bass adversely affects the low-end sound of the snare.

Overhead Cymbals Two types of overhead cymbals are the ride, which produces ring and shimmer, and the crash, which has a splashy sound. In miking either cymbal, the definition of the characteristic sounds must be preserved. To this end capacitors usually work best; for stereo pickup the coincident, near-coincident (see 15-1), or spaced pair can be used (see 15-12 ; see also "Off-Miking with Stereo Microphone Arrays" later in this chapter). When using the spaced pair, remember to observe the three-to-one rule to avoid phasing problems.

Because the overhead microphones usually blend the sounds of the entire drum set, they must be at least a few feet above the cymbals. If they are too close to the cymbals, the drum blend will be poor and the mics will pick up annoying overtones that sound like ringing or gonging, depending on the narrowness of the mic's pickup pattern. If blending the drum sound is being left until the mixdown, and it is important to isolate the cymbals—roll off the low frequencies reaching the cymbal microphones from the other drums.

ACOUSTIC STRING INSTRUMENTS

Acoustic string instruments derive their sound from stretched strings, held taught in a frame, that are set into vibratory motion by being bowed, plucked, or struck. As strings do not produce much loudness, the frame, which also vibrates with the strings, serves to amplify and radiate sound. Three variables help determine the pitch of a vibrating string: length, tension, and mass, or thickness.

Plucked String Instruments

Plucked string instruments include the guitar, the banjo, and the mandolin.

Characteristics

Because the six-string guitar is clearly the most popular of the plucked string instruments, it is considered here. The guitar's six strings are stretched across a hollow body with a flat top and sound hole that resonates the fundamental frequencies and harmonics of the vibrating strings. Fundamental frequencies range from 82 to 988 Hz, with harmonics extending from 1 to 13 kHz.

The guitar has a fingerboard with raised metal frets that divide the effective length of the strings into exact intervals as the strings are pressed down onto the frets. Where the guitar string is plucked affects sound quality because of the relationship between the distance from the point of contact to the ends of the strings. For example, a string plucked close to the bridge contains more high-frequency energy due to the relatively short distance between the point of contact and the bridge. A string plucked farther from the bridge produces a warmer sound due to the presence of longer wavelengths and, therefore, lower frequencies.

Overall, most high frequencies are near the bridge. The joint between the neck and body produces more lower frequencies. The most lower frequencies are resonated by the back of the guitar and are generated from the sound hole.

What the strings are made of and what is used to pluck them also affect a guitar's sound quality. For example, metal strings tend to sound brighter than nylon, and a string plucked with a pick will be brighter than one plucked with the finger.

Miking

Because most of a guitar's sound radiates from the front of the instrument, centering a microphone off the middle of the sound hole should, theoretically, provide balanced sound. If a mic is too close to the hole, however, sound is bassy or boomy. If it is moved closer to the bridge, detail is lost. If it is moved closer to the neck, presence is reduced; if it is moved farther away, intimacy is affected. On the other hand, if a guitar lacks bottom, mike closer to the sound hole; if it lacks highs, mike closer to the bridge; to increase midrange, aim a mic at the neck.

Plucking creates quick attacks. Using a dynamic mic, which has slower transient response than a capacitor microphone, can slow the attacks and diminish detail, particularly in the guitar's bass frequencies. But if a capacitor mic brings out too much crispness, a good moving-coil microphone can reduce it. Dozens, perhaps hundreds, of methods have been used to mike the guitar. A few general techniques are discussed here, but keep in mind that many factors affect a guitar's sound, as just noted.

One way to achieve a natural, balanced sound is to position the microphone about 1 to 3 feet from

the sound hole. To set a more high- or low-frequency accent, angle the mic either down toward the high strings or up toward the low strings. To brighten the natural sound, place the microphone above the bridge and even with the front of the guitar, because most high-frequency energy is radiated from a narrow lobe at right angles to the top plate (see 15-13 and 15-14). Miking off the

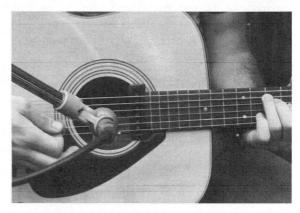

15-13 Miking an acoustic guitar. Aiming a microphone at the center of the guitar hole 2 to 3 feet away produces a sound with balanced highs, middles, and lows.

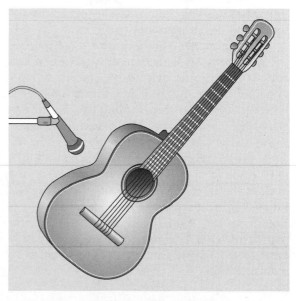

15-14 Miking an acoustic guitar. A microphone placed about 6 inches above the bridge and even with the front of the guitar brightens the natural sound of the instrument.

twelfth fret, across the strings, produces a sound rich in harmonics.

Another way to achieve natural sound is to place a microphone about 8 to 12 inches above the guitar, 1 to 2 feet away, aimed between the hole and the bridge. A good-quality capacitor mic reduces excess bottom and warms the sound.

A microphone perpendicular to the sound hole about 8 inches away reduces leakage from other instruments but adds bassiness. Rolling off the bass creates a more natural sound, but be careful not to take the guitar's important bass frequencies with the roll off.

A microphone about 4 to 8 inches from the front of the bridge creates a warm, mellow sound, but the sound lacks detail; this lack is beneficial if pickup and string noises are problematic.

For a classical guitar, which requires acoustic interaction, place the microphone more than 3 feet from the sound hole. Make sure mic-to-source distance is not too great, or the subtleties of the instrument will be diminished.

Clipping a microphone to the tip of the sound hole facing in toward the center or placing the microphone inside the guitar gives good isolation and added resonance. A mic attached inside the sound hole also reproduces a more closed, bassier sound and less string noise.

A natural part of the sound of most plucked string instruments is the screechy, rubbing noises called *fret* sounds caused by the musician's fingering. Fret noises usually bring to a head the issue of whether they should be part of the recording. Personal taste is the determining factor. If you do not care for the fret sounds, mike farther from the instrument or use a supercardioid or hypercardioid mic placed at a slight angle to the neck of the instrument. This puts the mic's dead side facing the frets. Make sure the mic's angle is not too severe, or the sound from the instrument will be off-mic. There are also strings specially designed to reduce finger noises and sprays to reduce friction.

Bowed String Instruments

The well-known bowed string instruments are the violin, the viola, the cello, and the bass.

Characteristics

Bowed string instruments are similar to plucked string instruments in that their strings are stretched across a fingerboard and hollow body, which resonates the vibrating strings. But bowed instruments have only four strings and no metal frets on the fingerboard; intervals are determined by the placement of the musician's fingers on the fingerboard. Another difference is that the strings are vibrated by a bow drawn across them, thereby generating a smoother attack than that of a plucked string. The bridge in a bowed instrument is connected to a top plate through a sound post to the back plate. It is important to overall sound, as are the F-holes in the top plate that allow the air inside the body to resonate. The dynamic range of bowed string instruments is not as wide as that of most other orchestral instruments, nor is their projection as strong (see 15-15).

Violin The four violin strings are tuned to perfect fifths and have a fundamental frequency range of 196 to 3,136 Hz, with harmonics that extend from 4 to 13 kHz. The violin radiates lower frequencies in a roughly spherical pattern. As frequencies get higher, the violin radiates frequencies about evenly in the front and back, as both the top plate and the back plate are designed to resonate with the strings. The highest frequencies are radiated upward from the top plate.

Viola The viola is essentially a larger, lower-pitched version of the violin. The strings are tuned a fifth lower than the violin's; their fundamental frequency range is 131 to 1,175 Hz, with harmonics that extend from 2 to 8.5 kHz. The radiating pattern is similar to that of the violin, but is less directional due to its lower frequency range.

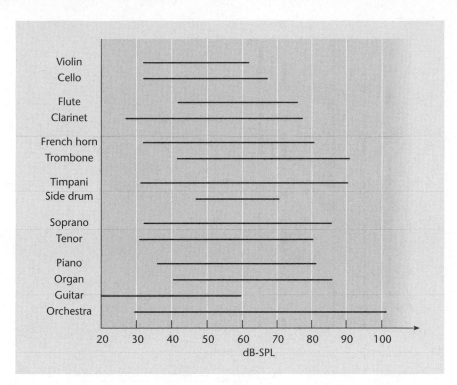

Cello The cello's strings are tuned a full octave below the viola, with a fundamental frequency range of 65 to 698 Hz and harmonics that extend from 1 to 6.5 kHz. The cello's radiating pattern is more omnidirectional than directional, but it is affected by the playing position. The cello rests on a rubber- or plastic-tipped spike that is set on the floor. Hence, vibrations are transmitted to the floor, which reflects and absorbs the sound waves to some degree, depending on the sound absorption coefficient of the flooring material.

Bass The bass strings are tuned in fourths rather than fifths and have a fundamental range from 41 to 294 Hz, with harmonics extending from 1 to 5 kHz. It radiates sound omnidirectionally and, because it is positioned like the cello, the sound is affected by the flooring material.

Miking

Because the dynamic range of bowed string instruments is not wide, sound has to be reinforced by using several instruments or multiple miking, or both, depending on the size of the sound required. Overdubbing is another method used to reinforce string sound. The need for reinforcement is compounded by the dearth of competent string players in many communities, to say nothing of the cost of hiring very many of them where they do exist in sufficient numbers.

Individually, miking a violin or viola a few feet above the instrument, aiming the mic at the front face, produces an open, natural sound, assuming fairly live acoustics, which are essential to recording a good string sound (see 15-16). Although sound radiation is uniform up to 500 Hz, depending on the microphone, a single mic may not hear

15-16 Miking a violin or viola. (a) Placing the mic several feet above the instrument, aimed at the front face, tends to produce an open, natural sound. (b) To produce a country fiddle sound, place the microphone closer to the bridge but not close enough to interfere with the bowing.

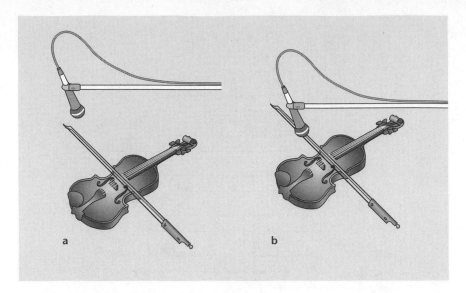

15-17 Enlarging the sound of a violin or viola. Place one microphone several feet above the instrument(s) and one below the instrument(s). This tends to make one instrument sound like a few and a few sound like several.

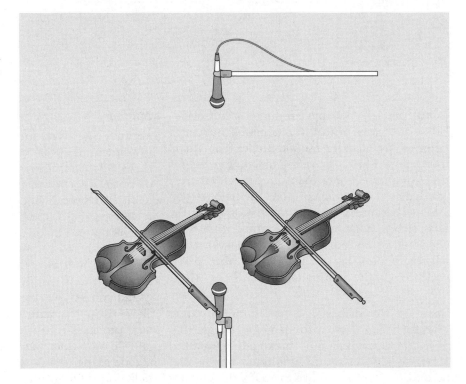

sufficient low end and therefore not reproduce a robust sound. Miking "over and under" ensures that the highs, which are concentrated above 500 Hz and radiate perpendicularly to the sound board, are picked up from above the instrument and the lows are picked up from both above and below. This technique also tends to make one instrument sound like a few and a few sound like several (see 15-17).

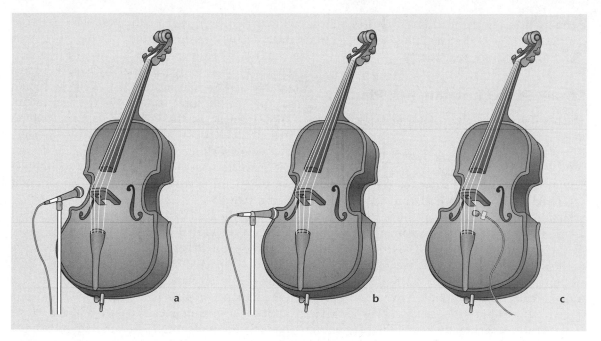

15-18 Three ways to mike a cello or bass. (a) Off the bridge produces a brighter sound. (b) Off the *f*-hole produces a fuller sound. (c) A contact mic behind the strings, near or at the bridge, taped to the body of the instrument, produces a more resonant sound, which could also be dull and devoid of harmonics.

Assuming that the acoustics are drier than what is usually required to record a good string sound, overdubbing will accomplish this, usually with greater effectiveness.

Miking a few inches from the side or above the strings of a violin produces a country fiddle sound; the closer a microphone is to the strings, the coarser or scratchier the sound. But take care not to interfere with the musician's bowing when close-miking over bowed instruments.

Generally, for either the cello or the acoustic bass, miking off the bridge 2 to 3 feet produces a brighter sound, and miking off the F-hole produces a fuller sound. The right contact mic placed behind the bridge produces a tight, robust sound (see 15-18). The wrong contact mic can produce a closed, dull sound.

With a plucked bass, used in jazz, some producers like to clip a mic to the bridge or F-hole for a more robust sound. A danger with this technique is getting a thin, midrange-heavy sound instead. Close-miking a plucked bass picks up the attack. If close miking also produces too boomy a sound, compress the bass slightly or roll off some of the low end, but beware of altering the characteristic low-frequency sound of the instrument.

Capacitor and ribbon microphones work particularly well with bowed string instruments. Capacitor mics enrich the string sound and enhance detail. Ribbon mics produce a resonant, warm quality, although there may be some loss of high-end detail. As for plucked strings, capacitors are preferred because of their excellent transient response.

Clip-on and contact microphones are other alternatives in miking bowed string instruments. Assuming the musician does not mind having a mic attached to the instrument, clip-on and contact mics tend to produce a harsher sound when placed near the bridge and a resonant, but closed, sound when attached to the body of the instrument. A better approach to this type of miking is the so-called *symphonic microphone system,* a noninvasive system designed to put a mic inside string instruments, connected through the end pin. The air motion inside the instrument creates a more natural sound than does a clip-on or contact mic vibrating against the instrument.

Struck String Instruments: Piano

The best-known example of a struck string instrument is the piano.

Characteristics

The piano's strings are stretched across a bridge attached to a soundboard that resonates in sympathy with the vibrating strings after they are struck. The strings are struck by hammers controlled by the keys on the keyboard. The strings continue to vibrate until the key is released and a damper stops the vibration of the string. The piano's fundamental frequency and dynamic ranges are quite wide (see inside front cover and Figure 15-15).

Radiation is generally perpendicular to the soundboard, primarily upward in a grand piano. The lower-frequency strings are more omnidirectional; the higher-frequency strings are located closer to an axis perpendicular to the sound board. The lid is also a factor in a piano's sound radiation, but directionality depends on the angle at which the lid is open.

Because of the percussive nature of the key striking the strings, timbre is affected by how hard the string is struck. Higher harmonics are more present in strings that are struck hard. Strings struck more gently produce a warmer sound.

Miking

The piano offers almost unlimited possibilities for sound shaping. Perhaps more than with many other instruments, the character of the piano sound is dependent on the quality of the piano itself. Smaller grand pianos may have dull, wooden low-end response. Old or abused pianos may sound dull or ring or thump. Steinways, generally, are built to produce a lyrical sound. Yamahas produce crisp sound with more attack. The Bosendorfer aims for additional sonority by adding semitones in the bass range. Mic technique and signal processing cannot change a piano's voicing from dull to bright, from thin to rich, or from sharp to smooth, but they can alter a piano's existing sound.

Another factor in piano miking is the music. Classical music and jazz generally require a more open sound, so mic placement and pickup should capture the full sonic radiation of the instrument. Popular music, such as rock and country, requires a more closed sound, so mic placement and pickup are generally closer and tighter.

There are several common miking techniques for the grand piano (see 15-19) and the upright piano (see 15-20). The techniques displayed in Figure 15-19 are examples, however; they do not address the fact that you have to be some distance from the piano to get its full sound—close distances yield only partial sound—because its dynamic range can be so wide. In studio recording there is the additional problem of leakage in the piano mics from other instruments, thus necessitating closer mic-to-source distances. Because there is more piano sound across the bridge–rail axis than horizontally along the keyboard, miking along the piano instead of across it reproduces a more spacious, full-bodied sound (see 15-21). But a clear low-end/high-end stereo image is sacrificed because the sound is more blended.

WOODWINDS

Just as the vibrating string is the acoustical foundation of string instruments, a vibrating column of air is the foundation of woodwind (and brass) instruments. All wind instruments have in common a tube, or cone, through which air is blown, generating a standing wave of vibrating air within. In woodwinds the vibrations are produced in the clarinet and saxophone using one reed, in the oboe and bassoon using a double reed, and in the flute and piccolo by blowing across the air hole.

Characteristics

The sounds of woodwinds are determined by the length of the tube, whether the tube is open at one end (clarinet) or at both ends (flute), and by the opening and closing of the holes in the tube. A tube

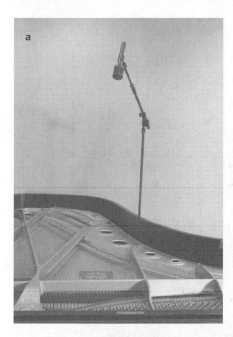
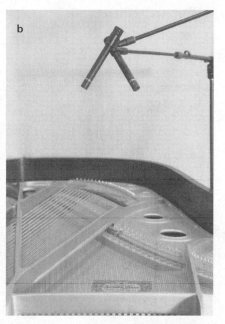
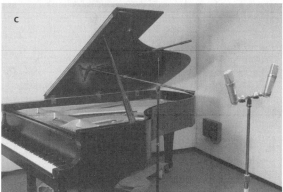
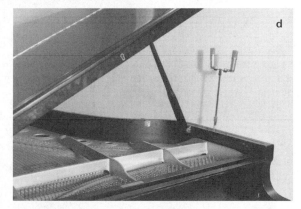

15-19 Miking a grand piano. (a) A middle-side (M-S) microphone high over the sound board, with the lid off, and aimed toward the midrange strings picks up the piano's direct and indirect radiations in a balanced and relatively spacious low-end to high-end stereo image (assuming proper acoustics). (b) For a more spacious stereo image, an X-Y pair of near-coincident mics can be employed. One popular coincident microphone technique is the *ORTF* (Office de Radiodiffusion-Television Française, the French broadcasting system) *array*. It spaces the X-Y pair just under 7 inches apart at a 110-degree angle, 55 degrees to the left and right of center. Whatever the distance between the mics, the imaging from the low to midrange to high frequencies must be balanced. (c) When the piano lid remains attached, in addition to the main microphone array, off-miking can be used to pick up more of the indirect reflections from the bounce off the lid. The off-mics can be spaced, which reproduces a more spacious stereo image than the near-coincident array, or they can be arrayed in an X-Y pattern. (d) If acoustics permit, the off-mics placed several feet from the piano can serve as the main pair. A problem with using spaced microphones is that the wider the spacing, the less mono-compatible the sound. In all of these arrays, a few insurance mics placed on the floor under the piano's sound board can help ensure that the full range of the instrument's radiations is captured.

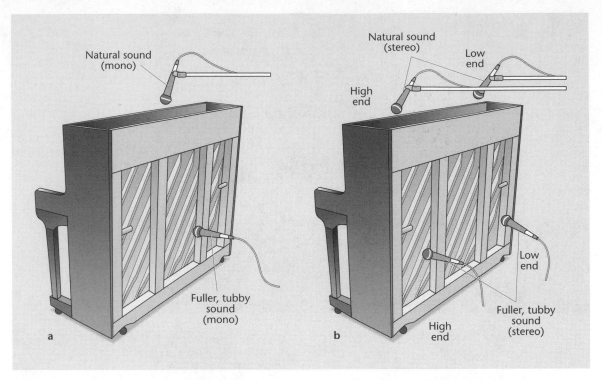

15-20 Miking an upright piano. (a) For mono, position a mic over an open top for a natural sound, or behind the sound board for a fuller, tubby sound. (b) For stereo, position two microphones, one for low-end pickup and the other for high-end pickup, over an open top or behind the sound board. Mics also can be placed inside the piano to pick up the hammer sound. When spacing the mics, remember the three-to-one rule.

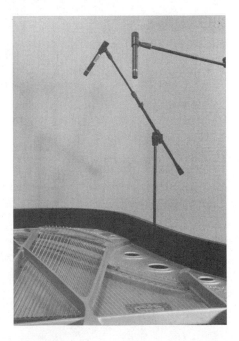

15-21 Miking across the bridge–rail axis. This produces a spacious, full-bodied sound but at the expense of low-end/high-end stereo imaging.

open at one end has odd-number harmonics: third, fifth, seventh, and so on. A tube open at both ends, and flared or conical tubes (oboe and bassoon), has the normal harmonics: second, third, fourth, fifth, and so on. The vibrating reed and sound holes generate their own overtones. In general, higher frequencies radiate from the bell, and lower frequencies radiate from the holes.

Flute The flute is a tube that is held horizontally. The musician blows air across a sound hole and controls pitch and timbre by varying the blowing force. Pitch is also determined by opening and closing the holes in the side of the instrument. Sound radiates from the sound hole, the side holes, and the end of the flute. Fundamental frequencies range from 261 to 2,349 Hz, and harmonics extend from 3 to 8 kHz. Its dynamic range is limited.

Clarinet The clarinet is a single-reed tube played almost vertically, with the bell pointed toward the floor. Its fundamental frequency range is 165 to 1,568 Hz, with harmonics extending from 2 to 10 kHz. Sound is generated from the mouthpiece and reed, the side holes, and the bell. Reflections from the floor also may affect the clarinet's sound.

Oboe and Bassoon The fundamental frequencies of the oboe and bassoon are 261 to 1,568 and 62 to 587 Hz, with harmonics extending from 2 to 12 kHz and 1 to 7 kHz, respectively. Both instruments, despite their relatively narrow frequency response and limited dynamic range, are comparatively rich in harmonics and overtones. The oboe's sound emanates from the mouthpiece and reed, sound holes, and bell. Like the clarinet, it is played aimed at the floor and may also be affected by sound that is absorbed by and/or reflected from the floor. The bassoon curves upward at its bottom, pointing toward the ceiling. If the ceiling is high enough, the bassoon's overall sound is usually not affected.

Saxophone The family of saxophones includes the soprano, alto, tenor, and baritone. Saxophones have a conical shape with a bell that curves upward (except for the soprano saxophone, which may be straight). The saxophone's sound radiates mostly from the bell, but the sound holes also generate significant detail. Fundamental frequency ranges are roughly as follows: soprano—200 to 1,100 Hz; alto—138 to 820 Hz; tenor—100 to 600 Hz; and baritone—80 to 400 Hz.

Miking

Woodwind instruments, such as the flute, clarinet, and oboe, are among the weaker-sounding instruments and have a limited dynamic range. Alto, tenor, and baritone saxophones are stronger sounding. But the higher-pitched woodwinds—flute, clarinet, and soprano saxophone—can cut through the sound of more-powerful instruments if miking and blending are not properly attended to (or if the sound designer intends it).

Because most woodwinds are not powerful instruments, the tendency is to close-mike them, but, due to their sound radiation, this results in an uneven pickup. They should be miked far enough away so that the pickup sounds blended and natural.

Because the flute and piccolo (a smaller, higher-pitched version of the flute) radiate sound in shifting patterns sideways and from the instruments' end holes, close miking, or, worse, contact miking, tends to miss certain frequencies and emphasize others. Moreover, dry, less reverberant sound can distort some tonalities.

For the flute, mic-to-source distance depends on the music. For classical it should be about 3 to 8 feet; for pop, about 6 to 24 inches. Microphone positioning should start slightly above the player, between the mouthpiece and the bell. To add the breathy quality of the blowing sound, mike toward the mouthpiece—how close depends on how much breath sound you want. If breath noise is a problem regardless of where the mic is placed, and you want to eliminate it, try placing the microphone behind the player's head, aiming it at the finger holes (see 15-22). This technique also reduces high-frequency content. A windscreen or pop filter reduces unwanted breath noise too. In miking a flute or any woodwind, be careful not to pick up the sound of the key action.

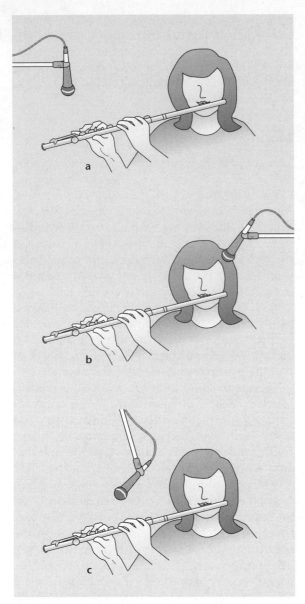

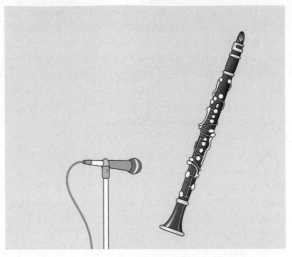

15-23 Miking clarinet and oboe. Place a microphone over the finger holes toward the bottom third, because most of the sounds come from this part of the instrument. In miking the keys of any instrument, avoid close mic-to-source distances; otherwise, the sound of the moving keys may be heard.

Microphone positioning for the clarinet and oboe must take into account the narrowing of high frequencies radiating in the vertical plane in front of the player, as well as floor reflections from the bell being aimed downward. Close miking tends to emphasize these disparities. If close miking is unavoidable, position the mic to the side of the bell rather than straight at it. This should smooth most of the sonic anomalies. Miking off the bell also tends to reduce leakage and makes the sound brighter and harder. Another possibility is to mike toward the bottom third of the instrument and far enough away to blend the pickup from the finger holes and bell (see 15-23).

Saxophones radiate more sound from the bell and some sound from the holes. But the proportion of sound radiating from holes and bell constantly changes as the keys open and close. Miking saxophones off the bell produces a bright, thin, hard sound. Miking too close to the bell further accentuates the high frequencies, making the sound piercing or screechy. Miking off the finger holes adds fullness, presence, and warmth. Aiming a

15-22 Miking flute and piccolo. (a) Placing a microphone over the finger holes near the end of the instrument picks up most of the sounds these instruments emit and does not pick up the breathy sounds that miking the mouthpiece produces. (b) Some producers feel that these sounds are part of the instruments' overall aural character, however, and mike the mouthpiece to produce a thinner-textured sound. (c) If unwanted breath sounds persist, place the microphone behind the musician's head, aimed at the finger holes.

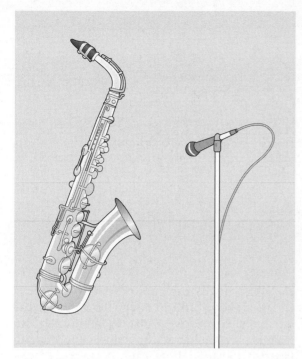

15-24 Miking a saxophone. Aiming a microphone at the holes from above the bell produces a natural, blended sax sound. Miking too close to the instrument may pick up blowing, spit, or key sounds.

microphone at the holes from above the bell produces a natural, more blended sound (see 15-24).

BRASS

Brass instruments—trumpet, trombone, baritone, tuba, and French horn—generally are conical and have a cup-shaped mouthpiece that acts as a vibrating "reed" when the musician blows into it. They are the loudest acoustic musical instruments with the widest dynamic range (see 15-15).

Characteristics

Trumpet The fundamental frequency range of the trumpet is 165 to 988 Hz, with harmonics extending from 1 to 7.5 kHz. In addition to the sound control by lip pressure and tension at the

mouthpiece, a series of three valves is used to vary the tube length and, hence, the pitches. Most of the sound radiates from the bell, with higher frequencies located on an axis closer to the center of the bell.

Trombone The trombone is the orchestra's most powerful instrument. Its distinctive feature is a slide that is moved in and out to vary the length of the tube and change pitches. (Some trombone models use valves instead of a slide.) The fundamental frequency range is 73 to 587 Hz, with harmonics and a radiation pattern similar to that of the trumpet.

Tuba The tuba is the lowest-pitched of the brass instruments, with a fundamental frequency range of 49 to 587 Hz and harmonics extending from 1 to 4 kHz. It uses valves to vary its effective length and emits sounds upward from a wide, curved bell. Higher-frequency harmonics are present at the axis of the bell although, to a live audience, they are not a recognizable component of the tuba's sound because they are generated upward. Most of a tuba's distinctive bass sound is radiated omnidirectionally.

French Horn The French horn is a curved, cone-shaped tube with a wide bell and valves that is played with the bell pointed to the side, or behind, the musician, often with the musician's hand inside the bell for muting. The instrument's sound is therefore not closely related to what the live audience hears. Its fundamental range is relatively narrow—87 to 880 Hz, with harmonics extending from 1 to 6 kHz—but the French horn's sound can cut through the sound of louder instruments with wider frequency response.

Miking

Brass instruments require care in microphone placement and careful attention in adjusting levels at the console, because of their loudness and dynamic range. They also emit the most directional sound; high-frequency harmonics radiate directly

15-25 Miking off the bell. Mike trumpets, trombones, baritones, and tubas at an angle to the bell for a natural, mellower sound, being careful to avoid close mic-to-source distances so that airflow and spit sounds are not heard. Miking in front of the bell produces a brighter sound.

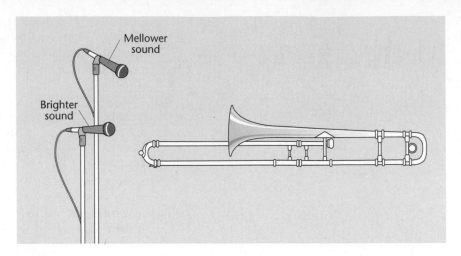

Mellower sound

Brighter sound

out of the bell. But the most distinctive frequencies of the trumpet and trombone are around 1,200 Hz and 700 Hz, respectively, which are radiated from the sides of the bell. Below 500 Hz, radiation tends to become omnidirectional. Therefore, close-miking brass instruments with a directional microphone does not quite produce their full frequency response. A directional mic close to and in front of the bell produces a bright, biting quality. Miking at an angle to the bell or on-axis to the side of the bell produces a more natural, mellower, more hornlike sound (see 15-25).

About 1 to 5 feet is a starting point to capture a good working mic-to-source distance. Closer placement gives a tighter sound, although miking too close to a brass instrument could pick up spit and valve sounds. More-distant placement makes the sound fuller and more emphatic.

For the French horn, a mic-to-source distance of at least 5 feet is recommended. It is not the most powerful brass instrument but, as noted previously, it can cut through and overwhelm louder instruments, and its levels fluctuate considerably. To increase control and minimize French horn leakage, move the instrument away from the ensemble (see 15-26).

In miking brass sections, trumpets and trombones should be blended as a chorus. One microphone for each pair of instruments produces a natural, balanced sound and provides flexibility in the mixdown. If you try to pick up more than two trumpets or trombones with a single mic, it has to be far enough from the instruments to blend them, and the acoustics have to support the technique. Of course, leakage will occur. Mike baritones and tubas individually from above (see 15-27).

The type of microphone you use also helps shape the sound of brass. The moving coil can smooth transient response; the ribbon can add a fuller, warmer tonality; and the capacitor can produce accurate transient response.

ELECTRIC INSTRUMENTS

Electric instruments—bass, guitar, and keyboards—generate their sounds through an electric pickup that can be sent to an amplifier or directly to the console. Three techniques are generally used to record an electric instrument: (1) plugging the instrument into an amplifier and placing a mic in front of the amp's loudspeaker, (2) *direct insertion (D.I.),* or plugging the instrument directly into the mic input of the console through a direct box, or (3) both miking the amp and using direct insertion.

Electric instruments are usually high impedance, whereas professional-quality audio equipment is

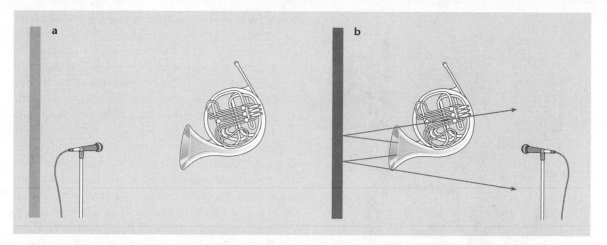

15-26 Miking the French horn. (a) To control leakage place the musician away from the ensemble and the microphone near a soft baffle pointing at the bell. (b) If this arrangement creates a blending problem due to the French horn's lack of presence, placing a hard baffle a few feet from the bell should carry the sound to the mic in sufficient proportions.

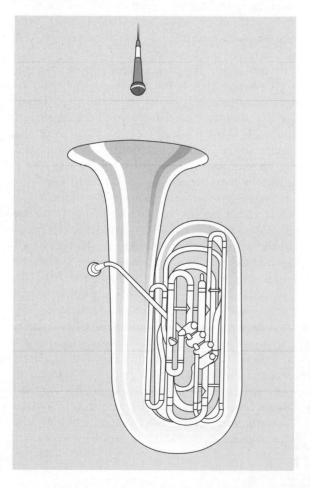

15-27 Miking the baritone and tuba from above the bell

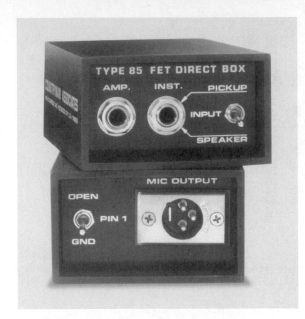

15-28 Direct box. A direct box has an isolated transformer that is less vulnerable to damage, distortion, grounding problems, volume loss, and changes in tone quality. This particular direct box can be battery- or phantom-powered. To further improve sound quality, many direct boxes are transformerless.

low impedance. Not surprisingly, high- and low-impedance equipment are incompatible and produce sonic horrors if connected. The direct box is a device that matches impedances, thus making the output of the instrument compatible with the console's input (see 15-28).

Although this chapter deals with the close-miking technique, it is important to know the differences between miking an amp and going direct. Deciding which method to use is a matter of taste, practicality, and convenience (see Tables 15-1 and 15-2).

When miking an amp loudspeaker, the moving-coil mic is most often used because it can handle loud levels without overloading. With the bass guitar, the directional moving coil is less susceptible to vibration and conductance, especially with a shock mount, caused when the instrument's long, powerful wavelengths are amplified. Due to its

powerful low end, the bass is usually recorded direct to obtain a cleaner sound. The fundamental frequency range of the electric bass is 41 to 300 Hz, with harmonics extending from 1 to 7 kHz.

Recording electric bass presents a particular challenge. If there is too much bass, the mix will sound muddy. This could mask the fundamentals of other instruments and result in a thickening and weighing down of the overall sound. Among the ways to improve clarity are to have the bassist increase treble and reduce bass on the guitar or to equalize in the control room by attenuating around 250 Hz and boosting around 1,500 Hz.

Compression is commonly used in recording the electric bass. It helps reduce noise, smooth variations in attack and loudness, and tighten the sound. Be careful in setting the compressor's release time. If it is too fast in relation to the decay rate of the bass, the sound will be organlike. A slower release time maintains the natural sound of the instrument; too slow a release time muddies the sound.

With an electric guitar, a directional moving coil adds body to the sound. But if it is necessary to reproduce a subtler, warmer, more detailed sound, try a capacitor or one of the more rugged ribbon mics. The fundamental frequency range of the electric guitar is 82 to 1,319 Hz. When amplified the harmonics extend from 1 to 3.5 kHz; going direct the harmonics range from 1 to 13 kHz.

As for placement, the main challenge is understanding the dispersion pattern of the amplifier's loudspeakers. Miking close to and head-on the amp produces a strong central lobe which has considerable high-frequency content within the bandwidth of the instrument itself (see 15-29a). Off-axis miking reduces high-frequency content, and backing the mic farther from the amp produces a more blended, balanced sound (see 15-29b). Also, the decrease in highs gives the impression of a heavier, bassier sound. Hanging a small microphone over the amp emphasizes a guitar's midrange and reduces leakage. If leakage is not a problem, and even if it is, close miking with an omni works well. An omnidirectional microphone has no proximity effect—its response is uniform; it will therefore pick

Table 15-1 Advantages and disadvantages of miking an amplifier loudspeaker

Advantages	Disadvantages
Adds interaction of room acoustics to sound	Could leak into other mics
Captures more midbass for added punch	Could be noisy due to electrical problems with amp
Creates potential for different sound textures	Level of amp can make it difficult for musicians to hear less powerful instruments
Gives musician greater control over an instrument's sound output	Distortion
Permits other instrumentalists more chance to hear what the electric instruments are playing so that the acoustic players can interact better with the electric instruments	

Table 15-2 Advantages and disadvantages of direct insertion

Advantages	Disadvantages
Has a cleaner sound	Has a drier sound—no room ambience
Captures more high and low frequencies	May use a transformer, which adds another electronic device to the sound chain
Allows more sound control at the console	Too present
Eliminates leakage	
Does not require an amp	

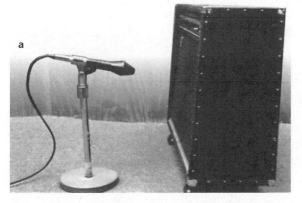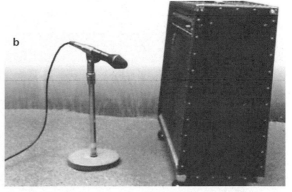

15-29 Miking an amplifier loudspeaker. (a) Aiming a directional microphone at the loudspeaker produces a brighter sound. (b) Aiming a directional microphone at an angle to the loudspeaker produces a fuller but less bright sound.

up various aspects of the loudspeaker dispersion pattern, and the inverse square law takes care of the leakage problem, because you are essentially force-feeding the mic from an amp that is producing a high sound-pressure level at a short mic-to-source distance. Use an omni capacitor or ribbon with fast response.

Producers also record both amp loudspeaker and direct insertion feeds simultaneously. This technique combines the drier, unreverberant but crisp sound of direct insertion with the acoustic coloring of the amplified sound. The amp and D.I. signals should be recorded on separate tracks. This provides more flexibility in the mixdown when the

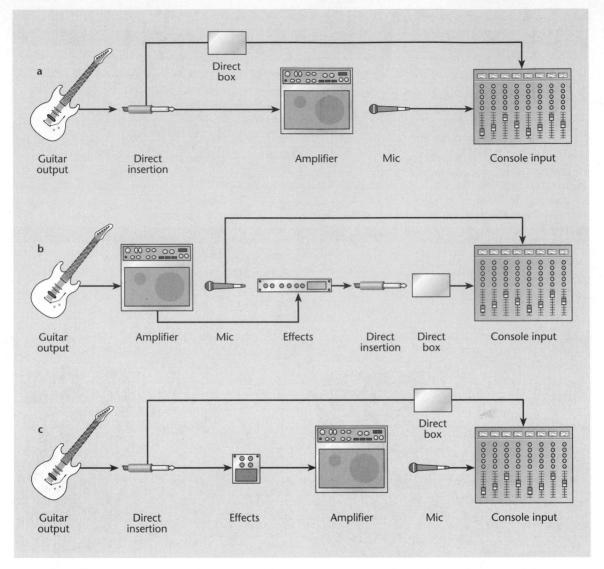

15-30 Techniques used to record direct and amplified signals simultaneously. (a) The signals are recorded on separate tracks. Special-effects boxes can be used for: (b) the usual technique or (c) an alternate technique.

two sounds are combined, or if you decide not to use one of the tracks.

It should be noted that direct recording of guitars does not necessarily guarantee a leakage-free track. If a guitar pickup is near or facing a loud instrument, it will "hear" the vibrations. By turning the musician away from the direct sound waves or by putting a baffle between the instruments, leakage is reduced.

With the electric guitar, special-effects boxes are often used to add to the sonic possibilities (see 15-30). Here too the various signals should be recorded on separate tracks, if possible, to allow flexibility in the mixdown.

Musicians' Amplifiers

An amp often produces annoying hum. Using a microphone with a *humbuck* coil can help reduce hum but not always enough. It also helps to turn up the loudness control on the guitar and turn down the volume on the amp and to use guitar cables with extra shielding. Moving the musician around the studio until a spot is located where the hum is reduced or disappears is another solution. If possible, convince the musician to use a smaller, lower-powered amp than is used in live concerts. There may be a problem here, however, because the change in amp produces a change in sound.

A device that avoids the variety of sound and electrical problems that often beset a miked amplifier is the *Mic Eliminator.*™ The Mic Eliminator delivers the combined mic/speaker sound of a miked amp direct from an electric instrument, preamp, or speaker output, without a microphone. It has two tone color settings—brite *(sic)* and dark— providing a choice between the bright, punchy sound of a mic directly in front of a speaker's center and the warm, rounder sound achieved by placing a mic off-center at the speaker's edge.

Leslie Loudspeaker Cabinet

The Leslie amplifier loudspeaker, most often used with an electric organ, is almost an instrument in itself (see 15-31). It is not a loudspeaker in the normal sense but is designed especially to modify sound. It contains a high-frequency loudspeaker (the tweeter) in the upper portion and a low-frequency loudspeaker (the woofer) in the lower portion. The two loudspeaker systems rotate, creating a vibrato effect. (*Vibrato* is short and repeating fluctuation in the pitch of a sound, not to be confused with *tremolo,* which is a rapid fluctuation in the amplitude of a sound.)

VOCALS

At its most basic level, the human voice acts like a wind instrument. The lungs expel air through the vocal cords, which vibrate and act like a double reed. The voice is then radiated through the larynx

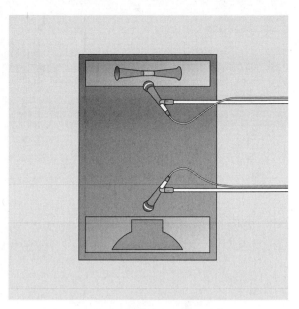

15-31 Miking a Leslie amplifier loudspeaker. One way is with two directional microphones, one to pick up the highs and the other to pick up the lows. The greater the mic-to-source distance, the less the chance of picking up the rotor sounds and increased tremolo and the better the sound blend. To record stereo, use either a top and bottom pair of mixed mics left and right, or just single mics panned toward the left and right. If the sound of the rotating horn is desired, place a boundary microphone inside the cabinet.

and mouth and out into the air. Sound is modified by movement of the tongue, jaw, and lips and the rate of exhalation. Pitch is determined primarily by the vocal cords and larynx, but mouth, lip, and tongue movements change timbre. The wide-ranging and complex harmonics and overtones of the human voice are a product of the mouth, nasal cavity, and chest cavity.

Although the speaking voice has a comparatively limited frequency range, the singing voice does not, and it can place a severe test on any microphone (see 15-32). The singing voice is capable of almost unlimited and subtle variations in pitch, timbre, and dynamic range. There are also plosives and sibilance—annoying popping and hissing sounds— to deal with.

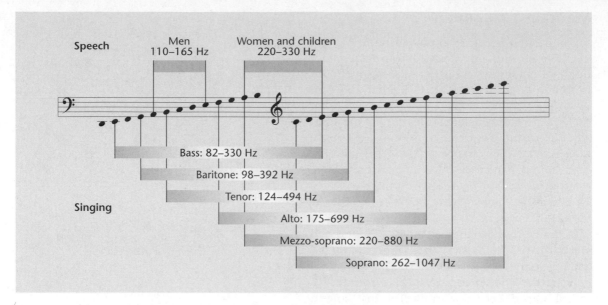

15-32 Fundamental frequency ranges for speech and singing in the human voice. Harmonics in the male singing voice extend from 1 to 12 kHz and in the female singing voice from 2 to 12 kHz.

Timbre

In choosing a vocal mic, the most important consideration is the singer's timbre—how edged, velvety, sharp, mellow, or resonant the voice sounds. The microphone should enhance a voice's attractive qualities and minimize the unattractive. Usually, assuming there are no serious problems with tone quality, most producers prefer to use capacitor microphones for vocals, because they can better handle the complicated pattern of harmonics and overtones in the human voice, and overall sound quality is the most natural.

Dynamic Range

Controlling the dynamic range—the quietest to loudest levels a sound source produces—is another tricky problem. Well-disciplined singers can usually control wide fluctuations in the dynamic range themselves. But many singers cannot—their voices barely move the needle on the VU meter during soft passages and pin it during loud ones. In miking these vocalists, a producer has three alternatives: (1) ride the level, (2) adjust the vocalist's micro-

phone position, or (3) use compression. There is a fourth alternative: record the vocal on two tracks.

Riding the level works but it requires an engineer's full attention, and this may be difficult considering everything else that goes on in a recording session. Also, less-gifted singers may handle dynamic range differently each time they sing, which means that riding the level is a matter more of coping than of aiding.

The preferred methods are to use microphone technique to adjust for irregularities in a vocalist's dynamic range or to use compression, or both. In pop music vocals are often compressed 10 to 13 dB. But to do so requires that a recordist know how to compensate after compression.

One placement technique is to situate the singer at an average distance from the mic relative to the loudest and softest passages sung; the distance depends on the song and the power of the singer's voice. From this average distance, you can direct the singer how closely to move to the mic during quiet passages and how far for the loud ones. The success of this technique depends on the vocalist's microphone technique—the ability to manage the song and the movements at the same time.

If these techniques do not work, try recording the vocal on two tracks with one track 10 dB down. If there is overload or a problem with the noise floor, the undistorted or less noisy sections of each recording can be intercut.

Breathing, Popping, and Sibilance

The closer to a microphone a performer stands, the greater the chance of picking up unwanted breathing sounds, popping sounds—plosives—from *p*'s, *b*'s, *k*'s, and *t*'s, and sibilance from *s*'s. If the singer's vocal projection or the type of music permits, increasing the mic-to-source distance significantly reduces these noises. Windscreens also help, but they tend to reduce the higher frequencies, although clearly some high-frequency loss is preferable to sibilance, plosives, or breathiness. Other ways to reduce popping and sibilance are to have the singer work slightly across mic but within the pickup pattern or to position the mic somewhat above the singer's mouth (see 15-33). If this increases nasality, position the mic at an angle from slightly below the singer's mouth. If leakage is no problem, using an omnidirectional mic permits a closer working distance because it is less susceptible to breathing, popping, and sibilant

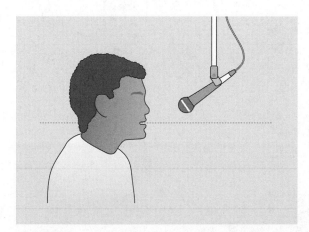

15-33 Eliminating unwanted vocal sounds. Positioning the microphone slightly above the performer's mouth is a typical miking technique used to cut down on unwanted popping, sibilance, and breathing sounds.

sounds. The sound may be less intimate, however, because an omni mic picks up more indirect sound waves than does a directional mic; but the closeness of the singer should overcome the larger amount of indirect sound picked up.

Although capacitors are almost always the microphone of choice for vocals, they do tend to emphasize sibilance because of the mid- to treble-range response of many models. In such cases, and when other techniques fail to eliminate sibilance, a first-rate dynamic mic usually takes care of the problem. Another reason to consider a dynamic mic for vocals is the harshness of some capacitors when used in digital recording (see "Miking Music for Digital Recording" later in this chapter).

Mic-to-Source Distance Versus Style

Generally, the style of the music sets the guidelines for mic-to-source distance. In popular music vocalists usually work close to the mic, from a few inches to a few feet, to create a tight, intimate sound. Classical and jazz vocalists work from a few feet to several feet from the mic to add room ambience, thereby opening the sound and making it airy.

When close miking be careful of proximity effect. Rolling off the unwanted bass frequencies may be one solution, but it almost certainly will change the delicate balance of vocal harmonics unless it is carefully and knowledgeably effected. It should be emphasized that, unless a mic is specifically designed for it, positioning the mic just about touching the lips, as some vocalists are seen doing on television and which unfortunately is imitated in the recording studio, rarely produces ideal sound. Indeed, if the microphone is not up to it, such mic technique rarely produces usable sound. If the distortion does not get you, the oppressive "lack of air" will.

Backup Harmony Vocals

Once the lead vocal is recorded, the accompanying backup harmony vocals are overdubbed. Often this involves a few vocalists singing at the same time. If they each have their own microphone, mic-to-source distances are easier to balance, but this also means more mics to control and could require using extra tape tracks. Another technique groups the vocalists around a bidirectional or omnidirectional microphone. This reduces the number of microphones and tape tracks involved, but requires greater care in balancing and blending harmonies. Backup vocalists must be positioned to prevent any one voice or harmony from being too strong or too weak.

MIKING STUDIO ENSEMBLES

This discussion of close miking has centered mainly on the individual instrument. There are studio situations, however, in which ensembles record as a group but are divided into smaller sections to control leakage. This requires isolating them as much as possible to avoid sonic confusion, yet blending them so that they sound cohesive. Figures 15-34, 15-35, and 15-36 display a few ways to mike studio ensembles.

15-34 Miking a jazz band when all voicings are recorded at the same time. Notice that trumpets and trombones are miked with bidirectional microphones and that the piano, acoustic bass, and drums are miked with boundary mics. Bidirectional mics are particularly useful in reducing leakage. For example, by facing the mic straight down in front of each saxophone, each mic's nulls are directed toward sound coming from the sides and rear. This is especially effective when woodwinds, or other weak instruments, are in front of brass or other strong instruments. A high ceiling is necessary for this technique to work, however.

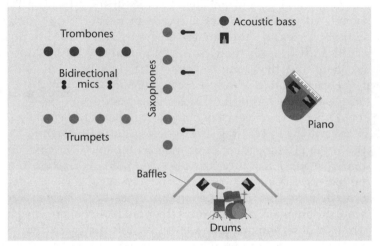

15-35 One way to position and mike a mixed ensemble when all voicings are recorded at once

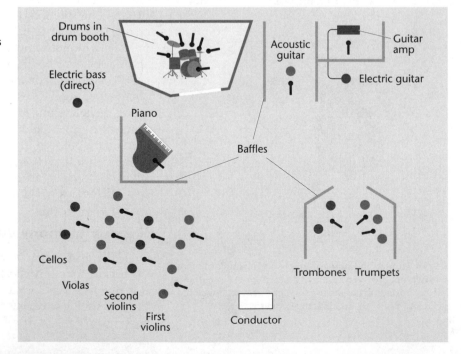

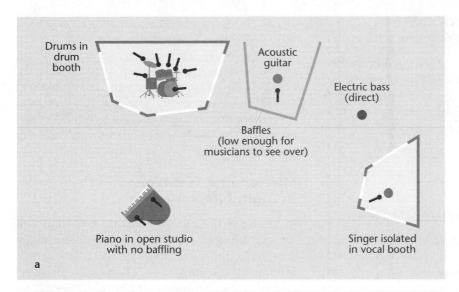

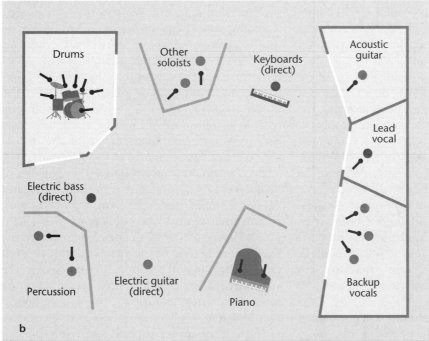

15-36 Two ways to arrange musical groups for studio recording. (a) Musicians are isolated from one another to prevent sound from one instrument from leaking into the microphone of another instrument, yet are still able to maintain visual contact. It is possible in this arrangement that the acoustic guitar sound will leak into the piano mics and vice versa. Leakage can usually be reduced, however, by supercardioid mics' on both instruments rejecting sound from the sides and rear, the piano lid's blocking of sound coming from the front guitar baffle, and the guitarist's body blocking the piano sound coming from the back of the studio. (b) Another example of arranging a musical group in a studio to control leakage.

MIKING MUSIC FOR DIGITAL RECORDING

As clear and noise-free as digital sound can be, there are valid complaints about digital recordings: that the high end is strident, thin, and shrieky, or that there is too much unwanted noise from amplifiers, pedals, keys, bows, tongue, teeth, lips, and so on. Many of these problems can be traced to two causes: the microphones and the miking techniques that were used.

Microphones in Digital Recording

Many microphones used in analog recording are selected for their rising high-end response; these mics help deal with problems associated with analog reproduction, the most serious being the potential loss of high-frequency information during disc mastering and copying. There is little such loss in digital recording, copying, or mastering. (Uneven quality in the manufacture of CDs is, alas, another story altogether.) Therefore, using such mics for digital recording only makes the high frequencies more biting and shrill. To avoid this problem, use microphones with smooth high-end response. Recordists have returned to tube-type equipment in the signal chain—microphones, amplifiers, equalizers—to help warm the sound, offsetting the edge in digital reproduction.

Capacitor microphones have preamplifiers, which generate noise. In analog recording, this noise is usually masked. In digital recording, if preamp noise is loud enough, it will be audible. High-quality, large-diaphragm capacitors are therefore preferred, because their self-generated preamp noise is very low level.

Modern ribbon microphones are popular in digital recording. Their response is inherently nontailored, smooth, warm, and detailed, without being strident. Microphones used in digital recording should be linear—that is, output should vary in direct proportion to input. The mic should not introduce unwanted sonic information because, in digital sound, chances are it will be audible. Of course, this is the case in analog recording as well; it is just more critical in digital recording.

Furthermore, mics used in digital recording should be of the highest quality, carefully handled, and kept in clean, temperature- and humidity-controlled environments. The dust, moisture, and rough handling that may not perceptibly affect mic response in an analog recording may very well sully a digital recording.

Microphone Technique in Digital Recording

In analog recording, close miking was employed virtually pro forma, because vinyl records usually smoothed the rough spots resulting from close miking by burying some of the harshness in background surface noise. In digital recording, no such masking occurs. For example, in analog recording, when close-miking an acoustic guitar, no one is concerned about noise that might be generated by the guitarist's shirt rubbing against the instrument; in digital recording, on the other hand, the rubbing sound may be audible if the guitar is close-miked. In addition, in analog recording, noise from a musician's amplifier may get lost in tape hiss; that will not be the case in digital recording, regardless of the mic used.

Even if mic-to-source distance is acceptable in digital recording, microphone placement may not be. For example, the upper harmonics of a violin radiate straight up in two directions. If a microphone is placed directly in one of these paths, the digital sound could be too crisp and shrieky, even though the mic is at an optimal distance from the violin. By placing the mic more in the path of the lower-frequency radiations, the digital sound should flatten.

High frequencies of brass instruments are radiated straight ahead in a relatively narrow beam. Placing a microphone directly in front of the bell may produce a harsh digital recording. Placing the mic at more of an angle to the bell, to pick up a better blend of the lower frequencies, should smooth the sound.

OFF-MIKING WITH STEREO MICROPHONE ARRAYS

The purpose of off-miking, when mixed with sound from the close mics, is to add airier, more ambient sound to the overall recording. The microphone arrays used in off-miking are often stereo arrays similar to those employed in distant miking. They are: coincident, near-coincident, and spaced.

Coincident Miking

Coincident miking, also called *X-Y miking,* employs two matched, directional microphones mounted on a vertical axis—with one mic diaphragm directly over the other—and angled apart to aim approximately toward the left and right sides of the sound source. The degree of angle, the mics' pickup pattern, and the distance from the sound source depend on the width of the stereo image you want to record (see 15-37).

A stereo pair must be matched to ensure a uniform sound, and the mics should be capacitors. Miking at a distance from the sound source, particularly with classical music, requires high-output, high-sensitivity microphones, and capacitors are the only type of microphone that meets this requirement. Moreover, the microphone preamps should be high gain, low noise.

The stereo microphone provides the same coincident pickup as the stereo pair but with two directional microphone capsules housed in a single casing. The upper element can rotate up to 180 degrees relative to the lower element. Some stereo mics enable control of each capsule's polar pattern (see 4-14).

Coincident microphone arrays produce level (intensity) differences between channels and minimize differences in arrival time. This has the advantage of being mono-compatible because the two microphones occupy almost the same space, meaning that their signals are in phase at all frequencies.

Near-Coincident Miking

Near-coincident miking angles two directional microphones, spaced horizontally, a few inches apart (see 15-38). The few inches' difference between the near-coincident and coincident arrays adds a sense of warmth, depth, and "air" to sound compared with the coincident array. The mics are close enough to retain intensity differences between channels at low frequencies, yet far enough apart to have sufficient time delay between channels for localization at high frequencies. The stereo spread can be increased or decreased with the angle or space between the mics. The time delay between

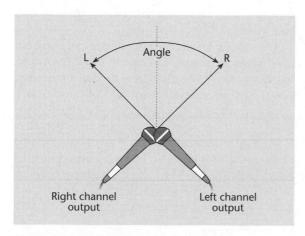

15-37 Coincident miking technique

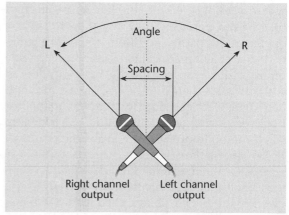

15-38 Near-coincident miking technique

channels creates a problem, however: The greater the delay, the less the chance of stereo-to-mono compatibility.

Spaced Miking

Spaced miking employs two matched microphones several feet apart, perpendicular to the sound source, and symmetrical to each other along a centerline. They reproduce a more spacious, lusher, bigger sound than any of the near-coincident arrays—but at a cost. Stereo imaging is more diffused and, therefore, less detailed. Also, because so much of the sound reaching the mics derives its directional information from time differences (in addition to intensity differences), stereo-to-mono compatibility is unreliable.

If studio acoustics and the music permit, spaced omnidirectional microphones are preferred to directional mics because they have less off-axis coloration and flatter overall response, especially in the low frequencies. Capacitors are almost always used. Spacing is determined by the desired width of the stereo image. With omnis, of course, spacing has to be wide enough to reproduce a stereo image. If it is too wide, however, separation may be exaggerated; if spacing is too narrow, the stereo image may lack breadth.

Spaced cardioid mics are arrayed similarly to spaced omnis, but their directionality produces a different sonic outcome. Used with an ensemble, spaced cardioids tend to emphasize the voicings that are most on-axis. They also show the effects of coloration, particularly from any studio ambience. Placement is critical to producing acceptable results with any spaced miking, but even more so with cardioids than with omnis. Spaced cardioids do provide a better chance for mono compatibility, however, because each microphone is picking up less common information, reducing the chance of phase cancellations.

Spaced nondirectional boundary microphones used for off-miking, particularly in relatively dry studios, are another possibility. Their pickup is similar to that of omnidirectionals, although around the boundary surface the polar pattern is hemispheric.

Stereo-Miking an Ensemble

When a stereo microphone array—coincident, near-coincident, or spaced—is used for the primary pickup, the configuration affects the image location of the sound source. Figure 15-39 displays examples of those effects.

RECORDING FOR SURROUND SOUND*

There are a few ways to handle a music recording for surround sound. One is to use the miking techniques already discussed in this chapter and apply the surround-sound imaging during the mix, through panning. Another is to mike for surround sound in the recording session. Using a combination of the first two approaches may be considered a third technique. (Mixing music for surround sound is covered in Chapter 19.)

In miking for surround during recording, there are two basic means of handling selection and placement. One is to use direct and ambient miking, the other is to take the direct approach.

With *direct/ambient surround-sound miking*, either one of two stereo arrays—near-coincident or spaced—will do as a basis for the left-right frontal pickups, then add a center mic for the center channel. Because of the center mic, the angle or space between the stereo mics should be wider than usual. The surround microphones are used mainly for ambience and are pointed away from the sound source to the rear or rear-side of the studio or hall (see 15-40).

The microphones' spacing and pickup pattern depend on the size of the ensemble and the music. For example, large ensembles, such as orchestras, bands, and choruses, usually call for more widely spaced arrays than do small jazz and country music groups. Also, because of the rooms in which they are usually recorded, the larger ensembles ordinarily take omnidirectional mics, whereas directional mics may work better with smaller groups. These generalities assume good acoustics, however. For example, omni surround mics may not work in very

---

*This discussion assumes the 5.1 surround-sound format.

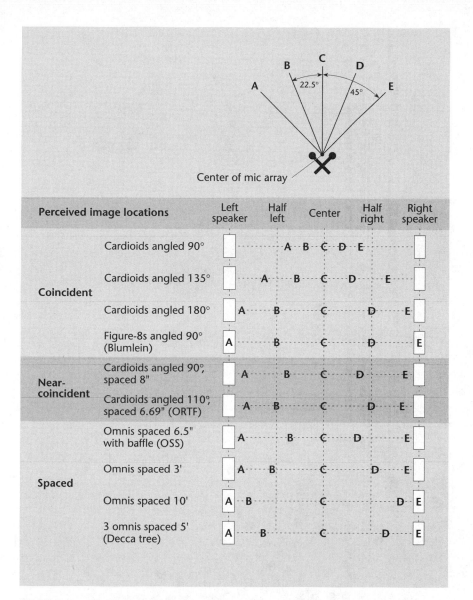

Perceived image locations		Left speaker	Half left	Center	Half right	Right speaker
Coincident	Cardioids angled 90°			A B C D E		
	Cardioids angled 135°		A	B C D	E	
	Cardioids angled 180°		A	B C D	E	
	Figure-8s angled 90° (Blumlein)	A		B C D		E
Near-coincident	Cardioids angled 90°, spaced 8"		A	B C D	E	
	Cardioids angled 110°, spaced 6.69" (ORTF)		A	B C D	E	
Spaced	Omnis spaced 6.5" with baffle (OSS)		A	B C D	E	
	Omnis spaced 3'		A B	C	D E	
	Omnis spaced 10'	A	B	C	D	E
	3 omnis spaced 5' (Decca tree)	A	B	C	D	E

15-39 Stereo localization. The upper portion shows the locations of sound sources A through E. The bottom portion indicates the positions in which listeners perceive them to be. The *Blumlein technique* uses two coincident bidirectional microphones positioned at a 90-degree angle. *OSS = optimal stereo signal,* also known as the *Jecklin disk.* This technique separates two omnidirectional mics with a sound-absorbing disk (or baffle). The *Decca Tree* technique mounts three spaced omni mics at the ends of a T-shaped frame.

From Bruce and Jenny Bartlett, *On-Location Recording Techniques* (Boston: Focal Press, 1999).

15-40 Examples of surround-sound miking.
(a) Surround-sound miking for a small ensemble. This microphone array consists of directional mics.
(b) Surround-sound miking for an orchestra. In this example the surround mics are middle-side (M-S) microphones.

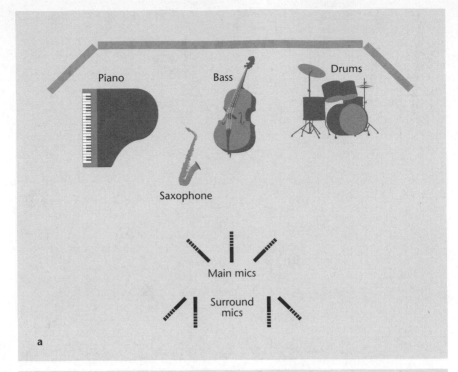

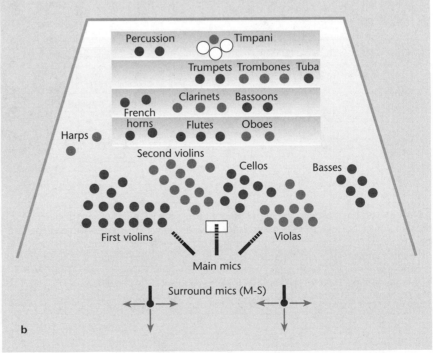

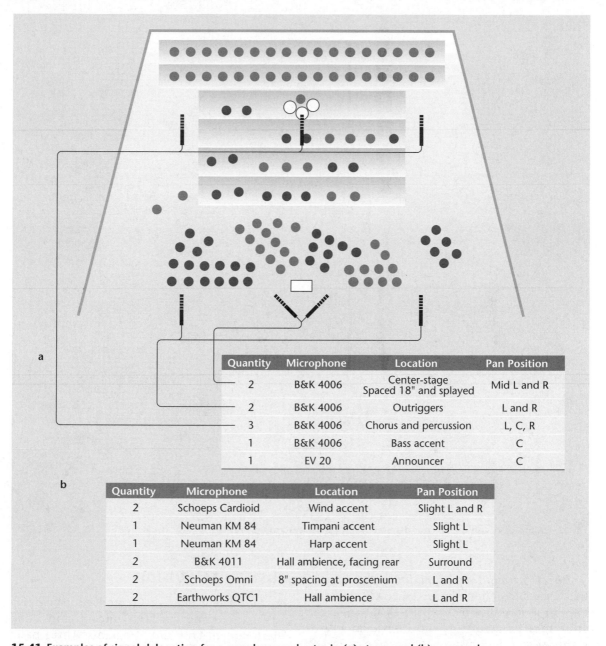

Quantity	Microphone	Location	Pan Position
2	B&K 4006	Center-stage Spaced 18" and splayed	Mid L and R
2	B&K 4006	Outriggers	L and R
3	B&K 4006	Chorus and percussion	L, C, R
1	B&K 4006	Bass accent	C
1	EV 20	Announcer	C

Quantity	Microphone	Location	Pan Position
2	Schoeps Cardioid	Wind accent	Slight L and R
1	Neuman KM 84	Timpani accent	Slight L
1	Neuman KM 84	Harp accent	Slight L
2	B&K 4011	Hall ambience, facing rear	Surround
2	Schoeps Omni	8" spacing at proscenium	L and R
2	Earthworks QTC1	Hall ambience	L and R

15-41 Examples of signal delegation for a symphony orchestra in (a) stereo and (b) surround

live venues, or directional surround mics may pick up too concentrated a sound in drier rooms.

Direct/ambient surround-sound recording may use more than the three front and two surround mics. If fact, several different configurations may be needed. You do what it takes to get the sound you want. But with whatever number of microphones are employed, pay careful attention to how their signals are delegated, otherwise the sonic results could be a mishmash (see 15-41).

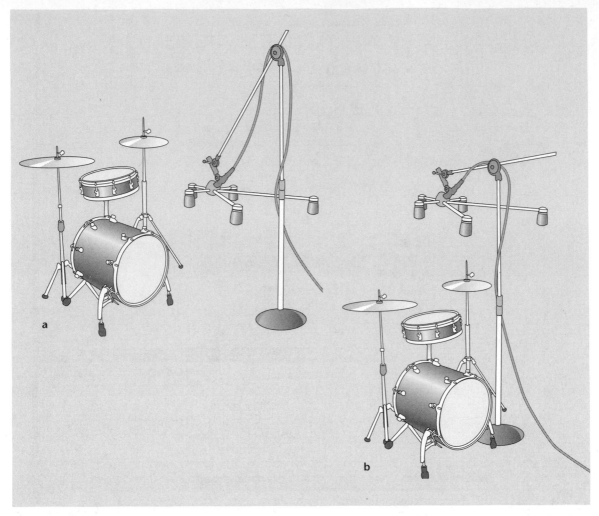

15-42 Examples of using a surround-sound microphone system on drums

Direct surround-sound miking is an approach that uses microphone arrays especially designed for surround-sound pickup (see Chapter 4). The array may be used to record individual instruments or groups of instruments, or to pick up the sound of an entire ensemble (see 15-42). Direct miking tends to center the listener more "inside" the music by placing the voicings side-to-side across the front and from the front speakers to the surrounds. Or the spatial imaging may be in a horseshoe shape, with the listener centered at or somewhat inside its base.

MUSIC IN TELEVISION

Several different types of TV productions use live music, including variety, concert, and some entertainment-type talk programs. Three basic considerations are involved in miking all of them: (1) whether the musicians are seen on-camera, (2) the acoustics, and (3) the type of music.

Musicians On- or Off-Camera

Getting the best possible sound is the primary goal of every recordist. But if the musicians are seen on-camera, it can be disturbing to an audience to have them blocked by, and the picture cluttered with, microphones. Mics have become an accepted part of the TV picture, but unless they are selected and positioned with care, they can ruin a shot. Fortunately, a variety of mics that produce excellent sound are also good-looking. Even windscreens and cables come in various colors.

If musicians are off-camera, mike them in whatever way is best, with little concern for appearance. Keep in mind that the musicians have to be able to see the conductor, if there is one.

Whether musicians are on- or off-camera, you will most likely use directional mics to cut down not only on leakage but also on feedback. Many large studios and theaters have loudspeakers so that the audience can better hear the performance. Singers need loudspeakers on-stage to hear the music blend, especially when they are not near the accompanying ensemble. With loudspeakers and microphones in the same vicinity, not only are directional mics almost a necessity to avoid feedback, but so are directional loudspeakers.

This problem is alleviated when performers use noise-canceling mics (see Chapter 4) and in-the-ear monitoring. *In-the-ear monitoring* employs small headphones instead of stage monitors to feed the music blend to the performer. A noise-canceling mic may be attached to the headset.

Acoustics

Because the types of studios used for large-scale TV productions, particularly with an audience present, are acoustically adequate for speech but sometimes not so for music, most recordists use the close-miking instead of the distant-miking approach. Sound control is much better. Even if the acoustics are excellent, much of today's popular music requires close miking.

Type of Music

The type of music can influence TV miking. Classical music audiences may not care to see a symphony orchestra, or string quartet for that matter, draped with microphones, but they tolerate it. They are accustomed to hearing music in excellent acoustic settings where mics are not necessary to carry the sound. Their objection is not so much that mics are in the picture but rather that mics are being used at all.

This is one reason why concert broadcasts typically originate from concert halls and not from studios. In controlled acoustic environments, the recordist can hang a few mics to achieve a natural sound blend and also keep the mics out of the picture. Even so, some of the newer concert halls have been designed with electronic enhancement built-in. Loudspeakers are strategically placed either to make up for certain response deficiencies at various locations in the hall or to make frequency and loudness response uniform throughout.

Popular music usually requires a mic for each sound source (or direct insertion) plus electronic enhancement. It would be impractical to use only a few mics to pick up, say, a rock band, because it would change the entire character of the sound, to say nothing of the difficulty in matching the loudness of acoustic and electric instruments.

Miking Music in Television

For some of the common techniques used in miking music for television, see Figures 15-43 to15-46. It is important to note that an ensemble must first be arranged to be pleasing to the eye and then miked within the constraints established by visual requirements.

MUSIC IN FILM

The microphone techniques used in recording music for film are similar to those used in conventional music recording. Ensembles are miked using the distant- or close-miking approach, stereo or surround techniques, or a combination of all of these. It all depends on the film's release formats. A major consideration in miking music for underscoring is that it be blended; no single voicing or group of voicings should be apparent, unless it is intended, nor should the music and the elements therein draw attention away from the picture.

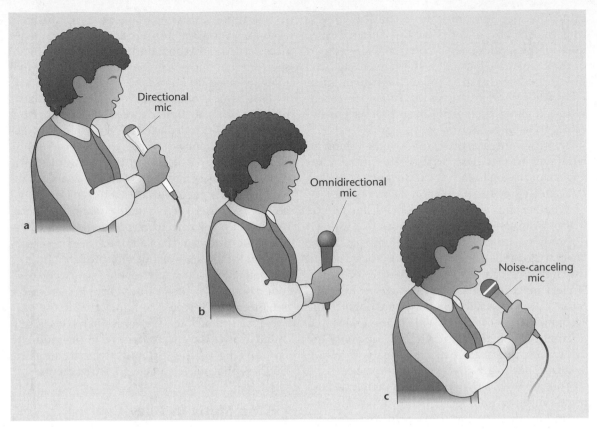

15-43 Miking vocals for TV. (a) A singer using a handheld directional microphone should hold it at about a 45-degree angle to the mouth to stay within the pickup pattern but not block the face. (b) Handheld omnidirectional mics can be held at chest level. A handheld microphone should contain a pop filter and be shock resistant, easy to hold, and good-looking. (c) If the vocalist uses a noise-canceling microphone, the mic must be close to, and pointed directly at, the mouth.

15-44 Miking an instrumentalist. The customary approach in miking an instrumentalist who also sings is to use two directional mics: one to pick up the voice and the other to pick up the instrument. This technique can be obtrusive, however, when conventional mics on mic stands are employed. A better-looking approach, and one that also provides reasonably good sound, is to use a clip mount or an electric pickup on the instrument.

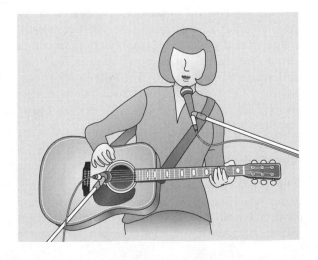

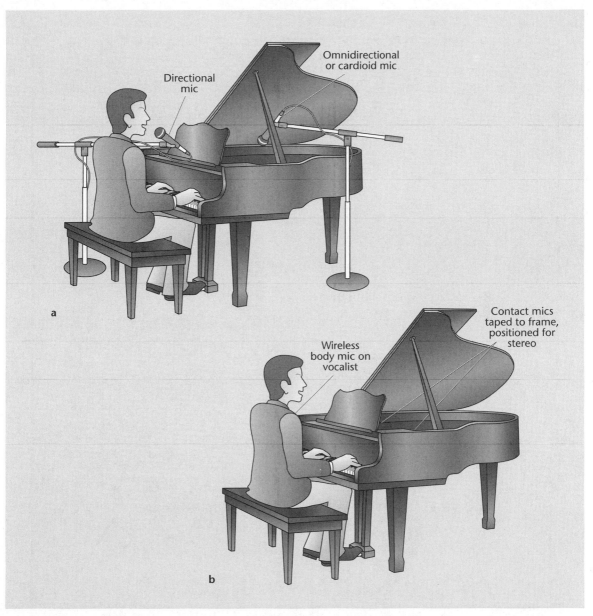

15-45 Miking a singer-pianist. (a) The conventional way to handle this situation has been to mount microphones on stands and mike the vocalist with a directional mic and the piano with either an omnidirectional or a cardioid mic, depending on its proximity to the sound board. This approach not only places the mics squarely in the picture, but also runs the risk of having them jarred. Therefore, less obtrusive and safer microphone techniques have become more popular. (b) The vocalist may use a small headset microphone system or a wireless body mic. For a stereo piano, boundary or contact mics can be taped to the inside of the frame, one near the high strings, the other near the low strings (making sure that the midrange is also in the pickup). For mono a boundary or contact mic can be taped to the piano lid over the intersection of the high and low strings, facedown. Still another technique is to place the piano mic in a clip mount and attach it to the piano frame a few feet above the sound board and equidistant between the high and low strings.

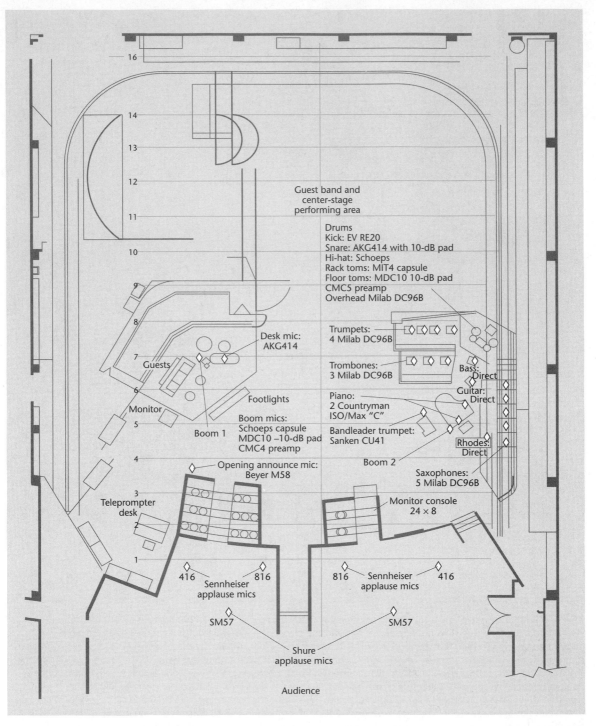

15-46 Example of a stage and microphone setup for a television variety/talk show

▶ Distant miking uses a stereo array for principal pickup and additional microphones, as needed, to record an entire ensemble.

▶ Close miking places a microphone relatively close to each sound source or group of sound sources in an ensemble.

▶ Because close miking involves miking most of the instruments in an ensemble, it means that (1) the three-to-one rule, or an appropriate variation of it, should be observed to avoid phasing problems; (2) mic-to-source distances are usually close, thus reducing the interaction of music with acoustics and requiring the addition of artificial reverberation; and (3) each sound source usually requires a separate recorder channel to better control the various microphone inputs.

▶ The closer a microphone is to a sound source, the more detailed, drier, and, if proximity effect is a factor, bassier the sound is. The farther a microphone is from a sound source, the more diffused, open, and reverberant the sound is.

▶ The underlying concept of distant miking is often used in-studio along with the close-miking technique to enhance a recording with a more acoustically natural, open sound. This technique is referred to as off-miking.

▶ No single close-miking technique is necessarily better than another. Microphone selection and positioning depend on many factors: the music, the musician, the quality of the instrument, the acoustics, the blend, and so on.

▶ The higher the frequency, the more directional the sound wave; the lower the frequency, the more omnidirectional the sound wave.

▶ In recording drums, tuning the drum set is critical if they are to sound good.

▶ Although the drum set consists of several different-sounding instruments, it must be miked so that they sound good individually and blend as a unit.

▶ Because most of an acoustic guitar's sound radiates from the front of the instrument, centering a microphone off the middle of the sound hole should, theoretically, provide a balanced sound. But if a mic is too close to the hole, sound is bassy or boomy. If it is moved closer to the bridge, detail is lost. If it is moved closer to the neck, presence is reduced. If it is moved farther away, intimacy is affected.

▶ Because the dynamic range of bowed string instruments is not wide, sound has to be reinforced by using several instruments or multiple miking, or both, depending on the size of the sound required.

▶ The piano offers almost unlimited possibilities for sound shaping. Perhaps more than with many other instruments, the character of the piano sound is dependent on the quality of the piano itself.

▶ Because most woodwinds are not powerful instruments, the tendency is to close-mike them. Due to their sound radiation, however, this results in an uneven pickup. They should be miked far enough away so that the pickup sounds blended and natural.

▶ Because of their loudness and dynamic range, brass instruments require care in microphone placement and careful attention in adjusting levels at the console.

▶ Some electric instruments, such as the bass and guitar, can be recorded either by miking their amplifier loudspeaker or by direct insertion—plugging the instrument into the console—or a combination of both.

▶ Recording a vocalist is a severe test for any microphone, because the mic must be able to handle the nuances of the vocalist's timbre and dynamics as well as any breathy, popping, and sibilant sounds. Mic selection and placement depend on voice quality, style of music, and microphone presence.

▶ The microphone arrays used in off-miking are often stereo arrays similar to those employed in distant miking. They are: coincident, near-coincident, and spaced.

▶ Coincident miking, also called X-Y miking, employs two matched directional microphones mounted on a vertical axis—with one mic diaphragm directly over the other—and angled apart to aim approximately toward the left and right sides of the sound source.

- Near-coincident miking angles two directional microphones, spaced horizontally, a few inches apart.

- Spaced miking employs two matched microphones—uni- or omnidirectional—several feet apart, perpendicular to the sound source, and symmetrical to each other along a centerline.

- There are basically two ways to handle a music recording for surround sound: (1) to use conventional miking techniques during recording and apply the surround-sound imaging during the mix; and (2) to mike for surround sound during recording and feed the signals directly to the surround-sound channels.

- In miking surround sound during recording, two basic ways to handle mic selection and placement are using the direct/ambient and direct surround-sound approaches.

- Because digital recording often reproduces sounds not audible in analog, the microphones used for digital recording must be of very high quality, generate very low self-noise, be carefully handled, and be kept in clean, temperature- and humidity-controlled environments.

- A major consideration in miking music for underscoring is that it be blended; no single voicing or group of voicings should be apparent, unless it is intended, nor should the music and the elements therein draw attention away from the picture.

16

Internet Production

Computer technology in general and the Internet in particular have provided the means to produce and disseminate audio on an unprecedented scale. What was once a relatively closed medium practiced by professionals in studio-based environments is now accessible to practically anyone and with the potential to reach a worldwide market at the touch of a button. Opportunities abound. They include producing audio for an online company, recording online sessions interactively, promoting and selling your own work, hiring out your production services to others, Webcasting, producing sound for Web pages, and creating audio just for the fun of it. In producing sound for professional purposes, however, it serves to rephrase avant-garde writer Gertrude Stein's famous line "A rose is a rose is a rose is a rose." Audio production is audio production is audio production.

As the methods of producing sound change, that is sometimes forgotten. How audio is produced is only the means to the end. The basic principles related to that end are similar regardless of where production is carried out—in a major production facility with all types of sophisticated gear or in a project studio with only a computer. The end is always to produce a high-quality product, technically and aesthetically. The point can be made in another way: Whether writing with a pen,

Table 16-1 Changes in audio quality in relation to connection speed

Connection Speed (Kbps)	Mode	Audio Quality	Bandwidth (kHz)	Application
128–150	Stereo	CD quality	20	Intranets
96	Stereo	Near CD quality	15	ISDN, LAN
56–64	Stereo	Near FM quality	12	ISDN, LAN
24–32	Stereo	Boombox FM quality	7.5	28.8 modem
16	Mono	AM quality	4.5	28.8 modem
12	Mono	SW quality	4	14.4 modem
8	Mono	Telephone sound	2.5	Telephone

ISDN = Integrated Services Digital Network; LAN = local-area network.

a typewriter, or a computer, it is not the medium that creates the poetry, it is the poet.

Because the world of computers and the Internet changes almost hourly, the approach to this chapter is generic, dealing with the processing of audio in a general way and avoiding, as much as possible, proprietary references and detailed operational information. This material also assumes some experience with computers and the Internet.

AUDIO FIDELITY

Achieving digital-quality sound transmission over the Internet is chancy. The ability to process high-end audio in computer systems varies widely, as does the quality of the loudspeakers. Some systems have fast modems and broad bandwidth capabilities, whereas others do not. Some systems use high-quality loudspeakers; others use only the low-quality in-board computer speaker. Then there is the problem of trying to squeeze a large amount of sound through a small pipeline. For example, a four-minute song on a CD in 16 bit and 44.1 kHz would take 42 MB. Encoded to a 128-Kbps MMP-3 file, the song is reduced to just 3.84 MB. Even under favorable conditions, reproducing the CD's original sound quality after downloading is uncertain. The main factors that influence audio fidelity on the Internet are connection speed, reducing file size by manipulation, and data compression.

Connection Speed

The greater the connection speed, the higher the audio quality. Connection speed is measured in kilobits per second (Kbps). For example, a connection speed of 150 Kbps produces a bandwidth of 20,000 Hz and stereo CD–quality sound. A connection speed of 8 Kbps produces a bandwidth of 2,500 Hz and mono telephone–quality sound (see Table 16-1).

File Manipulation

Another way to improve Internet sound is by reducing the size of audio files, because size reduction facilitates transmission or transfer of a file from one computer to another. This can be done through manipulation and compression. (Compression is covered in the next section.) There are different ways to handle this by manipulation, such as reducing the sampling rate, reducing the word length, reducing the number of channels, reducing playing time by editing, and, with music, using instrumental, rather than vocal-based tracks (see Table 16-2).

Reducing the Sampling Rate

Some sounds, such as a solo instrument, a sound effect, and straight narration, to name just a few, do not require a high sampling rate, say, of 44.1 kHz. For these sounds 32 kHz may suffice.

Table 16-2 Approximate file sizes for one minute of audio recorded at differing sampling rates and resolutions (1,000 KB = 1 MB)

Word Length/Sampling Rate	44.1 kHz	22.05 kHz	11.025 kHz
16-bit stereo	10 MB	5 MB	2.5 MB
16-bit mono/8-bit stereo	5 MB	2.5 MB	1.26 MB
8-bit mono	2.5 MB	1.26 MB	630 KB

Reducing the Word Length

Audio with a narrow dynamic range, such as speech, simple sound effects, and certain instruments (see Figure 15-15) does not require longer word lengths. An 8-bit word length should support such sound with little difficulty. Of course, wider dynamics require longer word lengths—16-bit and higher. But a given audio recording does not comfortably fit into either a narrow or a wide dynamic range. It almost always includes both. One technique used to counter the adverse effects caused by having too short a word length to handle a changing dynamic range is to use a *sliding window*—selecting an 8-bit format that moves up and down on the 16-bit scale, depending on whether the sound level is high or low.

Reducing the Number of Channels

Stereo audio uses twice as much data as mono. If an audio file can be handled in mono, it makes sense to do so. Sound effects are usually produced in mono; effects in stereo do not provide as much flexibility to the editor, mixer, and rerecordist in postproduction, because the spatial imaging has already been committed. Speech and vocals can be monaurally imaged because they are usually centered in a mix. Music is the one sonic element that requires fuller spatial imaging and, hence, stereo.

Reducing Playing Time by Editing

Obviously, reducing playing time reduces file size. Of course, this is not always feasible or desirable, but when the opportunity does present itself,

editing the file will help. In this case, editing refers to eliminating extraneous bits of data, rather than to conventional editing discussed in Chapter 18. Three ways to handle such editing is through compression, noise reduction, and equalization.

Compression (in relation to dynamic range) reduces the distances between the peaks and troughs of a signal. This raises the level of the overall signal, thereby overriding background noise.

Noise reduction is best handled by listening to the silent parts of a file to check for unwanted noise. If it is present, that section of the file can be cleaned, taking care not to get rid of desirable sound.

Equalization comes in handy to add the high frequencies that are usually lost in codec compression (data reduction).

Using Instrumental Music Instead of Vocal-Based Tracks

Reducing the data of instrumental music is easier than that of vocal-based music backed by an accompanying ensemble. Therefore it is another way to eliminate unwanted bits, so long as production requirements make it feasible to do so.

Compression

Compression is the most common way to reduce the size of large audio files by removing psychoacoustically unimportant data. The process is facilitated by a *codec* (*c*ompression-*dec*ompression) device, which computes enormous mathematical calculations (called algorithms) to make data compression possible.

Compression can be either lossless or lossy. In *lossless compression* the original information is preserved; in *lossy compression* it is not. Lossless compression preserves binary data bit-for-bit and does not compress data at very high ratios. The codec does not articulate audio data well because its operations are based on strict mathematical functions which are more conducive to handling video. Lossy compression delivers high compression ratios. The lossy codec compression approximates what a human ear can hear and then filters out frequency ranges to which the ear is insensitive.

There are several compression formats: Adaptive Differential Pulse Code Modulation, a-law and μ-law, RealAudio, MPEG, MPEG-2 layer 3 technology, and MPEG-2 AAC.

Adaptive differential pulse code modulation (ADPCM) uses the fact that audio is continuous in nature. At thousands of samples per second, one sample does not sound much different from another. ADPCM records the differences between samples of sound rather than the actual sound itself. This technique reduces the sampling rate from 16 bits to 4 bits, compressing original data to one-fourth its size.

A-law and *μ-law* constitute an 8-bit codec format developed for sending speech via digital telephone lines. It uses the principle of redistributing samples to where sound is loudest—during speech—from where it is softest, during pauses in speech. μ-law is used in North America and Japan; a-law is used in the rest of the world.

RealAudio is a proprietary system using a compression method called *CELP* at low bit rates for speech. For music it uses Dolby Digital codec with higher bit rates. The Dolby system is known as *AC-3* (the AC stands for *audio coding*) (see Chapter 19).

MPEG stands for the *Moving Pictures Experts Group*. It was established by the film industry and the International Standards Organization (ISO) to develop compression software for film. MPEG uses an analytical approach to compression called *acoustic masking*. It works by establishing what the brain perceives the ear to be hearing at different frequencies. When a tone, called a *masker,* is at a particular frequency, humans cannot hear audio on nearby frequencies if they are at a low level. Based on this principle, MPEG developers determined various frequencies that could be eliminated. They use perceptual coders that divide the audio into multiple frequency bands, called *filterbanks,* each one assigned a masking threshold below which all data is eliminated.

MPEG-2 layer 3 technology is commonly known as *MP-3*. It is considered an excellent system for sound effects, speech, and most types of music. It ranges from 16 to 128 Kbps. On a 28.8 modem, it sounds like AM radio; at 128 Kbps it produces digital-quality sound.

MPEG-2 AAC (Advanced Audio Coder) is the latest coding system from MPEG. It is approximately a 30 percent improvement over the MPEG-2 layer 3 technology and 100 percent better than AC-3.

File Formats

Programs that play digital audio need to recognize the files before they can play them. Therefore files that are converted into digital audio must be saved in a particular format. The process adds an *extension* (a period followed by a two- or three-letter descriptor) to the file name identifying it as a sound file. It also adds *header information,* which tells the playback program how to interpret the data. File identifiers specify the name of the file,

Table 16-3 Common file formats and their associated extensions

File Formats	Extension(s)
WAV	.wav
AIFF	.aif, .aiff
AIFC	.aifc, .aic
Sun/NeXT Audio File (AU)	.au, .snd
MPEG Audio	.mp2, .mp3, .mpa
Real Audio	.ra
Liquid Audio	.la1

AIF = Audio Interchange File.

file size, duration, sampling rate, word length (bits), number of channels, and type of compression used. A large number of formats are available on the Internet, and they come and go; a few, however, have been in relatively widespread use for a while (see Table 16-3).

Downloadable Nonstreaming Formats

Downloadable nonstreaming formats require that the user first download the entire file and store it on the computer's hard disk. A program helper then plays the file. No specific server (transmitter) software is needed. The difference between nonstreaming and streaming is that streaming allows audio data to be sent across a computer network so that there are no interruptions at the receiving end for what appears to be continuous audio playback. In practice, however, interruptions do occur with slower connections.

Downloading nonstreaming data is usually slow when the files are even relatively large. Because a WAV (waveform) file with one minute of digital-quality sound—16-bit, 44.1 kHz, stereo—will occupy roughly 10 MB of disk space, these formats are generally used for audio of a minute or so. Table 16-4 provides an idea of the various formats' ease of use, quality versus size, and portability.

Downloadable Streaming Formats

The principle behind streaming technologies is *buffering*. As the player receives data, it stores it in a buffer before use. (The *player* is built into or added onto a user's Web browser.) After data builds a

Table 16-4 Common downloadable formats in relation to ease of use, quality versus size, and portability (its support across different platforms, such as Windows, Macintosh, and UNIX)

	Ease of Use	Quality Versus Size	Portability
AU	Good	Good	Excellent
MPEG (MP-3)	Poor	Excellent	Fair
WAV/AIFF	Excellent	Poor	Good
	Strengths		
AU	Can be used across all platforms		
MPEG (MP-3)	High compression ratios that can shrink CD files to one-tenth their size with no apparent loss of quality		
WAV/AIFF	Because these are the default audio type for all operating systems, they are extremely easy to use on all systems and applications		
	Recommendation: Use in . . .		**Reasons**
AU	Short audio clips (<30 seconds), background sound tracks, sound effects, and voice clips		High portability; good sound with small file sizes
MPEG (MP-3)	Audio that requires CD quality		Highly compressible; extremely popular
WAV/AIFF	Short audio clips of voice and solo instrumental music		Files too large; non-portable if compressed

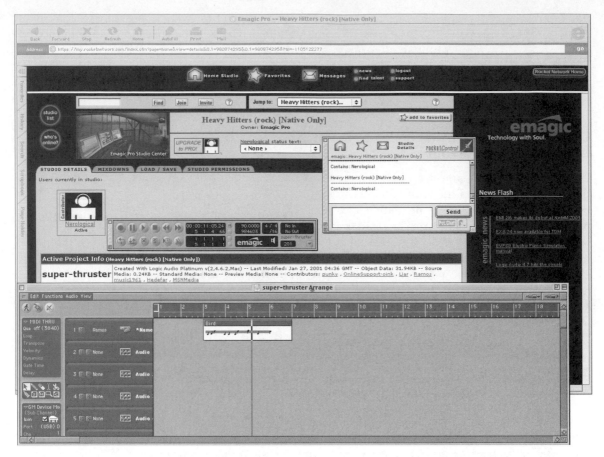

16-1 Screen of one "virtual studio" software program. The dialog boxes in the lower part of the screen facilitate communication among participants in the remote locations.

substantial buffer, the software player (such as RealPlayer) begins to play it. All incoming data is first stored in the buffer before playing. Thus the player is able to maintain a continuous audio output despite the changing transmission speeds of the data. Sometimes the buffer runs empty, and the player has to wait until it receives more data, in which case the computer displays the message, "Web congestion, buffering."

Data is sent over the Internet in *packets*. Each packet bears the address of the sender and the receiver. Because the Internet is lossy and non-deterministic, it means that the packets may get lost and that they arrive at different times. One company has developed a system that allows audio to flow even if packets are lost or appear later. Nonetheless, streaming technologies come closest to approximating traditional broadcast.

Transmission

With streaming technology the transmission process passes through the encoder, the server, the Internet, and the player. The encoder is responsible for translating the original audio signal to one of the data compression formats. The compressed audio bit stream is then sent to a server. Sometimes the encoder and the server can run on the same computer, but this is not usually the case for high-capacity servers or encoders running at high bit rates. The server is responsible for repackaging the bit stream for delivery over the Internet, sending the same bit stream to multiple users. This link is the weakest in the chain, because the Internet was not designed with real-time streaming applications in mind. At the receiving end is the user's computer with the appropriate applications software to play the audio file. This player unpacks the streaming data from the server, recovers the compressed audio bit stream, and decodes it back into an audio signal.

THE VIRTUAL STUDIO: ONLINE COLLABORATIVE RECORDING

Integrated Services Digital Network (ISDN) made it possible to produce a recording session in real time between studios across town or across the country (see Chapter 7). Now it is possible to do collaborative audio production online, such as music recording; *automated dialogue replacement (ADR);* spot announcements with voice-over, music, and effects; and film and television sound tracks. Users can record to their local systems, edit and process the audio, then post their tracks to the "virtual studio" for delivery to other participants in the session (see Figure 16-1). There is, however, no opportunity for those involved in the session to collaborate on the audio simultaneously. Dealing with the virtual studio is analogous to doing a multitrack session. The various tracks are recorded at different times rather than having, in a music session, for example, all the musicians playing at once.

MAIN POINTS

▶ Achieving digital-quality sound transmission over the Internet depends on several factors, not the least of which are a computer and loudspeakers capable of delivering the high-quality audio.

▶ Among the factors relevant to high-quality audio are the connection speed and reducing file size.

▶ Reducing file size can be done by file manipulation or data compression.

▶ File manipulation includes reducing sampling rate, word length, number of channels, playing time, and, with music, using instrumental instead of vocal-based tracks.

▶ Playing time can be reduced by editing through compression of the dynamic range, noise reduction, and equalization.

▶ Compression can be either lossless, preserving the original information, or lossy, with high compression ratios where some data is filtered out.

▶ Protocols used for data compression include: adaptive differential pulse code modulation (ADPCM); a-law and μ-law; RealAudio; Dolby AC-3; MPEG-2 layer 3 technology (MP-3); and MPEG-2 AAC (Advanced Audio Coder).

▶ File formats facilitate the saving of digital audio files.

▶ The difference between streaming and non-streaming is that streaming allows audio data to be sent across a computer network with no interruptions at the receiving end, although, in practice, interruptions do occur with slower connections.

▶ Downloading nonstreaming data is usually slow and, therefore, limited to small files.

▶ The principle behind streaming technologies is buffering.

▶ With streaming technology the transmission process passes through the encoder, the server, the Internet, and the player.

▶ Now it is possible to do collaborative audio production online, such as music recording; automated dialogue replacement (ADR); spot announcements with voice-over, music, and effects; and film and television sound tracks in a "virtual studio."

17

Learn more at *http://communication.wadsworth.com/*

Dialogue, Sound Effects, and Music in Postproduction

Most of the finished product that you *hear* in theatrical film and television is recorded in postproduction. Dialogue, frequently, is difficult to record during shooting. Even when acceptably performed and technically usable dialogue is obtained during shooting, directors often make refinements in post, where they have more sonic control than they do on the set. Most sound effects are more easily produced away from the set and the demands of production recording. Underscored music is often not selected or composed until production is fairly well along or completed. Moreover, music cannot be synched to picture until editing is finished.

AUTOMATED DIALOGUE REPLACEMENT

In *automated dialogue replacement (ADR)*, also known as *automatic dialogue replacement* and *looping*, dialogue is recorded or rerecorded, depending on the outcome of the production recording or the director's aesthetic preference, or both. Generally, there are two schools of thought about ADR.

Some directors believe that an original performance is preferable to a re-created one and that the background sounds that are part of the dramatic action are a natural part of the sonic environment, just as shadow is a natural part of light. They therefore prefer to use the dialogue and other sounds recorded during production, assuming that pickup is tight enough so that the intelligibility of the dialogue and the sonic balances are acceptable. Other directors prefer dialogue recorded with a minimum of background sound. They want to control the ambience and other elements, separately in postproduction, where they can also hone an actor's performance. Regardless of preference, however, there are times when ADR is the only way to capture dialogue, as it usually is in far-flung battle and chase scenes, scenes involving considerable actor movement, and scenes that require several microphones, for example.

Purpose and Process

Automated dialogue replacement is done in a dialogue recording studio, a relatively dry room (reverberation time is about 0.4 second for average-sized studios) with a screen, microphone(s), and an audio control panel (see Figure 17-1). As the picture is displayed on the screen, the performer, wearing headphones, stands before a microphone and synchronizes the dialogue to his or her mouth and lip movements on the screen. Relatively dry rooms are necessary so that the background sound added later can be laid in with as little prerecorded ambience as possible. Too dry a studio, however, absorbs the vitality of an actor's performance and could create a claustrophobic feeling.

Not only is ambience kept to a minimum in ADR, but audio enhancements are also minimal to give the sound editor and rerecording mixer the most latitude possible. Compression or a microphone pad may be applied to keep a signal from overmodulating. Sometimes spare equalization is employed to smooth intercut dialogue and transitions.

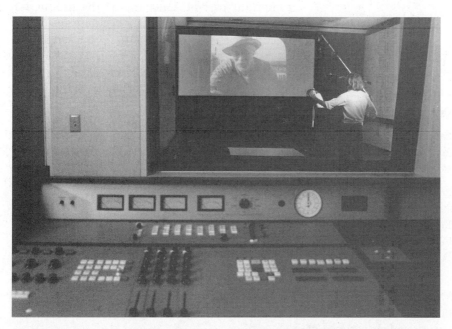

17-1 Automated dialogue recording studio and control room. The console is specially designed for ADR (and Foley recording). Among its unique features are a high number of monitor/assign channels and a low number of input channels; a room mic that solos automatically in rewind so communication is never lost; an auxiliary bus system with its own solo to enable isolating a track for the talent only and then returning them to their previous mix; Ahead/In/Past matrices for the editor, actor, studio, and control room that are time code driven; record/rehearse/playback mode selection; and spotting software.

The *automated* in automated dialogue replacement refers to the computer-controlled aspect of the procedure. The equipment is programmed to start, shuttle between cue points, and stop automatically. The computer also puts the recorder in *record* or *playback* and selects the desired playback track(s) in a multitrack recording. Cue points are designated in time code or feet and frames.

Dialogue rerecording is also referred to as *looping*, because the process once involved putting the dialogue sequences into short film loops so they could be repeated again and again without interruption. Each short section was rehearsed until the actor's dialogue was in sync with the picture and then recorded. Today the procedure is still the same, only it is automated and the picture medium may be videotape or computer.

In rerecording dialogue there are a few points and procedures worth remembering:

☑ Screen and analyze the scenes to be recorded and break them down line by line.

☑ Study the actor's tone, pitch, and emotion in the production recording.

☑ Note such things as dialogue that is to be shouted, whispered, and so on.

☑ Get to know what the performer sounds like speaking normally, because voice quality is quite different between a first take early in the day and a take 12 hours later.

☑ Another reason to get to know what the performer sounds like speaking normally is to gauge scenes calling for projected or quiet delivery. Then you have an idea of what adjustments to make in microphone placement.

The ADR studio is a sterile setting for a performance. The acoustics are dry, there is no set to help create a mood or establish a sense of environment, and there is rarely interaction among actors—they usually record their dialogue one at a time.

When it comes to ADR, the distinction is made between performers and trained actors. Performers often have a problem becoming the character in the absence of people on the set and a camera to play to. A trained actor, on the other hand, has an easier time adjusting to ADR's sterile environment.

For all talent, but particularly for the performers in ADR, listen carefully to delivery in relation to believability and how a performance will sound after background audio is added. For example, if a scene calls for an actor to talk loudly over the noise of, say, a race car, the dialogue's force and accentuation have to be convincing. Also, the dialogue may sound sufficiently loud in the quietness of the studio, but once the race car sound is added the delivery may not be forceful enough.

Adding the sound of a scene's background environment to the actor's headphone mix sometimes helps enliven performance. It may not be possible to use the precise background called for in the picture, but adding some presence helps counteract the sterility of the studio.

Recordkeeping is an often overlooked but very important part of ADR (and of the production process in general). Keeping accurate records of track assignments and making notes about each take is not only necessary to avoid confusion but of immeasurable help to the editors and mixers, who will be working with the dialogue tracks later in postproduction. A director may choose the reading of a particular line even though the beginning of a word may not be as crisp as it should be. By noting that in the record, an editor can try to find the same sound, delivered more crisply, elsewhere in the recording and edit it in, or the mixer may be able to use equalization to add the desired amount of crispness—all with the director's approval, of course.

The five elements generally considered to be most important in ADR are: pitch, tone, rhythm, emotion, and sync. The goals are to maintain consistency and to make the dialogue sound as though it was the original.

Microphone Selection and Technique

Keeping in mind that there are as many opinions about how to deal with mics and miking technique as there are ADR supervisors, it is generally agreed that the microphone used on the set does not have to be the same in ADR. Because the purpose of ADR is to record the clearest, cleanest dialogue (in a good, synched performance, of course), only the finest mics are chosen. The particular mic will vary according to the situation. For example, recording an intimate, warm sound may call for a large-diaphragm capacitor. If the tone is not sufficiently robust, a second mic may be positioned between the mouth and the sternum to add a chestier sound. Extremely tight dialogue may require a shotgun to close down the dry acoustics even more. Screams may necessitate a moving-coil mic.

Ordinarily, ADR involves straight-on recording. Such elements as perspective and signal processing are added later. Movement, however, may be attended to through mic positioning or by having the actor move. These techniques are used more to move the voice around a bit for level to achieve some of the naturalness of the production recording. For example, if on the set an actor walks into a scene and then comes through the camera, in ADR the actor can start a bit off-mic and then walk to the mic.

Loop Groups

In scenes calling for background voices, called *walla*, loop groups are used. Walla consists of spoken words to create ambient crowd sound usually without anything discernible being said. A *loop group* comprises everyone from professional actors who do walla for a living, or some part thereof, to anyone who happens to be around and is hired by the postproduction or ADR supervisor.

The function of a loop group is to provide whatever type of background sound the script calls for, from moans and kisses to all types of crowd audio for restaurant scenes, mobs, sports events, office hubbub, and so on. Using a loop group is far less expensive than paying principal actors to do what is, essentially, making sounds.

During actual shooting, a loop group will mouth the words, instead of actually saying them so their background does not interfere with the actors' production recording. The loop group adds the words in ADR. Usually, whatever is being said is kept at a low level just to convey a sense of location and atmosphere.

When certain words are designed to come through, these *callouts* are edited into holes where there is no dialogue or into shots with little visual or aural action. For example, in a fight scene when the favorite has his opponent against the ropes, the callout may be "Knock him out!" Or if the champ is on the canvas, the callout may be "Get up, you bum!" In a restaurant scene, in addition to the background conversational walla, you may hear callouts such as, "Would you care for another cup of coffee?" or "Thank you, come again."

A common loop group assignment is to cover nonspecific sounds for an actor, such as breaths, groans, and grunts. Again, it is much cheaper than having an A-list actor do them.

Dialogue Rerecording: Pros and Cons

Dialogue rerecording frees picture from sound and gives the director more flexibility and control. When there is a choice between using the original dialogue or rerecording it, directors and sound designers disagree about the benefits of looping. The question becomes: Are the added sonic control and assurance of first-rate audio quality and refined performance worth the loss of spontaneity and the unexpected?

On the one hand, regardless of the subject and style of the material, art is illusion, so there is no reason not to use whatever means necessary to produce the most polished, well-crafted product possible. Every sonic detail must be produced with the same care and precision as every visual detail. Anything less than excellent sound (and picture) quality reduces the effect of the illusion.

On the other hand, quality of performance is more important than quality of sound; "natural" is more realistic and, hence, more effective. Because actors, as a rule, do not like to re-create their performances in a rerecording studio, dialogue looping is rarely as good as the original performance recording. Even though lines sound different as a shooting day goes on, because the actor's voice changes, the difference between a production line and a looped line is always much greater than the difference between two production lines.

Actors generally prefer the natural environment and interactions on the set to the sterile environment of the ADR studio. As good as postproduction can be, many believe that it cannot quite capture the dozens of tiny sounds that correspond to physical movements, such as soft gasps of anxiety, a sniff, or the rustle of a newspaper page against the edge of the table. Although ADR gives directors complete control and often saves time and money, most actors agree that it is no substitute for the real thing.

SOUND EFFECTS

There are two sources of *sound effects* (abbreviated *SFX*): prerecorded and produced. Prerecorded sound effects are distributed on digital disc or can be downloaded via the Internet (see Chapter 16). Produced SFX are obtained in four ways: They can be (1) created and synchronized to picture in postproduction in a studio often specially designed for that purpose; (2) recorded on the set during shooting; (3) collected in the field throughout production or between productions; (4) generated electronically using a synthesizer or computer. Sound effects are also built using any one or a combination of these approaches. In the interest of clarity, each approach is considered separately here. Regardless of how you produce sound effects, an overriding concern is to maintain sonic consistency.

Prerecorded Sound-Effect Libraries

Sound-effect libraries are collections of recorded sounds that can number from several hundred to many thousand, depending on the distributor. The distributor has either produced and recorded the original sounds or collected them from other sources and obtained the rights to sell them, or both.

Advantages of Sound-Effect Libraries

A major advantage of sound-effect libraries is that for one buyout fee you get many different sounds for relatively little cost, compared with the time

Subject	Category	Section
Cable car bell	Bells, buzzers, whistles	4
Café	Backgrounds	3
Calf	Animals—barnyard	2
Camera	Hits, impacts	14
Campfire	Backgrounds	3
Canary	Birds, insects	5
Cannon	Guns, explosions	13
Cards	Sports, games	23
Carillon	Bells, buzzers, whistles	4
Carnival	Backgrounds	3
Car doors	Doors, gates, windows	10
Car horns	Horns, sirens	15
Carriage	Stagecoach, wagons	24

17-2 (a) Examples of categories and effects in a recorded sound-effect library.

and expense it would take to produce them yourself (see 17-2). *Buyout* means that you own the library and have unlimited, copyright-cleared use of it. Even better, there are Internet sources that provide copyright-cleared sound effects for downloading either free or for a modest charge.

Most broadcast stations and many production houses use libraries because they have neither the personnel nor the budget to assign staff to produce sound effects. Think of what it would involve to produce, for example, the real sounds of a jet fly-by, a forest fire, a torpedo exploding into a ship, or stampeding cattle. Moreover, SFX are available in mono, stereo, and surround sound, depending on the library.

Sound quality, or the absence thereof, was a serious problem with prerecorded sound effects before the days of digital audio, when they were distributed on tape and long-playing (LP) record. The audio was analog, dynamic range was limited, tape was noisy, LPs got scratched, and too many effects sounded lifeless. Frequently, it was easy to tell that the SFX came from a recording; they sounded "canned." The sound effects on digital disc have greatly improved fidelity and dynamic range; that is, those that were digitally recorded or transferred from analog to digital with widened

Catalog Number	Subject	Description	Time
6-046	Ship's deck	Large type—anchor chain down quickly	:05
6-047	Coast Guard cutter	Operating steadily—with water sounds	:41
6-048	Water taxi	Start up—steady run—slow down	:47
6-049	Water taxi	Steady run—slow down—rev ups—with water sounds	1:25
6-050	Fishing boat	Diesel type—slow speed—steady operation	:36
6-051	Tugboat	Diesel type—slow speed—steady operation	:38
6-052	Tugboat	Diesel type—medium speed—steady operation	:38
6-053	Outboard	Fast run-by	:32
6-054	Naval landing craft	Medium speed—steady operation	:50

17-2 *(continued)* **(b) Example of a detailed list of sound effects by category.**

dynamic range and sans noise. Be careful, however, of analog EFX transferred to digital disc without noise processing. Two other benefits of sound effects on digital disc are faster access to tracks and the ability to see a sound's waveform on-screen.

The great advantage of libraries is the convenience of having thousands of digital-quality sound effects at your fingertips for relatively little cost. There are, however, disadvantages.

Disadvantages of Sound-Effect Libraries

Sound-effect libraries have three conspicuous disadvantages: (1) You give up control over the dynamics and timing of an effect; (2) ambiences vary, so in editing effects together they may not match one another or those you require in your production; and (3) the effect may not be long enough for your needs. A fourth potential disadvantage is in downloading sound effects, when compression may degrade sound quality.

Dynamics and Timing One reason why sound editors prefer to create their own effects rather than use libraries is to have control over the dynamics of a sound, particularly effects generated by humans. For example, thousands of different footstep sounds are available in libraries. But you might need a specific footfall that requires a certain-sized woman walking at a particular gait on a solidly packed road of dirt and stone granules. Maybe no library can quite match this sound.

Timing is another reason why many sound editors prefer to create their own effects. To continue our example, if the pace of the footfall has to match action on the screen, trying to synchronize each step in the prerecorded sound effect to each step in the picture could be difficult.

Ambience Matching ambiences could present another problem with prerecorded sound effects. Suppose in a radio commercial you need footsteps walking down a hall, followed by a knock on a door that enters into that hallway. If you cut together two different sounds to achieve the overall effect, take care that the sound of the footsteps walking toward the door has the same ambience as the knock on the door. If the ambiences are different, the audience will perceive the two actions as taking place in different locales. Even if the audience could see the action, the different ambiences would be disconcerting.

To offset this problem, some sound-effect libraries provide different ambiences for specific applications: footsteps on a city street with reverb to put you in town among buildings, and without reverb to put you in a more open area; or gunshots with different qualities of ricochet to cover the various environments in which a shot may be fired. Some libraries provide collections of ambient environments, allowing you to mix the appropriate background sound with a given effect (see 17-3). In so doing be sure that the sound effect used has

	Title	Description	Time
01	Crowd, indoor	Small crowd: small room, light conversation	3:00
02	Crowd, indoor	Small crowd: large room, general walla	3:00
03	Crowd, indoor	Medium crowd: adults and children, general walla	3:00
04	Crowd, indoor	Medium crowd: adults, heavy voice walla	3:00
05	Crowd, indoor	Medium crowd: reception area, heavy walla	3:00
06	Crowd, indoor	Medium crowd: concrete foyer, general ambience, intensity varies	3:00
07	Crowd, indoor	Medium crowd: foyer, general ambience	3:00
08	Crowd, indoor	Medium crowd: general ambience	3:00
09	Crowd, indoor	Medium crowd: general ambience, light walla	3:00
10	Crowd, indoor	Large crowd: heavy walla	3:00
11	Crowd, indoor	Large crowd: wooden hall, crowd entering seating area	3:00
12	Crowd, indoor	Large crowd: entering cathedral-style building, low crowd ambience	3:00
13	Crowd, indoor	Large crowd: large open hall, general ambience	3:00
14	Crowd, indoor	Large crowd: large concrete hall, adults and children, general ambience	3:00
15	Crowd, indoor	Large crowd: filing by, heavy footsteps, hard surface	3:00
16	Crowd, outdoor	Medium crowd: general ambience	3:00
17	Crowd, outdoor	Medium crowd: general ambience, under concrete overhang	3:00
18	Crowd, outdoor	Medium crowd: general ambience, voices, footsteps	3:00
19	Crowd, outdoor	Large crowd: adults and children, general ambience	3:00
20	Crowd, outdoor	Large crowd: general crowd ambience, busy city	3:00
21	Crowd, outdoor	Large crowd: crowd passing by, heavy walla, footsteps	3:00
22	Crowd, outdoor	Ski resort: general ambience at the bottom of a ski hill	3:00
23	Crowd, outdoor	Large crowd: street party—large celebration	3:00
24	Crowd, outdoor	Large crowd: street party—victory celebration, heavy horns, cheering	3:00

	Title	Description	Time
01	Crowd, angry	Indoor: medium crowd—parliamentary dispute	3:00
02	Crowd, concert	Indoor: large theater—energetic crowd cheering for an encore	3:00
03	Harbor, marina	Small marina: general ambience—light boats, water lapping, loons	3:00
04	Harbor, port	Large port: general ambience—ship horns, seagulls, etc.	3:00
05	Hockey, ice	Indoor: adults—game ambience, no crowd	3:00
06	Hospital	Nurses station: general ambience, P.A. announcements	3:00
07	Hospital	Nurses station: general ambience, no announcements	3:00
08	Hospital	Intensive care room: heart monitor, ventilator, E.E.G.	3:00
09	Household, kitchen	Kitchen ambience: rinsing dishes, loading dishwasher, turning on dishwasher	3:00
10	Household, dining room	Dining room: general dish noise at dinner table	3:00
11	Industry, sawmill	Indoor: general ambience	3:00
12	Industry, steelyard	Exterior: general ambience	3:00
13	Industry, winery	Bottling area: general ambience	3:00
14	Laundromat, washers	Washing area: coin slots, loading, washing	3:00
15	Laundromat, dryers	Drying area: coin slots, dryers running	3:00
16	Library	Quiet library: light voices	3:00
17	Lobby	Hotel lobby: medium crowd—voices, telephone, elevator bell	3:00
18	Lobby	Hotel lobby: medium crowd—voices, light music	3:00
19	Market	Indoor: medium crowd—general ambience	3:00
20	Market	Outdoor: medium crowd—general ambience	3:00
21	Office foyer	Large office foyer: hard surface, footsteps, light voices	3:00
22	Office foyer	Large office foyer: footsteps, voices, elevator bells	3:00
23	Parade	Various bands passing, general crowd walla	3:00
24	Parade	No music, crowd applause and cheering, various horns, sirens	3:00

17-3 Examples of ambience sound effects

very little, or no, ambient coloration of its own. Otherwise, the backgrounds will be additive or clash, or both.

Fixed Length of Sound Effects Library SFX have fixed lengths. You need a sound to last 15 seconds, but the effect you want to use is only 7 seconds long. What to do?

If the effect is continuous, crowd sound or wind, for example, it can be looped (see "Looping" later in this chapter). If it is not continuous, such as a dog barking and then growling, you are stuck unless you can find two separate effects of the same-sounding dog barking and growling. If it is possible to edit them together to meet your timing needs, be careful that the edit transition from bark to growl sounds natural.

Manipulating Library Sound Effects

Once a sound effect has been recorded, any number of things can be done to alter its sonic characteristics, thereby extending the usefulness of a library.

Altering Playing Speed Because pitch and duration are inseparable parts of sound, it is possible to change the character of any recording by varying its playing speed. This technique will not work with all sounds; some will sound obviously unnatural— either too drawn out and guttural or too fast and falsetto. But for sounds with sonic characteristics that do lend themselves to changes in pitch and duration, the effects can be remarkable.

For example, the sound effect of a low-pitched, slow, mournful wind can be changed to a ferocious howl of hurricane force by increasing its playing speed. The beeps of a car horn followed by a slight ambient reverb can be slowed to become a small ship in a small harbor and slowed still more to become a large ship in a large harbor. Hundreds of droning bees in flight can be turned into a squadron of World War II bombers by decreasing the playing speed of the effect, or turned into a horde of mosquitos by increasing playing speed.

Decreasing the playing speed of cawing jungle birds will take you from the rain forest to an eerie world of science fiction. A gorilla can be turned into

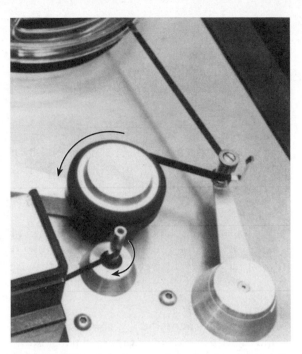

17-4 Threading technique used to play tape backward

King Kong by slowing the recording's playing speed. The speeded-up sound of chicken clucks can be turned into convincing bat vocalizations. The possibilities are endless, and the only way to discover how flexible sounds can be is to experiment.

Playing Sound Backward Another way to alter the characteristics of a sound is to play it backward. Many hard-disk recorders have a *reverse* command that rewrites the selected region in reverse, resulting in a backward audio effect. Some tape recorders have a *reverse play* function. On those that do not, you can play a tape backward by threading it around the capstan and pinch roller so that the tape feeds from right to left (see 17-4).

Looping Sometimes you may need a continuous effect that has to last several seconds, such as an idling car engine, a drum roll, or a steady beat. When the sound effect is shorter than the required time, it can be looped. In hard-disk systems, the *looping* command will continuously repeat the selected region. It is also possible to use a cartridge recorder or digital sound repeater for looping.

When looping make sure that the edit points are made so that the effect sounds continuous, not repetitious. That said, even well-edited loops run the risk of sounding repetitious if they are played too long.

Another looping technique that can sometimes be used to lengthen an effect is to reverse-loop similar sounds against themselves. When done right this technique also has the advantage of sounding natural.

Loops can also be designed to create a sound effect. For example, taking the startup sound of a motorcycle before it cranks over and putting it into a half-second repeat can be used as the basis for the rhythmic sound of a small, enclosed machine area.

Using Signal Processing By signal-processing a sound effect using delay, flanging, pitch shifting, and so on, it is possible to create a virtually infinite number of effects. For example, flanging a cat's meow can to turn it into an unearthly cry, adding low frequencies to a crackling fire can make it an inferno, and chorusing a bird chirp can create a boisterous flock.

Signal processing also helps enhance a sound effect without actually changing its identity—for example, adding low frequencies to increase its weight and impact, or beefing it up by pitch-shifting the effect lower and then compressing it (bearing in mind that too much bottom muddies the overall sound and masks the higher frequencies).

Choosing Sounds from the Titles

Titles in sound libraries are often not precise enough to be used as guides for selecting material. For example, what does "Laughter," "Washing Machine," "Window Opening," or "Polite Applause" actually tell you about the sound effect, besides its general subject and application? Most good libraries provide short descriptions of each effect to give an idea of its content (see 17-2b). Even so, always listen before you choose, because nuance in sound is difficult to describe in words.

LIVE SOUND EFFECTS

Although prerecorded sound libraries are readily available—some are quite good—most audio designers prefer to produce their own effects, because doing so allows complete control in shaping a sound to meet a precise need. In addition, if the effect is taken from the actual source, it has the advantage of being authentic. Then too sound designers are sometimes called on to create effects that do not already exist, and they prefer to build these from live sources.

Live sound effects are collected in three ways: (1) by creating them in a studio, (2) by recording them on the set during shooting, and (3) by recording them directly from the actual source, usually in the field, sometimes during production.

Foley Sound Effects

Creating sound effects in the studio goes back to the days before television, when drama was so much a part of radio programming. Surrounded by the "tools of the trade"—door frames, telephone ringers, bells, buzzers, water tubs, car fenders, cutlery, cellophane, coconut shells, virtually anything that made a sound—the effects people, usually situated in the same studio with the performers, produced many of the sounds called for in the script. (Effects that were difficult to produce in a studio were taken from recordings.) Many ingenious ways were devised to create effects in the studio. For example: The sound of a gunshot was created by closing a book smartly or slamming it on a hard, solid surface; clapping coconut shells in a box of dirt produced the sound of hoof beats; crinkling cellophane effected fire; the "vision" of a moving sailboat was generated by twisting the resined screw handle of a broom into and out of a socket and flapping a cloth lightly; and squeezing cornstarch in a gloved hand simulated walking in snow.

The term now applied to this technique is *Foley recording*, named for Jack Foley, a sound editor with Universal Pictures for many years. Given the history of radio drama and the fact that other Hollywood sound editors had been producing effects in the studio for some time, clearly Jack Foley did not invent the technique. His name became identified with it in the early fifties when he had to produce the sound of paddling a small survival raft in the ocean. Instead of going out and recording the real sound, he did it in the studio and in sync with the picture. The inventiveness and efficiency he showed in producing this and several other effects and simultaneously recording them to picture—saving the sound editor considerable postproduction time—impressed enough people that Foley's name has become associated with the technique ever since. Today the primary purposes of Foley recording are: (1) to produce sound effects that are difficult to record during production, such as far-flung action scenes or large-scale movement of people and materiel; (2) to create sounds that do not exist; and (3) to produce controlled sound effects in a regulated studio environment.

This is not to suggest that "Foleying" and sonic authenticity are mutually exclusive. Producing realistic Foley effects involves much more than pointing a microphone at a sound source on a surface that is not a real surface in an acoustic space that has no natural environment. A door sound cannot be any door. Does the scene call for a closet door, a bathroom door, or a front door? A closet door has little air, a bathroom door sounds more open, and a front door sounds solid, with a latch to consider. In a sword fight, simply banging together two pieces of metal adds little to the dynamics of the scene. Using metal that produces strong harmonic rings, however, creates the impression of swords with formidable strength. Recording a basketball game in a schoolyard will have a more open sound with different types of ball bounces on asphalt, rim noises, and ball handling than the sound of a basketball game in an indoor gymnasium, which will differ from the sounds of a basketball game played in an indoor arena.

Generally, Foley effects are produced in an acoustically dry, specially designed sound studio known as a *Foley stage* (see 17-5). It is acoustically dry, not only because, as with dialogue rerecording, ambiences are usually added later, but because

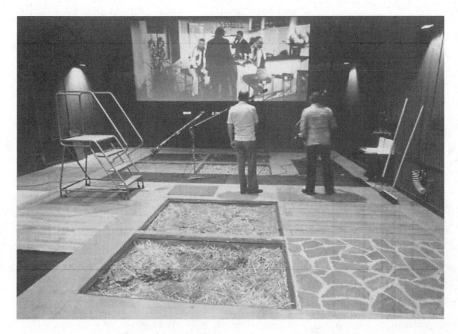

17-5 A Foley studio setup. The two Foley walkers are using the various pits and equipment to perform, in sync, the sounds that should be heard with the picture.

reflections from loud sounds have to be kept to a minimum. That said, Foley recording is sometimes done on the actual production set to take advantage of its more realistic acoustic environment.

Foley effects are usually produced in sync with the visuals. The picture is shown on a screen in the studio, and when a foot falls, a door opens, a paper rustles, a floor squeaks, a man sits, a girl coughs, a punch lands, or a body splashes, a Foley artist generates the effect at the precise time it occurs on-screen. Such a person is sometimes called a Foley walker, because Foley work often requires performing many different types of footsteps. In fact, many Foley artists have been dancers.

Important to successful Foleying is having a feel for the material—to become, in a sense, the actor on the screen by, among other things, recognizing body movements and the sounds they generate. John Wayne, for example, did not have a typical walk; he sort of strode and rolled. Other actors may clomp, shuffle, or glide as they walk.

Also important to creating a sound effect is studying its sonic characteristics and then finding a sound source that contains similar qualities. Take the sound of a growing rock. There is no such sound, of course. But if there were, what would it be like? Its obvious characteristics would be stretching and sharp cracking sounds. One solution is to inflate a balloon and scrape it with your fingers to create a high-pitched scraping sound. If the rock is huge and requires a throatier sound, slow down the playing speed. For the cracking sound, shellac an inflated rubber tube. Once the shellac hardens, sonically isolate the valve to eliminate the sound of air escaping and let the air out of the tube. As the air escapes, the shellac will crack. Combine both sounds to get the desired effect.

There are thousands of examples of created sounds. Here are a few:

■ Using a feather duster in the spokes of a spinning bicycle wheel to create the sound of gently beating wings or flapping a leather glove to generate a more aggressive wing sound

■ Twisting stalks of celery to simulate the sound of tendons being stretched

■ Bending a plastic straw to simulate the sound of a moving joint

■ Scraping a metal guitar pick or can opener over a block of ice for the sound of ice-skating

■ Scraping dry ice on metal to create the sound of a moving glacier

■ Wiping dry glass to use as the basis for a squeak from a large mouse

■ Lightly tapping safety pins on linoleum to simulate a mouse's footsteps

■ Inserting a mini-mic up the nose to create the perspective of hearing breathing from inside the head

■ Taking the rubber ball from a computer mouse and dragging it across the face of a computer monitor to help create the sound of a bat

■ Putting a dry soil conditioner on a piece of cloth and sliding a board around to simulate the sound of skiing

■ Whipping a thin, flexible stick through the air and overdubbing it several times to create the sound of arrows whooshing through air

■ Using the slurpy, sucking sound of a bathtub drain as the basis for the sound that emphasizes a whirlpool or someone sinking into quicksand

■ Discharging compressed air in a lot of mud to create the dense bubbling sound of a molten pit

■ Pushing a plunger in a sandbox to simulate horses walking on sand

■ Pulling a fist in and out of a watermelon to produce the sound of a monster taking the heart from a living person

■ Using the venting and exhaust sounds from a cylinder of nitrogen as the basis for the sound of a freeze gun

■ Holding a cassette recorder outside the window of a moving car to record a deep, grating rumble to reinforce the sound of a rocket launch

■ Banging on a metal canoe in a swimming pool and dropping the canoe into the water above an underwater microphone to produce the sounds of explosions beating on the hull of a submarine

Often it takes two, three, or more sounds plus electronic processing to come up with the appropriate sound effect:

■ The helicopter sound at the beginning of *Apocalypse Now*—the blade thwarp, the turbine whine, and the gear sound—were created by synthesizing the sounds of a real helicopter.

■ In *Back to the Future III,* the basic sound of galloping horses was created using plungers on different types of surfaces. The sound was then rerecorded and processed in various ways to match the screen action.

■ The sound of the giant boulder careening toward the frantically running Indiana Jones in *Raiders of the Lost Ark* was the processed audio of a car rolling down a gravel road, in neutral, with the engine off.

■ The sound of the insects coming out of the heat duct in *Arachnophobia* was produced by recording Brazilian roaches walking on aluminum. The rasping sound a tarantula makes rubbing its back legs on the bulblike back half of its body was created from the sound of grease frying mixed with high-pressure air bursts.

■ The alien voices in *Cocoon* were made up of the crystal tones of champagne glasses and a flute with all the tone gone.

■ The roar of a Los Angeles freeway recorded through a vacuum cleaner pipe served as the basis for the sound of Luke Skywalker's land speeder in *Star Wars*.

■ The sounds of the spaceship *Millennium Falcon* in *Star Wars* included tiny fan motors, a flight of World War II torpedo planes, a pair of low-frequency sine waves beating against each other, variably phased white noise with frequency nulls, a blimp, a phased atom bomb explosion, a distorted thunderclap, an F-86 jet firing afterburners, a

Phantom jet idle, a 747 takeoff, an F-105 jet taxiing, and a slowed-down P-51 prop plane pass-by. Various textures were taken from each of these sounds and blended together to create the engine noises, takeoffs, and fly-bys.

■ In *Jurassic Park* the sounds of the tyrannosaurus were made up of the trumpeting sound of a baby elephant, an alligator growl, and the growls of 15 other creatures, mostly lions and tigers. The inhale of T. Rex's breathing included the sounds of lions, seals, and dolphins; the exhale included the sound of a whale's blowhole. The smashing, crashing sound of trees being cut down, particularly Sequoias, was used to create the footfalls of the larger dinosaurs. The sounds of the reptilian dinosaurs were built from the sounds of lizards, iguanas, bull snakes, a rattlesnake (flanged), and horselike snorts. A Synclavier was used to process many of these sounds, including some of the dinosaur footsteps and eating effects. (A Synclavier is a highly sophisticated synthesizer; but unlike most synthesizers, which have sounds already programmed in, sounds have to be fed into a Synclavier before they can be programmed, processed, and sampled.)

■ In the film *PageMaster,* the dragon's sound was produced vocally and reinforced with tiger growls to take advantage of the animal's bigger and more resonant chest cavity.

■ The spinning and moving sounds of the main character going from place to place in *The Mask* were created by twirling garden hoses and power cables to get moving-through-air sounds, layering them in a Synclavier, routing them through a loudspeaker, waving a mic in front of the loudspeaker to get a Doppler effect, and then adding jets, fire *whooses,* and wind gusts.

■ The multilayered sound of the batmobile in *Batman and Robin* was made up of the sounds of an Atlas rocket engine blast, the turbocharger whine of an 800-horsepower Buick Grand National, a Ducati motorcycle, and a Porsche 917 12-cylinder racer.

- In *St. Elmo's Fire,* which is a phenomenon caused when static electricity leaps from metal to metal, signal-processing the sound of picking at and snapping carpet padding emulated the effect.

- For the final electrocution scene in *The Green Mile,* the sound of metal scraping, human screams, dogs barking, pigs squealing, and other animals in pain were integrated with the idea of making the electricity's effect like scratching a chalkboard.

- In *Star Trek Insurrection,* there are little flying drones, basically a robot with wings. Their sound was created by running vinyl-covered cable down a slope, tying a boom box to it on a pulley, and putting a microphone in the middle to get the Doppler effect. A series of different-quality steady-state tones were played back from the boom box's cassette to create the basic effect. All the sounds were then processed in a Synclavier.

- Many different processed sounds went into creating the effects for the hovercraft *Nebuchad-nezzar* in *The Matrix*. To help create the low metal resonances heard inside the ship, the sound of a giant metal gate that produced singing resonances was pitch-shifted down many octaves.

Vocalizing sound effects has been done since the days of radio drama. Today a popular signal processor called a *vocoder* is used to help create vocalized effects, which are often combined with a physical sound to achieve a contoured effect. It is worth noting, however, that vocalized effects work only when they do not sound like a human voice generated them.

Components and Context of a Foley Sound Effect Being ingenious in creating a sound effect is not enough. You also have to know the components of the effect and the context in which the effect will be placed. Let us use two examples as illustrations: a car crash and footsteps.

The sound of a car crash generally has six components: (1) the skid, (2) a slight pause just before impact, (3) the impact, (4) the grinding sound of metal, (5) the shattering of glass just after impact, and (6) silence.

The sound of footsteps consists of three basic elements: (1) the impact of the heel, which is a fairly crisp sound, (2) the brush of the sole, which is a relatively soft sound, and sometimes (3) heel or sole scrapes.

But before producing these sounds, you need to know the context in which they will be placed. For the car crash, the make, model, and year of the car will dictate the sounds of the engine, the skidding, and, after the impact, the metal and glass. The type of tires and road surface will govern the pitch and density of the riding sound; the car's speed is another factor that affects pitch. The location of the road—for example, in the city or country—will help determine the quality of the sound's ambience and reverb. A swerving car will require tire squeals. Of course, what the car crashes into will also affect the sound's design.

As for the footsteps, the height, weight, gender, and age of the person will influence the sound's density and the heaviness of the footfall. Another influence on the footfall sound is the footwear itself—shoes with leather heels and soles, pumps, spiked heels, sneakers, sandals, and so on. The choices here may relate to the hardness or softness of the footfall, and the attack of the heel sound, or lack thereof. Perhaps you would want a suction-type or squeaky-type sound with sneakers; maybe you would use a flexing sound of leather for the sandals. The gait of the walk—fast, slow, ambling, steady, or accented—will direct the tempo of the footfalls. The type of walking surface—concrete, stone, wood, linoleum, marble, or dirt—and whether it is wet, snowy, slushy, polished, or muddy will be sonically defined by the sound's timbre and envelope. The amount of reverberation added to the effect depends on where the footfalls occur.

Miking and Perspective in Foley Recording

The capacitor microphone is most frequently used in recording Foley effects because of its ability to "hear" subtleties and capture transients—fast bursts of sound, such as door slams, gunshots, breaking glass, and footsteps—that constitute so much of Foley work. Tube-type capacitors help smooth harsh transients and warm digitally recorded effects.

Directional capacitors—super-, hyper-, and ultracardioid—are preferred because they pick up concentrated sound with little ambience. These pickup patterns also provide more flexibility in changing perspectives. Moving a highly directional microphone a few inches will sound like it was moved several feet.

Factors such as dynamic range and the noise floor require a good microphone preamp. Recording loud bangs or crashes or soft nuances of paper folding or pins dropping requires the capabilities to handle both a wide variety of dynamics and considerable gain with almost no additional noise. Many standard in-console preamps are not up to the task. Limiting and compression are sometimes used in Foley recording; except for noise reduction, processing is usually done during the final stages of postproduction.

Microphone placement is critical in Foleying, because the on-screen environment must be replicated as closely as possible on the Foley stage. In relation to mic-to-source distance, the closer the microphone is to a sound source, the more detailed, intimate, and drier the sound. When the microphone is farther from a sound source, the converse of that is true, but only to a certain extent on a Foley stage, because the studio itself has such a short reverberation time. To help create perspective or openness, or both, in the latter instance multiple miking is often used. Nevertheless, if a shot calls for a close environment, baffles can be used to decrease the room size. If the screen environment is more open, the object is to operate in as open a space as possible.

It is important to know how to record sound at a distance. Equalization (EQ) and reverb can only simulate distance and room size. Nothing is as authentic as recording in the appropriately sized room with the microphones matching the camera-to-action distance.

A critical aspect of Foley recording cannot be overstated: Make sure the effects sound consistent and integrated and do not seem to be outside, or on top of, the sound track. When a sound is recorded at too close a mic-to-source distance, in poor acoustics, or with the wrong equipment, it is unlikely that EQ, reverb, or other signal processing will save it.

Production Sound Effects

Some directors prefer to capture authentic sounds either as they occur on the set during production or by recording them in the field separately, or both. These directors are willing to sacrifice, within limits, the controlled environment of the Foley stage for the greater sonic realism and authenticity of the actual sound sources produced in their natural surroundings. Or they may wish to use field sound as a reference for Foley recording, or take advantage of a sound's authenticity and use it as the basis for further processing. Still, a number of factors have to be taken into consideration to obtain usable sounds.

If sounds are recorded with the dialogue as part of the action—a table being thumped, a match being struck, a toaster being popped—getting the dialogue is always more important than getting the sound effect; the microphone must be positioned for optimal pickup of the performers.

When a director wants sound recorded with dialogue, the safest course of action is to record it with a different mic than the one being used for the dialogue. If the dialogue mic is a boom, use a plant (stationary) mic for the sound effect; if the dialogue microphone is a body mic, use a boom or plant mic for the sound. This facilitates recording sound and dialogue on separate tracks and, therefore, provides flexibility in postproduction editing and mixing.

If for some reason only one mic is used, a boom would be best. Because its mic-to-source position changes with the shot, there is a better chance of capturing and maintaining perspectives with it than with a body or plant mic. Moreover, in single-camera production a scene is shot at least a few times from different perspectives, so there is more than one opportunity to record a usable sound/dialogue relationship.

This point should be emphasized: It is standard in single-camera production to shoot and reshoot a scene. For each shot time is taken to reposition camera, lights, and crew, to redo makeup, primp wardrobe, and so on. During this time the sound crew also should be repositioning mic(s). Take advantage of every opportunity to record audio on the set. The more takes of dialogue and sound effects you record, the greater the flexibility in editing and mixing. Even if dialogue or effects are unusable because of mediocre audio quality, it is still wise to preserve the production recording because it is often useful in dialogue rerecording and Foleying as a reference for timing, accent, and expressiveness.

You never want to mask an actor's line with a sound effect, or any other sound for that matter, or to have a sound effect call attention to itself (unless that is the intent). If sound effects are recorded on the set before or after shooting rather than with the action, try to do it just before shooting. Everyone is usually in place on the set, so the acoustics will match the acoustics of the take. If an effect has to be generated by the actor, it can be. And all sounds should be generated from the sound source's location in the scene.

When recording the effect, there has to be absolute quiet; nothing else can be audible: a dog barking far in the distance, an airplane flying overhead, wind gently wafting through trees, crockery vibrating, lights buzzing, crew shuffling, actors primping. The sound effect must be recorded "in the clear" so that it carries no sonic baggage into postproduction.

This brings us back to the question: If all these added concerns go with recording sound effects on the set, why bother? Why not save time, effort, and expense and simply Foley them? Some directors do not care for the controlled acoustics of the Foley studio or for artificially created sound. They want to capture the flavor or "air" of a particular location and preserve the unique characteristic of a sound an actor generates, or fuse the authenticity of and interaction among sounds as they occur naturally.

This creates considerable challenge in moving-action scenes, such as chases, that take place over some distance. These scenes are usually covered by multiple cameras; and although multiple microphones may not be positioned with the cameras,

using them will capture the sounds of far-flung action. The mics can be situated at strategic spots along the chase route with separate mixer/recorder units at each location to control the oncoming, passing, and fading sounds. In addition, a mic mounted on the means of conveyance in the chase can help greatly in postproduction editing and mixing. For example, on a getaway car, mics can be mounted to the front fender, level with the hubcaps, and aimed at a 45-degree angle toward where the rubber meets the road; or a fishpole boom can be rigged through the rear window and rested on a door for support. In a horse chase, a mic can be mounted outside the rider's clothing or fastened to the lower saddle area and pointed toward the front hooves.

Another advantage to multiple-miking sound effects is the ability to capture various perspectives of the same sound. To record an explosion, for example, positioning mics, say, 25, 50, 100, and 500 feet away provides potential for a number of sonic possibilities when editing and mixing. Another reason it is a good idea to record extremely loud sound from more than one location is that the sound can overmodulate tape to the point that much of it may not record. With a digital recording, tape or disk, remember that there is no headroom. That is why, for example, the sound of loud weaponry is compressed—to create a more percussive sound that otherwise might be distorted or sound thinner and weaker than the actual sound.

The obvious microphone to use in many of these situations may seem to be the wireless because of its mobility. As good as wireless systems can be, however, they are still subject to interference from radio frequencies, telephone lines, and passing cars, which causes spitting and buzzing sounds. A directional capacitor microphone connected to a good mic preamp is the most dependable approach to take here. In these applications use very strong shock mounts and tough windscreens. And do not overlook the importance of wearing ear protection when you are working with loud sounds. Do not monitor these sounds directly—use your eyes and the VU (or ppm) meter instead of your ears.

Collecting Sound Effects in the Field

Live sound recorded away from the set for a specific production or between productions to build effects libraries is usually collected in the field. As with most field recording, utmost care should be taken to record the effect in perspective, with no unwanted sound. It cannot be overemphasized that any recording done away from the studio also requires first-rate, circumaural headphones for reliable monitoring.

As with most sound-effect miking, the directional capacitor is preferred for reasons already noted. That said, the parabolic microphone system, using a capacitor mic, is also employed for recording sounds in the field for a long-reach, highly concentrated pickup. This is particularly important when recording weaker sounds, such as insects, certain types of bird calls, or rustling leaves. Parabolics are essentially midrange instruments, so it is probably unwise to use them on sound sources with significant defining low or high frequencies.

For stereo, the middle-side (M-S) and stereo mics are most common because they are easier to set up than coincident or spaced stereo microphones and are more accurate to aim at a sound source. In fact, spaced stereo mics should be avoided, because in reproducing it the sound image will jump from one loudspeaker to the other as the effect passes. M-S mics are particularly useful because it is often difficult to control environmental sounds. With an M-S mic, it is possible to keep the environmental sound separate from the principal sound and either not use it or combine the two sounds in the mix. When recording moving stereo sound effects, be careful if the sound image passes across the mic in a straight line as it moves toward the center of the pickup. In certain instances it becomes disproportionately louder compared with its left and right imaging, particularly if the mic array is close to the path of the sound source. Also, the closer the stereo mic-to-source distance, the faster the image will pass the center point. Keep in mind that accurately monitoring stereo requires stereo headphones.

With any directional microphone, is it worth remembering that changing the mic-to-source angle only a few degrees will change the character of the sound being recorded. This can be advantageous or disadvantageous, depending on the effect you are trying to capture.

Also important in field-recording sound effects are having excellent microphone preamps and the right recording equipment. Recorders vary in robustness and in their ability, for example, to deal with subtle sounds, percussive sounds, and dynamic range.

A key to collecting successful live effects in the field is making sure that the recorded effect sounds like what it is supposed to be, assuming that is your intention. Placing a mic too close to a babbling brook could make it sound like boiling water or liquid bubbling in a beaker. Miking it from too far a distance, on the other hand, might destroy its liquidity. A flowing stream miked too close could sound like a river; miking it from too far away could reduce its size and density. A recording of the inside of a submarine could sound too cavernous. Applause might sound like rain or something frying. A spraying fountain might sound like rain or applause. In fact, a spraying fountain often lacks the identifying liquid sound. To get the desired audio, it might be necessary to mix in a watery-type sound, such as a river or a flowing, rather than babbling, brook. A yellow jacket flying around a box could sound like a deeper, fuller-sounding bumblebee if miked too close, or a mosquito if miked too far. A gunshot recorded outdoors, in open surroundings, sounds like a firecracker; some types of revolvers sound like pop guns.

Keep four other things in mind when recording sounds in the field: Be patient, be persistent, be inventive, and, if you really want authenticity, be ready to go anywhere and to almost any length to obtain an effect.

For the film *Hindenburg,* the sound designer spent six months researching, collecting, and producing the sounds of a dirigible, including sonic perspectives from a variety of locations inside the ship and from on the ground to someone hearing a dirigible passing overhead.

In the film *Glory,* the sound designer wanted the effects of Civil War weaponry to be as close to authentic as possible, even to the extent of capturing the sound of real Civil War cannonballs and bullets whizzing through the air. Specially made iron cannonballs were shot from cannons forged for the film; this was recorded at 250 yards and a quarter-mile downrange. These locations were far enough from the initial explosion that it would not contaminate the sound of the projectile going by. The two distances provided a choice of whiz-by sounds and also the potential for mixing them, if necessary. Because the cannons could not be aimed very well at such distances, not one acceptable whiz-by was recorded during an entire day of taping. For the bullet whizzes, modern rifles would not have worked, because the bullet velocity is not slow enough to produce an audible air whiz-by. Using real Civil War bullets, a recordist sat in a gully 400 yards downrange and taped the whiz-bys as the live rounds flew overhead. In the end the cannonball whiz-bys had to be created by playing the bullet whiz-bys in reverse and slowed down.

Finally, when collecting sounds in the field, do not necessarily think literally about what it is you want to capture. Consider a sound's potential to be built into another effect. For example, the basic sound of Chewbacca the Wookee in *Star Wars* was the growl of a real bear. Among the many different laser sounds in the film, some incorporated the buzz of inductance recorded by passing a microphone behind a television set or the guy wire twang of a transmitter tower. Other examples of transforming sound effects are cited throughout this chapter.

ELECTRONICALLY GENERATED SOUND EFFECTS

High-quality sound effects can be generated electronically with synthesizers and computers and by employing MIDI. This approach is also referred to as *electronic Foley*. Its advantages are cost-efficiency, convenience, and the unlimited number of sounds that can be created. Its main disadvantage is that electronically generated sound effects sometimes lack the "reality" directors desire.

Synthesized Sound Effects

A *synthesizer* is an audio instrument that uses sound generators to create waveforms. The various ways these waveforms are combined can synthesize a vast array of sonic characteristics that are similar to, but not exactly like, existing sounds and musical instruments. They can also be combined to generate a completely original sound. In other words, because the pitch, amplitude, timbre, and envelope of each synthesizer tone generator can be controlled, it is possible to build synthesized sounds from scratch.

In addition to being able to create synthesized effects, preprogrammed sound from libraries designed for specific synthesizer brands and models are available. These collections may be grouped by type of sound effect—such as punches, screams, thunder—or by instrument category, such as drum, string, brass, and keyboard sounds (see 17-6). These libraries come in various formats, such as floppy and hard disk, plug-in memory cartridge, and computer files available as separate software or by downloading.

One complaint about synthesized sound has been its readily identifiable electronic quality. With considerably improved synthesizer designs and software, this has become much less of a problem, however. But take care to make sure that the synthesizer and sound library you use produce professional-quality sound—many do not, particularly those available through downloading, because of the adverse effects of data compression.

The operational aspects of synthesizers and their programs are beyond the purview of this book. Even if they were not, it is extremely difficult to even begin to describe the sonic qualities of the myriad effects a synthesizer can generate. Suffice it to say, almost anything is possible. The same is true of computer-generated sound effects.

Computer-Generated Sound Effects

A principal difference between the synthesizer and the computer is that the synthesizer is a device

Sampling

An important sound-shaping capability of many electronic keyboards and computer software programs is *sampling,* a process whereby digital audio data representing a sonic event, acoustic or electroacoustic, is stored on disk or into electronic memory. The acoustic sounds can be anything a microphone can record—a shout, splash, motor sputter, song lyric, trombone solo, whatever. Electroacoustic sounds are anything electronically generated, such as those a synthesizer produces. The samples can be of any length, as brief as a drumbeat or as long as the available memory allows.

A *sampler,* which is basically a specialized digital record and playback device, may be keyboard-based, making use of musical keyboard controllers to trigger and articulate sampled audio; or it may be a rack-mountable unit, without a keyboard, which is controlled by an external keyboard or a sequencer. A *sequencer* is a device that stores messages, maintains time relationships among them, and transmits the messages when they are called for from devices connected to it. The sampler system may also be computer-based.

With most sampling systems, it is possible to produce an almost infinite variety of sound effects by shortening, lengthening, rearranging, looping, and signal-processing the stored samples. A trombone can be made to sound like a saxophone, an English horn, or a marching band of "76 trombones." One drumbeat can be processed into a thunderclap or built into a chorus of jungle drums. The crack of a baseball bat can be shaped into the rip that just precedes an explosion. Chirping birds can become a gaggle of geese. A metal trash can being hit with a hammer can provide a formidable backbeat for a rhythm track. The squeal of a pig can be transformed into a human scream.

In solid-state memory systems, such as *ROM (read-only memory)* or *RAM (random-access memory),* it is possible to instantly access all or part of the sample and reproduce it any number of times. The difference between ROM- and RAM-based samplers is that ROM-based samplers are factory-

Note	Drum Kit 1 (Total Kit)
34	•
35	046: Orch Crash
36	000: Fat Kick
37	005: Real Kick
38	002: Ambient Kick
39	012: Syn Kick 3
40	007: Gated Kik
41	018: Piccolo Snare
42	019: Soft Snare
43	027: Gated Snare
44	029: Syn Snare 1
45	014: Snare 1
46	036: Side Stick
47	026: Rock Snare
48 (C3)	059: Tom Lo
49	060: Process Tom
50	059: Tom Lo
51	060: Process Tom
52	058: Tom Hi
53	048: Tite HH
54	051: Close Syn HH
55	048: Tite HH
56	052: Open Syn HH
57	049: Open HH
58	085: Tambourine
59	050: Pedal HH
60 (C4)	040: Crash Cym
61	040: Crash Cym
62	054: Ride Edge
63	055: Ride Cup
64	082: Syn Maracas
65	081: Cabasa
66	094: Hand Claps

(C2 is at note 36)

17-6 Selected example of one synthesizer's soundfiles in the drum category

specifically designed to create and produce sounds; the computer is not. The computer is completely software-dependent. With the appropriate software, the computer, like the synthesizer, can also store preprogrammed sounds or create them from scratch, or both. Many computer sound programs make it possible not only to call up a particular effect but to see and manipulate its waveform and, therefore, its sonic characteristics (see Chapter 18).

programmed and reproduce only; RAM-based samplers allow you to both reproduce and record sound samples. The number of samples you can load into a system is limited only by the capacity of the system's storage memory.

The Samplefile

After a sample is recorded or produced, or both, it is saved to a storage medium, usually a floppy disk, hard disk, compact disc, or DVD. The stored sound data is referred to as a *samplefile*. Once stored, of course, a samplefile can be easily distributed. As a result, samplefiles of sounds are now available to production facilities in the same way that sound-effect libraries are available. Other storage mediums are also used for samplefile distribution, such as CD-ROM, erasable and write-once optical discs, and online.

You should take two precautions before investing in a samplefile library. First, make sure that the samplefiles are in a format that is compatible with your sampler. There has been increased standardization of samplefile formats for computer-based systems. Second, make sure that the sound quality of the samples is up to professional standards; too many are not, particularly those obtained online.

Tips for Recording Samples

In recording samples from whatever source—acoustic or electronic—it is vital that the sound and reproduction be of good quality. Because the sample may be used many times in a variety of situations, it is disconcerting (to say the least) to hear a bad sample again and again. Moreover, if the sample has to be rerecorded, it might be difficult to reconstruct the same sonic and performance situation.

Miking

The same advice that applies to miking for digital recording (see Chapter 15) also applies to miking for sampling. Only the highest-quality microphones should be used, which usually means capacitors with a wide, flat response; high

sensitivity; and an excellent self-noise rating. If very loud sound recorded at close mic-to-source distances requires a moving-coil mic, it should be a large-diaphragm, top-quality model with as low a self-noise rating as possible.

The challenge is to avoid tonal coloration of the sample. A noisy sample audibly shifts in pitch as you play different keys on the keyboard. Close miking with a directional mic helps reduce any room sound. Any recorded ambience, as with any unwanted noise, becomes part of the sample.

In recording samples in stereo, imaging and room size are significantly affected by the miking technique, because the interchannel delay varies with the pitch shift. The only way to know which technique will work best for a given application is to experiment with the various stereo microphone arrays—coincident, near-coincident, and spaced—before deciding.

ORGANIZING A SOUND-EFFECT LIBRARY

It is not unusual for an audio facility to have thousands of sound effects in its collection. Although prerecorded libraries come with an index, timing information, and, often, descriptions of the cues, and sound effects produced in-house are also catalogued, it can be time-consuming to locate and audition an effect. Database systems are available that enable you to search, locate, and audition a sound effect in seconds.

Generally, the search feature provides four ways to find an effect: by category, word, synonym, and catalog number. The database system can be interfaced with a multidisc player so that once an effect has been located, it can be auditioned from the start of the track or cued to within a split second anywhere in the track.

For example, by punching in "thunder," the user finds out that there are 56 versions of thunder available, the time of each version, and a short description of what type of thunder it is. In some systems the computer will unload the disc and play back the thunder effects called for (see 17-7).

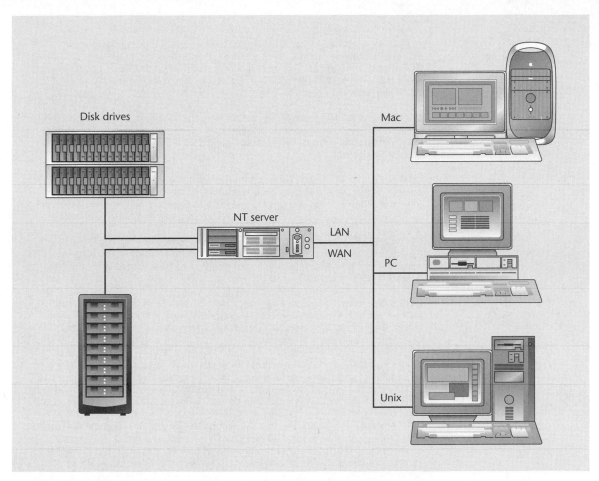

17-7 Example of one CD server's architecture. This system allows the user to search, audition, and download sound effects from a Windows NT server to any PC, Macintosh, or Unix-based computer. LAN = local-area network; WAN = wide-area network.

MUSIC

Music for productions can be obtained in three ways: (1) by having it composed and recorded for a particular piece; (2) by choosing it from a prerecorded music library; or (3) by selecting it from a commercial CD. Because Chapter 11 covers composing music for underscoring and Chapter 15 deals with music recording, the following section considers the use of prerecorded music libraries and commercial music on digital disc.

Prerecorded Music Libraries

Prerecorded music libraries, like prerecorded sound-effect libraries, are convenient and less expensive alternatives to commissioning the music to be composed and recorded. Music libraries are used for commercials, promos, bumpers, and drama. They provide original music composed to evoke a wide range of human emotions and information: happiness, conflict, melancholy, liveliness, danger, the future, the eighteenth century, the Far East, the bustling city, and countless others.

CD 71 **"Sailing"**—Light jazz and other relaxed contemporary backgrounds characterize this new release, with a variety of uses from leisure activities and travel to cosmetics and fashion. The orchestrations are mostly acoustic and feature saxophone, guitar, and piano. This disc contains 17 full-length themes plus 22 broadcast edits.

CD 72 **"Hard Rock"**—From heavy metal to grunge to thrash, this disc captures the hot licks and high energy of the rock-and-roll sounds of the nineties. The 19 full-length themes range from Pearl Jam to The Red Hot Chili Peppers. 24 broadcast edits are included.

CD 73 **"Zapfile 2"**—We've packed more than 150 logos, bumpers, zaps, sweepers, percussion effects, and bulletin boards into one of the single most useful discs in any music library. Seven sections include Bulletin Boards, News, Contemporary Logos, Traditional Logos, Special Effects, Percussion, and Tags and Transitions.

CD 74 **"New Generation"**—This disc contains 17 contemporary pop music tracks for "Generation X," ranging from quasi-rap urban funk to lush, melodic guitar ballads. The 22 broadcast edits included on the disc make it perfect for fashion, cosmetics, teen culture, or any other young subject.

CD 75 **"Precision"**—The pace and urgency of today's business combine with the excitement and wonder of technology in this disc, which features 17 different full-length themes and 22 broadcast edits. Applications extend to any production that deals with today's work environment.

CD 76 **"Da Capo"**—This disc features 18 well-known classical themes orchestrated in a variety of styles, ranging from jazz combo to rock orchestra. Tracks include the slightly serious, the cool contemporary, and outright slapstick. Famous composers include Bach, Beethoven, Mozart, and Grieg. 21 broadcast edits are also included.

CD 77 **"Passport"**—Ethnic music from around the world, including the Far East, Middle East, southern Europe, Mexico, South America, and Africa. This mostly contemporary disc features many authentic and exotic instruments. It's ideal for those productions that require an instant "location" identifier. 24 broadcast edits are also included.

17-8 Example of selected contents in one CD music library

Music libraries provide music in a variety of styles and textures. Compositions are arranged for orchestras of various sizes, dance and military bands, rock and jazz groups, solo instruments, synthesizers—virtually any voicing or combination of voicings necessary to evoke an idea or emotion (see 17-8). Music cues are also subdivided by length and version. A disc may have cuts of 0:29, 0:59, 1:30, and 2:30 minutes, and tag edits, each with a full orchestral mix and just a rhythm track for underscoring an announcer. There are also entire music libraries recorded with reduced dynamic range for the sole purpose of music underscoring. The reduced dynamic range permits music to accompany an announcement or narration without overwhelming or competing with it.

Avoiding the "Canned" Music Sound

The problems with sound quality that used to plague analog music libraries have been eliminated for the most part with digital-quality audio. Those problems resulted in the "canned" sound—

deficiencies, such as thin, raspy sound, not enough presence or brilliance, too much midrange, limited dynamic range, and so on.

Although those characteristics of canned sound have been largely eliminated in today's music libraries, you still have to be wary of another facet of the "canned" sound: stilted and mechanical performances and mediocre composing and arranging, which has nothing to do with the analog or digital format. Because music libraries vary in creative and sonic quality, listen to a demonstration disc before you buy. In addition to sound quality, good performance, and creative composing and arranging, also listen for true stereo imaging, realistic acoustics or ambience, and music that is not so invasive that it could draw attention away from the narrative.

Customized Music Libraries

Prerecorded music libraries have the same limitations as sound-effect libraries: fixed cues and times. Computer programs are available that customize music cues. They help you assemble a jingle or a sound track in a number of ways: by designating openers, finales, accents, and backgrounds to times that can be specified to tenth-of-a-second accuracy. It is also possible to choose from a variety of musical styles and describe the effect you want the music to have. The editing function breaks soundfiles into moveable blocks for positioning in any order. It may also be possible for the nonmusician to "compose" music; if assembled pieces do not fit together musically, the system may convey a warning and provide a function for smoothing transitions between blocks.

Copyrights

By law any recorded material with a copyright may not be played over the air, copied (dubbed), or used for most nonprivate purposes without permission from the licensor—that is, the company or individual(s) holding the rights to the recorded material. Broadcasters, for example, pay fees to such major licensors as Broadcast Music, Inc. (BMI) and the American Society of Composers, Authors, and Publishers (ASCAP) for the right to play commercially recorded music on the air.

The rights to music libraries, however, usually belong to the companies that distribute them. Fees are paid to these companies. There are a variety of licensing and payment options. Some libraries are buyout-based and some charge by the region, media, length of cut, or length of use.

There are three rights to consider: mechanical, synchronization, and public performance. Mechanical rights permit rerecording the music from a purchased digital disc. Synchronization rights allow the music to be put into a time relationship with a picture. Public performance rights authorize commercial use of the music.

Generally, when you buy a music library, you pay an annual set fee for it. (You may have the option of buying all or part of a collection, including discs added to the collection during the contract period.) Your right to use that library for profit or public performance is another matter. Depending on the distributor, you acquire usage rights for another fee determined either on the basis of *needle,* or *laser, drops*—the number of times you use music from any selection or any portion of a selection—or a fee that gives you unlimited usage rights for one or a number of years (see 17-9). (*Needle drop* was the term coined when music libraries were available on vinyl.) Sometimes the laser-drop fee may be applied to the buyout cost. When the buyout cost has been paid in laser-drop fees, unlimited long-term usage is granted.

If you are paying on the basis of laser drops, you must fill out a clearance form listing all the laser drops used in your production. You pay whatever fee the licensor's rate card indicates. The licensor then sends you written permission to use its music, for profit, in your production. If you use any of the same music in another production, you have to pay another laser-drop fee.

Often a production contains so many laser drops that the copyright fee is prohibitively expensive. In such cases, many licensors charge a flat rate, which has become the most common way of charging usage fees.

For those clients whose production schedules do not justify an annual blanket license, Omnimusic may be used and licensed on a laser-drop basis. The multiple laser-drop license covers the use of an unlimited number of drops within a single production.

	Non-Broadcast	*Broadcast*
Single Laser-Drop License	$ 50.00	$ 75.00

Multiple Laser-Drop License
(Fees based on total production length)

	Non-Broadcast	*Broadcast*
Production of 5 minutes or less	$ 100.00	$ 150.00
Production of 10 minutes or less	150.00	225.00
Production of 15 minutes or less	200.00	300.00
Production of 20 minutes or less	250.00	375.00
(Each additional 5 minutes)	(50.00)	(75.00)

Commercials and PSAs
(Rates are per laser drop)

	Local/Regional	*National*
Television or radio spot	$ 60.00	$ 100.00
Public service announcement	60.00	60.00

Duplication and Retail Sale Surcharges
(Retail sale rates include duplication)

	Duplication Only (per laser drop)	*Retail Sale* (per laser drop)
Up to 100 copies	no charge	no charge
Up to 1,000 copies	$ 5.00	$ 10.00
Up to 10,000 copies	10.00	25.00
Up to 50,000 copies	25.00	50.00
Up to 100,000 copies	50.00	75.00
Each additional 100,000 copies	150.00	300.00

Prices are subject to change without notice or obligation. Licenses are not valid for the use of our music in any production where the music constitutes the primary value of the production, or where the music is offered as a separate and distinct element for reuse by others, or in adult-entertainment productions.

"Broadcast" includes commercial broadcasting stations, commercial networks, and satellite and microwave networks. Productions created for company-owned networks used exclusively for non-commercial company business are considered "Non-Broadcast." "Educational" rates are available only to accredited institutions.

Multiple-use facilities, network broadcasters, cable programmers, and music wholesalers may be subject to additional license fees.

17-9 (a) Example of a laser-drop licensing rate schedule

Some organizations, such as educational institutions, small production companies, and many broadcasting stations, do not generate enough in copyright fees to make the rental of a music library worthwhile to the licensor. Therefore many licensors rent their libraries to such organizations for a lower, flat, annual rate. This clears the music for royalty-free blanket use. Such an arrangement may be renewed each year; when it terminates, most licensors require return of the library. Some Internet licensors provide royalty-free music libraries regardless of a broadcast or production facility's amount of usage. Of course, there is some fee involved in obtaining such rights.

The Omnimusic Broadcast Blanket

This annual synchronization license covers music use by radio and television broadcasters or producers, ad agencies, and others whose productions will be broadcast (including cable, microwave, satellite, etc.). Non-broadcast rights are included. New CD releases are included at no additional charge. $2,500.00

The Omnimusic Non-Broadcast Blanket

This annual synchronization license covers use by multimedia companies, corporate AV or video departments, film companies, and others producing corporate or educational communications not intended for broadcast. New CD releases are included at no additional charge. $2,000.00

The Omnimusic Educational Blanket

This annual synchronization license covers broadcast and non-broadcast use by accredited colleges, universities, and school districts. New CD releases are included at no additional charge. $1,500.00

Other Omnimusic Blankets

	Broadcast	*Non-Broadcast*	*Educational*
Omni Select 50 Blanket	$ 1,800.00	$ 1,500.00	$ 1,200.00
Omni Select 25 Blanket	$ 1,500.00	$ 1,200.00	$ 900.00
Omni Select 10 Blanket	$ 850.00	$ 750.00	$ 650.00

New CD releases are not included in the Select Blankets, but upgrades are available at any time. Ask our sales representatives for details.

Multiple-year contracts for all blanket clients are available on request.

17-9 *(continued)* **(b) Example of a blanket licensing rate schedule**

Using Music from Commercial Recordings

Using music from commercial recordings, such as CDs, SACDs, and DVDs, for underscoring should be carefully considered. It carries emotional baggage and, in theatrical film and television, it is expensive.

Familiar music tends to trigger memories associated with it, which could compete with or distract from the main information. Familiar music usually does not compel the attention on the part of the listener that unfamiliar music does, which could reduce the overall impact of the communication.

Sometimes using familiar music is justified and effective, however. For example, in a story set in the 1950s, music from that era can set the appropriate tone; or in a drama about the social upheavals caused by the Vietnam War, incorporating music from the late 1960s can have additional impact. But the decision to use familiar music should come only after careful consideration. It should not be used simply because it is an easier way to provide informational or emotional enhancement. That said, some film and TV producers are less concerned with familiar music not furthering the story line or adding to the drama than they are with its commercial potential and taking advantage of the opportunity to sell more CDs in record stores with sound tracks made up of popular or potentially popular songs.

Another problem with using familiar music, for the budget conscious, is that it usually comes from commercially released recordings, so obtaining copyright release could be costly. The copyright fee is definitely much more expensive than using library music and often higher than the cost of commissioning and recording original music.

Whatever the advantages and disadvantages of using prerecorded music for underscoring, directors generally prefer original to derivative music. It can be more carefully crafted to fulfill a production's dramatic goals.

Using Music from Sample CDs and the Internet

Sample CDs of music are available in all types of styles and instrumentations. Musical style may be hip-hop, rap, general purpose, pop rock, and so on. Samples may be of drum loops, bass and voices, funky guitar, synthesizer, keyboards, music indigenous to a particular region, and so on. A bank of samples may have several variations, such as short release, darker, and octave stacks. Rhythm samples come in a variety of *beats per minute (bpm)*.

Samples are also designed for use with particular synthesizer platforms. Accompanying manuals provide instructions for sample manipulation, which may include ways to produce alternate envelope shapes, alternate velocity curves, EQ balances, phase shifts, and stereo imaging.

A countless number of samples are also available online. As with any audio material that is downloaded, acceptable sound quality cannot be assumed. It is dependent on how the samples were produced, the data compression scheme used, and the quality of your retrieval and sound system. The convenience, and often nominal cost, of downloading data cannot be disputed but the sheer volume of audio available on the Internet means the range of sound quality is very wide. Be careful!

Music Sampling and Copyright

The issue of sampling and copyright is a thorny one, because a sample is so easy to produce and hide in a recording. Moreover, there are myriad samples available from sample libraries and the Internet.

Suppose that a production company leases a music library and in that library are portions of selections—accents, phrases, beat combinations—that are particularly suitable for sampling. The company redesigns them to make a new music cue. The new music cue sounds nothing like the work from which it was taken, and the samples used were only fractions of a second. Has copyright been violated? If so, who pays what to whom?

The letter of the law is straightforward: It is illegal to make derivative works of another person's copyrighted material without their express permission. In this example, clearing usage of a sample requires the permission of the copyright owner of the original composition (the composer or publishing company) and the owner of the copyright of the master (record company, music library, or other distributor).

There are other considerations in negotiating a sample clearance as well: the territory of your authorized use of the sample; cost of the sample; whether there will be an ongoing royalty for as long as the sample is in use; what credits are to be given to the original copyright holder; who owns the new work; and whether new permissions must be given for other uses of the sample.

Sampling has made it possible to take any recorded sound, process it, and use it for one's own purposes. The practice has become so widespread that it has created a major controversy about royalty and copyright infringement, and millions of dollars have already been awarded for such infringement.

Using the copyrighted work of others without their permission for your own financial gain, no matter how little of that material you use, is unethical and illegal. If you take it, you have to pay for it. Consider your reaction if someone took credit for and profited from material you created without sharing any of the earnings with you.

Organizing a Music Library

To better organize and more speedily retrieve the thousands of selections an audio facility may have in its music collection, database systems are available similar to those used for sound-effect collections. A user can call up a music cue by library, category, keyword, instrumentation, tempo, and version. Some computer systems allow auditioning and editing of any number of musical segments instantly.

For example, a user needs a particular music cue to last 25 seconds. The system finds, say, seven versions of that cue and plays those you wish to hear. If there are similar music cues but in varying times of 15, 33, 45, and 66 seconds, they too can be called up, auditioned, and, with some systems, edited to conform to your timing needs.

MAIN POINTS

▶ In automated dialogue replacement (ADR), also known as automatic dialogue replacement and looping, dialogue is recorded or rerecorded, depending on the outcome of the production recording or the director's aesthetic preference, or both.

▶ ADR is done in a dialogue recording studio, a relatively dry room with a screen and a microphone.

▶ ADR frees picture from sound and gives the director more flexibility and control. On the other hand, it involves re-creating a performance, which is not as natural or as authentic as the real thing.

▶ In scenes calling for background voices, called walla, loop groups are used.

▶ The two primary sources of sound effects (SFX) are prerecorded and produced.

▶ Prerecorded sound effects that can number from several dozen to several thousand are available in libraries. The major advantage of sound-effect libraries is that for relatively little cost many different, perhaps difficult-to-produce, sounds are at your fingertips. The disadvantages include the lack of control over the dynamics of the effects,

possible mismatches in ambience, and the possibility that the effects may sound canned.

▶ Sound-effect libraries (and any recorded sound) can be expanded by a variety of methods, such as varying a sound's playing speed, altering it through signal processing, playing it backward, and looping it.

▶ Producing live sound effects in the studio goes back to the days of radio drama but is commonly known as Foleying, after former film soundman Jack Foley.

▶ The keys to creating a sound effect are analyzing its sonic characteristics and then finding a sound source that contains similar qualities, whatever it may be.

▶ The capacitor microphone is most frequently used in recording Foley effects because of its ability to "hear" subtleties and capture transients. Tube-type capacitors help smooth transients and warm digitally recorded effects.

▶ A critical aspect of Foley recording is making sure that the effects sound integrated and do not seem to be outside, or on top of, the sound track.

▶ Some directors shun using studio-created effects, preferring to capture authentic sounds either as they occur on the set during production or by recording them separately in the field, or both.

▶ Sound effects can also be generated electronically with synthesizers and computers and by employing MIDI—an approach called electronic Foley. A synthesizer is an audio instrument that uses sound generators to create waveforms. Computer sound effects can be generated from preprogrammed software or software that allows sounds to be produced from scratch.

▶ An important sound-shaping capability of many synthesizers and computer software programs is sampling, a process whereby a section of digital audio representing a sonic event, acoustic or electroacoustic, can be signal-processed into a different sound or expanded to serve as the basis for a longer sonic creation.

▶ In recording samples it is important to take your time and record them with the highest fidelity; if a sample has to be rerecorded, it might be difficult to reconstruct the same sonic and performance situation.

- ▶ Sound-effect collections can be organized into databases to facilitate cataloging, locating, and auditioning them.

- ▶ Music for productions can be obtained in three ways: (1) by having it composed and recorded for a particular piece; (2) by choosing it from a prerecorded music library; or (3) by selecting it from a commercial music recording.

- ▶ Prerecorded music libraries provide a relatively inexpensive way to use original music to underscore the ideas and emotions in a script.

- ▶ Most recordings are copyrighted and may not be used unless a fee is paid to the licensor. In the case of music libraries, the fee is charged on a flat-rate use or is based on the number of needle, or laser, drops in a production.

- ▶ Sampling has made it possible to take any recorded sound, including copyrighted material, process it, and use it for one's own purposes. Using any copyrighted material without permission is illegal.

- ▶ Be wary of downloading samples, or any audio material for that matter, from the Internet. Acceptable sound quality cannot be assumed.

- ▶ Like sound libraries, music libraries can be organized into databases to facilitate cataloging, locating, and auditioning them.

18

Editing

The art of editing requires the ability to see a whole and build toward it while it is still in parts. It calls for a good "ear," coordination, and sensitivity to the aesthetics of sound. Yet with these abilities, the editor seldom gets recognition, except professionally; an effective edit does not call attention to itself. Hence the audience is usually not aware of it.

There are several reasons for editing. Program segments may need to be rearranged, shortened, or cut out altogether. Directors commonly record elements of a program out of sequence; editing makes this possible. It also makes it possible to transpose parts of words; "recompose" music; change the character of a sound effect; improve the quality of dialogue; take out noises such as clicks and pops; eliminate mistakes, long pauses, coughing, "ahs," "ers," "ums," and other awkwardness; record a segment several times and choose the best parts of each take; change the relationship of characters in a drama; create the pace; establish timing; and even redirect an entire story line.

EDITING METHODS

Most editing today is accomplished digitally using the nonlinear method. *Nonlinear editing* allows the assembly of disk-based material in or out of sequence, taken from any part of a recording, and placed in any other part of the recording almost instantly, at the touch of a few buttons. It is possible to audition the edit at any stage in the procedure, adjust levels, add signal processing, and restore any change in the edited material to its original waveform at any time, quickly and seamlessly—all without endangering the master audio. Still another advantage of disk-based editing is the ability to see the waveform of the sound being edited, thereby making it much easier to deal with sustained sounds having no attack, such as vowels and legato strings (see 18-6).

The term *random-access editing* is often used synonymously with *nonlinear editing*. Of course, all editing, nonlinear and linear, is random access. You access a sound in one part of a recording, then you go to another sound in another part of the recording, and so on. What is usually meant by *random access* when it applies to nonlinear editing is quick access to randomly selected points in a recording. This is not to quibble with terminology but to clarify more precisely what nonlinear editing is.

In *linear editing*, the procedure used with tape and magnetic film, audio is edited successively by taking one section at a time from one part of a recording and either physically *cutting and splicing* it to another part or *electronically editing* it in one of two ways: by punching in or transferring—*dubbing*—the audio from one recorder to another. The material may be edited sequentially or inserted at a particular point in the tape.

Linear editing is much slower, more cumbersome, and far less flexible than nonlinear editing and it lacks the formidable power of computer processing and data storage. Even though a significant amount of recording today is still done using tape and magnetic film, the audio is usually transferred to hard disk for editing. Hence, cut-and-splice editing has become obsolete. Linear editing electronically is still practiced to some extent, however, and therefore warrants some coverage here.

LINEAR ELECTRONIC EDITING

Electronic editing of audiotape is accomplished using one or two tape recorders. When it is necessary to insert material only by punching in, one tape recorder will do. *Insert editing* replaces a particular segment on a tape without altering the other recorded material and can also be accomplished using two recorders. *Assemble editing*, dubbing each program segment from a "master" to a "slave" tape in sequential order, requires two machines.

Punching In

If something goes wrong during a take in a recording session and there is no extra tape track to try recording again, there is not enough time, or another take would not improve the overall performance, rerecording just the subpar section is possible by an insert-editing technique called *punching in*—rerecording any portion of any multitrack tape without affecting the rest of the recording.

Punching in is done by putting the recorded tracks into **Sel Sync** (a trademarked term, short for *selective synchronization*); playing them back to the performer(s) through headphones; and, when it is time to rerecord over the problem portion of a track, switching that track to *record*. After the appropriate section has been rerecorded, the track can be taken out of record mode manually either by stopping the machine or by switching the track back into Sel Sync or play mode; with modern tape recorders, these functions can be handled automatically.

Punching in is a clean way to edit electronically. It is quick and usually leaves no extraneous sound pulses on the tape. Although time code helps considerably in hitting the cue points precisely, the timing has to be perfect to avoid erasing good material. Remember too that levels must match between punched-in and retained material, unless the intention is otherwise.

Punching in can also be used to erase material. But if the material is brief, such as a click or pop, timing and operational functions must be precise and coordinated to avoid erasing wanted material.

Automatically Controlled Electronic Editing

With electronic editing using two or more recorders, the tape recorder you dub from—called the *master*—contains the original material; and when the recorders are synchronized, the master also controls the tape recorder(s) you are dubbing to—called the *slave(s)*. Synchronizers lock the transports of the master and slave recorders, allowing automatic control of the editing functions (see Chapter 8). Although synchronizers vary in sophistication and performance features, most carry out the same basic operations. They direct: (1) the operations of the master and slave machines, (2) the place where the edit points punch in and out, (3) the preroll starting point, and (4) preroll, forward, and reverse speeds. They also enable assemble and insert edits.

Given the many advantages of hard disk-editing, it is reasonable to ask why one would use electronic editing. In classical music, for example, 48 or more tracks may be recorded, and some producers find it easier to do tape-to-tape editing, to say nothing of locating a computer-based editing system that can successfully handle such an editing demand. When modular digital multitrack recorders are involved, it is often more convenient to do electronic editing, because the units are linked and can run synchronously (see Chapter 7). In news, where time is of the essence, it is often faster to

edit the taped material electronically than to spend time transferring it to hard disk and then back to tape again, assuming tape is the playback medium for broadcast.

EDIT DECISION LIST

An essential part of editing is the *edit decision list (EDL)*. This step-by-step list, generated during editing, contains the edit-in and edit-out points of a shot or audio segment, the nature of the transitions, the duration of the edit, and, if needed, the source reel numbers or addresses. The format of an EDL may be charted in whatever arrangement is most functional to a production and editing system (see Figure 18-1). Coding is usually in time code, but with film it can also be in film frame numbers. EDLs are computer-generated but can be handwritten if need be.

Because an EDL is produced at the outset of editing, it serves as the guide to subsequent editing sessions, during which it is revised and refined until final editing. By keeping an accurate record of all editing events, the EDL is indispensable both for control and as a timesaver.

No.	Reel	Source	Type	A time in	A time out	Comment	Cue name	Track	Time in	Time out
0			C			In court with the defense	Scene 1	0		
2	012	4	C	07:00:10:24:20	07:01:22:05:16		fill	4	02:00:00:03:40	02:00:00:28:24
3	008	4	C	07:00:10:24:20	07:01:22:05:16		fill	4	02:00:00:28:20	02:00:01:02:76
2	006	1	C	06:12:24:10:00	06:12:30:14:00			1	02:00:01:12:00	02:00:01:25:62
3	006	2	C	06:12:24:10:00	06:12:30:14:00			2	02:00:01:12:00	02:00:01:25:62
3	006	1	C	06:07:08:18:00	06:07:12:00:00			1	02:00:01:25:62	02:00:02:09:04
4	006	1	C	06:06:12:22:00	06:06:22:12:00			1	02:00:02:09:44	02:00:02:23:26
5	006	1	C	06:24:10:23:00	06:24:15:00:00			1	02:00:02:23:26	02:00:03:07:08
9	004	4	C	07:00:15:04:40	07:00:43:09:36	If Mr. Kipner wishes to	Lawyer	4	02:00:06:16:00	02:00:16:01:48
7	020	3	C	07:00:24:02:00	07:00:48:25:36	Sustained, ...	judge	3	02:00:14:04:20	02:00:30:15:36
11	028	5	C	07:00:38:14:60	07:00:58:23:16		mvmnt	5	02:00:30:15:40	02:00:38:29:00
12	000	15	C	07:00:21:00:00	07:01:55:04:76	Intro Music	7M1	15	02:00:30:17:20	02:01:44:18:14
13	016	16	C	07:00:21:00:00	07:01:55:04:76	Intro Music	7M1	16	02:00:30:17:20	02:01:44:18:14
6	013	1	C	07:00:45:26:00	07:00:58:19:36	Hi, Carolyn, where have	MIKE@	1	02:00:38:19:40	02:00:39:27:21
7	019	1	C	07:00:45:28:00	07:00:58:12:36	Mike, what happened to	Carolyne	1	02:00:38:28:60	02:00:39:24:15
8	011	1	C	07:00:45:28:00	07:00:58:29:36	Where is Brad	MIKE@	1	02:00:38:29:20	02:00:40:04:10
9	010	1	C	07:00:45:28:00	07:00:58:19:36	He disappeared from...	Carolyne	1	02:00:41:00:40	02:00:42:19:37
10	005	1	C	07:00:45:28:00	07:00:58:12:36	Oh! My god	MIKE@	1	02:00:41:05:20	02:00:42:21:26
11	031	1	C	07:00:45:26:00	07:00:58:29:36		MIKE*	1	02:00:41:05:60	02:00:42:26:50

18-1 Example of an edit decision list

NONLINEAR EDITING

Nonlinear editing allows the retrieval, assembly, and reassembly of disk-based material quickly and in any order, regardless of the material's location on the disk. Using a disk-based system for editing also affords the convenience of allowing any digital recording—from DAT, CD, DVD, MDM, and so on—to be transferred and coded (or re-coded, if necessary) in the process. Even audio from analog tape can be dubbed to hard disk, which both digitizes the signal and facilitates its coding. In performing such transfers, however, it is critical to make sure that when frame rates are involved between the input source and the hard-disk system they are compatible (see Chapter 8). Once editing, and often mixing, is completed at the computer, the audio is transferred back to its mastering or distribution medium.

Several different types of disk-based editing systems are on the market. Most are multitrack and multipurpose—capable of not only editing, but of recording, digital signal processing, and MIDI. They use either PC or Macintosh platforms or their own proprietary hardware/software interface.

Editing systems may be either block editors or waveform editors, or some combination of the two. A *block editor* manipulates the beginning and end points of a virtual segment within an audio file without changing the content of that disk file. Block editors are so called because all segments related to a particular track are displayed as blocks of information and handled as such. In some systems a graphic waveform is shown within the block. A *waveform editor* processes samples of audio, making changes directly to the disk files. It usually allows more surgical editing of sound files, even to the extent of creating samples (see "Sampling" in Chapter 17).

The following section is a distillation of the basic functions found in most hard-disk editing systems. It is intended to give you an operational overview of nonlinear editing. Although all the terms are explained, some are more common than others. In some cases, their familiarity may depend on your knowledge of a particular editing system.

Overview of Hard-Disk Nonlinear Editing

In a hard-disk editing system, audio that is encoded onto the disk takes the form of a *soundfile*. The soundfile contains information about the sound such as amplitude and duration. When the soundfile is opened, that information is displayed on the monitor, usually within the overall features of the edit screen (see 18-2).

The waveform displays the profile of a sound's amplitude over time. By being able to "see" a sound, it is easy to spot its dynamics (see 18-3). It is also possible to see greater detail in a waveform by zooming in, a feature that facilitates extremely precise editing (see 18-4). Once the soundfile is retrieved and its waveform is displayed, it can be auditioned to determine which of its sections is to be defined for editing.

As a sound is played, a play cursor, or playbar, scrolls the waveform, enabling the editor to see precisely the part and shape of the sound that is playing at any given moment. When the soundfile is longer than the screen can display, as the scroll moves to the end of the visible waveform, approaching the off-screen data, the screen is either redrawn, or *refreshed,* showing the entire updated waveform, or it continues scrolling to the end of the track.

When the editor determines the part of the sound to be edited, the segment is highlighted in what is known as a *defined region.* Once a region is defined, the selected edit is performed only in that section of the waveform (see 18-4). The region can be cut from the waveform display or moved and/ or copied to another part of the waveform or to another waveform. It can also be inverted, changed in level, envelope, frequency, and so on, up to the limits of the system.

A *marker* or *identification flag* can be placed anywhere in the waveform to facilitate jumping the play cursor at will to the desired marker points. The marker can be a graphic identifier using a number, a letter, or text (see 18-2).

Anytime in the editing process, the soundfile can be auditioned in a number of ways: from beginning

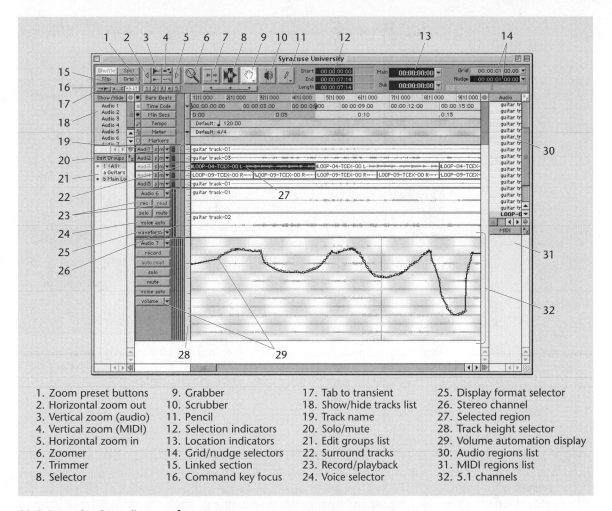

18-2 Example of an edit screen*

1. Zoom preset buttons
2. Horizontal zoom out
3. Vertical zoom (audio)
4. Vertical zoom (MIDI)
5. Horizontal zoom in
6. Zoomer
7. Trimmer
8. Selector
9. Grabber
10. Scrubber
11. Pencil
12. Selection indicators
13. Location indicators
14. Grid/nudge selectors
15. Linked section
16. Command key focus
17. Tab to transient
18. Show/hide tracks list
19. Track name
20. Solo/mute
21. Edit groups list
22. Surround tracks
23. Record/playback
24. Voice selector
25. Display format selector
26. Stereo channel
27. Selected region
28. Track height selector
29. Volume automation display
30. Audio regions list
31. MIDI regions list
32. 5.1 channels

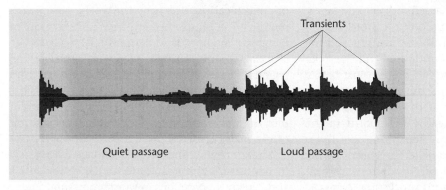

18-3 Dynamics of a waveform

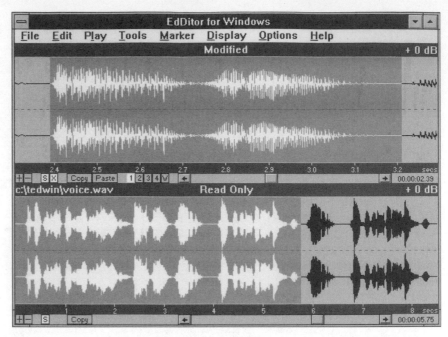

18-4 Zoom function. The section from 2.4 seconds to 3.2 seconds in the Read Only soundfile is detailed in the Modified window. The lighter sections are the *defined regions,* that is, the part of the waveforms selected for editing. The zoomed section is a "Harrumph" that interrupted a sentence in a speech.

to end, from the defined region, from marker to marker, and at increased or decreased speed in either direction. This latter operation is called scrubbing.

Scrubbing lets you move, or rock, the play cursor through the defined region at any speed and listen to the section being scrubbed at the same time. With scrubbing you can audibly and visibly locate the in- and out-points of a defined region.

Suppose you want to pinpoint a chord located in one section of a soundfile and use the same chord at the end of the soundfile to end the song. By moving the play cursor to an area just before the chord, you can slowly scrub the area until you find the precise location at the beginning of the first sound. This will be the first point in the defined region. Continue scrubbing until you locate the precise end point of the chord's decay and mark it as the end of the defined region. Then, as you would in word processing, copy the defined region and paste it at the proper point near the end of the scene.

Some operations in nonlinear editing are similar to those in word processing, such as when you delete a word entirely or cut or copy it from one part of a sentence and paste it elsewhere in the same sentence or into another sentence. This is known as *cutting and pasting.* Once a region is defined, the *Cut* command removes it from its original location and copies it to the computer's memory for temporary storage. This section of computer memory is sometimes referred to as the *clipboard.* Using the *Copy* command, the defined region is added to the clipboard but is not cut from its original position. The *Paste* command copies the defined region from the clipboard and inserts it into the waveform immediately after the position of the play cursor.

There are also Shuffle and Replace commands in nonlinear editing that are similar to the Insert and Typeover operations in word processing. *Shuffle* moves the audio that originally followed the play cursor to a point immediately following the newly inserted segment. *Replace* overwrites the audio immediately following the play cursor.

Example of an Edit Screen

It may be useful to outline the functions of the edit screen in Figure 18-2 to give you an idea of one system's approach. (See Chapter 7 for the Mix and Transport windows in the system shown in 18-2.)

Mode Buttons

Shuffle Mode In this mode the defined regions "snap" to other regions like magnets, with no gap or overlap between them.

Slip Mode In this mode a defined region can be moved freely with spaces preceding or following it, or it can overlap a portion of another region.

Spot Mode In this mode a defined region can be placed into a specific time code location by simply clicking it with the grabber (see "Grabber" later in this section).

Grid Mode In this mode a defined region can be automatically lined up at a precise interval. For example, in a music recording, if the nudge/grid units selector has been set to quarter-note increments, dragging a defined region to a new location in a track will cause it to snap to the nearest quarter-note location.

Display Scale Arrows

Display scale arrows allow adjustment of the track view. The *up arrow* expands the waveform view upward, making the waveform taller. The *down arrow* performs the opposite function. The *right arrow* expands the track to the right. The *left arrow* zooms out from the waveform, compressing the track view to show more of its duration.

Cursor Control Keys

Zoomer This tool magnifies the portion of the track you wish to view.

Scrubber This tool locates a precise point in the track by moving, or "rocking," the cursor through it at a speed that is manually controlled.

Trimmer This tool trims a defined region by shortening or expanding it to a desired length.

Selector This tool selects the defined region for editing.

Grabber This tool moves a defined region to a new track location. The grabber is used in conjunction with the four mode buttons.

Start/End/Length Buttons, Current Position Indicators, and Current Time Display

The *start box* gives the start point of the current selection. The *end box* gives the end point of current selection. The *length box* gives the duration of the current selection. The *data indicator boxes* can be displayed in time code, minutes and seconds, bars and beats, or feet and frames.

The current time display indicates the current point of the play cursor in a track.

Nudge/Grid Units Selector

This menu selects the value of the grid mode and defines the amount that a defined region can be nudged, forward or backward, into place on a track—for example, milliseconds in time code; quarter-note or eighth-note in bars and beats; and quarter-frame or sub-frame in feet and frames.

In addition to the edit screen, there is the standard Edit menu found in word processing, except in hard-disk editing systems, of course, the Edit commands such as Cut, Copy, Paste, Delete, and so on are applied to the audio material on a track.

Editing Example

Let's go through a short editing procedure with a specific example, using the edit screen in Figure 18-2. The edit example in Figure 18-5 is guitar strums. The peaks in the waveform are where the volume goes up, and the valleys are where the volume goes down. Different types of

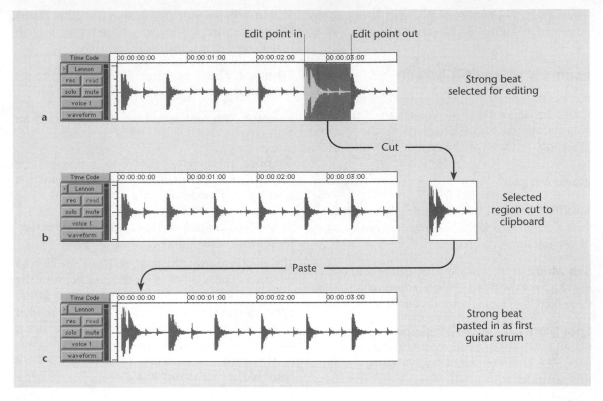

18-5 Editing example. Guitar strums must be edited to move the fifth beat to the first by (a) selecting the area to edit, (b) cutting it to the clipboard, and (c) pasting it into the first position.

sounds produce different types of waveforms. Vowel sounds in speech and wind sounds, for example, produce waveforms with less pronounced peaks and valleys, because they have softer attacks and longer decays (see 18-6).

Notice that the accents in the fifth beat, which begins at roughly 02:45, are played more strongly compared with the accents in the previous four beats. The challenge is to move this stronger strum from the fifth beat to the first and still maintain

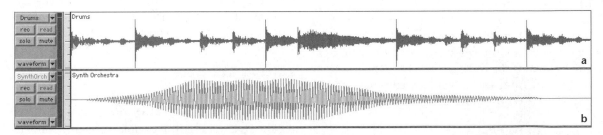

18-6 Waveforms showing percussive and sustained sounds. Editing percussive sounds (a) is easier than editing sustained sounds (b), because percussives usually have distinct breaks in the audio.

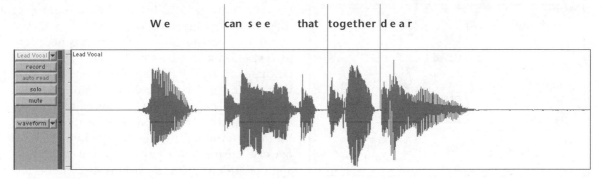

18-7 Editing before the dynamic. The best places to edit in this example are just before the hard consonants in the words "can," "together," and "dear."

the 4/4 time. Whenever possible, define a region precisely before a volume peak and end it immediately before another volume peak. In this case, that would be from the instant before the fifth beat begins, at about 02:45, to the tail end of the beat sequence at what would be about 04:00.

The editing procedure would be as follows: Scrub the region to be edited until you are sure of the in and out edit points. If necessary, use the zoomer for a more precise look at the in- and out-points. These points can be verified using the current position indicator. Click on the selector and drag the cursor from the in- to the out-point, thereby defining the region to be edited. Once defined, clicking on the Edit menu Cut command removes the edit and places it on the clipboard.

To replace the edited region at the beginning of the track, position the cursor there and click on the Edit menu Paste command. Another method of making the move is to select the shuffle mode, assuming the edit has to snap to another region, and use the grabber to actually move the defined region. If placement of the edit is critical to maintaining the beat, the grid mode may be the one to use.

Editing Tips

As with any creative activity, there are about as many approaches as there are players. From the various techniques used in hard-disk editing, the following are a few generally accepted guidelines.

▨ It is physically easier and sonically cleaner to select the in and out edit points at silent spots in the track.

▨ If there is no silent spot, listen and look for the attack of a dynamic, such as a hard consonant, percussive hit, or other transient sound. The best place to edit is just before the dynamic. The quick burst of its onset usually provides enough separation from the preceding sound (see 18-7).

▨ If it is not possible to find a silent or well-defined point in the track, start and end the edit at zero crossings. A *zero crossing* is the point where the waveform crosses the center line. It denotes a value of zero amplitude and divides the positive (upper) and negative (lower) parts of the waveform. This technique brings little unwanted audio to the edit when segments are pasted together.

▨ If the zero-crossing technique still yields too much unwanted sound at the edit point, crossfading should make the edit less noticeable. A *crossfade* fades out one segment while fading in another (see 18-8). Crossfades can vary in length from a few seconds to a few milliseconds. The audibility of a crossfade of a few milliseconds is virtually imperceptible.

▨ Avoid using time-based effects, such as reverb and delay, during recording. It makes pasting sections from different tracks difficult, because they may not match. Dry tracks are far easier to edit, because they provide a more uniform sound.

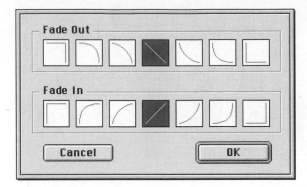

18-8 Examples of a Fades dialog. This Fades command allows seven different fade out/fade in curves from which to choose in crossfading between two adjoining regions.

Destructive and Nondestructive Editing

Still another advantage of hard-disk editing is that the edits you make can be nondestructive. *Nondestructive editing* does not alter the original soundfile regardless of what editing or signal processing you effect. **Destructive editing**, on the other hand, permanently alters the original soundfile by overwriting it.

This raises the question: Why employ destructive editing when you can process a soundfile in any way you wish and still preserve the original? There are three answers: (1) The editing program itself may be destructive, that is, changes to the files on the disk are temporary until the file is saved; (2) destructive editing may be necessary when memory is limited—it is easier to save a single soundfile than both the original and duplicate soundfiles; and (3) it's necessary when the edited soundfile has to be downloaded to another system.

ORGANIZING THE EDIT TRACKS

The approach to organizing edit tracks obviously depends on the number of individual sound tracks involved. If only a few tracks are to be edited, which may be the case in, say, an interview, the procedure is apparent: Intercut the questions and answers so the continuity is logical. But when a number of sound tracks are involved, which is likely in drama and music recording, for example, it is necessary to devise a system whereby they are organized to facilitate editing and mixing. There is no definitive way of doing this; sound editors use various approaches. The point is: Before any editing begins, catalog all the sounds and keep a running log throughout the editing process, otherwise mixups, or worse, are inevitable. List each sound and include appropriate information, such as its content; reel location; time code address; film frame number; any special instructions for editing, signal processing, or mixing; and any problems with the sound, such as noise, change in ambience, sudden dropout, a fluff in pronunciation, and so on.

In productions with dialogue, music, and sound effects, first group the sound by category (often referred to, appropriately enough, as the *DME tracks*). Then further group them in each category. For example, the dialogue tracks may be arranged by character and then divided into dialogue from the production recording and dialogue from the automated dialogue replacement (ADR). Sound effects can be categorized as Foley, ambience, and cut sound effects. A *cut sound effect*, such as a splash or car ignition being turned on, requires little adjustment in editing to remain in sync with the picture.

Another way that production sound tracks are grouped is by microphone pickup. In a multicamera program, for example, the sound pickup may be from two boom, two plant, and four audience mics, each one recorded on a separate track.

In music recording takes can be grouped by passage, for example, the first 32 measures, the final section of a movement, or a song verse. In noting each take, it saves time to indicate whether the take is worth considering for editing or should be rejected.

Once sounds have been grouped, assign them to individual tracks. In so doing decide to the extent you can those sounds that do and do not have to overlap. This not only facilitates editing but also affects a sound's placement in a track. For example, if a transition from one scene to another calls for a dissolve (gradually fading one scene out as the next scene fades in) and the accompanying music has to crossfade from one theme into another, the two different pieces of music must be placed on separate tracks. On the other hand, a cut sound effect can be placed on one track.

In editing a music selection, the best parts of several music takes are usually combined to make the composite final version, a practice called *comping*. Each take is therefore assigned to a separate track (see "Comping" later in this chapter).

DRIVE MANAGEMENT

The details involved in most productions are formidable, making accurate recordkeeping essential if chaos is to be avoided. This is especially so with computers, because of their ability to process and store such large amounts of data. Therefore drive management during production is imperative. Devise whatever system works for you, but keep track of which disk drives contain which files and what soundfiles are where. It seems like obvious advice, but too frequently the obvious is overlooked.

TECHNIQUES AND AESTHETIC CONSIDERATIONS

As the examples cited earlier suggest, editing involves more than just cutting, copying, and pasting: It establishes correlations, juxtapositions, coherence, and pace. Therefore, beyond the operational skills it takes to edit speech, sound effects, and music, there are techniques and aesthetic considerations to bear in mind.

Differences Between Editing Sound and Editing Picture

Editing picture is one-dimensional; one shot is cut, dissolved, or faded out and in to another shot. Once the transition has been made, in terms of editing, little happens until the next transition.

Editing sound is multidimensional. Sounds are layered within each shot, so editing audio becomes more than attending to transitions. In a scene an actor may be speaking to another actor with traffic outside, a clock ticking, a bath running in another room, footsteps moving back and forth, and music underscoring the action. All these elements have to be edited so that the various sonic layers are properly matched and synchronized and the perspectives are maintained.

Editing Speech

Among the considerations basic to editing speech are recognizing the sounds that make up words; cutting together similar and dissimilar sounds; handling emphasis and inflection; matching ambience (or room tone); and taking corrective action with problem tracks.

Identifying Sounds That Make Up Words

In scrubbing a sound, some sounds are easier than others to recognize. The easiest are those with striking power, such as *d, k, p,* and *t*—sounds with a pronounced attack identified sonically by a click or pop and visually by a spike in the waveform. A voiced (hard) consonant such as *v, g, z,* or *b* is formed of vocal tone as well as breath; a voiceless (soft) consonant such as *f, k, s,* or *p* is formed only of breath. The presence or absence of vocalization creates less of a spike in the waveform but is detectable when the waveform is scrubbed at a slower speed. The vowels *a, e, i, o,* and *u* are the most difficult to identify and separate, because they lack any attack and usually blend with the other sounds in a word. When vowels begin phrases in connected speech, their sound is more readily apparent when scrubbed at a slower speed.

One way to locate vowels, or any sound that is difficult to perceive, is to listen for differences in pitch or look for a change, however slight, in the waveform. Suppose you had to cut between the *o* and *i* in "anoint." In pronouncing the word, the *oi* combination is usually sounded as "oy" (as in "toy" or "boy"), with the pitch going from lower to higher. Therefore, the cut can be made just before or at the pitch change.

Sometimes sounds are run together and cannot be separated in the usual way. If the word *deem* were mispronounced "dreem," you would have to delete the *r*. But scrubbed forward, the sound of the *r* runs into the sound of the *e* and is difficult to hear clearly. The waveform might show a slight rise at the *r*, but by scrubbing the sound backward, the point where the "ee" changes to the lower-pitched and more guttural "r" may be more apparent. If cutting between sounds is still a problem, then try the crossfade technique.

Editing Similar and Dissimilar Sounds

Editing dissimilar sounds in speech is easier than editing similar sounds, because they are usually distinct and flow more naturally. Consider the sentence "Sound is both challenging and creative." If we delete *both,* the edit will be made after *is* and before *challenging*. The *s* will be pasted to the *ch* and, because they are different sounds, the rhythmic transition between *is* and *challenging* is natural and distinct.

Such is not the case with speech sounds that are similar. Suppose a speaker says, "I am, as you already know, more than happy to be here," and you want to remove *as you already know*. At first glance, after the *am* and before *more* appear to be the edit points. But this could alter natural speaking rhythm, because most people do not pronounce separately adjacent words that begin and end with the same letter, such as "am more." The tendency is to slur them together so, in effect, one *m* serves both the "a" and the "ore": "amore." (Test this by saying "and Donna" or "Joe's soda.") Therefore, one of the *m*'s should be dropped to maintain the natural sound and rhythm. Probably the best place to edit is in the word *am*, just after the "a" and before the lips come together to form the "m" sound. Cutting between the *m* and *o* in *more* would be difficult and awkward.

This example assumes that the speaker enunciated the "I" and "am" distinctly. What if the two words were run together and the beginning of the "a" sound is inaudible? So long as it does not change the speaker's style, cut the *m* in "am," making the contraction "I'm" sound more natural.

You can think of this technique as *editing on,* or *to, the same sound*. Another way to handle similar sounds that are adjacent is to *cut within a sound*. Suppose someone says, "Nothing means more to me than my muse, or, I should say, music." Obviously, the intention was to say, "Nothing means more to me than my music." A quick look at the problem points to a cut between *my* and *muse* as the simplest edit. For the sake of illustration, let's assume "my muse" is so slurred that there is no way to cut between the words. By editing within the sound common to both words—"zi"—you can maintain the natural sound and rhythm. Cut through the *s*'s in *muse* and *music,* and paste "mus" to "sic." Clearly, the "mu" sound in both words helps make this edit possible.

If that approach does not work, another would be to listen if the speaker made a "zi" sound somewhere else in the recording. Assuming inflection, ambience, and tonal quality match the "s" sound in "muse" and "music," this may be a suitable alternative.

Slurring, generally, can be a problem with non-professional speakers. When possible, slightly extending a consonant that has some sonic attack can give a word added clarity and bite.

You can also edit by taking advantage of the mind's ability to hear what it expects to hear, rather than what is actually there. For example, if you continually repeat the word "tress"—the old name for a lock of hair—other words start to appear, such as "stress" and "rest," and even though there is no "d" sound, you also hear "dress" and "stressed." Suppose a speaker says, "products and," but slurs the two words so there is no space between them and it comes out "productsand." The audio cue must end on the word "products." If there is not another usable "s" sound to edit in, by taking, say, a final "f" sound from a word like "belief," the edit will work. The reason is that both the "s" and "f" sounds are produced in the same way, by forcing air through a constricted mouth and teeth (see "Changing Words" later in this chapter). This technique was developed years ago by audio pioneer Tony Schwartz, who called it *mnemonic editing.*

Emphasis and Inflection

Another common problem for the sound editor is dealing with emphasis and inflection. Suppose the speaker says, "How are you?" with the emphasis on "you" to express concern. For some reason the "you" is garbled, and without this word it is not possible to use the phrase. If it is unimportant, there is no problem; but if it has to be kept, there are three alternatives: (1) ask the person to deliver the line again, which may be impractical if not impossible; (2) go through the recording to hear whether the person said "you" elsewhere with the same or almost the same inflection; or (3) construct the word from similar sounds the speaker uttered.

To construct the word, you would have to listen for a "yoo" sound. Perhaps, with luck, the speaker may have said the word "unique," "unusual," or "continue." The "yoo" sound is part of each word, and if the emphasis, audio level, and ambience match, one of these "yoo's" may suffice.

As for inflection, suppose two characters exchange these lines:

> Character 1: Does it have to be that way? It doesn't have to.
> Character 2: I just don't know.
> Character 1: Well, it shouldn't have to be that way.

The director decides that character 1 should not ask a question first but make a definite statement: "It doesn't have to be that way." Character 1 has already said, "It doesn't," so we need a "have to be that way." Character 1 says "have to" three times. To take it from character 1's question and add "be that way" would mismatch the intended inflection and keep the statement a question—and an awkward one. To take the second "have to" would also sound unnatural because the *to* would probably be pronounced "tu." The third *to* would most likely be pronounced "tə," which is more natural. So the final edit would butt the "It doesn't" from character 1's first statement and the "have to be that way" from character 1's second statement.

Ambience

Ambience is background sound. Other terms used synonymously are **room tone** and **presence**. The British call it **atmos**, short for *atmosphere*. Some people draw a distinction between these terms: *ambience* being any background sound that is part of a recording or has been added in postproduction; and *room tone* or *presence* being background sound recorded during actual production to provide the sound editor with the material to assemble sonically consistent backgrounds.

Editing speech recorded in different acoustic environments requires not only maintaining continuity of content but also matching the background sounds. For example, in the sentence "Good evening [breath] [cough] [breath], ladies and gentlemen," the cuts should be made after the first breath and before "ladies." Why not cut after "evening" and before the second breath? A breath would still be there to preserve the rhythm. Does it matter which breath we use?

The difference is in the ambient sounds of the two breaths. For one thing, the cough is percussive whereas "evening" is not. Thus the reverberation after the first breath sounds different from the reverberation after the second breath. If "evening" were pasted to the breath after the cough, it would sound unnatural; the ambience does not match.

In editing two statements from the same speech when one was delivered over applause and the other over silence, or when one was delivered in a room full of people and the other was delivered after most of the audience had left, the edit will be obvious unless something is done to match the different backgrounds.

One technique used to make the transition from one statement/background to the other is by diverting the listeners' attention. In the second of the preceding examples, if the ambience during one statement was quiet when the room was filled with people, and the ambience during the second statement was reflectant when the room was almost empty, you could try to locate in the recording a cough, a murmur, someone accidentally hitting the microphone, or some other distraction. Paste the distractor between the two statements (the distractor would also contain some room background) so attention momentarily is called to it instead of to the obvious change in background sound.

Another technique used to match backgrounds is to mix one background with another to even them out. This assumes that they were recorded "in the clear" before or after the event, which, by the way, should be standard procedure.

Still another approach that works well in dialogue editing is the *backfill technique.* Assume that a scene cuts from a close-up (CU) of character 1 to a CU of character 2, then back to a CU of character 1, with a noticeable change in background sound in the second CU. Say the drone of a plane, audible in shots 1 and 3, drops out in shot 2. The in-and-out effect of the edit will draw attention to the change in sound.

To remedy this problem, you could go through the dialogue tracks until you find the same sound with no one talking. Use time compression or expansion so that it conforms to the length of shot 2. Take a modulated section of a soundfile and paste it to the beginning and end of the noise track for shot 2 so that the total track length equals that of the three shots. Take the original dialogue track containing the background sound and paste an unmodulated section of a track the exact length of shot 2 between shots 1 and 3. Paste a third "strip" of unmodulated track for shot 1, the dialogue without the background sound for shot 2, and blank track for shot 3. Then mix all three tracks with picture so that the same background sound is continued through the scene (see 18-9).

If there are rhythmic sounds in the background, such as a motor or a clock, take care to preserve these rhythms when editing. You may need a *chug*

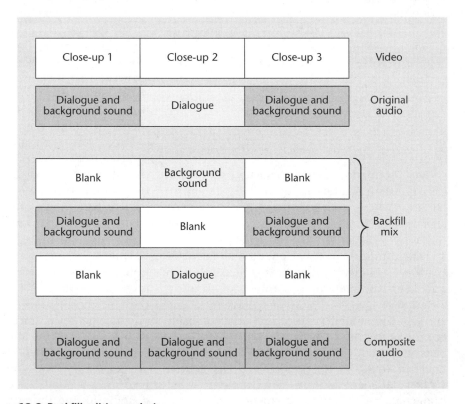

18-9 Backfill editing technique

or a *tick* from another part of the recording to prevent any noticeable break in the background rhythm or, if it is possible, loop the sound (looping is address later in this discussion). Again, try to record the background sound separately to provide flexibility in editing.

A technique frequently used to smooth a potentially awkward transition between two ambiences is to have the sound and picture cut at slightly different places in the shot change. For example, a man and woman in two different rooms (say, a bathroom and an adjoining bedroom) are talking to each other. Cutting the audio and picture from the man to the woman at the same time would sound abrupt, if not jarring, given the obvious differences in ambience between the two rooms. To smooth the transitions, the shot of the man can begin slightly before the woman stops talking, and the dialogue of the woman can begin slightly before she is shown (see 18-10). This technique is referred to as *split editing* (see also Figures 18-11 and 18-25).

Another technique used to handle background sound is *looping*. When background sound, such as crowd, wind, or room tone, is continuous, particularly through lengthy scenes, running a continuous track could be unwieldy or take up unnecessary memory, or both. Selecting the automatic loop command in a hard-disk editor solves this problem. But remember: *To be effective a loop must sound continuous, not repetitive.*

In broadcasting, field reporting is so common that the audience, to some extent, has grown used to abrupt changes in background sound and levels within the same program. Nevertheless, change should be motivated and not unnecessarily jarring. With dialogue, however, audiences are more apt to be annoyed by uneven background sound. The best thing to do during the recording is to *anticipate the editing.*

Ambience is a concern not only in editing speech; it is also an important factor when editing sound effects and music. In all three domains, ambience—background sound—is usually not effective without foreground sound. The two together bring perspective, environment, and size to a scene.

Changing Words

Films shown on television often have dialogue changed to eliminate profanity or for legal reasons. Trying to match lip movements to the word changes is a challenge; too often it is obvious that they are not consistent with the words being heard. One technique to help remedy the problem is to look for labials, dentals, and fricatives, because within each group lip movements are interchangeable.

Labials—*m, b,* and *p*—you close your lips to say. Dentals—*c, d, s,* and *t*—you speak through the teeth. Fricatives—*f, v, s,* and *z*—are produced by forcing air through a constricted mouth and teeth.

Composite Dialogue

It is not unusual for a line of dialogue to be built from different takes in the production recording or from the ADR, or both. A director may prefer three words from take 4, one word from take 7, two from take 8, and a breath from take 11. These "best"

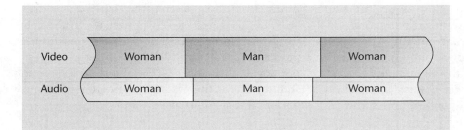

18-10 Split editing smoothes the difference in ambience by cutting sound and picture at slightly different times

takes are then combined into what becomes the optimal dialogue track. Of course, this technique assumes that the various takes, when combined, flow naturally in relation to delivery, synchronization with picture, and ambience (see also "Comping" later in this chapter).

Dialogue Processing

In processing production dialogue, four problems typically occur: (1) ring-off, (2) additive ambience, (3) defective or unusable dialogue, and (4) synchronizing dialogue to picture.

Ring-off occurs when a dialogue line ends with the ambient ring of a room, and another line begins with that ring decaying under it. This can be a problem, for example, when someone is entering a room and the ring-off is decaying under the line of the entering actor. In editing cut the ring-off and either mix it with digital reverb on a controlled basis, thereby trying to blend the ambient qualities of the two dialogue lines so that continuity is maintained underneath, or drop the ring-off and create the appropriate background values using digital reverb only. If, when cutting to the entering actor, ring-off of the old word is still perceptible under the new word, even with doctoring of the digital reverb, use a sound effect to cover the transition or the crossfade technique, with the director's concurrence, of course.

Additive ambience occurs when several actors are recorded at the same time on separate tracks of a multitrack recorder and the multiple room tones become cumulative when the tracks are mixed. To avoid additive ambience, in the editing cut from one track to another to keep the single room sound on each track. In the case of overlapping dialogue, try to close down the room sound through digital reverb. Failing that, or if too many voices overlap, making the digital reverb processing sound too unnatural, dialogue rerecording is probably the alternative.

Defective or unusable dialogue occurs when, for example, actors are body-miked and stand very close to one another or hug, covering words; or when an unwanted sound, such as clothes rustling, an object being bumped, or the voice "cracking," masks a word. If there is no time to retake a scene, or if these problems go unnoticed and reediting the material is not worth the time or expense, there are alternatives. Editing in the same syllable(s) or word(s) from another part of the track is one alternative. Another is to expand the syllable(s) or word(s) so that they overlap the defect. In both cases, ambience has to be processed so that it matches the original. If the dialogue track was produced in ADR, ambience, of course, is not a problem.

To facilitate editing dialogue, split-edit the dialogue track into two or more separate tracks. This makes it easier to extend lines that may have been cut too short during picture editing, to compress lines that are too long to sync with picture, to overlap voices, and to carry over lines from one scene to the next. "Splitting off" dialogue also makes it easier to adjust levels in the mix (see 18-11).

Synchronizing dialogue to picture is a common problem when the dialogue being edited is not from the production recording but from the ADR. What frequently happens is that when the ADR is matched against the picture, it is not always in sync with the lip and mouth movements of the actors. Therefore, ADR tracks have to be processed to be brought in sync with the tracks of production dialogue which, of course, are in picture sync. A number of tools are used to accomplish this. Two of the most common are digital time compression and expansion, which can shorten or lengthen a dialogue line without affecting its pitch, loudness, or timbre. Using the words "He does," Figures 18-12 through 18-21 illustrate the synchronization of the ADR dialogue with the production recording dialogue using time compression and expansion. The top line in the screen shot represents the production recording, and the bottom line is the ADR.

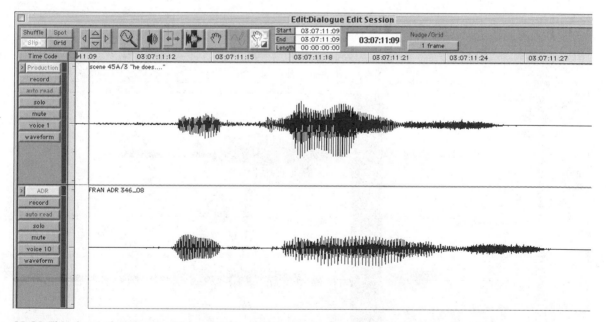

18-11 Split-editing dialogue. (a) The dialogue of characters 1 and 2 as recorded during production recording. (b) Splitting off their dialogue to facilitate overlapping the lines. (c) Splitting off their dialogue to extend a line.

18-12 This shows that the word "does" in the ADR is out of sync with the production recording

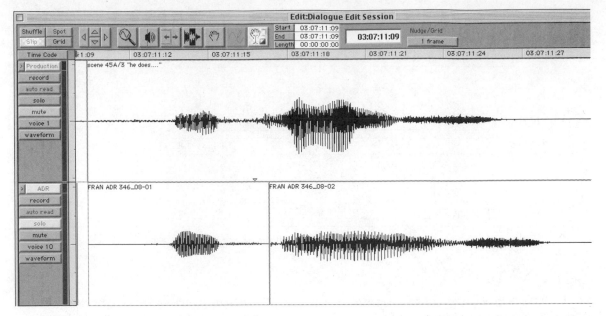

18-13 To bring the word "does" in the ADR track in sync with the production track, a sync point (▽) is put in the production track

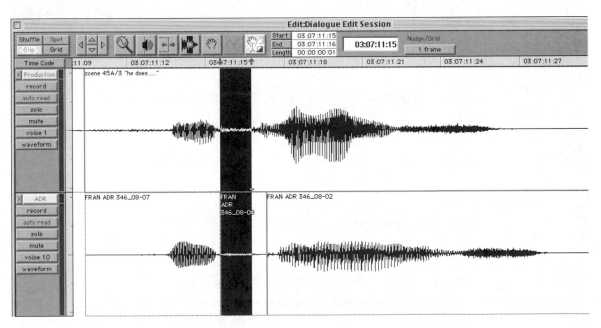

18-14 The differences in length between "he" and "does" in the production and ADR tracks

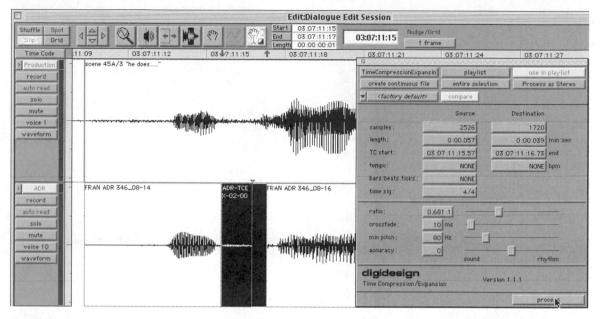

18-15 The end of the word "he" in the ADR track is shortened with the hard-disk editing system's time compression/expansion tool

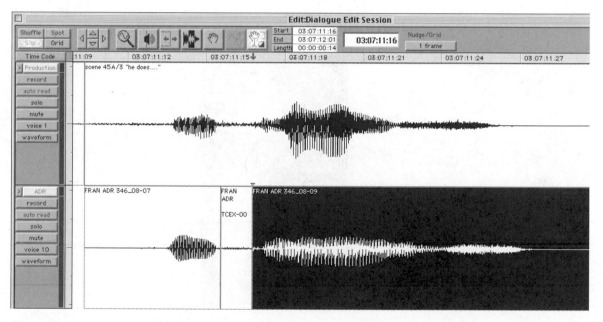

18-16 The word "does" in the ADR track is brought up and aligned with the production track

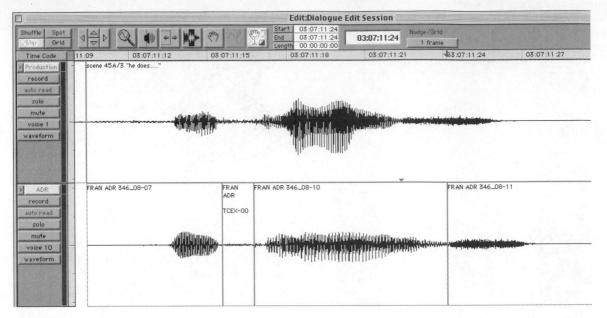

18-17 To sync the trailing "s" in the word "does" in the ADR track with the production track, a sync point (▽) is placed just before the "s" begins

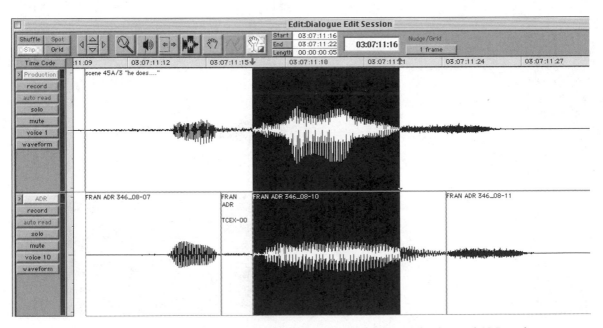

18-18 This shows the differences in length of the word "does" between the production and ADR tracks

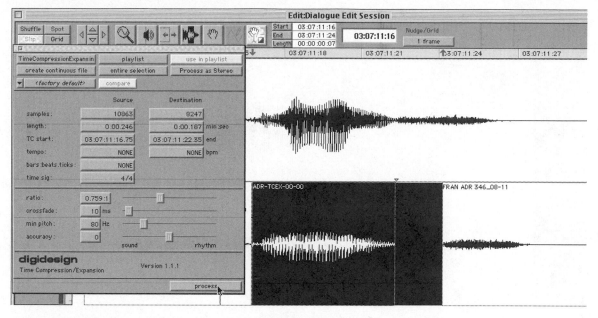

18-19 The head of the word "does" is compressed on the ADR track

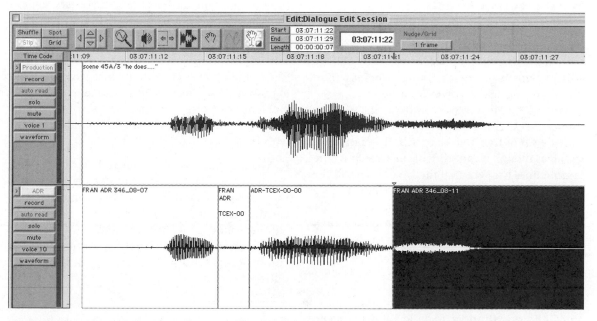

18-20 The head end of the "s" in "does" in the ADR track is brought up to sync with the production track

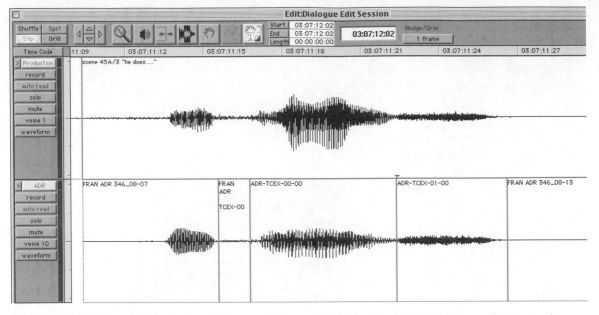

18-21 The "s" in "does" in the ADR track is expanded to match the length of the "s" in the production track

Editing Sound Effects

Many of the techniques used in dialogue editing are also used in editing sound effects. If there is an essential difference between the two, dialogue editing mostly involves fixing, whereas sound effects editing also involves creating.

One of the most basic considerations in editing sound effects is matching perspective. In editing the screech of tires to a car crash, the crash has to sound as though it came out of the screeching tires. It sometimes happens that the screech is heard close up and the crash far away, as if the sounds, although related, occurred in two different locations. The same thing happens in editing a police car or ambulance siren to the sounds of a screech and stop. The siren is heard in one perspective and the screech and stop are heard in another, because either the levels or the ambiences are different.

Another example is editing rain and wind, or wind, rain, and thunder, to build a storm sequence. Storms have various intensities, and the force of

each component should match the others; violent thunder and wind hardly go with a drizzle. Here are a few other guidelines that may prove helpful in editing sound effects:*

☑ Cut the effect as close to the first point of sound as possible. The effect may be preceded by low-level ambience or noise, the audible rush of a channel being opened, or some extraneous sound associated with the effect.

☑ Most sounds have a natural decay or tail. A sound may start at once but does not stop that way; even transient sounds have some trail-off. Cutting into the tail will be noticeable unless another sound comes in over it and "washes it out," or it is crossfaded with another sound, or if the cutoff occurs with a shot change to an entirely different scene.

---

*Some material is based on Marvin A. Kerner, *The Art of the Sound Effects Editor* (Boston: Focal Press, 1989).

☑ When editing in a sound effect that occurs off-screen, it is usually distracting to lay it over dialogue. Spot the effect between two lines of dialogue.

☑ Some sounds are difficult to sync with picture, such as horse's hooves. All four hooves cannot be synched. Generally, editors follow the first front leg and then establish the horse's rhythm.

☑ In "Editing Music to Picture" later in this chapter, it is suggested that an abrupt sound cut will not be as jarring if it is covered by an equally abrupt picture cut. Some sound-effect editors prefer to avoid such a sharp change in sound by overlapping a split second or two of background on either side of the transition.

☑ In fight scenes it is not uncommon to see an actor's head-jerk occur before the attacker's fist is close enough to the face. The choice is to match the sound of the chin sock to the head-jerk or at the point where the fist is closest to the chin. Neither choice will be completely satisfactory. The sound effect should therefore be placed on the basis of where it looks best. Also, the sound of the hits should vary. A punch to the face sounds different than a punch to the head, upper body, lower body, and so on.

Editing Music

A good music editor is usually a trained musician. This is particularly helpful in working with the composer. That said, editing music is difficult to discuss in any detail, because it involves using one language—the printed word—to explain another language—the notes, chords, rhythms, and other features of abstract, temporal sound. Although there is some similarity between editing speech and editing music, such as consideration of space, rhythm, loudness, and inflection (intonation), there are also differences. Music contains so many simultaneous sonic elements that matching sounds is more complex and slight mistakes in editing are more easily detected. In music editing you have to

consider cutting on the right accent to maintain rhythm, tonality, relative loudness, and style. If any of these elements are aurally incompatible, the edit will be obvious.

A few guidelines and techniques may be helpful. Generally, edits that heighten intensity cut together well, such as going from quiet to loud, slow to fast, or nonrhythmic to rhythmic. A transition from a seemingly formless or meandering phrase to one that is obviously structured and definite also tends to work.

Cutting to Resolution

Perhaps one of the most useful guidelines is to cut before an accent, downbeat, or resolution. Think of the final chord in a musical phrase or song. Although it resolves the music, it is the chord before it that creates the anticipation and need for resolution; it sets up the last chord. Edit on the anticipatory note—the one requiring some resolution, however brief—so that it leads naturally to the note being joined.

Preserving Tempo

Most Western music has a *time signature*—2/4 ("two-four" not "two-fourths"), 3/4, 4/4, 3/8, 6/8, and so forth. The first numeral indicates the number of beats in each measure; the second indicates the value of the note that receives each beat. For example, in 4/4 time there are four beats to a measure and each quarter-note receives a whole beat; in 3/8 time there are three beats to the measure and each eighth-note receives a beat. In editing music you have to preserve the beat, or the edit will be noticeable as a jerk or stutter in the tempo. If you cannot read music or no sheet music exists, pay close attention to the waveform of the music to discern the tempo. Listen to the beat and look for the resulting spike in the waveform.

Regardless of the number of beats in a measure, some beats are strong and some are weak. When you tap your foot to a song, it usually comes down on the strong beat, or downbeat, and lifts on the weak beat, or upbeat. A song in 3/4 time, known as waltz time, is characterized by a strong beat followed by two weak beats—*one,* two, three, *one,* two, three. Beats in 2/4 time follow a *one,* two, *one,* two, strong beat/weak beat pattern. This is a rudimentary explanation of a complex subject, to be sure. The point is that when editing tempo, you have to be aware of preserving the number of beats per measure as well as the accents. In a piece in 3/4 time, if you cut after the first beat in a measure, the beat you cut to should be a weak beat, and another weak beat should follow; if you cut after the third beat in a measure, you would cut to a strong beat with two weak beats to follow.

Repetitive Measures

One way to shorten or lengthen audio material through editing is to use repetitive measures in the music. These measures can be cut out to shorten material, which is obvious. Lengthening the audio using a hard-disk system is relatively straight-forward: Repetitive measures can be extended by copying and pasting them to the music track or by digital time expansion.

Preserving the tempo in music editing is not an isolated consideration. There are other factors, such as key signature, comping, and musical style and texture.

Key Signature

Just as most music has a time signature to regulate its tempo, it also has a key signature—E major or B minor, for example—that determines its overall tonality. Some keys are compatible; when you change from one to the other, it sounds natural or "in tune" (see 18-22). Other keys are not, and pasting them together is jarring or sounds "out of tune," like the editing in some of the album offers on TV. Unless it is for effect, or if the picture justifies the change (discussed later in this chapter), edited music should sound consonant so as not to be noticed. Another way to cover a bad key change in an edit is with pitch shifting. Usually, it is easier to

Music in this key will segue with →	First choice	Second choice	Third choice	Fourth choice
A	A	D	E	F#/G♭ minor
A# (B♭)	A# (B♭)	D# (E♭)	F	G minor
B	B	E	F#	G#/A♭ minor
C	C	F	G	A minor
C# (D♭)	C# (D♭)	F# (G)	G# (A♭)	A#/B♭ minor
D	D	G	A	B minor
D# (E♭)	D# (E)	G# (A)	A# (B♭)	C minor
E	E	A	B	C#/D♭ minor
F	F	B♭	C	D minor
F# (G♭)	F# (G♭)	B	C# (D♭)	D#/E♭ minor
G	G	C	D	E minor
G# (A♭)	G# (A♭)	C# (D♭)	D# (E♭)	F minor

18-22 Compatible or consonant music keys

try bringing one of the offending keys into musical compatibility with the other key than it is to look for a sonic compromise between the two. Using an attention-grabber in the dialogue such as a cough or a distracting sound effect can also cover an unmusical edit, but consider this approach only when there is no alternative.

Comping

Comping takes the best part(s) of each recorded track and combines them into a composite final version. In theory comping music seems straightforward: Edit together all the best takes of every note, phrase, section, lyric, or whatever. In practice, however, that approach often does not work because, overall, the music may lack coherence, sound too mechanical, or result in a part from one take not making sense when played next to a part from another take. Maintaining perspective is critical if comping is to be aesthetically successful. It is analogous to a painter who has to work close to a canvas on a detail but must step back to view the entire painting to determine if the detail works (see 18-23).

Style and Texture

Each type of music and musical group has a unique style and texture. This distinguishes the style of jazz from rock, or the texture of one voice from another although both may have identical registers, or one group from another although both may play the same instruments and music.

Editing from the same piece of music usually does not present a problem in matching style and texture so long as you follow the other guidelines for editing. But if the music is from different sources, matching elements can be a problem. Normally, you would not edit different styles—a piece of classical music to rock music just because they had the same tempo, or a dance band to a military band just because they were playing the same song. The differences in sound would make the edits conspicuous and distracting.

Editing Music to Picture

In editing music to picture, the audio has to have a purpose. Ordinarily, it is to complement what is being shown. But as pointed out in Chapter 11, it can also supplement or counterpoint the picture.

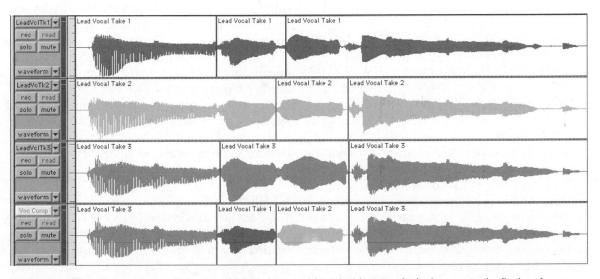

18-23 Comping. Fragments from takes 1 and 2 have been combined with most of take 3 to create the final performance.

The suggestion of editing loud, fast symphonic music to that of a soft, quiet trio is disconcerting, but if a picture cuts from a scene of violent destruction to one of desolation, the edit makes sense. In fact, it would make sense to cut from loud, jarring music to silence.

Changing from a dull tonality to a bright one, or vice versa, is not recommended generally, but if the edit is played behind a change from night to day, or day to night, the picture could justify it.

Editing two different styles, perhaps the most awkward type of change, is acceptable if the picture covers it. Cutting from Mozart to the Beatles normally offends our sensibilities, but not if the picture cuts from a shot of eighteenth-century Vienna to mid-twentieth-century London.

Another consideration in editing music to picture (or any sound for that matter) is that it not mask dialogue and sound effects (See "Mixing Versus Layering" in Chapter 19). Sometimes, however, a smooth music edit is difficult to make. In such instances a common technique is to keep the music level under another sound to mask the problem in the edit.

Transitions

Sequencing two sounds (or shots) involves creating a transition, which helps establish pace. In audio three techniques are used to make transitions: (1) segue (pronounced "seg-way") or cut, (2) crossfade, and (3) fade-out/fade-in.

Segue and Cut

Segue is a musical term that means "follow on." In radio it has come to refer to the playing of two or more recordings with no live announcing in between or live announcing over the segue. In a broader sense, segue is analogous to the term *cut* used to describe transitions in TV and film. In this context cutting from one element to another means establishing a picture or sound immediately after the previous picture or sound stops, and doing it

at once, not gradually. In discussing the effects of this particular type of transition, we will use the broader term *cut*.

The *cut* is standard language for a small related change within the same time, place, or action, such as cutting from someone waking up, to washing, to eating breakfast; or cutting from a striking match and the eruption of a flame to an alarm sounding at a fire station. Cutting creates transitions that are sharp and well defined, picking up the rhythm of sequences and giving them a certain briskness. Cutting also tightens the pace of a production, because the change from one sound (or picture) to another is quick. Due to its aesthetic value, the cut is also used for larger transitions, such as cutting from a person walking out the door in the morning to coming back in at dinnertime, or from the eruption of flames to charred remains.

The cut, in effect, butts two different sounds or groups of sounds together; in that regard it is like an edit. Like the edit, you have to give some thought to whether the effect is natural. Cutting from a fast, loud sound to one that is very slow and quiet, or vice versa, may be too abrupt; segueing two songs in keys that are incompatible may create a transition that has unwanted dissonance; or cutting from a program about folks living in poverty to a commercial for a disinfectant may raise questions of taste.

Dramas and documentaries provide more of an opportunity to make unnatural cuts, because the action or picture can cover the transition, like cutting from a furious storm to the quiet calm of its aftermath, or from a deeply moving love scene to a raucously funny bachelor party. The cut has both an informational and an aesthetic function, and either purpose justifies its use.

Crossfade

The *crossfade,* in addition to its corrective uses in editing, is used as another type of transition for smaller changes in time, locale, and action, although you can vary the length of these changes somewhat by increasing or decreasing the duration of the crossfade (see 18-24). Informationally, the crossfade accomplishes the same thing as the fade-out/fade-in, but aesthetically it is softer, more fluid, and more graceful. It also maintains, rather than breaks, rhythmic continuity and pace.

You can produce the crossfade in a number of ways, depending on the crossfade times and loudness levels of the sounds when they cross. Usually, it is more aesthetically satisfying to cross the sounds at the moment they are at full and equal loudness. This keeps audience attention "stage-center" with no loss of focus or gap in continuity, which could occur if the crossfade were made at lower levels. Crossfading at too low a level could sound like a sloppy fade-out/fade-in. These suggestions assume that the crossfade is not being used for the type of corrective purposes discussed earlier in this chapter.

Fade-Out/Fade-In

The *fade-out/fade-in* transition is used to make a clearly defined change from one time, place, and action to another. Aesthetically, it is gentler than the cut and it gives a stronger sense of finality to a scene that is ending and a sense of new possibilities to the scene that is beginning.

In TV and film, the rate of the fade-out/fade-in depends on the picture. Generally, the type of fade used provides not only an aesthetic effect but an informational one as well. A slow fade-out and fade-in with silence between suggests a complete break from one action to another. The change is rather marked, because it so obviously and deliberately stops one scene and starts another and also because it changes the pace or rhythm of the material. You could use this type of transition to bridge the time between a student going off to college as a freshman and his graduation, or to link a police car's hot pursuit of bank robbers and the thieves being booked at the police station. Faster fades suggest shorter lapses of time, smaller changes of location, or fewer events in a series of actions. They still provide a definite break in the presentation, but their quicker rate implies that less has happened.

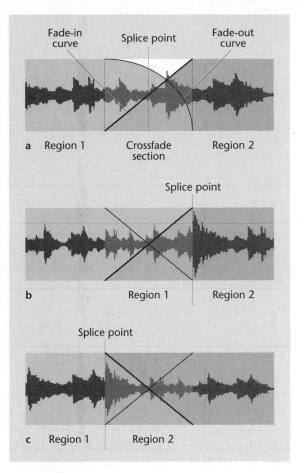

18-24 Common types of crossfades. (a) Standard, or centered, crossfade on both sides of the splice point. In this example the fade-in curve is linear and smooth, and the fade-out curve is gradual, reducing level steadily. (b) Pre-crossfade creates a crossfade before the splice point, thus maintaining the level of the beginning of region 2 instead of fading across it. Pre-crossfade is useful if there is a strong percussive downbeat or loud sound at the beginning of region 2. (c) Post-crossfade generates the crossfade after the splice point. It is useful in maintaining the level of region 1 until it ends, to keep, for example, a strong upbeat or an exclamatory sound that occurs at the end of region 1.

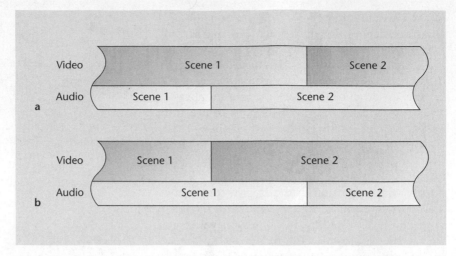

18-25 (a) Audio-leading-video split edit; (b) video-leading-audio split edit

You should not, however, consider these guidelines as prescriptive. There are no formulas for how long transitions should be relative to the scenes they bridge; it is a matter of what "feels" right.

Audio-Leading-Video and Video-Leading-Audio

Transitions involving sound and picture often do not occur at the same time for dramatic or technical reasons. When there is a picture transition, the sound transition may not be simultaneous or vice versa; the audio or video leads or lags a portion of the previous edit (see 18-25). These are split-editing techniques known as *audio-leading-video* and *video-leading-audio.*

When the sound of the incoming scene starts before the corresponding picture appears, the audio is leading the video. For example, the picture shows a boy building a model airplane as the sound of a jet fighter fades in. The picture then cuts to a shot of the grown-up boy as the pilot.

When the picture of a new scene starts before the sound of the old scene has finished, the video is leading the audio. An example: the audio of a romantic song in a scene showing a couple who has just met carries into the next scene, showing the couple dancing on their honeymoon.

Listening Fatigue

Editing for long periods of time can create *listening fatigue*—reduced ability to perceive or remember the nuances of sound. In computer editing, the problem can be compounded by eyestrain and physical discomfort (see Chapter 3). If you suffer from listening fatigue during editing, such features of sound as tempo, inflection, and tonality are continually mismatched, cuts are slightly off, and it is difficult to keep track of what should be edited to what.

One way to postpone listening fatigue is to work in a quiet acoustic environment with no predominance of midrange frequencies, because they tend to tire the listener faster. If a recording or loudspeaker system has too much midrange, equalize the monitor playback by slightly boosting the lower frequencies anywhere between 50 and 150 Hz and the frequencies above 10,000 Hz. This balances the sound and reduces its harshness and intensity. You can also attenuate the frequencies between 1,000 and 3,500 Hz, although this may reduce intelligibility. It is also important to remember to bring down playback gain after turning it up, as is often required, to hear an edit point better. Finally, take regular breaks to rest the ears and anything else that needs relaxation.

▶ Editing permits the rearranging, shortening, or deleting of elements in a production. It allows elements to be recorded out of sequence and as often as necessary.

▶ The process of editing is either linear—the edits are made successively—or nonlinear—they can be made in any order.

▶ Two ways to edit sound linearly are cutting and splicing, which has become obsolete, and electronic editing—transferring information from one tape to another or punching-in material.

▶ Electronic editing can be accomplished using one or two recorders. One recorder will do when inserting material by punching in. But to assemble-edit, dubbing each program segment from a master to a slave recording in sequential order requires two machines: one to play back and one to record and play back.

▶ In automatic electronic editing, the master and slave recorders are programmed to start and stop on cue and perform the edit.

▶ An essential part of editing is the edit decision list (EDL), a step-by-step list generated during editing of the edit-in and edit-out points of a shot or audio segment, the nature of the transitions, the duration of the edit, and, if needed, the source reel numbers or time code addresses.

▶ Nonlinear editing allows the retrieval, assembly, and reassembly of disk-based material quickly and in any order, regardless of the material's location on the disk.

▶ Audio encoded onto a hard disk takes the form of a soundfile, which is displayed in a waveform. A waveform displays the profile of a sound's amplitude over time.

▶ The waveform segment highlighted for editing is called the defined region.

▶ Scrubbing the waveform to locate an edit point precisely is similar to rocking tape in the cut-and-splice editing method.

▶ In nonlinear editing there are operations similar to those in word processing, such as cut, copy, paste, delete, insert, and typeover. The precise terms for these operations may differ among hard-disk editors.

▶ Destructive editing permanently alters the original soundfile by overwriting it. Nondestructive editing does not alter the original soundfile regardless of what editing or signal processing you effect.

▶ Before editing begins, organize the edit tracks by cataloging all the sounds and keep a running log throughout the editing process. Also employ drive management: Keep track of which disk drives contain which files and what soundfiles are where.

▶ Editing picture is one-dimensional: One shot is cut, dissolved, or faded out and in to another shot; little happens until the next transition. Editing sound is multidimensional: Sounds are layered within each shot, so editing audio becomes more than attending to transitions.

▶ Among the considerations basic to editing speech are recognizing the sounds that make up words; cutting together similar and dissimilar sounds; handling emphasis and inflection; matching ambience (or room tone); and taking corrective action with problem tracks that may suffer from such things as ring-off, additive ambience, and defective or unusable dialogue, and synchronizing dialogue to picture.

▶ A fundamental consideration in editing sound effects is to match perspective.

▶ In editing music attention must be paid to cutting to resolution, preserving tempo, repetitive measures, matching keys, comping, and matching style and texture.

▶ Generally, edits that heighten intensity will work, such as cutting from quiet to loud, nonrhythmic to rhythmic, slow to fast, formless to structured, or atonal to tonal.

▶ Comping takes the best part(s) of each recorded track and combines them into a composite final version.

▶ Mismatching of sound makes an edit obvious, unless the sound is being edited to a picture and the picture justifies the edit.

▶ Transitions used in audio editing include the segue or cut, the crossfade, and the fade-out/fade-in.

▶ Transitions involving sound and picture may employ the audio-leading-video or the video-leading-audio technique, where sound and picture transitions do not occur at the same time.

▶ Editing for long periods of time can cause listening fatigue. Take regular "ears" breaks.

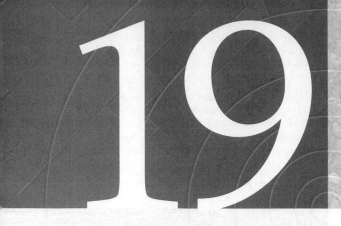

Mixing and Rerecording

Up to now, the elements that go into producing audio have been considered separately. But audiences are usually not aware of ingredients; they hear only the final product, the result of the last phases in the production process—mixing and rerecording. The procedure in getting to the final stages in production may differ among the media, but the purpose is the same: to combine the parts into a natural and integrated whole.

The term *mixing* is used generally in radio, television, and music recording to describe the process of combining individual audio tracks into two (stereo) or more (surround sound) master tracks. *Sweetening* is another popular term. In theatrical film and TV, by the time the dialogue, sound effects, and music tracks reach the rerecording stage, they have already been premixed. Hence, the term **rerecording** refers to the process of combining them into their final form—stereo or surround sound.

Regardless of terminology, mixing and rerecording have the same purposes:

▓ To enhance the sound quality and style of the existing audio tracks through signal processing and other means

▓ To balance levels

▓ To add special effects

▓ To create the acoustic space, artificially if necessary

- To position the sounds within the aural frame

- To establish aural perspective

- To maintain the sonic integrity of the audio, overall, regardless of how many sounds are heard simultaneously

MAINTAINING AESTHETIC PERSPECTIVE

The general purposes of mixing and rerecording notwithstanding, the overriding challenge is to maintain aesthetic perspective. The ears have an uncanny ability to focus on a single sound in the midst of many sounds. You may have noticed that in a room with several people talking in separate conversations at once, you can "focus" on hearing one conversation to the exclusion of the others. This capability is known as the *cocktail party effect.* In mixing and rerecording, it can be both a blessing and a curse.

Mixing and rerecording require that as you pay attention to the details in a recording, you never lose aesthetic perspective of the overall sound. That is easier said than done. Aural perception changes over time. What sounds one way at the outset of a mixing session often sounds quite another way an hour or so later, to say nothing of the listening fatigue that inevitably sets in during a long session. To make matters worse, the ear tends to get used to sounds that are heard continuously over relatively short periods of time. The effects are manifested in a few ways. In what sensory researchers call *accommodation,* the ear may fill in, or resolve, sounds that are not actually there. The ear may tune out certain sounds and, therefore, not pay attention to them. This is particulary the case when the focus is on another sound. As a mixer, because all the sounds are competing for your attention, it becomes necessary to concentrate on those that require processing at any given time. While attending to the details, it is possible to lose the perspective of how those details fit into the overall mix. The more you listen to the fine tunings, the greater the danger of drifting from the big picture.

What to do? (1) Be aware of the problem. (2) Take a checks-and-balances approach: After attending to a detail, listen to it within the context of the overall mix. (3) Seek another opinion. (4) As with any lengthy audio session, take regular and frequent "ears" breaks. When there are no union regulations in place that prescribe break times, if a client balks tactfully explain the problem of listening fatigue: that by trying to use every second of studio time just because it is paid for will reach a point of diminishing aesthetic returns.

MIXING FOR VARIOUS MEDIA

Another purpose of the mix (and rerecording) to add to those listed earlier is to keep all essential sonic information within the frequency and dynamic ranges of the medium for which it is being made. In other words, you have to take into consideration what type of delivery system will be used to reproduce the audio, because it is difficult to create one mix suitable for all systems.

Radio

In doing a mix for radio, two considerations are the frequency response of the medium—AM or FM—and the wide range of receivers the listening audience uses, from the car radio to the upscale stereo component system. Although AM radio may transmit in stereo and play music from compact discs, its frequency response is mediocre—roughly 100 to 5,000 Hz. The frequency response of FM is considerably wider, from 20 to 20,000 Hz. Therefore it would seem that mixing for AM requires care to ensure that the essential sonic information is within its narrower frequency band and that in mixing for FM there is no such problem. Both statements would be true if it were not for the broad assortment of radio receivers that vary so greatly in size and sound quality, and for the variety of listening conditions under which radio is heard. There is no way to do an optimum mix, for either AM or FM, to satisfy listeners with a boom box, a portable radio the size of a hand, or car stereos that run the gamut from mediocre to excellent and are played against engine, road, and air-conditioner noise.

The best approach is to mix using loudspeakers that are average in terms of frequency response, size, and cost and to keep the essential sonic information—speech, sound effects, and music—within the 150- to 5,000-Hz band, which most radio receivers can handle. With AM radio's limited frequency response, it often helps to compress the sound to give it more power in the low end and presence in the midrange. For FM mixes a sound check on high-quality loudspeakers is wise to make sure that the harmonics and overtones beyond 5,000 Hz are audible to the listener using a high-quality receiver.

Another factor that may influence a music mix, if not at the mixdown session then in the way it is handled for broadcast, is when a station runs a tight board. A *tight board* is radio parlance for having no dead air and playing everything at a consistent level. Because most radio stations compress and limit their output, running a tight board tends to raise the level of music with soft intros, back it off as the song builds, and then let compression and limiting do the rest. Songs ending in a fade are increased in level as the fade begins, until the music segues evenly with the next song or spot announcement.

Videotape and Television

The frequency response of analog videotape can be as wide as 40 to 15,000 Hz; the frequency response of digital audio on videotape is even wider. Moreover, conventional TV audio transmission goes to 15,000 Hz. High definition television (HDTV), which transmits digital audio, is 20 to 20,000 Hz. But in television as in radio, mixing has to conform to the limitations of the home TV receiver.

There is also the reality that TV viewing does not usually take place in a quiet, focused environment: One parent is getting the meal together, another is talking on the phone, the kids are playing. To ensure that subtle or low-level sounds are heard, it is necessary to bring the levels above the noise floor. But TV has a comparatively narrow signal-to-noise ratio, because most conventional television sets cannot play very loud without distortion.

Although digital sound on videotape does not appreciably degrade with dubbing, sound on analog videotape does. Important information (dialogue and effects as well as music) should be mixed between roughly 150 and 5,000 Hz. Boosting around 700 Hz should tighten the bass, and at around 4,000 to 5,000 Hz should enhance clarity and presence. Gentle limiting, to prevent over-modulation, and/or compressing overall sound is often a good idea, especially with digital sound, which has no headroom.

Monitor on average-type bookshelf loudspeakers most of the time. For overall referencing, occasionally switch to the big loudspeakers and small mono loudspeakers. For television, the mono loudspeaker mix is crucial, because this is what much of the TV audience still listens to. Also make sure that the quality and imaging of a surround-sound mix are suitable for reproduction of home entertainment TV systems. This requires discriminating mixing on high-quality loudspeakers.

Mixing for television and radio is different from mixing for digital disc (see the following section). Few people listen to TV and radio on decent stereos the way they do CDs and DVDs. Avoid going for a big, deep low end or for tingly, shimmery high-end sounds, because most viewers will not hear them. Make sure the essential sonic information is clear on stereo and mono loudspeakers.

For TV and also for radio, keep the stereo mix mono-compatible by not hard-panning anything to the extreme left and right. If reverb is used, make it wetter in the mix than normal, because TV transmission diminishes reverb.

The top priority in television is what is on the screen. If there is a close-up of a singer or lead guitarist, this is what the audience expects to hear front and centered; do not be afraid to exaggerate these or other featured elements. In surround sound the audio usually carried in the surround channels is supplementary to the principal audio, such as ambience, crowd sound, environmental sound effects, and so on (see "Surround Sound" later in this chapter).

Film

Dynamic range is less on an optical sound track than on videotape, particularly in 16-mm film. Although 35-mm film sound is better than 16 mm, it is still not as good as sound on videotape—analog and digital. That said, in theatrical films, with the various digital stereo formats, surround sound, and the improved theater audio systems, the sound quality of audio on film is remarkable compared with what it was not too long ago.

In mixing music for film, it may be best to do a partial mix and let the rerecording mixer make the final adjustments when dialogue and effects are added. To this end one approach is not to restrict too severely low-end and high-end roll-offs and leave some play for adjustments in processing. Another approach has been the "unisound" mix, which cuts out all sound below 100 to 200 Hz and above 5,000 to 6,000 Hz. This technique was preferred by some mixers, because there is not much work to do and there are fewer problems with rumble and hiss. With vastly improved production and reproduction technology, however, there is less concern about employing such a narrow frequency response. Typical mixes for 16-mm optical sound should be between 150 and 5,000 Hz, with a dynamic range of 15 to 20 dB.

Digital Disc

In mixing an album for compact disc, three important factors are digital edge, distortion, and total playing time of the music. There may be other considerations as well, such as applying the Red Book and Orange Book standards (see Chapter 7).

Digital edge is the overly bright sonic byproduct of the digital recording process that too often spoils the sound quality on a CD. It is usually the result of either improper miking and recording techniques (discussed in Chapter 15) or inappropriate EQ during mixing, or both. It may also be the result of poor CD mastering, but that discussion is beyond the scope of this book.

In analog sound reasonable boosts in the upper midrange and lower treble ranges may turn out to be sonically satisfactory. But due to the clarity of digital sound, the same boosts in EQ in the same ranges may result in making these frequencies overly apparent to the point of annoyance.

Distortion can be another problem in mixing digital sound. As pointed out there is no headroom in digital recording; levels have to be watched carefully. Once you reach zero-level, you have run out of headroom—there is no place to go. In analog recording, assuming the use of high-output tape, there is headroom above zero-level.

Trying to pack too much program material onto a music compact disc can create problems in mastering and reproduction. A CD can hold more than 70 minutes of data, and in today's marketplace discs sell on the basis of length as well as content. On a CD that has much more than 60 minutes of material, the spiral traces of the data track are pushed closer together, which makes laser tracking more difficult and can cause skipping.

Generally, a compact disc is mixed with one of three types of playback systems in mind: (1) a high-quality system with amplifier and loudspeakers capable of reproducing wide dynamic range and frequency response; (2) a medium-quality system capable of reproducing a fairly wide frequency response and dynamic range; or (3) a low-quality system with limited dynamic range and frequency response.

For CDs being prepared for radio airplay, another consideration is doing a radio-friendly mix. In an album mix, most important are the integrity of the song, how the song fits within the CD, and the artist's vision. What's important in doing an alternative mix for radio is making sure the CD's dynamic range and EQ are suitable for the medium and adding compression to the overall mix to make it stand out.

Music on audio DVDs and the Super Audio Compact Disc (SACD) can be qualitatively superior to music on compact disc (see Chapter 7). But here again the improved data storage and sonic fidelity can be realized only with an excellent reproduction system. It can be said, however, that the music mixed for DVD-A and SACD, in particular, assumes the audiophile as the primary market.

Multimedia

Even though digital sound has extremely wide dynamic range and most of it is mastered in 16, 20, or 24 bit, the reproducing medium remains a factor. Mixing for multimedia is like mixing for TV: You do not know what the end user has for playback.

Multimedia usually means that the product is heard (and seen) on a computer. Many computers out there still produce only 8-bit audio, which is worse than mediocre analog sound. In producing audio for multimedia, the essential information must therefore be mixed and mastered so that it can be heard within this range. Another factor is the data compression and expansion that is so much a part of computer signal processing. Even with high-end computers capable of 16-bit audio, the consideration is still the quality of the loudspeaker being used for playback. This means that audio information below 100 or 200 Hz and above 7 or 8 kHz might not be heard.

MIXING VERSUS LAYERING

Not to quibble about semantics, but *mixing* suggests a blend in which the ingredients lose their uniqueness in becoming part of the whole. Although such blending is important, in relation to a mix the term *layering* may be more to the point.

When sounds are combined, there are four essential objectives to keep in mind:

■ To establish the main and supporting sounds to create focus or point of view

■ To position the sounds to create relationships of space and distance

■ To maintain spectral balance so that the aural space is properly weighted

■ To maintain the definition of each sound without losing definition overall

These considerations come closer to the definition of layering than they do of mixing. The following discussion notwithstanding, *mixing* is the term in popular use.

Layering

Layering involves some of the most important aspects of aural communication: balance, perspective, and intelligibility. When many sounds occur at once, unless they are layered properly it could result in a loud sound drowning out a quiet sound; sounds with similar frequencies muddying one another; sounds in the same spatial position interfering with focus; and sounds that are too loud competing for attention.

Usually, when elements in a mix are muddled, it is because too many of them are sonically alike in pitch, tempo, loudness, intensity, envelope, timbre, or style, or there are too many sounds playing at once. Imagine the sound track for a gothic mystery thriller. The scene: a sinister castle on a lonely mountaintop high above a black forest, silhouetted against the dark, starless sky by flashes of lightning. You can almost hear the sound: rumbling, rolling thunder; ominous bass chords from an organ, cellos, and double basses; the low-pitched moan of the wind.

The layering seems straightforward, depending on the focus: music over wind and thunder to establish the overall scariness; wind over thunder and music to focus on the forlorn emptiness; and thunder over wind and music to center attention on the storm about to break above the haunting bleakness. But with this particular mix, setting the appropriate levels may be insufficient to communicate the effect. The sounds are so much alike—low pitched and sustained—that they may cover one another, thereby creating a combined sound that is thick and muddy, lacking clarity and definition. The frequency range, rhythm, and envelope of the sounds are too similar: low pitched, continuous, weak in attack, and long in sustain.

One way to layer them more effectively is to make the wind a bit wilder, thereby sharpening its pitch. Instead of rolling thunder, start it with a sharp crack and shorten the sustain of the rumble to separate it from any similar sustain in the music. These minor changes make each sound more distinctive, with little or no loss in the overall effect on the scene.

This technique also works in complex mixes. Take a far-flung battle scene: soldiers shouting and screaming, cannons booming, rifles and machine guns clattering, jet fighter planes diving to the attack, explosions, and intense orchestral music dramatically underscoring the action. Although there are several different elements, they are distinctive enough to be layered without losing their intelligibility.

The pitch of the cannons is lower than that of the rifles and machine guns; their firing rhythms and sound envelopes are also different. The rifles and machine guns are distinct because their pitch, rhythm, and envelope are not the same either. The explosions can be pitched lower or higher than the cannons; they also have a different sound envelope. The pitch of the jets may be within the same range as that of the rifles and machine guns, but their sustained, whining roar is the only sound of its kind in the mix. The shouting and screaming soldiers have varied rhythms, pitches, and tone colors. As for the music, its timbres, blend, and intensity are different from the other sounds. Remember too that the differences in loudness levels and positioning in a stereo or surround-sound frame will help contribute to the clarity of this mix. Appropriate signal processing is usually employed as well.

In relation to loudness and the frequency spectrum, two useful devices in maintaining intelligibility are the compressor and the equalizer. Compressing certain sounds increases flexibility in placing those sounds, because it facilitates tailoring their dynamic ranges. This is a more convenient and sonically better way to place sounds than by simply using the fader. Through modest and deft equalization, attenuating, or boosting, sounds can cut or fill holes in the aural frame, thereby also facilitating placement without affecting intelligibility.

Some scenes are so complex, however, that there are simply too many sonic elements in the SFX and music to deal with separately. In such instances try grouping them and playing no more than three or four groupings at the same time, varying levels as you go. For example, in the previous battle scene the different elements (other than the voices) could

be put into four groups: canons, guns, planes, and music. By varying levels and positioning groups in the foreground, background, side-to-side, and front-to-rear, and moving them in, out, or through the scene, you avoid the sound track's collapsing into a jumble. (The movements cannot be too sudden or frequent, however, or they will call attention to themselves and distract the audience.)

Another approach to scenes densely packed with audio effects is to use only the sounds that are needed—perhaps basing their inclusion on how the character perceives them or to counterpoint intense visual action with relatively spare sound. For example, it is opening night at the theater: There is the hubbub of the gathering audience, the last-minute preparations and hysteria backstage, and the orchestra tuning up; the star is frightfully nervous, pacing the dressing room. By dropping away all the sounds except the pacing, the star's anxiety becomes greatly heightened.

Focusing sonically on what the audience is seeing at the moment also works. In the war scene described earlier, in a tight shot of, say, the cannons booming, play to that sound. When the shot is off the cannons, back off their sound. In a wider shot with the soldiers firing their rifles in the foreground and explosions bursting in the background, have the levels of the soldiers' actions louder than the sound of the explosions.

Another reason not to play too many sounds at once, particularly loud sounds, is that if they stay constant, the effect is lost; they lose their interest. Contrast and perspective are the keys in keeping complex scenes sonically interesting.

It is also unwise to play too many loud sounds at the same time, because it is annoying. In a scene with thunderclaps, very heavy rain, a growling monster crashing through a city or countryside on the attack, kids yelling, people screaming, and cars crashing, there is no sonic relief. It is loud sound on loud sound; every moment is hard. The rerecording mix can be used to create holes in the constant loudness without diminishing intensity or fright and can provide relief from time to time throughout the sequence. For example, the rain could be used as a buffer between two loud sounds.

After a crash or scream, bring up the rain before the next loud sound hits. Or use the growl, which has low-frequency relief, to buffer two loud sounds.

Be wary of sounds that "eat up" certain frequencies. Water sounds in general and rain in particular are so high-frequency intense that they are difficult to blend into a mix, and the presence of other high-frequency sounds only exacerbates the problem. Deep, rumbly sounds like thunder present the same problem at the low end of the frequency spectrum. One means of handling such sounds is to look for ways to change their perspectives. Have the rain fall on cars, vegetation, pavement, and in puddles. Make the thunder louder or quieter as the perspective of the storm cloud changes in relation to the people in the scene.

In music recording, an ensemble often has a variety of instruments playing at once. Their blend is important to the music's structure, but not to the extent that violins become indistinguishable from cellos, or the brass drowns out the woodwinds, or a screaming electric guitar makes it difficult to hear the vocalist.

Perspective

In layering, some sounds are more important than others; the predominant one usually establishes the focus or point of view. In a commercial the announcer's voice is usually louder than any accompanying music or effects, because the main message is likely to be in the copy. In an auto-racing scene, with the sounds of speeding cars, a cheering crowd, and dramatic music defining the excitement, the dominating sound of the cars focuses on the race. The crowd and the music may be in the middleground or background, with the music under to provide the dramatic support. To establish the overall dramatic excitement of the event, the music may convey that point of view best. Therefore, the speeding cars and cheering crowd might be layered under the music as supporting elements.

In music recording, it is obvious that a vocalist should stand out from the accompaniment, or that

an ensemble should not overwhelm a solo instrument. When an ensemble plays all at once, there are foreground instruments—lead guitar in a rock group, violins in an orchestra, or piano in a jazz trio—and background instruments—rhythm guitar, bass, woodwinds, and drums. Whatever the combination of effects, establishing the main and supporting sounds is fundamental to good mixing, indeed, to good dramatic technique and musical balances. *Foreground does not mean much without background*. But because of the psychological relationship between sound and picture, perspectives between what is heard and seen do not necessarily have to match but rather complement one another. In other words, you can "cheat" in handling perspective.

For example, take a scene in which two people are talking as they walk in the countryside and stop by a tree. The shot as they are walking is a long shot (LS), which changes to a medium close-up (MCU) at the tree. Reducing the loudness in the LS to match the visual perspective could interfere with comprehension and be annoying, because the audience would have to strain to hear and the lip movements would be difficult to see. When people speak at a distance, the difficulty in seeing lip movements and the reduced volume inhibit comprehension. It may be better to ride the levels at almost full loudness and roll off low-end frequencies, because the farther away the voice, the thinner the sound. Let the picture also help establish the distance and perspective. Psychologically, the picture establishes the context of the sound. This also works in reverse.

In the close-up there must be some sonic change to be consistent with the shot change. Because the close-up does not show the countryside but does show the faces better, establish the environment by increasing ambience in the sound track. In this case, the ambience establishes the unseen space in the picture. Furthermore, by adding the ambience, the dialogue will seem more diffused. This creates a sense of change without interfering with comprehension, because the sound is louder and the actors' lip movements are easier to see.

MIXING FOR RADIO

Many of the techniques used in mixing for radio are also applicable to TV, film, music recording, and multimedia audio, and vice versa, although some techniques may be more frequently employed in one medium than another.

Voice-Over Background Music or Sound Effects

An announcement or narration is recorded and eventually mixed with other elements in a production so that it is voiced over them. In recording spot announcements such as commercials and promos, an announcer often voices-over music or effects, or both. Because the announcement is usually short, the sonic elements may be mixed at one sitting.

A typical spot may call for music to be attention-getting at the open, then faded under during the announcement, returned to the opening level when the spoken part of the announcement concludes, and then either faded out or played to its conclusion. This format is called a *donut*—fading the music after it is established to create a hole for the announcement and reestablishing the music later at its former full level.

The problem with fading music, or any sound, is that the high and low frequencies and overall ambience are faded as well, thus dulling the music. Using equalization it is possible to cut a hole (instead of fading a hole) in the music by attenuating the midrange frequencies that clash with or mask the announcer. This creates sonic room for the announcer while maintaining the music's presence, low- and high-end response, and ambience.

The procedure involves selecting the band of frequencies in the music that conflicts with the announcer's intelligibility, when they are at the same level, and attenuating the conflicting frequencies the necessary amount. When the announcer speaks, the music EQ is switched in; when the announcer is not speaking, it is switched out.

Another technique used to balance levels between an announcer and music, or between an announcer and other sounds such as crowd noise or traffic, is to feed each sound through a limiter and set one limiter to trigger the response of the other. In the case of a voice-over-music announcement, the limiter controlling the music would be set to reduce the music level to a preset point when it is triggered by the limiter controlling the announcer's sound. As soon as the announcer speaks, the limiters' actions automatically reduce the music level. When the announcer stops speaking, the announcer's limiter triggers the music's limiter to restore the music to its preset louder level. This can also be done with a limiter and a compressor. This practice has been used for years, but you have to be careful when setting the limit levels. If they are not precise, you will hear the limiters' annoying pumping action as they increase and decrease levels.

To facilitate balances between the announcer and the music bed, music libraries produced for use with spot announcements may include cuts with reduced dynamic range. Thereby giving a producer a choice of supporting music with either full or limited dynamic range.

When an announcer or narrator is mixed with background music or sound effects, the copy is the most important element. This is why the performer's voice is in the foreground. If the music or effects become as loud as, or louder than, the performer, it forces the audience to struggle to focus attention on one of the competing elements, thereby inhibiting communication. This does not mean that the music and effects must remain in the background. During a pause in the copy, the background can be increased in level or, if it is kept under the announcer, it can be varied to help accent the message, thereby providing sonic variety to heighten interest and pace. In audio production it is worthwhile to remember that *sonic variety attracts the ear*. In fact, whether it is audio or video, the human perceptual system likes change. Shifts in focus, directed by the production, hold audience attention. This is not to suggest that confused, cluttered, frenetic production is advised. Obscuring the message with production pyrotechnics is poor communication practice.

For example, instead of using the stale donut approach to production, take time to produce the spot. It makes the station sound better and the client happier.

Using Compression

Using compression as a production tool in radio is almost as common as using equalization. It enhances the spoken word by giving it clarity and power. It also helps keep speech from being overwhelmed by sound effects or music and brings it forward in the mix. With analog sound, compression facilitates recording at a hotter level, thereby reducing distortion and noise, particularly at low levels. Compressing in the digital domain improves bit processing. In an overall mix, compression adds more cohesion and balance.

Compression also has limitations: Too much of it dulls sound and makes it lifeless. It can also accentuate sibilance. Heavy compression may produce the annoying pumping sound of the compressor's action and also increase, rather than decrease, noise.

Like for most aspects of audio production, there are no prescribed rules for employing compression, but a few guidelines provide a starting point for experimentation.* It is also worth noting that it may take time to perceive the effects of compression, because they can be subtle.

■ In close-miking speech, try a compression ratio of 2:1 or 3:1 and adjust the threshold until there is a 3 or 4 dB gain reduction. Use a fast attack time and a slow release time. With this, and all of the following guidelines, use the makeup gain to restore any lost level.

■ Using a music bed, start with a 2:1 ratio and a fast attack time. Adjust the threshold until there is a 4 to 6 dB gain reduction.

---

*From Loren Alldrin, "The Joys of Compression," *Radio World,* July 21, 1999, p. 55.

■ With sound effects, which (1) may not need compression, and (2) can be considerably changed with it, experiment with a ratio range of 3:1 to 6:1. Set gain reduction at 6 dB. Use a fast attack time and a medium release time.

■ Dealing with room tone and ambience usually requires only light compression: a ratio of 1.5:1 or 2:1, 2 to 4 dB gain reduction, and fast attack and medium release times.

■ Compressing the overall mix is better processed using a low ratio, 3 to 6 dB gain reduction, a medium to medium-fast attack time, and a medium release time.

Backtiming and Deadpotting

Using prerecorded music to underscore or end a spot announcement, narrative, dialogue, or a program theme song may involve backtiming and deadpotting to ensure that it ends at the appropriate time. Prerecorded material has a fixed total time; it may be 3:13, 1:22.5, 0:11, or something else. Suppose in a commercial that the section of music used to end a spot is 18 seconds long but only the last 11 seconds of it are needed. To get the music to end when the commercial ends, assuming a 30-second spot, the music has to start 12 seconds into the commercial. Subtracting the time of an individual element from the total time of a program or program segment is known as *backtiming*.

Deadpotting, also known as *deadrolling,* refers to starting a recording with the fader turned down all the way. To get the music to end when the spot ends, begin playing the music 12 seconds after the spot begins, just do not raise the fader. The music recording will deadpot—play with no sound feeding through—until you are ready for it. At that point, fade it in; because it started at the right time, it will also end on time. And ending music is usually a more effective close than fading it out. Of course, computers and automation can handle operations automatically once the data has been entered.

MUSIC MIXDOWN

There is a common misunderstanding about the music mixdown, namely, that it is the stage in music production when everything that went wrong in the recording session is put right. No doubt this unfortunate notion has been nurtured in recording sessions that have not met expectations when producers have glibly reassured clients, "Don't worry, we can fix it in the mixdown."

The mixdown certainly is very important to the finished product, but keep its significance in perspective. The mixdown cannot change a mediocre performance into a good one, compensate for poor microphone technique, or make a sloppy recording precise. In most instances it is the quality of the recording session that determines the overall quality of the mix.

Nevertheless, the mixdown should not be taken too lightly. A good mix cannot salvage a bad recording, but a poor mix can ruin a good one.

Keeping the significance of the mixer's role in perspective is also important to the outcome of a recording. Whatever the mixer does should be music driven; *a mixer's responsibility is to serve the music,* not the other way around.

Auditioning the Rough Mix

It is poor policy to do a mix on the same day that you finish the recording. Regardless of what you may think it sounds like immediately after the session, in a day or so it will sound different. Taking some time to regain perspective and renew "ears" is essential. Therefore before beginning a mix or making any final decisions about approach, signal processing, positioning, special effects, and so on, refamiliarize yourself with the recording by auditioning it as often as needed to get a handle on what to do.

Ideas about the mix usually begin forming during recording and crystalize during mixing. However your vision develops, its outcome should be appropriate to the music. Different types of music employ different instrumentation and blends of that instrumentation. The handling of foreground, background, and side-to-side voicings vary with musical style. For example, in music with a lyric, the vocal is usually the defining element. But in heavy rock, it is often mixed as another lead "instrument" rather than in front of the accompaniment. Country music is mixed with the vocal prominent, no other instrument can distract from it. Generally, the vocal is handled in the same way in popular music, but with the tendency to give other elements in the ensemble more discernible roles.

Before doing any listening, it is vital to make sure that the controls are set to *off, zero,* or *flat* and the equipment has been checked out.

1. If tape recorders are involved, demagnetize and clean the heads and align both the heads and the recorder(s).

2. Test the monitoring system with a sound-pressure-level meter and a pink noise source to make sure the stereo and surround-sound loudspeaker distributions are what they should be. Test measurement tapes and discs are available to help with this procedure (see Bibliography).

3. Calibrate the meters in the signal path—console, recorders, signal processors, and so on. With hard-disk systems, use a meter-measuring plug-in. A signal generator with several types of noise and waveforms in the appropriate bit resolution is also very helpful in making sure no sonic anomalies are present in the hard-disk system.

In refamiliarizing yourself with the recording, try not to make any detailed adjustments. Focus on the big picture first. Set relative levels and basic panning. Before any mixing begins, it is usually obvious that in the final mix certain voicings will be louder than others and that some elements in the ensemble will be positioned toward the front, rear, left-side, and so on. These basic adjustments allow the opportunity to evaluate what you have without the clutter of additional processing. In other words, simply set the relative level and location of each voicing to achieve approximate, but satisfactory, overall loudness and positional balances.

Here is one approach:

1. Set the level of the loudest or most prominent sound first, leaving plenty of headroom on the VU meter. For example, if the loudest sound is a support voicing, such as the bass drum, set the level at –10 VU; if the sound is a prominent lead voicing, such as a vocal, set the level higher, at, say, –5 VU. Leaving headroom is important because mixing almost always involves adding level during signal processing through EQ, reverb, and so on. (As discussed later in this section, too much boosting without compensating attenuation can create a number of sonic problems.)

2. Turn up the monitor level so it is comfortably loud; 85 dB-SPL is usually considered optimal. Because what is considered comfortably loud depends on personal taste, musical style, and hearing acuity, however, 85 dB-SPL is at least a good place to start. It is critical to not set the monitor level too loud. Loud levels desensitize hearing or, in the vernacular of audio, "fry" ears, to say nothing of the potential for hearing loss. Once monitor loudness is set, try not to change it; otherwise, the reference you are using to determine sonic values and proportions will change as well.

3. Add all other tracks relative to the level of the first voicing. If you started with drums, add bass, the rest of the drum set, the other accompanying instruments, and the vocal(s). If you started with the lead or most prominent instrument, bring in the other tracks one at a time, starting with the rhythm instruments, followed by the rest of the accompaniment. Another approach is to set all instruments equally loud, then increase levels of the lead voicings and decrease levels of the support instruments.

4. Position each instrument in the stereo or surround space approximately where you plan to put it in the final mix.

5. Readjust fader levels to compensate for loudness changes resulting from these positional alignments.

6. If something is not working, do not force it. Maybe it is not needed. That applies, for example, to parts of a song, control settings, signal processing, and, if necessary, even to an entire instrumental track.

Once you have refamiliarized yourself with the recording and have reconfirmed its design, you are ready to do the actual mixdown. It is likely that during the mix, as various sonic alterations are made, many of your original decisions will change. This is natural. Be flexible. Do not be afraid to experiment or go with your instincts. In fact, it is not unusual to want to make changes even after the mix has been mastered.

Signal Processing

Signal processing is so much a part of music recording that sound shaping seems impossible without it. Yet overdependency on signal processing has created the myth that just about anything can be done with it to ensure the sonic success of a recording. These notions are misleading. Unless special effects are required or MIDI is involved, signal processing in the mixdown should be used to touch up the aural canvas, not repaint it. The greater the reliance on signal processing in the mixdown, the more likely the poorer the recording session. Nevertheless, signal processing is important—and often critical. Recordists who proudly proclaim that they can do without it are foolish. The purpose of this section is only to suggest possibilities and techniques. It is not intended to imply that because signal processing offers so many options to the recordist, most of them should be used. Remember: *Less is more.*

Equalizing: How Much, Where, and When?

One question often asked of a recordist is: "What kind of a sound will I get on this instrument if I equalize so many decibels at such and such a frequency?" The question suggests that there are ways to predetermine equalization. There are not! Consider the different things that can affect sound. For example, for a guitar you might ask: "What is it made of? Is it acoustic or electric? Are the strings steel or plastic, old or new, played with a metal or plastic pick or with the fingers? Is the guitarist heavy- or light-handed? Are there fret sounds? Is the guitar miked and, if so, with what type of microphone? How are the acoustics? What type of song is being played? What is the spatial placement of the guitar in the mix?" These influences do not even include personal taste, the most variable factor of all.

The best way to approach equalization is to (1) know the frequency ranges of the instruments involved, (2) know what each octave in the audible frequency spectrum contributes to the overall sound, (3) listen to the sound in context, (4) have a good idea of what you want to achieve before starting the mixdown, and (5) decide whether EQ is needed on a particular sound.

Also remember the following:

▓ Equalizing alters a sound's harmonic structure.

▓ Very few people, even under ideal conditions, can hear a change of 1 dB or less, and many people cannot hear changes of 2 or 3 dB.

▓ Large increases or decreases in equalizing should be avoided.

▓ Equalizing should not be used as a substitute for better microphone selection and mic placement.

▓ Only a certain number of tracks in the same frequency range should be increased or decreased. For example, on one channel you may increase by 4 dB at 5,000 Hz the sound of a snare drum to make it snappier, then on another channel you increase 2 dB at 5,000 Hz to make a cymbal sound crisper, and on a third channel you increase 3 dB at 5,000 Hz to bring out a vocal. If you consider each channel separately, there has been little equalizing at 5,000 Hz, but the cumulative boost at the same frequency, which in this example is 9 dB, could unbalance the overall blend.

▓ Equalizing often involves boosting frequencies, and that can mean more noise, among other problems. Therefore be careful, particularly when increasing some of the unpleasant frequencies in the midrange and high end, especially with digital sound.

▓ Because boosting frequencies on one track often necessitates attenuating frequencies somewhere else, consider *subtractive equalization* first. For example, if a sound is overly bright, instead of trying to mellow it by boosting the appropriate lower frequencies, reduce some of the higher frequencies responsible for the excessive brightness.

▓ Frequencies above and below the range of each instrument should be filtered to reduce unwanted sound and improve definition. Be very careful not to reduce frequencies that are essential to the natural timbre of an instrument.

▓ To achieve a satisfactory blend, the sounds of individual elements may have to be changed in ways that could make them unpleasant to listen to by themselves. For example, the frequencies between 1,000 and 3,500 Hz make most vocals intelligible. One way to improve the clarity of a vocal and make it stand out from its instrumental accompaniment while maintaining the overall blend is to boost it a few decibels in the 1,000- to 3,500-Hz range and decrease the accompaniment a few decibels in the same range. Together they should sound quite natural. Separately, however, the vocal will be somewhat harsher and thinner and the accompaniment will sound a bit dense and lifeless.

▓ If a voice is powerful and rich with harmonics in the 5,000-Hz range, the sound is usually clear and full. Male singing voices, particularly in opera, have this sonic characteristic; female vocals usually do not.

Voices deficient in the 5,000-Hz range can be enhanced by a boost of several decibels in this area. Not only is the definition of such sounds as "t," "s," "ch," and "k" increased, but a 6-dB increase at 5,000 Hz gives an apparent increase of 3 dB to the overall mix. When mixing digital sound using these EQ values, be wary of digital edge—that overly bright sonic byproduct of the digital recording process that too often spoils sound quality on a CD.

■ Use *complementary equalization* to help define instruments and keep masking to a minimum. Many instruments have comparable frequency ranges, such as the bass guitar and kick drum, or the keyboard, guitar, and female vocal. Because physical law states that no two things can occupy the same space at the same time, it makes sense to equalize voicings that share frequency ranges so that they complement, rather than interfere with, one another (see Figures 19-1 and 19-2).

■ An absence of frequencies above 600 Hz adversely affects the intelligibility of consonants; an absence of frequencies below 600 Hz adversely affects the intelligibility of vowels.

■ Equal degrees of equalizing between 400 and 2,000 Hz are more noticeable than equalizing above or below that range, especially in digital sound (remember the equal loudness principle; see Chapter 2).

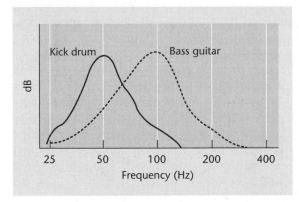

19-1 Complementary EQ for bass instruments

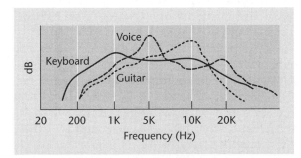

19-2 Complementary EQ for midrange instruments

■ Most amplified instruments do not have ranges higher than 7,500 Hz; boosting above that frequency usually adds only noise.

■ Each sound has a naturally occurring peak at a frequency or band of frequencies that contains more energy than surrounding frequencies and which, by being boosted or cut, enhances or mars the sound. In other words, the naturally occurring peak can become a *sweet spot* or a *sore spot*. The peaks are caused by natural harmonics and overtones or by formants. A *formant* is the resonance band in a vibrating body that mildly increases the level of specific steady-state frequencies in that band.

To find the resonance area, turn up the gain on the appropriate section of the equalizer and sweep the frequency control until the voicing sounds noticeably better or worse. Once you find the sweet or sore spot, return the equalizer's gain to zero and boost or cut the enhancing or offending frequencies to taste.

Equalization and Semantics

A major problem in equalization is describing what it sounds like. What does it mean, for example, when a producer wants "sizzle" in a cymbal sound, "fatness" in a snare sound, "brightness" in an alto saxophone sound, or "edge" to a vocal? Not only is there a problem of semantics, but you must identify the adjustments needed to achieve the desired effect. Then, too, one person's "sizzle" and "fatness" may be another person's "bite" and "boom." The following may be of some help in translating the verbal into the sonic.

■ Twenty to 50 Hz is considered the "rumble zone," and a subwoofer or full-range loudspeaker is required to reproduce it accurately. Even so, it does not take much of a boost in this range to add unwanted boom to the sound, which also eats up headroom.

■ The range from about 60 to 80 Hz adds punch to sound. It can also give sound impact, size, power, and warmth, without clouding, depending on the instrument and amount of EQ. The range is also bassy enough to eat up headroom with too much of a boost.

A boost between 200 and 300 Hz can add warmth and body to a thin mix, but too much of an increase makes sound woody or tubby. It can also cloud sound, making the bass, in particular, indistinct.

Generally, boosting below 500 Hz can make sound fat, thick, warm, or robust. Too much can make it muddy, boomy, thumpy, or barrel-like.

Flat, extended low frequencies add fullness, richness, or solidity to sound. They can also make sound rumbly.

Low-frequency roll-off thins sound. This can enhance audio by making it seem clearer and cleaner, or it can be detractive by making it seem colder, tinnier, or weaker.

Mid-frequency boost between 500 Hz and 7 kHz (5-kHz area for most instruments, 1.5 to 2.5 kHz for bass instruments) can add presence, punch, edge, clarity, or definition to sound. It can also make sound muddy (hornlike), tinny (telephonelike), nasal or honky (500 Hz to 3 kHz), hard (2 to 4 kHz), strident or piercing (2 to 5 kHz), twangy (3 kHz), metallic (3 to 5 kHz), or sibilant (4 to 7 kHz). Between 500 and 800 Hz, too much boost can cause a mix to sound hard or stiff.

Flat mid-frequencies sound natural or smooth. They may also lack punch or color.

Mid-frequency boost (1 to 2 kHz) improves intelligibility without increasing sibilance. Too much boost in this range adds unpleasant tinniness.

Mid-frequency dip makes sound mellow. It can also hollow (500 to 1,000 Hz), muffle (5 kHz), or muddy (5 kHz) sound.

The 2- to 4-kHz range contains the frequencies to which humans are most sensitive. If a sound has to cut through the mix, this is the range to work with. But too much boosting across these frequencies adds a harshness that brings on listening fatigue sooner rather than later.

High-frequency boost above 7 kHz can enhance sound by making it bright, crisp, etched, or sizzly (cymbals). It can also detract from sound by making it edgy, glassy, sibilant, biting, or sizzly (voice). Most vocal sibilance is in the range of 5 to 10 kHz.

Extended high frequencies in the range of roughly 10 kHz and higher tend to open sound, making it airy, transparent, natural, or detailed. Too much boost makes a mix sound brittle or icy.

High-frequency roll-off mellows, rounds, or smooths sound. It can also dull, muffle, veil, or distance sound.*

In relation to specific instruments, the equalization values in Table 19-1 may help refine the semantics. Note that frequencies and frequency ranges listed in the table are general and intended only to provide a point of departure for more-refined sound shaping.

Compression

Sounds are compressed to deal with the dynamic ranges of certain instruments so that they better integrate into the overall mix. Like any other signal processing, it is not a panacea for corrective action; it is more a sound-shaping tool and, as such, is to be used when aesthetically justified. The type of voicing with which compression is generally used is one tending to have a transient attack, a wide dynamic range, or a frequency response that can cut through a mix, such as drums, vocals, bass guitar, French horn, and piano.

Certain styles of music have also developed a tradition as to the amount of compression that is employed. For example, much of popular music has more compression than most country and punk rock music. Jazz, generally, uses light compression. In classical music compression varies widely depending on the music's dynamic range.

Chapter 9 covered a number of reasons why compression is used in sound shaping. Here are some general guidelines for applying compression to (1) selected areas of the frequency spectrum and (2) instruments that are commonly compressed. These are only a point of departure and should not

---

*Some of this material is adapted from Bruce Bartlett, "Modern Recording and Music," *Modern Recording and Music Magazine,* November 1982. Used by permission.

Table 19-1 Approximate equalization values for selected instruments

Instrument	Equalization values
Bass drum	Bottom ranges between 60 and 80 Hz; attenuating between 300 and 600 Hz reduces dullness, thuddiness, and cardboardlike sound; boosting between 1,600 and 5,000 Hz adds brightness, attack, and snap.
Low (floor) tom-tom	Fullness ranges between 80 and 120 Hz; brightness and attack are in the 4,000-Hz range.
High (rack) tom-tom	Fullness ranges between 220 and 240 Hz; brightness and attack are in the 5,000-Hz range.
Snare drum	Bottom ranges between 120 and 160 Hz; fatness ranges between 220 and 240 Hz; crispness ranges between 4,000 and 5,000 Hz.
Cymbals	Dullness—clank and gong—ranges between 200 and 240 Hz; brilliance, shimmer, and brightness range from 7,000 Hz and up.
Bass guitar	Bottom ranges between 60 and 80 Hz; cutting around 250 Hz adds clarity; attack ranges between 700 and 1,200 Hz; string noise is around 2,500 to 3,500 Hz.
Electric guitar	Fullness ranges between 210 and 240 Hz; edge or bite ranges between 2,500 and 3,500 Hz; upper harmonic limits do not range much beyond 6,500 Hz.
Acoustic guitar	Bottom ranges between 80 and 140 Hz; fullness and body range between 220 and 240 Hz; clarity ranges between 1,600 and 5,000 Hz, with sound becoming thinner as these frequencies get higher. Steel strings are 5 to 10 dB louder than nylon strings.
Piano	Bass ranges between 80 and 120 Hz; body ranges between 65 and 130 Hz; clarity and presence range between 2,000 and 5,000 Hz, with sound becoming thinner as these frequencies get higher. The most robust sound is obtained from a concert grand; sound is less robust in a baby grand and least robust in an upright.
Strings	Generally, sound from the bridge of a violin, viola, cello, or acoustic bass is brighter compared with sound coming from the F-holes, which is fuller. Bowing close to the bridge produces a less brilliant, gentler tone. Fullness ranges between 220 and 240 Hz; edge or scratchiness ranges between 7,000 and 10,000 Hz.

be followed without careful listening and experimentation. It is worth repeating that some compression effects are subtle and take experience to handle.

■ **Bass** (80 to 150 Hz). To tighten the low end—*ratio:* 2.5:1; *attack time:* 20 ms; *release time:* 150 ms; *threshold:* fairly low. Makeup gain should be just enough to compensate for the gain lost in compression.

■ **Low midrange** (150 to 600 Hz). To tighten the mix—*ratio:* 3:1; *attack time:* 20 ms; *release time:* 150 ms; *threshold:* set to trigger regularly. Makeup gain should be just enough to compensate for the gain loss in compression, or a bit more for added warmth.

■ **Midrange** (600 to 1,500 Hz). To add punch to a mix—*ratio:* 6:1; *attack time:* 10 ms; *release time:* 150 ms; *threshold:* set fairly low. Add 4 to 6 dB makeup gain for lost gain and adding solidity.

■ **Upper midrange** (1,500 to 6,000 Hz). To add clarity and presence—*ratio:* 3:1; *attack time:* 10 ms; *release time:* 150 ms; *threshold:* set to trigger regularly. Add 1 to 3 dB of gain for clarity and presence.

■ **High end** (6 to 14 kHz). To reduce harshness without losing brilliance—*ratio:* 2:1; *attack time:* 10 ms; *release time:* 150 ms; *threshold:* set high enough to trigger when harshness is present. Add 1 to 2 dB gain makeup to compensate for brilliance lost in compression.*

Here are some specific applications of compression on selected instruments.

---

*From Rob McGaughey, "Using a Multi-band Compressor on a Mix," *Keyboard,* June 1999, p. 64.

■ **Drums.** *Ratio:* 2:1 to 3:1 or 4:1 to 8:1; *attack time:* fast; *release time:* medium to fast; *threshold:* set to compress loudest peaks 4 to 6 dB or 6 to 8 dB. Compressing drums allows you mix them at a lower level and still retain their impact.

■ **Bass.** *Ratio:* 4:1; *attack time:* medium; *release time:* medium to fast; *threshold:* set to compress loudest peaks 2 to 4 dB. One main reason why recordists compress the bass is because its low-frequency energy tends to eat up much of the mix's overall headroom. One cautionary note: Watch out for distortion that can be introduced by overly quick release times.

■ **Rhythm instruments** (guitar, sax, synthesizer). *Ratio:* 4:1 to 6:1; *attack time:* medium; *release time:* medium; *threshold:* set to compress loudest peaks 3 to 5 dB. Moderate compression can enrich texture and help make rhythm instruments forceful without dominating the mix.

■ **Vocals.** *Ratio:* 3:1 to 4:1; *attack time:* fast to medium; *release time:* medium to fast; *threshold:* set to compress loudest peaks 3 to 6 dB. The amount of compression on a vocalist depends on the singer's technique; that is, does the singer back off slightly when hitting loud notes and lean in slightly to compensate for softer ones—which is good technique—or does the singer not compensate for dynamic range or, worse, "eat" the microphone? If the music track is dense and the vocals need to be heard, compression will have to be more aggressive. For delicate singers use more-sensitive threshold levels and smaller ratios. For screamers you may need to compress 6 to 8 dB to get the proper texture. Beware that high compression levels bring out sibilance and background noise.

Here are some other effects of compression on selected instruments:

■ **Drums.** A long-to-medium attack time reduces the percussive effect. A short release time and wide ratio create a bigger or fuller sound.

■ **Cymbals.** Medium-to-short attack and release times and an average ratio reduce excessive ringing.

■ **Guitar.** Short attack and release times and a wide ratio increase the sustain.

■ **Keyboards.** A medium-to-long attack time, a medium-to-short release time, and a wide ratio give a fuller sound.

■ **Strings.** Short attack and release times and an average ratio add body to the sound.

■ **Vocals.** Medium-to-short attack and release times and an average ratio reduce sibilance.

There are many other approaches to compression. The suggestions listed here are not intended to imply that compression should be used just because it is available or that most voicings should be compressed. If you do employ compression, these suggestions may be good starting points.

Reverberation: Creating Acoustic Space

Due to the common practice of miking each sound component separately (for greater control) and closely (to reduce leakage), many original multitrack recordings lack a complementary acoustic environment. In such cases the acoustics are added in the mixdown by artificial means using signal-processing devices such as reverb and digital delay (see Chapter 9).

If you add acoustics in the mixdown, do it after equalizing (because it is difficult to get a true sense of the effects of frequency changes in a reverberant space) and after panning (to get a better idea of how reverb affects positioning). Avoid giving widely different reverb times to various components in an ensemble, or it will sound as though they are not playing in the same space, unless that is your intention for special effect.

The quality of the reverberation depends on the musical style. Most types of popular music work well with the sound of digital reverb or a reverb plate. Jazz usually requires a more natural-sounding acoustic environment; classical music definitely does.

In determining reverb balance, adjust it one track at a time (on the tracks to which reverb is being added). Reverb can be located in the mix by panning; it does not have to envelop an entire recording. Reverb in stereo mixes should achieve a sense of depth and breadth. In surround sound it should not overwhelm or swallow the mix, nor should reverb from the front loudspeakers be the same as it is from the rear-side (or rear) loud-speakers. In acoustic conditions the audience sitting closer to an ensemble hears less reverb than does the audience sitting farther away.

With reverberation some equalizing may be necessary. Because plates and chambers tend to generate lower frequencies that muddy sound, attenuating the reverb between 60 and 100 Hz may be necessary to clean up the sound. If muddiness is not a problem, boosting lower frequencies gives the reverb a larger and more distant sound. Boosting higher frequencies gives the reverb a brighter, closer, more present sound.

Less expensive reverberation systems lack good treble response. By slightly boosting the high end, the reverb will sound somewhat more natural and lifelike.

If any one voicing is inevitably assigned to reverb, it is the vocal. Yet there is often the danger that the reverb's midrange will interfere with the harmonic richness of the vocal's midrange. Attenuating or notching out the reverb's competing midrange frequencies can better define the vocal and help make it stand out.

Other effects, such as *chorusing* and *accented reverb*, can be used after reverberation. By setting the chorus for a delay between 20 and 30 ms and adding it to the reverb, sound gains a shimmering, fuller quality. Patching the reverb output into a noise gate and triggering the noise gate with selected accents from a percussive instrument such as a snare drum, piano, or tambourine can heighten as well as unify the rhythm.

Before making a final decision about the reverb you employ, do an A-B comparison. Check reverb proportions using large and small loudspeakers to make sure the reverb neither envelops sound nor is so subtle that it defies definition.

Digital Delay: Enhancing Acoustic Space

Sound reaches listeners at different times, depending on where a listener is located relative to the sound source. The closer to the sound source you are, the sooner the sound reaches you, and vice versa. Hence, a major component of reverberation is delay. To provide more-realistic reverberation, therefore, many digital reverbs include *predelay*, which sets a slight delay before reverb. If a reverb unit does not include predelay, the same effect can be generated by using a digital delay device before reverb. Predelay adds a feeling of space to the reverberation. In either case, predelay should be short—15 to 20 ms usually suffices. (A millisecond is equivalent to about a foot in space.) On some delay devices, the longer the delay time, the poorer the signal-to-noise ratio.

Post-delay—adding delay after reverb—is another way to add dimension to sound, particularly to a vocal. In the case of the vocal, it may be necessary to boost the high end to brighten the sound or to avoid muddying it, or both.

Synchronizing delay to tempo is another effect that can heighten sonic interest. This technique involves adjusting rate of delay to the music's tempo by dividing the tempo into 60,000—the number of milliseconds per measure to which the digital delay is set.

It is also possible to create *polyrhythms*—simultaneous and sharply contrasting rhythms—by using two delays and feeding the output of one into the input of the other. Varying delay time of the second unit generates a variety of spatial effects.

In using a digital delay, there is one precaution: It should have a bandwidth of at least 12 kHz. But given the quality of sound being produced today, 15 kHz and higher is recommended.

Two features of digital delay—feedback and modulation—can be employed in various ways to help create a wide array of effects with flanging, chorusing, doubling, and slapback echo. *Feedback*, or *regeneration*, as the terms suggest, feeds a proportion of the delayed signal back into the delay line, in essence, "echoing the echo." *Modulation* is controlled by two parameters: width and speed. Width dictates how wide a range above and below the chosen delay time the modulator will be allowed to swing. You can vary the delay by any number of milliseconds above and below the designated time. Speed dictates how rapidly the time delay will oscillate.

Electronic Sounds

There are three basic kinds of electronic sounds: samples or emulations of music; samples or emulations of real-world (nonmusical) sounds; and completely artificial sounds. Trying to place these elements in an acoustic environment using the same rationale you would in placing musical instruments is not called for. There are no templates. Because an electronic sound is used for its own uniqueness and not as an attempt to replicate the sound of a musical instrument, it can be manipulated in any way and placed anywhere in a mix so long as it makes sense aesthetically.

SPATIAL IMAGING OF MUSIC

Almost from the beginning of recorded sound, attempts have been made to increase the dimensionality of sonic reproduction. Years before stereo, recordists were experimenting with miking techniques to make sound more spacious. Binaural recording has been around for decades, but still requires playback through headphones to appreciate its full three-dimensional effect. Several years ago the commercially failed quadraphonic sound increased the depth of sonic space by using loudspeakers to the rear as well as in front of the listener. Formats are available that augment the stereo image by effectively bringing the depth and width of the aural frame to the outermost edges of the sound field on a plane with the listener. In short, a number of approaches applied during recording or mixing have been, or are being, used to bring sound reproduction closer to the live listening experience. Of those, so far stereo and surround sound have proved to be the most commercially viable.

Stereo

In multitrack recording, each element is recorded at an optimal level and on a separate track. If all the elements were played back in the same way, it would sound as though they were coming from precisely the same location, to say nothing about how imbalanced the voicings would be. In reality, of course, this is not the case. You therefore have to position each musical component in an aural frame by setting the levels of loudness to create front-to-rear perspective, or depth, and panning to establish left-to-right perspective, or breadth. In setting levels, the louder a sound, the closer it seems to be; and, conversely, the quieter a sound, the farther away it seems. Frequency and reverb also affect positioning. In panning stereo there are five main areas: left, left-center, center, right-center, and right.

There are many options in positioning various elements of an ensemble in an aural frame, but three factors enter into the decision: (1) the aural balance, (2) how the ensemble arranges itself when playing before a live audience, and (3) the type of music being played. Keep in mind that each musical style has its own values. Popular music is usually emotional and contains a strong beat. Drums and bass therefore are usually focused in the mix. Country music is generally vocal-centered with the accompaniment important, of course, but subordinate. Jazz and classical music are more varied and require different approaches. The mixer must have a clear idea of what the music sounds like in a natural acoustic setting before attempting a studio mix.

Sounds and where they are placed in aural space have different effects on perception. In a stereo field, these effects include the following: (1) The sound closest to the center and nearest to the listener is the most predominant; (2) a sound farther back but still in the center creates depth and a balance or counterweight to the sound that is front and center; (3) sound placed to one side usually requires a similarly weighted sound on the opposite side or else the left-to-right aural space will seem unbalanced; and (4) the more you spread sound across the aural space, the wider the sound sources will seem.

This is not to suggest that all parts of aural space must be sonically balanced or filled at all times; that depends on the ensemble and the music. A symphony orchestra usually positions first violins to the left of the conductor, second violins to the left-center, violas to the right-center, and cellos to the right. If the music calls for just the first violins to play, it is natural for the sound to come mainly from the left. To pan the first violins left to right would establish a stereo balance, but it would be poor aesthetic judgment and would disorient the listener. To illustrate aural framing in a stereo field, see Figures 19-3 through 19-10.

Surround Sound

Sound is omnidirectional; our natural acoustic environment is 360 degrees. Surround sound provides the opportunity to come far closer to reproducing that experience than stereo by enabling the music and the listener to occupy the same space. With stereo the audio is localized wide and deep in front of the listener, whereas surround increases the depth of the front-to-rear and side-to-side sound images, placing the listener more in the middle of the aural event. In stereo two discrete channel signals are reproduced separately through two loudspeakers, creating phantom images between them. In surround sound discrete multichannel signals are reproduced separately, each through a dedicated loudspeaker.

There are two basic ways of handling surround sound. One is to use a number of audio processors to synthesize a multichannel signal from two-channel stereo. The other is to build a multichannel mix from the outset. Because the latter is the preferred way, it is considered here.

At this writing the surround-sound format in widespread use is 5.1. Formats in 6.1, 7.1, up to 10.2 have also been developed. The first number

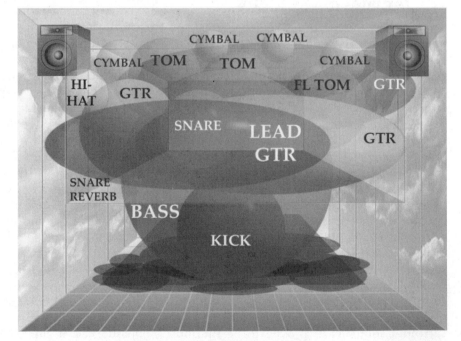

19-3 Rock mix. Quite full with lots of fattening and overlapping sounds. The lead guitar is spread in stereo with a rhythm guitar behind it and another stereo guitar in the background. The low end is clean, with a strong kick drum and bass. (In this figure and Figures 19-4 through 19-10, the size of the globes indicates the relative loudness of the voicings.)

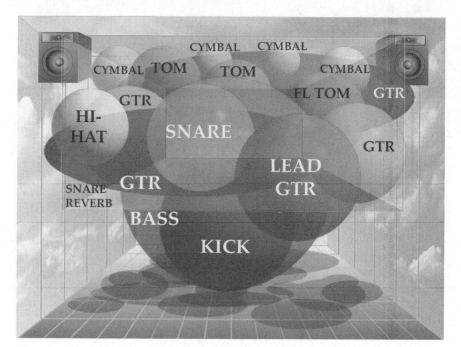

19-4 Heavy metal mix. A full, busy mix yet with a clear low end (kick and bass). The hi-hat, snare, and lead guitar are out in front. There are multiple guitar parts with a few panned in stereo. The overall effect is a wall of sound.

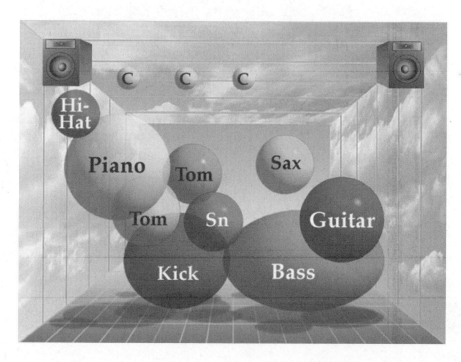

19-5 Jazz mix. Overall, a clean and clear mix with the guitar, piano, and hi-hat in front and the kick drum atypically loud for a jazz mix.

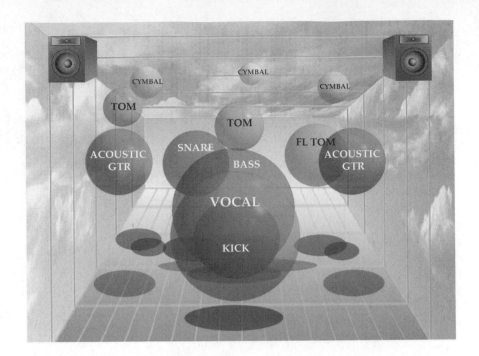

19-6 Folk music mix.
A loud vocal in front of a clean, clear, spacious mix of the ensemble.

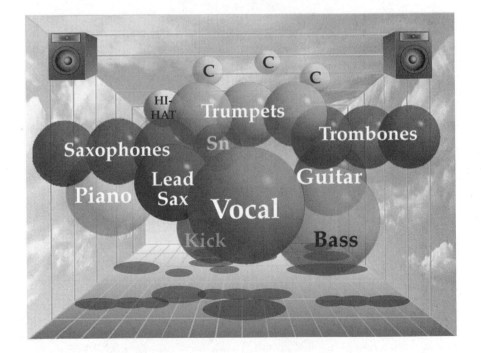

19-7 Big band mix.
The vocal and horns are the prominent features of this mix.

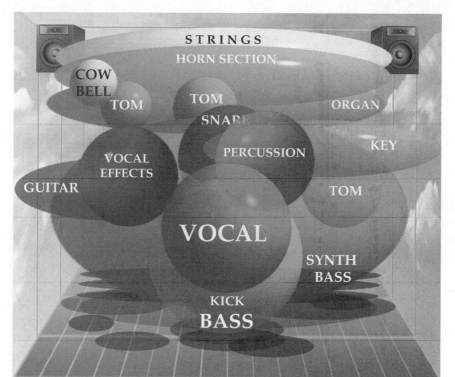

19-8 The mix on the song "Blinded Me with Science" from the album *Wireless* by Thomas Dolby

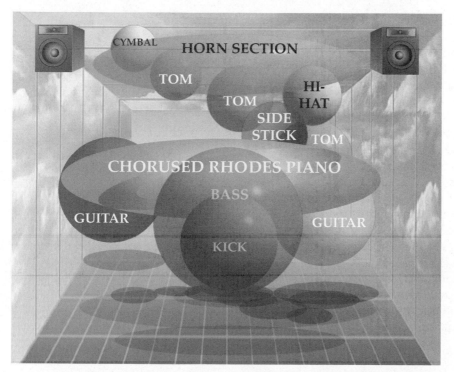

19-9 The mix on the song "Babylon Sisters" from the album *Gaucho* by Steely Dan

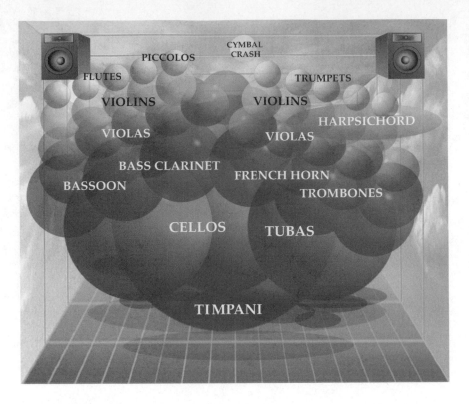

19-10 A mix of "The Four Seasons" by Antonio Vivaldi

refers to the discrete channels of full-bandwidth audio and the array of loudspeakers used to reproduce it. The full-bandwidth channels are 20 Hz to 20 kHz. The second number refers to the channel(s)/subwoofer(s) used for *low-frequency enhancement (LFE)*. (The *E* is also referred to as *effects*.) The LFE channel has a frequency response rated from 5 to 125 Hz. Because few subwoofers can produce sounds lower than 15 to 20 Hz, their range more realistically begins around 30 to 35 Hz.

In the 5.1 surround-sound format, audio from the five channels is sent to loudspeakers positioned frontally—left, center, and right—and to the left and right surround loudspeakers. LFE audio feeds to the subwoofer, which may be positioned between the left and center or center and right frontal loudspeakers (see Chapter 10). Sometimes two subwoofers are used to reproduce the mono LFE signal, ordinarily positioned behind and outside the left- and right-front speakers.

Basic Equipment for Mixing Surround Sound

To produce a surround-sound mix, a few basic types of equipment are required. These requirements assume the 5.1 format (see 19-11): (1) A console or hard-disk system with the capability to pan sounds among the six surround-sound channels; (2) loudspeakers and amplification to reproduce five full-bandwidth channels and one low-frequency channel; (3) a recorder to record the six surround channels; and (4) depending on the delivery format the mix is for, an encoder to compress the data.

There are a handful of delivery formats in the surround-sound market. *Dolby Digital*, *Digital Theater System (DTS)*, *DVD-Audio (DVD-A)*, and the *Super Audio Compact Disc (SACD)*. DVD-Audio and the SACD were covered in Chapter 7. Dolby Digital and DTS are addressed here.

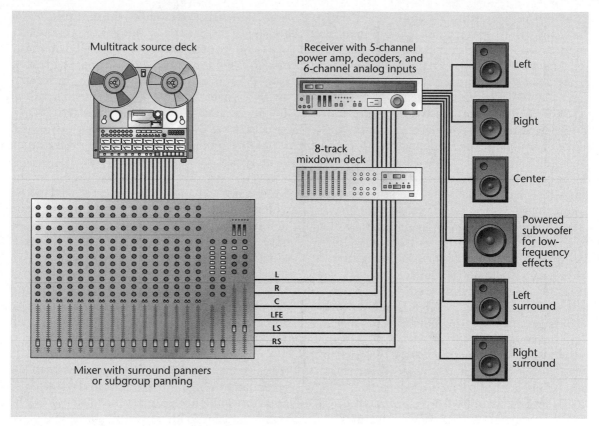

19-11 Example of the basic types of equipment needed to produce surround sound

Uncompressed audio at 44.1 kHz with 16-bit resolution requires a bandwidth of about 700 Kbps. Therefore the six channels in the 5.1 format require 4.2 megabits per second (Mbps). Dolby Digital uses a lossy data compression and an encoding algorithm called *AC-3* (the *AC* stands for *audio coding*) to reduce the required bit rate to roughly 400 kilobits per second (Kbps). DTS also uses lossy compression, although its compression is less extreme than Dolby's; its bandwidth requirements are about 1.4 Mbps.

Mixing for Surround Sound

Mixing for surround sound opens up a new world of aesthetic options in dealing with sound localization. But by so doing, it also creates new challenges in dealing with those options. Among them are handling the center channel and the surround channels, reverberation, and bass management.

The Center Channel Because there is no center channel or loudspeaker in stereo, the center image is a psychoacoustic illusion; in surround sound it is not. Because there is a discrete center channel and speaker in surround sound, if you are not careful about delegating the signal(s) there, it could unbalance the entire frontal imaging. This is particularly important in a music mix. For TV and film, the center channel must be used because it is necessary for the dialogue (see "Surround Sound" under "Spacial Imaging in Television" later in this chapter).

There is no single recommended way of handling the center channel; it depends on producer preference and the music. Generally, dealing with the center channel can be divided into two broad approaches: delegating little if anything to it or using it selectively.

Those who use the center channel little or not at all believe that handling the center image is better done by applying the stereo model: letting the left and right loudspeakers create a phantom center. By having too much audio sent to the center channel, there is a greater build in the middle of the frontal sound image. This makes the voicings coming from the center speaker more dominant than they should be, thereby focusing attention there to the detriment of the overall musical balance. Another consideration is that many home surround systems do not come with a center loudspeaker; if they do, either it is positioned incorrectly or not set up at all. Hence, they have no way of reproducing any center channel audio.

Producers who prefer to use the center channel take various approaches. One technique creates a phantom center between the left and right loudspeakers, along with a duplicated discrete center channel several dBs down. This adds depth and perspective to the center voicings without overly intensifying their image.

In a typical pop song, the bass and kick drum are positioned center-rear to anchor the mix. If they are delegated to the center channel, it may be necessary to diffuse their center channel impact. Their signal can be reduced in level and also fed to the left and right loudspeakers, then panned toward the center.

Producers who take full advantage of the center channel do so because they want that emphasis in their mix. Their point is that in stereo, when a voicing is put in the center, it is not really in the center—it is a phantom image created from the left and right channels. Why do the same thing with surround? Use the discrete center channel to create a truer spatial spectrum that will add more depth and power to the frontal imaging.

The type of music also has something to do with how the center channel is used. Classical music and large jazz bands, for example, take advantage of it because of the size and breadth of the ensembles.

In dealing with the center channel, pop music producers tend to center such voicings as the bass, snare drum, kick drum, and vocal but are careful not to delegate too many instruments to it, nor to delegate a voicing solely to the center channel without some duplication elsewhere in the mix. As for the problem with surround-sound home systems not having a center loudspeaker, their feeling is: Why bother mixing for surround if the music is not going to be played in the medium for which it is intended? Take advantage of what surround sound provides and mix for those who have the systems to hear the music the way it should be heard.

The Surround Channels How the surround channels are used comes down to what the music calls for or producer preference, or both. It is an artistic decision—there are no rules.

Some music mixes, such as classical and live concerts, may take a more objective approach. The presentation is mainly frontal, with the surrounds used for ambience to place the listener in the venue's audience. Other types of more studio-based music, such as pop and, perhaps, jazz may take a more subjective approach and place the listener in the middle of the music. For example, a jazz combo with lead piano may be mixed to center the listener at or near the piano, with the rest of the ensemble and ambience surrounding him or her. Or an approach may be a combination of the objective and subjective. In the previous example, instead of centering the listener inside the ensemble, the mix would arc to the listener's sides, filling out the surrounds with some signal duplication and ambience. Regardless of the approach, in any music mix, surround or otherwise, it always helps to remember that what you do should primarily serve the music.

In panning sounds between the front and surround channels, two perceptual effects are worth noting: (1) The frequency response between the front and surrounds is different, and (2) sound panned halfway between the front and surrounds draws some attention forward and some attention behind; this instability creates a separation or split in the sound.

Reverberation The presence of the center channel calls for some precautions when using reverberation. Just as putting too much of any voicing in the center channel focuses the ear on it, the same is true with reverberation. There are also the added concerns of phasing problems with the reverb in other channels, particularly the left and right, and if the music is played back on systems without a center loudspeaker, or a center loudspeaker not positioned correctly.

The current wisdom is to leave the center channel dry and put reverb in the left and right channels, continuing it in the surrounds. Any reverb placed in the center is very minor and usually different from what is in the other channels.

Bass Management The advantage of the LFE channel is that it provides more headroom below 125 Hz, where the ear is less sensitive and requires more boost to perceive equal loudness with the midrange. By providing this headroom, bass enhancement can be used without its eating up other frequencies. Generally, the LFE channel is for low-end effects such as rumbles, explosions, thunder, gunshots, and the very lowest notes of the lowest bass instruments. In music mixes low-end instruments are usually assigned to the full-frequency range channels, not the LFE, because of the LFE channel's limited frequency response. Most bass instruments have ranges that go beyond 125 Hz. That said, the LFE channel may be used as a bass extender to reproduce the very low content of the main channels. Another use for the LFE is that by taking a good deal of the bass out of the surround speakers, it can enhance their clarity and help reduce distortion.

In working with the LFE channel, it helps to add a bass management and volume controller to the system. This assists in giving a better idea of how the low end will sound on different-quality reproduction systems, such as a typical home system or an upscale unit. For example, sounds such as plosives and breath blasts from a vocalist may be picked up by a high-quality mic but not heard through a small speaker. But if they are mixed to, say, a DVD, those sounds would be routed automatically to the LFE channel via the bass management filters in the receiver and, therefore, be quite audible. Keep in mind that with any .1 surround-sound format, the LFE is a monaural channel. Any bass that requires stereo must be delegated to the main channels.

Track Assignment

Although there is no agreed-upon protocol for assigning surround-sound tracks, the International Telecommunications Union (ITU) has suggested that the track assignments be as follows: track 1–front left; track 2–front right; track 3–front center; track 4–subwoofer; track 5–left-rear surround; and track 6–right-rear surround. Other groupings are also used (see 19-12). Whichever mode of assignment you use, make sure that the mix tape or file is clearly labeled as to which tracks are assigned where.

Downmixing to Stereo

Given the fact that radio broadcasting and most home music systems are stereo, it is likely that a surround-sound mix may have to be *downmixed* to stereo. In such instances some producers prefer to do the stereo mix first and then make the adjustments for surround afterward in a separate pass. There may also be a mono mix, because many people still listen to radio and television in mono.

Generally, downmixing surround sound to stereo is relatively straightforward. Center channel audio is added equally to the left- and right-front channels, as is the audio from the left and right surrounds. In some cases the LFE channel is added to the stereo channels, but economically, to ensure that the bass does not overwhelm the rest of the mix. In other cases, the LFE channel is just dropped. For mono mixes all channels except LFE are delegated to the center loudspeaker.

As straightforward as a downmix may be, there are potential problems to watch out for. For example, if there is delay between the left-front and

19-12 Six common modes in assigning surround-sound channels to tape or disk. Tracks 7 and 8 are the left and right stereo downmix.

Track	1	2	3	4	5	6	7	8
Mode 1	L	R	Ls	Rs	C	LFE	Lt	Rt
Mode 2	L	C	R	Ls	Rs	LFE	Lt	Rt
Mode 3	L	Ls	C	Rs	R	LFE	Lt	Rt
Mode 4	L	R	C	LFE	Ls	Rs	Lt	Rt
Mode 5	L	C	Rs	R	Ls	LFE	Lt	Rt
Mode 6	C	L	R	Ls	Rs	LFE	Lt	Rt

left-surround channels or the right-front and right-surround channels, significant phasing could occur when the channels are combined. Reverberation values may also change. A lot of high end that sounds good in a surround mix may not translate well when downmixed to stereo due to the effects of cancellation.

Keeping a Record

Keeping a record of settings for EQ levels, reverb send, reverb return, compression, limiting, track assignments, and so on in a mixdown is essential. It often takes several sessions to complete a mix, and any adjustments previously made must be reset precisely. Moreover, perceptions of a mix have a strange way of changing from one day to the next, so being able to reference the sound to the setting is critical.

Information in automated and computer-assisted mixdowns is stored automatically. It may be recalled for visual display or printed out in hard copy. This convenience notwithstanding, it is always wise to make a backup copy of all computer-encoded information.

TELEVISION AND FILM

The process of combining the *dialogue, music, and sound effects (DME)* tracks for television and film is accomplished, generally, during the premixing and rerecording stages. *Premixing* is when the various tracks are blended and smoothed into composite dialogue and sound effects. Music tracks produced from prerecorded libraries may also be premixed. If the underscoring is original, and therefore recorded live, the music is mixed down separately. The *rerecording* mix is the final stage in postproduction, when the premixed tracks—dialogue, sound effects, and music—are combined into stereo or surround sound. The differences in technology and release formats between television and film may account for differences in the sequence and type of operations during mixing and rerecording, but the purposes of both stages are the same for each medium: to produce a finished sound track.

In postproduction improving the already recorded audio, adding necessary material, and signal processing is also known as *sweetening*. Again, depending on the medium and the release format, the operational stages differ somewhat. Dialogue and sometimes sound effects from an edited master are transferred to multitrack, along with time code. This stage is sometimes referred to as *layover* or *laydown*. Other audio tracks, such as music and additional sound effects, are added to the multitrack as needed. These tracks are then premixed and, in the *layback*, either transferred back to the edited master or to composite audio tracks for rerecording. Though the procedures used for television do not differ much from those used for film, there is a distinct set of problems and constraints related to the materials and distribution formats of each medium.

MIXING FOR TELEVISION

Of the factors that influence mixing sound for television, three important ones are how the audio is heard in most homes, TV's emphasis on the spoken (and sung) word, and how screen size and program type affect spatial imaging.

Mixing Audio for the Home TV Receiver

It was pointed out earlier in this chapter that a large percentage of the TV audience still hears the audio in mono through small loudspeakers. (Even with the advent of HDTV, it will be some time before most viewers invest in an HDTV receiver.) These small loudspeakers not only reproduce little or no bass, they accentuate sound that resides in the upper midrange, producing an unpleasant hard, raspy sound and sonically unbalancing the audio overall. To avoid potential problems caused by the small TV speakers, switch back and forth during a mix between the upscale full-frequency loudspeakers and the smaller TV-type loud-speakers. Although the larger speakers are used for the bulk of the mixing, referencing the mix through the smaller ones helps ensure that (1) essential low-end audio is not lost when played back through those speakers, and (2) midrange harshness has been neutralized.

Mixing the Word

The centerpiece of television audio is the spoken and sung word. Whether it is an announcer, voice-over narrator, newscaster, actor, variety show performer, or a singing commercial, in a small-screen medium, and given the fidelity of so many home receivers, the words have to be delivered "loud and clear." When music is part of the mix, it is still essential that the speech stand out. Consequently, take care to make sure that the music is not too loud in relation to the speech or that any lead instrument does not interfere with the intelligibility of the words. Even if the lead voicing is a singer or a group of singers, the lyrics should stand out from the accompaniment.

In mixing for TV, the following guidelines may be helpful:*

☑ Monitor at low levels to simulate the average listening environment.

☑ Switch back and forth between full-frequency loudspeakers and TV-type speakers. Be wary of equalizing on the smaller speakers, because their limited frequency response can be misleading.

☑ Keep the dynamic range relatively small.

☑ In a music mix that is to be combined with a voice-over or dialogue, keep the lead elements lower than normal.

☑ Make sure the mix is mono-compatible (see "Stereo-to-Mono Compatibility" later in this chapter).

Spatial Imaging in Television

Another important factor to deal with in a mix for TV is the spatial placement of the various elements.

Stereo

Natural assumptions in placing elements in a stereo mix for television and film are that dialogue and effects are positioned in relation to their on-screen locations and that music, if there is no on-screen source, fills the aural frame from the left to the right. For the most part, these assumptions are imprecise. Placement depends on the screen format, the reproduction system, and the type of material being produced.

The aesthetic demands of television and film differ because of the differences between their screen sizes and, hence, their sonic and pictorial dimensions. Clearly, film has more space in which to place and maneuver the aural and visual elements than does television. Nevertheless, when it comes to sound, the *localization*—placement—of dialogue, sound effects, and music in the stereo frame is similar in both media.

---

*Based on Mike Levine, "Mixing for the Small Screen," *Electronic Musician,* November 1998, p. 79.

The aesthetic challenges in mixing for stereo television are twofold: scale and perspective.

Scale Until the advent of stereo TV, the television loudspeaker was smaller than the screen, but, together, the scale of picture and sound images have seemed proportional. No doubt conditioning has had something to do with this perception.

With stereo TV, loudspeakers are mounted in two ways: either attached to the left and right sides of the set, or detached. Permanently attached speakers can be no farther apart than the width of the TV set. This is a limiting factor in creating a stereo image, because the aural space is so narrow. Detachable speakers can be situated an optimal distance apart; 6 feet is usually recommended to reproduce a more realistic stereo image. In fact, when sound is more spacious because of stereo, the picture seems bigger: *What we hear affects what we see.*

Perspective Despite the trend toward larger screens, television for most viewers is still a small-screen medium. It relies on close-up shots to enhance impact and to show detail that otherwise would be lost. Speech (and song lyrics), therefore, is concentrated in the center. Trying to match sound with movement would be chaotic.

Localization of Talk and Dialogue

In television talk and dialogue are usually kept at or near the center of the stereo frame. Unless the shot remains the same, trying to match a performer's sonic location to that person's on-screen position can disorient the audience.

For example, if in a variety show a wide shot shows (from the viewer's perspective) the host in the center, the announcer to the left, and the band leader and band to the right and the shot does not change, the audio can come from these locations in the stereo space. If the host and announcer exchange remarks, and the shot cuts to the host on the right and the announcer to the left in a two-shot, and the shot stays that way, the host's sound can be panned toward the right and the announcer's sound can be panned toward the left. If during their interchange, however, the shots cut back and forth between one-shots of the host and the announcer, the left and right stereo imaging becomes disconcerting, because the image of either the host or the announcer is in the center of the frame when the sound is toward the left or right. When frequent shot changes occur, therefore, the best approach is to keep the overall speech toward or at the center (see 19-13).

When a performer is moving in a shot, say, from left to right, and the camera-to-source distance

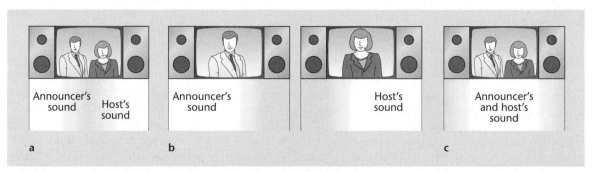

19-13 Speech localization in a two-shot. (a) In this example, so long as the announcer and host remain positioned left and right in a medium shot (MS) and the shot does not change, their sounds can be panned toward the left and right, respectively, with no dislocation. (b) If the shot changes, say, to a medium close-up (MCU) of the announcer followed by an MCU of the host and the stereo imaging remains the same, it will create a Ping-Pong effect. (c) If one-shots of the announcer and the host are planned, the sound in the original two-shot should be centered for both of them and carried through that way throughout the sequence. Panning the sound with the shot changes is even more sonically awkward than the Ping-Pong effect.

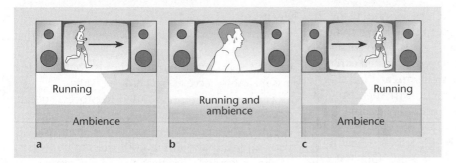

19-14 Sound localization in a moving shot. (a) If a subject is, say, running across the screen from left to right and the shot does not change, the stereo imaging can also move from left to right without dislocation. (b) Should the shot cut to a close-up (CU) to show perspiration on the runner's face, in which case the across-screen movement would be reflected in the moving background, the subject's sound would have to be centered. If the sound continued moving left to right in the CU, the difference between the visual and aural perspectives would be disorienting. (c) Cutting from the CU back to the wide shot, the sound once again can move across the screen with the runner without disorientation, because the perspectives match. If throughout the runner's across-screen movement there were a few cuts from the wide shot to the CU, however, the sound in the wide shots would have to be more centered to avoid the Ping-Pong effect.

remains the same, the stereo image can be panned to follow the performer's movement without audience disorientation. But if the performer's camera-to-source distance changes due to cutting from wider shots to closer shots or vice versa, or intercutting another actor into the frame even though the first performer's momentum is clearly left to right, the dialogue has to be centered to avoid dislocation (see 19-14).

Sound Effects The handling of sound effects also should be conservative. Obvious movement should be selective and occur mostly with effects that make pronounced crossing movements. The extent of the movement has to be carefully controlled so that it is not greater than the physical dimension of the screen (unless it is surround sound).

Ambiences in stereo television certainly can be fuller than they are in mono TV. Undoubtedly, the significant perceptible difference between mono and stereo TV is in the fullness and depth of the ambience.

Music Underscored music is mixed across the stereo field with the left and right sides framing the overall stereo image. Generally, in the mix of dialogue, music, and sound effects, underscored music is the one element that is usually in stereo.

Surround Sound

How sonic elements are placed in a surround-sound mix for television depends to a considerable extent on the program, except for speech (and lyrics). In the small-screen medium of TV, the word, spoken or sung, is delegated to the center channel. Sometimes to give the sound source some spread, or to avoid too much center channel buildup, the speech may be panned a bit left and right of center. Surround sound notwithstanding, the two main objectives of mixing speech are to make sure it is clear and to avoid dislocation.

As for sounds and music, taste and the program type affect placement. For example, in a talk show, the audience sound may be panned to the left, right, and surround loudspeakers. In sports the crowd may be handled in the same way, or the action sounds may be mixed into the left and right imaging, with the crowd in the surrounds. Music underscoring for a drama may be handled by sending it to the left, right, and surround speakers, or just to the left and right speakers and using the surrounds for the ambience of the setting. In music programs delegating the audio is often related to the type of music being played. As noted earlier in this chapter, with classical music the mix is primarily left, center, and right, with the surrounds used for ambience. Pop music may approach the mix by taking more advantage of the surrounds to place voicings. Or because it is television, with the picture showing an ensemble front and centered, the surrounds may be used for audience sound, if there is one, and ambience.

Then too with any surround-sound mix you must consider how it will translate on a stereo or mono TV receiver. Therefore, throughout the mixdown or rerecording session back-and-forth monitoring is essential. A few years ago, a music program was mixed for stereo, but the announcer was inadvertently recorded in mono. Those in the listening audience hearing the broadcast in stereo were unable to hear the announcer, because his audio, being in mono, was canceled.

MIXING FOR FILM

Whereas television audio is usually handled in two distinct mixes—the music mix and the post (rerecording) mix in which the narration or dialogue, sound effects, and music are combined—the procedure in film audio differs somewhat. Music is recorded and mixed separately. The dialogue and sound effects are premixed, and the three elements are then combined in the rerecording mix. Of course, the distinction between the way audio is handled in postproduction for TV and film can be somewhat artificial. For example, a made-for-TV drama may be postproduced using the film model. The distinctions made here are to make the discussion more manageable and to not lose sight of the differences in approach that do exist.

Premixing the Film Sound Track

The *premix* is the stage in film postproduction during which dialogue, sound effects, and, to some extent, music are prepared for the final rerecording mix.

Dialogue

In most situations dialogue (or any speech for that matter) must be prominent and clear, whether it is by itself or mixed with other sounds; that is, unless it is meant to serve as background walla.

Various techniques are used to process speech, depending on the medium, voice quality, and competing sounds. Regardless of which techniques you employ, maintaining both the sonic integrity of the voice and intelligibility of the speech are most important.

Clear dialogue begins with a good master recording, whether it is the production recording or the ADR recording. That means using the highest-quality microphones and recording equipment. In addition, the value of recording as noise free as possible cannot be overstated. The other techniques include the familiar signal processing of equalization, filtering, compression, limiting, and so on.

In addition to the familiar uses of equalization in dialogue premixing—to make speech intelligible and agreeable sounding—it can be employed to smooth or match any differences between dialogue on different tracks or reels. It helps overcome anomalies in frequency response due to varying microphone techniques used during production, body microphones hidden under clothing, proximity effect, the recording system, or dubbing. Equalization also helps improve the imbalance in reverberation when the reverb time in the bass is longer than it is in the midrange and treble. Filtering helps reduce system and background noise.

Compression and limiting are commonly used to ensure that the dialogue stays within the dynamic range of the reproducing system. Remember that in recording and mixing, the important factor is how the audience will hear the sound, not the sonic capabilities of the recording or transmitting systems. Compression is also used to keep dialogue above the ambience and the noise floor of the combined dialogue tracks. Compression helps keep other sonic elements, such as sound effects and music, from interfering with the dialogue's intelligibility. It is better to compress individual tracks, rather than the overall dialogue mix, because the risk of distortion, audible pumping, and a clustered, blurred sound is considerably less.

De-essing smoothes the sibilance in speech, which can be a boon in digital recording. It also helps optical-track sound when sibilant distortion results from problems in lab processing.

Noise gates help reduce ambient noise and keep dialogue tracks relatively free of leakage from other dialogue lines and sound sources. But using too many noise gates might add, rather than reduce, noise; and if they are not top-of-the-line units or are set improperly, their gating actions will be audible.

Reverberation, in addition to its familiar use of providing acoustic definition to a space, helps match the reverberant characteristics of different ambiences that may be part of the various dialogue tracks. One type of reverberation is known as *worldizing*, whereby a microphone and loudspeaker are set up in a room in a way that is similar to their arrangement in an acoustic reverberation chamber. The room sound is recorded to add the sound of that space to a dry recording or to enhance or smooth ambient backgrounds that are already part of a dialogue track. Or the room sound is recorded in the same space in which the dialogue was recorded.

The aural exciter can add clarity to a dialogue track and help the voice stand out at a quieter level. Short delays can add depth and apparent loudness to the voice, but be careful here: It takes only a bit more delay than necessary for the delay to become obvious and, if it is inappropriate to the narrative material, ludicrous.

Sound Effects

The same considerations that pertain to premixing dialogue apply to premixing sound effects, although the degree and application of signal processing often differs. For example, it is more likely that sound effects will be manipulated to a greater extent than dialogue. Using a significant amount of EQ boost or cut on dialogue would change voice character dramatically, whereas with a sound effect dramatic alteration may be quite appropriate. More liberties can be taken with sound effects, because they are not as familiar to our ears as is the human voice, particularly those that emanate from science fiction situations. But paying attention to sonic clarity, preventing distortion, and keeping an effect within the prescribed dynamic range are no less important for sound-effect premixing than they are for dialogue premixing. This is sometimes easier said than done, because sound effects tend to be mixed "hot." There are other notable differences between dialogue and sound-effect premixing.

Sound-effect premixing usually includes handling most, or all, of the fades. It sometimes also includes setting the relative differences in level that are to occur in the final mix. Dialogue in film and television normally is centered in the stereo and surround-sound mixes, and underscored music is mixed left, center, and right. In surround it may be arced more toward the left and right sides as well. These operations are done in the rerecording mix. Sound effects are often placed in a particular screen space or, if there is no danger of dislocation, moved with the action in the picture. A sound effect is normally done in mono; it is the reverb that gives it the stereo imaging or feel. With surround sound too mixers are placing and signal-processing primarily with mono effects. Any panning of sound effects is done in the premix.

Music

Music is handled differently than dialogue and sound effects in a premix in that very little, if anything, is done at that stage to prepare it for rerecording. Musical knowledge is integral to music mixing, and not all sound people have that foundation. Of the three elements in the sound track—dialogue, sound effects, and music—music is the most structurally complex and spectrally and dynamically varied. Another reason that little premixing is done with music is that by the time a music track is ready for the premix, most of what a premix would accomplish has already been done. If the music undergoes any processing at the premix stage, it may be some high-end boosting to compensate for high-frequency loss during subsequent processing, and compression if the music is conflicting with the dialogue that it is underscoring.

The Rerecording Mix

There is one thing about the rerecording process involving film that differs from mixing for TV that you cannot get around: Because film is played in a large room, it is necessary to rerecord it in a large room to be sure of what you are doing. It comes down to the acoustics; things happen in a large room that do not happen in a small room.

That said, the purpose of the rerecording mix is to blend the premixed DME tracks into a seamless stereo or surround-sound recording. Depending on market level, budget, and union regulations, rerecording may be handled by the same people who recorded, edited, or premixed the sound, or by people who have not yet heard the track or seen the picture.

On one hand, the rerecording mix should be relatively straightforward, assuming the premix has been well produced. Gross changes should be unnecessary. On the other hand, if the rerecording mix is unsuccessful, all of the previous work goes just about for naught.

It is particularly important, therefore, that the premixed tracks are free of technical problems so that the rerecording mixer(s) can concentrate on aesthetic points. (There may be one, two, three, or more rerecording mixers, depending on the scale and complexity of the material. Two mixers usually divide duties between dialogue/music and effects; three mixers handle each component separately. The dialogue mixer is usually in charge of rerecording.)

All extraneous sounds should be deleted during editing, and certainly no later than the premix. The three composite tracks should be clean at the beginning and end of each sound or sequence. Each track should be cut as close to the beginning and end of a sound as possible without cutting off soft attacks or decay.

In addition, in- and out-points of each cue must be precise—a rerecording mixer cannot be expected to pinpoint cues. A well-laid-out cue sheet is mandatory (see 19-15).

Spatial Imaging in Film

The larger screen size of motion pictures allows somewhat greater flexibility in locating dialogue, but not that much more when frequent shot changes position the actors at different camera-to-source distances. There is more opportunity to take advantage of the stereo and surround-sound spaces with sound effects and, to some extent, music. But even here, whatever is done should serve the audience's attention to the story, rather than create sonic fireworks.

Stereo

Conventional stereo sound tracks in 35-mm film are reproduced on three channels—left, center, and right. At least three channels are necessary because of the screen width and the size of the audience area. Without a center channel, people sitting at the left and right would hear only the loudspeaker closest to them and receive no stereo effect.

Dialogue As a general rule, on-screen dialogue is placed in the center. If a character moves about and there are several cuts, as in television, it can become annoying to have the sound jump around, particularly if more than one character is involved. On the other hand, if characters maintain their positions in a scene, even though shots change from wide to close-up or vice versa, stereo imaging can be effected without disorienting the audience.

Sound Effects Sound effects also tend to be concentrated toward the middle. If they are stationary or move across a wide distance, they may be located and panned without distracting. But too much movement muddles the sound. Sometimes, to create the sense that an effect is positioned relative to the action, the effect is

RERECORDING CUE SHEET									
Track No.		Track No.		Track No.		Track No.		Track No.	
Reel No.		Reel No.		Reel No.		Reel No.		Reel No.	

< Fade in > Fade out + Raise – Lower ∟ Crossfade

19-15 Rerecording cue sheet

reverbed. Most of the dry effect is placed at or near screen-center, and the wet part is used to convey its placement in the frame.

Music Music is distributed in stereo. It is usually mixed so that it frames dialogue and effects. If there is no music (and sometimes when there is), background sounds and ambience are mixed to the left and right to create overall tone.

Surround Sound

The traditional approach to surround sound for film has been to delegate the principal audio—dialogue, sound effects, and music—to the left, center, and right channels and the nonessential sound, such as ambience and background effects, to the surround channels. Specifically, with the addition of the center and surround channels to conventional stereo reproduction, it creates a stable center and background imaging. The center loudspeaker provides more-precise localization, particularly of dialogue. This is more important with television sound than it is with film sound, because the TV image takes up a smaller space in the field of view. Hence, the center loudspeaker helps localize dialogue toward the center of the screen.

As audio producers become more accustomed to working with surround sound and audiences grow more comfortable with it as part of the overall viewing experience, the surround channels are being used for more than just ambience and additional environmental effects, when the situation warrants. The thinking is that sound is omnidirectional and our natural acoustic environment puts it all around us all the time, so why not do the same thing with surround sound, the caveats being so long as it contributes to or furthers the story and does not call attention to itself, distracting the audience.

In these types of surround mixes, the dialogue of a character walking into a scene may be heard first from the side or rear and panned to the front-center as he appears on-screen. Music from a band playing behind a character seated in a venue with lots of people and hubbub may be heard in the surround speakers, with the dialogue frontally centered and the walla of the hubbub panned from the front speakers to the surrounds. A battle scene may have the sound of explosions, firing weaponry, and the shouts of soldiers coming from the front and surround speakers, placing it in the middle of the action.

In general, when mixing in surround sound, it may be useful to consider the following guidelines:

☑ The main purpose of surround sound is to provide an expanded, more realistic sense of aural space.

☑ Do not pull the audience's attention from the screen or try to overwhelm them with directional pyrotechnics in the surround-sound channels. Never try to rival what is on-screen.

☑ When the surround channels consist of long arrays of loudspeakers, as they do in theaters, for example, sounds do not localize as well as they do through the frontal loudspeaker array.

☑ Because localization is poor at low frequencies, it is not a good idea to try to focus a sound source using the LFE channel.

☑ The frequency response between the front speakers and the surrounds is different.

☑ Sound panned halfway between the front and surrounds draws some attention forward and some attention behind. This instability creates a separation or split in the sound.

☑ Mix to the visual perspective on the screen.

☑ Keep in mind the edges of the medium for which you mixing and place the elements within that frame.

☑ Dialogue goes center channel and is usually not panned, unless the on-screen action justifies it.

☑ Principal sound effects may be centered and/or placed somewhat left and right of center. If there are environmental or nonessential effects, they are delegated to the surrounds.

☑ Ambience is usually treated as fill or surround sound. Sometimes it may be music to add more dimension to the frontal music spread.

☑ Before doing the surround mix, do the left, center, and right mixes first.

☑ When using compression or limiting on dialogue, do not process any additional ambience signal through the same compressor-limiter. This reduces the potential for the dominant sound to cause the ambience to "pump."

☑ When using signal processing, use separate processing devices for each element. Using the same processor for more than one element could, among other things, smear sonic imaging.

☑ When background sound distracts from dialogue, it helps to widen the voice by panning it toward the surround-sound position. If the material is recorded and it is possible to work with separate tracks, the best thing to do is change the mix.

☑ When the visual action justifies them, moving sounds not only support on-screen elements passing by the audience, but they also support a moving point of view.

☑ Unless it makes sense in relation to the on-screen action or it is for special effect, placing major program elements to the side and/or behind the audience is usually disconcerting. Being gimmicky only calls attention to itself and does little, if anything, to further the story line or maintain the audience's attention.

All in all, the advantages of multidimensional manipulation of sound far outweigh its problems: (1) Dialogue and sound effects can be accurately localized across a wide or small screen for almost any audience position; (2) specific sound effects can be localized to the surround-sound loudspeakers; (3) ambience and environmental sounds can be designed to reach the audience from all directions; and (4) panning of sound can occur across the front sound stage and between front and surround locations.

Downmixing

As is the case with mixing music, a surround-sound mix for film or television may not be reproduced on a surround-sound system. To provide a compatible playback format for other types of systems, the film and TV surround mix is generally downmixed to other formats (see 19-16).

CUE SHEETS

Cue sheets are essential throughout any production in any medium, but they are indispensable during the premix and rerecording mix stages. The forms vary from studio to studio; they may be handwritten or computer-generated, but they must contain at least the information outlined in the following list (see 19-17, 19-18, and 19-19).

A column of time cues. This may be designated in time code, real time, or footage, depending on the medium and format. By using one column to serve all tracks, it is easy to see at a glance the relationship of cues.

What the sound is. Each cue must be identified. Identification should be both brief to avoid clutter and precise to give the mixer certainty about what the cue is.

When a sound starts. The word or words identifying a sound are written at the precise point it begins. With dialogue or narration, in-points may be indicated by a line or the first two or three words.

How a sound starts. Unless otherwise indicated, it is assumed that a sound starts clean; that is, the level has been preset before the sound's entry. If a cue is faded in, faded in slowly, crossfaded with another sound, and so on, that must be indicated on the cue sheet.

The duration of a sound. From the point at which a cue begins to the point at which it ends is its duration. The simplest way of indicating this is to draw a straight line between the two points. Avoid using different-colored markers, double and triple lines, or other graphic highlights. The cue sheet or screen should be clean and uncluttered. If the cues are handwritten, pencil is better than ink, in case changes have to be made.

When a sound ends. This can be indicated by the same word(s) used at the entry cue accompanied by the word *out* or *auto* (for automatically). This tells the mixer that the end cue is clean and has been handled in the premix.

How a sound ends. If a sound fades, crossfades, and so on, this should be indicated at the point

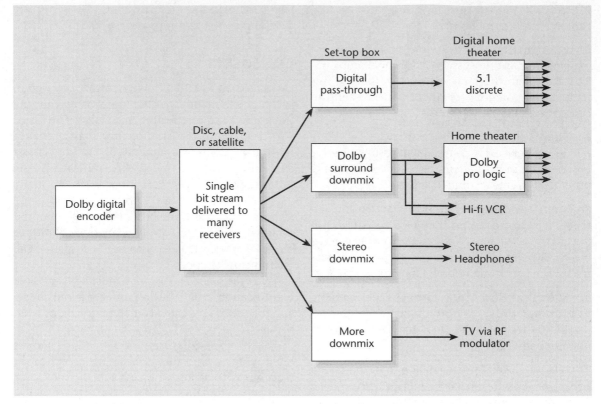

19-16 Example of downmixing from a 5.1 channel surround digital encoder to a variety of formats

when the sound must be out or crossfaded. The mixer then has to decide when to begin the out-cue so it has been effected by the time indicated.

STEREO-TO-MONO COMPATIBILITY

Although *stereo-to-mono compatibility* is not the problem it once was, because stereo is the format of the day, it does warrant some attention here. In surround sound stereo-to-mono compatibility is even less of a concern, because most systems in use are mono-compatible.

Stereo discs, radio, TV, film, and multimedia notwithstanding, except for home component music systems and visits to the motion picture theater, enough people still receive mediated information in mono so that with much of what is stereo-mastered monophonic compatibility is a consideration.

Stereo-to-mono compatibility must be checked and rechecked throughout a mix. What sounds good in stereo may be less than acceptable in mono. A wide and satisfactorily balanced stereo recording played in mono may be too loud. For example, a 0 VU reading at the extreme left and right in stereo is equivalent to +6 in mono. Anything assigned to the center in the stereo mix may be too loud in mono and out of context with the rest of the sound. Moreover, placing voicings extreme left or right in stereo results in a 3-dB or greater loss in their level(s) relative to the rest of the spectrum when played in mono.

So the problem of stereo-to-mono compatibility is twofold: too much sound in the center and not enough at the left and right. The reason, briefly stated, is that signals that are in phase in stereo add in mono, and signals that are out of phase in stereo cancel in mono.

19-17 Example of a cue sheet used for automated dialogue replacement

ADR

ELECTRONIC POST SYNC
AUTOMATED DIALOGUE RECORDING

CUE SHEET

REEL # _____ ¼ REEL # _____ PAGE # _____

PRODUCER _____ EDITOR _____

PRODUCTION _____

JOB # _____ PROD # _____ DATE _____

CHARACTER	FOOTAGE START STOP	MIXER NOTES	CHANNELS				DIALOGUE
			1	2	3	4	

SOUND EFFECTS — (Foley FX)

Triplicate: Editor — Mixer — Recordist

Production Number		Reel		Time				FX Editor	Telephone

Cue No.	Mixer Notes	Footage Start & Stop		Channels			Detailed Description and Remarks		
				1	2	3			
		Start							
		Stop							
		Start							
		Stop							
		Start							
		Stop							
		Start							
		Stop							
		Start							
		Stop							
		Start							
		Stop							
		Start							
		Stop							
		Start							
		Stop							
		Start							
		Stop							
		Start							
		Stop							
		Start							
		Stop							
		Start							
		Stop							
		Start							
		Stop							
		Start							
		Stop							
		Start							
		Stop							
		Start							
		Stop							

19-18 Example of a cue sheet used for recording Foley effects

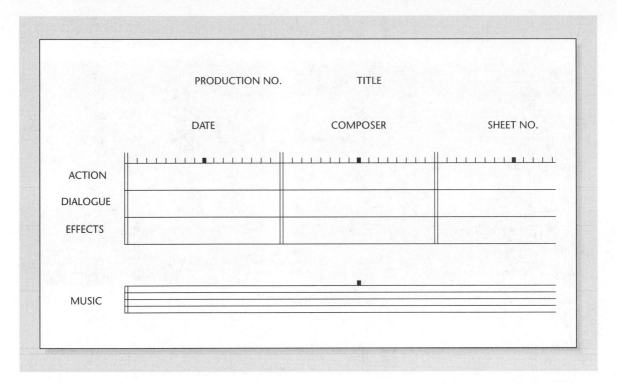

19-19 Example of a cue sheet used for music underscoring

Certain devices, such as the phasing analyzer or stereo display processor, are used to indicate stereo-to-mono compatibility during a mix (see 19-20). Many of today's pan pots are designed with either a 3-dB– or a 6-dB–down notch that facilitates mono compatibility.

Two other techniques are also used. One is not to put anything dead center or at the extreme left or right in a stereo mix. About three and nine o'clock are usually recommended. This reduces both center channel buildup and loss of some of the left and right information when playing stereo recordings in mono. But the stereo image may not be as wide as it should be, and center imaging could be awkward.

The better technique is to be very careful of in-phase and out-of-phase signals during recording and signal processing, especially with reverb, and to constantly A-B between stereo and mono playback during a mix, using both your ears and a phasing analyzer. In the A-B comparisons, always check to make sure that nothing is lost due to phase,

that nothing stands out inordinately, and that the overall blend is maintained.

EVALUATING THE FINISHED PRODUCT

What makes good sound? Ask 100 audio specialists to evaluate the same sonic material and undoubtedly you will get 100 different responses. That is one of the beauties of sound: It is so personal. Who is to tell you that your taste is wrong? As a listener, if it satisfies you, that is all that matters. When sound is produced for an audience, however, professional "ears" must temper personal taste. To this end, there are generally accepted standards that audio pros agree are reasonable bases for artistic judgment.

Before discussing these standards, a word about the monitor loudspeakers is in order. Remember that the sound you evaluate is influenced by the loudspeaker reproducing it. You must therefore be thoroughly familiar with its frequency response and how it otherwise affects sonic reproduction. If a

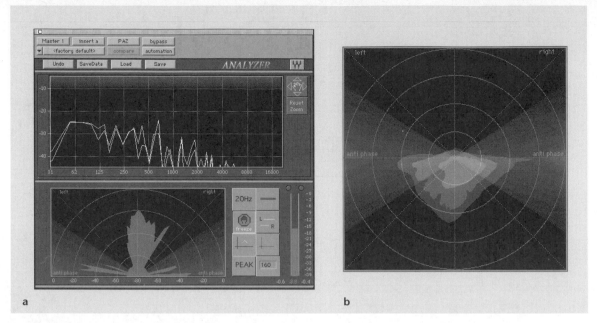

19-20 Real-time analyzer. (a) This model provides frequency analysis, a stereo position display, and loudness/peak meters. The stereo position display in this figure shows a mono-compatible stereo signal. A skewing to the left or right indicates a left-heavy or right-heavy stereo signal, respectively. (b) Stereo position display showing a badly out-of-phase stereo signal.

sound is overly bright or unduly dull, you have to know whether that is the result of the recording or the loudspeaker. Remember, a good way to familiarize yourself with a loudspeaker's response is to take a few test discs and well-produced commercial recordings with which you are thoroughly familiar and listen to them on the monitor system until you are confident about its response characteristics.

Intelligibility

It makes sense that if there is narration, dialogue, or song lyrics, the words must be intelligible. If not, meaning is lost. But when working with material over a long period of time, the words become so familiar that it might not be apparent that they are muffled, masked, and otherwise difficult to distinguish. In evaluating intelligibility it is therefore a good idea to do it with fresh "ears," as if you were hearing the words for the

first time. If that does not give you the needed distance from the material, ask someone else if the words or lyrics are clear.

Tonal Balance

Bass, midrange, and treble frequencies should be balanced; no one octave or range of octaves should stand out. Be particularly aware of too much low end that muddies and masks sound; overly bright upper midrange and treble that brings out sibilance and noise; absence of brilliance that dulls sound; and too much midrange that causes the harshness, shrillness, or edge that annoys and fatigues.

The timbre of the voice, sound effects, and acoustic instruments should sound natural and realistic. Music and sounds generated by electric and electronic instruments do not necessarily have to sound so, unless they are supposed to.

Ensemble sound should blend as a whole. As such, solos or lead voicings should be sonically proportional in relation to the accompaniment.

Spatial Balance and Perspective

All sonic elements in aural space should be unambiguously localized; it should be clear where various sounds are coming from. Their relationships—front-to-back and side-to-side—should be in proper perspective. Dialogue spoken from the rear of a room should sound somewhat distant and reverberant; an oboe solo should be distinct yet come from its relative position in the orchestra; a vocal should not be too far in front of an ensemble or buried in it; background music should not overwhelm the announcer; crowd noise should not be more prominent than the sportscaster's voice.

Positional and loudness changes should be subtle and sound natural. They should not jar or distract by jumping out, falling back, or bouncing side-to-side (unless the change is justified in relation to the picture).

Definition

Each element should be clearly defined—identifiable, separate, and distinct—yet, if grouped, blended so that no one element stands out or crowds or masks another's sound. Each element should have its position in, and yet be a natural part of, the sound's overall spectral range and spatial arrangement.

Dynamic Range

The range of levels from softest to loudest should be as wide as the medium allows, making sure that the softest sounds are easily audible and the loudest sounds are undistorted. If compressed, sound should not seem squeezed together, nor should it surge from quiet to loud and vice versa.

Clarity

A clear recording is as noise- and distortion-free as possible. Hum, hiss, leakage, phasing, smearing, blurring from too much reverb, and harmonic, intermodulation, and loudness distortion—all muddle sound, adversely affecting clarity.

Airiness

Sound should be airy and open. It should not sound isolated, stuffy, muffled, closed-down, dead, lifeless, overwhelming, or oppressive.

Acoustical Appropriateness

Acoustics, of course, must be good, but they must also be appropriate. The space in which a character is seen and the acoustic dimension of that space must match; classical music and jazz sound most natural in an open, relatively spacious environment; acoustics for rock-and-roll can range from tight to open. A radio announcer belongs in an intimate acoustic environment.

Source Quality

When a recording is broadcast, downloaded, or sent on for mastering, there is usually some loss in sound quality. This occurs with both analog and digital sound. For example, what seems like an appropriate amount of reverb when listening to a scene or a song in a studio may be barely discernible after transmission or transfer. Therefore, as a general guideline, be aware that a source recording should have higher resolution than its eventual release medium.

PRODUCTION VALUES

The degree to which you are able to develop and appraise production values is what separates the mere craftsperson from the true artist. Production values relate to the material's style, interest, color, and inventiveness. It is the most difficult part of an evaluation to define or quantify, because response is qualitative and intuitive. Material with excellent production values grabs and moves you. It draws you into the production, compelling you to forget your role as objective observer; you become the audience. When this happens, it is not only the culmination of the production process, but its fulfillment.

▶ Mixing and rerecording are the phases of postproduction when the separately recorded elements are combined into a natural and integrated whole.

▶ The general purpose of mixing and rerecording notwithstanding, the overriding challenge is to maintain aesthetic perspective.

▶ In proceeding with a mix, it is necessary to know on what type of delivery system it will be reproduced. Radio, television, film, digital disc, and multimedia have different sonic requirements.

▶ In layering sound it is important to: establish the main and supporting sounds to create focus or point of view; position the sounds to create relationships of space and distance; maintain spectral balance so that the aural space is properly weighted; and maintain definition of eachsound.

▶ To help maintain definition as well as intelligibility in a mix, the various sounds should have different sonic features. These features can be varied in pitch, tempo, loudness, intensity, envelope, timbre, style, and so on.

▶ In layering sounds it is also important to establish perspective. Some sounds are more important than others; the predominant one usually establishes the focus or point of view.

▶ One procedure in voicing-over recorded music is called a donut—fading the music after it is established and reestablishing it later at its former full level to create a hole for the announcement.

▶ When voicing-over music or sound effects, try to vary the background dynamics to help direct focus and create interest through sonic variety.

▶ Compression is a commonly used production tool in radio; it helps enhance the spoken word by giving it clarity and power and it keeps speech from being overwhelmed by sound effects or music.

▶ Subtracting the time of an individual item from the total time of a program or program segment is known as backtiming.

▶ Playing sound with the fader off is known as deadpotting.

▶ In a music mixdown, one procedure is to evaluate the positive and negative attributes of the recording, working with one track at a time but building on the tracks already processed. When each track sounds acceptable in the context of the overall mix, blend and balance the sounds together. This may involve changing individual settings in favor of the overall mix.

▶ When equalizing avoid large increases or decreases in EQ, do not increase or decrease too many tracks at the same frequency, and do not use equalizing as a substitute for better microphone selection and placement. Try subtractive, instead of additive, equalization and use complementary EQ to keep masking to a minimum. Equalizing between 400 and 2,000 Hz is more noticeable than equalizing above and below that range. Be sure to equalize with an awareness of the frequency limits of the medium in which you are working.

▶ The quality of reverberation added to a recording in the mix depends, to a considerable extent, on musical style. Classical, jazz, and some types of folk music usually require natural-sounding acoustics; various reverberant environments may be appropriate for popular music.

▶ Do not add artificial reverberation until after signal processing and panning, because it is difficult to get a true sense of the effects of frequency and positional change in a reverberant space. Also, avoid giving widely different reverb times to the various components in an ensemble or sound track unless they are supposed to sound as though they are in different acoustic environments.

▶ Factors involved in placing musical components in the stereo frame are the aural balance, the arrangement of the ensemble when performing, and the type of music being played.

▶ Surround sound comes far closer than stereo to reproducing our natural acoustic environment by enabling the music and the listener to occupy the same space. It increases the depth of the front-to-rear and side-to-side sound images.

▶ Surround sound can be produced by synthesizing a multichannel signal from two-channel stereo or by building the multichannel mix from the outset, which is the preferred way.

- The 5.1 surround format uses five full-bandwidth channels and a low-frequency channel for sounds below 125 Hz.

- In mixing for surround sound, four important elements to manage are the center channel, the surround channels, reverberation, and the low-frequency enhancement (LFE).

- Recordkeeping, whether handwritten or entered into a computer memory, is important in any type of mixing and rerecording. You never know if it will be necessary to redo a part of the mix or the entire thing.

- The process of combining the dialogue, sound effects, and music (DME) tracks for television and film is accomplished, generally, during the premixing and rerecording stages.

- The premix is the stage during which dialogue, sound effects, and, to some extent, music are prepared for the final rerecording mix.

- The purpose of the rerecording mix is to blend the premixed dialogue, sound effects, and music into a seamless stereo or surround-sound recording.

- Of the factors that influence mixing sound for television, three important ones are how the audio is heard in most homes, TV's emphasis on the spoken (and sung) word, and how screen size and program type affect spatial imaging.

- Stereo placement in film and TV usually positions dialogue and sounds in the center, and music to the left, in the center, and to the right. Large-screen film positions dialogue in the center with limited lateral movement, sound effects across a somewhat wider space but still toward the center, and music left, center, and right. The reason for such placement is to avoid disorienting the audience in relation to the on-screen sources of sound and image.

- Surround sound produces a soundfield in front of, to the sides of, and behind the listener.

- Generally, the left, center, and right channels contain the principal audio—dialogue, sound effects, and music—and are reproduced by the frontal loudspeakers. The center channel is used for dialogue. The surround-sound channel is dedicated to background sound(s) and reproduced by the side or rear loudspeakers, or both. Although, as producers and the audience grow more accustomed to surround sound, the surround channels are being used for secondary audio in addition to ambience and environmental effects.

- However surround sound is mixed, the main imperative is to not pull the audience's attention from the screen.

- Cue sheets are essential throughout the production process, but they are indispensable during the premix and rerecording mix stages.

- In mastering stereo sound that may be reproduced on monophonic systems, the material must be mono-compatible.

- In evaluating a final product, factors that should be considered include intelligibility, tonal balance, spatial balance and perspective, definition, dynamic range, clarity, airiness, acoustical appropriateness, and source quality.

- Production values relate to the material's style, interest, color, and inventiveness.

Appendix A:
Occupations in Audio

This list of occupations is intended to provide a sense of the breadth of available jobs in audio and a few audio-related fields. It is not inclusive, nor are these positions mutually exclusive. Depending on the type of production and the assignment, one or more of these functions may be incorporated. The job descriptions are generalized and differ from studio to studio.

Job responsibilities in given markets also vary. A person in a smaller audio production house may have more than one duty to perform. In a large market, union regulations may proscribe that members perform a designated job and may not perform other tasks also credentialed to that union or to other unions.

In the audio marketplace, a college education; a background in production, music, engineering, computers, or some combination of the four; and "ears" are distinct advantages. Of considerable importance too is the ability to get along with people.

assistant, setup, or second engineer In music recording, sets up the studio and control room before a session, checks and readies the equipment, and assists the engineer during production.

audio educator Teaches audio courses in a junior or senior college, university, or trade school. In colleges and universities, audio courses are located in various departments, such as broadcasting, television and radio, and film, and in the schools of music, engineering, and communications.

audio engineer Depending on the medium—radio, television, or music recording—maintains the audio equipment, operates the console and other control room gear, and performs the recording, editing, and mixing functions.

audio for video postproduction editor Edits audio materials for video in television postproduction. May also do the mixing.

audio for video postproduction mixer Mixes audio materials for video in television postproduction. May also do the editing.

audio production engineer In radio and television, equipment operator and producer of audio materials.

audio software designer/producer Creates, designs, and produces audio software for computers, games, and Internet production.

automated dialogue replacement (ADR) editor Edits the ADR recording.

automated dialogue replacement (ADR) producer In charge of the ADR recording session and postproduction editing.

board operator Operates the console and other control room equipment during a broadcast and production session.

boom operator Operates the boom microphone during a broadcast and production recording.

concert sound reinforcement engineer Sets up, tests, and operates the sound equipment for live concerts.

dialogue editor Edits the production dialogue and postproduction ADR recordings.

duplication technician Duplicates client audio recordings, determines if material is suitable for duplication, handles packaging, and checks and readies the record and playback equipment.

entry-level trainee Does whatever is asked in the execution of studio and control room activities and in helping during a production session; performs routine housekeeping duties; takes the opportunity to observe and learn.

Foley artist Creates and performs sound effects in the Foley studio.

Foley editor Edits the Foley-produced sound effects. May also record and mix the Foley effects.

Foley mixer Mixes the Foley-produced sound effects. May also record and edit the Foley effects.

Foley recordist   Records the sound effects during Foley production. May also mix and edit the Foley effects.

librarian   Receives, catalogs, files, and mails a studio's audio materials; obtains appropriate authorization for recordings' release.

machine room operator   In film, loads and operates the magnetic film recorder/playback machines. In television, handles the loading and operation of the recorders.

maintenance engineer   Maintains the audio equipment to keep it up to working specifications, including the alignment and calibration of recorders; DSP calibration; real-time analysis of the monitor system; finding sources of noise; and performing emergency repairs.

maintenance technician   Diagnoses problems and repairs audio and other electronic equipment.

mastering engineer   Processes and records the tape, disc, or vinyl masters from the production master recordings.

music editor   Edits the recording of the music score.

music premixer   Mixes the music score to prepare it for the rerecording mix.

music producer   Has creative charge of the music production; may be affiliated with a record company, film company, or the performing artist.

production recordist/mixer   Records and, if necessary, mixes dialogue on the set.

radio production engineer/producer   Operates the equipment and produces audio materials, such as spot announcements, promos, jingles, and station IDs.

remote broadcast engineer   Maintains the audio equipment on location; may also handle the recording.

remote broadcast mixer   Records the audio on location.

rerecording mixer   Mixes the composite dialogue, sound effects, and music tracks to stereo or surround sound; may be handled by one, two, or three mixers.

scoring mixer   Mixes the film or video music sound track.

sound assistant   Assists the principal audio production personnel in whatever ways they wish, including packing and carrying equipment, setting up the studio and control room, doing light maintenance, organizing the paperwork, and getting coffee.

sound designer   Creates, directs, and is usually involved in the production of the overall sonic character of a work, such as a film, video, television program, spot announcement, game, CD-ROM, Web page, theatrical play, or musical.

sound-effect editor   Edits the sound effects; may collect, record, and produce them as well.

sound transfer engineer   Transfers audio from one recording medium to another, usually from tape or disk to magnetic film.

technical writer   Writes about audio equipment, technology, production techniques, trends, and news in the various media of the audio world.

television postproduction editor/mixer   Edits and mixes the production audio plus the music and any additional sound effects in postproduction.

theater sound designer for plays and musicals   Records, edits, and mixes the audio for plays and musicals; handles the audio at the theater's mixing console during performances.

Appendix B:
Selected Audio-Related Web Sites

Acoustical Products and Architectural Materials

Acoustic Sciences Corp.   www.tubetrap.com

Acoustic Systems, Inc.   www.acousticsystems.com

Acoustic Technologies   www.acoustic-tech.com.au

Acoustical Solutions   www.acousticalsolutions.com

Acoustics First Corp.   www.acousticsfirst.com

Apogee Sound, Inc.   www.apogee-sound.com

ASC-Tube Trap   www.tubetrap.com

Auralex Acoustics Inc.   www.auralex.com

Industrial Acoustics Co.   www.industrialacoustics.com

Klippel GmbH   www.klippel.de

Level Control Systems   www.LCSaudio.com

Renkus-Heinz   www.renkus-heinz.com

Rohde & Schwarz   www.rsd.de

RPG Diffusor Systems   www.rpginc.com

Sellmark Electronics
    audiomation@sellmark.octagon.co.uk

Wenger Corporation   www.wengercorp.com

WhisperRoom   www.whisperroom.com

Amplifiers and Preamplifiers

Alesis Studio Electronics   www.alesis.com

Amek   www.amek.com

AMS Neve PLC   www.ams-neve.com

Aphex Systems   www.aphex.com

Applied Research & Technology, Inc.
    www.artproaudio.com

Automated Processes, Inc. (API)   www.apiaudio.com

Avalon Design, Inc.   www.avalondesign.com

Bang & Olufsen   www.bang-olufsen.com

Behringer International   www.behringer.de

Bellari   www.bellari.com

Bryston Ltd.   www.bryston.ca

C Audio   www.c-audio.com

Carvin   www.carvin.com

Carver Professional   www.carverpro.com

Chevin Research   www.chevin-research.com

Cirrus Logic/Crystal Audio   www.cirrus.com

CraneSong, Ltd.   www.cranesong.com

Crest Audio   www.crestaudio.com

Crown International   www.crownaudio.com

Dale Pro Audio   www.daleproaudio.com

Demeter Amplification   www.demeteramps.com

Geoffrey Daking & Co, Inc.   www.daking.com

dbx Professional Products   www.dbxpro.com

Demeter Amplification
    www.demeteramps.com/proaudio.html

D&R Electronica   www.d-r.nl

Dredge-Tone Audio   www.dredgetone.com

D. W. Fearn   www.dwfearn.com

Earthworks   www.earthwks.com

Electro-Voice Professional Audio Products
    www.electrovoice.com

Focusrite   www.focusriteusa.com

Gibson/Opcode   www.gibson.com

Grace Design   www.gracedesign.com

Great River Electronics   www.greatriverelectronics.com

Groove Tubes   www.groovetubes.com

GT Electronics   www.gtelectronics.com

Hafler   www.hafler.com

HHB Communications USA LLC   www.hhbusa.com

Hoontech Co, Ltd.   www.hoontech.com

JBL Professional   www.jblpro.com

Joemeek   www.joemeek.com

The John Hardy Company   www.johnhardyco.com

Lexicon Inc.   www.lexicon.com

Mackie Designs, Inc.   www.mackie.com

Manley Laboratories, Inc.   www.manleylabs.com

Millennia Media, Inc.   www.mil-media.com

QSC Audio Products   www.qscaudio.com

Presonus Audio Electronics   www.presonus.com

Raven Labs   www.raven-labs.com

Requisite Audio Engineering   www.requisiteaudio.com

Roland Corporation U.S.   www.rolandus.com

Universal Audio   www.uaudio.com

Samson Technologies Corp.   www.samsontech.com

Sound Devices   www.sounddevices.com

STK Professional Audio   www.stkpro.com

Summit Audio   www.summitaudio.com

Symetrix Professional   www.symetrixaudio.com

THAT Corporation   www.thatcorp.com

TOA Electronics   www.toaelectronics.com

Tsunami Technologies   www.tsunamitechnologies.com

Yamaha Corp.   www.yamaha.com

Yorkville Professional Audio Products
www.yorkville.com

Audio and Acoustical Measurement Equipment

Apogee Sound, Inc.   www.apogee-sound.com

Audio Control Industrial   www.audiocontrol.com

Audio Precision   www.audioprecision.com

Audiomatica SRL   www.mclink.it/com/audiomatica

Beyerdynamic   www.beyerdynamic.com

Channel D Corp.   www.channld.com

Sound Alignment Systems by Checkpoint
www.checkpoint3d.com

Dorrough Electronics   www.dorrough.com

Earthworks   www.earthwks.com

Furman Sound   www.furmansound.com

Group One Ltd.   www.g1ltd.com

JBL Professional   www.jblpro.com

Josephson Engineering   www.josephson.com

Klippel GmbH   www.klippel.de

Lake DSP   www.lakedsp.com

LinearX   www.linearx.com

Listen, Inc.   www.listeninc.com

Logitek   www.logitekaudio.com

Metric Halo   www.mhlabs.com

Meyer Sound Labs   www.meyersound.com

Neutrik USA   www.neutrikusa.com

Opticom   www.opticom.com

Rhode & Schwarz   www.rsd.de

RPG Diffusor Systems, Inc.   www.rpginc.com

Sam Ash Professional Audio Group
www.samashmusic.com

Siasoft   www.siasoft.com

Soundsmith   www.sound-smith.com

Tektronix   www.tek.com

Terrasonde   www.terrasonde.com

Walters-Storyk Design Group   www.wsdg.com

Wohler Technologies   www.wohler.com

Audio Archiving

Alesis Studio Electronics   www.alesis.com

Arboretum Systems Inc.   www.arboretum.com

ATR Service Company   www.atrservice.com

BIAS: Berkley Integrated Audio Software, Inc.
www.bias-inc.com

Dale Pro Audio   www.daleproaudio.com

dB Technologies c/o AID   www.dbtechno.com

Digigram Inc.   www.digigram.com

GML/ Massenburg Design Works c/o AID
www.gmlinc.com

Mitsui Advanced Media   www.mitsuicdr.com

mSoft, Inc.   www.msoftinc.com

The Museum of Sound Recording   www.mosr.org

Nagra USA, Inc.   www.nagra.com

Sam Ash Professional Audio Group
www.samashmusic.com

Sonic Foundry   www.sonicfoundry.com

Sonifex Limited   www.sonifex.co.uk

Audio Restoration

Algorithmix Advanced DSP Devices
www.algorithmix.com

Arboretum Systems, Inc.   www.arboretum.com

Audio Intervisual Design   www.aidinc.com

BIAS: Berkley Integrated Audio Software, Inc.
www.bias-inc.com

Cedar Audio USA   www.independentaudio.com

dB Technologies c/o AID   www.dbtechno.com

DARTECH Inc.   www.dartpro.com

Diamond Cut Technologies   www.diamondcut.com

digidesign   www.digidesign.com

Enhanced Audio   www.enhancedaudio.com

GML/Massenburg Design Works c/o AID
www.gmlinc.com

Independent Audio   www.independentaudio.com

JVC Disc America   www.jvcsdiscusa.com

The Museum of Sound Recording   www.mosr.org

Quantegy Inc.   www.quantegy.com

SADiE, Inc.   www.sadie.com

Sam Ash Professional Audio Group
www.samashmusic.com

SEK'D America   www.sekd.com

Sonic Foundry   www.sonicfoundry.com

Sonic Solutions   www.sonicsolutions.com

SPL Electronics GmbH   www.spl-electronics.com

Steinberg North America   www.steinberg.net

Syntrillium Software Corp.   www.syntrillium.com

Toroid Corp. of Maryland   www.toroid.com

Broadcast Mixing Consoles

Arrakis Systems, Inc.   www.arrakis-systems.com

ATI-Audio Technologies, Inc.   www.atiguys.com

Calrec Audio Ltd.   www.calrec.com

CM Automation   www.cmautomation.com

Cooper Sound Systems, Inc.   www.coopersound.com

Dale Pro Audio   www.daleproaudio.com

DHD Deubner Hoffman Digital GmbH
www.dhd-audio.de

Dolby Labs   www.dolby.com

Euphonix   www.euphonix.com

Generalmusic Corp.   www.generalmusic.com

Harrison   www.glw.com

Level Control Systems   www.lcsaudio.com

Logitek   www.logitekaudio.com

Mackie Designs, Inc.   www.mackie.com

Metric Halo   www.mhlabs.com

Millennia Media, Inc.   www.mil-media.com

Oram Professional Audio   www.oram.co.uk

Penny & Giles Controls, Inc.
www.penny-giles-controls.co.uk

Roland Corporation U.S.   www.rolandus.com

Rolls Corp.   www.rolls.com

Sam Ash Professional Audio Group
www.samashmusic.com

Scharff Weisberg, Inc.   www.swinyc.com

Solid State Logic Ltd.   www.solid-state-logic.com

Sonifex Ltd.   www.sonifex.co.uk

Sony Electronics, Inc.   www.sony.com/proaudio

Soundcraft   www.soundcraft.com

Stage Tec GmbH   www.stagetec.com

Studer North America   www.studer.ch

Turner Audio   www.turneraudio.com

Ward-Beck Systems   www.ward-beck.com

Wheatstone/Auditronics/Audio Arts
www.wheatstone.com

CD/DVD Authoring, Duplication, and Production Equipment

Alesis Studio Electronics   www.alesis.com

ATI-Audio Technologies, Inc.   www.atiguys.com

Audio Intervisual Design   www.aidinc.com

Dale Pro Audio   www.daleproaudio.com

dB Technologies c/o AID   www.dbtechno.com

Denon Electronics   www.del.denon.com

digidesign   www.digidesign.com

Disc Makers   www.discmakers.com

Fairlight USA   www.fairlightusa.com

Fostex Corp. of America   www.fostex.com

G Prime   www.gprime.com

Gefen, Inc.   www.gefen.com

Glyph Technologies, Inc.   www.glyphtech.com

HHB Communications USA LLC   www.hhbusa.com

JVC Disc America   www.jvcsdiscusa.com

Media Stream Technologies   www.mediastream.com

MediaFORM, Inc.   www.mediaform.com

Mediatechnics Systems   www.mediatechnics.com

Microboards Technology
www.microboardsproaudio.com

Oasis   www.oasisCD.com

Panasonic Broadcast & Television Systems Company
www.panasonic.com

Philips   www.philips.com

Rimage Corporation   www.rimage.com

Roland Corporation U.S.   www.rolandus.com

Roxio (Adaptec)   www.roxio.com/index.html

SADiE, Inc.   www.sadie.com

Sam Ash Professional Audio Group
www.samashmusic.com

Scharff Weisberg, Inc.   www.swinyc.com

Sonic Solutions   www.sonicsolutions.com

Sonorus, Inc.   www.sonorus.com

Sony Electronics, Inc.   www.sony.com/proaudio

SPL Electronics GmbH   www.spl-electronics.com

Studer North America   www.studer.ch

Synchronous Systems   www.syncsystems.com

Tascam   www.tascam.com

ThinKware   www.thinkware.com

Turner Audio   www.turneraudio.com

Z-Systems   www.z-sys.com

Digital Recording and Processing Equipment

Akai Musical Instrument Corp.   www.akaipro.com

Alesis Studio Electronics   www.alesis.com

Allen & Heath   www.allen-heath.com

Antares Audio Technologies   www.antarestech.com

Apogee Electronics Corp.   www.apogeedigital.com

Apogee Sound, Inc.   www.apogee-sound.com

Applied Research & Technology, Inc.
www.artproaudio.com

Audio Intervisual Design   www.aidinc.com

Audio Processing Technology   www.aptx.com

Audio Science, Inc.   www.audioscience.com

Arboretum Systems, Inc.   www.arboretum.com

Beyerdynamic   www.beyerdynamic.com

BSS Audio   www.bss.co.uk

Cakewalk Music Software   www.cakewalk.com

Circuit Research Labs, Inc.   www.crlsystems.com

Cirrus Logic   www.cirrus.com

CM Automation   www.cmautomation.com

Crane Song Ltd.   www.cranesong.com

Crown International   www.crownaudio.com

Cutting Edge   www.nogrunge.com

Cycling '74   www.cycling74.com

Dale Pro Audio   www.daleproaudio.com

dB Technologies c/o AID   www.dbtechno.com

dbx Professional   www.dbxpro.com

DCS Ltd.   www.independentaudio.com

Denon Electronics   www.del.denon.com

digidesign   www.digidesign.com

Dolby Labs   www.dolby.com

Drawmer-Transamerica Audio
www.transaudiogroup.com

DSP North America   www.dsppl.com.au

EMU-ENSONIQ   www.emu.com

Eventide Inc.   www.eventide.com

Fairlight USA   www.fairlightusa.com

Focusrite Audio Engineering/Group One Ltd.
www.focusriteusa.com

Fostex Corp. of America   www.fostex.com

Frontier Design Group   www.frontierdesign.com

G Prime   www.gprime.com

Generalmusic Corp.   www.generalmusic.com

Gibson/Opcode   www.gibson.com

GML/Massenburg Design Works c/o AID
www.gmlinc.com

Group One Ltd.   www.g1ltd.com

HHB Communications USA LLC   www.hhbusa.com

Innovative Electronic Designs, Inc.   www.ieaudio.com

Junger Audio Studiotechnik GmbH
www.junger-audio.com

JVC Disc America   www.jvcsdiscusa.com

Klippel GmbH   www.klippel.de

Korg USA, Inc.   www.korg.com

Kurzweil Music Systems
www.kurzweilmusicsystems.com

Lake DSP   www.lakedsp.com

Lectrosonics, Inc.   www.lectrosonics.com

Lexicon, Inc.   www.lexicon.com

Lighthouse Digital Systems, Inc.
www.lighthousedigital.com

Mackie Designs, Inc.   www.mackie.com

Metric Halo   www.mhlabs.com

Merging Technologies   www.merging.com

Mitsui Advanced Media   www.mitsuicdr.com

Mytek Digital   www.mytekdigital.com

Nagra USA, Inc.   www.nagra.com

Momentum Data Systems   www.mds.com

Monster Cable Products   www.monstercable.com

Motorola   www.dspaudio.motorola.com

Orban, Inc.   www.orban.com

Otari Corporation   www.otari.com

Outboard Electronics Ltd.   www.outboard.co.uk

Pacific Microsonics Ltd.   www.hdcd.com

Panasonic Broadcast and Television Systems Company   www.panasonic.com

Peavey Electronics Corp.   www.peavey.com

PMC Monitors   www.pmcloudspeaker.com

Presonus Audio Electronics   www.presonus.com

Prism Sound   www.prismsound.com

Roland Corp. U.S.   www.rolandus.com

SADiE, Inc.   www.sadie.com

Sam Ash Professional Audio Group   www.samashmusic.com

Scharff Weisberg   www.swinyc.com

Schoeps/Posthorn Recordings   www.posthorn.com

SeaSound   www.seasound.com

SEK'D America   www.sekd.com

Sonic Sense, Inc.   www.sonicsense.com

Sonic Solutions   www.sonicsolutions.com

Sonifex Limited   www.sonifex.co.uk

Sonorus, Inc.   www.sonorus.com

Sony Electronics, Inc.   www.sony.com/proaudio

Sounds Logical   www.soundslogical.com

Soundscape Digital Technology   www.soundscape-digital.com

SPL Electronics GmbH   www.spl-electronics.com

Studer North America   www.studer.ch

Superscope Technologies/Marantz Professional   www.superscope-marantzpro.com

Symbolic Sound Corporation   www.symbolicsound.com

Symetrix   www.symetrixaudio.com

Syntrillium Software Corp.   www.syntrillium.com

Tascam   www.tascam.com

ThinKware   www.thinkware.com

360 Systems   www.360systems.com

Turner Audio   www.turneraudio.com

Weiss   www.weiss.ch

White Instruments   www.whiteinstruments.com

Wohler Technologies/Panoramadtv   www.wohler.com

XTA Electronics/Group One Ltd.   www.xta.co.uk

Yamaha Corp.   www.yamaha.com

Z-Systems   www.z-sys.com

Disc Playback Systems

BIAS: Berkeley Integrated Audio Software, Inc.   www.bias-inc.com

Dale Pro Audio   www.daleproaudio.com

Digital Audio Research   www.dar.uk.com

Euphonix   www.euphonix.com

Fairlight USA   www.fairlightusa.com

HHB Communications USA LLC   www.hhbusa.com

Roland Corp. U.S.   www.rolandus.com

Sonifex Ltd.   www.sonifex.co.uk

Sony Electronics, Inc.   www.sony.com/proaudio

Hearing

H.E.A.R.   www.hearnet.com

House Ear Institute   webmaster@hei.org

National Hearing Conservation Assoc.   www.nhca.com

Precision Laboratories   www.precisionweb.com

Headsets

AKG Acoustics   www.akg-acoustics.com

Audio-Technica U.S., Inc.   www.audio-technica.com

Beyerdynamic   www.beyerdynamic.com

Clear-Com Intercom Systems   www.clear-com.com

Denon Electronics   www.del.denon.com

Jensen Music Industries   www.recoton.com

Quart Professional   www.radialeng.com

Roland Corp. U.S.   www.rolandus.com

Turner Audio   www.turneraudio.com

Internet Audio Production

AKM Semiconductor, Inc.   www.akm.com

Arboretum System, Inc.   www.arboretum.com

Audio Intervisual Design   www.aidinc.com

BIAS: Berkeley Integrated Audio Software, Inc.   www.bias-inc.com

Cakewalk Music Software   www.cakewalk.com

Connectsound, Inc.   www.connectsound.com

Cutting Edge   www.nogrunge.com

dB Technologies c/o AID   www.dbtechno.com

Digibid.com   www.digibid.com

Dolby Labs   www.dolby.com

EMU-ENSONIQ   www.emu.com

Fostex Corp. of America   www.fostex.com

Fraunhofer Institute IIS
    www.iss.fhg.delamm.index.html

Gefen, Inc.   www.gefen.com

Global Groove   www.globalgroove.org

Liquid Audio   www.liquidaudio.com

Management Data Media Systems
    www.mdata-us.com/index.htm

Merging Technologies   www.merging.com

mSoft, Inc.   www.msoftinc.com

OMT Technologies   www.mediatouch.net

Real Audio   www.realaudio.com

Rocket Network, Inc.   www.rocketnetwork.com

SEK'D America   www.sekd.com

Sonic Foundry   www.sonicfoundry.com

Sonorus, Inc.   www.sonorus.com

Sorenson Media   www.sorenson.com

Steinberg North America   www.steinberg.net

Syntrillium Software Corporation
    www.syntrillium.com

Telos Systems   www.zephyr.com

360 Systems   www.360systems.com

Waves   www.waves.com

Virtual Mixing Company   www.virtualmixer.com

Zandar Technologies   www.zandar.com

Location Sound and Recording

Comrex   www.comrex.com

The J-Lab Company   www.j-lab.com

JK Audio   www.jkaudio.com

Marti Electronics   www.martielectronics.com

Loudspeakers and Monitoring

AKG Acoustics   www.akg-acoustics.com

Alesis Studio Electronics   www.alesis.com

Ambiance Acoustics Loudspeakers   www.calcube.com

ATC Loudspeaker Technology 1272   www.atc.gb.net

ARX Systems   www.arx.com.au

Audix Corporation   www.audixusa.com

Bag End Loudspeakers   www.bagend.com

Behringer International   www.behringer.de

Bose   www.musicwest.com/sponsors/bose

Carvin   www.carvin.com

Celestion   www.celestion.com

D.A.S. Sound Products   www.dasaudio.com

Dynaudio Acoustics   www.dynaudioacoustics.com

EAW   www.eaw.com

FBT Electronics   www.fbt.it

Fostex Corp. of America   www.fostex.com

Fundamental Acoustic Research   www.far-audio.com

Genelec   www.genelec.com

Hafler   www.hafler.com

HHB Communications USA LLC   www.hhbusa.com

Hot House Professional Audio   www.hothousepro.com

JBL Professional   www.jblpro.com

Klein & Hummel GMBH   www.klein-hummel.de

Korg USA   www.korg.com

KRK Systems   www.krksys.com

Mackie Designs, Inc.   www.mackie.com

Musikelektronik Geithain GmbH
    www.home.t-online.de/home/musikelectronic-gelthain

Meyer Sound Labs, Inc.   www.meyersound.com

Miller & Kreisel Professional
    www.mkprofessional.com

NHT Professional   www.nhtpro.com

PMC Monitors   sales@promonitor.co.uk

Quested Monitoring Systems   www.quested.com

Spirit by Soundcraft   www.spiritbysoundcraft.com

Studer   www.studer.ch

TAD-Pioneer   www.TAD-Pioneer.com

Tannoy   www.tannoy.com

Truth Audio   www.truthaudio.com

Westlake Audio, Inc.   www.westlakeaudio.com

Velodyne   www.velodyne.com

Vergence Audio   www.vergenceaudio.com

Yamaha Corp. of America   www.yamaha.com

Yorkville   www.yorkville.com

Microphones

ACO Pacific, Inc.   www.acopacific.com

ADK Professional Microphones   www.adk.cc

Advanced Sonic Concepts
    www.advancedsonicconcepts.com

AKG Acoustics   www.akg-acoustics.com

Alesis Studio Electronics   www.alesis.com

Alesis/GT Electronics   www.gtelectronics.com

Apex Electronics   www.apexelectronics.com

Applied Microphone Technology
   www.appliedmic.com

Astatic Commercial Microphones   www.astatic.com

Audiocontrol Industrial   www.audiocontrol.com

Audio Engineering Associates   www.wesdooley.com

Audio Intervisual Design   www.aidinc.com

Audio Ltd./MacArthur Group
   macarthurgroup@erols.com

Audio-Technica U.S., Inc.   www.audiotechnica.com

Audix Corp.   www.audixusa.com

Azden Corporation   www.azdencorp.com

Bell Labs   www.bell-labs.com

Behringer International   www.behringer.de

Benson Audio Labs   www.bensonaudiolabs.com

Beyerdynamic   www.beyerdynamic.com

BLUE   www.bluemic.com

BPM Microphones   www.pmiaudio.com

Brauner of Germany/Transamerica Audio
   www.transaudiogroup.com

Bruel & Kjaer   www.danishproaudio.com

CAD Professional Microphones   www.cadmics.com

Carvin   www.carvin.com

Cascade Audio   www.cascade-audio.com

Coles/Audio Engineering Associates
   www.wesdooley.com

Countryman Associates, Inc.   sales@countryman.com

Crown International   www.crownaudio.com

Curtis Technology & Trade, Inc.
   www.curtis-technology.com

Dale Pro Audio   www.daleproaudio.com

DPA Microphones/TGI North America, Inc.
   www.dpamicrophones.com

Earthworks   www.earthwks.com

Elation   www.ropnet.ru/pages/elation/elation.htm

Electro-Voice   www.electrovoice.com

G Prime   www.gprime.com

Gold Line/TEF   www.gold-line.com

Group One Ltd.   www.g1ltd.com

HEAD Acoustics GmbH   www.head-acoustics.de

High Definition Audio   www.highdefaudio.com

Holophone   www.holophone.com

Independent Audio   www.independentaudio.com

Jensen Music Industries   www.recoton.com

Joemeek   www.joemeek.com

Josephsen Engineering   www.josephson.com

K & K Sound Systems   www.kksound.com

Lawson, Inc.   www.lawsonmicrophones.com

Lectrosonics, Inc.   www.lectrosonics.com

Manley Laboratories, Inc.   www.manleylabs.com

MBHO-Haun Microphones   www.mbho.de

Microflown Technologies   www.microflown.com

Microtech Gefell   www.microtechgefell.de

Minami Audio Equipment Company, Ltd.
   www.ecm-speaker.com

MIPRO Electronics   www.mipro.com.tw

MXL Professional Microphones   www.MXLmics.com

Nady   www.nadywireless.com

Neumann/USA   www.neumannusa.com

Peavey Electronics Corp.   www.peavey.com

PMI Audio Group   www.pmiaudio.com

Precision Labs, Inc.   www.precisionweb.com

Rising Sun Productions LTD   www.theholophone.com

Rode Microphones   www.rodemicrophones.com

Roland Corp. U.S.   www.rolandus.com

Royer Labs   www.royerlabs.com

Sabine, Inc.   www.sabineusa.com

Sam Ash Professional Audio Group
   www.samashmusic.com

Samson Technologies Corp.   www.samsontech.com

Sanken Audio Systems c/o AID   www.sas-mk.co.jp

Scharff Weisberg, Inc.   www.swinyc.com

Schoeps/Posthorn Recordings   www.posthorn.com

Sennheiser Electronic Corp.   www.sennheiserusa.com

Servoreeler Systems   www.servoreelers.com

Shure Brothers, Inc.   www.shure.com

SIB Systems   www.sib-drumsystems.com

Sony Electronics, Inc.   www.sony.com/proaudio

Soundelux Microphones   www.soundelux.com/mics

Soundfield/Transamerica Audio   www.soundfield.com

SPL Electronics GMBH   www.spl-electronics.com

Studiomaster   www.studiomaster.com

Superscope Technologies/Marantz Professional
   www.superscope-marantzpro.com

ThinKware   www.thinkware.com

Turner Audio   www.turneraudio.com

Vega   www.vegawireless.com

Xedit Corporation   www.servoreelers.com

MIDI Equipment

Akai Musical Instrument Corp.   www.akaipro.com

Alesis Studio Electronics   www.alesis.com

Antares Audio Technologies   www.antarestech.com

BSS Audio   www.bss.co.uk

Cakewalk Music Software   www.cakewalk.com

CM Automation   www.cmautomation.com

Crookwood   www.crookwood.com

EMU-ENSONIQ   www.emu.com

Fostex Corp. of America   www.fostex.com

Frontier Design Group   www.frontierdesign.com

Generalmusic Corp.   www.generalmusic.com

Gibson/Opcode   www.gibson.com

Korg USA, Inc.   www.korg.com

Kurzweil Music Systems
www.kurzweilmusicsystems.com

Lexicon, Inc.   www.lexicon.com

Mark of the Unicorn   www.motu.com

Peavey Electronics Corp.   www.peavey.com

Rolls Corp.   www.rolls.com

Roland Corp. U.S.   www.rolandus.com

Sam Ash Professional Audio Group
www.samashmusic.com

SeaSound   www.seasound.com

Sellmark Electronics
audiomation@sellmark.octagon.co.uk

Sonorus, Inc.   www.sonorus.com

Soundscape Digital Technology
www.soundscape-digital.com

Studiologic by Fatar
www.musicindustries.com/fatar/fatar-menu.htm

Symbolic Sound Corporation
www.symbolicsound.com

Synchronous Systems   www.syncsystems.com

ThinKware   www.thinkware.com

The Virtual Mixing Co./California Recording Institute
www.virtualmixer.com

Music Synthesizers

Access Music Electronics   www.access-music.de

AKM Semiconductor, Inc.   www.akm.com

Alesis Studio Electronics   www.alesis.com

Arboretum Systems, Inc.   www.arboretum.com

Clavia Digital Musical Instruments   www.clavia.se

CM Automation   www.cmautomation.com

EMU-ENSONIQ   www.emu.com

Future Retro Synthesizers   www.future-retro.com

Kurzweil Music Systems
www.kurzweilmusicsystems.com

Oberheim   www.oberheim.com

Peavey Electronics Corp.   www.peavey.com

Purple Audio, Inc.   www.purpleaudio.com

Quasimidi   www.quasimidi.com

Roland Corp. U.S.   www.rolandus.com

Sam Ash Professional Audio Group
www.samashmusic.com

Sounds Logical   www.soundslogical.com

Studio Electronics   www.studioelectronics.com

Symbolic Sound Corporation
www.symbolicsound.com

ThinKware   www.thinkware.com

Waldorf Electronics   www.waldorf-gmbh.de

Noise Reduction Systems

Arboretum Systems, Inc.   www.arboretum.com

Behringer International   www.behringer.de

BIAS: Berkeley Integrated Audio Software, Inc.
www.bias-inc.com

Circuit Research Labs, Inc.   www.crlsystems.com

Dale Pro Audio   www.daleproaudio.com

dbx Professional   www.dbxpro.com

digidesign   www.digidesign.com

Dolby Labs   www.dolby.com

Drawmer/Transamerica Audio
www.transaudiogroup.com

GML/Massenburg Design Works c/o AID
www.gmlinc.com

Precision Labs, Inc.   www.precisionweb.com

Sam Ash Professional Audio Group
www.samashmusic.com

Sonic Solutions   www.sonicsolutions.com

Sounds Logical   www.soundslogical.com

THAT Corporation   www.thatcorp.com

Whisper Room, Inc.   www.whisperroom.com

Patchbays

dbx Professional   www.dbxpro.com

Behringer International   www.behringer.de

Fostex Corp. of America   www.fostex.com

Gibson/Opcode   www.gibson.com

Neutrik   www.neutrik.com

Penny & Giles Controls, Inc.
   www.penny-giles-controls.co.uk

Signal Transport   www.sigt.com

Switchcraft Inc.   www.switchcraft.com

Z-Systems   www.z-sys.com

Periodicals

The Absolute Sound   www.theabsolutesound.com

Audio Amateur Inc.   www.audioXpress.com

Audio Engineering Society (AES) Journal
   www.aes.org/journal

Audio Media/AM Publishing Ltd.
   www.audiomedia.com

AV Video Multimedia Producer   www.kipinet.com

BE Radio   www.beradio.com

Broadcast Engineering
   www.broadcastengineering.com

Broadcaster   www.broadcastermagazine.com

Digital Producer   www.digitalproducer.com

Electronic Musician   www.emusician.com

EQ Magazine   www.eqmag.com

Film & Video   www.filmandvideomagazine.com

Home Recording   www.homerecordingmag.com

Keyboard   www.keyboardmag.com

Internet Audio   www.mixonline.com/internetaudio

Millimeter   www.millimeter.com

Mix Magazine   www.mixmag.com

Mixdown   www.mixdown.com

One to One   www.prostudio.com/oto/index.html

Post   www.postmagazine.com

Pro Audio Review   www.proaudioreview.com

Pro Sound News   www.prosoundnews.com

Professional Sound   www.vaxxine.com/ps

Radio World   www.rwonline.com

Recording Engineers Quarterly   www.recordingeq.com

Recording Magazine   www.recordingmag.com

Remix   www.remixmag.com

SMPTE Journal, The
   www.smpte.org/publ/journal.html

Sound and Communications
   www.soundandcommunications.com

Sound and Video Contractor
   www.intertec.com/forms/subforms/svc.htm

Sound On Sound   www.sospubs.co.uk

Studio Sound   www.prostudio.com/studiosound

Surround Professional   www.surroundpro.com

Tape Op   www.tapeop.com

Tapeless Studio, The   www.tapeless.com

Video Systems   www.videosystems.com

Videography   www.videography.com

World Broadcast Engineering   www.wbeonline.com

Recording and Synchronization

Magnetic Tape Manufacturers

BASF/EMTEC Pro Media   www.emptec-usa.com

Quantegy   www.quantegy.com

Tape-Based Recorders (digital and analog)

Alesis Studio Electronics   www.alesis.com

ATR Service Company   www.atrservice.com

Denon   www.del.denon.com

Panasonic Broadcast and Television Systems Company
   www.panasonic.com

Fostex Corp. of America   www.fostex.com

HHB Communications USA LLC   www.hhbusa.com

JRF Magnetic Sciences   www.jrfmagnetics.com

Nagra USA, Inc.   www.nagra.com

Otari Corp.   www.otari.com

Sony Electronics, Inc.   www.sony.com/proaudio

Studer   www.studer.ch

Superscope Technologies/Marantz Professional
   www.superscope-marantzpro.com

Tascam   www.tascam.com

Yamaha Corp. of America   www.yamaha.com

Digital Audio Workstations and Hard-Disk Systems (including software-only packages)

Aardvark   www.aardvark-pro.com

Akai Musical Instrument Corp.   www.akaipro.com

Alesis Studio Electronics   www.alesis.com

BIAS: Berkeley Integrated Audio Software, Inc.
www.bias-inc.com

Bitheadz Inc. www.bitheadz.com

Cakewalk Music Software www.cakewalk.com

M Automation www.cmautomation.com

Creamware U.S., Inc. www.creamware.com

Creative Labs www.creaf.com

Dale Pro Audio www.daleproaudio.com

dbx Professional www.dbxpro.com

digidesign www.digidesign.com

digidesign Development Partners
www.digidesign.com

Digigram Inc. www.digigram.com

Digital Audio Labs www.digitalaudio.com

Digital Audio Research www.dar.uk.com

DSP Media www.dspmedia.com

DSP North America www.dsppl.com.au

EGO Systems, Inc. www.egosys.net

Emagic www.emagic.de

EMU-ENSONIQ www.emu-ensoniq.com

Euphonix www.euphonix.com

Event Electronics www.event1.com

Fairlight USA www.fairlightusa.com

Fostex Corp. of America www.fostex.com

Gadget Labs www.gadgetlabs.com

Gefen, Inc. www.gefen.com

Gibson/Opcode www.gibson.com

JVC Disc America www.jvcsdiscusa.com

Korg USA www.korg.com

Lake DSP www.lakedsp.com

Lexicon Inc. www.lexicon.com

Innovative Quality Software www.iqsoft.com

iZ Technology Corp. www.izcorp.com

Mackie Designs, Inc. www.mackie.com

Mark of the Unicorn www.motu.com

M-Audio www.m-audio.com

Merging Technologies www.merging.com

MIDIMAN www.midiman.net

Minnetonka Audio Software
www.minnetonkaaudio.com

mSoft, Inc. www.msoftinc.com

Mytek Digital www.mytekdigital.com

Nemesys Music www.nemesysmusic.com

Otari Corp. www.otari.com

Roland Corporation U.S. www.rolandus.com

Rorke Data, Inc. www.rorke.com

SADiE, Inc. www.sadie.com

Seasound www.seasound.com

SEK'D America www.sekd.com

Spectral, Inc. www.spectralinc.com

Sonic Solutions www.sonic.com

Sonifex Ltd. www.sonifex.co.uk

Sonorus, Inc. www.sonorus.com

Sony Electronics www.sony.com/proaudio

Soundscape Digital Technology
www.soundscape-digital.com

Soundtracs USA, Inc. www.soundtracs.com

Steinberg www.steinberg.de

Studer North America www.studer.ch

Symbolic Sound Corp. www.symbolicsound.com

Syntrillium Software Corp. www.syntrillium.com

Tascam www.tascam.com

TC Electronics www.tcworks.de

360 Systems www.360systems.com

Turtle Beach www.tbeach.com

X-VISION AudioUS Ltd. www.xvisionaudio.com

Synchronization Products
(and related information)

Aardvark www.aardvark-pro.com

Alesis Studio Electronics www.alesis.com

Audio Intervisual Design www.aidinc.com

Brainstorm Electronics c/o AID
www.brainstormtime.com

CB Electronics/AEA www.colinbroad.com

Dale Pro Audio www.daleproaudio.com

digidesign www.digidesign.com

Emagic www.emagic.de

Frontier Design Group www.frontierdesign.com

Gibson/Opcode www.gibson.com

HHB Communications USA LLC www.hhbusa.com

Mark of the Unicorn www.motu.com

Roland Corporation U.S. www.rolandus.com

Sam Ash Professional Audio Group
www.samashmusic.com

Society of Motion Picture and Television Engineers
www.smpte.org

Sonorus, Inc. www.sonorus.com

Synchronous Systems www.syncsystems.com

Syntrillium Software Corp. www.syntrillium.com

Tascam www.tascam.com

ThinKware www.thinkware.com

360 Systems www.360systems.com

Timeline Vista, Inc. www.timelinevista.com

The Virtual Mixing Co./California Recording Institute
www.virtualmixer.com

Waveframe www.waveframe.com

Recording Consoles and Software Control Surfaces

AKM Semiconductor, Inc. www.akm.com

Alesis Studio Electronics www.alesis.com

Allen & Heath www.allen-heath.com

Amek Technology Group www.amek.com

AMS Neve www.ams-neve.com

API Audio www.apiaudio.com

Arrakis Systems, Inc. www.arrakis-systems.com

Audient audioind@inexpress.net

Audio Independence, Ltd. audioind@inexpress.net

Behringer International www.behringer.de

Calrec Audio Ltd. www.calrec.com

Carvin www.carvin.com

CM Automation www.cmautomation.com

Cooper Sound Systems, Inc. www.coopersound.com

Dale Pro Audio www.daleproaudio.com

DDA www.ddaconsoles.com

digidesign www.digidesign.com

D&R Electronica www.d-r.nl

Euphonix www.euphonix.com

Fairlight USA www.fairlightusa.com

FBT/MIPAD www.fbt.it

Focusrite Audio Engineering/Group One Ltd.
www.focusriteusa.com

Fostex Corp. of America www.fostex.com

Generalmusic Corp. www.generalmusic.com

GML/Massenburg Design Works c/o AID
www.gmlinc.com

Harrison www.glw.com

HHB Communications USA LLC www.hhbusa.com

Innovasion www.mediacomaudio.de/s1/NEU/seiten/
Hersteller/innovason.htm

Mackie Designs, Inc. www.mackie.com

Martinsound, Inc. www.martinsound.com

Midas Consoles www.midasconsoles.com

Millennia Media, Inc. www.mil-media.com

Oram Professional Audio www.oram.co.uk

Otari Corp. www.otari.com

Panasonic Broadcast & Television Systems Company
www.panasonic.com

Peavey Electronics Corp. www.peavey.com

Radikal Technologies www.radikaltechnologies.com

Roland Corp. U.S. www.rolandus.com

Sam Ash Professional Audio Group
www.samashmusic.com

Samson Technologies Corp. www.samsontech.com

Scharff Weisberg, Inc. www.swinyc.com

SeaSound www.seasound.com

Shep Associates Ltd. www.shep.co.uk

Solid State Logic Ltd. www.solid-state-logic.com

Sony Electronics Inc. www.sony.com/proaudio

Soundcraft www.soundcraft.com

Soundtracs USA, Inc. www.soundtracs.co.uk

Spirit www.spiritbysoundcraft.com

Studer North America www.studer.ch

Studiomaster www.studiomaster.com

Tascam www.tascam.com

Turner Audio www.turneraudio.com

The Virtual Mixing Co./California Recording Institute
www.virtualmixer.com

Yamaha Corp. of America www.yamaha.com

Zaxcom Inc. www.zaxcom.com

Signal Processing

Alesis Studio Electronics www.alesis.com

Antares Audio Technologies www.antarestech.com

Anthony DeMaria Labs www.adl-tube.com

Aphex Systems www.aphexsys.com

Apogee Sound, Inc. www.apogee-sound.com

Applied Research & Technology
www.artproaudio.com

ARX Systems www.arx.com.au

ATR Service Company www.atrservice.com

Audient   audioind@inexpress.net
Audiocontrol Industrial   www.audiocontrol.com
Audio Independence, Ltd.   audioind@inexpress.com
Audio Intervisual Design   www.aidinc.com
Avalon Design, Inc.   www.avalondesign.com
BBE Sound   www.bbesound.com
Behringer International   www.behringer.de
BSS Audio   www.bss.co.uk
Circuit Research Labs, Inc.   www.crlsystems.com
CLM Dynamics   www.pmiaudio.com
Crown International   www.crownaudio.com
Cutting Edge   www.nogrunge.com
Geoffrey Daking & Co, Inc.   www.daking.com
Dale Pro Audio   www.daleproaudio.com
dbx Professional   www.dbxpro.com
Demeter Amplification
   www.demeteramps.com/proaudio.html
Digitech   www.digitalvision.se
digidesign   www.digidesign.com
Dolby Labs   www.dolby.com
Drawmer/Transamerica Audio
   www.proaudio.co.uk/drawmer.htm
D. W. Fearn   www.dwfearn.com
Electro-Voice   www.electrovoice.com
Element 78 by Summit Audio, Inc.
   www.element-78.com
Eventide Audio, Inc.   www.eventide.com
FMR Audio   www.fmraudio.com
Focusrite Audio Engineering/Group One Ltd.
   www.focusriteusa.com
Furman Sound   www.furmansound.com
G Prime   www.gprime.com
Gefen, Inc.   www.gefen.com
GML/Massenburg Design Works/Group One Ltd.
   www.gmlinc.com
Gold Line/TEF   www.gold-line.com
Grace Design   www.gracedesign.com
Group One Ltd.   www.g1ltd.com
HHB Communications USA LLC   www.hhbusa.com
JBL Professional   www.jblpro.com
Joemeek   www.joemeek.com
Junger Audio Studiotechnik GmbH
   www.junger-audio.com

Klark Teknik   www.klarkteknik.com
Klippel GmbH   www.klippel.de
Korg USA, Inc.   www.korg.com
Kurzweil Music Systems
   www.kurzweilmusicsystems.com
L.A. Audio   www.laaudio.com
Lectrosonics, Inc.   www.lectrosonics.com
Lexicon Inc.   www.lexicon.com
Manley Laboratories, Inc.   www.manleylabs.com
Marquette Audio Labs   www.marquetteaudiolabs.com
Metric Halo   www.mhlabs.com
Meyer Sound Labs, Inc.   www.meyersound.com
Millennia Media, Inc.   www.mil-media.com
Oram Professional Audio   www.oram.co.uk
Pendulum Audio, Inc.   www.pendulumaudio.com
PreSonus Audio Electronics   www.presonus.com
QSC Audio Products, Inc.   www.qscaudio.com
QSound Labs   www.qsound.ca
Rane   www.rane.com
RDL Radio Design Labs   www.rdlnet.com
Retrospec, Inc.   www.retrospec.com
Rolls Corp.   www.rolls.com
Roland Corp. U.S.   www.rolandus.com
Sabine, Inc.   www.sabineusa.com
Sam Ash Professional Audio Group
   www.samashmusic.com
Samson Technologies Corp.   www.samsontech.com
Scharff Weisberg, Inc.   www.swinyc.com
Shep Associates Ltd.   www.shep.co.uk
Shure Brothers, Inc.   www.shure.com
Sounds Logical   www.soundslogical.com
Sonic Solutions   www.sonic.com
Sony Electronics Inc.   www.sony.com/proaudio
Spatializer Audio Laboratories   www.spatializer.com
SPL Electronics   www.spl-electronics.com
Stage Accompany USA   www.stageaccompany.com
Studio Technologies, Inc.   www.studio-tech.com
Summit Audio, Inc.   www.summitaudio.com
Symetrix   www.symetrixaudio.com
TC Electronic   www.tcelectronic.com
THAT Corporation   www.thatcorp.com

Turner Audio   www.turneraudio.com

Ultrafunk   www.ultrafunk.com

Universal Audio   www.uaudio.com

Wave Distribution   www.wavedistribution.com

Waves   www.waves.com

White Instruments   www.whiteinstruments.com

XTA Electronics/Group One Ltd.   www.xta.co.uk

Yamaha Corp. of America   www.yamaha.com

Z–Systems, Inc.   www.z-sys.com

ZOOM   www.samsontech.com/zoom

Sound Effect/Music Libraries

Abaco Music Library   www.abacomusic.com

Behringer International   www.behringer.de

BIAS: Berkley Integrated Audio Software, Inc.
www.bias-inc.com

dbx Professional   www.dbxpro.com

EMU-ENSONIQ   www.emu.com

HHB Communications USA LLC   www.hhbusa.com

The Hollywood Edge   www.hollywoodedge.com

Hollywood Sound Factory
www.hollywoodsoundfactory.com

IMPACT Music Library   www.studioland.com

Killer Tracks   www.killertracks.com

Kurzweil Music Systems
www.kurzweilmusicsystems.com

Megatrax   www.megatrax.com

mSoft, Inc.   www.msoftinc.com

Music Bakery   www.musicbakery.com

Network Music, LLC   www.networkmusic.com

Omnimusic   www.omnimusic.com

Pro Creation   www.procreation.co.za

Promusic   www.promusic-inc.com

Rarefaction   www.rarefaction.com

Roland Corp. U.S.   www.rolandus.com

Sam Ash Professional Audio Group
www.samashmusic.com

Scharff Weisberg, Inc.   www.swinyc.com

Signal Transport   www.sigt.com

Sonic Foundry   www.sonicfoundry.com

Sound Dogs   www.sounddogs.com

Sound Effects Library, Ltd.
www.sound-effects-library.com

Sound Ideas   www.sound-ideas.com

Sounds Logical   www.soundslogical.com

Symbolic Sound   www.SymbolicSound.com

ThinKware   www.thinkware.com

Valentino Production Music and Sound Effects Library
www.tvmusic.com

Surround-Sound Products

Alesis Studio Electronics   www.alesis.com

Apogee Electronics Corp.   www.apogeedigital.com

Crookwood   www.crookwood.com

Denon Electronics   www.del.denon.com

Dolby Labs   www.dolby.com

DSP North America   www.dsppl.com.au

DTS   www.dtsonline.com

Fairlight USA   www.fairlightusa.com

Hot House Professional Audio   www.hothousepro.com

Human Machine Interfaces/Wave Arts Inc.
www.humanmachine.com

JBL Professional   www.jblpro.com

Kind of Loud Technologies   www.kindofloud.com

Lake DSP   www.lakedsp.com

Leitch, Inc.   www.leitch.com

Metric Halo   www.mhlabs.com

Meyer Sound Labs, Inc.   www.meyersound.com

Millennia Media, Inc.   www.mil-media.com

Miller & Kreisel Sound Corp.
www.mkprofessional.com

Momentum Data Systems, Inc.   www.mds.com

Outboard Electronics Ltd.   www.outboard.co.uk

SADiE, Inc.   www.sadie.com

Schoeps/Posthorn Recordings   www.posthorn.com

Sony Electronics, Inc.   www.sony.com/proaudio

Sounds Logical   www.soundslogical.com

Soundfield/Transamerica Audio
www.transaudiogroup.com

Soundtracs USA, Inc.   www.soundtracs.com

Studio Technologies, Inc.   www.studio-tech.com

Tannoy/TGI North America   www.tannoy.com

Yamaha Corp. of America   www.yamaha.com

Trade Associations

AES (Audio Engineering Society)   www.aes.org

AMPS (Association of Motion Picture Sound)
www.amps.net

The Audio History Library   www.audiohistory.com

APA (Audio Publishers Association)
www.audiopub.org/apa

APRS (Association of Professional Recording
Services)   www.aprs.co.uk

IEEE (Institute of Electrical and Electronics Engineers, Inc.)
www.ieee.org

MPEG (Moving Picture Experts Group)
www.cselt.it/mpeg

The Museum of Sound Recording   www.mosr.org

MPGA (Music Producers Guild of the Americas)
www.mpga.org

NAB (National Association of Broadcasters)
www.nab.org

NAMM (National Association of Music Merchants)
www.namm.com/namm

The Recording Academy   www.grammy.com

SMPTE (Society of Motion Picture and Television
Engineers)   www.smpte.org

SPARS (Society of Professional Audio Recording
Services)   www.spars.com

Other Web Sites

Altermedia *(studio management software)*
www.studiosuite.com

Digital Media NET *(a community of digital content creators,
including pro audio)*   www.digitalmedianet.com

Film Sound *(dedicated to motion picture sound with
many links)*   www.filmsound.org

Harmony Central *(gear and recording-related news, as well
as classified-ad services)*   www.harmony-central.com

ProRec.com *(resources and news for the recording
professional)*   www.prorec.com

365proaudio.com *(news and links updated regularly)*
www.365proaudio.com

The World Studio Group *(a consortium of studios from
around the globe)*   www.worldstudio.com

Glossary

μ-law An 8-bit codec compression format for sending speech via digital telephone lines; used in North American and Japan. *See also* **a-law.**

5.1 The surround-sound format incorporating five discrete full-frequency audio channels and one discrete channel, the subwoofer, for low-frequency enhancement.

AC-3 The encoding algorithm used in Dolby Digital data compression. *AC* stands for *audio coding. See also* **Dolby Digital.**

ACN *See* **active combining network.**

acoustical phase The time relationship between two or more sound waves at a given point in their cycles.

acoustic pickup mic *See* **contact microphone.**

acoustics The science that deals with the behavior of sound and sound control. The properties of a room that affect the quality of sound.

active combining network (ACN) An amplifier at which the outputs of two or more signal paths are mixed together before being routed to their destination.

Adaptive Array microphone system A microphone consisting of five mic elements—a shotgun interference tube and four cardioids, housed in a single casing—designed to increase long-distance pickup while substantially reducing background (unwanted) sound.

adaptive differential pulse code modulation (ADPCM) Compression format that records the differences between samples of sound rather than the actual sound itself, compressing original data to one-fourth its size.

ADAT One of two formats used in modular digital multi-track tape recorders. It uses S-VHS videocassette tape. *ADAT* stands for *Alesis Digital Audio Tape* recorder. *See also* **digital tape recording system.**

ADAT Optical A proprietary digital-connection format designed for use with the Alesis modular digital multitrack (MDM) tape recorder.

additive ambience When the ambience of each track becomes cumulative in mixing a multitrack recording.

ADPCM *See* **adaptive differential pulse code modulation.**

ADR *See* **automated dialogue replacement.**

ADSR *See* **sound envelope.**

AES/EBU Internationally accepted professional digital audio interface transmitted via a balanced-line connection using XLR connectors, specified jointly by the Audio Engineering Society (AES) and the European Broadcast Union (EBU). *See also* **SPDIF.**

a-law An 8-bit codec compression format for sending speech via digital telephone lines, used worldwide, except in North American and Japan. *See also* **μ-law.**

ambience Sounds such as reverberation, noise, and atmosphere that form a background to the main sound. Also called *room tone* and *presence* and, in Great Britain, *atmos.*

amplifier A device that increases the amplitude of an electric signal.

amplitude The magnitude of a sound wave or electric signal, measured in decibels.

amplitude processor A signal processor that affects a signal's loudness. Also called *dynamics processor.*

analog recording A method of recording in which the waveform of the recorded signal resembles the waveform of the original signal.

analytical listening The evaluation of the content and function of sound. *See also* **critical listening.**

anechoic chamber A room that prevents all reflected sound through the dissipation or the absorption of sound waves.

assemble editing Dubbing segments from one tape or tapes to another tape in sequential order.

atmos Short for *atmosphere*, the British term for ambience. *See* **ambience.**

Atmos 5.1 surround microphone system A microphone system for surround-sound pickup consisting of an adjustable surround-sound microphone and a control console for controlling the output assignment and panning of the various surround configurations.

attack (1) The way a sound begins—that is, by plucking, bowing, striking, blowing, and so on. (2) The first part of the sound envelope.

attack time The length of time it takes a limiter or compressor to respond to the input signal.

audio-leading-video When the sound of the incoming scene starts before the corresponding picture appears. *See also* **video-leading-audio**.

automated dialogue replacement (ADR) A technique used to rerecord dialogue in synchronization with picture in postproduction. The picture is automatically replayed in short "loops" again and again so that the performers can synchronize their lip movements with the lip movements in the picture and then record the dialogue. Also known as *automatic dialog recording* and *looping*. *See also* **dialogue recording studio**.

azimuth Alignment of the record and playback heads so that their centerlines are parallel to each other and at right angles to the direction of the tape motion passing across the heads.

backtiming Method of subtracting the time of a program segment from the total time of a program so that the segment and the program end simultaneously.

balanced line A pair of ungrounded conductors whose voltages are opposite in polarity but equal in magnitude.

band-pass filter A filter that attenuates above and below a selected bandwidth, allowing the frequencies between to pass.

bandwidth The difference between the upper and lower frequency limits of an audio component. The upper and lower frequency limits of AM radio are 535 and 1,605 kHz; therefore, the bandwidth of AM radio is 1,070 kHz.

bandwidth curve The curve shaped by the number of frequencies in a bandwidth and their relative increase or decrease in level. A bandwidth of 100 to 150 Hz with 125 Hz boosted 15 dB forms a sharp, narrow bandwidth curve; a bandwidth of 100 to 6,400 Hz with a 15-dB boost at 1,200 Hz forms a more sloping, wider bandwidth curve.

bass The low range of the audible frequency spectrum; usually from 20 to 320 Hz.

bass roll-off Attenuating bass frequencies. The control—for example, on a microphone—used to roll off bass frequencies.

bass tip-up *See* **proximity effect**.

bass trap *See* **diaphragmatic absorber**.

bias The inaudible DC or AC signal added to an audio signal to overcome nonlinearities of amplification or the medium. In magnetic-tape recording, ultrasonic AC bias is used to linearize the tape medium, which would otherwise be highly distorted.

bias current An extremely high frequency AC current, far beyond audibility, added during a tape recording to linearize the magnetic information.

bidirectional microphone A microphone that picks up sound to its front and back and has minimal pickup at its sides.

binaural hearing Hearing with two ears attached to and separated by the head.

binaural microphone head Two omnidirectional capacitor microphones set into the ear cavities of an artificial head, complete with pinnas. This arrangement preserves binaural localization cues during recording and reproduces sound as humans hear it—three-dimensionally. Also called *artificial head* or *dummy head stereo*.

blast filter *See* **pop filter**.

blocking Plotting performer, camera, and microphone placements and movements in a production.

board Audio mixing console.

boundary microphone A microphone whose capsule is mounted flush with or close to, but a precise distance from, a reflective surface so that there is no phase cancellation of reflected sound at audible frequencies.

bulk eraser A demagnetizer used to erase an entire roll of magnetic tape without removing it from its reel. Also known as a *degausser*.

bus A mixing network that combines the outputs of other channels.

calibration Adjusting equipment—for example, a console and a tape recorder—according to a standard so that their measurements are similar. *See also* **electronic alignment**.

camcorder A handheld video camera with a built-in or dockable videotape recorder.

capacitor microphone A microphone that transduces acoustic energy into electric energy electrostatically.

capstan The shaft that rotates against the tape, pulling it across the heads at a constant speed.

cardioid microphone A unidirectional microphone with a heart-shaped pickup pattern.

CD-R *See* **recordable compact disc.**

CD-RW *See* **rewritable CD.**

center frequency In peak/dip equalizing, the frequency at which maximum boost or attenuation occurs.

chorus effect Recirculating the doubling effect to make one sound source sound like several. *See also* **doubling.**

clapslate A slate used in synchronizing sound and picture during filming and editing. The slate carries such information as scene and take number, production title, location of shot—e.g., indoors or outdoors—and time code. A pair of hinged boards on top of the slate—called *clapsticks*—clap together, producing the sound that is used to synchronize picture and sound.

clipping Audible distortion that occurs when a signal's level exceeds the limits of a particular device or circuit.

close miking Placing a microphone close to a sound source to pick up mostly direct sound and reduce ambience and leakage. *See also* **distant miking.**

cocktail party effect A psychoacoustic effect that allows humans to localize the sources of sounds around them.

codec A device that encodes a signal at one end of a transmission and decodes it at the other end. The word *codec* is taken from en*cod*er/*dec*oder.

coercivity The magnetic force field necessary to reduce a tape from saturation to full erasure. This value is expressed in oersteds.

coincident miking Employing two matched microphones, usually unidirectional, crossed one above the other on a vertical axis with their diaphragms. *See also* **X-Y miking.**

comb-filter effect The effect produced when a signal is time-delayed and added to itself, reinforcing some frequencies and canceling others, giving sound an unnatural, hollow coloration.

commentative sound Descriptive sound that makes a comment or interpretation. *See also* **descriptive sound** and **narrative sound.**

compander A contraction of the words *compressor* and *expander* that refers to the devices that compress an input signal and expand an output signal to reduce noise. Also known as a *noise reducer.*

companding A contraction of the words *compressing* and *expanding* that refers to wireless mics' increasing dynamic range and reducing noise inherent in a transmission system.

comping Taking the best part(s) of each recorded track and combining them into a composite final version.

complementary equalization Equalizing sounds that share similar frequency ranges so that they complement, rather than interfere with, one another.

compression (1) Reducing a signal's output level in relation to its input level to reduce dynamic range. (2) The drawing together of vibrating molecules, thus producing a high-pressure area. *See also* **rarefaction.**

compression ratio The ratio of the input and output signals in a compressor.

compression threshold The level at which a compressor acts on an input signal and the compression ratio takes effect.

compressor A signal processor with an output level that decreases as its input level increases.

condenser microphone *See* **capacitor microphone.**

console An electronic device that amplifies, processes, and combines input signals and routes them to broadcast or recording.

constructive interference When sound waves are partially out of phase and partially additive, increasing amplitude where compression and rarefaction occur at the same time.

contact microphone A microphone that attaches to a sound source and transduces the vibrations that pass through it. Also called *acoustic pickup mic.*

contextual sound Sound that emanates from and duplicates a sound source as it is. *See also* **diegetic sound.**

contrapuntal narration Juxtaposes narration and action to make a statement not carried by either element alone.

cordless microphone *See* **wireless microphone system.**

coverage angle The off-axis angle or point at which loudspeaker level is down 6 dB compared with the on-axis output level.

cps *See* **hertz.**

critical listening The evaluation of the characteristics of the sound itself. *See also* **analytical listening.**

crossfade Fading in one sound source as another sound source fades out. At some point the sounds cross at an equal level of loudness.

crossover frequency The frequency at which the high frequencies are routed to the tweeter(s) and the low frequencies are routed to the woofer(s).

crossover network   An electronic device that divides the audio spectrum into individual frequency ranges (low, high, and/or mid) before sending them to specialized loudspeakers such as the woofer(s) and tweeter(s).

crosstalk   Unwanted signal leakage from one signal path to another.

crystal synchronization   Synchronizing the operating speeds of a film camera and an audiotape recorder by using a crystal oscillator in both camera and recorder. The oscillator generates a sync pulse tone. *See also* **double-system recording.**

cue sheet   Any type of form used in recording, editing, or mixing audio that lists dialogue, sound effects, or music cues and their in- and out-times.

cut   (1) An instantaneous transition from one sound or picture to another. (2) To make a disc recording. (3) A decrease in level.

cycles per second (cps)   *See* **hertz.**

DASH format   *See* **Digital Audio Stationary Head format.**

DAT   *See* **digital audiotape.**

DAW   *See* **digital audio workstation.**

dB   *See* **decibel.**

dBm   An electrical measurement of power referenced to 1 milliwatt as dissipated across a 600-ohm load.

dB-SPL   A measure of the pressure of a sound wave, or sound-pressure level (SPL), expressed in decibels (dB).

dBu   A unit of measurement for expressing the relationship of decibels to voltage—0.775 volt.

dBv   *See* **dBu.**

dBV   A measure of voltage with decibels referenced to 1 volt.

DCA   *See* **digitally controlled amplifier.**

deadpotting   Starting a recording with the fader turned down all the way. Also known as *deadrolling.*

decay time   *See* **reverberation time.**

decibel (dB)   A relative and dimensionless unit to measure the ratio of two quantities.

de-esser   A compressor that reduces sibilance.

degausser   *See* **bulk eraser.**

delay   The time interval between a sound or signal and each of its repeats.

delay time   The amount of time between delays. In a digital delay, delay time regulates how long a given sound is held.

descriptive sound   Describes sonic aspects of a scene not connected to the main action. *See also* **commentative sound** and **narrative sound.**

destructive editing   Permanently alters the original sound or soundfile. *See also* **nondestructive editing.**

destructive interference   When sound waves are partially out of phase and partially subtractive, decreasing amplitude where compression and rarefaction occur at different times.

dialogue recording studio   A studio in which dialogue is recorded and synchronized to picture. *See also* **automated dialogue replacement.**

diaphragmatic absorber   A flexible panel mounted over an air space that resonates at a frequency (or frequencies) determined by the stiffness of the panel and the size of the air space. Also called *bass trap.*

diegetic sound   Sound that comes from within the story space, such as dialogue and sound effects. *See also* **contextual sound** and **nondiegetic sound.**

diffraction   The spreading or bending around of sound waves as they pass an object.

diffusion   The scattering of sound waves.

Digital Audio Stationary Head (DASH) format   A format agreed to by Sony, Studer, and Tascam to standardize digital recording.

digital audiotape (DAT)   The cassette tape used with the rotary-head digital audiotape recorder (R-DAT). It is about ½ inch wide, about ¼ mil thick, and about one-fourth the length of an analog cassette audiotape.

digital audio workstation (DAW)   A multifunctional hard-disk production system, controlled from a central location, that is integrated with and capable of being networked to other devices, such as audio, video, and MIDI sources, within or among facilities.

digital cartridge disk system   An audio recorder and/or playback system that uses a compact, magneto-optical, or mini disc or a hard disk as the recording medium.

digital delay   An electronic device designed to delay an audio signal.

digital news gathering (DNG)   Reporting and gathering news from the field using digital equipment.

digital recording   A method of recording in which samples of the original analog signal are encoded on tape as pulses and then decoded during playback.

digital signal processing (DSP) Provides various manipulations of sound in a digital format. The term is generally used to refer to signal processing using computer software.

digital tape recording system (DTRS) One of two formats used in modular digital multitrack tape recorders. It uses Hi8 videocassette tape. *See also* **ADAT**.

Digital Theater System (DTS) A lossy data compression format that reduces the bit rate to roughly 1.4 megabits per second.

digital versatile disc (DVD) A compact disc providing massive data storage of digital-quality audio, video, and text.

digitally controlled amplifier (DCA) An amplifier whose gain is remotely controlled by a digital control signal.

direct/ambient surround-sound miking A surround-sound miking technique using a stereo microphone array for the left-right frontal pickups, plus a center mic for the center channel, and the surround microphones mainly for ambience. *See also* **direct surround-sound miking**.

directional microphone Any microphone that picks up sound from one direction. Also called *unidirectional microphone*.

direct narration Describes what is being seen or heard.

direct sound Sound waves that reach the listener before reflecting off any surface. *See also* **early reflections**.

direct surround-sound miking A surround-sound miking approach that uses a microphone array especially designed for surround-sound pickup. *See also* **direct/ambient surround-sound miking**.

distant miking Placing a microphone(s) far enough from the sound source to pick up most or all of an ensemble's blended sound including room reflections. *See also* **close miking**.

distortion The appearance of a signal in the reproduced sound that was not in the original sound. *See also* **harmonic distortion**, **intermodulation distortion**, **loudness distortion**, and **transient distortion**.

diversity reception Multiple-antenna receiving system for use with wireless microphones. *See also* **non-diversity receiver**.

DNG *See* **digital news gathering**.

Dolby Digital A lossy data compression format that reduces the bit rate to roughly 400 kilobits per second. *See also* **AC-3**.

donut In mixing audio for a spot announcement, fading the music after it is established to create a hole for the announcement and reestablishing the music later at its former full level.

Doppler effect The perceived increase or decrease in frequency as a sound source moves closer to or farther from the listener.

double-system recording Filming sound and picture simultaneously but separately with a camera and a recorder. *See also* **crystal synchronization**.

doubling Mixing slightly delayed signals (15 to 35 ms) with the original signal to create a fuller, stronger, more ambient sound. *See also* **chorus effect**.

dropout (1) A sudden attenuation of sound or loss of picture due to an imperfection in the magnetic coating. (2) Sudden attenuation in a wireless microphone signal due to an obstruction or some other interference.

dry sound A sound devoid of reverberation. *See also* **wet sound**.

DSP *See* **digital signal processing**.

DTRS *See* **digital tape recording system**.

DTS *See* **Digital Theater System**.

dub Transferring sound from tape or disk to another tape or disk.

DVD *See* **digital versatile disc**.

DVD-A *See* **DVD-Audio**

DVD-Audio (DVD-A) A digital versatile disc format with extremely high quality audio.

dynamic microphone A microphone that transduces energy electromagnetically. Moving-coil and ribbon microphones are dynamic.

dynamic range The range between the quietest and the loudest sounds that a sound source can produce without distortion.

dynamics processor *See* **amplitude processor**.

early reflections Reflections of the original sound that reach the listener within about 40 to 50 ms of the direct sound. Also called *early sound*. *See also* **direct sound**.

early sound. *See* **early reflections**.

echo Sound reflections delayed by 35 ms or more that are perceived as discrete repetitions of the direct sound.

edit decision list (EDL) A list of edits, computer-generated or handwritten, used to assemble a production.

EDL *See* **edit decision list.**

EFP *See* **electronic field production.**

eigentones The resonance of sound at particular frequencies in an acoustic space. May add unwanted coloration to sound. More commonly known as *room modes*.

elasticity The capacity to return to the original shape or place after deflection or displacement.

electret microphone A capacitor microphone which, instead of requiring an external high-voltage power source, uses a permanently charged element and requires only a low-voltage power supply for the internal preamp.

electroacoustics The electrical manipulation of acoustics.

electronic alignment The adjustment of electronic and mechanical characteristics of a tape recorder to a defined standard specified by the manufacturer or by international industry bodies such as the Audio Engineering Society (AES), the National Association of Broadcasters (NAB), or the International Electrotechnical Commission (IEC). *See also* **calibration.**

electronic editing Using one tape recorder and inserting—punching in—material, or transferring material from one tape recorder (the master) to another (the slave).

electronic field production (EFP) Video production done on location, involving program materials that take some time to produce.

electronic Foley Creating sound effects electronically using devices such as synthesizers and computers.

electronic news gathering (ENG) News production done on location, sometimes taped and sometimes live, but usually with an imminent deadline.

ENG *See* **electronic news gathering.**

enharmonic In music two different notes that sound the same, for example, C# and D♭, G# and A♭.

EQ Equalization. *See* **equalizer.**

equalizer A signal-processing device that can boost, attenuate, or shelve frequencies in a sound source or sound system.

equal loudness principle The principle that confirms the human ear's nonlinear sensitivity to all audible frequencies: that midrange frequencies are perceived with greatest intensity and that bass and treble frequencies are perceived with lesser intensity.

erase head Electromagnetic transducer on a tape recorder that automatically demagnetizes a tape before it reaches the record head when the recorder is in the record mode.

ergonomics Designing an engineering system with human comfort and convenience in mind.

expander An amplifier whose gain decreases as its input level decreases.

fade-in Gradually increasing the loudness of a signal level from silence (or from "black" in video).

fade-out Gradually decreasing the loudness of a signal level to silence (or to "black" in video).

fade-out/fade-in A transition usually indicating a marked change in time, locale, continuity of action, and other features.

fader A device containing a resistor that is used to vary the output voltage of a circuit or component. Also known as an *attenuator*, a *gain* or *volume control*, or a *pot* or *potentiometer*.

feedback When part or all of a system's output signal is returned into its own input. Feedback can be acoustic or electronic. A common example of acoustic feedback is the loud squeal or howl caused when the sound from a loudspeaker is picked up by a nearby microphone and reamplified. Electronic feedback is created in digital delay devices by feeding a proportion of the delayed signal back into the delay line. Also called *regeneration*.

filter A device that removes unwanted frequencies or noise from a signal.

fixed-frequency equalizer An equalizer with several fixed frequencies usually grouped in two (high and low) or three (high, middle, and low) ranges of the frequency spectrum.

fixed mic *See* **plant microphone.**

flanging Combining a direct signal and the same signal slightly delayed and continuously varying their time relationships.

flat Frequency response in an audio system that reproduces a signal between 20 and 20,000 Hz (or between any two specified frequencies) that varies no more than ±3 dB.

flutter Frequency changes in an analog tape recording resulting from slower variations in the speed of the tape transport. *See also* **wow.**

flutter echoes Echoes between parallel walls that occur in rapid series.

FM microphone *See* **wireless microphone system.**

foldback The system in a multichannel console that permits the routing of sound through a headphone monitor feed to performers in the studio.

Foley recording Producing and recording sound effects in the studio in synchronization with picture.

formant The resonance band in a vibrating body that mildly increases the level of specific steady-state frequencies in that band.

four-way system loudspeaker A loudspeaker system with three crossover networks.

frame rate The number of film frames that pass in 1 second of real time—frames per second (fps).

freewheel A mode in a synchronizer that allows stretches of poorly encoded time code to be passed over without altering the speed of the slave tape recorder's transport.

frequency The number of times per second that a sound source vibrates. Now expressed in hertz (Hz); formerly expressed in cycles per second (cps).

frequency response A measure of an audio system's ability to reproduce a range of frequencies with the same relative loudness; usually represented by a graph.

full coat Magnetic film in which the oxide coating covers most or all of the film width. *See also* **stripe coat**.

fundamental The lowest frequency a sound source can produce. Also called *primary frequency* and *first harmonic*.

gauss A unit of magnetic density.

graphic equalizer An equalizer with sliding controls that gives a graphic representation of the response curve chosen.

guard band The space between tracks on an audiotape recorder head to reduce crosstalk.

Haas effect *See* **precedence effect**.

hard-disk recording Using a hard-disk computer system as the recording medium, which is more versatile than tape because data storage and retrieval is random, quick, and nonlinear; storage capacity is far greater; and data is nondestructive.

hard knee compression Abrupt gain reduction at the start of compression. *See also* **knee** and **soft knee compression**.

hardwired Description of pieces of equipment wired to each other. *See also* **patch bay**.

harmonic distortion Nonlinear distortion caused when an audio system introduces harmonics to a signal at the output that were not present at the input.

harmonics Frequencies that are multiples of the fundamental.

headroom The amount of increase in loudness level that a tape, amplifier, or other piece of equipment can take, above working level, before overload distortion.

headset microphone A microphone attached to a pair of headphones; one headphone channel feeds the program and the other headphone channel feeds the director's cues.

headstack A multitrack tape head.

height One of the adjustments made when aligning the heads on an audiotape recorder. This adjustment aligns the height of the heads with the recording tape.

helical scanning Using one or more rotating heads that engage the tape wrapped at least partially around the head drum.

Helmholtz absorber A resonator designed to absorb specific frequencies depending on size, shape, and enclosed volume of air. The enclosed volume of air is connected to the air in the room by a narrow opening, or neck. When resonant frequencies reach the neck of the enclosure, the air inside cancels those frequencies. Also called *Helmholtz resonator*.

hertz (Hz) Unit of measurement of frequency; numerically equal to cycles per second (cps).

high end The treble range of the frequency spectrum.

high-output tape High-sensitivity tape.

high-pass (low-cut) filter A filter that attenuates frequencies below a selected frequency and allows those above that point to pass.

Holophone microphone system A microphone used for surround-sound pickup consisting of seven miniature omnidirectional microphone elements housed in a $7\frac{1}{2}$-by-$5\frac{7}{10}$-inch fiberglass epoxy ellipsoid shaped like a tiny teardrop.

humbuck circuit A circuit built into a microphone to reduce hum pickup.

Hz *See* **hertz**.

IEC standard The time code standard for R-DAT recording, established by the International Electrotechnical Commission (IEC).

IFB *See* **interruptible foldback system**.

IM *See* **intermodulation distortion**.

impedance The measure of the total resistance to the current flow in an AC circuit; expressed in ohms.

indirect narration Describes something other than what is being seen or heard.

indirect sound Sound waves that reflect from one or more surfaces before reaching the listener.

infrasonic The range below the frequencies audible to human hearing.

inharmonic overtones Pitches that are not exact multiples of the fundamental.

initial decay In the sound envelope, the point at which the attack begins to lose amplitude.

in-line console A console in which a channel's input, output, and monitor functions are placed in line and located in a single input/output (I/O) module. *See also* **split-section console** and **input/output module**.

inner ear The part of the ear that contains the auditory nerve, which transmits sound waves to the brain.

input/output (I/O) module On an in-line console, a module containing input, output, and monitor controls for a single channel.

input section On a console the section into which signals from a sound source, such as a microphone, feed and are then routed to the output section.

insert editing In electronic editing, inserting a segment between two previously dubbed segments. Also, electronic editing segments out of sequential order.

Integrated Services Digital Network (ISDN) A public telephone service that allows inexpensive use of a flexible, wide-area, all-digital network for, among other things, recording simultaneously from various locations.

intermodulation distortion (IM) Nonlinear distortion that occurs when different frequencies pass through an amplifier at the same time and interact to create combinations of tones unrelated to the original sounds.

interruptible foldback (IFB) system A communications system that allows communication from the producer or director and selected production personnel with the on-air talent. *See also* **mix-minus**.

in-the-ear monitoring Using small headphones to feed the sound blend to on-stage performers instead of stage monitors.

in the mud Sound level so quiet that it barely "kicks" the VU meter.

in the red Sound level so loud that the VU meter "rides" over 100 percent of modulation.

inverse square law The acoustic situation in which the sound level changes in inverse proportion to the square of the distance from the sound source.

I/O module *See* **input/output module**.

ISDN *See* **Integrated Services Digital Network**.

jack Receptacle or plug connector leading to the input or output circuit of a patch bay, tape recorder, or other electronic component.

jam sync A mode in a synchronizer that produces new time code during dubbing either to match the original time code or to regenerate new address data.

knee The point at which a compressor starts gain reduction. *See also* **hard knee compression** and **soft knee compression**.

lavalier microphone Microphone that used to be worn around the neck but is now worn attached to the clothing.

layback Dubbing the composite audio track from the multitrack tape to the edit master tape, or the dialogue, sound effects, and music tracks to separate reels of magnetic film. *See also* **layover**.

laydown *See* **layover**.

layering When many sounds occur at once, layering involves making sure that they remain balanced, in perspective, and intelligible in the mix.

layover Dubbing the audio from the edit master tape or audiotape, or both, to a multitrack recorder for premixing. Also called *laydown*. *See also* **layback**.

limiter A compressor with an output level that does not exceed a preset ceiling regardless of the input level.

linear editing Nonrandom editing. *See also* **nonlinear editing**.

linearity Having an output that varies in direct proportion to the input.

listening fatigue A pronounced dulling of the auditory senses, inhibiting perceptual judgment.

localization (1) Placement of a sound source in the stereo or surround-sound frame. (2) The direction from which a sound source seems to emanate in a stereo or surround-sound field. (3) The ability to tell the direction from which a sound is coming.

longitudinal time code (LTC) A high-frequency signal consisting of a stream of pulses produced by a time code generator used to code tape to facilitate editing and synchronization. Also known as *SMPTE time code*.

loop group   People who provide the background sound for a crowd scene.

looping   *See* **automated dialogue replacement**.

lossless compression   A data compression process during which no data is discarded. *See also* **lossy compression**.

lossy compression   A data compression process during which data that is not critical is discarded during compression. *See also* **lossless compression**.

loudness distortion   Distortion that occurs when the loudness of a signal is greater than the sound system can handle. Also called *overload distortion*.

low bass   Frequency range between roughly 20 and 80 Hz, the lowest two octaves in the audible frequency spectrum.

low end   The bass range of the frequency spectrum.

low-frequency enhancement (LFE)   In a surround-sound system, using a separate channel and subwoofer loudspeaker to reproduce low-frequency sounds.

low-output tape   Low-sensitivity tape.

low-pass (high-cut) filter   A filter that attenuates frequencies above a selected frequency and allows those below that point to pass.

LTC   *See* **longitudinal time code**.

MADI   *See* **Multichannel Audio Digital Interface**.

magnetic film   Sprocketed film containing sound only and no picture. See also **full coat** and **stripe coat**.

magneto-optical (MO) recording   Disc-based, optical recording medium that uses tiny magnetic particles heated to extremely high temperatures.

makeup gain   A compression control that allows adjustment of the output level to the desired optimum. Used, for example, when loud parts of the signal are so reduced that the overall result sounds too quiet.

masking   The hiding of some sounds by other sounds when each is a different frequency and they are presented together.

master   (1) The original recording. (2) The final tape or disc recording that is sent to the CD mastering house or to distribution.

master fader   The fader that controls the combined signal level of the individual input channels on a console.

master section   In a multichannel production console, the section that routes the final mix to its recording destination. It usually houses, at least, the master controls for the mixing bus outputs, reverb send and reverb return, and master fader.

maximum sound-pressure level   The level at which a microphone's output signal begins to distort, that is, produces a 3 percent total harmonic distortion (THD).

MD™   *See* **mini disc**.

MDM   *See* **modular digital multitrack recorder**.

microphone   A transducer that converts acoustic energy into electric energy. Also called *mic*.

microscopic microphone   A microphone that measures the velocity of air particles across tiny, resistive strips of platinum or silicon nitride, instead of measuring fluctuating air pressure as conventional mics do. The sensor strips are too small to be seen with the naked eye.

middle ear   The part of the ear that transfers sound waves from the eardrum to the inner ear.

middle-side (M-S) microphone   Consists of two mic capsules housed in single casing. One capsule, usually cardioid, is the mid-position microphone. The other capsule, usually bidirectional, has each lobe oriented 90 degrees laterally.

MIDI   *See* **Musical Instrument Digital Interface**.

MIDI time code (MTC)   Translates SMPTE time code into MIDI messages that allow MIDI-based devices to operate on the SMPTE timing reference.

midrange   The part of the frequency spectrum to which humans are most sensitive; the frequencies between roughly 250 and 4,000 Hz.

mil   One-thousandth of an inch.

milking the audience   Boosting the level of an audience's sound during laughter or applause and/or reinforcing it with recorded laughter or applause.

mini disc™ (MD™)   Magneto-optical disc 2½ inches wide that can store more than an hour of digital-quality audio.

mini-mic   Short for *miniature microphone*. Any extremely small lavalier microphone designed to be unobtrusive on-camera and which can be easily hidden in or under clothing or on a set.

mix-minus   A program feed through an interruptible foldback (IFB) circuit minus the announcer's voice. *See also* **interruptible foldback system**.

mixdown The point, usually in postproduction, when all the separately recorded audio tracks are sweetened, positioned, and combined into stereo or surround sound.

mixer A small, highly portable device that mixes various elements of sound, typically coming from multiple microphones, and performs limited processing functions.

MO *See* **magneto-optical recording.**

mobile unit A car, van, or tractor-trailer equipped to produce program material on location.

modular digital multitrack (MDM) recorder An audio-tape recorder that uses a videocassette transport with videocassette tape. It can record up to eight channels and, linked to multiple MDMs, can expand track capability in eight-channel increments.

monitor section The section in a console that enables the signals to be heard. The monitor section in multichannel production consoles, among other things, allows monitoring of the line or recorder input, selects various inputs to the control room and studio monitors, and controls their levels.

morphing The continuous, seamless transformation of one effect (aural or visual) into another.

moving-coil loudspeaker A loudspeaker with a moving-coil element.

moving-coil microphone A microphone with a moving-coil element. The coil is connected to a diaphragm suspended in a magnetic field.

MP-3 *See* **MPEG-2 layer 3 technology.**

MPEG Stands for *Motion Picture Experts Group.* A compression format for film established by the film industry and the International Standards Organization (ISO). Uses an analytical approach to compression called *acoustic masking.*

MPEG-2 AAC (Advanced Audio Coder) Compression format that is approximately a 30 percent improvement over the MPEG-2 layer 3 technology (MP-3), considered 100 percent better than AC-3.

MPEG-2 layer 3 technology Compression format considered excellent for sound effects, speech, and most music. Commonly known as *MP-3.*

ms Milliseconds.

M-S microphone *See* **middle-side microphone.**

MTC *See* **MIDI time code.**

mult *See* **multiple.**

Multichannel Audio Digital Interface (MADI) The standard used when interfacing multichannel digital audio.

multidirectional microphone Microphone with more than one pickup pattern. Also called *polydirectional microphone.*

multipath In wireless microphones, when more than one radio frequency (RF) signal from the same source arrives at the receiver's front end, creating phase mismatching.

multiple (1) On a patch bay, jacks interconnected to each other and to no other circuit. They can be used to feed signals to and from sound sources. Also called *mults.* (2) An amplifier with several mic level outputs to provide individual feeds, thereby eliminating the need for many. Also called a *press bridge* or a *presidential patch.*

multiple-entry-port microphone A microphone that has more than one opening for sound waves to reach the transducer. Most of these openings are used to reject sound from the sides or back of the microphone through phase cancellation. Each port returns a different frequency range to the mic capsule out of phase with sounds reaching the front of the mic.

Musical Instrument Digital Interface (MIDI) A protocol that allows synthesizers, drum machines, sequencers, and other signal-processing devices to communicate with or control one another, or both.

narrative sound Sound effects that add more to a scene than what is apparent and so perform an informational function. *See also* **commentative sound** and **descriptive sound.**

NC *See* **noise criteria.**

near-coincident miking A stereo microphone array in which the mics are separated horizontally but the angle or space between their capsules is not more than several inches. *See also* **X-Y miking.**

near-field monitoring Monitoring with loudspeakers placed close to the operator, usually on or just behind the console's meter bridge, to reduce interference from control room acoustics at the monitoring position.

noise Any unwanted sound or signal.

noise-canceling microphone A microphone designed for use close to the mouth and with excellent rejection of ambient sound.

noise criteria (NC) Contours of the levels of background noise that can be tolerated within an audio studio.

noise gate An expander with a threshold that can be set to reduce or eliminate unwanted low-level sounds, such as room ambience, rumble, and leakage, without affecting the wanted sounds.

noise processor Originally, a signal processor that reduces tape noise; with the added power of digital signal processing, may also be designed to reduce or eliminate pops, clicks, and background noises.

noise reducer *See* **compander**.

noise reduction coefficient (NRC) *See* **sound absorption coefficient**.

nondestructive editing Editing that does not alter the original sound or soundfile, regardless of what editing or signal processing is effected. *See also* **destructive editing**.

nondiegetic sound Sound that is outside the story space, such as music underscoring. *See also* **diegetic sound**.

nondirectional microphone *See* **omnidirectional microphone**.

nondiversity receiver Single-antenna receiving system used with wireless microphones. *See also* **diversity reception**.

nonlinear The property of not being linear—not having an output that varies in direct proportion to the input.

nonlinear editing Instant random access to and easy re-arrangement of recorded material. *See also* **linear editing**.

notch filter A filter capable of attenuating an extremely narrow bandwidth of frequencies.

octave The interval between two sounds that have a frequency ratio of 2:1.

oersted A unit of magnetic force.

off-mic Not being within the optimal pickup pattern of a microphone; off-axis.

off-miking Miking technique that employs microphones farther from the sound source than the close mics to add more-ambient, airier sound to the overall recording.

ohm A unit of resistance to current flow.

omnidirectional microphone Microphone that picks up sound from all directions. Also called *nondirectional microphone*.

on-mic Being within the optimal pickup pattern of a microphone; on-axis.

open-reel audiotape recorder A tape recorder with the feed reel and takeup reel not enclosed in a cartridge, requiring that they be mounted manually.

oscillator A device that generates pure tones or sine waves.

outer ear The portion of the ear that picks up and directs sound waves through the auditory canal to the middle ear.

output section In a mixer and console, the section that routes the signals to a recorder or broadcast, or both.

overdubbing Recording new material on a separate tape track(s) while listening to the replay of a previously recorded tape track(s) to synchronize the old and new material.

overload Feeding a component or system more amplitude than it can handle and thereby causing loudness distortion.

overload distortion *See* **loudness distortion**.

overload indicator On a console, a light-emitting diode (LED) that flashes when the input signal is approaching or has reached overload and is clipping.

overroll Recording ambience after recording narration or dialogue by letting the recorder continue to run.

overtones Harmonics that may or may not be multiples of the fundamental. Subjective response of the ear to harmonics.

pad An attenuator inserted into a component or system to reduce level.

pan pot A volume control that shifts the proportion of sound from left to right between two output buses and, hence, between the two loudspeakers necessary for reproducing a stereo image, or among the six (or more) surround-sound channels, and loudspeakers, necessary for reproducing a surround-sound image. *Pan pot* is short for *panoramic potentiometer*.

parabolic microphone system A system that uses a concave dish to focus reflected sound into a microphone pointed at the center of the dish.

paragraphic equalizer An equalizer that combines the features of a parametric and a graphic equalizer.

parametric equalizer An equalizer in which the bandwidth of a selected frequency is continuously variable.

patch bay An assembly of jacks to which are wired the inputs and outputs of the audio components in a console and/or sound studio. Also called *patch panel*. *See also* **hardwired**.

patch cord A short cord or cable with a plug at each end, used to route signals in a patch bay.

peak program meter (ppm) A meter designed to indicate transient peaks in the level of a signal.

percentage of modulation The percentage of an applied signal in relation to the maximum signal a sound system can handle.

perspective miking Establishing through mic-to-source distance the audio viewpoint in relation to the performers and their environment in screen space.

PFL *See* **solo.**

phantom power Operating voltage supplied to a capacitor microphone by an external power source or mixer, thereby eliminating the need to use batteries.

phase The time relationship between two or more sounds reaching a microphone or signals in a circuit. When this time relationship is coincident, the sounds or signals are in phase and their amplitudes are additive. When this time relationship is not coincident, the sounds or signals are out of phase and their amplitudes are subtractive.

phase shift The phase relationship of two signals at a given time, or the phase change of a signal over an interval of time.

phasing An effect created by splitting a signal in two and time-delaying one of the signal portions.

phon A dimensionless unit of loudness level related to the ear's subjective impression of signal strength.

phone line (PL) system *See* **private line system.**

pickup pattern *See* **polar response pattern.**

pin When the needle of the VU meter hits against the peg at the right-hand corner of the red. Pinning is to be avoided because it indicates too high a loudness level and it could damage the meter.

pinch roller On a tape recorder, the spring-loaded, free-spinning rubber wheel that holds the tape against the capstan. Also called *capstan idler* and *pressure roller.*

pink noise Wideband noise that maintains constant energy per octave. *See also* **white noise.**

pitch The subjective perception of frequency.

pitch shifter A signal processor that varies the pitch of a signal.

PL system *See* **private line system.**

plant microphone A stationary mic positioned on the set to cover action that cannot easily be picked up with a boom or a body mic or to provide fill sound. Also referred to as a *fixed mic.*

playback head Electromagnetic transducer on a tape recorder that converts magnetic energy into electric energy.

polarity The relative position of two signal leads—the high (+) and the low (–)—in the same circuit.

polarity reversal The control on a console that inverts the polarity of an input signal 180 degrees. Sometimes called *phase reversal.*

polar response The indication of how a loudspeaker focuses sound at the monitoring position(s).

polar response pattern The graph of a microphone's directional characteristics as seen from above. The graph indicates response over a 360-degree circumference in a series of concentric circles, each representing a 5-dB loss in level as the circles move inward toward the center. Also called *pickup pattern.*

polydirectional microphone *See* **multidirectional microphone.**

pop filter Foam rubber windscreen placed inside the microphone head. Particularly effective in reducing sound from plosives and blowing. Also called *blast filter.* *See also* **windscreen.**

porous absorber A sound absorber made up of porous material whose tiny air spaces are most effective at absorbing high frequencies.

pot Short for *potentiometer. See* **fader.**

potentiometer *See* **fader.**

ppm *See* **peak program meter.**

precedence effect The tendency to perceive the direct and immediate repetitions of a sound as coming from the same position or direction even if the immediate repetitions coming from another direction are louder. Also known as the *Haas effect.*

predelay The amount of time between the onset of the direct sound and the appearance of the first reflections.

prefader listen (PFL) *See* **solo.**

premix The stage in postproduction sweetening when dialogue, sound effects, and music are prepared for final mixing.

presence Perception of a sound as being close and realistic. Also called *ambience* and *room tone. See* **ambience.**

presidential patch *See* **press bridge.**

press bridge An amplifier with several mic level outputs to provide individual feeds, thereby eliminating the need for many. Also called a *presidential patch.*

primary frequency *See* **fundamental.**

print-through Unwanted transfer of a magnetic signal from one tape layer to an adjacent tape layer.

private line (PL) system An intercom system consisting of a headset with an earpiece and a small microphone used during production to connect production and technical personnel. Also called *phone line system*.

production recording Dialogue recording on the set, thereby preserving the sonic record of a production, regardless of whether the dialogue is to be rerecorded.

production source music Music that emanates from an on-screen singer or ensemble and is produced live during shooting or in postproduction.

proximity effect Increase in the bass response of some mics as the distance between the mic and its sound source is decreased. Also known as *bass tip-up*.

psychoacoustic processor Signal processor that adds clarity, definition, overall presence, and life or "sizzle" to recorded sound.

psychoacoustics Study of the perception of sound stimuli.

punching in Linear electronic insert-editing method whereby just the subpar section of a multitrack tape recording is rerecorded, without affecting the rest of the recording.

pure tone *See* **sine wave**.

quantization Converting a waveform that is infinitely variable into a finite series of discrete levels.

radio microphone *See* **wireless microphone system**.

rarefaction Temporary drawing apart of vibrating molecules, causing a partial vacuum to occur. *See also* **compression** (2).

R-DAT *See* **rotary-head digital audiotape recorder**.

read mode Mode of operation in an automated mixdown when the console controls are operated automatically by the data previously encoded in the computer. Also called *safe mode*. *See also* **update mode** and **write mode**.

RealAudio Proprietary system that uses a compression method called CELP at low bit rates for speech. For music it uses the AC-3 codec developed by Dolby with higher bit rates.

real-time analyzer A device that shows the total energy present at all audible frequencies on an instantaneous basis.

record head Electromagnetic transducer on a tape recorder that converts electric energy into magnetic energy.

recordable compact disc (CD-R) A CD format allowing users to record one time but to play back the recorded information repeatedly.

recovery time *See* **release time**.

reflected sound Reflections of the direct sound that bounce off one or more surfaces before reaching the listener.

regeneration *See* **feedback**.

release The time and manner in which a sound diminishes to inaudibility.

release time The length of time it takes a limiter or compressor to return to its normal level after the signal has been attenuated or withdrawn. Also known as *recovery time*.

remnance The residual magnetization from a previous recording after erasure.

remote Any broadcast done away from the studio.

rerecording The process of combining individual dialogue, sound effects, and music tracks into their final form—stereo or surround sound.

resonance Transmitting a vibration from one body to another when the frequency of the first body is exactly, or almost exactly, the natural frequency of the second body.

retentivity Measure of a tape's ability to retain magnetization after the force field has been removed. Retentivity is measured in gauss—a unit of magnetic energy.

reverberation Multiple blended, random reflections of a sound wave after the sound source has ceased vibrating. Also called *reverb* and *reverberant sound*.

reverberation time The length of time it takes a sound to die away. By definition: the time it takes a sound to decrease to one-millionth of its original intensity, or 60 dB-SPL. Also called *decay time*.

rewritable CD (CD-RW) A CD format that, as with tape, can be recorded on, erased, and used again for another recording.

ribbon microphone A microphone with a ribbon diaphragm suspended in a magnetic field.

ride the gain Continually adjusting controls on a console or other audio equipment to maintain a more or less constant level.

ring off When a dialogue line ends with the ambient ring of a room and another line begins with that ring decaying under it.

room modes   *See* **eigentones.**

room tone   Another term used for *ambience*. Also called *presence*. *See* **ambience.**

rotary-head digital audiotape (R-DAT) recorder   Specifically, a digital cassette audiotape recorder with rotary heads. *See also* **stationary-head digital audiotape recorder.**

SACD   *See* **Super Audio Compact Disc**

safe mode   *See* **read mode.**

SA system   *See* **studio-address system.**

sampler   An audio device that records a short sound event—such as a note or a musical phrase—into computer memory. The samples can be played by triggering them with a MIDI signal from a MIDI controller or a MIDI sequencer.

sampling   (1) Examining an analog signal at regular intervals defined by the sampling frequency (or rate). (2) A process whereby a section of digital audio representing a sonic event, acoustic or electroacoustic, is stored on disk or into a memory.

sampling frequency   The frequency (or rate) at which an analog signal is sampled. Also called *sampling rate*.

scrape flutter filter   A cylindrical, low-friction, metal surface installed between the heads to reduce the amount of unsupported tape, thereby restricting the degree of tape movement as it passes across the heads. It reduces flutter.

scrubbing   In hard-disk editing, moving the playbar cursor through the defined region at any speed to listen to a sound being readied for editing.

SCSI   *See* **Small Computer Systems Interface.**

S-DAT   *See* **stationary-head digital audiotape recorder.**

segue   (1) Cutting from one effect to another with nothing in between. (2) Playing two recordings one after the other, with no announcement in between.

Sel Sync™   A propietary system of selective synchronization—changing the record head into a playback head to synchronize the playback of previously recorded material with the recording of new material.

selective synchronization   *See* **Sel Sync.**

self-noise   The electrical noise, or hiss, an electronic device produces.

sensitivity   (1) Measurement of a tape's output level capability relative to a standard reference tape. (2) Measurement of the voltage (dBV) a microphone produces, which indicates its efficiency. (3) The sound-pressure level directly in front of the loudspeaker, on-axis, at a given distance and produced by a given amount of power.

sequencer   An electronic device that can be programmed to store and automatically play back a repeating series of notes on an electronic musical instrument such as a synthesizer.

shelving   Maximum boost or cut at a particular frequency that remains constant at all points beyond that frequency so the response curve resembles a shelf.

shock mount   A device that isolates a microphone from mechanical vibrations. It can be attached externally or built into a microphone.

shotgun microphone   A highly directional microphone with a tube that resembles the barrel of a rifle.

signal-to-noise ratio (S/N)   The ratio, expressed in decibels (dB), of an electronic device's nominal output to its noise floor. The wider the signal-to-noise ratio, the better.

silent film   Film carrying picture only.

sine wave   A pure tone or fundamental frequency with no harmonics or overtones.

single-D™ microphone   *See* **single-entry-port microphone.**

single-entry-port microphone   A directional microphone that uses a single port to bring sounds from the rear of the mic to the capsule. Because these sounds from the rear reach the capsule out of phase with those that reach the front of the capsule, they are canceled.

single-system recording   Recording picture and sound in a film or video camera simultaneously.

slap back echo   The effect created when an original signal repeats as distinct echoes that decrease in level with each repetition.

slate   The part of a talkback system that feeds sound to tape. It is used to record verbal identification of the material being taped, the take number, and other information just before each recording.

slave   The tape or disk to which the material on a master recording is transferred.

Small Computer Systems Interface (SCSI)   The standard for hardware and software command language that allows two-way communication between, primarily, hard-disk and CD-ROM drives. Pronounced "scuzzy."

SMPTE time code   A high-frequency signal consisting of a stream of pulses produced by a time code generator used to code tape to facilitate editing and synchronization. Also known as *longitudinal time code*.

S/N *See* **signal-to-noise ratio**.

soft knee compression Smooth gain reduction at the start of compression. *See also* **knee** and **hard knee compression**.

solo A control on a multitrack console that automatically cuts off all signals feeding the monitor system except those signals feeding through the channel that the solo control activates. Sometimes called *prefader listen (PFL)*.

Sony/Philips Digital Interface (SPDIF) The consumer version of the AES/EBU interface calling for an unbalanced line using phone connectors. *See also* **AES/EBU**.

sound absorption coefficient A measure of the sound-absorbing ability of a surface. This coefficient is defined as the fraction of incident sound absorbed by a surface. Values range from 0.01 for marble to 1.00 for the materials used in an almost acoustically dead enclosure. Also known as *noise reduction coefficient (NRC)*.

sound chain The audio components that carry a signal from its sound source to its destination.

sound design The process of creating the overall sonic character of a production (usually in relation to picture).

sound designer The individual responsible for a production's overall sonic complexion.

sound effect Anything sonic that is not speech or music. Abbreviated *SFX*.

sound envelope Changes in the loudness of a sound over time, described as occurring in four stages: attack, initial decay, sustain, and release (ADSR).

SoundField microphone system Four capacitor microphone capsules shaped like a tetrahedron, enclosed in a single casing, that can be combined in various formats to reproduce sonic, depth, breadth, and height.

soundfile A sound stored in the memory of a hard-disk recorder/editor.

sound film Film carrying both picture and sound.

sound frequency spectrum The range of frequencies audible to human hearing: about 20 to 20,000 Hz.

sound-pressure level *See* **dB-SPL**.

sound transmission class (STC) A rating that evaluates the effectiveness of barriers in isolating sound.

sound wave A vibrational disturbance that involves mechanical motion of molecules transmitting energy from one place to another.

source music Background music from an on-screen source, such as a stereo, radio, or jukebox.

spaced miking Two, sometimes three, microphones spaced from several inches to several feet apart, depending on the width of the sound source and the acoustics, for stereo recording.

SPDIF *See* **Sony/Philips Digital Interface**.

spectrum processor A signal processor that affects a sound's spectral range.

split editing (1) Editing the same sound into two or more separate tracks to facilitate control of its length and in editing transitions. In dialogue, for example, this makes it easier to extend lines that may have been cut too short during picture editing, to overlap voices, and to carry over lines from one scene to the next. (2) A type of transition where the audio or video leads or lags a portion of the previous edit.

split-section console Multichannel production console in which the input, output, master, and monitor sections are separate. *See also* **in-line console**.

split-track recording Recording two separate sound sources on two separate tracks of a stereo recorder or VCR with two audio tracks.

spotting Going through a script or work print and deciding on the placement of sound effects and music.

spotting sheet Indicates the sound effect, or music, cue and whether it is synchronous or nonsynchronous, its in- and out-times, and its description.

stationary-head digital audiotape (S-DAT) recorder A fixed-head digital audiotape recorder. *See also* **rotary-head digital audiotape recorder**.

STC *See* **sound transmission class**.

stereo One-dimensional sound that creates the illusion of two-dimensional sound.

stereo-to-mono compatibility Ensuring that a recording made in stereo is reproducible in mono without spatial or spectral distortion.

stereophonic microphone Two directional microphone capsules, one above the other, with separate outputs, encased in one housing.

stripe coat Magnetic film that contains two stripes of oxide coating, a wide stripe for recording single-track mono and a narrow balance stripe to ensure that the film wind on reels is smooth. *See also* **full coat**.

studio-address (SA) system An intercom system used like a public-address system to communicate with people in the studio not connected to the private-line system, such as the performers, and for general instructions to all studio personnel. Also called *talkback*.

subcode Recorded data that is independent of the audio.

subtractive equalization Attenuating, rather than boosting, frequencies to achieve equalization.

Super Audio Compact Disc (SACD) Sony's proprietary, extremely high quality CD audio format intended for the audiophile market.

surround sound Multichannel sound, typically employing six or more channels, each one feeding to a separate loudspeaker that expands the dimensions of depth, thereby placing the listener more in the center of the aural image than in front of it.

sustain In the sound envelope, the period during which the sound's relative dynamics are maintained after its initial decay.

sweet spot In control room monitoring, the designated listening position which is the optimal distance away from and between the loudspeakers.

sweetening Enhancing the sound of a recording in postproduction through signal processing and mixing.

synchronization The ability to lock two or more devices that have microprocessor intelligence so that they operate at precisely the same rate.

synchronizer Device that regulates the operating speeds of two or more recorders so they run in sync.

sync tone The tone or pulse that synchronizes tape recorder speed and film camera speed in double-system recording.

system microphone Interchangeable microphone capsules of various directional patterns that attach to a common base. The base contains a power supply and a preamplifier.

system noise The inherent noise that an electronic device or a system generates.

tails out Having the end of the material on a tape or film at the head of the reel.

talkback Studio-address intercom system that permits communication from a control room microphone to a loudspeaker or headphones in the studio.

tangency One of the adjustments made when aligning the heads of an audiotape recorder. This adjustment aligns the forwardness of the heads so that the tape meets them at the correct pressure.

tape transport system The mechanical portion of the tape recorder, mounted with motors, reel spindles, heads, and controls, that carries the tape at the constant speed from the feed reel to the takeup reel.

Tascam Digital Interface Format (TDIF) A proprietary digital audio format that carries eight channels of digital audio bidirectionally.

TDIF *See* **Tascam Digital Interface Format**.

temporal fusion When reflected sound reaches the ear within 10 to 20 ms of the original sound, the direct and reflected sound are perceived as a single sound. This effect gradually disappears as the time interval between direct and reflected sound increases from roughly 30 to 50 ms.

three-to-one rule A guideline used to reduce the phasing caused when a sound reaches two microphones at slightly different times. It states that no two microphones should be closer to each other than three times the distance between one of them and its sound source.

three-way system loudspeaker A loudspeaker system with two crossover networks.

threshold of hearing The lowest sound-pressure level (SPL) at which sound becomes audible to the human ear. It is the zero reference of 0 dB-SPL.

threshold of pain The sound-pressure level at which the ear begins to feel pain, about 140 dB-SPL, although levels of around 120 dB-SPL cause discomfort.

tie line Facilitates the interconnecting of outboard devices and patch bays in a control room or between studios.

timbre The unique tone quality or color of a sound.

time code address The unique SMPTE time code number that identifies each $\frac{1}{30}$ second of a recording.

time compression Shortening the time (length) of material without changing its pitch.

time expansion Increasing the time (length) of material without changing its pitch.

time processor A signal processor that affects the time interval between a signal and its repetition.

tinnitus After prolonged exposure to loud sounds, the ringing, whistling, or buzzing in the ears, even though no loud sounds are present.

TL *See* **transmission loss**.

transducer A device that converts one form of energy into another.

transient A sound that begins with a sharp attack followed by a quick decay.

transient distortion Distortion that occurs when a sound system cannot reproduce sounds that begin with sudden, explosive attacks.

transmission loss (TL) The amount of sound reduction provided by a barrier such as a wall, floor, or ceiling.

transmitter microphone *See* **wireless microphone system**.

treble Frequency range between roughly 5,000 and 20,000 Hz, the highest two octaves in the audible frequency spectrum.

trim (1) To attenuate the loudness level in a component or circuit. (2) The device on a console that attenuates the loudness level at the microphone/line input.

tube microphone A capacitor microphone using a tube circuit in the preamp.

tweeter The informal name of a loudspeaker that reproduces high frequencies. *See also* **woofer**.

two-way system loudspeaker A loudspeaker system with one crossover network.

ultrasonic Frequencies above the range of human hearing.

unbalanced line A line (or circuit) with two conductors of unequal voltage.

underscore music Nondiegetic music added to enhance the informational or emotional content of a scene.

unidirectional microphone A microphone that picks up sound from one direction. Also called *directional microphone*.

upcut When the board operator is late in responding to the first few utterances of a speaker, thereby missing the words or having them barely audible.

update mode Mode of operation in an automated mixdown when an encoded control can be recorded without affecting the coding of the other controls. *See also* **read mode** and **write mode**.

upper bass Frequency range between roughly 80 and 320 Hz.

upper midrange Frequency range between roughly 2,560 and 5,120 Hz.

variable-D™ microphone *See* **multiple-entry-port microphone**.

variable-speed control Device on an audiotape recorder that alters the playing speed to various rates of the recorder's set speeds.

VCA *See* **voltage-controlled amplifier**.

velocity The speed of a sound wave: 1,130 feet per second at sea level and 70 degrees Fahrenheit.

vertical interval time code (VITC) Time code that is recorded vertically on videotape and within the video signal, but outside the picture area.

video-leading-audio When the picture of a new scene starts before the sound of the old scene has finished. *See also* **audio-leading-video**.

virtual track In hard-disk recording, a track that provides all the functionality of an actual track but cannot be played simultaneously with another virtual track.

VITC *See* **vertical interval time code**.

V.O. *See* **voice-over**.

voice-over (V.O.) An announcement or narration to which other materials, such as sound effects, music, and visuals, are added, usually at later time.

voltage-controlled amplifier (VCA) An amplifier used to decrease level. The amount of amplification is controlled by external DC voltage.

volume unit (VU) meter A meter that responds to the average voltage on the line, not true volume levels. It is calibrated in volume units and percentage of modulation.

VU *See* **volume unit meter**.

walla A nonsense word that used to be spoken by film extras to create ambient crowd sound without anything discernable actually being said.

waveform A graphic representation of a sound's characteristic shape displayed, for example, on test equipment and hard-disk editing systems.

wavelength The length of one cycle of a sound wave. Wavelength is inversely proportional to the frequency of a sound; the higher the frequency, the shorter the wavelength.

weighting network A filter used for weighting a frequency response before measurement.

wet sound A sound with reverberation or signal processing. *See also* **dry sound**.

white noise A wideband noise that contains equal energy at each frequency. *See also* **pink noise**.

windscreen Foam rubber covering specially designed to fit over the outside of a microphone head. Used to reduce plosive and blowing sounds. *See also* **pop filter**.

wireless microphone system System consisting of a transmitter that sends a microphone signal to a receiver connected to a console. Also called *radio, FM, transmitter,* or *cordless microphone*.

woofer Informal name for a loudspeaker that produces the bass frequencies. *See also* **tweeter**.

word clock A synchronization signal that is used to control the rate at which digital audio data is converted or transmitted.

worldizing Recording room sound to add the sound of that space to a dry recording or to use it to enhance or smooth ambient backgrounds that are already part of the dialogue track.

wow (1) Starting a recorded sound before it reaches full speed. (2) Frequency changes in an analog tape recording resulting from faster variations in the speed of the tape transport. *See also* **flutter**.

wrap One of the adjustments made when aligning the heads of an audiotape recorder. This adjustment aligns the head so that it is in full physical contact with the tape.

write mode The mode of operation in an automated mixdown during which controls are adjusted conventionally and the adjustments are encoded in the computer for retrieval in the safe mode. *See also* **read mode** and **update mode**.

XLR connector Commonly used male and female microphone plugs with a three-pin connector.

X-Y miking Coincident or near-coincident miking that places the microphones' diaphragms over or horizontal to one another. *See also* **coincident miking** and **near-coincident miking**.

zenith One of the adjustments made when aligning the heads of an audiotape recorder. This adjustment aligns the vertical angle of the heads so they are perpendicular to the tape.

zero crossing The point in a waveform denoting a value of zero amplitude. It divides the positive (upper) and negative (lower) parts of the waveform.

Selected Bibliography

Books

Adam, Thomas, and Peter Gorges. *FX: 100 Effects Settings for Sound Design and Mix.* New York: Schirmer Books, 1999.

Alldrin, Loren. *The Home Studio Guide to Microphones.* Emeryville, Calif.: MixBooks, 1998.

Alkin, Glyn. *Sound Recording and Reproduction.* Oxford: Focal Press, 1996.

Alten, Stanley. *Audio in Media: The Recording Studio.* Belmont, Calif.: Wadsworth Publishing, 1996.

Altman, Rick, ed. *Sound Theory/Sound Practice.* New York: Routledge, 1992.

Amyes, Tim. *The Technique of Audio Post-Production in Video and Film,* 2nd ed. Oxford: Focal Press, 1999.

Bartlett, Bruce. *Stereo Microphone Techniques.* Boston: Focal Press, 1991.

Bartlett, Bruce, and Jenny Bartlett. *Practical Recording Techniques,* 3rd ed. Boston: Focal Press, 2002.

———. *On Location Recording.* Boston: Focal Press, 1999.

Baskerville, David. *Music Business Handbook,* 7th ed. Thousand Oaks, Calif.: Sage Publications, 2001.

Berendt, Joachim-Ernst. *The Third Ear: On Listening to the World.* New York: Henry Holt, 1992.

Blauert, Jens. Trans. by John S. Allen. *Spatial Hearing.* Cambridge, Mass.: MIT Press, 1983.

Borwick, John. *Microphones: Technology and Technique.* Oxford: Focal Press, 1990.

Borwick, John, ed. *Sound Recording Practice: A Handbook,* 4th ed. New York: Oxford University Press, 1995.

———. *Loudspeaker and Headphone Handbook,* 3rd ed. Oxford: Focal Press, 2000.

Bregman, Albert. *Auditory Scene Analysis.* Cambridge, Mass.: MIT Press, 1990.

Brown, Royal. *Overtones and Undertones: Reading Film Music.* Berkeley: University of California Press, 1994.

Carlin, Dan, Sr. *Music in Film and Video Productions.* Boston: Focal Press, 1991.

Chion, Michael. Trans. by Claudia Gorbman. *Audio-Vision: Sound on Screen.* New York: Columbia University Press, 1994.

Crich, Tim. *Assistant Engineer's Handbook.* Emeryville, Calif.: MixBooks, 1995.

Crocker, Malcolm. *Handbook of Acoustics.* New York: John Wiley & Sons, 1998.

Davis, Richard. *Complete Guide to Film Scoring: The Art and Business of Writing Music for Movies and TV.* Boston: Berklee Press, 2000.

Davis, Steve, ed. *SPARS Time Code Primer.* Lake Worth, Fla.: Society of Professional Audio Recording Services, 1997.

Derry, Roger. *PC Audio Editing from Broadcasting to Home CD.* Boston: Focal Press, 2000.

DeSantis, Jayce. *How to Run a Recording Session,* 2nd ed. Emeryville, Calif.: MixBooks, 2000.

Deutsch, Diana, ed. *The Psychology of Music.* Orlando: Academic Press, 1982.

Dorritie, Frank. *Essentials of Music for Audio Professionals.* Emeryville, Calif.: MixBooks, 2000.

Dowling, W. J., and D. L. Harwood. *Music Cognition.* Orlando: Academic Press, 1986.

Eargle, John. *Handbook of Recording Engineering,* 3rd ed. New York: Van Nostrand Reinhold, 1996.

———. *Loudspeaker Handbook.* New York: Chapman & Hall, 1996.

———. *The Microphone Handbook.* Plainview, N.Y.: ELAR, 1981.

———. *Music, Sound, and Technology,* 2nd ed. New York: Van Nostrand Reinhold, 1995.

Eisenberg, Evan. *The Recording Angel: Explorations in Phonography.* New York: McGraw-Hill, 1987.

Essex, Jeff. *Multimedia Sound and Music Studio.* New York: Random House, 1996.

Everest, F. Alton. *Master Handbook of Acoustics,* 4th ed. New York: McGraw-Hill, 2001.

Everest, F. Alton, and Ron Streicher. *The New Stereo Soundbook,* 2nd ed. Pasadena, Calif.: Audio Engineering Associates, 1998.

Fletcher, Neville, and Thomas Rossing. *The Physics of Musical Instruments.* New York: Springer-Verlag, 1991.

Gayford, Michael. *Microphone Engineering Handbook.* Oxford: Focal Press, 1994.

Gibson, Bill. *The AudioPro Home Recording Course,* Vols. 1–3. Emeryville, Calif.: MixBooks, 1996–1999.

Gibson, David. *The Art of Mixing.* Emeryville, Calif.: MixBooks, 1997.

Gorbman, Claudia. *Unheard Melodies: Narrative Film Music.* Bloomington: Indiana University Press, 1987.

Gross, Lynne, and David Reese. *Radio Production Worktext: Studio and Equipment,* 3rd ed. Boston: Focal Press, 1997.

Gross, Lynne, and Larry Ward. *Electronic Moviemaking,* 4th ed. Belmont, Calif.: Wadsworth Publishing, 2000.

Hagen, Earle. *Scoring for Films.* Sherman Oaks, Calif.: Alfred Publishing, 1989.

Handel, Stephen. *Listening: An Introduction to the Perception of Auditory Events.* Cambridge, Mass.: MIT Press, 1989.

Hansen, Brad. *The Dictionary of Multimedia.* Chicago: Franklin Beedle, 1997.

Harris, John. *Tips for Recording Musicians,* 2nd ed. New York: Cimino Publishing Group, 1999.

Hausmann, Carl, Philip Benoit, and Lewis O'Donnell. *Modern Radio Production,* 5th ed. Belmont, Calif.: Wadsworth Publishing, 2000.

Helmstetter, Anthony, and Ron Simpson. *Web Developer's Guide to Sound & Music.* Scottsdale, Ariz.: Coriolis Group Books, 1996.

Holman, Tomlinson. *Sound for Film and Television.* Boston: Focal Press, 1997.

———. *5.1 Surround Sound Up and Running.* Boston: Focal Press, 2000.

Howard, David, and James Angus. *Acoustics and Psycho-acoustics.* Oxford: Focal Press, 1996.

Huber, David, and Robert Runstein. *Modern Recording Techniques,* 5th ed. Boston: Focal Press, 2001.

Huber, David Miles, and Phillip Williams. *Professional Microphone Techniques.* Emeryville, Calif.: MixBooks, 1998.

Kalinak, Kathryn. *Settling the Score: Music and the Classical Hollywood Film.* Madison: University of Wisconsin Press, 1992.

Kamichik, Stephen. *Practical Acoustics.* Indianapolis: Prompt Publications, 1998.

Karlin, Fred. *Listening to Movies.* New York: Schirmer Books, 1994.

Karlin, Fred, and Rayburn Wright. *On the Track: A Guide to Contemporary Film Scoring.* New York: Schirmer Books, 1990.

Kenny, Tom. *Sound for Picture,* rev. ed. Vallejo, Calif.: Artistpro.com, 1999.

Kerner, Marvin A. *The Art of the Sound Effects Editor.* Boston: Focal Press, 1989.

LoBrutto, Vincent. *Sound-on-Film: Interviews with Creators of Film Sound.* Westport, Conn.: Praeger Publishers, 1994.

Lyver, Des. *Basics of Video Sound,* 2nd ed. Oxford: Focal Press, 1999.

MacDonald, Laurence. *The Invisible Art of Film Music.* New York: Ardsley House, 1998.

McLeish, Robert. *Radio Production,* 4th ed. Oxford: Focal Press, 1999.

Mansfield, Richard. *Studio Basics.* New York: Watson-Guptill, 1998.

Martin, George. *All You Need Is Ears.* New York: St. Martin's Press, 1979.

Massey, Howard. *Behind the Glass.* San Francisco: Backbeat Books, 2000.

Molenda, Michael. *What's That Sound? The Audible Audio Dictionary.* Milwaukee: Hal Leonard, 1998.

Moore, Brian C. J. *An Introduction to the Psychology of Hearing.* San Diego: Academic Press, 1990.

Mott, Robert. *Sound Effects: Radio, TV, and Film.* Boston: Focal Press, 1990.

Moylan, William. *The Art of Recording.* New York: Van Nostrand Reinhold, 1992.

Music Producers, 2nd ed. Emeryville, Calif.: MixBooks, 2000.

Newall, Philip. *Recording Spaces.* Oxford: Focal Press, 1998.

Olson, Harry. *Music, Physics, and Engineering.* New York: Dover, 1967.

Owsinski, Bobby. *Mixing Engineer's Handbook.* Vallejo, Calif.: Artistpro.com, 1999.

Pasquariello, Nicholas. *Sounds of Movies: Interviews with the Creators of Feature Film Soundtracks*. San Francisco: Port Bridge Books, 1996.

Pohlmann, Kenneth. *Principles of Digital Audio,* 4th ed. New York: McGraw-Hill, 2000.

Prendergast, Roy. *Film: A Neglected Art*. New York: W. W. Norton, 1992.

Ratcliff, John. *Time Code: A User's Guide,* 3rd ed. Oxford: Focal Press, 1999.

Recording Industry Sourcebook. Los Angeles: Recording Industry Sourcebook, 2001 (annual).

Rossing, Thomas. *The Science of Sound,* 2nd ed. Reading, Mass.: Addison-Wesley, 1990.

Rumsey, Francis, and Tim McCormick. *Sound and Recording: An Introduction,* 3rd ed. Oxford: Focal Press, 1997.

Rumsey, Francis, et al., eds. *Acoustics and Psychoacoustics*. Oxford: Focal Press, 1996.

Schafer, Murray. *The Tuning of the World*. New York: Alfred A. Knopf, 1977.

Schelle, Michael. *The Score: Interviews with Film Composers*. Los Angeles: Silman-James Press, 1999.

Schwartz, Tony. *The Responsive Chord*. Garden City, N.Y.: Anchor, 1974.

SMPTE Made Simple: A Time Code Tutor. San Marcos, Calif.: TimeLine Vista, 1996.

SPARS Occupational Handbook. Lake Worth, Fla.: Society of Professional Audio Recording Services, 1992.

Talbot-Smith, Michael. *Audio Explained*. Oxford: Focal Press, 1997.

———. *Broadcast Sound Technology,* 2nd ed. Oxford: Focal Press, 1995.

———. *Sound Assistance,* 2nd ed. Oxford: Focal Press, 1999.

———. *Sound Engineer's Pocket Book,* 2nd ed. Oxford: Focal Press, 2000.

Talbot-Smith, Michael, ed. *Audio Engineer's Reference Book,* 2nd ed. Oxford: Focal Press, 1999.

Thomas, Tony. *Film Score: Art and Craft of Movie Music*. Burbank, Calif.: Riverwood Press, 1991.

———. *Music for the Movies,* 2nd ed. Los Angeles: Silman-James Press, 1997.

Truax, Barry. *Acoustic Communication*. Norwood, N.J.: Ablex, 1984.

Watkinson, John. *The Art of Digital Audio,* 3rd ed. Oxford: Focal Press, 2000.

———. *Audio for Television*. Oxford: Focal Press, 1997.

———. *The Art of Sound Reproduction*. Oxford: Focal Press, 1998.

Yewdall, David Lewis. *Practical Art of Motion Picture Sound*. Boston: Focal Press, 1999.

Weis, Elisabeth. *The Silent Scream*. Rutherford, N.J.: Farleigh Dickinson, 1982.

Weis, Elisabeth, and John Belton, eds. *Film Sound: Theory and Practice*. New York: Columbia University Press, 1985.

White, Ira. *Audio Made Easy,* 2nd ed. Milwaukee: Hal Leonard, 2000.

White, Paul. *The Sound on Sound Book of Music Technology: A Survivor's Guide*. London: Sanctuary Publishing Limited, 1997.

———. *Recording and Production Techniques*. London: Sanctuary Publishing Limited, 1997.

Zettl, Herbert. *Sight, Sound, Motion: Applied Media Aesthetics,* 3rd ed. Belmont, Calif.: Wadsworth Publishing, 1999.

Periodicals

The Absolute Sound

Audio Engineering Society (AES) Journal

Audio Media

BE Radio

Broadcast Engineering

Broadcaster

Electronic Musician

EQ

Film and Video

Home Recording

Home and Studio Recording

International Recording Equipment and Studio Directory

Millimeter

Mix

Mix Annual Master Directory of Recording Industry Facilities and Services

Mixdown

One to One

Post

Producer

Professional Sound

Pro Audio Review

Pro Sound News

Radio World

Recording

Remix

S & VC (Sound & Video Contractor)

SMPTE Journal

Sound and Communications

Sound on Sound

Surround

Studio Sound

Tape Op

Videography

Tapes and CDs

Everest, F. Alton. *Critical Listening and Auditory Perception.* Emeryville, Calif.: MixBooks, 1997.

Gehman, Scott. *From Tin to Gold: Train Your Ears to Golden Standards.* Houston: Gehman Music, 1996.

Gibson, Bill. *Killer Demos: Hot Tips & Cool Secrets.* Federal Way, Wash.: Bill and Bob's Excellent Productions, 1991.

Gibson, Bill, and Peter Alexander. *Hit Sound Recording Course.* Newbury Park, Calif.: Katamar Entertainment Corporation, 1992.

Hernandez, John. *Miking the Drum Set.* Claremont, Calif.: Terence Dwyer Productions, 1992.

Kramer, Eddie. *Adventures in Modern Recording.* San Francisco: Premium Entertainment, 1994.

Lubin, Tom. *Shaping Your Sound.* Los Angeles: Acrobat, 1988–1991.

Moulton, Dave. *Golden Ears.* San Diego: KIQ Productions, 1993.

Swedien, Bruce. *Recording with Bruce Swedien,* vol. 1. San Francisco: AcuNet Corporation, 1997.

Wadhams, Wayne. *Sound Advice: The Musician's Guide to the Recording Studio.* New York: Schirmer, 1990.

CD-ROMs

Begault, Durand. *The Sonic CD-ROM for Desktop Audio Production.* San Diego: Academic Press, 1996.

Sides, Alan. *Alan Sides' Microphone Cabinet.* Emeryville, Calif.: EM Books, 1995.

Sterling, Christopher (gen. ed.), and Stanley Alten, et al. (eds.). *Focal Encyclopedia of Electronic Media.* Boston: Focal Press, 1998.

Reference CDs and CD-ROMs

Anechoic Orchestral Music Recording. Denon PG-6006.

Mix Reference Disc: Deluxe Edition. Emeryville, Calif.: MixBooks.

The Sheffield Drum Record/The Sheffield Track Record. Sheffield Lab CD-14/20.

Sound Check, Vols. 1 and 2. Compiled by Alan Parsons and Stephen Court. dbx.

Studio Reference Disc. Prosonus SRD.

TMH Digital Audio Test Discs. Produced by TMH Corporation and Tomlinson Holman. Hollywood Edge.

Index